Mirror Images

Reading and Writing Arguments

Anne M. Machin
Aims Community College

Russ Ward
Aims Community College

PEARSON
Longman

New York San Francisco Boston
London Toronto Sydney Tokyo Singapore Madrid
Mexico City Munich Paris Cape Town Hong Kong Montreal

Acquisitions Editor: Lauren A. Finn
Senior Marketing Manager: Sandra McGuire
Production Manager: Denise Phillip
Project Coordination, Text Design, and Electronic Page Makeup: Electronic Publishing Services Inc., New York City
Cover Design Manager: Wendy Ann Fredericks
Cover Designer: Base Art Co.
Cover Photo: ©Jutta Klee/Corbis
Photo Researcher: Jody Potter
Senior Manufacturing Buyer: Alfred C. Dorsey
Printer and Binder: R. R. Donnelley & Sons/Harrisonburg
Cover Printer: R. R. Donnelley & Sons/Harrisonburg

For permission to use copyrighted material, grateful acknowledgment is made to the copyright holders on pp. 449–455, which are hereby made part of this copyright page.

Library of Congress Cataloging-in-Publication Data
Machin, Anne Marie.
    Mirror images : reading and writing arguments/
  Anne M. Machin, Russ Ward.—1st ed.
    p. cm.
    Includes bibliographical references and index.
    ISBN 978-0-205-53073-1
    1. English language—Rhetoric. 2. Persuasion (Rhetoric) 3. College readers.
  I. Ward, Russ. II. Title.

PE1431.M334 2008
808'.0427—dc22   2007042689

Copyright © 2008 by Pearson Education, Inc.

All rights reserved. No part of this publication may be reproduced, stored in a retrieval system, or transmitted, in any form or by any means, electronic, mechanical, photocopying, recording, or otherwise, without the prior written permission of the publisher. Printed in the United States.

Please visit us at www.ablongman.com

ISBN-13: 978-0-205-53073-1
ISBN-10:   0-205-53073-7

1 2 3 4 5 6 7 8 9 10—DOH—10 09 08 07

Contents

Preface to the Instructor   xi
Preface to the Student   xv

PART I   Analyzing Argument

1   A Brief Introduction to Argument 3

Argument as a Thought Process   7
Some of the Many Contexts for Argument   8
   Argument in a Personal Business Context   8
   Argument in an Advertising Context   11
   Argument in a Social Commentary Context   14
   "Road Tests for Seniors," *Mike Rosen*   15
   "Poetry Is Dead. Does Anybody Really Care?," *Bruce Wexler*   17
   Argument in an Art Context   18
   "Assault on Precinct 13," *Mike Pearson*   19
   "Analysis of *Self-Portrait with Cropped Hair*," *Sarah M. Lowe*   20
What Argument Should Do for Us   22
Trying to Remain Flexible in Your Thinking   23
Rogerian Argument   24
A Note on Organization: Writing as a Process   25
   "Border Calling," *James Reel*   28
   "Not Giving Up on Immigration Control," *Kurt Williamson*   31
Students at Work: Putting Argument to Use   34
Discovering Your Own Arguments: Arguments in Everyday Life   37
Reflections on the Chapter   39

2 Traditional Means of Establishing Context and Discovering Your Argument 40

The Appeal to Personal Credibility (the Ethical Appeal) 42
 What Do You Bring to an Argument? 44
The Appeal to Emotions (the Pathetic Appeal) 45
The Appeal to Reason (the Logical Appeal) 47
Students at Work: Thinking About Persuasive Appeals 49
Inductive Reasoning 51
 Seeking a Reliable Induction Conclusion 51
Deductive Reasoning 54
Seeking the Valid Deductive Conclusion 56
 The Toulmin System 57
Using the Toulmin System to Analyze an Argument 61
 Discovering Your Own Arguments: Using the Classical Appeals 63
Reflections on the Chapter 64

3 An Argument's Anatomy 65

The Thinking Behind an Argument 66
The Rhetorical Triangle and the Argument Concept 67
The Thinking Within an Argument 69
The Claim 69
 Types of Claims 70
Reasons and Evidence 72
Concessions and Rebuttals 75
Students at Work: Analysis of the Structure of a Student Argument 79
Discovering Your Own Arguments: Using the "Parts" of Arguments 82
Reflections on the Chapter 83

4 Using the Argument Concept to Analyze an Argument's Plan 84

The Argument Concept 86
 The Argument Concept and How It Can Work for You 87
 The Argument Concept in Both Reading and Writing 87
How the Topic's Focus Influences an Argument's Design 89
How the Potential Reader Influences an Argument's Design 91
How the Intended Purpose Influences an Argument's Design 96

Altering Any Part of the Context   99
Students at Work: Using the Argument Concept   100
The Move from Argument Concept to the
  Argument's Claim   102
*Discovering Your Own Arguments: Arguments from Refined Argument
  Concepts   104*
Reflections on the Chapter   105

5   The Potential Problems in Arguments   107
Insufficient Evidence   110
Atypical Evidence   112
Citing Improper Authorities   113
Subjectivism   114
Appeal to a Majority   115
Personal Attack on the Opposition   116
False Cause   117
Begging the Question   118
Non Sequitur   119
False Dilemma (Either/or Fallacy; Black/White Fallacy)   120
*Students at Work: Reexamining an Argument for
  Potential Fallacies   124*
*Discovering Your Own Arguments: Keeping an Eye
  Out for Fallacies   125*
Reflections on the Chapter   126

6   Using the Argument Concept to Read the
     Arguments of Others   127
An Example of the Need for Critical Reading   128
*Students at Work: Pete Asks Critical Questions
  About His Source   132*
Causes of Superficial, Less Than Critical Reading   133
"Active" Versus "Passive" Reading Practices   134
"Reversing" the Argument Concept   136
  "There's No Future in Lady Luck," Linda Chavez   138
  "Margaret Fuller Slack," Edgar Lee Masters   143
  "College Brings Alienation," John Gonzales   144
  "A Hanging," George Orwell   146
  "Severing the Human Connection,"
    H. Bruce Miller   150

"Hollywood Poison Factory," *Michael Medved*   154
"Erosion," *Terry Tempest Williams*   160
Discovering Your Own Arguments: An Overall Analysis
   of Arguments   162
Reflections on the Chapter   162

PART II   Developing Researched Arguments

7   Looking in the Mirror and Beyond—Generating Topics   165
How to Generate a Productive Topic for an Argument   167
Methods to Inspire Writers' Choices   170
   Clustering   171
   Free Writing   175
   Looping   176
Discovering Your Own Arguments: Topic Exploration   177
Reflections on the Chapter   177

8   Seeking, Sorting, and Selecting Outside Source Material   178
Turning to "Outside" Sources for Support   179
How to Select the Best Outside Sources for
   Your Argument   180
Sources Other than Databases   183
How to Select the Best Sources   184
   "About Trout," *Robert Behnke*   187
"Triangulation"—An Attempt at Validity   190
Discovering Your Own Arguments: A Status Report   194
Reflections on the Chapter   194

9   Envisioning the Complete Argument as a Prewriting Process   195
The Need for a Plan   196
   An Ineffective Approach: Pasting Together
      a "Report"   197
A Writer's Guide to the Envisioned Plan   198
   The Envisioning Process   200
   Considering Your Reader's Potential Knowledge   206

Considering Your Readers' Established Values   208
Considering Your Readers' Opposition to Your Claim   210
Deciding What to Include   211
Adjusting Your Envisioned Plan   220
Discovering Your Own Arguments: Envisioning
 Your Argument   221
Professional Sample of an Envisioned Plan and
 Final Argument   222
"Mentally Retarded Don't Belong on Death Row," *Jamie Fellner*   224
Students at Work: A Student's Plan and
 Corresponding Argument   226
"Minimum Wage vs. Living Wage," *Debbie Stewart*   227
Reflections on the Chapter   233

10 Refining the Purposes for Your Argument   235

Arguing for the Quality of a Product, Behavior, or
 Work of Art   237
"Los Lobos Sing of Immigrants' Hopes, Heartbreaks,"
 Agustin Gurza   240
Do Evaluative Arguments Allow for Fairness?   242
How Evaluative Arguments Are Often Organized   242
Students at Work: The Primarily Evaluative
 Purpose   243
Arguing Solutions to Problems   244
Recognizing and Identifying a Problem   246
Exploring and Evaluating the Possible Solution(s)
 to a Problem   247
Do Problem/Solution Arguments Allow
 for Fairness?   249
Selecting and Defending a Solution to a Problem   249
Students at Work: The Primarily Problem/
 Solution Purpose   249
Arguing Causes(s) and Effect(s)   250
Do Cause-and-Effect Arguments Allow
 for Fairness?   253
Students at Work: The Primarily
 Cause/Effect Purpose   255
Arguing to Maintain or Change a Policy   256
Do Policy Arguments Allow for Fairness?   258

"Tort Reform at Gunpoint," *Anna Quindlen* 260

Students at Work: The Primarily Policy Purpose 262

Discovering Your Own Arguments: Refining Your Envisioned Plan 264

Reflections on the Chapter 264

11 Drafting the Sections of Your Argument—Illustration, Detail, and Outside Sources 265

The Need for Support—Getting Your Reader to "Buy In" 266

The Power of Illustration 268

Types of Examples 268

"The Impact of Extended Example from Savage Inequalities," Jonathan Kozol 273

Examples from Personal Experience 275

Integrating Outside Source Material with Your Argument 277

Using Summary, Paraphrase, and Direct Quotation 277

Writing an Accurate and Adequate Summary 278

Creating a Paraphrase 279

Using Direct Quotations 280

Guidelines for Integrating Source Material 283

"Surfing's Up and Grades Are Down," Rene Sanchez 285

Discovering Your Own Argument: Practice in Integrating Outside Source Material with Your Voice 289

Discovering Your Own Argument: Drafting Your Argument 289

Reflections on the Chapter 291

PART III Documenting and Polishing Arguments

12 Documenting Outside Sources 295

The Purposes of Documentation 296

An Important Caution About Documentation 300

The Basic Processes of Documenting Sources 301

External Documentation (Bibliographical Information) 305

The Three Responsibilities of Documentation 306

External Documentation of Electronic Sources 309

Internal (In-Text) Documentation 313

Students at Work: Sample MLA and APA Papers 318

Discovering Your Own Arguments: Reviewing and Revising Your Source Use 328
Reflections on the Chapter 328

13 Revising Your Written Argument 329

Basic Revising Advice 330
Revising the Focus on Reader and Purpose 334
    Students at Work: Revision Begins 335
    Students at Work: Second Draft 336
Revising the Amount and Quality of Evidence 337
    Students at Work: Revising the Evidence 338
Revising Organization 339
    Students at Work: Revising Organization 341
Top Ten Editing Errors to Avoid 344
    Students at Work: Revising for Language Correctness 351
Discovering Your Own Arguments: Examining Drafts for Language Correctness 352
Reflections on the Chapter 352

PART IV Additional Readings for Analysis

Unit 1 Business Ethics 355

"The Ethics of Business Schools," Katherine S. Mangan 356
"They Call Their Boss a Hero," Michael Ryan 359
"Executive Decisions," Russell Mokhiber and Robert Weissman 363
"Greed Despoils Capitalism," Barbara Wilder 366
"The Upside of Downsizing," Art Buchwald 368
Questions to Guide Analysis 369

Unit 2 Our Body Images 371

"I'm a Barbie Girl," Karen Epstein 373
"Wearing Tights," from *Real Boys' Voices* 375
"Fat Girls (Don't) Dance," Sharleen Jonasson 377
"Just One Look," Kim Campbell 379
"The Muscle Mystique," Barbara Kingsolver 382
Questions to Guide Analysis 385

Unit 3 Poverty and Wealth 387

"Wealth Statistics Stack Up Unevenly,"
  Rick Montgomery   388
"What Is Poverty?," Jo Goodwin Parker   392
"Helping Binyam, When His Mother Won't,"
  Nicholas D. Kristof   396
"The Singer Solution to World Poverty," Peter Singer   398
"Are You Too Rich If Others Are Too Poor?,"
  Marjorie Kelly   403
Questions to Guide Analysis   405

Unit 4 Visual Rhetoric 407

"An Argument for the Superiority of Printed Media over Visual
  Media," Scott Aniol   408
"A Modern Perspective on Graffiti," Killian Tobin   409
"Learning to Love PowerPoint," David Byrne   412
"PowerPoint Is Evil," Edward Tufte   414
"Visual Culture and Health Posters: Anti-Smoking
  Campaigns," from *Profiles in Science*   416
Cartoons from the Time of the Spanish-American War   421
"American Progress," John Gast   424
Questions to Guide Analysis   425

Unit 5 Working in America 427

"All Work, No Play," Claudia Smith Brinson   428
"The Work Addict in the Family," Diane Fassel   431
"Other Factors More Important in Job Stress,"
  Melissa C. Stöppler   435
"A Working Community," Ellen Goodman   436
"Good-bye to the Work Ethic," Barbara Ehrenreich   438
From "*Nickel and Dimed: On (Not) Getting By in America*,"
  Barbara Ehrenreich   441
Questions to Guide Analysis   447

Credits   449
Index   457

Preface to the Instructor

Mirror Images: Reading and Writing Arguments addresses a practical trend in teaching college students about writing. The shift is to a more rhetorical approach: reading *and* writing arguments in varied contexts. To do so, the book acknowledges that arguments are not simply imposed on a reader, but that meaning is negotiated between reader and writer.

We understand the nature of reading and writing as mirror images of each other and believe students will benefit from a more intentional connection of these two processes than is available in most current argument texts. Using the method of analysis we offer, students can learn to analyze the written arguments of others by detecting the argument's rhetorical foundations and then, using the same process, learn to construct arguments in varied contexts for their own needs.

All writing falls within what might be described as a "transactional to expressive" continuum from the most informal of arguments (a job memo, for example) to moderately formal arguments (say, a letter to the editor of a newspaper) to more formal arguments (such as academic writing) even to more sophisticated narrative forms. To illustrate this range, we vary the examples of argument in the chapters—some are visual, some are humorous, some are very businesslike, some are academic, some are professional, and some are news related. We hope such diverse readings help students more readily transfer their experience of analyzing arguments in a classroom environment to the many critical arguments they will face in their personal and career settings.

To help students learn how comprehending a written argument in a particular context mirrors the manner in which its author composed it, we apply what we call the Argument Concept to analysis and development of arguments. The Argument Concept explicitly states, in very specific terms, the Focus, Reader, and Purpose of a given argument. Students will learn that writers make decisions concerning the structure and development of any piece of writing by carefully considering the focus for the piece, its intended reader, and its purpose (why the argument is written in the first place). Doing so, readers may then mirror this process when they *read* by identifying the Argument Concept (rhetorical foundations) of any given argument. The organization of the book is intended to help students create strong and convincing arguments (Part II) by first reading and analyzing them carefully (Part I), always emphasizing that the two processes are mirror images of each other.

xii *Preface*

STRUCTURE OF MIRROR IMAGES

Part I: Analyzing Argument

- Characterizes argument in a variety of contexts;
- Explains the necessity of focus, reader attention, and purpose in the context of argument by demonstrating the Argument Concept process;
- Explains classical approaches to argument (the classical "appeals," induction, deduction, and the Toulmin system);
- Demonstrates how arguments are typically constructed and how to avoid the pitfalls (specifically fallacies) that can discredit an argument;
- Provides extensive practice in analyzing written argument.

Part II: Developing Researched Arguments

- Offers extensive advice about selecting significant topics and modifying them to fit specific contexts;
- Provides suggestions and cautions associated with specific purposes of argument: arguing solutions, arguing for causes and/or effects, arguing quality, and arguing to maintain or change a policy;
- Demonstrates the process of envisioning a coherent argument and the sections necessary to satisfy the Argument Concept;
- Discusses methods, such as illustration, of developing sections of the argument and the use of outside source material, including a demonstration of integrating such material smoothly within the text;
- Discusses how to develop each section according to its specific purpose.

Part III: Documenting and Polishing an Argument

- Illustrates the difference between informal and formal documentation;
- Shows students how to make in-text citations and reference entries in both APA and MLA styles;
- Guides students through a careful process of deep revision;
- Provides a concise "punch list" for editing an argument for the most frequent grammatical and mechanical errors.

Part IV: Additional Readings for Analysis

- Includes five units of thematically organized readings. Readings are not pro-con, although a variety of perspectives are included. More than opposing arguments, the sets of readings illustrate the wide range of "angles" from which a writer might choose, given an interest in the general topic.

DISTINGUISHING FEATURES OF *MIRROR IMAGES*

- The book begins by demonstrating how argument fits into the scope of human communication, illustrating with examples from the most transactional of purposes (a business letter) to the very expressive and inferential

(narrative). Included in this introductory material are cartoons, pictures, and a discussion of art that provokes visual argument.
- To emphasize the reading/writing connection, this book uses a common process and vocabulary for both analysis and development of arguments, providing an explicit link between the two activities. The book weaves reading and writing together in the study of rhetoric.
- This text includes writing instruction in the context of argument, not as isolated skills.
- The concept of an active, not a passive, reader is central to the book's method. The student is introduced to the idea that reader and writer are negotiating meaning in an argument, that a reader is not an inert audience to which an argument is just "presented." Instead, the student learns how the writer must look at the potential reader as a partner in drawing conclusions about the topic and the argument. The book includes discussion of claims, evidence, reasons, opposition, concession, warrants, and fallacies of logic, but always with the emphasis on how these aspects of argument relate to an active reader's ability and willingness to comprehend the argument and to the tendency to interpret the argument in light of his or her own frame of reference.
- Students learn how to summarize various types of arguments by "reversing" the Argument Concept that the original writer used, resulting in a truly analytical summary rather than just a "narration" of the author's points.
- Students learn to categorize and/or define the different sections authors use to support their claims and to envision their own arguments by creating similar sets of sections.
- *Mirror Images* encourages the use of outside sources from the perspective of the *need demanded by specific purposes* rather than offering a "standalone" chapter on source use. However, the text includes detailed and illustrated sections on how to integrate material smoothly into text: when/why/how to quote, to paraphrase, and to summarize.
- A broad range of arguments (including student writing) throughout the text illustrates different purposes and methods of argument, from the ubiquitous political and popular cartoons to academic writing and sophisticated creative nonfiction.

PEDAGOGICAL FEATURES OF *MIRROR IMAGES*

Each chapter offers learning tools useful to students' comprehension of the chapter's main points:

- Chapter opening apparatus to help students read critically:
  - **Introductions** explain how analytical skills connect to and aid composing skills. These introductions also include connections to previous chapters.
  - **"Terms and Concepts to Watch For"** lists critical terms that students will encounter in each chapter. Within the chapter text, these terms are called out and defined.

- ○ **"Questions to Guide Your Reading"** alerts students to the significant chapter concepts.
- **Students at Work** in many chapters shows how students have grappled with argument concepts and strategies in their own writing practice.
- **Exercises** throughout each chapter offer opportunities for individual practice and mastery of each chapter's concepts as well as collaborative group activities.
- **Also Note . . .** boxes provide additional explanation of concepts and recursive connections to other parts of the text. Students learn additional skills and read specific examples of the book's primary concepts.
- **Argument in Action** boxes provide sample arguments (often on contemporary issues and narrative in structure) to enrich or offer alternative perspectives to samples within the text.
- **Discovering Your Own Arguments** writing prompts appear at the close of each chapter and encourage writing of varying length and complexity. In Part I, these move from short transactional suggestions to more academic arguments; in Part II, these further the development of major research-based arguments.
- **Reflections on the Chapter** concludes each chapter by highlighting the importance of the chapter's concepts to students' own writing processes and by previewing the next chapter's topics.

SUPPLEMENTS

- The Instructor's Manual that accompanies *Mirror Images*, written by the authors, features an introductory pedagogical section with hints on teaching argument, suggestions for introducing each chapter, chapter overviews with suggested enhancement activities, brief discussions of the projects included in each chapter, and suggested responses to the exercises in the text. The authors also provide two sample syllabi, one following the order of the text and one demonstrating additional options for course organization.
- MyCompLab is a Web application that offers comprehensive and integrated resources for every writer. With MyCompLab, students can learn from interactive tutorials and instruction; practice and develop their skills with grammar, writing, and research exercises; share and collaborate their writing with peers; and receive comments on their writing from instructors and tutors. Go to http://www.mycomplab.com to register for these premiere resources and much more!

Preface to the Student

We contend that the analysis and writing of arguments (as mirror images of one another) frame one of the central and most productive of human endeavors. You will find as the chapters of this textbook unfold that argument occurs in myriad contexts, from business letters to political cartoons, to critiques of art, to formal academic writing. Truly, we are surrounded by argument in our everyday lives, and our efforts to understand the arguments of others and to create arguments as we need them are important to become educated citizens.

Mirror Images: Reading and Writing Arguments will show you that reading and writing are mirror images of one another in the quest that is human communication. This textbook shows you how to use both processes in an integrated manner to understand what you read and to compose with vitality and power.

Whether you realize it, reading and writing are not fundamentally different processes. Think of reading and writing as business transactions. As a reader, you read what an author says, but you do not merely "buy" or adopt the author's ideas without first comparing them to what you already know about the author's topic and analyzing the soundness of the author's presentation. In a sense, then, you actually *compose* meaning even as you read. Thus, you accept or reject the author's ideas. In other words, an author does not (and really cannot) just lay out his or her ideas with the expectation that you will automatically accept them. Instead (and this is a crucial concept within this text), you *negotiate* meaning with the author: accepting some points, rejecting others, considering counter arguments. In the end, you will have formed some relationship with the author with varying degrees of understanding, agreement, or disagreement.

As a writer, then, you learn that to produce sound arguments, you must carefully consider not only what you think and believe about your topic, but also how to present your ideas to a reader in a negotiated manner. What does my reader know already and value about my issue? What evidence might I offer that best supports the conclusions I have drawn? What opposing viewpoints may I have to acknowledge (negotiate) to assure my reader of how reasonable and fair I am when it comes to my issue? And believe it or not, you will improve your abilities to answer such questions by thoroughly understanding how argument works by reading the arguments of others.

To help you gain expertise in reading and writing arguments, we will show you how the Argument Concept allows you to analyze the logical foundations of any argument you read and then how to write your own arguments with similar techniques. The Argument Concept states very explicitly just what the focus of an argument is, who the intended reader is, and what the purpose is—in both the arguments you read and in those you write. In other words, the best reading and writing advice anyone can offer you is to approach your communication tasks by never losing sight of *what the main point is, for whom it is meant, and why.* Every decision you make—from the evidence an argument presents, to the examples it offers, to the very tone of its language—is guided by the Argument Concept that serves as the argument's basis.

So, *Mirror Images* begins by defining argument and how it works and then moves to showing you how to analyze arguments of all types. Then, we show you how to find meaningful topics in your life and how to apply your understanding of arguments to those you will write yourself. We show you how to envision the "whole picture" of an argument, how to develop it in reasonable and interesting manners, how to avoid the thinking errors that lurk in everyone's mind, and then how to polish that argument so that it presents your ideas with accuracy, clarity, and reason. Understanding argument is a journey, to be sure. But we will guide you as you define your goals and begin to understand the steps it will take to achieve them.

ACKNOWLEDGMENTS

We would like to thank the following reviewers for their frank and professional advice about *Mirror Images*. The book simply would not be the same without their guidance and suggestions: Jeffrey Andelora, Mesa Community College; Jo Ann Buck, Guilford Technical Community College; Michael A. Burke, Southern Illinois University Edwardsville; Vincent Casaregola, Saint Louis University; Emily Crawford, University of South Carolina; Paula Eschliman, Richland College; Phyllis Frus, Hawaii Pacific University; Judith G. Gardner, University of Texas at San Antonio; Diana C. Gingo, Collin County Community College; Kay Heck, Walters State Community College; Sarah A. Quirk, Waubonsee Community College; Efstathia A. Siegel, Montgomery College; Patricia Webb, Arizona State University; and Sue Carter Wood, Bowling Green State University.

Also, we appreciate our competent—and cheerful!—editors and production staff, particularly Lauren Finn, who stuck with us from beginning to completion, Lisa Kinne, and two very skilled and patient permissions coordinators, Jody Potter and Caroline Gloodt.

Our work together has been a pleasure; we are grateful for our continuing friendship and good humor throughout the project. This congenial spirit could not have existed without the support of our families, and we recognize and appreciate their unflinching encouragement.

Anne M. Machin
Russ Ward

PART I

Analyzing Argument

Part I of this text illustrates that arguments are all around us. We are not talking about the heated words exchanged between you and the person who crashed into your new car, or the confrontation you had with a coworker about whose turn it was to take the late shift. Instead, Part I will demonstrate that real, productive argument occurs when differing, *though reasonable*, viewpoints intersect: in your personal and professional lives, with family and friends, and even within your own mind as you attempt to draw significant conclusions about our ever-changing world.

Thus, Part I of this textbook demonstrates a number of ways to understand the nature of real argument, how it is typically constructed, and how to analyze arguments in a variety of contexts. This entire section will help you read arguments better as you prepare to write (and speak) arguments that you will face in future personal, academic, and professional venues.

CHAPTER

1

A Brief Introduction to Argument

Chapter 1 defines what *argument* is and what it is not. It will help you see that not only is argument an integral part of all of our lives all of the time, but also that it serves as a method to better our understanding of the significant issues we face. Perhaps the world would be an easier place if all people agreed on everything. But they don't. Based on their own experiences, values, education, and other factors, people form differing perspectives—sometimes vastly differing—about how the world should work. We hope you learn that expecting and accepting such differences will actually *increase* your power to think critically and to write powerfully. And, after all, isn't the world a more interesting place when people form varying conclusions about the exact same issue?

TERMS AND CONCEPTS TO WATCH FOR
- Argument
- Perspective
- Confrontation

QUESTIONS TO GUIDE YOUR READING
- How does argument differ from confrontation?
- How do people identify significant issues, form claims, and defend those claims?
- Can you discern argument in various contexts?

3

- Why is it important to recognize varied perspectives on an issue?
- Is there a "rubric" or "plan of action" useful to analyzing arguments?

When Hurricane Katrina battered the southern coast of the United States in 2005, it destroyed entire cities and the lives of those cities' residents. For a heart-wrenching five days, the residents of New Orleans and other cities endured floodwaters as high as 20 feet; watched their houses wash away; worried about the well-being of loved ones; and suffered without adequate food, water, power, and shelter. Where, the desperate survivors wondered, were the rescuers to snatch them from rooftops or whisk them to dry ground? Why was it taking federal and local agencies so long to provide needed food and water? Why did it take five days before anyone seemed to care?

So, the argument began.

Some people argued that because most of Katrina's victims were poor, African American, or both, federal and local rescue efforts were not deemed high priority. These people asserted that had those stranded in the hurricane's aftermath been wealthy, for example, rescue teams would have shown up overnight with boatloads of food and water, electrical generators, and the like.

ARGUMENT IN ACTION   **How to Deal with the Aftermath of Hurricane Katrina**

Many people like Louisiana Governor Kathleen Blanco and Mayor Ray Nagin, pictured here offering suggestions on what should be done shortly after Hurricane Katrina hit New Orleans, argued for different plans to help citizens and reconstruct the city.

Others argued that the Federal Emergency Management Agency's (FEMA) delayed response exposed glaring inadequacies in the country's ability to deal with large-scale emergencies. Such lack of planning and organization on the part of federal and local officials, they claimed, even pointed to the country's true lack of preparedness in the event of terrorist strikes.

Some people argued that the top five officials of FEMA were only political cronies, not professionally capable of handling emergencies on the scale of Katrina. The FEMA officials' jobs, some said, were more political gifts than acknowledgment of their skills in organizing the supplies, personnel, and money that Katrina victims needed quickly.

Still others argued that the response from FEMA and local authorities was not politically or socially motivated (or even unorganized), but that the sheer scale of the destruction left by Katrina was incomprehensible, so much so that few, if any, people really knew *how* to respond.

The debate will likely continue into the future, but the point here is that all four viewpoints above demonstrate *argument in action*: a significant issue or problem arises, and different people reach different conclusions (and viewpoints) about resolving it. Arguments such as this occur all around us. And until ample debate has occurred—and sufficient evidence gathered—no one viewpoint will take center stage. In fact, it is quite possible in significant argumentative issues that people will reach some compromise of viewpoints in a fair and reasonable manner.

Visual Rhetoric...
AN EMERGING FIELD

Visual rhetoric is a newly established field of study focusing on how images communicate in similar and different ways than spoken or written texts. The study of visual rhetoric is a currently emerging field, although the power of images has long been recognized, from the mesmerizing prehistoric cave paintings in Lascaux, France, to the contemporary interest in Japanese anime. Visual *language* comes in many different forms: cartoons, business diagrams, flowcharts, advertising images, animation, streaming video—an ever-widening array of moving and still images. You may be speaking this "language" when you pick a particular font to represent an idea in a certain way, or to appeal to your specific reader; the font has a certain personality that you want to project.

The study of visual rhetoric includes asking many critical questions of this language such as the following:

- Can images represent feeling we can't put into words?
- Do images communicate more or less clearly than word text?
- What is left out in an image, and what does that signify?

- How believable are images?
- What different cultural interpretations are possible of a given image?
- What is the publication context of an image, and what does that have to do with the meaning?
- How is background used to focus the message of an image?
- How does writing change in a contemporary, visually oriented society?
- What role do images play in a particular field of study?

Throughout this book, you will see occasional images in "Visual Rhetoric" boxes. The associated text will ask you to think of the nature of the message and how the image communicates that message. Also, the articles and questions in Unit 4 in Part IV (pp. 407–426) investigate some issues in the field of visual rhetoric. This attention to the power and method of images in your environment may help you "read" your world more critically. The images around you are making arguments.

Although we have provided this cartoon as an example of the natural inclination for people to argue, there are other messages in this image also. What does the apparent age and relationship difference between the two characters imply about arguing? Note the body language of each character. What message is that sending? Is it meaningful that the dad is working and the son is not, and if not, why did the artist draw them this way? What other questions might you ask about the messages in this image?

To be fair, we acknowledge that the context of some arguments encourages a desire to "win." For example, opposing attorneys in a trial, politicians running for office, or people writing letters of complaint—to name a few—present their arguments with the intent that others will acquiesce and agree with the arguer's point of view. Nonetheless, we hope you approach argument with the sense that it is a process of understanding the varied perspectives any significant issue allows. After all, no prosecuting attorney in a murder case, for example, would enter a courtroom without a thorough understanding of what the defense team for the accused person intended to do. As in all arguments, such preparation helps you not to be one-sided or naïve as you work toward your conclusions. Then, once you believe your conclusions are reasonably sound, you can defend them as well as you can.

ARGUMENT AS A THOUGHT PROCESS

> **ARGUMENT** is a means of determining a reasonable perspective and supporting it effectively.

You may find over the course of your in-class experiences that argument serves as one of the main tools of your learning. In reasonable discussions of issues, you get the chance to "try out" your ideas and opinions in an atmosphere of classmates and professors. Let's say that in a media course, the discussion turns to whether journalists, aside from opinion columnists, have the right to insert their own opinions into news stories. You argue that since journalists are only human—and are often required to get information quickly in order to meet a deadline—occasional opinions on their part are acceptable. But then you listen to others arguing that the news media in this country are powerful and may possess the means to influence public opinion on important political and social matters instead of merely reporting the "facts" of a story. Perhaps the "journalists are only human" argument begins to sound a little flimsy, and you think that maybe you need to think further about your stance. If so, you have discovered one of the highlights of reasonable argument—that the consideration of differing viewpoints helps us understand issues better. In his essay, "The Beauty of Argument," John Leo contends that "arguing can rescue us from our own half-formed opinions." So, in the classroom and elsewhere, you find that argument opens a door to understanding. In his book, *The Revolt of the Elites*, Christopher Lasch once said that only through argument do "we come to understand what we know and what we still need to learn" and that "we come to know our own minds only by explaining ourselves to others" through reasonable debate. Ultimately, for example, the intense and long debate about the response (or lack thereof) to Hurricane Katrina will help us to form future policies about responding to large-scale emergencies.

> A **PERSPECTIVE** is a personal or group view about (or interpretation of) an issue; generally, multiple perspectives exist for any significant issue.

The *thinking* process of argument, therefore, requires you to discover issues that need your attention, to gather and examine evidence on those issues, to draw reasonable conclusions from the evidence, and then to defend those conclusions by revealing the evidence to others. The *writing* (or speaking) of an argument is similar. You alert your reader to an issue's importance (much as it came to your own attention), state your conclusion (often referred to as a "claim" in written argument), and then provide your reader with the evidence that led you to your claim—in other words, defending your stance as reasonable.

SOME OF THE MANY CONTEXTS FOR ARGUMENT

Let's examine some of the contexts in which argument swirls around you. Our point here is to illustrate just how pervasive argument is in everyday life. Humans find numerous motives to argue because, we contend, argument is a central human endeavor. To analyze the arguments they encounter regularly, many people use a reasonably straightforward approach, some form of "rubric" or "plan of action." For example, they may ask questions like these:

- What focus on what issue does the arguer pinpoint? (*Focus*)
- What audience does the arguer target? (*Reader*)
- What does the arguer wish to accomplish? (*Purpose*) To sell a product? To support a particular political stance? To move others to action on a social issue? To right a wrong? And so forth.
- How effective are the arguer's reasons and evidence to support his or her focus and to achieve his or her purpose for the intended audience?

Put another way, all of us plan or analyze an argument by first understanding its three primary components: focus, reader, and purpose. Then, we must take the next step in our planning or analysis by evaluating the *quality* of the argument's support—its reasons, evidence, examples, use of authorities, and so forth. Such a four-step plan of action gives us the tools we need to devise our own arguments and to assess the quality of those put together by others. As this textbook proceeds, you will note our emphasis on the first three components (we call this the *Argument Concept*), but we will also provide you with the necessary means to evaluate any argument's persuasive appeal: the qualities of its claim, reasons, evidence, concessions, and rebuttals.

What follows next, then, are samples of arguments from varied contexts and examples of how the previous questions (the "plan of action" for analysis) will help you analyze the arguments you encounter, followed by opportunities for your own personal practice.

Argument in a Personal Business Context

Ms. Marcia Tomlinson, Director, Customer Service
NewSouth Communications
4182 West 111th Street
Fort Worth, Texas

Dear Ms. Tomlinson,

1   I wish to challenge the charges on my recent cell phone bill from your company. In March of this year, I received a bill for $317.00. This sharply contrasts with my usual monthly rate of $52.59. Your company

alleges that I exceeded my purchased minutes and made calls outside of my roaming area. Both allegations are false. So, after repeated conversations with your billing representations and receiving no satisfaction, I am writing to you.

2   My current cell phone contract with NewSouth (account #N4331-65998) allows me 1000 minutes per month either in phone or text messages. I hardly could have exceeded the 1000 minutes in March since I was in the hospital for 17 days (without access to my cell phone) and used the phone sparingly the rest of the month. My own records show that I called my mother three times and made a number of other personal calls, but taken together, these calls amount to fewer than 120 minutes for the entire month. How is it possible that your company claims I made more than 1000 minutes in calls?

3   NewSouth also claims that a number of my calls in March occurred outside of my roaming area. However, since I traveled very little during March (I was in the hospital, remember) and only twice made calls outside of the Fort Worth area—both well within the roaming area cited in the brochure that came with my cell phone when I purchased it—I fail to see how I was outside my allowable roaming area. I have included a copy of the brochure with this letter as well as the locations from which I made the two calls.

4   Ms. Tomlinson, surely you can understand my frustration with your company's latest charges. Please review my billing record and correct the situation, or I will be forced to contact the FCC and drop my account with NewSouth. I look forward to your reply.

Sincerely,

Thomas J. Frankel

> **CONFRONTATION** and **PERSUASION** *are not necessarily the same thing. An argument need not be confrontational to be persuasive. An argument is forceful when it provides well-documented evidence in a civil tone and clear presentation. Confrontation can often be uncivil and emotional rather than reasoned, subverting the writer's efforts.*

- What focus on what issue does the arguer pinpoint? (*Focus*)

Frankel focuses his letter on what he believes to be incorrect charges on his cell phone. Note that he sticks to this focus throughout; he does not wander into other issues connected to his cell phone use: quality of the phone itself, demeanor of NewSouth's customer service representatives, difficulty of obtaining online help, and so forth.

- What audience does the arguer target? (*Reader*)

Frankel has an obvious audience in mind. He now writes specifically to the director of customer service for NewSouth. His decision to focus upon this reader comes from a lack of satisfactory response from lower-level customer representatives. The decision is appropriate, since Marcia Tomlinson appears to be the next person in the "command chain" at NewSouth.

- What does the arguer wish to accomplish? (Purpose) To sell a product? To support a particular political stance? To move others to action on a social issue? To right a wrong?

Frankel's purpose in his letter is to complain about what he believes are exorbitant and miscalculated charges on his monthly cell phone bill. But his purpose extends beyond mere complaint; he wants the charges reduced to reflect his use of the phone in accordance with the company's written policies on roaming and minutes used (in other words, to right a wrong).

- How effective are the arguer's reasons and evidence to support his or her focus and to achieve his or her *purpose* for the intended audience?

Frankel's reasons and evidence are quite specific: His phone use was limited by his hospital stay (he even cites the number of days) and the calls alleged as outside the roaming area were actually within his cell phone contract. Note, too, that he uses an emotional appeal in his letter by pleading "you can understand my frustration." Such use of specific evidence (and a sincere, mature tone) to support his claim of unfair phone charges makes Frankel's letter effective and likely to serve his purpose.

Exercise 1
Collaborative Analysis: Analyzing an Argument in a Business Context

Read the following letter and analyze its effectiveness by applying the four-part "plan of action" demonstrated above. Be prepared to discuss your analysis with the class.

July 12, 2007
Mr. Marshall Langdon, Director
Financial Aid Services

Dear Mr. Langdon,

1   At the end of Fall semester 2006, I was placed on academic probation, and my scholarship was suspended because my GPA had dropped to 1.9. To keep my scholarship, I must maintain at least a 3.0. Problems with my family's business and a nasty breakup with my

2   During the Spring semester of 2007, I earned three A's and one B in my courses and raised my overall GPA to 3.15; however, when I checked to see if my scholarship would be reinstated, I was told by one of your employees, Marilyn Fansco, that no decision had been made to reinstate my scholarship and wouldn't be until a meeting on October 15 of this year. But since classes begin in late August, a meeting on October 15 will be too late to allow my scholarship money to help me pay for Fall semester tuition and fees, and I cannot afford school without that money.

3   I am asking that you reconsider my scholarship reinstatement before classes begin this August. My only options would be to delay attending classes until Spring term (if my money is reinstated) or to attend another college with cheaper tuition and fees, neither of which do I really want to do. Is it possible that you and your staff (with the exception of Ms. Fansco, who I thought was really rude on the phone) could consider my situation in time for Fall classes? I have worked hard to raise my GPA and think I should regain my scholarship. I would appreciate your looking into this for me and letting me know either by phone or email what your decision is. Thank you.

Sincerely,
Jessica Olivares

Argument in an Advertising Context

When you think about it, advertisements of all types are actually mini-arguments, fast and furious attempts to get your attention, claim the merits of a product, and then offer reasons (primarily, perhaps, of the emotional variety) why you should buy a product or service. One idea advertisements make clear is that evidence can be primarily visual. Advertisers often spend little space providing concrete, written evidence to support their claims that you should purchase their products, preferring instead to let visual images do the work. Since we live in such a visual society, such evidence can be potent indeed. Convincing or not, advertisements are yet another form of argument. Recognizing them as such allows you to evaluate an advertisement's appeals and to form your own response to them.

Consider the following advertisement for the Sony Walkman W800i, one of the precursors of the more advanced iPod and iPhone. At the time the Walkman was first marketed, the Sony Corporation quite naturally touted it as the latest thing in music storage and retrieval, focusing its advertising on what was then new and exciting technology. We have applied the four-part "plan of action" to analyze the ad. When you get to Exercise Two, follow the four-part plan in a way similar to our analysis of the Walkman ad.

12 Chapter 1 *A Brief Introduction to Argument*

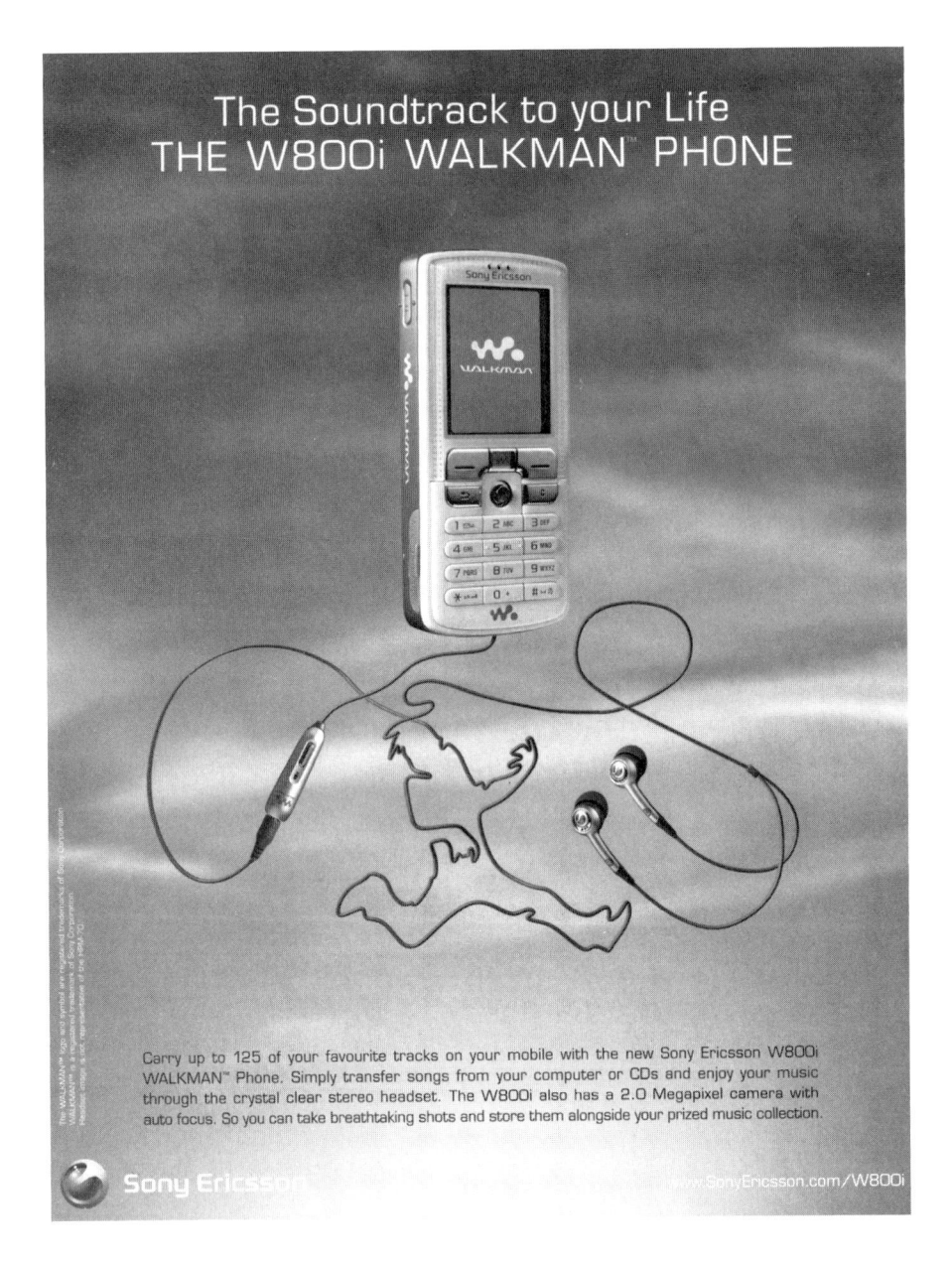

> **The Soundtrack to your Life**
> **THE W800i WALKMAN™ PHONE**
>
> Carry up to 125 of your favourite tracks on your mobile with the new Sony Ericsson W800i WALKMAN™ Phone. Simply transfer songs from your computer or CDs and enjoy your music through the crystal clear stereo headset. The W800i also has a 2.0 Megapixel camera with auto focus. So you can take breathtaking shots and store them alongside your prized music collection.
>
> Sony Ericsson www.SonyEricsson.com/W800i

- What focus on what issue does the arguer pinpoint? (*Focus*)

The Sony Walkman ad focuses on the current and growing desire for people to have easy and portable access to their favorite music and photography.

- What audience does the arguer target? (*Reader*)

This ad targets anyone who wants convenient access to music, but probably more specifically, the ad pinpoints younger people, those who Sony may believe will have the most interest in and purchasing potential for such a device. The focus on younger people is most evident in the air guitar player outlined within the Walkman's wire.

- What does the arguer wish to accomplish? (*Purpose*) To sell a product? To support a particular political stance? To move others to action on a social issue? To right a wrong? And so forth.

The purpose of most advertising, of course, is to sell something, and the Sony Walkman ad intends to do just that. The company wants you to believe that the Walkman is the "Soundtrack to your Life" and will serve your portable music needs better than other electronic devices produced by other companies. Note, as well, that advertisements of this type often imply a problem-solution purpose, too. You have a need for easily accessed music? We have the solution.

- How effective are the arguer's reasons and evidence to support his or her focus and to achieve his or her purpose for the intended audience?

The primary evidence for purchasing a Sony Walkman attempts to give you a feeling of "science" or "numbers." For example, the ad mentions that you can store 125 songs on the W800i and also has a 2.0 Megapixel camera.

Some of the language in this ad is interesting as well, especially from its attempts at appealing to the emotions (see Chapter 3). The ad says you can "simply" transfer songs from a computer or CD to the Walkman to enjoy "your" music through a "crystal clear" headset. The camera feature offers "auto focus" so you can take "breathtaking" photos to store with your "prized" music collection. While such emotionally tempting language is common in advertising, you should note that it doesn't really provide any concrete evidence for purchasing a product.

Visual Rhetoric...
IMAGES IN THE SONY WALKMAN AD

The visual argument is interesting in this advertisement, too. In written and spoken language, we often use similes ("The wind howled *like* a demon through the night") and metaphors ("The wind was a demon howling through the night") to compare things we are explaining to other things that might be more familiar to our audience. Visual images use the comparisons, also. In the Sony Walkman ad, an air guitarist is formed by the device's sound wire. It would seem that the ad wants you to believe that when you listen to your favorite music on the Walkman that the device, music, and person become "one." (Many people might recognize too that the air guitarist also suggests the ad's targeted audience.) The theme of "oneness" is likewise suggested by the blurring of earth and sky in the ad's background color scheme. What other aspects of the visual language in this ad do you find interesting?

14 Chapter 1 *A Brief Introduction to Argument*

Exercise 2
Collaborative Analysis: Arguments in Advertising
In small groups, analyze the following advertisement using the four-part plan modeled above. Discuss your findings with the class.

> NOTHING MAKES YOU THINK OF THE
> FUTURE LIKE HOLDING IT IN YOUR ARMS.
> WE LIVE WHERE YOU LIVE.

The wonder of being a new parent includes wondering how to plan for your new family's future. Do you have the life insurance coverage you need? To help you be absolutely sure, look to someone who's been there for you right from the start.

LIKE A GOOD NEIGHBOR   STATE FARM IS THERE.™

Providing Insurance and Financial Services

For life insurance, call your neighborhood State Farm agent, or visit *statefarm.com*®

Argument in a Social Commentary Context
Truly one of the most common forms of argument is that which expresses a need for social change, a judgment about social trends and values, or the causes and effects of particular social problems. You encounter such arguments in newspaper editorials, journal columns, classroom lectures and discussions about social and political movements, books about political trends and politicians, and so forth.

Exercise 3
Individual Analysis and Practice: Responding to Social Comment
Mike Rosen is an editorial writer for *The Rocky Mountain News* in Denver, Colorado. When you read this editorial, use the four-step process demonstrated previously to analyze what Rosen attempts to accomplish and his effectiveness in

> **Visual Rhetoric...**
> ARGUMENT IN A SOCIAL COMMENTARY CONTEXT
>
> [Graph showing index values (1973 = 100) from 1973 to 2003 for five education levels: Advanced degree, College, Some college, High school, Less than high school. Y-axis ranges from 75 to 125.]
>
> This graph from the Economic Policy Institute appears on the Web site of the Federal Reserve Bank of San Francisco. (Other graphs and further information on income inequality in the United States are also available at the Bank Web site: www.frbsf.org.) What arguments might be generated from this data regarding income and education levels?

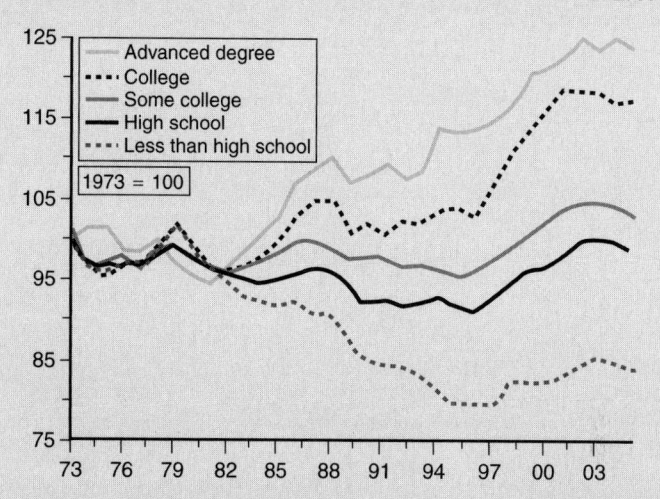

doing so. Note, too, that he acknowledges the argument of those who may oppose his stance on senior citizens' driving rights.

Write a short response to Rosen's editorial in which you counter his argument about senior citizens and their driving. Offer reasons and evidence that Rosen's solution is biased, mistaken, or shortsighted—even if you essentially agree with what he says.

Road Tests for Seniors
Mike Rosen

1   Last week, 86-year-old Russell Weller lost control of his car and plowed into a busy Santa Monica, Calif., farmers market, killing 10 people and injuring dozens more. Weller apparently stepped on the gas pedal instead of the brake, became confused and continued to mow down pedestrians for two-and-a-half blocks before his car came to a halt.

2   By all accounts, Weller is a wonderful old gent, beloved by all. Although, in recent years, he's had several run-ins with a neighbor's retaining wall and his own garage. This tragic accident has renewed calls for periodic road testing of aging drivers. Such a proposal failed in the California legislature three years ago amid protests from powerful senior citizen groups.

3   Opposition from that quarter is not surprising. Their concerns for the public safety could be expected to take a back seat to the interests of their dues-paying members who would be directly affected. Now don't get me wrong. I have nothing against seniors, as I hope to be one myself some day. In fact, I'm a lot closer to 65 than 25. I can also appreciate the value of a driver's license to a 75- or 80-year-old, tenaciously holding on to his mobility and independence. I know, in similar circumstances, I wouldn't want to surrender mine.

4   On the other hand, middle-aged children of octogenarians have agonized over the ordeal of separating granddad from his car when it becomes obvious that, behind the wheel, he's a hazard to himself and everyone else on the road—or sidewalk for that matter.

5   Twenty-one states currently have some kind of age-based restrictions on driver's licenses for the elderly, including special renewal requirements, vision testing and mandatory road tests. The point isn't to ban all or even most seniors from the road, just to weed out the relative few who don't have the good sense to ban themselves. It seems like a perfectly reasonable policy.

6   In Illinois and New Hampshire, those over 75 must take a road test when renewing their licenses. Some seniors claim it's illegal to discriminate based on age. Of course it isn't. The airlines, for example, legally enforce a mandatory retirement age. At the other end of the scale, 14-year-olds aren't allowed to drive, drink or vote.

7   Age-based discrimination is illegal only when it's arbitrary. Common sense tells us that reflexes and judgment deteriorate with age. A periodic test of driving skills beyond a specified age could objectively determine this. No one is saying that driver's licenses should be yanked capriciously just because of advancing age.

8   Some individual 80-year-olds are, no doubt, more competent and skillful drivers than some 20-year-olds. But driving on the public roadways isn't a constitutionally protected right. Under the law, it's regarded as a regulated privilege administered by the states. We also legally and rationally discriminate against blind people who might like to drive.

9   The American Association of Retired Persons (AARP) opposes the singling out of super seniors for road tests. Others demand that if seniors must take such tests, everyone should, too, especially younger drivers who generally have higher rates of traffic violations and accidents.

10   Interesting, but unworkable. We already have a process to revoke the licenses of drivers who accumulate too many moving violations. Given the already long lines at motor vehicle offices, imagine adding the burden of regularly road testing *every* driver in the country. It would be too expensive, too time consuming and not effective, in any event.

11   The AARP advocates targeted road-testing of drivers in a number of proven risk categories. That wouldn't work either. Your typical reckless driver would simply contrive to be on his best behavior while accompanied by a Department of Motor Vehicles agent during the five-minute road test, and then revert to his worst practices when returning to the highway with his freshly renewed license.

12   The point, here, is to test for discernible, impaired physical competence, not temporarily disguisable bad attitude.
13   If you're still not persuaded, spend a week driving in south Florida and get back to me.

Exercise 4
Collaborative Analysis: Responding to Social Comment

In his *Newsweek* commentary, "Poetry Is Dead. Does Anybody Really Care?" author Bruce Wexler argues that poetry, as a means of literary expression and format for social change, has run its course in American culture. Read the article using the four-step process and find Wexler's reason for the decline of poetry. As a class, be prepared to discuss whether or not you agree. Note, too, where he concedes points to those who may disagree with his stance.

Poetry Is Dead. Does Anybody Really Care?
Bruce Wexler

1   It is difficult to imagine a world without movies, plays, novels and music, but a world without poems doesn't have to be imagined. I find it disturbing that no one I know has cracked open a book of poetry in decades and that I, who once spent countless hours reading contemporary poets like Lowell and Berryman, can no longer even name a living poet.

2   All this started to bother me when heiress Ruth Lilly made an unprecedented donation of $100 million to *Poetry Magazine* in November. An article published on the Poetry International Web site said critics and poets agreed that the gift "could change the face of American poetry."

3   Don't these critics and poets realize that their art form is dead? Perhaps not. They probably also don't realize that people like me helped kill it.

4   In high school, I, like most of my classmates, hated the poetry unit in English class that surfaced annually with the same grim regularity as the gymnastics unit in physical education. Just as I was a good athlete who detested the parallel bars, I was an avid reader who despised rhymed and rhythmic writing. Plowing through tangled symbol and allusion, I wondered why the damn poets couldn't just say what they meant.

5   Then I went to college and at some point, I got it. Maybe it was when I was infatuated with some girl and read "I Knew a Woman" by Theodore Roethke: "I knew a woman, lovely in her bones/When small birds sighed, she would sigh back at them." Or maybe it happened when I read Keats's odes or Eliot's "Prufrock" or that haunting line in Frost: "I have been one acquainted with the night." For the next 10 years or so, I was hooked. I read poetry, wrote it and recited verse to impress dates.

6   And then my interest waned. On the surface, I suppose it was because I had other interests that demanded my time and attention: I got married, had children, pursued my career, bought a house. With

apologies to Frost, I began to find more relevance in articles about interest rates than essays on the sprung rhythm of Hopkins.

7   Society, too, was changing in a way that did not favor the reading of poetry. From the Me Generation of the '70s to the get-rich-quick '80s, our culture became intensely prosaic. Ambiguity, complexity and paradox fell out of favor. We embraced easily defined goals and crystal-clear communication (Ronald Reagan was president, presiding over the literalization of America). Fewer politicians seemed to quote contemporary poets in speeches, and the relatively small number of name-brand, living American poets died or faded from view.

8   By the '90s, it was all over. If you doubt this statement, consider that poetry is the only art form where the number of people creating it is far greater than the number of people appreciating it. Anyone can write a bad poem. To appreciate a good one, though, takes knowledge and commitment. As a society, we lack this knowledge and commitment. People don't possess the patience to read a poem 20 times before the sound and sense of it takes hold. They aren't willing to let the words wash over them like a wave, demanding instead for the meaning to flow clearly and quickly. They want narrative-driven forms, stand alone art that doesn't require an understanding of the larger context.

9   I, too, want these things. I am part of a world that apotheosizes [glorifies] the trendy, and poetry is just about as untrendy as it gets. I want to read books with buzz—in part because I make my living as a ghostwriter of and collaborator on books—and I can't remember the last book of poetry that created even a dying mosquito's worth of hum. I am also lazy, and poetry takes work.

10   In my worst moments, I blame the usual suspects for my own failings: the mainstream media, the Internet, the fast-food mentality. If it weren't for the pernicious influence of blah, blah, blah . . . Ultimately, though, there's no one to blame. Poetry is designed for an era when people valued the written word and had the time and inclination to possess it in its highest form.

11   I really do believe that poetry is the highest form of writing. Read Yeats's "The Wild Swans at Coole," Whitman's "When Lilacs Last in the Dooryard Bloom'd," Thomas's "Fern Hill," and you'll experience the true power of art. They touch the heart and the head in ways that moviemakers (our current artistic high priests) can only dream of.

12   April was National Poetry Month, a fact I know only because it was noted in my younger daughter's school newsletter. I celebrated by finding out the name of our poet laureate (Billy Collins) and reading one of his poems. This may not seem like much, but I have television shows to watch, best sellers to read and Web sites to visit before I sleep.

Argument in an Art Context

In his weekly column for *The Rocky Mountain News* (Denver), critic Mike Pearson reviews the movie *Assault on Precinct 13*. You will note that Pearson offers his readers, as do most critics of various art forms, a brief review of the movie's plot and characters. He even uses an analogy of a wagon train under attack to give readers a sense of the drama and action in the film. Note, then, where Pearson's actual critique (*argument*) of the movie begins with his defense of the quality of the edgy action in it. Where does Pearson offer a concession about the quality of the movie? Use the four-step process to analyze Pearson's evaluation of the movie. If you have seen this film, would you agree or disagree with Pearson's assessment? Why?

"Assault on Precinct 13"
Mike Pearson

1. Looking for a movie that embraces ferocity over finesse?
2. Check out *Assault on Precinct 13*, a visceral remake of the 1976 John Carpenter thriller about a big-city police station under siege on New Year's Eve. Ethan Hawke is the police captain charged with shutting down the old station. He's expecting a smooth transition, until a snowstorm forces a police transport to detour to Precinct 13, and temporarily deposit the city's most wanted man (Laurence Fishburne). He's a drug dealer extraordinaire. He's also in bed with some corrupt cops, which means just when Hawke and crew think the night can't get any worse, people start shooting at them. People with badges.
3. Think of a wagon train pinned down by hostiles and you get the tone of *Assault*, which never defers to a scalpel when a machete is handy. Everything is over-the-top. Which was clearly the point of Carpenter's original B-movie (set in Los Angeles and featuring gang member villains not cops), here given a steroid injection.
4. Hawke's cop is fidgety yet heroic. Fishburne's drug lord is dapper and vicious. John Leguizamo as an unstable con, and Brian Dennehy as a crusty desk sergeant anchor the large supporting cast.
5. The central conceit: How long before the outgunned cops inside the station arm their prisoners?
6. Granted, they're not doing Shakespeare (the dialogue is formula at best), and there's nothing nuanced about the acting. Somebody told the performers to emote like it's the last job of their lives and they complied.
7. On the other hand, things get blown up real good. Once the shooting starts, *Assault on Precinct 13* doesn't let up for nearly an hour. Throw in the claustrophobia factor—this jail has too many entry points—and you find yourself more entertained than you might expect. Forget subtlety; director Jean-Francois Richet is all about relentless. If you like your cop dramas violent and profane, you'll like this one a lot.

In 2002, the movie *Frida* was nominated for several Academy Awards. The movie documented the life and art of Frida Kahlo, a Mexican artist and powerful woman of the early 1900s who dealt with great pain and suffering from a terrible bus accident, and who had a tempestuous relationship with her husband, Diego Rivera, himself an important artist. Study the following painting and the argument excerpt that follows.

You will see that the assessment of the painting is clearly a statement about Kahlo, not just a neutral analysis of the work.

Analysis of *Self-Portrait with Cropped Hair*
Sarah M. Lowe

1   Kahlo . . . explores the social construct of "woman" in *Self-Portrait with Cropped Hair* from 1940. She puts forth not an analysis of her own identity, but an exegesis of the cultural definition of femininity. For what Kahlo eliminates from her self-image are the social trappings of womanhood: long hair, dresses, and even modest posture. In light of the proscription against cross-dressing that dates at least to Biblical scripture

Frida Kahlo The Museum of Modern Art, New York

[Deuteronomy 22:5], and in light of the claim of social anthropologists that clothing not only grants, but produces social meaning, this image of transgression is astoundingly daring. Wearing an oversized man's suit, holding a pair of scissors where a "lady" would hold a fan, looking directly at the viewer, Kahlo challenges the viewer to see her as a woman. Ever conscious of the meaning of costume, Kahlo's deliberate refusal to acquiesce to conventional modes of dress signals her declaration of independence. By adapting the trappings of authority, she readily acknowledges the power such a masquerade confers. Kahlo's images invert traditional expectations and thus question the viability of constructing a female self using male-created forms of expression. The lines from a popular song painted above the figure of Kahlo point out how women's status relies upon elements of social signification (clothing, conduct, physical beauty), and how resistance to prescribed modes of behavior is rewarded with, in this case, emotional disenfranchisement.

> Look, if I loved you, it was for
> your hair,
> Now that you're bald, I no longer
> love you.

2   The animation of Kahlo's sheared tresses, as they twist and slither around her, as if energized by their new-found freedom, inevitably recall the roots and veins that appear with regularity in Kahlo's work. She often painted tendrils, roots, and veins, imagery derived, in part, from her physiological knowledge: veins carry blood, and roots bring nourishment just as nerves transmit pain. Where in other cases, for example *Self-Portrait on the Border Between Mexico and the United States*, *The Dream*, *Self-Portrait as a Tehuana*, *Two Nudes in the Jungle*, and *Roots*, roots signify a groundedness, an interconnection with all life, here, severed from their origin, the tendrils of hair are rendered incapable of providing stability or nurture. Nothing grounds the figure except Kahlo's unyielding gaze with which she engages the viewer.

3   The immobile face characteristic of *Self-Portrait with Cropped Hair*, and almost every self-portrait, reads as a mask, an interpretation Kahlo not only acknowledged but courted. Her calculated effort to disguise her emotions and hide her feelings while she relentlessly depicts her life on canvas produces an ever-present tension in her images. . . .

Because you have the option of agreeing or disagreeing with this interpretation of Kahlo's painting, you find yourself in an argument. For example, do you agree that Kahlo attempts to declare her own and other women's declaration of independence from male-created perceptions of women, a bold move in 1940? That the painting challenges a one-sided, traditionally accepted view that women should dress and behave in certain manners? That the work—perhaps especially the pair of scissors, the "unyielding gaze," and the man's suit—represents Kahlo's determination to be seen as a strong and independent woman? In other words, even a painting can symbolize an "issue," and thus be open to differing opinions about its importance and meaning.

WHAT ARGUMENT SHOULD DO FOR US

As you can see, the need for and use of argument is vast. We should not underestimate its importance in our daily lives, so in this textbook and in your college courses, you will find both the motivation for and instruction about argument, how to avoid its pitfalls, and how to write convincing arguments to meet your needs.

People who think critically about significant issues in their lives use the process of argument to examine their own perspectives on those issues and to evaluate whether their perspectives need further study or alteration. Such people recognize that they may indeed not know all the facts about problems they encounter—such as a falling economy, bullying in the public schools, or rising insurance rates—and so they consciously and reasonably seek additional information, the opinions of experts, and pertinent examples before drawing conclusions that serve their needs. They see argument as a means of reasonable decision making, reaching conclusions in which they can honestly and ethically believe. Such critical thinkers also know that any conclusion drawn or decisions made now may change when they encounter additional evidence in the future and understand an issue more clearly.

ARGUMENT IN ACTION   Assertion vs. Argument

During a recent local election in our hometown, many residents made *assertions* about how others should vote on several hotly debated issues. Signs in yards proclaimed the following:

NO on #1.

Yes on # 1.
Repeal the Grocery Tax

Yes on #3! For Good Streets.
Tax Renewal

Stop Fluoride in Our Water.
Vote Yes on #2.

How convincing do you think these signs should be to their viewers? Should people be persuaded to vote "NO" on "1"? Is the "Good Streets" tax renewal a good idea? Should voters repeal the grocery tax? Why shouldn't we fluoridate our drinking water?

As you evaluate and create arguments, think about the difference between a valid argument—a *supported* stance—and an assertion—an *expressed* stance. Often, writers try to persuade their readers to accept their opinions simply because they believe them deeply. Certainly commitment is an important feature of effective writing, but don't confuse passion and dedication for reason.

TRYING TO REMAIN FLEXIBLE IN YOUR THINKING

Perhaps you would agree that for many people, particular issues in their lives are what might be called "blood boilers." For whatever reason, certain issues and topics just "set them off." For example, we have witnessed otherwise calm and quiet students suddenly engage in heated outbursts when gun control, abortion, immigration, or other perennially divisive topics come up in class. Such outbursts are likely fueled by these students' experiences, family backgrounds, reading, and values. And passion about an issue can be a powerful instigator of argument indeed. However, our point is to encourage you to be flexible in your thinking, to discover and evaluate multiple perspectives on important issues in order to inform your passions and to evaluate their reasonableness.

Let's consider the issue of whether same-sex marriage should be acceptable and legal. Right away, we can reasonably assume that at least two perspectives exist: those who believe same-sex marriage should be legal and those who believe that it should be illegal. We can see the reason(s) behind both perspectives. Some people believe same-sex marriage should be illegal because, they argue, it is immoral and will lead to the downfall of the traditional family. Others who believe same-sex marriage should be legalized argue that if two people love each other and desire to create a committed family relationship, then their sexual orientation is irrelevant. People who are reasonable expect—and accept—such a dichotomy in thinking because multiple views offer the opportunity to consider a significant issue carefully before jumping to conclusions that may later prove faulty.

In another example, consider the issue of drilling for oil in environmentally fragile areas. What multiple perspectives seem likely? Those who support the drilling will argue that the oil is necessary to fuel our economy, the oil is available, drilling will decrease our dependence on foreign oil sources, and so forth. Opponents will assert that such drilling permanently damages some of the last wild country in the world, harms the ecosystem for endangered and other animals, and creates an ugly scar on the landscape. Now, if faced with arguments such as the same-sex marriage or oil drilling issues, you take on a challenging task: that of remaining flexible and open-minded enough to "hear" both sides of the argument accurately.

Many people have distinct *feelings* about one side of multisided issues (they encounter issues with preset values and conclusions), and sometimes those feelings lead them to conclusions that are biased or at best merely the result of "following the crowd." For instance, if your best friend's brother is gay and would like to marry one day, you may lean toward the pro-same-sex marriage perspective more than you realize, and perhaps, even more problematic, without real evidence for such an opinion. But our challenge to you is to concentrate more on the *thinking* behind the various sides of the issues you face in life. Consider the evidence on all sides, weigh the varying arguments against each other, think about the source of the evidence you confront—and then make up your mind. In short, choose the best course of action from the known possibilities.

Perhaps you are beginning to see that argument is a *method* of examining issues, evaluating solutions, understanding causes and effects, and so forth.

Another likely discovery you may make is that the so-called "pro" and "con" sides are often not as polarized as they may seem on the surface. You might learn, for instance, that some oil companies may understand the environmental impacts that drilling causes and would agree to minimize the ecological problems wherever possible. Even though you may lean toward one side or another, a true understanding of how argument works allows you to be flexible enough to consider carefully the varying perspectives (perhaps several) on any issue.

ROGERIAN ARGUMENT

Arguing does not necessitate *confrontation*. The purpose of argument is not always to "win." Carl Rogers (1902–1987) was one of the most prominent figures in modern psychology. Two of his concepts—*positive regard for self and others*, and *openness to experience* (the opposite of defensiveness)—are central to the type of argument that carries his name. Rogers was always willing to state his own position clearly, then listen carefully to the opinion of another. Always he asked, "Can we learn from each other?" To craft a Rogerian argument, the writer looks at ideas that challenge his or her claim as opportunities to understand the issue more fully.

On the other hand, Saul Bellow, an American novelist, said, "The only way to defeat the enemy is to write as well as you can." In the type of argument Bellow suggests, you may examine opposing arguments, but primarily with the agenda of defeating them. Rogers would hold that you have much to gain by trying to understand the value of other perspectives, integrating the thinking of others into your own when appropriate, appreciating the values and belief systems that underlie differing opinions, and trying to find common ground.

Think of an issue—say, whether or not the United States should have gone to war in Iraq in 2003. Maybe you and a friend disagreed on the war's merits, but instead of a reasonable discussion, you found yourself in a shouting match. You stood toe to toe, hoping that by raising your voice you could "convince" your friend to see the light, the sheer reasonableness of your stance. Your friend possibly used a similar tactic. But your friend is larger, louder, more

This aggressive use of Rogerian argument isn't quite what Rogers had in mind, but Hagar provides yet another reason to consider the views of your opponent thoroughly.

experienced in political issues, more threatening in all sorts of ways—so later, you found yourself confused, angry, and even more unwilling to change your mind. How did you feel? That the issue of the war had been equitably discussed? That both perspectives had been considered and perhaps a reasonable compromise found? That your friend made the stronger argument? Probably not, because neither you nor your friend engaged in real argument, only a misguided, defensive confrontation.

Now, think of the argument in a wider context: When countries disagree over borders, over political control, over the sharing of resources, over economic sanctions—they face important, life-changing decisions. Such decisions will ultimately affect the lives of their citizens. What happens if instead of arguing reasonably, perhaps through mediated negotiations, they confront each other? They arm themselves and go to war. Doing so violates the very nature of reasoned argument in which multiple perspectives are considered, compromise likely occurs, and both sides find an agreeable, *albeit not perfect*, means to resolve an issue. And surely seeking reasonable means to avoid conflict and settle differences serves all people more than angry concessions to pride and confrontation.

A NOTE ON ORGANIZATION: WRITING AS A PROCESS

To this point, this chapter has described argument and its most basic pattern. Developing a full-blown argument is a process of defining an issue, forming a claim, and defending that claim in a manner that will allow the argument to function as an integrated whole, just like the body's anatomy functions in a holistic manner.

As you read through the rest of the book, remember that creating a written argument is a *process*, not just a product. Although the parts of argument structure must necessarily be discussed in some reasonable order, they are more aptly explained as *recursive*. Recursive means *returning to an earlier thought or stage*. Visually, this idea is often represented by a Mobius strip. A line drawn on the strip would continuously turn back on itself.

Mobius strip

Skilled writers do not hope to sit down, write out a topic, create a claim, develop an outline, write a draft one time through, fix the spelling, and be done—in that order. Instead, an accomplished writer understands that the writing *process* is one that will turn back on itself . . . that to create a sound and compelling argument will entail returning to earlier stages of thinking and writing, and thus rethinking and rewriting.

Sometimes, for instance, a wise writer may recognize that the first plan for the argument's main points is flawed. But instead of doggedly sticking with that plan and trying to force it to work, sometimes the best thing is to go back and totally reconceive the argument, even to the point of reconsidering its original focus and intent. Doing otherwise is like trying to fix a poorly constructed wooden structure by pounding more nails into it. Eventually, the structure will fall apart because of all the holes you've made in it: You've compromised the integrity of the original structure. The wise thing to do is to tear it apart, get some new wood, and draw up a better plan.

We invite you to use this book recursively. Return to sections that can help you rethink your stance, find more convincing evidence, create more convincing examples, or reorganize the pattern of your argument.

A book has to start somewhere and end somewhere else, and therefore the organization of this text appears to be a step-by-step walk toward understanding and writing argument. The reality of writing is that seldom will different individuals and/or various projects follow the same straight line to success. As you learn more about your argument by getting into the thick of it, you can better evaluate and revisit earlier decisions.

This text is organized to reflect the mirror images of reading and writing argument:

- Part I offers discussion and practice in *reading*, *analyzing*, and *writing argument*;
- Part II launches you into the recursive experience of *writing researched argument*;
- Part III provides guidance on *polishing the surface* of your argument;
- Part IV includes groups of essays with multiple perspectives and analysis questions to practice *creating* and *critiquing* argument.

Exercise 5
Individual Analysis and Practice: Arguments in the News

Locate a newspaper with a wide circulation. Find the editorials section and do one of two tasks:

1. Select an editorial written by the newspaper's editors. Define as concisely as possible what the issue seems to be. Why have the editors chosen this issue at this time? What claim (or stance) do the editors take? In your opinion, is

the argument well defended? Organized? In a short written argument, respond to the editorial. What would you support or refute about the editors' argument?

2. Wide-circulation newspapers, such as *USA Today* and *The Miami Herald*, often have a "Pro–Con" or "Point–Counterpoint" section in which two authors provide their views on opposing sides of a significant issue. See if your newspaper prints such a section. After reading both "sides" of the issue, discuss what viewpoints the two sides share in common. What seem to be the most fiercely contested points? Does each author seem fair in his or her argument? What about the issue might make it difficult for you or others to read the arguments with an open mind?

Exercise 6
Collaborative Analysis: Analyzing Multiple Perspectives on a Topic

Here is yet more practice in analyzing arguments, using the four-part process discussed earlier in this chapter. Use the following questions and information to help you complete your analyses.

This chapter has emphasized the idea that there are many different contexts for arguments and a wide variety of perspectives from which arguments emerge. For example, the recent attention to illegal immigrants is an issue that often prompts a wide range of perspectives. Although this issue might be addressed in innumerable other ways as well, the sample arguments that follow represent a few of the angles that might be taken on this highly controversial issue. These essays give you the opportunity to think about the agenda, mindset, and values of the writers and how those affect their arguments.

The four essays in this collection are designed to help you start thinking about focusing the context of an argument you might want to make and understanding the perspective from which it comes. Too often, when novice writers approach the task of argument, the personal excitement of arguing about a topic about which they are passionate makes it difficult to think about honing down the topic. They might say, "I can't talk only about the border patrol, because the new legislation about building a wall on the border is just as important." Or, "I can't talk only about the expense of emergency health care for immigrants without talking about what brings them here in the first place." Of course, most aspects of immigration are related. But again, remember a good argument can't be everything to everyone. All of these ideas and many, many more are important about immigration. A writer cannot possibly hope to cover all these interrelated topics adequately. Here, in this array of opinions regarding immigration, you will be able to see how a more experienced and effective writer conceives his or her argument in much narrower terms.

Chapters 2 and 3 will focus on defining the context of argument more specifically. When you can begin to see the structure of an argument, you are beginning to analyze, or break down, the argument into its constituent parts for clearer understanding. Think of a chemistry experiment in which you break down a complex compound into its basic components. When you do this, you know more clearly how it is put together, how the components interact. Analysis of this same kind is a critical part of the reading/writing connection. Analysis helps you understand, write, and evaluate arguments. This exercise asks you to apply the ideas in this chapter to a set of arguments, to analyze them.

In small groups of three or four, examine the perspectives presented in the essays. Read the selections carefully, marking clues you see about the writer's issue and intent. Analyze the essays by addressing the following tasks:

- Look for *claims* in the arguments, at least one sentence that points out precisely what the writer wants the reader to glean from the argument. Sometimes claims will be explicit—clearly spelled out for the reader in very clear terms. Often, however, the claim is implicit—left for the reader to piece together from the evidence provided. Are the various claims in these essays explicit or implicit? Which do you prefer? Which makes the analysis of an argument easier for reader? (Much more about claims in Chapter 3.)
- Note the many different *perspectives* these writers have taken on the immigration issue. Is each focused, limited satisfactorily, or is the writer biting off too much for such a short essay?
- Why do you think the author, with the limited information you have on each, might have chosen his or her particular focus? Does any of the information you know about the writer give you any clues to understanding his or her particular perspective on the issue?
- What kind of *defense* is the writer offering? What evidence in the argument is most convincing to you and which is least persuasive? Why?
- Find the sections where the writer identifies and/or seems to address the values, beliefs, and/or the arguments of a potential *reader*. What assumptions about immigration does each writer believe his or her reader will hold?

Sample 1:

"Border Calling" first appeared in the March 2005, issue of *Sojourners Magazine*. James Reel is a freelance writer from Tucson, Arizona.

Border Calling
James Reel

1 Annunciation House reaches out to the undocumented with faith and hospitality.

2   The only thing separating El Paso, Texas, from Ciudad Juãrez, Mexico, is a canal that a child could wade across. That, plus a gross disparity in

job availability, wages, and quality of life. Not to mention official U.S. border policies designed to keep undocumented guest workers out, even while unofficial economic policies all but encourage American farms, restaurants, and hotels to hold consumer prices down by hiring undocumented laborers for the roughest, most menial work.

3   And so every year perhaps up to 4,000 people—no one is sure exactly how many—wade north across the canal when they think the Border Patrol isn't looking, or wedge themselves into the nooks of cars or vans crossing one of the congested bridges linking the cities across the Rio Grande, or pay coyote and pollero—people-smugglers, the latter term meaning "chicken wranglers"—to sneak them across by some other means. Today, 8 to 12 million undocumented immigrants are in the United States, many of them living in hiding and in poverty.

4   Yet they needn't live without a home. Since the late 1970s, El Paso's Annunciation House has opened its doors to immigrants and refugees on the U.S.-Mexico border. The 20-volunteer organization includes a residence for immigrants trying to get on their feet, as well as separate facilities for those seeking political asylum and for women and children, and a building in a Juárez squatters' neighborhood that provides support and space for community-building efforts. Sometimes the Border Patrol looks the other way; sometimes it arrests Annunciation House volunteers. In early 2003, an agent shot and killed a 19-year-old guest who was running away with a pipe in his hand.

5   The work can be discouraging, but it's an essential component of its founders' faith. "We're working with an unequivocal certitude that for God there is no such thing as an illegal human being," says Ruben Garcia, Annunciation House's director. "And God would have no problem providing hospitality to these people."

6   In 1976, Garcia was running the youth department of the Catholic Diocese of El Paso. "The young adults I worked with wanted to buy into something that had depth and substance," he says, but they didn't know exactly what that might be. During weekly meetings over the next several months, the group reflected on how its members could live lives with meaning, and do so in a substantive way.

7   "As we reflected on scripture," he recalls, "we realized that the God we believe in is one who first and foremost identifies with people who are oppressed, people who are enslaved, the stranger in our midst, the poor. We realized what we needed to do was place ourselves among the poor in our own area."

8   In early 1978, five members of the group gained rent-free access to the second floor of a building owned by the diocese, still without a clear notion of what to do. "We started trying to understand where it was that the poor would take us," says Garcia.

9   The group had no money, and initially its members circulated through El Paso's impoverished neighborhoods, connecting people with social service agencies. Eventually they realized that the city's two

homeless shelters would not accept undocumented immigrants. That's when the volunteers of Annunciation House discovered their mission.

10   By word of mouth, people began to hear about the house and guests began to arrive, seeking the very basic food and shelter Annunciation House could offer. There were only four or five at first, but within a few years the organization was offering hospitality to 120 people at a time. Garcia estimates that over the past quarter-century, Annunciation House has hosted more than 80,000 immigrants, refugees, and undocumented workers.

11   Although the origin of Annunciation House coincided with the Sanctuary movement, in which many American congregations declared their churches to be sanctuaries for people fleeing political upheaval in Latin America, Garcia's group stood apart from that effort.

12   "These churches would go through a long process of discernment to make the decision to declare sanctuary and take in a single family," says Garcia. "I'd tease them and say, 'You've gone through this long process to take in four people, but at Annunciation House we already have 100 people. You've got the theology, but we've got the bodies!'"

13   In truth, theology—or, more precisely, faith—lies at the heart of the work at Annunciation House. "The God that we believe in," says Garcia, "is a God who says, 'I am first and foremost in among the widow and the orphan, the stranger in a strange land.' So if we are to recognize that in our own work, it requires us to trust in the providence of God, to live simply, to make ourselves available to people without charging anything and without expecting anything in return."

14   "We said at the beginning that we should shy away from funding sources or resources that would try to control us or make us be something different from what we were trying to be. Almost 27 years later, Annunciation House continues to be sustained by the spontaneous commitment and generosity and solidarity of people, and of course by a volunteer staff. Individuals come from all over the United States and from six or seven countries to commit to living and working in our houses for one to three years at a time, with no financial help."

15   The ideal volunteer, says Garcia, can "walk on water and multiply loaves and fishes and turn water into wine." Short of that, he'll accept someone like Kansas-born Megan Hope, who first worked at Annunciation House when she was 22 and now, nine years later and after getting a master's in Latin American studies, is completing a second year with the organization.

16   "You don't know from one day to the next if you'll be helping somebody get medical assistance or get hooked up with a lawyer, or if you'll be running some errand, or talking to the Mexican consulate, or unclogging a toilet," she says.

17   "The difficult part is on an emotional basis. The first time I was here, I was really the only volunteer at one of the houses, with 15 guests. I came into Ruben's office crying, saying I hadn't done a very good job of meeting the needs of the guests, and that I sometimes felt incapable of doing anything worthwhile for them. He said he suspected I was experiencing my own poverty. What that means is sort of being broken up and made

to realize how limited our capacity is for so many things, and realizing we don't have the power to change people's realities; sometimes we don't even have the ability to comfort people in the way we'd like to.

18   "Like our guests, all of us are on our own solitary journeys, with moments of doubt and loneliness and isolation and frustration, and with an incredible need for faith and hope."

19   Garcia's advice to other communities interested in starting an organization like Annunciation House is simple: "You don't need money and connections to make this succeed," he says. "You need trust. There has to be some sense of belief in what is calling you; even if it doesn't make sense, you continue to walk down the road."

Sample 2:

"Not Giving Up on Immigration Control" by Kurt Williamson appeared in the October 2005 issue of *The New American*, a magazine published by the John Birch Society.

Not Giving Up on Immigration Control
Kurt Williamson

1   The assertion that we can't curtail exploding illegal immigration is based on the false notions that our government is already doing the best it can to control the problem, that our borders are too long to be effectively controlled, and that finding and evicting the illegals would demand too much of an investment in terms of time and money to be worthwhile. But these assumptions are flawed, and the government can solve the immigration mess as soon as it decides to do so.

2   Yes, our borders are long, but we can secure them without putting a guard on every square foot of territory. Barriers such as walls and fences, and technology that alerts border patrollers to the presence of illegals, can radically reduce the need for manpower. Moreover, we don't have to catch and expel every illegal attempting to sneak into the United States in order to solve the problem. We can also reduce the flow by getting rid of the incentive to come here, including limiting the ability of illegals to obtain employment.

3   However, instead of honestly trying to solve the problem, Democrats cater to illegals to get the Hispanic vote, and Republicans cater to them to get businessmen's votes—Hispanics provide cheap labor. Despite the cries from many politicians that the border is virtually uncontrollable, the deployment of a multifaceted approach on immigration that sought to hinder the freedom of illegals near the border and in the interior of our country could surely remedy this problem.

Implementing Change

4   The first step that would need to be taken is to implement changes at the border so that crossing into our country is much more difficult. The

Minuteman Project showed that this could be done effectively if some manpower is added to the border. By hiring more border patrol officers and building barriers at highly used crossing points, we could effectively contain and stop border crossings if the number of would-be crossers is held to moderate levels....

5   As part of making life as an illegal alien untenable, cities deemed "sanctuary cities" for illegals—like Chicago, Denver, and Los Angeles—which do not report illegal immigrants to the federal government, must be required to detain illegals for deportation. Pressure brought to bear on state legislators could bring about this result. To enlist the aid of local law enforcement personnel in deporting illegals, statewide standards need to be set for what does and does not constitute racial profiling (to prevent the ACLU from suing cities for doing their duty), and the Bureau of Immigration and Customs Enforcement needs to do its job.

6   A report by the Center for Immigration Studies, entitled "Officers Need Backup," lists numerous instances when immigration officials either refuse to pick up illegals from local law enforcement or turn them free after they pick them up. In fact, illegals end up in our legal system constantly, only to be released. When European, Asian, and African illegals are caught at the southern border, unless they are suspected terrorists, they are immediately released because Mexico will not take them—they are not Mexican nationals—and Customs considers it too costly to fly them home. When Hispanics get caught in our country, they are usually given a "notice to appear" at a future court date, and they are let free. Over 88 percent don't show up for hearings. In cities near the border the no-show rate is often over 98 percent.

7   To make immigration controls work, we must lock up the illegals (in tent cities, if necessary) until it is time to deport them, and we must end or greatly simplify the appealing of deportations by illegals, by which illegals clog the federal holding facilities and bring deportations to a virtual standstill. Only the federal government can make the Bureau of Immigration do its job, and so congressional representatives need to hear that we know about this.

8   Also, many more immigration officers need to be hired to patrol the interior of our country to arrest businessmen who hire illegals and do not report the workers for tax purposes, breaking tax laws. To stop employers from hiring illegals who have managed to obtain forged identification documents, thereby giving employers who hire them the veneer of legality, and to catch illegal aliens, immigration officers should investigate every company that turns in an invalid Social security number on tax forms because most illegals who have forged immigration documents are using fake Social Security numbers.

Fouled Federal Policy

9   As an added method to foil the free movement of illegals through our society, the federal government and state governments must stop accepting foreign I.D. cards for important transactions: buying a house, taking out

loans, enrolling children in school, and getting a driver's license. There is no reason to accept them. If a foreigner is here legally, he has proper identification such as a passport or a green card.

10   The identification most often used by illegals from Mexico is the matricula consular card. These cards are so widely abused that illegals already in our country go to consulate offices and are basically handed a card. They are a completely insecure form of identification, and Congressman Tom Tancredo (R-Colo.) has testified that illegals have been caught with as many as four of these cards, all with their pictures on them but issued under different names. Almost unbelievably, under President Bush, the Treasury Department told banks to accept the cards as legal identification.

11   Without the enticement of employment opportunities to draw them or the ability to live here with impunity, illegal immigrants will be discouraged from coming to America. Likewise, the knowledge that they will be swiftly deported if they ever come in contact with a government official (think police) would also discourage many.

12   To further add to the effectiveness of our immigration policy, the citizenship lure must be used to our advantage, instead of our disadvantage. In the United States, if an illegal immigrant bears a child, that child is considered to be a citizen and immediately qualifies for welfare benefits—Medicaid and stipends under Supplemental Security Income and Disability Income. These babies are called "anchor babies" because the government seldom sends their families out of the country. Between 300,000 and 350,000 are born each year.

13   Congress can remedy this problem by clarifying the principle of the 14th Amendment (which is used as the justification behind giving citizenship to illegals) to, in essence, make the 14th Amendment "mean what it means." According to George Detweiler, a lawyer specializing in constitutional issues, the 14th Amendment was never intended to "extend citizenship to someone born in America to parents who are here illegally."

14   Congress can make the clarification about citizenship and then forbid the federal courts to hear cases dealing with similar legislation to stop the courts from becoming "activist" and reinterpreting the meaning of the 14th Amendment to suit its whims. As part of the carrot and stick approach to immigration, Congress should pass a law that says that no person who is caught in the United States illegally will ever be granted U.S. citizenship.

Visa Reform

15 Finally, we should eliminate several types of immigration visas—not create new types of visas, as many congressmen are proposing, whereby illegals can easily hop from one type of visa to another and essentially make their stay permanent by taking advantage of government bureaucracy.

16   A type of visa that should be eliminated entirely is the Diversity Visa. This type of visa allows 50,000 people annually to immigrate to the United States from countries where we do not usually get many immigrants. Its purpose is

strictly to enhance immigrant variety as to geographic regions, and it requires almost no real educational requirements. This is a foolish feel-good policy. Visas that the United States gives out should be based upon the idea that the immigrant will provide a real tangible economic benefit in a field where there truly is a shortage of qualified American workers.

17   One type of proposed visa that needs to be avoided, which has the support of the White House, is the "W" visa, short for World Visa, which would supposedly match willing workers from around the world with willing employers throughout the country. This is basically a visa that provides for unlimited immigration of low-wage workers so that employers can drive down wages in job markets.

18   Going hand in hand with limiting visas, immigration officials need to immediately follow up on people who have overstayed their visas to evict them. Before the present mass influx of illegal immigrants from our southern border, more illegals got into our country by overstaying their visas than by crossing our borders.

19   The fact that we need to regulate and limit immigration is common sense. Besides the present and future negative economic consequences of mass immigration, we have suffered the devastation of September 11, 2001, and know that various terrorist and criminal groups actively seek to attack our citizens.

20   Amnesty plans, like the one President Bush is pushing, leave our citizens extremely vulnerable by encouraging mass illegal immigration to such an extent that our border patrol cannot stop the human rush. Plus, the increased numbers of foreign-born residents provide myriad potential safe-havens for terrorists and criminals, making them hard to catch. These approaches to immigration are not in the best interests of the citizens of this nation.

STUDENTS AT WORK: PUTTING ARGUMENT TO USE

Sample 3:

This argument by Rubi Reyes, a student journalist at Texas A & M University at Kingville (TAMUK), was published in a tabloid edition of the student newspaper, the *South Texan* on October 24, 2006. This issue received a first place award from the Texas Intercollegiate Press Association for its coverage on immigration issues.

Children Born in the U.S. Serve as Means to Get Parents, Family Here
Rubi Reyes

1   The United States has now reached 300 million people, but how many were anchor babies—a child born in the United States to an illegal immigrant or other non-citizen?

2   Anchor baby births are allowed to happen because the 14th Amendment to the U.S. constitution reads in part: "All persons born or naturalized in the United States, and subject to the jurisdiction thereof, are citizens of the United States and of the state wherein they reside."

3   The majority of Texas A&M University-Kingsville students asked did not know what anchor baby meant. "I have mixed feelings because, one they are using government money and, two they are just trying to have a better life," Veronica Avila, TAMUK senior biology major said. "I don't think it is fair to those that are trying to go through the process legally," Joe Vasquez TAMUK junior bilingual education said.

4   Many immigrants travel to the U.S. to have their babies in order for their child to be a U.S. citizen, so they can have the same benefits that a U.S. citizen has. They travel to great lengths just so their babies can be U.S. citizens and so they, the parents, can become citizens in the future, thus the term anchor babies. Immigrants from Mexico and Central America are trying to make it into the states because if their baby is born on U.S. [soil], they feel it will help them with their citizenship as well, U.S. Border Patrol agents said. "On one night an eight-month pregnant woman attempted to cross three times," Jim Dorcy, with the San Diego Border Patrol said.

5   According to an MSNBC survey, the Census Bureau estimated that some 8.7 million people reside in the U.S. without proper documentation. About 60 percent of those crossed the U.S. border without permission.

6   An estimated 70 percent to 80 percent of the 10,587 births at Ben Taub General Hospital and Lyndon B. Johnson General Hospital, in Houston, last year were to undocumented immigrants, the *Houston Chronicle* reported, in 2006. The number of anchor babies being born keeps rising. In 1997 the General Accounting Office estimated that 165,000 children are born to undocumented aliens in the U.S. annually. Allowing immigrant mothers to have their babies on U.S. soil costs taxpayers hundreds of millions of dollars, say health officials. Many cross over because if they have their babies in places like Starr County in the Rio Grande Valley or free clinics, delivering a baby does not cost them a dime and their baby will be considered a U.S. citizen.

7   Starr County Memorial Hospital had $3.6 million in uncollected medical bills in 2005, up from $1.5 million in 2002 the *Houston Chronicle* reported. These numbers will keep rising throughout the years to come.

8   The Urban Institute estimates that the cost of educating an estimated 800,000 illegal alien school children was approximately $3.1 billion in 1993. Anchor babies that are allowed to stay give their relatives hope that they too can eventually crossover, *The American Resistance* reported. Anchor babies are not just hurting the U.S. in medical costs; they are also costing the school districts, experts claim. There will be no end to anchor babies if the U.S. hospitals, schools, and the government do not become more demanding with the immigrants' paperwork.

Sample 4:

Dr. Hector Avalos is a professor at Iowa State University. "Issue Looks Different Through Latino Eyes," published January 2, 2007, in the *Des Moines Register*, reflects on the history of immigration and what he calls "forced immigration" in the United States.

Iowa's Great Immigration Divide

Hector Avalos

1   If one were to see illegal immigration through Latino eyes, what might it look like?

2   We might begin by observing that the first illegal immigrants came from across the Atlantic. Somewhere around 1492, not counting some earlier errant Vikings, the trans-Atlantic invaders arrived in the Americas. By the 1620s, they had set up a permanent shop, in Massachusetts.

3   These invaders had no titles to land, but they did not seem to mind that. The fact that people were already here posed only a temporary obstacle—nothing a little case of genocide and ethnic cleansing could not cure.

4   Even before they had completely "pacified" all those natives, these immigrants and their descendants set up what they called "laws." These laws were not really established by a democratic process because the natives did not have much say in those laws, which were written by, and for the benefit of, the invaders from across the Atlantic. It was all very convenient.

5   Almost as soon as these invaders came in, some of them also decided that they needed free labor. So these now "law-abiding" citizens turned to "forced immigration," which otherwise involved kidnapping and slave-trading millions of souls from another continent called Africa.

6   Of course, such "forced immigration" into the United States is no longer a good practice because so much cheap or slave labor now is readily available elsewhere. But we don't hear much about that because we don't want Americans to get depressed about how they are still benefiting from slavery. "Out of sight, out of mind," as they say.

7   Sometime around the 1820s and '30s, many of these EuroAmerican invaders entered in droves into what was then Mexico. The laws of Mexico did not matter much to these invaders. There were so many of these "law-abiding" EuroAmericans who settled in Mexican territory that they started thinking it was no longer Mexico, but rather something called the Republic of Texas.

8   Mexicans who had owned farms and ranches for generations were none too happy about that. Who did these newcomers think they were in breaking Mexican law and expecting all sorts of services they never paid for? So a war was fought, and in 1848, the Anglo-Texan invaders managed, through superior firepower, brutality and excellent political maneuvering, to dispossess Mexicans who were born and owned land there.

9   As was a habit now, the EuroAmerican newcomers wrote their own laws, again without much input from the people they threw off the land. Actually, it was no longer "cheating" because you can't cheat someone out of land that the laws you made up say is yours now.

10   But it was not enough for these Anglo invaders to dispossess Mexicans. Now these Mexicans were told that they had to learn this confusing language called English. English proved ideal for settling any legal complaints the Spanish-speakers might raise.

11   Fast-forward to the 21st century, and apparently many of these EuroAmericans have overlooked how they are benefiting from the blood-soaked inheritance of invading ancestors who made it nice and legal for them to keep farms and land they had no right to have in the first place.

12   Nor should these upright citizens be surprised that Latin American people would be impoverished by the vast mineral and other land resources stolen from them by these transatlantic invaders. American citizens should not be surprised that people will seek to cross borders because of poverty their EuroAmerican ancestors helped to create.

13   Shouldn't these "citizens," who have been the primary beneficiaries of a country founded by "illegal" immigrants, be more merciful toward people who cross a border to feed their children?

14   Through Latino eyes, these American "citizens" should at least be honest enough to say that they are not really against all "illegal" immigration, but only against illegal immigration that does not benefit them.

DISCOVERING YOUR OWN ARGUMENTS: ARGUMENTS IN EVERYDAY LIFE

1. We have mentioned that one frequent use of argument is to resolve disputes. Think of a time when you felt you were treated unfairly, rudely, or unprofessionally. Try writing two short arguments that attempt to express your irritation and that call for reparation of some kind, no matter how small. In the first argument, use a confrontational approach. In the second, use a more reasoned—even Rogerian (see p. 24)—approach.

2. At the beginning of this chapter, we talked about the many arguments made regarding the response to Hurricane Katrina. Think of a time when you witnessed a challenging situation of some kind firsthand (students out of control at an athletic event, a potentially dangerous situation with a group of friends, etc.). Write an argument identifying *the one action* (we are asking you to *focus* your response here) that was most significant in your chosen experience that caused it to turn out poorly or well—with the purpose of helping others confronted with a similar problem. Use specific details of the incident as evidence for both the difficulty of the problem and the importance of the action you have selected.

3. Write an argument for first-time college students that might be included in orientation materials. The argument should point out the two most significant mistakes a first-year student often makes and also the two best decisions he or she can make.
4. One of the most common "everyday" uses of argument is a letter to the editor of a newspaper. Such letters are short and address issues of immediate concern in a community; they are often complimentary as well as critical. Write an argument about an issue or event in your college, local, or home community that might appear as a letter in that community's newspaper.
5. You have been commissioned to write an argument to buy a certain product. Your argument will be printed on an 8 × 10 flyer that will be

---

ALSO NOTE
SOURCE USE

At the end of most all chapters you will find a number of suggestions—"Discovering Your Own Arguments"—for writing projects that emphasize the concepts in the chapter. Sometimes you may want to use material you have seen, heard, or read to support your arguments in these writing projects. Often, instructors will want you to start using one or two sources rather quickly so that your experience with finding and using sources builds toward the focus of Part II of this book: the academic research paper. Different instructors will have different preferences about when to introduce source material and its documentation.

In the samples we have included in Part I, you will see informal documentation. In Part II, you will see both informal and formal academic documentation. As always, ask your instructor how he or she wants to have source material identified if you want to use outside sources before they have been assigned in class. Following are brief descriptions of the two types of documentation:

- *Informal documentation* (used for the most part in Part I of this text) refers to the kind of source identification you would find in popular, general interest sources such as magazine and newspapers. You can preview a paper with this kind of source identification in Chapter 3, p. 79.
- *Formal documentation* (appropriate for research-based writing emphasized in Part II of this text) refers to the academic practice of documenting papers according to an established style sheet. If your instructor wants you to begin immediately to acknowledge sources according to an accepted style sheet—usually APA or MLA documentation—you will want to preview Chapter 12 for those guidelines and sample papers.

attached to every door in your apartment building (dorm, neighborhood). The business owner has told you to use only three to five bullet points and two short paragraphs, one at the beginning and one at the end. Select a product you think is most appropriate for your targeted audience.

6. Think of a current issue you have heard a great deal about in the news, on campus, or in casual conversation with your friends and/or family. Use the Internet to identify at least two different argument perspectives on this issue. Explain, in a short paper, these two different arguments on the issue.

REFLECTIONS ON THE CHAPTER

We hope that Chapter 1 helps illuminate just how pervasive argument is in our lives. We see it all around us and learn to deal with it. As you reflect upon the main points of this chapter, begin to consider two things: How does argument affect your personal life at school, at work, and at home? And what issues in your life might you wish to explore further—say in a written argument? Finding issues that have direct bearing on and importance to you is the life-blood of an argument's appeal.

CHAPTER

2

Traditional Means of Establishing Context and Discovering Your Argument

Since arguments occur in varied contexts, the boundaries placed upon your arguments by their contexts provide you with a road map to reach your goals. This chapter provides you some traditional means by which to understand others' arguments and how to inform your own.

Over two thousand years ago, the Greek philosopher Aristotle concluded that people persuade each other to adopt new viewpoints, purchase products, change behaviors, and so forth by establishing their own credibility, by touching upon the audience's emotions, and by using the strength of reason. And as you will learn, these classical appeals may overlap in any one context. By learning Aristotle's three appeals, you will begin to recognize them in the arguments you read and hear, and you will grasp just how powerfully they play a role in your own arguments. Since Aristotle's original illumination of the three primary persuasive appeals, thinkers and writers have striven to put them to use in the contexts of their own arguments, sometimes by altering in minor ways the definition of or use of the three appeals. The

Argument Concept (review this in Chapter 1 or read more about it in Chapters 3 and 4) allows you to see, in a very down-to-earth manner, how to plan your own arguments and to analyze those of others in a manner of which we believe you will find useful.

In addition, this chapter discusses the two prevalent human thought patterns, induction and deduction, and introduces you to yet another, practical means of understanding how arguments are constructed—the Toulmin system.

TERMS AND CONCEPTS TO WATCH FOR
- Ethos
- Pathos
- Logos
- Deductive reasoning
- Inductive reasoning
- The Toulmin System

QUESTIONS TO GUIDE YOUR READING
- How are classical "appeals" used in argument?
- How can an argument be formed with deductive reasoning?
- How can an argument be formed with inductive reasoning?
- How do deduction and induction work together?
- How does the Toulmin system help you think through an argument?

Think for a moment about the arguments you have experienced in your life. How did you fare? Did you come across as fair and willing to listen to viewpoints contradictory to your own? Did you get angry? What about the manner in which you argued your case? From your point of view now, which of your actions and words worked for or against your perspective on the issue at the time? Like all of us, you will come to understand that constructing an argument involves a series of choices about its *context*: your intended *focus* on the issue; your intended *reader* or listener; and your intended *purpose*, why the perspective you have chosen is important and necessary to you and others. You choose every detail, indeed every word, in an argument based upon your understanding of that argument's context, sometimes in ways that arguers have employed for thousands of years.

As an example, let's say you mentally plan an argument such as this:

"*I will argue that* our college's accounting department should establish internships with local accounting firms *for* the chair of the accounting department *in order to* demonstrate that internships would provide legitimate, practical experience beyond that classroom for those intending to become professional accountants."

You must now decide how to proceed in a manner that will best produce the results you want. How will you best convince the accounting department chair that internships are reasonable and workable? You may decide, for instance, that a highly emotional appeal may fall flat since the accounting department chair is known as a rigid, no-nonsense person. But appeals to your own credibility (you are a serious, successful student who seeks practical experience in your chosen field) and appeal to logic ("real-world" accounting practice would enhance students' knowledge, several local accounting firms have already expressed interest in having interns, the program would cost the college little or nothing) would perhaps garner an appreciative, interested response. Thus, your argument, either written or spoken, would focus primarily on appeals to credibility and to reason. In other words, as you learn about these more traditional appeals, you will find that understanding the context of an argument allows you to select the style and appeals most likely to be effective for your purpose.

Since the goal of many arguments is to be persuasive, you must write in the most appealing manner possible to get your readers to believe and act as you would have them. Often, such persuasion requires that you consider the three primary means by which humans persuade one another: the appeal to personal credibility, the appeal to the reader's emotions, and the appeal to the logic (reasonableness) of your reasons and evidence. And as you will soon discover, these appeals often overlap in their usefulness.

THE APPEAL TO PERSONAL CREDIBILITY (THE ETHICAL APPEAL)

> **ETHOS** *is the appeal to one's personal credibility about an issue, the attempt to gain a reader's or listener's trust.*

Think for a moment about how hard it is to believe something a person says when you do not trust that person. We all know people who, for one reason or another, simply cause us to put up our protective "shields" when they begin one of their spiels. Perhaps you don't fully trust one of your roommates and so would never lend him or her money in spite of an impassioned plea for funds. Many of us distrust car salespersons, maybe because of unsatisfactory dealings with them in the past or because of societal stereotypes. Whatever the case, we find it difficult to accept the salesperson's pitch about a car when we distrust his or her motives, believing the salesperson has a sales commission more in mind than our personal automotive needs.

Your reader will find your argument less than persuasive, as well, if for some reason he or she believes you are not trustworthy. So, you must take care to establish your own credibility within your argument. One of the best ways to invite your reader's trust is to present a *fair* argument. You must not appear overly one-sided, unfairly attack viewpoints contrary to your own, or make fun of opposing arguments in an attempt to disparage them. Be sure that you carefully consider all viewpoints and to concede those that, while not supportive of your stance, still deserve some recognition. In many ways, conceding points empowers your position with your reader in that he or she will recognize that you know the various views your issue may foster and will recognize, too, that you are not afraid to be fair by recognizing opposing arguments. Thus, you generate trust.

Visual Rhetoric...
BRAD PITT, TOYOTA, AND AN APPEAL TO ETHOS

Often marketing specialists use a version of Aristotle's appeal to ethos when they use celebrities to add credibility to their arguments for a product. Using any of the Aristotelian appeals, however, can be risky if they are not coordinated with your reader's values and mindset. For example, in 2002, Toyota ran an ad in Malaysia where Brad Pitt was determined, by market research, to have strong appeal. You can view this ad and a story about the problem with this visual rhetoric at http://archives.cnn.com/2002/WORLD/asiapcf/southease/12/16/offbeat. malaysia.pitt/index.html, or by just putting "Brad Pitt Malaysia Ad" in your Web browser. Unfortunately for Toyota, the ad was banned because of Malaysian regulation. Malaysian Deputy Information Minister Zainuddin Maidin commented that "... Western faces in advertisements could create an inferiority complex among Asians ..." and that the advertisement "... was a humiliation against Asians ..."

Using one of these appeals demands that you do so thoughtfully with the impact on your reader in mind.

A second way to strengthen your credibility is to be *knowledgeable* about your issue. You must know what you're talking about. The reader should believe that you have completed a thorough and sincere analysis of the issue, have used the knowledge of experts when necessary, and have provided ample reasons and evidence for your stance. Again, ask yourself how often you are persuaded by people whose arguments amount to little more than puffs of "hot air." A reader is much more likely to trust your argument when it presents ample, relevant evidence and does not attempt to hide behind a smokescreen of anecdotes and incomplete research.

Third, your credibility with a reader also hinges upon your ability to *write clearly and correctly*. Your word choices, correct grammar and punctuation, organization, and spelling will go a long way to engender your reader's trust, even unconsciously. Imagine a writer's argument about nuclear waste, for example. Throughout the course of the argument, the author repeatedly spells *nuclear* as *nuklear*. Doesn't even such a minor error make you begin to question the author's credibility in that he or she does not correctly spell such a key word? The same holds true, of course, for your own writing. Be sure to revise, revise, revise—until your writing best represents what you wish to say and how to say it (see Chapter 13 for complete revision and editing tips). You would hate to lose your reader's trust in your hard work and thinking over minor, preventable errors.

44 Chapter 2 *Traditional Means of Establishing Context*

Visual Rhetoric...
ETHOS AND ADVERTISING

Moves by the Knowles. Body by milk.

Take it from my sister and me, when you look and feel your best, it shows. Some studies suggest teens who choose milk tend to be leaner, plus the protein helps build muscle. Staying active, eating right, and drinking 3 glasses a day of lowfat or fat free milk instead of soda helps you look your best. Talk about working it.

got milk?
www.bodybymilk.com

In what way does the "Got Milk?" campaign use images of major celebrities such as Beyonce Knowles and her younger sister Solange to argue for their product? How might this practice relate to Aristotle's idea of ethos? Is the campaign using the images effectively or not?

What Do *You* Bring to an Argument?

When you argue, perhaps even before deciding upon just what stance you will take on an issue, it is imperative that you do some self-reflection. As discussed previously you have a number of persuasive appeals with which you may inform your arguments, but ask yourself what lurks in the back of your mind concerning the issue you are about to confront. Do you have any biases, for example, that may cloud your perceptions of your issue? If so, might these biases affect how you research your issue or how you interpret the evidence you find? Is the stance you intend to take merely one of convenience or simplicity?

Perhaps a small analogy would help at this point. Have you ever taped your own voice and then listened to it? Were you surprised by how your voice sounded? Most people hear their recorded voice and say, "Is *that* what I sound like?" Others in the room will likely say yes, that is exactly how you sound. The point here is that our own perceptions of ourselves (how we sound, how we seem to "come across" to others, how we view the world) may differ from others' perceptions of us. Thus we have to be careful in our approaches to the claims we make and our defense of them.

Granted, it is hard for all of us to be completely open-minded and flexible about all issues; however, real and fair argument requires that you make every effort to examine your issues fairly, to research them fully, and to present your evidence in a fair and balanced manner. In the next section of this text, you will learn about two overlapping means of reasoning to conclusions. See if you can learn more about how your own conclusions are formed.

THE APPEAL TO EMOTIONS (THE PATHETIC APPEAL)

> **PATHOS** *is a deliberate appeal to a reader's or listener's emotions.*

A second type of persuasive appeal is one that writers and speakers alike have known for years: an appeal to an audience's emotions can be powerful indeed. The appeal to emotions generally means that a writer wants a reader to *feel* rather than to *think*—to respond with the heart, not the mind. Advertisements provide potent examples of such an appeal. Many ads, for example, associate babies, sex, money, or food with a product for sale. A few years ago, an automobile tire manufacturer regularly produced television ads that showed babies crawling through the tires. And everyone loves babies, right? But ask yourself exactly what babies might logically have to do with the quality or price of automobile tires. But logic (thinking) is not the point. Just the positive association encouraged between infants and tires creates a powerful emotional appeal that many find hard to resist.

We must caution you here, however, about the use of emotional appeals in arguments. Although you may be tempted to push the buttons of fear, joy, guilt,

Visual Rhetoric...
EMOTIONAL APPEALS

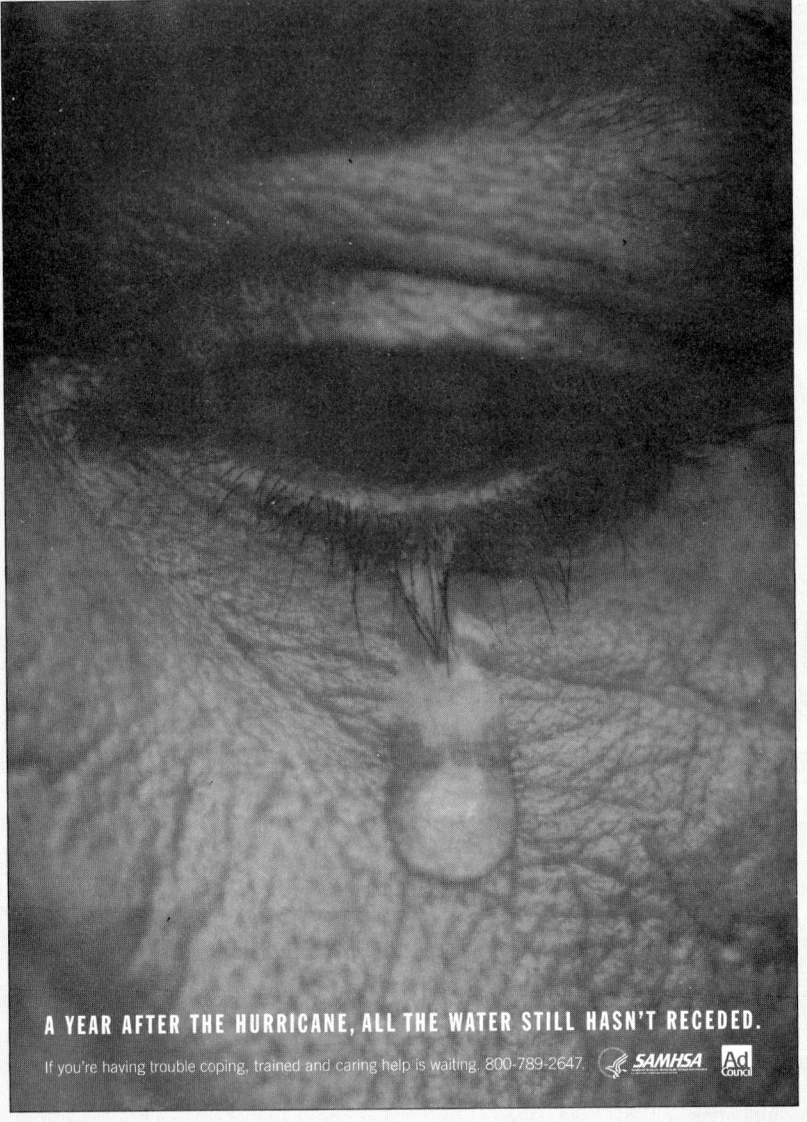

A YEAR AFTER THE HURRICANE, ALL THE WATER STILL HASN'T RECEDED.
If you're having trouble coping, trained and caring help is waiting. 800-789-2647. SAMHSA Ad Council

The images in this public service advertisement have obvious emotional appeal. The creators of this ad want to keep the public interested in the continuing plight of Hurricane Katrina victims. The image of the tear and the reference to water are an intended use of *pathos* to make a direct emotional connection and to recall the heartbreak of this disaster.

or sadness in your readers, you must be careful. Perhaps, for example, your argument concerns the unsanitary conditions of a local homeless shelter. You might use emotional appeal effectively in the introduction of your argument by describing the dirty floors, counters, and windows of the facility. This way, you inspire a sense of outrage in your reader in a quick, efficient manner. However, careful readers often resist continued attempts to "tug at their heart strings," preferring instead that the bulk of your argument consist of solid reasons and evidence that the homeless shelter deserves cleaning. Readers often weary of explicit emotional appeals, so let your evidence do the talking. Besides, citing that 167 homeless people became ill last year after a visit to the shelter provides solid evidence (a fact) that supports your overall argument and yet may cause an emotional response in the reader as well. Plus, the use of real evidence garners further trust in your viewpoint (note the overlapping usefulness of the appeals). Our point? Make careful decisions about the use of emotional appeals based upon your knowledge of your reader and the persuasive means you deem best.

THE APPEAL TO REASON (THE LOGICAL APPEAL)

> **LOGOS** *is a deliberate use of reasons and evidence to appeal to a reader's or listener's ability to think about an issue.*

How did you choose the college or university where you now study? Did you do so simply because the buildings looked "cool," the recruiter was good looking, and three of your friends enrolled here, too? Although such emotional and credibility appeals may have had some influence upon your decision, more than likely you selected your school because it offers the program you wish to pursue, reputable faculty, affordable tuition and housing, and so forth.

Thus, a third powerful appeal, of course, is to the logic of your argument. Although readers may find your credibility sound and your emotional ploys appealing, they still deserve reasons, evidence, and fairly portrayed depictions of opposing viewpoints—in other words, a carefully considered and evidenced presentation. The strength of your reasoning will go a long way toward persuading your audience that your viewpoint deserves their attention, perhaps even convincing them to change their minds. Thinking clearly, of course, is not always easy, but failure to try invites certain disaster.

Two classical, and overlapping, mental processes to discover and defend your claims are those of induction and deduction (discussed later in this chapter). The rest of this chapter (indeed the entire textbook) addresses more fully the means of preparing and defending an argument in a reasonable manner. But for now, try to recognize that readers respond well to your carefully researched and considered points, your use of apt authorities, your willingness to concede points to opposing arguments, your organization, and your avoidance of logical fallacies (see Chapter 5).

48 Chapter 2 *Traditional Means of Establishing Context*

Foreign language education spells success.

Improves academic performance. Raises SAT scores. Creates more opportunities for success in tomorrow's international economy. That's what learning another language can do for your child. So speak up for language education. Learn more at www.discoverlanguages.org.

Discover Languages®
Discover the World!
www.discoverlanguages.org

Sponsored by the American Council on the Teaching of Foreign Languages

You probably note in this advertisement that the primary appeal is to reason. The ad offers a short list of reasons to support foreign language study. Also note the use of blank space—the blackboard—as a visual rhetoric device to focus the attention of the reader/viewer on the central image of the student writing Chinese characters. Do you see any signs of other of Aristotle's appeals in this ad?

Exercise 1
Collaborative Analysis: Determining What Appeals May Work Best

Complete the following activities for the scenarios listed after the sample analysis:

A. In small groups, discuss what appeals to personal credibility, to emotions, and/or to logic would work best for each scenario.

B. Discuss which appeal, if any, might play a smaller role because of the issue's purpose and audience.

C. Based on your group discussions, select one of the scenarios and explain, in a short written analysis, what the writer's best plan of action might be toward this issue.

Here is an example: For your boss at the restaurant where you wait tables, argue that you would like more weekend hours because the wait staff makes better money on the weekends.

- Perhaps here, an appeal to the emotions would be effective. Explaining to your boss that between college tuition and books and having rent to pay,

Students At Work: Thinking About Persuasive Appeals   49

> [handwritten margin: E.1 one S. for Analysis]

ur financial situation has become dire. Your parents do not help with
llege expenses, so you need more money to stay afloat financially.

appeal to personal credibility, as well, might have some effect. You could
ind your boss that you have worked efficiently and loyally at the restau-
t for the past year and a half. You have never been late to work and treat
the restaurant's customers to respectful, fast service. You assure your boss
that your excellent work ethics would continue during weekend shifts.

- You might also use an appeal to reason. You might point out to your boss that weekend shifts allow wait staff to earn more because there is more business on those days. More business requires additional staff, especially those with proven work records. Adding you to the weekend staff would not cost the restaurant anything extra. Besides, you would not give up all of your Monday through Thursday shifts, so the boss would not face having to hire new employees. In other words, both you and your boss would win.

Scenarios for Analysis

1. For a selection of your college's administrators, argue that a greater percentage of student fees should be allocated to providing tutoring centers to help students improve their writing.

2. For members of your local chamber of commerce, argue that businesses should sponsor a college-wide "Employment Fair" to provide students opportunities to speak with employers specific to their respective majors or employment dreams.

3. For a group of concerned parents, argue that class sizes in a local elementary school should be reduced by half.

4. For doctors and nurses at your college's health clinic, argue that condoms should be readily available and free for college students who request them.

5. For your professor in an argument or composition course, argue that the required oral presentation should be dropped from the syllabus.

STUDENTS AT WORK: THINKING ABOUT PERSUASIVE APPEALS

In an in-class exercise, students were asked to write, even brainstorm if they wished, about a topic having personal significance to them and to discover how using their knowledge of Aristotle's three persuasive appeals might help them understand their argument. The following is student Tami's response, including random thoughts and a perhaps surprising conclusion on her part.

1   I guess the thing most on my mind right now is that I didn't make our school's volleyball team and I think I should have. I didn't get a scholarship to play when I graduated from high school so I was a walk-on, tried out and was cut. My argument should be something like "Walk-ons

getting an equal chance to make our school's volleyball team." Kinda lame but this might work.

2. How would I establish my credibility? Well, I have played volleyball since I was 11 and was a starter on my high school team three years in a row. One school scouted me for a scholarship so I must have at least some talent. I think I'm a team player and could have made a difference as a setter for our school's team.

3. What emotional appeals could I use? I don't think the coach gave me the same chance as some of the other girls because I was a walk-on. Maybe there's something I could say about fairness. Maybe I could point out that I tried out on my own and my ambition to play without a scholarship says something about me. I don't think the coach liked me because I graduated from a small high school. That ****es me off.

4. What reasons could I give? Just because I was a walk-on doesn't mean I can't play volleyball as well as the girls who got scholarships. I made all-conference my junior year in high school. At the try-outs for the team, the coach said she had room for three walk-ons so I should have gotten a chance.

5. Okay so how do I go about this? Now that I look at what I wrote, I don't think I can. The other day [professor's name] said that sometimes we pick topics that are too close to us. This whole thing about volleyball may be that for me. Just cause I played okay in high school doesn't give me credibility I don't think. And look at the emotional stuff I put down. It makes me look like a clown. How do I really know the coach didn't like me; she didn't say that. Maybe I'm just mad and that probably wouldn't help my argument. I hate this sometimes. My so-called logical reasons are lame too. Someone would probably say that the girls who got scholarships got them for a reason and that same reason is why I didn't. This whole idea is just about me. What did [professor's name] say—no reasons, no argument. If I try to use what I wrote, I think Aristotle would shoot me.

Exercise 2
Your Writing/Reading in Process: Using Appeals Effectively to Develop Arguments

Let's say that you intend to write an argument defending this claim: "Before they marry, an engaged couple should thoroughly discuss how they should handle their finances and raise their children." In groups of three or four, discuss what appeals (to credibility, to emotion, or to reason) might work best for the given audience. Do you see a need for all three types of appeals? What emotional appeals, for example, might be effective? How might you establish your credibility? What evidence might you have to present to defend your claim? Where might you find such evidence? Who, for instance, might you interview? And so forth.

Many articles have been written on similar topics dealing with premarital issues. If possible, locate one of them (perhaps on the Internet) and discuss which appeals appear in the piece. Are these appeals effective?

INDUCTIVE REASONING

> **INDUCTIVE REASONING** *is the drawing of a conclusion based upon specific pieces of evidence, such as observations, experiments, and experiences.*

Inductive reasoning is the process of drawing a conclusion *after* collecting pieces of evidence, observations, scientific experimentation, personal experience, and the like. In other words, instead of moving *from* a principle or generalization (as you will see with deductive reasoning), you move *toward* the forming of a new principle or generalization. We all know that standing in an open field during a lightning storm is dangerous, but how did we come to know this? After years of observations of the power of lightning and hearing stories of people being struck while in an open field, we concluded that the practice is dangerous. In other words, we derived this conclusion through induction.

Inductive reasoning is perhaps the most basic means by which humans learn. Think of a newly born child. That child is born with no conclusions whatever about how the world works, but throughout its lifetime, the child adds up the total of his or her experiences to draw conclusions about how things work, whom he or she can trust, how to do math, how to speak, and so forth. A simple example is this: Ask yourself how you learned not to touch a hot stove burner. Now, you were not born knowing this, but over time you added up pieces of information about hot stove burners (your parents' warnings, your own touching of hot burners in spite of those warnings), and concluded (formed a new principle in your mind) that touching hot burners is a bad idea.

When you think about it, much scientific research is inductive reasoning. Scientists will test the effects of a new drug over and over until they can reasonably conclude about its efficacy. Up to that point, they don't know if the drug will work. It must be analyzed many times before a reliable conclusion can be drawn. Or perhaps sociologists will gather statistics and observations about how poverty affects school performance and then—and only then—draw some conclusion(s) about this relationship. Before analyzing the effects of poverty on school performance (performing an inductive study), those sociologists could only hypothesize about any reasonable and reliable results.

Seeking a Reliable Inductive Conclusion

Some people find one aspect of inductive reasoning unsettling: inductive reasoning will generally produce conclusions that are to some degree only *probably* correct. Induction creates only probable results because rarely can you examine *all* the known samples or pieces of evidence possible for an issue. Think about this for a moment. If you were to study the sales techniques of clothing salespeople in the United States, how many thousands of possible "samples" might there be? You could never interview or analyze all of them. So, you analyze *some* of them and conclude about all. By necessity, then, conclusions drawn about all based only on some are to some degree *likely* but not necessarily *certain*. You must take two steps to increase the reliability of any inductive conclusion.

The first step to increase the likelihood that your conclusions are trustworthy is to study a *sufficient* number of pieces of evidence before concluding. A "sufficient number," though, varies according to the issue you study. If you know that all of the evidence you study is pretty much constant (such as studying the reaction of one chemical with another), then the necessary number of samples might be relatively small. However, should your evidence not be constant (such as studying the buying habits of college-aged men), then you must increase the number of samples analyzed. In either case, carefully consider what your evidence tells you. Concluding too quickly—such as drawing conclusions about all elderly drivers based on the behavior of two or three of them—will lead you to committing the fallacy of *hasty generalization* (see Chapter 5).

Second, since you will conclude about all based on a study of some, the "some" you study must be *representative* of the larger group. For instance, if you buy a bag of oranges and wonder if they are sweet, you could sample only one or two of them because the one or two samples will be very much like (representative of) the others in the bag. But should you be studying anything about human beings, finding representative samples is much harder. What is a "typical" human being? Let's say you want to predict how the members of your community will vote in the next school bond election. Statistics indicate that your community's 150,000 people can be categorized this way: 48% of voters are male, 38% of voters make more than $50,000 per year, 27% of voters are Hispanic, and so forth. Obviously, you could not interview all the voters in town, so you decide to interview 100 of them. These 100 voters (the "some") must represent as accurately as possible the whole community. So, 48 must be male, 38 must make more than $50,000 per year, and 27 must be Hispanic (keep in mind that one voter may actually represent all three variables). You hope that the sample of "some" will then at least somewhat accurately represent the whole—at least as far as the whole is defined. Even so, your conclusion will only be "probably" accurate.

Your overall goal in inductive reasoning is to draw the most reliable conclusions possible, a process that requires that you conduct careful research and think carefully about what your evidence suggests. Many people unfamiliar with induction tend to overstate in their conclusions what their evidence will support. Would you like it, for instance, if someone labeled your entire family as "the criminal type" based on the criminal history of only one of your uncles? Such a conclusion and social slap overstates what the evidence shows. Be careful in your own conclusion processes. (See the box on Weapons of Mass Destruction, p. 53.)

ARGUMENT IN ACTION   Weapons of Mass Destruction

One of the examples of *inductive reasoning* that will probably be used in agrument, rehtoric, and logic texts for years to come is the conclusion about weapons of mass destruction in Iraq prior to the war.

Barton Gellman is a *Washington Post* correspondent who reported from Iraq on the search for WMD. His assessment (in an online discussion: http://foi.missouri.edu/polinfoprop/hunt.html) of the strength of the case Secretary of State Colin Powell presented to the United Nations as justification to go to war was this: "*Evidence on display did not match the strength of the conclusions,*" a comment on the inductive process used to analyze the evidence.

Gellman explained that others argued prior to the war that the evidence was not strong including, most vocally, Senator Robert Byrd. A sampling of that dissent:

- Former CIA Director George Tenet tried to intervene in October 2002 with administration officials to have a questionable reference to an Iraqi purchase of uranium removed from a presidential speech, knowing that the documents supporting the assertion were obvious forgeries.
- Hans Blix, head of weapons inspection teams operating in Iraq prior to the war, expressed his doubt about the existence and extent of WMD: "We went to a great many sites that were given to us by intelligence, and only in three cases did we find anything— and they did not relate to weapons of mass destruction. That shook me a bit, I must say. I thought - my God, if this is the best intelligence they have and we find nothing, what about the rest?"

Gellman's colleague at the *Washington Post*, Dana Priest, wrote in 2004 that an investigation by the Senate Select Committee on Intelligence found that a document released to the public by the administration prior to the beginning of the war with Iraq "left out or watered down the dissent within the government about key weapons programs, and exaggerated Iraq's ability to strike the United States. . . . The report also notes that the White Paper dropped such qualifiers as 'we judge' and 'we assess,' making best estimates appear as fact."

In any inductive reasoning process, a thinker must at some point engage in an "inductive leap"– "leap" over unexamined evidence–because it is rarely possible to see all the potential evidence.

What were the beliefs and values of seasoned professionals that encouraged the inductive leap over unexamined evidence in this case? Was the conclusion about Iraq's possession of WMD reasonable?

How can *you* avoid making too quick a generalization about the evidence you are examining for your argument?

How should you qualify the strength of your conclusion to match the strength of your evidence (e.g., "we judge," and "we assess")?

What beliefs and values do you hold about your topic that might interfere with your ability to draw a sound inductive conclusion?

Exercise 3
Individual Analysis and Practice:
Forming an Inductive Conclusion

Assume that the following statements came from an inductive gathering of evidence. In small groups, select three of the statements and write down what evidence might exist for either the truth or falsehood of each. Consider as well what appeals to credibility and emotion each statement may require or induce.

- High school students should face higher standards in their math courses.
- Professional athletes should serve as positive role models for children.
- Private companies should provide free childcare for their employees who need it.
- Colleges should allow beer sales at sporting events.
- Prison inmates should be required to work for free.
- College general education course requirements should be abolished.
- Money is the root of all evil.
- Everyone has the right to own a handgun.
- Women who work outside of the home do not have their children's best interests at heart.
- Police officers should be required to be bilingual.

DEDUCTIVE REASONING

> **DEDUCTIVE REASONING** *is the act of moving* away from *an already formed conclusion to a new, more specific conclusion.*

Deductive reasoning differs from inductive reasoning in that instead of moving *toward* the formation of a new conclusion, deduction moves *away* from a conclusion we have formed some time in the past to a new, more specific conclusion. Remember how we inductively concluded that standing in an open field during a lightning storm was a dangerous act? Knowing that now, we can argue *from* that conclusion. If standing in an open field while it is lightning is dangerous, and I am in an open field right now and have seen some lightning—I am going to make a mad dash for cover. In a sense, then, think of arguments based upon observations, tests, and experiences as inductive (we form them after gathering evidence), whereas arguments based upon preformed laws, societal rules, principles of all types, and so on (we have formed these at some point previously) are deductive.

All arguments can be formed inductively or deductively, and most contain necessary overlapping of the two means of organization. In truth, you use both types every day in reaching the conclusions you draw about everything. But for now, let's examine how deductive reasoning works.

Deductive arguments form in three parts:

1. A generalization, rule, or accepted principle underlies the argument.
2. A specific example serves as a "test case" for the above principle.
3. A conclusion about the test case in relation to the principle is then drawn.

- People who drink and drive are dangerous to other motorists. (The principle formed sometime in the past that now underlies the entire argument.)
- Sarah drinks and drives (the specific "test case" for the above principle).
- Therefore, Sarah is dangerous to other motorists (the more specific conclusion drawn based upon the above two statements).

Here is a famous example:

- Countries that are politically and economically oppressed by another have the right, the duty to declare their independence from their oppressor.
- The U.S. colonies are politically and economically oppressed by the British.
- Therefore, the U.S. colonies have the right, the duty to declare their independence from Britain.

(This is the three-part skeletal argument used by Thomas Jefferson to form the Declaration of Independence.)

Here is an example a student might use to construct an argument:

- Behavior by adults who harm a child should be considered child abuse.
- A woman's use of crack cocaine during pregnancy is behavior by an adult who knowingly harms a child.
- Therefore, a woman's use of crack cocaine during pregnancy should be considered child abuse.

By forming this three-part argument, the student has established a valid, albeit skeletal, vision of a potential issue. The student will defend the claim that cocaine consumption during pregnancy should be considered child abuse *because* cocaine consumption during pregnancy harms the child's well-being *and because* harming a child's well-being is child abuse in general. The student's next step is to consider how to offer evidence for the first two statements. We offer this warning: Before leaping into a deductive argument's defense, consider the best way to phrase and reasonably defend the first two statements to ensure that you have fully considered the issue at hand and so do not attempt to prove more than you logically can.

Arguments of this type—however reasonable and valid they seem—must still be defended with reasons and evidence to convince a reader. To defend the first statement, your written argument would have to demonstrate fully *why* and *how* actions by adults who knowingly harm a child are, by definition, child abuse. But be extremely cautious here. Even though the three-part argument is valid, could you ever defend the first statement in a reasonable manner? Parents unfortunately harm a child on occasion, such as closing a car door on the child's finger. Now, a closed car door on a finger certainly harms the child, but is it *abuse*? The parent did not close the door on the child's finger deliberately. It was an accident. You would never be able to defend the first statement without first restating that the "behavior that harms a child" must be *intentional*. With this qualification, now you could offer reasons and examples drawn from your research and experience that demonstrate intentional harm caused to a child is child abuse.

Next, of course, you must provide reasons and evidence that a woman's use of crack cocaine during pregnancy is a deliberate act that harms a child. Much research certainly shows that cocaine consumed during a pregnancy has negative effects on a fetus's health.

You could effectively use such evidence in support of this statement. However, because of the change made to the first statement that harm to a child must be *intentional*, you would have to demonstrate that women who use cocaine during pregnancy do so with the full knowledge that their action is harmful to their fetus—that is, that their behavior is intentional. Possibly, you might assert that not knowing the harm created by cocaine use during pregnancy is no excuse, but doing so may not have much persuasive appeal. And what will you do about the occasional situations in which women were known to use cocaine while pregnant without significant harm to the child? In such cases, you will have to concede the point (see Chapter 3 about the nature of concessions to the opposing viewpoint) and then offer rebuttal that the majority of evidence still points to the harm caused a child if a mother uses cocaine during her pregnancy.

The final sentence of the three-part argument, of course, is the conclusion that will serve as your *claim*—and will likely appear somewhere in your argument's introduction. It is the conclusion drawn from the first two parts of the argument and thus must be defended in the manner described previously.

Seeking the Valid Deductive Conclusion

When you think correctly in a deductive manner, *a valid argument will produce a predictable and necessary conclusion*. The conclusion drawn is one that *must* be a result of the first two statements.

To illustrate the point about the necessary nature of conclusions, consider this example:

- People who are rich and famous are by nature hard workers.
- My chemistry professor is by nature a hard worker.
- Therefore, my chemistry professor is rich and famous.

Do you see that the conclusion in the above is not *necessarily* so? People who are hard workers make up a very large group, and not all of them are rich and famous. You certainly could point out many people in your life who work as hard as they can but who have never achieved wealth or status. So, your chemistry professor is not *necessarily* rich and famous, and the three-part argument is thus invalid. To reiterate, the conclusion *must* be a direct result of the first two sentences. Deductive arguments are everywhere and serve useful functions in our thinking processes, but we must all take care that the conclusions we draw are logical.

Deductive reasoning works from the three-part argument discussed previously. Based upon a defensible, already formed principle, you then cite a specific case that demonstrates the principle and draw a conclusion that is a logical result of the case compared to the principle. Forming the three parts (the "skeleton" of the argument), you can see how your conclusion is drawn and what evidence you must offer to persuade a reader when you flesh the argument out into its written form.

Exercise 4
Analysis and Practice: Constructing Deductive Arguments

Try to furnish the missing part in each of the following three-part arguments. Ask yourself if the conclusion in each case is a predictable and necessary one. In each example, (A) represents the overall, underlying principle or generalization, (B) represents the specific case to illustrate the underlying principle, and (C) represents the conclusion.

1.
   A. Children with ADHD display a lack of concentration on their schoolwork.
   B. Josh is a child with ADHD.
   C.

2.
   A.
   B. Professors Hartley and Garcia have training in writing theory and years of teaching experience.
   C. Professors Hartley and Garcia bring professionalism to the writing classroom.

3.
   A. Tax laws that favor the wealthy place an unfair tax burden on the middle class.
   B.
   C. Tax law HB-141 places an unfair tax burden on the middle class.

THE TOULMIN SYSTEM

> The **TOULMIN SYSTEM** appeals to a reader's or listener's sense of what is generally *true based upon evidence, personal experience, and commonly held beliefs.*

Philosopher Stephen Toulmin developed a method of critical thinking and argument that deserves some attention, particularly in his assertions about how people derive conclusions about issues and defend those conclusions. Toulmin believes that in ordinary, everyday arguments, people are persuaded by the general reasonableness of an argument based on the evidence they have, on their own experiences, and on commonly held beliefs and principles of a particular group of people. This concept reflects our ongoing emphasis on the importance of a reader's active involvement in an argument.

Toulmin believes that argument need not be a rigid system of rules; instead, people are often persuaded by what is *generally* true. Thus, a jury in a murder trial might convict the defendant if the evidence points to his or her guilt beyond a *reasonable* doubt even if the evidence does not point to guilt beyond *all* doubt.

Looked at another way, you may defend your argument's claim in a manner that people will probably believe. So, even if your argument does not reach any hard and irrefutable truths, your readers may be more willing than you think to accept it, nonetheless, if it is reasonable and familiar. Readers may not demand that you "prove" your claim beyond all doubt; they just want you to appeal to common sense and to the common experiences we all share in life.

Toulmin's manner of argument is based upon a skeletal system of parts, as shown in Table 2.1:

Table 2.1

Toulmin's Method	Toulmin's Terms
People form and assert a primary conclusion	Claim
from supportive, relevant examples	Evidence
by connecting that evidence to the claim	
with some shared, agreed-upon assumption	Warrant
Sometimes, the claim must be limited	
in its scope or force	Qualifier
or reasons and facts must be given	
for the warrant itself	Backing

As in other arguments, your *claim* serves as the primary assertion that your argument will defend as reasonable. Think of *evidence* as those specific pieces of information that lend direct support to the reasonableness of the claim. For example, let's say you and other students have gotten into credit card debt and face serious financial consequences. Based upon your experiences, you decide that college students probably should not have credit cards in their own names. So far, the argument would appear like this:

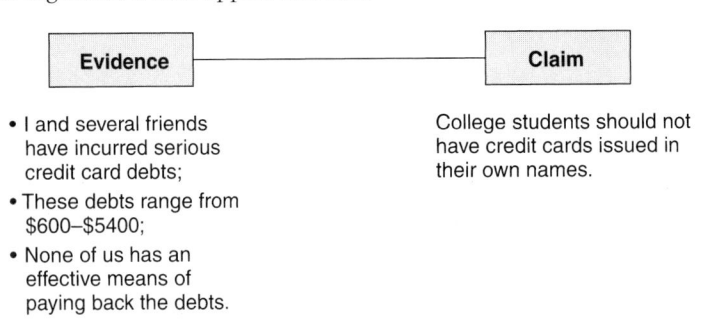

Evidence ———— **Claim**

- I and several friends have incurred serious credit card debts;
- These debts range from $600–$5400;
- None of us has an effective means of paying back the debts.

College students should not have credit cards issued in their own names.

But how did you move from this evidence to this claim? At this point, you need to understand an important connection (a "bridge" in Toulmin's thinking) between the evidence and the claim. Readers will want to know just how you are "allowed," indeed even "entitled," to assert the claim from the evidence in the first place. They want to know what the connection between evidence and claim is based upon. The connection that allows the claim to emerge from the evidence is the *warrant*, a shared assumption or general agreement that explains *why* the evidence supports the claim. For example, if you are stopped for speeding, you will eventually be fined in court (the judge's *claim* that you are guilty) because of your excessive speed (the *evidence* presented by the arresting officer), and the judge is authorized (given a *warrant*) to do so *because of the laws against speeding with which most of society agrees*. So, the judge's decision to fine you is warranted, or permitted, by the circumstances. When you speed (evidence), you will be fined (claim) because the law (warrant) allows this. In fact, laws serve as the warrants for punishment for any illegal activities.

Now, back to your credit card woes. You hope that your readers will agree with your claim that college students should not have credit cards because the evidence points to that direction. But why? What allows you to conclude that your evidence indeed supports your claim? What you are hoping is that your reader will allow you to state your claim from your evidence because that reader accepts something *fundamental* that forms the basis of your argument—the warrant. Your argument now looks like this:

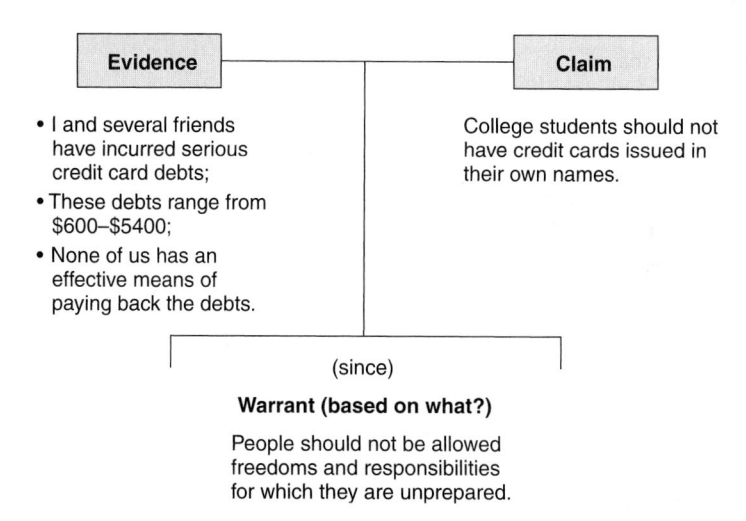

Evidence
- I and several friends have incurred serious credit card debts;
- These debts range from $600–$5400;
- None of us has an effective means of paying back the debts.

Claim
College students should not have credit cards issued in their own names.

(since)

Warrant (based on what?)
People should not be allowed freedoms and responsibilities for which they are unprepared.

Note that you state a claim and defend it with the specific evidence, but it is the more generalized warrant that allows your interpretation of the evidence.

Not all argumentative warrants need to be made explicit if the underlying reason for the claim's truth is apparent and accepted by the readers. Should you mention to someone, for example, that he or she should wear a heavy coat today (claim) because it is snowing outside (evidence), that person would not need you to make explicit the underlying warrant ("snowy weather makes people cold"). Nonetheless, even this simple warrant, like all others according to Toulmin, performs an integral function in the argument by providing the means by which you and your readers are entitled to connect evidence to claim.

> ### ALSO NOTE
> ### QUALIFIER OR "WEASEL WORD"?
>
> Just exactly what can you say about the strength of your argument, and how completely does your argument hold? Limiting the strength of your argument to its legitimate scope is smart and builds up your credibility with your reader. After thinking about the importance and meaning of good qualifiers, you may listen to and read advertising more critically. William Lutz, in his article, "With These Words I Can Sell You Anything," has his own argument about the way advertisers use "weasel words" to qualify away any responsibility for the effectiveness of their products.
>
>> Advertisers use weasel words to appear to be making a claim for a product when in fact they are making no claim at all. Weasel words get their name from the way weasels eat the eggs they find in the nests of other animals. A weasel will make a small hole in the egg, suck out the insides, then place the egg back in the nest. Only when the egg is examined closely is it found to be hollow. That's the way it is with weasel words in advertising. Examine weasel words closely and you'll find that they're as hollow as any egg sucked by a weasel. Weasel words appear to say one thing when in fact they say the opposite, or nothing at all.
>>
>> "Help"—The Number One Weasel Word
>> The biggest weasel word used in advertising doublespeak is "help." Now "help" only means to aid or assist, nothing more. It does not mean conquer, stop, eliminate, end, solve, heal, cure, or anything else. But once the ad says "help," it can say just about anything after that because "help" qualifies everything coming after it. The trick is that the claim that comes after the weasel word is usually so strong and so dramatic that you forget the word "help" and concentrate only on the dramatic claim. You read into the ad a message that the ad does not contain. More importantly, the advertiser is not responsible for the claim that you read into the ad, even though the advertiser wrote the ad so you would read that claim into it.
>
> Use your qualifers ethically, not as weasel words.

Now, let's examine how the other parts of Toulmin's system work. Perhaps, in your credit card argument, you begin to think that your claim may be somewhat overstated, that maybe your readers may not fully agree that "College students should not have credit cards issued in their own names" based on the experiences of only you and some of your friends. Maybe you need to alter the claim by the use of a *qualifier*, language that will limit the scope and force of your claim. Remember, Toulmin argues that people are persuaded by what is *generally* true. Also, you may decide that your warrant needs some *backing*—reasons for which the warrant itself is generally assumed to be true. So, you recast your argument:

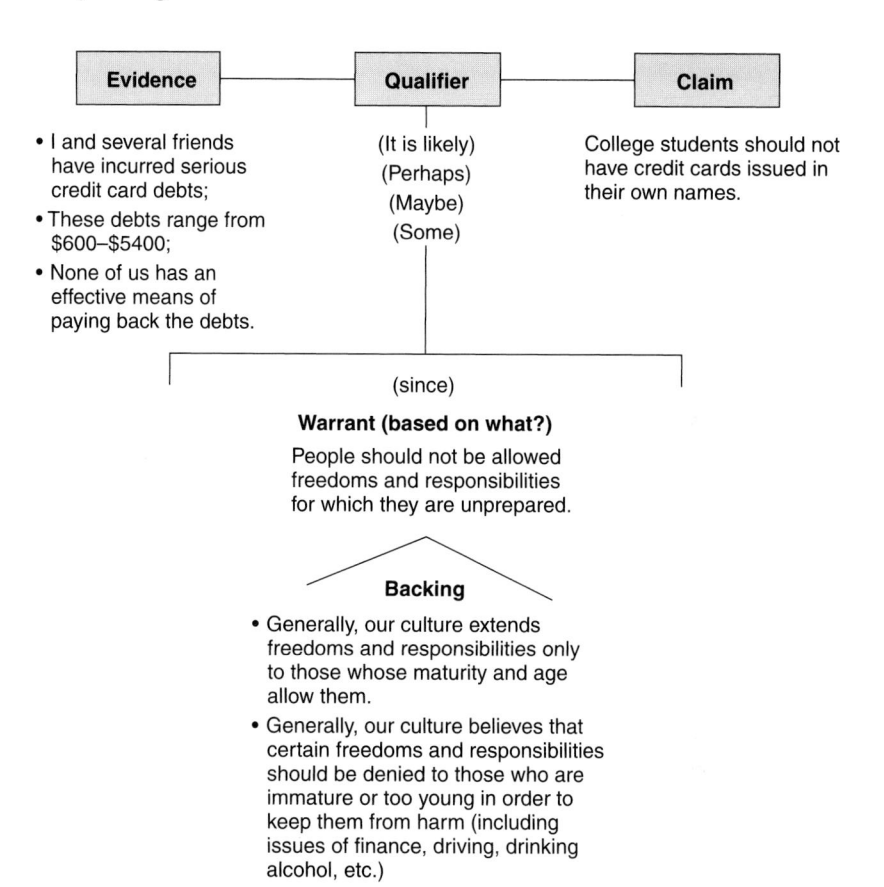

```
    Evidence  ─────  Qualifier  ─────  Claim
```

Evidence
- I and several friends have incurred serious credit card debts;
- These debts range from $600–$5400;
- None of us has an effective means of paying back the debts.

Qualifier
(It is likely)
(Perhaps)
(Maybe)
(Some)

Claim
College students should not have credit cards issued in their own names.

(since)

Warrant (based on what?)
People should not be allowed freedoms and responsibilities for which they are unprepared.

Backing
- Generally, our culture extends freedoms and responsibilities only to those whose maturity and age allow them.
- Generally, our culture believes that certain freedoms and responsibilities should be denied to those who are immature or too young in order to keep them from harm (including issues of finance, driving, drinking alcohol, etc.)

In this new form, you hope your readers agree that the claim seems generally acceptable now, although perhaps not absolutely so.

Using the Toulmin System to Analyze an Argument

To demonstrate how the Toulmin model of argument might work, consider the following newspaper article. The implied claim is that one member of a town's city council will probably vote against a proposed tax increase to fund a new jail. Read the article and then examine how the various parts of the Toulmin system can be extracted to analyze the argument.

Tax Increase for New Jail May Face Opposition

1   At a press conference on Tuesday, City Manager Nick Tomlinson stated that city council approval for funding a new city jail may be in

jeopardy. The jail, designed to house 300 inmates, would relieve overcrowding at the existing Anna P. Cowell Justice Center, but one powerful city council member, Juanita Alvarez, has questioned the necessary tax increase to fund the new facility.

2   Said Alvarez during last week's council meeting, "The tax burden on citizens is too high now, and approving a bond issue for a new jail may not be the smartest way to alleviate overcrowding at the current jail." Alvarez, however, declined to elaborate on other means of easing overcrowding.

3   Alvarez oversees the city's budget committee and, according to Tomlinson, has told him that the suggested tax proposal may not be significantly different from previous proposals for a new jail. Known as a fiscal conservative, Alvarez has voted against five of the last six tax increases brought before city council, and her approval for the jail bond initiative is seen as crucial for its passing. Tomlinson vowed to continue promoting the tax increase because the Cowell Justice Center now houses 450 inmates in a facility designed for 275.

A Toulmin Analysis of the Article's Argument

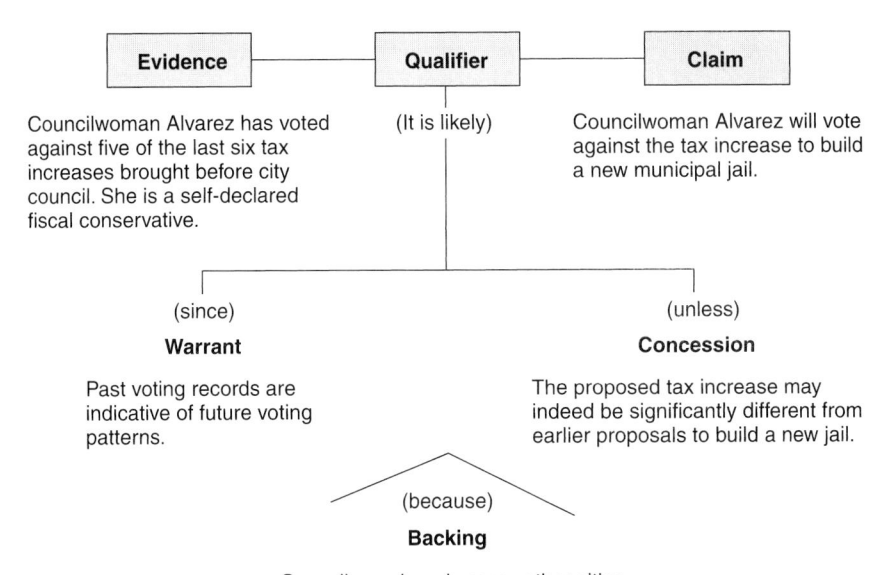

Evidence	Qualifier	Claim
Councilwoman Alvarez has voted against five of the last six tax increases brought before city council. She is a self-declared fiscal conservative.	(It is likely)	Councilwoman Alvarez will vote against the tax increase to build a new municipal jail.

(since)
Warrant
Past voting records are indicative of future voting patterns.

(unless)
Concession
The proposed tax increase may indeed be significantly different from earlier proposals to build a new jail.

(because)
Backing
Council members in many other cities, especially fiscal conservatives, tend to vote against tax increases of any kind. Political analyst Frederick Meyer notes in numerous studies that council members who have a pattern of voting against tax increases see doing so as a major responsibility of their office.

Exercise 5
Group Collaborative Analysis: Determining the Warrants that Underlie Arguments

In groups of three or four, discuss the following arguments. Locate the claim and the evidence for it in each argument. What warrant do you think allows the connection between claim and evidence? Does the warrant seem acceptable to you?

1. Professional athletes earn too much money for essentially just playing games that even children could play. When salaries range from $800,000 to $7.1 million per player, per year, it would seem that such salaries are excessive. Professional athletes receive such compensation even if they are injured and cannot play.

2. Our college's proposed increase in tuition for next year is excessive. When the national inflation rate sits at approximately 2.3% per year, how can the college justify raising our tuition by 12%? Many students already have student loan debts, must work outside of school, and have parents who cannot provide financial support. Perhaps the college could trim the proposed tuition hike by one-half or more.

3. Many political figures in this country have claimed that rap music advocates violence against women, the police, and other groups. They say that suggestive lyrics and the hard pounding beat of rap encourage violent behaviors. I disagree with such claims, and any politician's move to censor rap music should be challenged.

DISCOVERING YOUR OWN ARGUMENTS: USING THE CLASSICAL APPEALS

1. Write an argument to the appropriate reader (friend, parents, funding source, employer, etc.) for the purpose of gaining financial support for some endeavor—anything from money for a pizza to funds for a year's travel in Asia. Decide which Aristotelian appeal will work best for your chosen purpose and reader and emphasize that appeal in your argument.

2. Trust is one of the most important factors in electing officials of any kind. Write an argument either about someone you know quite well or someone about whom you have read a good deal who would make a good public official. Provide reasons and examples of his or her behavior that would establish the strong *ethos* of your candidate.

3. Choose a product and write three different advertisements targeting three different readers. In each ad, emphasize a different one of the three Aristotelian appeals.

4. Write an inductive argument about some practice you feel strongly about in bullet points. Each bullet should be a piece of appropriate evidence in sentence form, and you should provide a sufficient number of points to be convincing. After your list of evidence, write one concluding sentence, beginning with "Therefore." For example, your sentence might look like this: "Therefore, college students should not use credit cards for any purchase larger than they can repay at the end of the billing cycle" or "Therefore, parents should not give their children pets until the children are at least six years old" or "Therefore, owners of gas-guzzling SUVs should pay a luxury tax." Your task is to think about the necessary and sufficient evidence that would support your position fully and convincingly.

REFLECTIONS ON THE CHAPTER

You may be thinking after reading Chapter 2 that a thinker/writer sure has a lot to consider within an argumentative context. If so, you're right. But understanding how particular appeals and thinking strategies work will help you understand the arguments of others, plus help you discover the most effective means of arguing your own significant issues. You might start thinking, if you have some ideas about argument projects, just what warrants you and your readers may (or may not) share behind those issues and the kind of backing that would probably be acceptable for your claim. Are there some qualifiers you might need to use as you put your argument forward? After all, when you passionately (and justifiably) believe your claim, you want to defend it in whatever manner is most persuasive for your targeted reader. You not only want your reader to believe your claim, but you want that reader to share your passion.

CHAPTER

3

An Argument's Anatomy

Arguments work best when all their parts function together. As you read in Chapter 1, arguments occur in many forms and for many purposes. But if you read arguments carefully in any context, you will find that most have specific characteristics (working parts, if you will), each serving an important function in the argument's persuasive appeal. This chapter lays those parts on the work bench so you may study them separately, knowing all the while that they must eventually be put back together to form a working whole.

As you continue to consider issues in your life that are significant enough to analyze and argue, think about them in light of what you might claim, how you might defend that claim, and what you may have to concede. Chapter 3 shows you how this works.

TERMS AND CONCEPTS TO WATCH FOR
- Argument Concept
- Claim
- Reason
- Evidence
- Concession
- Rebuttal

QUESTIONS TO GUIDE YOUR READING
- What is the Argument Concept?
- What is the purpose of an argument's claim?
- What are the different types of claims?

- How do reasons and evidence differ? What is their purpose?
- What are concessions and rebuttals?

THE THINKING BEHIND AN ARGUMENT

First of all, let's agree that arguments do not come "out of the blue." You do not sit around a table and think to yourself, "You know, I think I'll argue something today since it's Tuesday." Rather, you often decide to argue an issue because you are provoked into doing so by what others say or do. Perhaps your father once stated that women have no place in the military, or a prominent senator believes tax breaks for the wealthy will stimulate the economy, or a friend decides to marry before she finishes her degree—all conclusions that may prompt you to respond. Some writers call such motives the "occasion" for the argument, the driving force pushing you forward.

Just how you will form your argumentative response (or, by extension, how you will analyze someone else's argument) depends on a number of factors. Writers and orators from Aristotle forward have recognized that effective arguments contain three primary elements, typically called the Rhetorical Triangle. The traditional view of the Rhetorical Triangle appears in this manner:

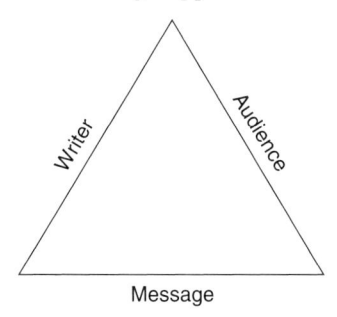

```
            /\
           /  \
          /    \
    Writer    Audience
        /        \
       /          \
      /_____\
         Message
```

All three points of the triangle exert influence over the others and are generally thought to correspond to Aristotle's three persuasive appeals (discussed in Chapter 2). In other words, a **writer** establishes his or her credibility and trustworthiness (*ethos*) by addressing the **audience's** values, needs, and concerns (*pathos*) and by composing a focused and logical **message** (*logos*). What the arguer wants to say, to whom, and why thus provides the guidelines (the rhetorical underpinnings, if you will) to produce an effectively persuasive argument. You will find that a thorough consideration of these three elements *before* you write an argument defines not only what you wish to say but suggests what your actual language choices should be.

In Chapter 1, we introduced a four-step "plan of action" that allows anyone to plan or to analyze an argument. It looks like this:

- What focus on what issue does the arguer pinpoint? (*Focus*)
- What audience does the arguer target? (*Reader*)
- What does the arguer wish to accomplish? (*Purpose*) To sell a product? To support a particular political stance? To move others to action on a social issue? To right a wrong? And so forth.

- How effective are the arguer's reasons and evidence to support his or her focus and to achieve his or her purpose for the intended audience?

The first three steps reflect the Rhetorical Triangle's importance for and influence on the effectiveness of any argument. In this chapter, we will add items to the fourth step to enhance your ability to compose and to analyze the quality of that argument. So, the fourth step in the "plan of action" will appear in this manner:

- How effective are the arguer's reasons and evidence to support his or her focus and to achieve his or her purpose for the intended audience?
    1. The quality of the argument's *claim*—its phrasing, placement, etc.
    2. The quality of the argument's *reasons and evidence*
    3. The quality of the argument's *concessions and rebuttals*

THE RHETORICAL TRIANGLE AND THE ARGUMENT CONCEPT

> The **ARGUMENT CONCEPT** is a matrix formed by an argument's focus, intended reader or listener, and purpose: what is the argument about, who it is for, and why?

Over the years, critical thinkers have conceived the three elements of the Rhetorical Triangle in slightly varying ways, but all address the necessities of successful arguments. In this text, we modify the traditional Rhetorical Triangle so that you can plan your argument in a down-to-earth manner, and we have witnessed hundreds of students put our version successfully into practice because according to Aristotle, successful rhetorical argument abides in "the ability, in each particular case, to see the available means of persuasion." Our plan for the thinking behind an argument is this:

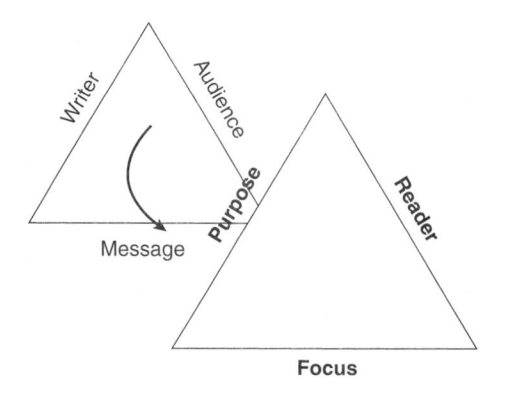

You note that our version of the Rhetorical Triangle replaces "writer" with "purpose," "message" with "focus," and "audience" with "reader." To our way of thinking, writers narrow a broad issue to a particular point (the "focus"), target a specific audience (the "reader," and your transaction with an audience occurs one reader at a time), and establish *why* the argument is significant in the first place (the "purpose" or what provoked your response). Like other versions of the rhetorical underpinnings of arguments, ours helps you plan your argument in a way that should establish your credibility as a sincere and trustworthy writer.

Our emphasis in this textbook is on how to incorporate the three underlying elements of persuasive argument into your *reading* of arguments and into the *writing* of your own, using what is in effect a "plan of action" that we call the **Argument Concept**, a matrix formed by an argument's focus, reader, and purpose:

I will argue about (Focus) *for* (Reader) *in order to* (Purpose).

Here is an example: *I will argue about* cell phone use while driving (Focus) *for* our community's lawmakers (Reader) *in order to* convince them that cell phone use while driving should be considered a factor when determining fines for reckless driving tickets (Purpose). Note that the Argument Concept gives your argument direction, boundaries, parameters, guidelines—however you wish to put it—*before* you craft an argument. Aimed at local lawmakers, your argument will demonstrate that cell phone use while driving is indeed a potential cause of reckless driving accidents and that increased fines for such phone use might deter its future practice.

The Argument Concept can likewise be "reversed," in that you can increase your understanding of another person's argument by identifying his or her focus,

---

ALSO NOTE
THE ARGUMENT CONCEPT AND DISCOVERY

Notice that on p. 67, we explain that the Argument Concept is a blueprint to use as you begin to *craft an argument*. The discussion of how to use the Argument Concept assumes you have a driving need for it. You have an issue you want to argue, and you need a systematic means of managing that task.

If you are not so driven, some preliminary free writing or a "discovery draft" may be in order to see just what you do know about, how you actually feel about, and how committed you are to an issue. Such writing should be unconstrained by structure as these limitations would defeat the purpose of discovery. We will discuss some other methods of issue investigation in Chapter 7 as we approach research-based arguments.

The value of the Argument Concept is that it helps you give form and substance to a general idea that is percolating in your mind. When you see its usefulness as you develop the shorter pieces of writing you may do in these early chapters, the Argument Concept system will become more comfortable and helpful as you approach "heavier" research-based arguments in Part II of this text.

reader, and purpose. In an advertisement for minivans, for example, you might recognize that the advertisers planned the ad/argument in this way: "We will promote our minivans for couples with children in order to convince them that our vans provide the most room and safety of any vehicle on the road." Of course, understanding others' Argument Concepts does not mean you necessarily agree with the arguments (and say, suddenly have the urge to buy a minivan), but you will have a better chance of comprehending just what they are up to and why.

In Chapter 4, you will see more concretely how the Argument Concept will help you plan your arguments and why doing so increases your chances of success.

THE THINKING WITHIN AN ARGUMENT

We all know that the anatomy of the human body is a series of interrelated and complex systems: respiratory, circulatory, muscular, skeletal, and so forth. All of these systems must work together to ensure health and vitality. Nonetheless, each of these systems may be analyzed separately to understand the unique function within the greater working of the body as a whole.

In like manner, an argument contains interlocking parts that when taken together form a convincing and reasonable discussion of important issues in our lives. We will examine each of these parts—claims, reasons, evidence, concessions, and rebuttals—to understand how each influences the others and how, like the parts of the human body, all must work as a team for the greatest effectiveness.

THE CLAIM

> The **CLAIM** is an assertion of an argument's main point, the argument's primary stance on an issue.

Some writers believe the primary **claim** to be an argument's most important sentence because it alerts the reader to the stance that the writer will take on a particular issue. The writer then selects every piece of information used in the argument according to how that information will advance the claim. Any reader should have no question about the issue at hand or the writer's view on the issue, and similarly no question about how and why any piece of information supports that view. Keep in mind, however, that various "subclaims" likely will appear within any argument as well—topic sentences within paragraphs, for example, are claims and must be supported with specific reasons and evidence.

Can you see in the following sentences that only one would serve as a primary claim?

- Should the United States abolish the penny?
- The penny is the most widely circulated of all U.S. coins.
- The United States should abandon the minting and circulating of the penny.

The first sentence cannot serve as a claim because, as a question, it takes no stance on the issue of whether the penny should be dropped from production. Questions work as effective instigators of research and argument but not as solid claims. The second sentence does not work either because it is a simple statement of fact. Most people agree that most facts themselves are not arguable, only how those facts are interpreted to form opinions. Only the third sentence may serve as a claim because it expresses the writer's perspective (formed after careful consideration of evidence, we hope) about the future of the U.S. penny. Like all effective claims, this one is *debatable*.

Types of Claims

Claims typically appear in one of four types. The first type is the claim of *fact*. Now, you might say, "I thought facts were not debatable," and in many cases you would be correct. For instance, saying "The American Civil War ended in 1865" is something anyone could look up and verify—and thus is not debatable. However, some claims that seem "factual" provoke disagreements among people:

> A college education is necessary to secure a good job.
>
> The September 11, 2001, attacks on the World Trade Center were preventable.
>
> Males are better than females in math and science.

To see how such "facts" may indeed be divisive, let's examine the first claim from above. Definitions of terms are crucial to factual claims. For example, the term *college education* could mean different things, such as a two-year versus four-year degree, a technical school education, a liberal arts versus occupational education, and so forth. And just what does a *good job* mean? One that provides a good deal of money? One that is interesting? One that works for social justice and change? You get the idea. Even claims of apparent "fact" can offer opportunity for reasonable argument.

A second type of claim is that of *cause and effect*, and these are often quite debatable:

> Listening to classical music enhances a person's IQ.
>
> Poverty leads to increased criminal behavior.
>
> Smoking marijuana increases the likelihood of later "hard" drug use.

In 2005, a University of Colorado professor, Ward Churchill, stirred a good deal of controversy when he claimed that years of aggressive U.S. foreign policies were a primary cause for the September 11, 2001, World Trade Center attacks. Claims of cause and effect, of course, require that you provide ample evidence to demonstrate a reasonable connection between the cause(s) and effect(s).

A third type of claim concerns *the quality of something*, often a product, a behavior, or a work of art:

> Chiropractic care is safer than standard medical care for back pain.
>
> Professional athletes serve as poor role models for children.
>
> Clint Eastwood's direction of *Flags of Our Fathers* deserved the Oscar.

As you will see in Chapter 10, claims about quality necessitate that you understand and illuminate for readers what criteria you used to conclude about the quality of a product, behavior, or work of art. What characteristics, for example, do those in the film industry use to evaluate a "good film director"?

Yet another type of claim is that of *solutions to problems:*

> Because of rising gasoline prices, commuting college students should use more public transportation.
>
> When a couple divorces, they can resolve their child custody differences by seeking court-sanctioned mediation.
>
> Cities can solve the problem of "red light runners" by installing cameras at all street intersections.

Perhaps you note in these examples that such claims both illuminate a problem and assert a specific solution for it. Naturally, the proposed solution must be reasonable and "do-able" within the context of the problem.

Exercise 1
Collaborative Analysis: Types of Claims

Analyze whether the following claims are those of fact, cause and effect, quality, or problem and solution.

1. Men are no less suited for the nursing profession than are women.

2. To ease traffic congestion in cities, freeways should have a lane designated just for large trucks.

3. Our university's online registration process makes registering for class too complicated.

4. ESPN should devote more airtime to women's professional basketball.

5. Spanking young children is an inappropriate means of discipline.

ALSO NOTE
LOOKING AHEAD

As you read about the parts, types, purposes, and claims of argument, you will no doubt be thinking about some arguments that have occurred to you.

We have discussed the act of *writing as a process*, not just a product, and have encouraged you to use this book recursively, previewing or reviewing sections when you *need* specific information.

If you are thinking about making an argument that involves solving a problem, for instance, now might be a time to thumb through Chapter 10 and glance over the section titled "Arguing Solutions to Problems." Some of the detail may be premature, but you may find the information helpful as you think about making claims of that type.

Exercise 2
Individual Analysis and Practice: Writing Possible Claims
Write two claims for each of the following topics. Do your claims give a straightforward, clear opinion?

- Television advertising
- The advantages or disadvantages of enlisting in the military
- Changing majors midway through college
- Legalizing medical marijuana
- Work-study opportunities at your school

REASONS AND EVIDENCE

> A **REASON** is any statement that defends a claim and so alerts a reader or listener to why you have asserted the claim. It is an explanation of your stance.

To expect a reader to believe a claim of any kind, you must provide ample support and such support comes in two types (or two levels of abstraction, if you will): **reasons** and **evidence**. You must have reasons, of course, for what you have claimed. Readers want to know, deserve to know, *why* you have claimed what you have. And you must have real evidence for those reasons, concrete information that you draw from research and/or experience.

For example, say you claim, "The United States should abandon the minting and circulating of the penny." Now, the reader understands your exact stance on the issue of future coinage but wonders why you have decided the United States should stop producing this long-accepted coin. So, you provide reasons at various points throughout your argument:

- The value of the penny has decreased over the years.
- Most Americans believe pennies to be nothing more than a nuisance.
- Pennies create problems for American businesses.

> **EVIDENCE** is any piece of concrete information that supports or defends a reason. It is generally drawn from research, observations, and experience.

A careful, thoughtful reader now wants more information, something he or she can "grab hold of" to understand why and how you formed your reasons and how they defend the claim. What evidence can you provide that the reasons have merit? Now your argument's structure may begin to look like this:

- The value of the penny has decreased over the years.
  - "Penny" candy no longer exists.
  - What a penny would purchase in the 1950s now takes a dime.
  - Pennies are not usable even in coin-operated vending machines.
  - Pennies are not even made strictly of copper anymore; instead, they are copper-plated discs worth far less.
- Most Americans believe pennies to be nothing more than a nuisance.
  - Most people simply throw pennies into a jar or piggy bank to get rid of them. Some estimates say that at least two-thirds of pennies end up this way.
  - Many people will not even pick up pennies they spy lying on the ground.
- Pennies create problems for American businesses.
  - One must consider the costs of producing 10 million pennies per day, including the labor costs.
  - Time and money are lost as employees must fish pennies out of cash registers (just to return one or two while shoppers impatiently wait), wrap them at day's end, and send them to a bank.
  - Many retailers now use a "leave a penny, take a penny" dish beside their cash registers to save time and energy giving change.

You probably noted in the previous examples that the evidence for each reason is quite specific. Rather than the more abstract, albeit necessary, reasons in defense of the claim, the statements of evidence give measurable, probable information that helps you answer a reader's call for you to "prove it!" In other words, you must follow the old writer's adage: "Show; don't just tell." By using concrete evidence, you "show" the reader the information that led you to construct the reasons in the first place.

As an illustration, how might a reader respond to your saying an event occurred "a long time ago"? Such an abstract "telling" might elicit guesses anywhere from "12 years ago" to "1200 years ago," depending on the reader's perceptions. As a writer, you have the obligation to "show" the reader what you mean. So, you specify the event occurred in 1878 so that "a long time ago" now has graspable, specific meaning. In your argument, for example, you couldn't merely tell a reader "Pennies create problems for American businesses" without showing that reader the evidence to back your reason.

"Evidence" comes in several overlapping options from which to choose:

- Statistics drawn from legitimate studies and surveys
- Opinions gleaned from authorities on the issue at hand
- Government-released facts and figures
- Examples that illustrate a point or show it in action
- Interviews with people personally experienced in the issue at hand
- Relevant personal experience in the issue at hand
- Actual names of people, places, events, concepts, etc.
- Specific descriptions of sizes, weights, colors, textures, distances, etc.

74 Chapter 3 *An Argument's Anatomy*

Using combinations of these options enriches your argument with more texture, more persuasive power, and certainly more interesting reading.

ARGUMENT IN ACTION **Reasons to Keep the Penny in Circulation**

The argument for abandoning the penny looks good. To check how strong the argument is and what others may say about the issue, there are many readily available Web sites to get you started. Visit the Americans for Common Cents Web site, for example, and you will find their argument, their "Top Ten Reasons to Keep the Penny":

1. The overwhelming majority of Americans want to keep the penny. . . .
2. Rounding transactions to the nickel—the alternative to the penny—simply can't be done fairly. . . .
3. The penny facilitates commerce. The U.S. Mint currently produces more than 8 billion pennies annually to meet broad public demand. . . .
4. Eliminating the penny would hurt charitable causes. Charities such as the Salvation Army, the Ronald McDonald House Foundation, and the Leukemia & Lymphoma Society rely significantly on these critical contributions. . . .
5. Abolishing the penny could erode consumer confidence in the economy. An A.P.- Ipsos poll conducted in November 2006 found that 71% of respondents fear that getting rid of the penny will spur vendors to round up their prices . . .
6. Elimination of the penny will hurt those who can afford it least—the poor and individuals on fixed incomes. Increased prices due to rounding would fall disproportionately on those who make cash purchases. . . .
7. Eliminating the penny would increase inflation. . . . According to Lombra, a conservative estimate of rounding translates into government outlays being close to $1 billion over five years.
8. The worldwide jump in metals prices has made the penny and other U.S. coins more expensive to produce (it costs almost 9 cents to make a nickel). Historical pricing data suggests that these jumps may be temporary. . . .
9. The penny is part of our nation's history and culture. . . .
10. A penny redesign law will honor President Lincoln in 2009. . . .

Exercise 3
Collaborative Analysis: Finding Reasons and Evidence for Issues

Granted, you may not have conducted much thinking or research about the topics in Exercise 2 (p. 72), but in this exercise, write the reasons you might offer to support one of the claims you developed in Exercise 2. Ask yourself if each reason supports the claim in a reasonable and direct manner.

Next, write the evidence you might offer (or what types of evidence you would need) to support the reasons you have discovered. Be prepared to have both potential reasons and evidence evaluated by the class. Might the claim you select along with the accompanying reasons and evidence work for a future written argument in this course or in another? Do your selected issue and potential support seem engaging and possibly divisive?

CONCESSIONS AND REBUTTALS

> A **CONCESSION** *is an acknowledgment of a point made by someone with a differing viewpoint about an issue, often necessary to be fair and trustworthy in an argument.*

Like most people, you probably find it difficult to believe, or even carefully listen to, arguments from people whom you do not trust. So when you write, it becomes necessary for your transaction with a reader that you establish yourself as trustworthy (more on this quality of ethical persuasion in Chapter 2). One of the most potent means of doing so is by being *fair* in your presentation of your argument. Few readers will seriously consider your arguments if they detect that you are biased in your providing of evidence or if you ignore, distort, or make light of the arguments counter to your own.

Remember from the early part of this textbook that the purpose of argument is to think carefully about the development of reasonable and defensible conclusions. Thus, in many argumentative contexts, you will find the need to offer **concessions** to those who would argue against your claim. You can fairly assume that most significant issues in our lives will generate differing perspectives. Just recall the issue of drilling for oil in environmentally sensitive areas, and you can see that even given the same evidence, different people will interpret that evidence differently—based, of course, on their knowledge of the subject, values, education, background, and so forth. And again you can assume that most people who disagree with you are nonetheless reasonable; they just don't agree with your interpretation.

First, of course, you must attempt to anticipate what objections someone might have to your claim. Just like in sports, you can establish your offense better if you understand how someone may defend against it. Concessions, then, are acknowledgments of the opposing reasons given for a claim counter to your own. You "grant" or "allow" that the arguments for a different perspective deserve some consideration, all in the name of a fair and equitable examination of the issue at hand. You may wonder at this point, "Won't acknowledging the other side's viewpoint damage the power of my own?" Actually, no. Thinking people recognize that all arguments have counter positions and that your acknowledgment of them signals the fact that you have studied the issue thoroughly: You know the varied perspectives and are prepared to address them. In short, you *increase* the power of your own argument (and the trust of your readers) by being fair and balanced.

Let's use the oil-drilling issue as an example. After examination of the available evidence, perhaps you conclude that drilling for oil in environmentally sensitive locations is not a good idea (your working claim). But you also recognize that those who support such drilling believe that it would decrease our country's dependence on foreign oil sources—an argument that seems reasonable and worthy of a concession. So, in your argument you concede the point: "Granted, drilling for oil in environmentally sensitive locations may decrease our country's dependence on foreign oil sources, however slightly." Doing so, you admit to your reader that although you may disagree *overall* with drilling for oil in Alaska and similar places, the opposing side has a reasonable point that should be brought into the open for fair consideration. Interestingly, offering concessions demonstrates certain courage. You don't fear an opposing argument; you merely disagree with it. Writers typically signal their use of concession with words like these:

- Granted
- Admittedly
- Although it may seem true that
- Although . . .
- Although some people believe
- I acknowledge

ALSO NOTE
OTHER POTENTIAL ARGUMENTS ABOUT THE ALASKAN WILDERNESS

The issue of drilling for oil in the Alaskan wilderness is complex. If you were intrigued and wished to take a first step to pursue this topic, you might want to visit the Alaska Wilderness League Web site, http://www.alaskawild.org/pressroom_mythsfacts.html. This nonprofit organization lists extensive information regarding what they call the "myths" about the benefits of oil development in the Arctic National Wildlife Refuge. They address such questions as the proportion of the Refuge that will be affected, the potential effect on U.S. oil and gas consumers, the impact on polar bear habitats, and many other aspects of this controversy. This information would help you find the many different perspectives on the issue and many of the points argued about drilling.

> A **REBUTTAL** is an "answer" to a concession that refutes a point made by someone with an opposing viewpoint.

In arguments, though, most of the time, when you offer a concession to the opposing point of view, you should respond to it with a **rebuttal**. You have admitted the counter argument has a point, but then you "answer" it with arguments of your own. For example, once you have conceded that drilling for oil in environmentally sensitive locations may decrease our country's dependence on foreign oil sources, you might respond by saying that we need not drill more, but could better conserve the oil we now produce. People might drive less, car manufacturers might produce cars with increased gas mileage, people might carpool, and so forth. In other words, although it is necessary for you to be fair and acknowledge a legitimate opposing point, you need not just let it hang in the air of your argument. Using a rebuttal, you show why you still believe your overall argument is defensible. Writers signal their use of rebuttal with words like these:

- However
- On the other hand
- Still
- Nonetheless
- But
- Another possibility exists
- Maybe X has not considered

Examine how a student writer, Jim Brennan, has written a personal essay that still has a broad audience. With some research into attitudes and experiences expressed on the Internet, Jim has answered a question many young men and women his age may wonder about. Notice how his essay demonstrates the different parts of the "anatomy of argument."

Prereading questions to consider as you read Jim's argument:

1. What do you think of the way Jim uses "I" in this argument? Is it effective? Would the essay be more relevant to his prospective reader if he wrote in third person instead of first? Why or why not? (This issue is discussed in Chapter 11.)

2. Has Jim provided *sufficient* evidence about the effects of getting a tattoo on getting a job? Is the evidence *typical*?

3. If Jim were to expand on this argument, what kind of more thorough research might he do?

4. Is Jim's choice to reserve his claim until the end of the essay effective? Why or why not?

78 Chapter 3 *An Argument's Anatomy*

Visual Rhetoric...
TATTOOS AT WORK

Arizona government employee Tim Hendrickson has tattoos on his arms, back, and shoulders. He also has black gauges in his earlobes. Hendrickson says he doesn't want people he interacts with at work to be distracted from what he's saying, so he wears long sleeves. This way he can express himself through his body art in his personal life but maintain a professional demeanor consistent with the policies in his employee handbook.

In what ways are tattoos a use of visual language? What are the different kinds of arguments that these images might make? Should employers be able to restrict this kind of language—argument—in the workplace?

STUDENTS AT WORK: ANALYSIS OF THE STRUCTURE OF A STUDENT ARGUMENT
Tagged on the Job
Jim Brennan

1   Many decisions people make during their youth don't seem to be a big deal when they make them, but later they reflect on that decision and wonder why they didn't think ahead — why they didn't think of how that decision might affect them in the future. I had just that experience when I was considering getting a tattoo a few weeks ago. I had seen one of my friends come home with a very artistic and bright-colored Chinese symbol of strength on his bicep, and, since I had frequently thought about this before, I decided I'd look into it further. I found an artist, went in and talked about the process and the cost, picked out a pattern (a Maori tribal symbol ringing the arm), made an appointment, and then made the mistake of telling my girlfriend.

2   While she never says what she thinks I should do, she asked me some questions that made me wonder if I had looked into the decision as far as I needed to. What if I change my mind and don't like it anymore? Can they be removed, and what does that cost? Most important, what will having a tattoo have to do with my getting a job now and later on? This was a dose of reality that I didn't really want to take, but she had a point. I was also planning on applying for a job at the local Lowe's home improvement store, so knowing how this decision might affect my chances was important.

3   My Chinese-tattooed friend works in the kitchen at a local restaurant, and he didn't have any trouble, but of course he wasn't dealing with the public. To figure out if there would be an impact on my plans for work, I looked on the Internet to see if people were talking about their experiences. It turns out that a lot of people have the same question I did. On the MacForums.com site, for example, 22 people, men and women who seemed about my age, were talking back and forth about "Tattoos and Jobs." One guy who identified himself as "electrofunk" said that he had "ink" all over his body, but that since his job was selling fiber optics, his tattoos are covered when he

Although the reader is not sure of Jim's final decision, the Argument Concept of the paper is clear at this point: Jim will argue about getting a tattoo for young people like him who may be trying to get a job in order to make them aware of the possible disadvantages they may face.

Note that Jim decides to reserve his final claim until the end of his argument. Here he provides reason and purpose for his investigation, a purpose with which his reader may identify.

*One **reason** not to get a tattoo is if there is evidence it will cause Jim trouble in the job market. Here he has provided **evidence** from those who have tattoos that, if he follows a few reasonable guidelines, there may not be a serious negative impact.*

80 Chapter 3 *An Argument's Anatomy*

goes into a bank or a hospital to try to make a sale. "OutThere," on the other hand, said she (he?) knew of a coworker who got fired for getting a "huge bleeding skull" on his forearm; it didn't "look good when you're serving ice cream and coffee." Another girl, "Shirley," said she was asked to cover up a small red rose on her arm with a "blue plaster," the British name for a band-aid, at work. She said, however, that the band-aid brought more attention from customers than the tattoo did. "User23" had some input that I might need to think about. He said,

> I've had corporate jobs where visible tattoos were never a problem. Only problem with tattoos I had was when I worked crappy retail jobs in my early 20s. They seem to care the most b/c their customer base is (generally) boring middle class types who don't understand that sort of thing . . . or, at least that is the excuse these jobs give as to why one must cover up, or get out.

4   This comment got my attention because that "crappy" retail job for someone in their 20s was exactly what I was headed for. From what these people were saying, it seemed like I would be safe if I got a moderate, not an outrageous, tattoo, and if I had it put high enough on my arm that I could easily cover it up during an interview and when I was at work if necessary.

*Notice that at the end of this section, Jim makes it clear what **inductive conclusion** (see p. 51) he wants his reader to draw from the evidence provided.*

5   The National Association of Colleges and Employers (NACE) must have thought this was a growing issue because they did a Job Outlook 2001 Annual Survey to find out what influences hiring decisions, available at www.valuereports.com. Employers ranked 10 different physical features of job candidates as to how much they would influence their hiring decisions. On a three-point scale (1 was no influence and 3 was a strong influence), employers rated obvious tattoos "2," but both "nontraditional attire" (2.3) and "handshake" (2.1) ranked higher. Marilyn Mackes, the Executive Director of NACE, says, "The best advice for new college graduates: Err on the side of caution."

*In this section, Jim is still working with his first **reason** to consider not to get a tattoo—that it will hurt him in the job market—but he offers **evidence** here from a different perspective: potential employers.*

6   I did find out, however, on the FindLaw. com site, that employers can set their own standards for work attire, and that includes most everything from makeup to tattoos and piercings. They can also fire employees who don't meet the requirements. An interesting case of this from the VeloNews Web site is the cyclist David

Again, Jim draws a conclusion from the evidence he has provided for his reader.

Clinger who was to be a new member of the Webcor cycling team. He showed up for the job with a face newly covered in tattoos and Webcor said "no deal." He is threatening to get legal help because of discrimination, but it doesn't look like the law is on his side in this one.

7   So, what if I do want a job in the future that might be a problem with a tattoo? It *is* possible to get them removed. A recent *60 Minutes* feature (November 5, 2006) covered the growing trend of tattooing. One man said his tattoo cost $140, but that he thought it was causing him problems in the job market, and it would cost $1200 to $1500 to remove. The *Howstuffworks.com* Web site has good, graphic information on how tattooing works and how they are removed. A physician quoted on the site estimates that over 50% of the people who get a tattoo later regret it and want it removed by one of several methods. There is *dermabrasion* where the skin is actually sanded down. *Cryosurgery* freezes the skin before it is removed, and *excision* is the process of cutting off the tattoo with a scalpel and then closing it up with stitches. None of those sound too good, but at least it is possible to correct a mistake.

*Jim has **conceded**, in the end of the previous paragraph and in the beginning of this one, that there may be some reason for him to avoid the tattoo. Then he provides a **rebuttal**: he can always have it removed if necessary.*

8   I haven't cancelled my appointment yet. One person on the *60 Minutes* program said she thought what was happening was a long-term change in attitude, not just a momentary fad, just like what people thought decades ago about women wearing pants. From what I've found, she may be right. *It sounds like acceptance may be growing, but if I want to be considered for jobs at all places, I'd better put my tattoo in a place that is not going to be conspicuous at work. Or I* can wait until I have a position where I can call all the shots.

*Now Jim shares his ultimate conclusion—his **claim**.*

▰▰ Exercise 4
Collaborative Analysis: Concessions and Rebuttals

Using the reasons and evidence you discovered in Exercise 3 (p. 74), now consider and write out what concessions to the opposing viewpoint you might need to offer. Why do you think such points deserve to be conceded? Then, write out how you might offer rebuttal of the concessions. What reasons you discovered in Exercise 3 might provide direct counter argument to the points you have conceded?

DISCOVERING YOUR OWN ARGUMENTS: USING THE "PARTS" OF ARGUMENTS

1. Think of a small problem at your school or at your workplace in which you are involved. Write an Argument Concept that would take a problem solving approach to the problem. Draft a memo to the person(s) most able to help with the solution. Include a concession and a rebuttal in your argument; also, include a claim in your argument that contains the essence of your Argument Concept.

2. Imagine that your home or school community has just received a multimillion-dollar grant from the state lottery commission. Write an Argument Concept that argues for the proper use of those funds (claim of policy). Draft a short letter to the local or school paper making this argument and including at least one concession and rebuttal. Include a claim in your argument that contains the essence of your Argument Concept.

3. Almost all of us have committed some act that seemed like a good idea at the time, but which we now regret, and for which we feel some need to apologize. Write an Argument Concept that argues why you regret the action, but why you feel you should be forgiven, given the motive for your action (a claim of cause and effect). Draft a short letter to the person to whom you owe an apology, including at least one concession and rebuttal. Include a claim in your argument that contains the essence of your Argument Concept.

4. Who has been your best role model? What are the features of a good role model, and how does that person meet, fall short of, or exceed all those features? Write an Argument Concept that argues for the quality of your role model, including a claim that contains the essence of your Argument Concept. Do you need to offer a concession and rebuttal in this argument? Are there actions of the person that might seem to disqualify her or him as a role model, but, nevertheless, their other actions outweigh those shortcomings? Is it necessary or helpful to include such a concession/rebuttal section in your argument? Why or why not?

5. Recently several large fast food operations (most notably Wendy's and Kentucky Fried Chicken) have begun using different kinds of cooking oils in order to eliminate some of the "trans fats" from their products. This change is largely in response to public outcry regarding the unhealthy nature of many fast foods. Is it the government's job to regulate the quality of products such as this that have a dramatic impact on the health of its citizens? In what ways are fast foods the same as or different from other products such as toys or even tobacco, for instance, which the government regulates for product safety? Design an Argument Concept that articulates a position on this question of governmental control. Think about the parts of an argument

you would need to consider for such an argument. What reasons for and against regulation can you think of? What kind of evidence would be necessary and sufficient to support your argument? What would be the strongest arguments against your position? What kind of concessions or rebuttal might you be able to offer to those opposing arguments? (Depending upon your instructor's requirements for using outside sources in your papers at this early stage, you might want to review a few Internet sites such as the following for more information on this topic: www.mindfully.org/Food/ Fast-Food-Nation.htm#1, which includes two reviews of Eric Schlosser's best-selling exposé, *Fast Food Nation*; or www.BestFoodNation.com, a site developed by food producers to argue against Schlosser's contentions.)

REFLECTIONS ON THE CHAPTER

Have you ever purchased something—a piece of furniture, for example—that had to be assembled when you got it home? Did you make sure all the parts were in the box and understand how they fit together before you started? If not, you may have nearly finished assembling the furniture only to learn that a crucial part was missing. Our purpose in this chapter, then, was to lay out all the "parts" of an argument so you can "see" them up front before you begin assembling that argument. Of course, like you hope for your furniture project, you want all of the parts to eventually create a whole something perhaps even greater than the sum of the parts. So, it may be about time to get out your toolbox. Consider some issues significant to you—remember, no passion, no paper—and prepare to argue.

CHAPTER

4

Using the Argument Concept to Analyze an Argument's Plan

Chapter 3 offered you a brief glimpse at what we call the Argument Concept. Now, Chapter 4 more fully acknowledges and discusses the importance of understanding an argument's focus, reader, and purpose. Not only will you read the arguments of others more analytically (because you will recognize how those arguments take aim at a particular focus for a particular audience for a particular purpose), but you will begin to appreciate how keeping your eye on the focus, reader, and purpose provides those same underpinnings in your own arguments. You will learn that you must stay focused on the point of your argument, for whom it is written, and why.

TERMS AND CONCEPTS TO WATCH FOR
- Context in communication
- Focus
- Reader
- Purpose

QUESTIONS TO GUIDE YOUR READING
- What is the Argument Concept?
- How can altering any of the three parts of the Argument Concept change an argument?

- Why is limiting the focus important to effective argument?
- Why is understanding a reader's needs important to effective argument?
- Why is establishing a clear purpose important to effective argument?
- How can the Argument Concept be used to both analyze and create arguments?
- How can using the Argument Concept help you know what your argument should include or exclude?
- How does an Argument Concept differ from an argument's claim?

Imagine standing in line at your college's bookstore one day when two people behind you get into an animated discussion. One of them says, "I'm getting really tired of women being told how their bodies should look. Why is only one type of body acceptable? What's wrong with my body, anyway? I hate all this pressure!" For a time, you stand there blinking and wondering what *that* was all about. Who tells women how they should look? How are they *supposed* to look? What pressure do women face about their body image?

What you lack in such "communication" is *context*, the background and occasion into which the communication fits. You lack knowledge about what has happened, reasons it has happened, who is involved, and why all of this is important. You justifiably feel like an outsider who has just walked in on a conversation.

All communications of any form—and this is particularly true of argument—require that they be placed snugly within a context that is known to and understood by all parties involved. Even if you write a list of food items before going to a grocery store, you do so within the context of who will need this information (you) and the purpose of the visit (to buy food). Everything on the list should relate to your food needs, and anything outside of that context becomes irrelevant at that point. Your list certainly would not contain such items as "must wash my car," or "remember my essay for political science on Wednesday."

> **CONTEXT IN COMMUNICATION** *is any necessary background information and the occasion for understanding and/or expressing information. It is, essentially, the who, what, where, when, and why of an occurrence or issue.*

> ### ALSO NOTE
> #### A FURTHER DISCUSSION OF BODY IMAGE
> If you are interested in the topic of body image and would like to pursue it further, look through the essays in Unit 4, Our Body Images, beginning on p. 407 of this text.

THE ARGUMENT CONCEPT

As we have suggested earlier in this text, the **context** of an argument includes three rhetorical elements:

- Focus
- Reader
- Purpose

So, the primary focal points of any argumentative context include the *reader* and the *purpose* for the communication. Of course, any context also includes your *focus* (the limits you place) on just what you intend to say. Keeping these three overlapping requirements in mind as you write and speak will make your communications with others much more clear, efficient, and purposeful. For example, a letter of application for a job focuses upon your reader (the potential employer), your focus (I want this particular position), and your purpose (to further my career goals with gainful employment). Everything thus included in your letter pertains to one or more of these qualities. You will address your potential employer with respect, explain your qualifications, discuss why this particular company and you will be a great match, and so forth. Defining the context also allows you one other advantage: knowing what to omit. Your letter of application, due to its particular context, disallows your including the type of car you drive, who will win the women's singles tennis title, what your parents do for a living—truly anything that makes your communication with your future employer confusing or less efficient. Put simply, any information considered "outside" of the context should be edited out.

Exercise 1
Individual Analysis and Practice: Identifying the Argument Concept in Specific Scenarios

Identify the particular focus, reader, and purpose within each of the following scenarios:

1. A recent college graduate asks his parents if he can move back with them until he finds a job, arguing that his current financial situation prevents him from living on his own.

2. A student with a disappointingly low grade in an economics class asks the professor to allow her to retake a failed exam.

3. A citizens' group approaches its city council to ask that a new stoplight be erected at a dangerous intersection.

4. A state governor in an election year seeks approval for a tax cut from the state's legislators.

5. Parents of a high school student threatened with expulsion for fighting sue a school district over the district's "zero tolerance" disciplinary policies.

6. A student in a teacher preparation program questions her supervisor about her having to submit to a criminal background check before she is allowed to do her student teaching.

The Argument Concept and How It Can Work for You

Any writer can formalize the context of an argument by using the Argument Concept:

> *I will argue about* __(Focus)__ *for* __(Reader)__ *in order to* __(Purpose)__ .

This statement defines the boundaries of any argument by making it clear just what the writer intends to do, for whom, and why. Here is an example:

> *I will argue about* our college's lack of adequate parking near classroom buildings *for* our college's administrators *in order to* persuade them to add such parking because close-in parking would save students time and make our campus more student friendly.

Note again that such a statement allows the writer to determine what to include in the argument and what to exclude. His or her evidence will be restricted to the parking situation close to classroom buildings (not parking all around the campus), will focus upon school administrators only (not professors, lab aides, etc.), and will argue for more convenience for students when attending class (not for more comfortable buildings, more student recreation, etc.).

The Argument Concept in Both Reading and Writing

What you will find is that understanding the nature of the Argument Concept and how it guides a writer will also help you, as a reader, analyze the arguments put forth by others. By "reversing" the Argument Concept, you can understand the context of any other writer's intent. When you *read* an argument, you should try to understand what the author is promoting (focus), for whom he or she is promoting it (the specific reader), and why (purpose). After all, that writer used an Argument Concept, or some form of it, to write his or her piece. So, as a reader, you enhance your comprehension of a piece by understanding the context within which it was written.

As a simple example, say you are walking down the hallway in one of your classroom buildings when you spot a poster advertising a textbook: "For Sale. Used Economics 233 textbook. $40. Call 555-1234." Even in this basic argument, you can understand the focus (sale of this book), the reader (any college student who needs an Economics 233 text for an upcoming term), and the purpose (buy this book from me and we'll both be ahead).

Our primary point here is to alert you to the notion that reading and writing arguments are not fundamentally different activities. While reading, you construct meaning from the author's ideas by connecting them to what you already know and have experienced. "Oh, I see what this writer means. The same thing happened to me." Or you might think, "The conclusion this writer has drawn about the causes of the Iraq War are similar to what Professor Wharton told us in history class the other day." In short, readers don't simply "lift" information from a page as though ideas are like food morsels offered on the writer's plate. Instead, readers

88   Chapter 4   *Using the Argument Concept to Analyze an Argument's Plan*

Visual Rhetoric...
STARBUCKS CARAMEL MACCHIATO

Caramel Macchiato
A DELICIOUS BLEND OF CARAMEL, VANILLA, MILK AND COFFEE.

The Caramel Macchiato may be the trendiest thing to be seen with this winter. But if you're riding one of those funny little kiddie scooters at the same time, it doesn't count.

Starbucks coffee shops may define the term "ubiquitous" because they are seen everywhere at the same time. The company's advertising plan, the Argument Concept for their product, is probably as responsible for its success as the proliferation of the shops. Advertisers focus heavily on their "target market"—their "reader." They also are careful to define the message (the purpose and focus of the ad) they are trying to put forward. In many cases such as this, the purpose of the advertiser's argument is not related to the product itself, but why you should have it. Very clear signals are in the copy of this ad about that reader: "trendiest," "to be seen with." The target market for this particular ad is probably not the woman getting up at 2:00 A.M. to catch a bus to her job cleaning high-rise offices.

> What is the Argument Concept of this ad? Do you think the intended reader will respond positively to this argument? Why or why not? What is the point of putting in the line about the "funny little kiddie scooters," and how does it further define Starbucks' target audience?

actually construct meaning by connecting the ideas on a page to their own thinking. This notion should explain that unsettling feeling you get when you attempt to read about a topic for which you have little previous experience or knowledge. You have little to connect with and so the piece of writing (perhaps about complex physics theory) seems "difficult." On the contrary, if you have extensive knowledge about home schooling, for instance, then reading a piece extolling the virtues of such education will seem familiar and easier to comprehend.

Like reading, writing is a process of constructing meaning as well. You select what you know and have feelings about and write in a manner you hope your readers find appealing. If you believe your audience will know little about your topic—thus limiting their comprehension—you will provide them with additional explanation and specific examples. So, reading and writing can be used to aid each other. *Both reading and writing well depend upon your understanding of the communication's context.*

You probably remember times when the context for particular college assignments was not made clear. "Why am I reading this," you wondered. "Just what does my professor expect me to learn? Is this piece written to inform me somehow or to persuade me into a different way of thinking?" Or maybe your boss assigned you to clean the company's storage room but didn't make the context obvious. Again, you may have pondered why the storeroom, rather than other areas of the store, needs cleaning (a question of "focus"), why you were chosen for the job (a question of "reader"), or why the storeroom needs cleaning right now (a question of "purpose"). So, when you write your own arguments in class or on the job, be sure to keep your focus, reader, and purpose clearly in your mind so that you do not leave readers scratching their heads, wondering just what you are trying to say.

Because each of the three elements in the Argument Concept are so critical in both analyzing the arguments of others and creating your own, and because all the processes of this text depend on this important method, the following sections discuss each of the three elements of the Argument Concept in detail and provide practice in recognizing and producing them.

HOW THE TOPIC'S FOCUS INFLUENCES AN ARGUMENT'S DESIGN

> **FOCUS** *is a narrowed, limited aspect of a broader issue. It is a deliberate choice to concentrate on a specific part of an argumentative issue out of wide-ranging possibilities.*

The possibilities that each topic or issue offers can often be endless. So, writers narrow, or limit, what they will discuss to a single, narrowed aspect of the topic—the *focus*. Think of focus this way: instead of writing about a whole forest, write about one of the trees.

For example, assume you are enrolled in a sociology course entitled "Marriage and the Family," and the professor gives one of those innocuous paper assignments such as, "Write about something related to this course in 20 to 25 pages with at least 10 outside sources." Granted, writing assignments like this rightfully cause students to reconsider a career in fast food because they are so broadly stated. After all, selecting from the possible topics suggested by "marriage and the family" is like standing in your father's workshop, staring at his 112 wrenches and wondering which to select after he has told you to, "bring me my best wrench."

All writers, then, must acknowledge that nearly all topics are too broad to pursue without first narrowing that topic to one possibility. Your sociology professor, perhaps by design, has only thrown open the door to a roomful of choices about "marriage and the family": proper disciplining of children, interfaith or interracial marriage, same-sex marriage, fair resolutions of spousal disagreements, family planning, dealing with aging parents, single-parent households, the divorce rate, dual-income families, mothers who stay home to raise children, day care solutions, abusive relationships, marriage counseling, prenuptial agreements, dealing with in-laws, paying for children's education, and on and on. This small list of possibilities alone offers you enough choices to continue writing long after your sociology professor's lifetime.

Even selecting one item from this list may not be limited enough to write a substantially defended argument in the time and space allotted. "Family planning" alone suggests arguing for college courses in the subject, differing religious perspectives on family planning, concerns about overpopulation, decisions about abortion or adoption, and so forth. In many ways, of course, having so many options allows you to select what interests you most, but select you must. Effective argument comes about only when the argument is sufficiently narrowed so that you can *fully* consider its development needs to offer full, rich evidence in defense of your claim.

When you form your Argument Concept, your chosen focus on the topic serves the purpose of defining that one focused aspect out of myriad options. With a clearly delineated focus, you better understand what to include and what to exclude in your upcoming argument. A not-very-useful Argument Concept might read:

> *I will argue about* marriage and the family *for* soon-to-be-married couples *in order to* tell them what a challenge marriage may be.

Note here that the overly broad focus influences the argument's purpose, which, as stated, is far too unfocused as well. With such an unlimited focus, you could include just about anything you wish about "marriage and the family" without realistic concern for your reader's needs. Such an argument would wander as aimlessly as a newcomer to New York City. A more focused Argument Concept might read:

> *I will argue about* effective alternatives to spanking children *for* parents of newborns *in order to* encourage them to use nonviolent disciplinary measures when confronting their children's future inappropriate behaviors.

Likewise, learning to pinpoint the specific focus of an article you read is the first step in fully understanding the writer's intent. For example, the essay by Rubi Reyes in Chapter 1 is not just an essay on immigration; it takes a specific stance on the issue of American-born children of immigrants. The author was wise enough to know that "immigration" is a life-long project, not the subject of a one-page essay.

Exercise 2
Collaborative Analysis: Focusing Topics from a Given List

Following are several unfocused topic possibilities. In groups of three or four, choose two of them and write at least three ways that you might narrow (focus) each. You are seeking a "focus" that might suffice for a five- to ten-page paper.

1. Costs of a college education
2. Working while in school
3. Illegal immigration
4. The airline industry
5. Women's professional sports
6. Fast food
7. Family holiday traditions

HOW THE POTENTIAL READER INFLUENCES AN ARGUMENT'S DESIGN

One of the most important concepts in both reading and writing arguments is understanding how a reader interacts with the text. In this book, we have intentionally chosen to use the word "reader" rather than "audience" to emphasize an important idea: readers are *active* participants in what they read. A reader personally (and individually) engages with an argument and makes meaning of it. Instead of thinking of the transaction between a reader and writer as the passive presentation of material to an audience, think of the process as a dynamic activity. Think of the complexity of actually communicating anything very accurately to another person.

> ### ALSO NOTE
> #### ENVISIONING A READER
>
> In her essay, "Mother Tongue," Amy Tan talks about her experience when she first started writing fiction. She began by writing what she thought were "wittily crafted sentences" to demonstrate that, as a Chinese-American writer, she was competent with the English language. She gives an example of the kind of lofty language she tried to use: "That was my mental quandary in its nascent state."
>
> Then, she realized her technique wasn't working. She did what this chapter encourages you to do—she considered her reader:
>
>> I later decided I should envision a reader for the stories I would write. And the reader I decided upon was my mother, because these were stories about mothers. So with this reader in mind—and in fact, she did read my early drafts—I began to write stories using all the Englishes I grew up with. . . . I wanted to capture what language ability tests can never reveal: her intent, her passion, her imagery, the rhythms of her speech and the nature of her thoughts.
>>
>> Apart from what any critic had to say about my writing, I knew I had succeeded where it counted when my mother finished reading my book, and gave me her verdict: "So easy to read."
>
> — Amy Tan (author of *The Joy Luck Club*)

> A **READER** *is anyone the writer has specifically targeted to react to and negotiate with what the writer says.*

First, a writer has an idea, and to illustrate this idea, we'll have to start with a very small and seemingly simple concept: a box. Let's say you walk up to a total stranger (and most of the time, for academic and business purposes, your reader's current mindset will be somewhat unknown) and pass her a note that says, "I need a box."

Think of the many ways your reader can go wrong.

First of all, she might turn and run, thinking that you are some kind of lunatic. She has no idea why you even approached her, what kind of a box you are looking for, why she should care, if she should get involved, and so forth.

You see her hesitance, and, afraid she won't cooperate, you slip her another quick note: "A small box." Now, of course, you think you've cleared everything up. But imagine how many new possibilities this has opened! Not only are all the things she was wondering about not satisfied (how could you ever imagine all of them), but she now has started forming pictures in her mind of what you want. She envisions a small, black velvet box with gold edges, the kind her grandmother used to keep her pearl earrings in: the kind, as a matter of fact, she now treasures as a keepsake from her grandmother. Who knew! But this concept of "a small box" is not what you had in mind at all.

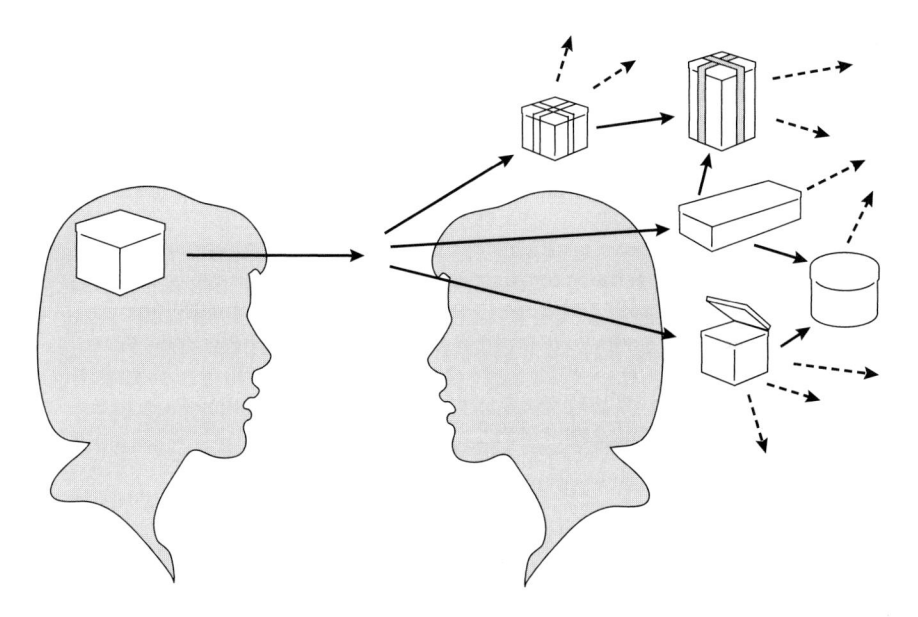

The point here is that, given any chance, a reader will often go wrong, even with the simplest of concepts. Why does that happen? We all have roles we fill, opinions we've formed in sometimes unknown ways, bits of information that may or may not be accurate, natural preferences, value-forming experiences, and personality quirks. All that we are goes into our interpretation of what we read. With thousands of possible interpretations, the chance that a unit of information you try to transmit, "box," will actually be received with any level of accuracy is slight. And that was just a box. Imagine, then, the complex nature of trying to communicate a sophisticated argument about, say, the ethics of CEO compensation to another person.

As a reader of argument, this active, two-way experience has happened as you read samples in the first chapters of this book. You might also, for instance, read an argument that a writer has constructed from his or her perspective about gun control. Now, just as you read that, didn't you have a reaction? Didn't you have some kind of "knee-jerk," automatic feeling on the issue that will color the way you read the argument? And where did that preset come from? Maybe you grew up in a family who hunted, and using guns safely and reasonably has always been part of your life. Maybe you read the article in *Time* years ago that showed a small picture of every single person killed one week by guns in America (464), and you remember that the number of people killed by guns in two years was larger than the number of people killed during the entire Vietnam War (that's true, by the way).* On the other hand, maybe you were accosted on your way back from a Kentucky Fried Chicken store by a man with a gun who then stole your chicken!

ARGUMENT IN ACTION   **Different Readers, Different Mindsets**

The death and legacy of President Gerald Ford (who rose to that position after the resignation of Richard Nixon) were the subject of an article in the January 15, 2007, issue of *Time*. In the next issue (February 5, 2007), two letters to the editor were printed regarding the article:

> 1. Shame on *Time* for insufficiently acknowledging the contributions of Gerald Ford, perhaps one of the most important American presidents of the 20th century—certainly one of the most decent. Ford deserved to be on *Times*' cover. He may not have been flashy or tested well with TV audiences, but he was a President with courage, wisdom, honesty, integrity, and compassion—in other words, a leader in whom we could place our trust. What other person could have done the hard but necessary work of leading the country out of, as President Ford himself put it, the long national nightmare of Watergate?
>
> 2. I don't buy the portrayal of Ford's pardon of President Richard Nixon as a reflection that "mercy and healing" were very much on Ford's mind at the time. Far from an act designed to help a poor beleaguered President and heal this nation's wounds caused by the Watergate affair, the pardon was a calculated political move. The pardon blocked application of the rule of law to a President who committed criminal acts while in office and was intended to save Nixon and the Republican Party from further legal scrutiny. It will forever sully Ford's record as President.

Here you readily see that each reader brought a different mindset to the reading of this article. One thought it was too hard on President Ford, and the other thought it made his political strategies appear heroic.

What other examples can you think of in your own experience when two or more people interpreted the same material—written, heard, or seen—in very different ways? What about their background, personalities, education, and so on, do you think accounted for the differences in interpretation?

What does the fact that your reader will bring a strong mindset to your argument mean to you as you think how to construct and develop it?

---

*Magnuson, Ed, Joyoc Leviton, and Michael Riley. "Seven Deadly Days." *Time* 17 July 1989: 30.

Whatever experience you've had, reading you've done, and conversations you've had helped establish your preset. *It is human nature that what we learn first, we believe as truth.* Everything else that comes to us is measured against that standard. It's as if our first perceptions take up arms and fight off any new ideas. The more educated and sophisticated you become as a reader, the more you will learn to disarm yourself and read to discover the argument rather than resist it, but that ability is a slowly learned skill and many or most readers to whom you will write will not yet have cultivated the skill.

As an argument *reader*, it is beneficial to monitor your response to what you are reading. Are you entering the negotiation, or is your preset going to rule? What experiences and background of yours have gone into that preset? Is the author aware of opinions and arguments that you and other readers might have as well as his or her own?

As an argument *writer*, then, you are part of this dynamic process of negotiating meaning. You are not just an organizer of objective and static information; instead, you are trying to engage your reader's mind in your process of thinking, to get the reader to see the "box" the way you do. To achieve any level of success, therefore, you have to think of your reader. Of course, you can't know in many cases precisely whether your reader is a hunter or the victim of a chicken thief. However, to write effective arguments, you must consider the fact that your readers are already loaded with perspective, whether they acknowledge it or not. If you hope to be effective in negotiating toward your claim with this active reader, you must think through the potential mindsets of your readers and consider them as you construct your argument, or your argument will be just one of those new ideas being fought off.

Exercise 3
Collaborative Analysis: Changing the Focus for Different Readers

Two broad topic areas are provided in this exercise. In groups of three or four, practice conceiving an argument's focus in terms of the targeted reader for each of these topic areas. Write an appropriate focus for each of the listed readers. Remember to be specific and detailed, not generic, as you develop your focus. For example, if you were to conceive an argument about mainstreaming special education students (including them in "regular" classrooms), you should pare that topic down to a manageable focus, targeting a reader with a certain mindset and addressing an explicit purpose. Remember, an argument can't be, and need not be, all things to all people.

Example of a poorly conceived focus and reader:

I will argue about mainstreaming *for* anyone interested.

Example of a well-conceived focus and reader:

I will argue about the process used in Valley Middle School to mainstream students with ADHD *for* parents of such students.

Topics for Practice

1. Leasing vs. buying new vehicles

    A. For new high school graduates who are headed to college
    B. For new car salespeople
    C. For owners of large real estate companies who need a fleet of nice cars to chauffeur potential buyers

2. Violence in movies on TV

    A. For parents of small children
    B. For those who advertise during these movies
    C. For reviewers of these movies in *TV Guide*

HOW THE INTENDED PURPOSE INFLUENCES AN ARGUMENT'S DESIGN

> The **PURPOSE** *is the specific reason* why *the writer is articulating the argument. It is what the writer hopes the reader or listener will gain from the argument.*

As you may suspect, an argument's purpose is its engine. The purpose for writing an argument is driven by *why* the writer decided to make a certain claim. And the question of "why?" is significant in the transaction with the reader. People are naturally drawn to the reasons others have for the opinions they assert; after all, if a friend should state, "I need to see a psychiatrist," wouldn't you immediately question the reasons, the motives behind such a claim? It's natural to seek understanding. Admittedly, you may not agree with the reasons your friend provides, but at least you now understand what drove your friend to such a startling statement.

When we discuss *purpose* in this textbook, we refer to more than the often generic definitions of the term: to inform, to entertain, to persuade, or to celebrate. Rather, we encourage you to define your argument's purpose more specifically, to give yourself more direction toward your goal. Doing so in the planning stages of your writing not only gives you a specific target, but later in your writing process helps you understand when your argument is "done" because you have fulfilled your purpose.

Purpose is an integral part of the Argument Concept and its function as a planning strategy. You simply could not say, "*I will argue* about genetically altered food *for* consumers who may not believe some of the food they consume has been altered in this manner." Your already somewhat dubious readers will automatically wonder *why* you have selected this topic for them. Readers will ask, "Why is the issue of genetically altered food significant to me?" or "Why should I concern myself about food of this type?" Should you not make your purpose clear—"so that consumers can make up their own minds about the safety of this food"—the reader has little reason to continue examining your argument.

Exercise 4
Individual Analysis and Practice: Different Purposes for the Same Issue

Practice conceiving arguments in terms of closely related focuses, audiences, and purposes for each of these topic areas. Write out an Argument Concept for each of the listed purposes. Of course, your audience may need to change, too, with the altered purpose. Remember to be specific and detailed, not generic, as you develop your Argument Concepts.

1. Raising the minimum wage

    A. In order to help wait staff make a livable wage
    B. In order to convince Congress not to raise it for small businesses
    C. In order to improve the quality of day care

2. Affirmative action (the rectifying of past injustice to identifiable groups by more open hiring and selection processes)

    A. In order to convince your employer to advertise more broadly for applicants
    B. In order to stop a medical school's practice of admitting some minority students with lesser scores on entrance examinations
    C. In order to convince Supreme Court Justice Samuel Alito to hire law clerks other than Ivy League graduates who have worked previously for a federal judge (A former Supreme Court Chief Justice, Rehnquist, actually had this hiring policy, which resulted in the hiring of only white males as his law clerks, the employees who do his research and write arguments for him.)

Exercise 5
Collaborative Analysis: Constructing Argument Concepts for Given Scenarios

Read the following scenarios (occasions that provoke a response) and then write Argument Concepts that you believe best reflect the context of the potential arguments. Read these aloud to classmates to see how similar or different your analyses are. One hint: The *purpose* part ("in order to") should be a real purpose—a specific opinion-altering or behavior-changing response—that you want from the reader. Try to avoid such "purposes" as ". . . in order to tell them about. . . ."

Scenario 1

A young man who has been home-schooled from sixth to twelfth grade enrolls in a college composition class, the first formal class he has taken since the fifth grade. He is quite bright, and he is confident he can meet the professor's standards for the assignments. He is apprehensive, however, because the syllabus clearly states that students are required to share their work with other classmates and comment in small groups on each other's work. Also, he sees that the last writing project is a collaboratively produced research project, and he will need to work in and out of class on the project with three other classmates. He has never participated in a team on academic projects; and as the term goes on, he becomes more and more anxious about this group work. The first time his group meets, he finds it difficult to contribute, particularly when the others jump in quickly to offer suggestions and divide up the work. He also notices that students in his other classes speak out frequently, and the teachers often let them argue points vigorously. In one class, several students have formed study groups, but he feels uncomfortable about asking to participate. Since he has been quiet in class, he assumes others think he probably doesn't want to join them. He survives the term, but afterward, as he reflects on the difficulty of his experience, he realizes he wasn't prepared for the social nature of contemporary classrooms because he only had independent learning experiences. He writes a detailed description of his experience in the hope it will be published on home-schooling Web sites.

Scenario 2

Christopher is sitting in the waiting room awaiting the return of his 12-year-old daughter from her appointment with the pediatrician. Nearly twenty minutes have passed, and he looks around for some reading material to occupy his time. He picks up a stack of magazines to thumb through and becomes more and more irritated as he proceeds. There are some old copies of *National Geographic* and a few very dated business magazines, but every magazine that would seem to appeal to his daughter is full of three things: diet information, cosmetic ads, and stories about how to be more attractive to the opposite sex. All of the advertising features scantily clad young women, usually being ogled by fully dressed men. Having never before seen this kind of magazine, he is appalled by the messages he believes are being sent to girls like his daughter about what it means to be female and how to be valued as a woman. Before leaving, he copies down the mailing addresses of several of the magazines, asks the receptionist to pass on his disbelief and disappointment that a doctor would display such magazines for young patients, and determines to register his opinion with the magazines.

Scenario 3

Leigh is an anthropology major at a large research university. She has been fortunate enough to spend two summers doing fieldwork at a recently discovered site that is beginning to yield important Native American artifacts. During her last summer, a serious controversy arose when the crew uncovered remains of what they believed to be ancestors of the local tribes. Word of the find circulated in the surrounding communities, and tribal leaders quickly demanded that the field team abandon the site and surrender the remains for reburial. Unprepared for such a dilemma, the team acquiesced and returned to campus, intent on finding a way to work out the misunderstanding so that the important work of documenting the history of this area and its people could go forward. Leigh is determined to research the situation and make the resolution of the conflict the subject of her senior thesis.

ALTERING ANY PART OF THE CONTEXT

Something you will soon learn in the process of writing your own arguments is that altering any of the three parts of the Argument Concept will change how you compose the argument. As a straightforward example, say you are writing a piece founded upon this Argument Concept:

> *I will argue about* home businesses *for* anyone seeking a second income *in order to* show that such businesses are often risky in terms of the initial investments required.

In such an argument, the focus, reader, and purpose are reasonably clear. The argument will focus only on home businesses, only on a reader seeking a second income, and only on the risky investment necessary. But let's say you decide to change the purpose of your argument so that your new Argument Concept reads this way:

> *I will argue about* home businesses *for* anyone seeking a second income *in order to* sound the alarm that home businesses often require far more time and effort than may be initially apparent.

Now this argument changes considerably. No longer will you focus on investment warnings (in fact, such information would be irrelevant to this piece), but you will now focus on the surprising amount of time and work involved in home businesses. Even though the focus and reader have not changed, your evidence and examples, because of the newly altered context, will strive to persuade your readers of time and work constraints—far different evidence and examples from advising your readers about investment pitfalls.

Or try changing the reader for your argument. Suppose you base a piece of writing on this Argument Concept:

> *I will argue about* the rising costs of college textbooks *for* new college students *in order to* encourage them to plan for the money needed in their collegiate budget.

Here again, the focus, reader, and purpose are apparent. You will alert new college students to a budgetary circumstance that they may not fully appreciate. Suppose, however, that you decide that new college students are not the group to whom you should address your argument, deciding instead to focus upon their parents. Your new Argument Concept reads this way:

> "*I will argue about* the rising costs of college textbooks *for* the parents of new college students *in order to* encourage them to plan for the money needed in their student's collegiate budget."

You should, of course, have significant reason for changing the intended reader. Perhaps you decide that many, if not most, new college students rely predominantly on their parents for textbook payments. And too, many parents who have not attended college, or did so many years ago, may not realize just how expensive textbooks have become. Thus, you concentrate on fulfilling the informational needs of the parents, altering your original argument to a degree. True, you may still use some of the evidence of rising textbook prices, but your intent now is to inform the *parents* that textbook prices have gone up so these parents do not experience sudden "sticker shock" or a financial heart attack.

STUDENTS AT WORK: USING THE ARGUMENT CONCEPT

Following are student Rebecca's three different examples of argument plans on the same general issue: college attendance policies. Notice how each plan (the sections and information intended) changes with varying focus, readers, and purposes as Rebecca explores a number of possibilities. Note, too, that although Rebecca can use some of the same information in various plans for her argument, she makes significant changes in what she intends to say based upon the needs of each changing reader.

Sample 1

> Argument Concept: *I will argue about* the lack of attendance policies in college classes *for* entering freshman students *in order to* explain how taking advantage of these policies will lead to disaster.

- An introductory section describing the loose attendance policies in my freshman classes, showing how easy it was to skip as many classes as a student might wish to skip
- A section giving the example of a large biology class in which there actually was a policy, but many students signed in for fellow classmates
- A section listing the excuses students can use to talk themselves into missing classes: "I need to sleep in," "I can just read the book," "the teacher doesn't know if I'm there or not," "I can get the notes from a buddy," and so on
- A section explaining what a college student is missing when he or she cuts class and how it's impossible to make up the work

- A section conceding the college students' age and level of responsibility allow them to make their own choices about attendance
- A final warning to the reader not to fall into the classic freshman "cut" trap

Sample 2

Argument Concept: *I will argue about* the lack of attendance policies in college classes *for* guidance counselors at my former high school *in order to* convince them to give workshops for high school students in preparation for this "freedom."

- An introductory section describing the loose attendance policies in my freshman classes, showing how easy it was to skip as many classes as a student might wish to skip
- A section giving the example of a large biology class in which there actually was a policy, but many students signed in for fellow classmates
- A section contrasting these college policies to those used in high school
- A section listing the excuses students can use to talk themselves into missing classes: "I need to sleep in," "I can just read the book," "the teacher doesn't know if I'm there or not," "I can get the notes from a buddy," and so on
- A section explaining how those excuses and rationale may have worked in high school, then showing how they do not work in the changed college environment that allows greater personal freedom, but demands greater personal responsibility as well
- A section suggesting how high schools could prepare students much better for this critical change in policy by offering workshops led by alumni of our high school who have experienced this problem and have suffered the consequences
- A section describing the potential content of such a workshop, focusing on methods that would best affect high school seniors.
- A final section suggesting a pilot program and offering help in developing such workshops

Sample 3

Argument Concept: *I will argue about* the lack of attendance policies in college freshman classes *for* instructors at our college *in order to* convince them to institute stronger policies.

- An introductory section describing the loose attendance policies in my freshman classes, showing how easy it was to skip as many classes as a student might wish to skip

- A section illustrating this problem with stories of several classmates who actually wanted to do well in school, but who just were not mature enough to handle the lack of structure during their freshman year
- A section of statistics comparing attendance policies to job responsibilities, arguing that attendance policies are not a matter of mere personal freedom, but of personal responsibility
- A section explaining that it is the instructor's job to help new students adjust to the rigors of college classes and that providing attendance policies is just part of that job
- A section conceding that students should take responsibility for their own attendance, eventually, in their later college years, and that self-motivation will develop after the students see how regular attendance can help them succeed
- A final section showing much more favorable dropout statistics from several comparable colleges that do have standard attendance policies for freshman courses

THE MOVE FROM ARGUMENT CONCEPT TO THE ARGUMENT'S CLAIM

We should restate that writing an Argument Concept to define the boundaries of an argument has value, of course, in the *planning* processes of writing that argument. But keep in mind that although an Argument Concept is a critical thinking tool—a blueprint, if you will, of that argument—it is not a statement of the argument's primary claim. An all-important sentence, an argument's claim, usually appears somewhere in your introduction—but sometimes in more emphatic locations—and tells your reader with clear, concise language what your issue is and where you stand on it.

Although Argument Concepts work primarily for the writer's planning needs, a claim serves both reader *and* writer. The reader, of course, knows from the claim just what the argument will do, its intent and promised outcome. But if you think about it, the claim works in a similar manner for the writer who knows he or she may not stray from the promises made in the claim. In the claim about purchasing college textbooks from the above Argument Concept ("In their budgets, parents of new college students should plan for the dramatically increasing prices of college textbooks"), you can see that you would be restricted from including anything in your argument other than specific evidence and examples concerning textbook prices. You could not include evidence about the history of textbooks, the size of your college's bookstore, the demeanor of bookstore employees, or the locations of other bookstores in the area. Although related to "college textbook," such examples are extraneous to the focused argument your claim asserts. You must stick to evidence about prices, why the books required in particular courses are more expensive than others, and so forth.

Of course, in many ways the Argument Concept and claim for an argument are as intertwined as a song's lyrics to its melody. Your first obligation is to ensure that your Argument Concept defines exactly how your argument will proceed; you have little question about what it is you intend to accomplish, for whom, and why. Such planning ahead of time sets the stage for your claim where you leave little doubt in your reader's mind about your paper's intent.

Your claim, then, is a logical outgrowth of your Argument Concept, but it varies from the Argument Concept in a few important ways:

- An Argument Concept is a generating and clarification device for *you*, the writer; a claim more directly clarifies your intent for you *and* your *reader*.
- A claim will never contain phrasing such as "*I will argue about. . . .*" Your reader knows you intend to "argue about" something, so there is little need to be redundant.
- Generally, compared to an Argument Concept, the claim will be a more compact, concise statement of your intent.
- Claims often contain persuasive language such as "should," "ought to," and "must." Such language signals the reader that he or she is approaching an argument.
- Claims are powerful, no-nonsense sentences that encourage the reader to ask, "Oh? Why is that?" or to respond with "Prove it!"

Let's examine the critical thought process in turning an Argument Concept into a claim. For example, consider this Argument Concept: "*I will argue about* spaying or neutering pets *for* people about to buy a new cat or dog *in order to* persuade them that spaying and neutering are positive means to help control the pet overpopulation problem." Although this Argument Concept defines the limits of this argument, it is too wordy and too indirect to convey the power of the argument. Readers may well grow impatient, waiting for the argument's point. But written as a claim, such as "New pet owners should spay or neuter their animals to help control the pet overpopulation problem," the sentence gets quickly and directly to the point of the argument. The reader has little doubt of the writer's intent, stance, and tone. Plus, the writer plants in the reader's mind the need to know "why?" and establishes that necessary anticipation that reasons for the claim are forthcoming. You might ask, at this point, why not just start the writing process with the claim itself. Our experience has shown that students just learning to craft arguments benefit from the process of honing their focus, reader, and purpose first, thus better understanding just what their claim will say and the overall goals of their argument. Without doing so, the three critical contextual pieces may not be clearly defined.

Consider a second example: An Argument Concept reads: "*I will argue about* toy safety during the holiday season *for* parents *in order to* persuade them to consider carefully a toy's potential hazards to their children." Again, the writer has defined the focus, reader, and purpose for his or her needs. Now the writer must sharpen the topic's intent into a claim: "This holiday season, parents must select toys they intend as gifts for their children by carefully evaluating any potential safety hazards the toys may have." *The claim now asks the reader to become an active participant in the argument.* It expects the reader to take some action both physically and mentally—"do" or "believe" this after "thinking about" this.

Exercise 6
Individual Analysis and Practice: Converting Argument Concepts into Claims

Convert the following Argument Concepts into claims. Try to be clear, direct, and concise.

1. *I will argue about* alternative high schools *for* parents seeking a different type of education for their children *in order to* reassure these parents that alternative high schools offer a comprehensive, credible curriculum.

2. *I will argue about* underground gasoline storage tanks *for* our city's health inspectors *in order to* assert that these tanks must be inspected for leaks at least annually.

3. *I will argue about* online college math courses *for* students who may not have access to a regular college campus *in order to* demonstrate the convenience and quality of this type of educational setting.

4. *I will argue about* hospitalized children *for* parents *in order to* show the parents steps to make the hospital stay less traumatic.

5. *I will argue about* current TV ads *for* women's clothing for teenage girls *in order to* persuade them that the body image promoted in such ads is unrealistic and potentially harmful.

6. *I will argue about* the press coverage of the Republican Convention *for* journalism students *in order to* demonstrate how the press misrepresented the Republican platform.

DISCOVERING YOUR OWN ARGUMENTS: ARGUMENTS FROM REFINED ARGUMENT CONCEPTS

1. Choose a well-known product and in a detailed paragraph write an advertisement to be read on the radio.
    A. Write one Argument Concept for a specific use of the product.
    B. Write another Argument Concept for a very different reader.
    C. Write a paragraph for each of the Argument Concepts, including the kind of reasons and evidence appropriate for each particular argument.

2. This chapter emphasizes that the writer and reader both bring a certain perspective to an argument and that the two parties are negotiating meaning. Imagine that you are going to write from this Argument Concept: "*I will argue about* the presence in the United States of illegal foreign workers *for* voters in my home county *in order to* convince them that such workers should (or should not) be allowed citizenship."

   A. Write a detailed explanation of the preconceptions you have about the issue prior to any research you might want to do on the topic. Explain how you think you developed that perspective—what experiences have you had that have given you a viewpoint before careful and thorough research?
   B. Write a second explanation of the preconceptions you might expect your reader(s) to have. Explain why you think they believe the way they do on the issue.

3. In many schools across the country, former athletes in the community are used in volunteer or low-paying positions to coach school sports, saving the school district a good deal of money. Write two Argument Concepts, one arguing for the use of community members as coaches in middle schools and high schools, and one against, being careful to adjust the reader and purpose for each of the Argument Concepts. Choose which Argument Concept you most want to develop and write a short argument that might appear in the editorial section of a newspaper or the letter-to-the-editor section of a magazine. (Remember the idea of concessions and rebuttals from Chapter 3.)

4. There is little doubt that the large number of low miles-per-gallon vehicles on U.S. streets and highways contributes to environmental pollution. For instance, according to a Sierra Club analysis, "SUVs have a dark side. They spew out 43 percent more global-warming pollution and 47 percent more air pollution than an average car." The U.S. Public Interest Research Group says that "If light trucks, SUVs and mini-vans met the same fuel economy standards as cars, oil consumption could have been reduced by about 336 million barrels—almost a million barrels per day, and global warming pollution could have been reduced by 187 million tons per year." Considering these points, write two Argument Concepts, one arguing for the passage of a special use tax for gas guzzlers, and one against such a tax. Choose which Argument Concept you most want to develop and write a short argument that might appear in the editorial section of a newspaper or the letter-to-the-editor section of a magazine. (Remember the idea of concessions and rebuttals from Chapter 3.)

REFLECTIONS ON THE CHAPTER

We believe that some of the best writing advice students can receive is reflected in this chapter. Paying close attention to your focus, reader, and purpose helps you in one of writing's most challenging processes: making decisions. By continually asking yourself if your evidence pertains directly to the focus, if the evidence and examples offer the most appealing argument for the chosen reader, and if you really know what you wish to accomplish, your own arguments have an excellent chance of being well received. Think carefully now about what issue or issues you intend to pursue in this course. Can you envision your focus, reader, and purpose? If so, you're well on your way to effective, accurate, passionate writing.

CHAPTER

5

The Potential Problems in Arguments

The first four chapters of this text demonstrated what argument is and is not, how it is typically structured, and how to plan what you need to do to compose a convincing piece, whether written or spoken. We have likewise encouraged you to consider the crafting of an argument as a *process* during which you consider an issue, reconsider it, change your mind, double back to earlier thinking, and perhaps scratch your head a number of times. All such actions are normal and expected. Think of crafting an argument as somewhat like a nature hike during which you have some destination in mind, but occasionally you must take a different path, double back to reread a directional sign, and so forth. And, of course, while you are admiring the beautiful scenery along your hike, you may trip over a rock or fall into a hole in the trail.

Like hiking, crafting an argument has its own rocks and holes, potential errors in the process of your reasoning that lead to indefensible or at least easily questioned conclusions. So during the process of your analyzing or composing an argument, take the time to think carefully about what you are about to say and look over your shoulder occasionally to review what you have previously concluded—all in the name of avoiding logical fallacies.

Once you have studied the following fallacies (errors in the *process* of reasoning), you will likely spot them in some arguments you read and hear. But, and this is a big *but*, you must also look in the mirror to detect any reasoning errors in your own written arguments. No one is perfect; we all make mistakes. Learning about the common fallacies, however, should make you more conscious of the means by which you draw conclusions.

TERMS AND CONCEPTS TO WATCH FOR

- Insufficient evidence
- Atypical evidence
- Improper authority
- Subjectivism
- Appeal to a majority
- Personal attack on the opposition
- False cause
- Begging the question
- Non sequitur
- False dilemma

QUESTIONS TO GUIDE YOUR READING

- How are reasoning errors (fallacies) generally a product of a poor reasoning *process*?
- How can various reasoning errors overlap? Can a thinking person commit more than one reasoning error at a time?
- Do you recognize any of your own reasoning errors in those discussed in this chapter? Were you aware of them?
- Do you understand that reasoning errors often occur due to our backgrounds, values, and desires for certain truths to be self-evident?
- Can you be flexible enough to admit errors when they occur and to try to avoid them in future thinking tasks?

Learning to form and write arguments requires that you take care to avoid the pitfalls common to argumentative thinking. Of course, everyone makes mistakes, but often your purpose in writing an argument is to be persuasive. You must convince your readers that your handling of evidence and the conclusions drawn from it are done so with care and without reckless disregard for proper and fair thought processes. Careful readers will question your credibility (*ethos*) should they detect fallacies in your reasoning.

You have undoubtedly witnessed people drawing unsound conclusions because those conclusions are easy, convenient, or based upon irrelevant outside influences. For example, a classmate commits this error when she concludes that a guest speaker must have Italian forebears because he often "speaks with his hands." Stereotypes of this form develop because somewhere in her life, your classmate was told—by parents, other friends, coworkers—that a trait common to people of Italian descent is their propensity to move their hands a good deal while speaking, and now she holds that conclusion because it is easy and requires no further thinking. However, if your classmate would think honestly about her conclusion, she would find that she has no real evidence for it. After all, many people use their hands in excitement or for emphasis when they speak; but even the classmate's neighbor, who is Italian by descent, rarely if ever uses his hands any time during conversations. Your classmate's uninformed conclusion could be further tested if you point out to her that she moves her hands sometimes when speaking, and so by her own reasoning she must be Italian!

Think about your own thinking for a moment. Have you formed conclusions without sufficient or exemplary evidence? For instance, have you argued with someone about America's terrorist threat without having read any documented examples or statistics? You may *believe* you have ample information, but is it only from anecdotes you have heard? Reports from only Republicans or only Democrats? Opinions spouted by a roommate or trusted friend? Or maybe you believe that all graduates in your major have excellent opportunities to make money in the current economy, but have you really investigated this? Have you spoken with people who work in your major field? Read government reports on employment in your career counseling center? Or have you just *heard somewhere* that your field is rich with possibilities? See the point? Be sure to ask yourself just what real support you have for the conclusions you draw.

Keep in mind as you study the potential problems in arguments that they indicate an improper reasoning *process*, not necessarily an incorrect conclusion. By sheer luck or coincidence, your classmate, for example, may actually be correct; the guest speaker may *be* Italian by descent. Nonetheless, her reasoning is still flawed. Drawing conclusions from insufficient or irrelevant evidence is risky at best. Throughout her lifetime, should she continue to base her conclusions on skimpy, untested information, she will make more mistakes than not.

Problems in argument occur when the connection between a conclusion and its supporting evidence is tenuous—slight or flimsy—in some manner. This chapter examines what these tenuous connections are and how to avoid them. Note in the following advertisement that the man's conclusion about student loans is not drawn from very solid reasoning. What would lead someone to conclude that a college's student loan office is a place to borrow a student? He is apparently confusing the idea of a student's *receiving* a loan for school expenses with a student's availability as a *loan* for personal use. But it is possible the man commits the fallacy of subjectivism (explained later in this chapter) in that he simply *wants* to believe that a student loan office lends students for various purposes. Of course, the fallacy is intentional by the cartoon artist, but it illustrates the idea that any move from evidence ("This *is* the student loan office, right?") to a conclusion based upon that evidence ("Then lend me a student") must be a sensible one. Consider this any time you gather evidence about your argumentative issues and then conclude about what the evidence will support.

Visual Rhetoric...
STUDENT LOAN "ARGUMENT"

© Mike Baldwin / Cornered

"Sorry, but no. I can't lend you a student to help clean up your yard."

The first and most important job of images in cartoons is to make you laugh. Often, any connection to the logic behind the laughter takes second place to the humorous outcome. What is the link between this image and the man's need for a "student loan"? Is such a link important or necessary in cartoons? What other examples do you remember seeing where the nature of the image has little to do with the reasoning behind the message?

INSUFFICIENT EVIDENCE

> **INSUFFICIENT EVIDENCE** *is the failure to provide enough evidence to support a claim or a reason, drawing a conclusion too hastily.*

Conclusions based upon insufficient evidence are often labeled *hasty generalizations* because you commit this error when you conclude or generalize too quickly. Your reader will not be convinced by thin presentations of evidence. The most egregious types of this error are stereotypes formed about groups with thousands of members but based upon only the actions of a few. Believing that blondes are dim-witted because you once knew an unintelligent blonde or because a few of your friends have told "blonde jokes" exemplifies this reasoning. The behaviors of only one or a few of a group certainly fail to speak for the group as a whole.

Let's say you intend to write an argument against online writing courses, with your primary reason being that because professors and students in these courses rarely meet face-to-face, students can readily submit plagiarized work. Now, a *strong* argument for this position would include many interviews with professors of online writing courses who have experienced cheating among their students, interviews with online students who admit the ease of submitting work other than their own, statistics from colleges that monitor their online courses, documented studies of online plagiarism, and so forth. Doing so, you would build a strong case for your stance. However, should you argue against online writing courses because someone you know bragged about his or her cheating, and dormmates told stories of others they had heard of, your argument will be weakened considerably. Granted, maybe some plagiarism occurs; and by default alone, your stance may be defensible. But careful readers would justifiably balk at a universal ban on online writing courses without the solid evidence mentioned previously. After all, anecdotal examples of cheating exist in the more traditional classroom as well. Should we thus ban all forms of classroom education? You should recognize, of course, that even a strongly evidenced argument might not convince some readers; nonetheless, you have an obligation to present your best case based upon sufficient information.

Exercise 1
Collaborative Analysis: Examining the Strength of Personal Opinions

For the following five issues, write down one opinion you hold. Then in small groups discuss your reasons and evidence for each. Do you have sufficient, concrete evidence for your opinions? Do your classmates agree? Might you have to modify your opinions?

- Gun ownership
- America as an English-only country
- Men as nurses or secretaries
- The quality of Japanese-made automobiles
- The usefulness of college speech courses

ATYPICAL EVIDENCE

> **ATYPICAL EVIDENCE** *is the use of evidence that is not representative of (has little direct bearing upon) the issue you are arguing.*

Although a less common error than using insufficient evidence, using atypical evidence means you may have used ample evidence but of the wrong kind. This mistake occurs when you conclude about an issue based upon evidence that has no direct bearing on the stance you take. To be honest, in most investigations of issues, you will never have the time or resources to study *all* of the evidence or examples possible (remember this problem from inductive reasoning in Chapter 2). Thus, you must study *some* of them, making sure that the "some" you study accurately reflect the characteristics of the whole. Clear and meaningful conclusions, especially about groups of things or people, must derive from an examination of examples that most represent the overall group. For instance, scientists testing the efficacy of a new drug must be certain that each sample of the drug used in their tests is *exactly* like the others: each sample must come from the same source, must be exactly the same amount, and must be tested in the same manner each time. Otherwise, the scientists introduce additional variables about the drug's effectiveness, and their conclusions are skewed. In other words, each tested drug sample must be *representative* of the overall group of samples possible.

A student once argued that American public schools should adopt the science and math curriculum of schools in India because examined Indian students tended to perform better on standardized tests and competed more efficiently against American graduates for college entrance. Evidence indeed shows that some Indian schools' students do remarkably in math and science. But the evidence here may be tainted by its lack of typicality.

Although the Indian math and science curriculum may be admirable, the problem occurs in comparing Indian to American students without qualification. Indian students who perform well in math and science, for one thing, do so because their school administrators have carefully screened and selected them for high intelligence and natural preference for math and science. Allowably then, the curriculum is challenging. American public school students face no such screening. Everyone is allowed to take math and science, indeed are required to do so, and the American public would decry any attempts to allow only the best math and science students to take these courses. So, saying that American schools should necessarily adopt the Indian pattern fails to acknowledge the differences in culture and school structure between the countries. Indian math and science students, although they are surely fine people, are "atypical" of their American counterparts, and using Indian students as equivalent examples for Americans' performance is unsound.

Be sure when drawing conclusions that your evidence and examples are representative of the issue at hand. Do not conclude about the tastiness of green apples after sampling a number of red ones. Do not conclude about the quality of your small, hometown school's computer accessibility based only on studies conducted on the computer accessibility in urban schools. What really defines a "representative" sampling of evidence for the issue you face?

Exercise 2
Collaborative Analysis: Discovering Representative Evidence
Consider the following argumentative scenarios. What types of evidence might prove most representative for an arguer to examine and use in the defense of a stance?

- Drug testing during the Olympics
- The safety of home birthing
- The safety of tanning salons
- The government monitoring private phone lines
- A general decrease in common courtesy in public

CITING IMPROPER AUTHORITIES

> **IMPROPER AUTHORITY** *is using the opinions of others who are not experts in or who are biased about the issue you are arguing.*

None of us can know everything, so by necessity in arguments we turn to authorities whose knowledge about issues exceeds our own. It just makes sense to support a stance with the views of experts in the issue. But you commit the error of improper use of authority if the experts you select fail to meet the requirements for credibility. Few readers will believe the arguments of experts whom they do not trust.

First of all, credible authorities must be experts in the exact issue of your argument. You cannot assume that people well informed on one topic are necessarily so on another. Just because Peyton Manning is a professional football quarterback (and thus an expert in professional football), he is not necessarily an expert in athletic footwear or breakfast foods, in spite of what advertisers would have us believe. Condoleezza Rice may indeed be an expert in U.S. foreign relations, but citing her in a paper on the morality of stem cell research would be absurd, in spite of how respected or well known she is.

You would hope, as well, that the authorities you cite are as objective as possible concerning your issue. Finding experts who are completely objective, of course, is difficult, but doing so remains your goal. Say your argument concerns a Republican president's new plan to return tax money to taxpayers to stimulate the economy. If you are tempted to argue against the plan by citing an article written by a powerful Democrat, you must first examine the background of this author to determine if he or she holds any political or economic bias toward the president's actions. Should you learn that the president and the Democratic author have long been political rivals on economic issues, the objectivity of the Democrat's article comes into question. Of course, the Democratic author may provide some insightful points, but you must be careful to examine them. Are they motivated purely by party affiliation? If so, careful readers may challenge this source's usefulness if they suspect that political rivalry—more than the economic interests of our citizens—may be at the root of the article. Citing a different article written by an author whose political well-being and salary are not tied to either a Republican or Democratic source might create a better argument.

Exercise 3
Collaborative Analysis: Evaluating Authorities
What types of authorities (not necessarily actual names, though you can include these if you know them) would serve best from whom to glean information for the issues given?

- The leeway public schools should have in disciplining students
- The effects of off-road driving on forests and deserts
- The practice of placing juvenile offenders in adult prisons
- Couples living together before marriage
- Parents "overscheduling" their children's time

SUBJECTIVISM

> **SUBJECTIVISM** *is an error committed when your personal belief in an issue is your sole reason for believing and defending it.*

You commit the error of subjectivism when you use your personal belief in some stance as the sole reason for its truth. Like many others, you may believe that since your opinions on most topics represent clear, reasonable thinking (or at least so you have always thought), then surely whatever you believe must be correct. But you must be careful. Just because you believe that San Francisco is the best city in the United States, that belief—by itself—does not make it so. You would have to provide other evidence (definitions of "best city," population numbers, educational opportunities, makeup of the workforce, municipal amenities, and so forth) before your reader would be convinced. And to be honest, *you* should have such evidence, too, before drawing such a conclusion.

Exercise 4
Individual Analysis and Practice: Detecting Subjectivism
Write how each of the following examples is subjectivist. What actual evidence could be offered to strengthen the conclusion in each?

- School board member Sheila Rothstein serves our students well. I believe this because she and I think the same way.
- Environmental science majors, like me, work to serve best the current needs of our society.
- Being Republican, I know that Democrats have a mistaken view of welfare benefits.

APPEAL TO A MAJORITY

> *An* **APPEAL TO A MAJORITY** *is an error committed when you assert something to be true based simply on the assertion that many people believe it.*

People commit this fallacy when they reason that simply because a large group of people believes a particular way, then that way must be right. Think of the appeal to a majority as the plural version of subjectivism discussed above. Believing that a certain musical group is the best in the land merely because it sells the most records (a good many people apparently think the group is good) illustrates this thinking error. Many of your friends may believe that smoking is not harmful, but this belief alone does not provide convincing proof of such a stance. Many Americans believe the public schools fail to teach history adequately, but merely believing so does not make it so. In all of these instances, a writer would have to cite statistics, examples, facts, interview results, and so forth before reasonable readers would accept them—or even listen to them, for that matter. To avoid committing this error, be sure you present sufficient information for your opinions, not merely a single group's preferences or biases.

> ### ALSO NOTE
> #### EINSTEIN AND THE MAJORITY
>
> Albert Einstein once said, "Common sense is the collection of prejudices acquired by age eighteen." We often appeal to *common sense*—what everybody thinks—as support for our conclusions. But what if Einstein had done so? His breakthrough theories of general and special relativity would not have emerged. Independent thinking has instigated the growth of human understanding, but such thinking is not always comforting or popular. (Remember Galileo was brought before the Inquisition and held under house arrest for the remainder of his life for suggesting something so outrageous as the idea that the sun is the center of the universe, not the earth, and that the earth moves within the universe.)
>
> Be careful about those "common sense" understandings you may be tempted to use as the basis of or as support for your argument.

Exercise 5
Collaborative Analysis: Appeal to Majority Problems

How does each of the following examples represent the fallacy of appeal to majority? How could the arguer's position be strengthened?

- Eat more lamb. All those wolves can't be wrong.
- We should reject Proposition 52 in the next election. It is not supported by our campus's members of the Young Republicans.
- Worldwide, more people drink Coke products than they do Pepsi products. Coke products are clearly better.

PERSONAL ATTACK ON THE OPPOSITION

> *A* **PERSONAL ATTACK ON THE OPPOSITION** *(ad hominem) is straying from an issue's actual arguments by attacking some personal characteristic of someone with an opposing viewpoint, attacking the arguer, not the argument.*

Perhaps one of the most difficult of all reasoning tasks is that of staying on the exact issue under discussion. People are easily distracted from the point of certain arguments, and one of the easiest means of distraction is to leave an issue by attacking anyone with an opposing viewpoint (this fallacy is formally called *ad hominem*, or argument "to the person"). Such attacks are unfair not only because they are irrelevant to the issue at hand but also because they often address some personal characteristic of the opposing arguer: appearance, intelligence, ethnicity, religion, gender, or birth origin. Your job in any argument is to stick to the issue and to present as fair and supportable a stance as possible, without getting personal.

Attacking a person may occur in three forms: a "crude form" in which you actually call someone a name (stupid, loser, radical, liberal, redneck); an unfair attack on a person's motives ("You only want the new park to be built near your house so that your property value will increase"); or a "You're the same way!" attack ("You nag me not to miss classes, but you miss all the time!"). All three types of attack indicate that you have left the issue under discussion and have assaulted the person offering a differing opinion.

Exercise 6
Collaborative Analysis: Detecting Unfair Attacks on Differing Viewpoints

Each of the following is an example of an unfair, personal attack on an opposing viewpoint. Which of the three forms of such attacks is represented by each example?

- "I know I borrowed your car just last week and need it again, but it's not like you never borrow anything of mine."
- "You just don't want to contribute to diabetes research because you don't have a family member suffering from the disease."
- "Only an idiot would listen to rap music."

ALSO NOTE
AN AD HOMINEM EXAMPLE

In November 2003, a filibuster was underway in the United States Senate. Some of President Bush's judicial appointees were considered by the Democrats to be idealogues—persons overly devoted to extreme doctrines—and therefore unfit for the judiciary. The filibuster was carried on to block a vote on these potential judges. When asked about the filibuster by a television reporter, Senator Ted Kennedy said that Democrats would continue to resist what he described as "any Neanderthal" the President nominated. Kennedy was taken to task for this comment, an *ad hominem* statement, not only by the opposition Republicans, but also by many members of his own party as well as by most representatives of the news media.

This characterization further divided the parties, making any kind of compromise or resolution nearly impossible.

FALSE CAUSE

> **FALSE CAUSE** *is citing an incorrect cause or insufficient causes for a particular effect.*

Many arguments require that you establish the causes of certain effects (see Chapter 10). How and why did Event A occur? Establishing a cause-and-effect relationship is not as easy as it may sound. Failing to get a job you have applied for may have a number of causes, from your lack of experience to nepotism to a clash of personalities with the interviewer. Do not be too hasty, though, to accept too readily that one or more of these conditions caused your failure. Maybe a poor interview actually disqualified you. Your lack of a sparkling performance may have harmed your chances for the job even without the other conditions in place.

Of course, some effects have direct causes: a sore thumb results from hitting it with a hammer, your car stops when out of gasoline, a hastily written essay results in its low grade. The relationship between cause and effect is recognizable and reasonable. Other effects, though, share only a time relationship with their cited cause, and basing an argument upon this time factor alone is risky. Reasoning errors of this type are called *post hoc, ergo propter hoc* fallacies, which means "after this, therefore because of this." What if you blamed your lack of getting the new job on the fact that your interview occurred the day after you lost money playing blackjack? Does your lack of card-playing talent truly contribute to failure of this type, or is the relationship between the game and your job loss only coincidental? If your argument requires that you establish a cause-and-effect relationship, be certain that the cause or causes you cite are sufficient and probable for the effect.

Likewise, you must be certain that the causes you cite for an effect tell the whole story. Many effects have multiple, coordinate causes, and if so, all of the causes must be illustrated to make your case. For example, if you write about why your state experienced tragic forest fires last year, you must provide all of the causes of the fires: years of continued drought; failure to thin trees in certain areas; a buildup of underbrush; lightning storms; and, of course, human carelessness with campfires, cigarettes, and fireworks. An argument that listed only one of the causes, for instance, would be woefully incomplete and lacking in argumentative weight.

Exercise 7
Collaborative Analysis: Issues with False Cause

In each example, point out just what *effect* occurs and then discuss the cited cause or causes. Are the given causes sufficient and probable for the effect?

- My brother dropped out of college because the professors disliked him.
- The U.S. economy slumped for three straight years because of corporate scandals.
- Smoking among teenagers actually increased after the federal government launched an antismoking program. Obviously, the program is to blame.

BEGGING THE QUESTION

> **BEGGING THE QUESTION** *is an error committed when you simply assume as true the very issue that you should be defending as true, asserting "it's true because it's true."*

People commit the error of begging the question when they *assume* as true an idea that they should be attempting to prove. Perhaps someone says, "The useless motorcycle helmet law should be repealed." Ask yourself, first of all, what the issue is that is implicit in the person's statement. Isn't the issue whether or not motorcycle helmet laws are useless? That being the case, you witness the person begging the question because he or she has already assumed the law is useless when that is the very issue to be proven. In fact, a good way to detect begging the question is to approach an issue by asking *whether or not* the issue is true; then, determine if one side of the issue is implied or assumed as true in your argument.

Non Sequitur

Begging the question: This experimenter's conclusion is already made in his request to borrow the cat!

Sometimes, people beg the question when their reasoning spins in a circle so that a conclusion and the reason for it are the same proposition: "The new sales tax law is fair because it treats everyone equitably." Note that "fair" and "treats everyone equitably" are essentially the same. The issue here is *whether or not* the new sales tax law is fair, but the arguer goes in a circle by essentially saying, "The new sales tax law is fair because it's fair." Shouldn't the arguer offer actual reasons he or she believes are in the law's fairness, rather than just assume it is because it is?

To avoid begging the question, evaluate the claims within your argument and consider how much real evidence you have offered for them. Does your defense of a claim take too much for granted as already true? Might both you and your reader be better served by providing information to support a stance rather than just assuming its truth because that would be easier?

Exercise 8
Individual Analysis and Practice: Detecting the Fallacy of Question Begging

For each example, first determine what the actual issue is: "whether or not X is true." Then, point out what the arguer has assumed as true and why the arguer cannot merely assume such a thing.

- Colleges around the country must continue their support of affirmative action in their admission policies since the program works so well.
- Our prisons cannot reduce the recidivism of prisoners because the prisoners continue committing crimes.
- Because college athletes are professionals, colleges should pay them a salary and allow them to accept endorsement deals.

NON SEQUITUR

> **A NON SEQUITUR** *is the offering of irrelevant evidence in support of a claim; the conclusion does not "follow" from the evidence provided.*

As you study argument, you will find that some people cannot stick to the issue at hand, or they present evidence that, while substantial and objective, is irrelevant to the issue. Doing so, they commit the error of *non sequitur* (meaning "it does not follow"). It makes sense to claim, "Day care providers must be licensed because the licensing procedure requires providers to obtain CPR and other health training." The reason for the licensing seems directly tied to the claim. But if you claim, "Day care providers must be licensed because then everyone will be happy," the stance simply does not follow the reason given. What does anyone's happiness have to do directly with whether or not day care providers should face licensure?

Non sequiturs also occur when the arguer fails to stick to the original issue. This form of non sequitur is called "diversion," because the arguer, consciously or not, wanders from the point of the argument. Politicians face public censure for such behavior all the time. During a press conference, when asked a question about her vote against same-sex marriages, a senator might divert by answering, "Well, before I explain my vote, I just want you to know that some of my best friends are gay. One friend is a computer engineer who has developed some amazing software for the security industry. You should see how efficient and cost effective that software is. . . ." Okay, but what does this anecdote have to do with the vote against same-sex marriages? The senator has attempted a diversion, perhaps because her "real" answer to the question might create even harder questions from the journalists she faces.

Exercise 9
Individual Analysis and Practice:
When Conclusions Don't "Follow"

In each scenario, first find the conclusion the arguer has drawn. Then, list the evidence cited for the conclusion. Discuss why the connection between the conclusion and its supporting evidence is illogical.

- I am uneasy having Dr. Lee operate on my knee since she was educated in China.
- Because it is a mere watercolor, the painting *Last Night in August* does not deserve the Best of Show prize.
- A married couple planning to have children should take parenting classes before the child's birth. That way, they will face less criticism from their own parents about how the child is raised. Less criticism means less stress on the couple's marriage, and certainly less stress in a marriage will help it last longer.

FALSE DILEMMA (EITHER/OR FALLACY; BLACK/WHITE FALLACY)

> A **FALSE DILEMMA** is the claim that only two alternatives exist (often opposites of each other) when other alternatives are known to exist, to say an issue is black or white when gray areas are distinctly possible.

Arguers commit the fallacy of false dilemma when they claim that only two alternatives (often polarized extremes) exist in an issue when, in reality, other alternatives exist. In other words, someone claims that only black or white options could be true when other arguers might point out many "gray" areas. If a person says, "You're either my friend or my enemy," he or she has committed this error. Surely, other possibilities exist in human relations besides friends and enemies. In fact, when you think about it, *most* of the relationships you have with other people are neither that of friend nor enemy.

Let's say that you believe that health care costs in the United States have become too high. So, you compose an argument about nationalized health care, making the claim that the United States either nationalizes health care (and adopts a system similar to that in Canada, for example) or thousands of people will die due to a lack of affordable health care. Doing so, you have created a false dilemma. Would not other choices besides nationalized health care or massive death counts be possible? For example, couldn't the U.S. government or private entities find the means to fund drug research to reduce drug costs? Couldn't the government or private entities support nonprofit medical clinics for indigent people? Couldn't the government enact restrictions on the rising costs of medical insurance so that more people could afford it? And so forth. The idea, of course, is not to claim that a complicated issue must have a "do it this way or else!" resolution when other, perhaps more reasonable options, might be studied.

Exercise 10
Collaborative Analysis: Issues with a False Dilemma

As a class, point out why the following examples are those of false dilemma. In each case, what other alternatives might be noted about the issue?

- To be successful in this society, women must be either brilliant or beautiful.
- Professor to student: "If you don't like the way I teach, then maybe you should just drop out of college."
- You must purchase only Japanese-made automobiles, or you're throwing your money away.
- Fast-food restaurants must be closed or everyone in this country will be obese.

Exercise 11
Collaborative Analysis: Detecting Reasoning Errors of Varied Types

Each of the following situations contains at least one of the errors discussed in this chapter. In small groups, discuss why the conclusion in each situation is improperly formed from the reasons and evidence given. What reasoning error or errors do you detect? Some examples may contain more than one fallacy.

1. The U.S. government should place tighter restrictions on immigrants to this country since tighter restrictions are necessary.

122 Chapter 5 *The Potential Problems in Arguments*

2. I think my low grade in calculus is unfair since I have always been a good mathematics student.

3. "Do you intend to submit that plagiarized essay to your professor?"

4. We should ignore Congresswoman Wilson's plea for more Medicaid funds since she has never been close to her own grandparents.

5. My friend believes that the students at this school are discourteous since he was nearly run down by one on a bicycle, and my friend witnessed another student smoking in one of the buildings.

6. Without a graduate degree, people will be ignorant and poor all of their lives.

7. My uncle believes that the public schools no longer do an adequate job of teaching basic reading skills. And he should know, since he has been a proofreader for the *Dallas Daily News* for nearly thirty years.

8. The looming professional baseball strike should be supported because most of the players in the league believe that the teams' owners have conspired to withhold salary increases.

9. Only those people who care little for the homeless oppose the legislature's new bill aimed at funding four homeless shelters in our state.

10. Phyllis Sanchez, our company's personnel director, was fired because she would not hire the CEO's niece as the company's new advertising consultant.

Exercise 12
Individual Analysis and Practice: Potential Problems in an Argument

Read the following argument and complete these steps:

1. Find the argument's primary claim (stance);

2. Determine what evidence and reasons the arguer provides for the stance;

3. Point out any possible reasoning errors and label them if you can.

Overall, do you think the argument is convincing? Why or why not?

Reading Ability: Why Males Fall Behind

1   Recently, studies around the United States have shown that, especially in grades three through seven, male students in our public schools demonstrate an ability to read quite below their female counterparts. Parents and educators are concerned, of course, and seek answers to this discrepancy. Since the ability to read well is crucial to all forms of education, we need to find the means to help male students improve their overall reading scores, which would lead to their increased performance in all other subjects that require a good deal of reading: science, history, physical education, and English. Where does the

problem lie? It has come to my attention that it is the teaching methods used by public school teachers that contribute to males' lack of reading ability.

2. Elementary school teachers, to this day, are by a great majority female. Surely this contributes to how students are taught. Female teachers tend to respond more favorably to female students, giving them more individual attention and responding more positively to their questions and answers. I remember a time in the fourth grade when my teacher asked this question: "How do plants make food?" My answer was that the sun shines on the plant and the green stuff in the plant turns the sunlight into food. My female teacher was less than enthusiastic, but when a female classmate raised her hand and shouted, "It's called 'photosynthesis,'" the teacher smiled and clapped her hands. Did I ever feel stupid and knew the teacher had it in for me.

3. Male students also soon learn that teachers are less interested in their academic performance than in their physical behaviors in the classroom. A female student can pass a note to another and when confronted say, "I was just asking a question about what we are studying," and get away with it. A male, on the other hand, gets caught throwing a rock on the playground, and the teacher comes unglued and accuses him of being a future juvenile delinquent! A professor at a well-known school in Kentucky validates my point. After interviewing nine teachers in his home state, he found that female teachers viewed male students, all of them, as potential troublemakers. One teacher even said, "I am always shocked when a young man remains in his seat during an entire math lesson." And everyone with half a brain knows that math is important and that males are better at it than females.

4. Besides, why would the fact that males are more physically active than females be a problem? My father told me once that males are genetically wired to like physical play and games more than females, and that is why males lean toward football, hockey, and basketball, where they excel. Americans love sports, paying millions of dollars each year to attend athletic events, so why are males in the public schools criticized for being themselves? Maybe many of these young men will turn out to be the next Michael Jordan or Tiger Woods. Surely that is to be admired as much as reading ability.

5. I believe that the concern about males falling behind females in reading ability also stems from the fact that reading has been emphasized by overly liberal teachers whose liberal college professors convinced them that reading ability contributes to a well-educated society. Well, so do lots of other things. I may not like to read that much, but I do like to fish and work with my hands. Don't these skills count in a well-educated society, too? Maybe teachers should find ways to encourage their male students to use their hands more and worry about their ability to read some stupid piece of literature less. Who needs literature in banking, sports, or business, which are primarily male-dominated professions, anyway? When I had to read *Where the*

Red Fern Grows, I wondered the whole time why this was necessary. I would rather have been reading something about a baseball player or watching a movie about photosynthesis.

6   When public school teachers begin to treat males more favorably, those males' reading scores will improve. Until then, I find any worry about reading scores less than significant.

■
STUDENTS AT WORK: RE-EXAMINING AN ARGUMENT FOR POTENTIAL FALLACIES

Student Kimberly Dillon (whose complete argument can be found on p. 318 of this text) drafted the following body paragraph in her argument against the No Child Left Behind (NCLB) program sponsored by the federal government. Kimberly reconsidered the paragraph, however, after studying the list of possible fallacies discussed in this chapter.

> The No Child Left Behind program is unworkable because it promotes a lack of creative and critical thinking in students. No "one-size-fits-all" educational program will ever allow students and teachers to learn what they need to know in our society because only a select group of governmental officials have decided what knowledge is important. This select group has decided that only certain prescribed math, science, and English skills matter in our consumer-driven culture. The narrow-minded people who designed the NCLB curriculum simply want to control what children learn so that they can increase the likelihood of these children being easily manipulated for the political and business powers that run the country and contribute to reelection campaigns. They obviously feel threatened by more creative and imaginative thinkers who might challenge their restrictive political and business agendas.

Kimberly thought about her paragraph and concluded that she may have formed an argument that would be easily attacked because of two potential fallacies within it. First, she committed the error of begging the question because she assumes the NCLB program is unworkable due to its design to limit students' creative thinking. But if a potential limitation on creative thinking is so imperative to her overall argument, she cannot merely assume such a consequence of NCLB without offering substantial proof. Also, Kimberly, perhaps in the "heat of the moment," commits a personal attack on the opposition by calling those who design curricula under NCLB guidelines "narrow-minded" and interested only in future political and financial control. After all, how does she know for sure that curriculum designers "obviously feel threatened" by creative, critical thinkers? Without evidence to defend such assertions, Kimberly risks alienating readers who prefer a less strident discussion of the issue. Thus, she reconsidered the information and tone of the paragraph and rewrote it as follows. Do you believe the paragraph now reads with more authority and reasonableness?

> One major flaw in NCLB is that it relies too heavily on a "one-size-fits-all" solution, which hurts those schools that are already achieving at an above-average rate. No Child Left Behind leaves no room for "higher-order thinking or creativity" (Guisbond and Neill 13). Many schools are already excelling far beyond the mandatory levels set by state governments; therefore, the Bush administration should not generalize a solution to a problem that for some is nonexistent. However, because of the new tests and laws implemented, educators have to go backward and work more on testing skills and the information on those tests instead of going forward to learn new things. Teachers and administrators now place less emphasis on subjects such as "art, music, social studies, and physical education" because the standardized tests do not cover those topics (Amrein and Berliner 2). Teachers all over the country voice their opinion that standardized tests put too much stress on the subject matter of the tests as opposed to other essential information children should be learning. Half of the teachers surveyed in a study done by anthropologist Lesley Bartlett at the University of North Carolina in 1998 said that they had spent at least 40% of the school year focusing on studying for end of the year tests (8).

DISCOVERING YOUR OWN ARGUMENTS: KEEPING AN EYE OUT FOR FALLACIES

1. Your task in the following is to write fallacies *deliberately*. Select two of the following situations and write a sentence or two in which you commit one or more of the fallacies discussed in this chapter. For example, if you select the fast-food scenario, you might write, "Most people in America believe that McDonald's makes the best French fries in the country, so their fries are definitely the best" (committing the error of *appeal to majority*), or "Anyone who doesn't believe McDonald's fries are the best is a fool" (committing the error of personal attack). By creating these fallacies intentionally, you will recognize them more readily when you come across them in arguments.

   - Fast food in America
   - Tuition and fees at this school
   - The environment
   - Minimum wage for service workers
   - Finding employment following graduation

2. Examine the arguments you composed in a previous chapter's "Discovering Your Own Arguments" section. Explain where you might find one or more of the potential problems mentioned in this chapter. Also, explain how you might address that problem, or problems, by modifying your argument.

REFLECTIONS ON THE CHAPTER

This chapter emphasizes just how careful all of us must be when we draw conclusions. It seems that our minds take some perverse pleasure in leading us astray, and that other people find equal pleasure in pointing out where our thinking has run into a ditch. After all, consider all "outside" influences each of us faces—other people, experiences, television programs, advertisements, and so forth—and it's no wonder we occasionally slip up. However, a careful study of the potential problems in arguments makes us more alert to and confident in avoiding reasoning errors. Just be sure to take time to evaluate each conclusion, large or small, that you draw in your arguments. Be honest with yourself when you suspect that your reasoning may be questionable.

CHAPTER

6

Using the Argument Concept to Read the Arguments of Others

Nowhere is the mirror image of writing and reading—the classic Rhetorical Triangle captured in the Argument Concept—more obvious and helpful than when you try to unravel an argument you come across, whether it is visual, literary, spoken, academic, or news related. At this stage in your process, after studying the basic structure of argument, classic approaches to argument as well as Toulmin's approach, and some of the most frequent problems in argument, you have accumulated a number of tools with which to read and take apart an argument. That's just what you're going to do in this chapter.

In Part II, which begins with the next chapter, you will be encouraged to discover your own research-based argument. The purpose of Chapter 6, however, is to concentrate on close, critical reading and analysis of the arguments of others. This is an invaluable skill in itself. The relationship of your practice in this chapter to the creation of your own arguments is that, after you have practiced using these tools on the arguments of others, what you will learn will reflect in your own writing. You will be able to read your own thinking and writing just as analytically, making you a more competent arguer.

128 Chapter 6 *Using the Argument Concept to Read the Arguments of Others*

> **TERMS AND CONCEPTS TO WATCH FOR**
> - Active, or critical, reading
> - Passive reading
> - "Reversing" the Argument Concept
>
> **QUESTIONS TO GUIDE YOUR READING**
> - How can the Argument Concept help you as you read, listen to, or see an argument?
> - What are three common problems people have in evaluating arguments?
> - What are some steps you can use to avoid being fooled by a faulty argument?

You have read in the first five chapters about the ways arguments are put together—the structure of arguments. We have stressed the crucial idea of the way writing and thinking mirror each other, with the promise that learning to think analytically will improve your writing, and, similarly, practicing the art of refining, organizing, and supporting a written argument will enhance your thinking skills. Earlier chapters have focused on the following skills related to arguing:

- Understanding Aristotelian appeals
- Understanding a variety of classic conceptions of argument
- Assessing the focus, reader, and purpose of argument
- Developing a claim
- Establishing the context of an argument
- Thinking about the general purposes of argument
- Recognizing the different parts of an argument
- Understanding that arguing is a process of negotiating meaning
- Considering the most frequent problems in arguments

Before moving on, in this last chapter of Part I you will rigorously apply these skills and concepts we've discussed by analyzing a wide range of arguments.

AN EXAMPLE OF THE NEED FOR CRITICAL READING

> **ACTIVE, or CRITICAL, READING** *is the attempt to analyze and draw inferences from a text. The critical reader realizes that a text provides one perspective on the issue and considers what the intention of the text is, what influence the position of the writer may have on that intention, what problems the text may present, and what the deeper and/or extended meaning of the text might be.*

An Example of the Need for Critical Reading **129**

But first, we will discuss a few important ideas about the actual reading of these arguments productively. Let's start with a very real example of one our students, Pete. Pete was a very intelligent, serious, nontraditional-age student who believed that colleges and universities are currently too narrowly focused on providing job skills and creating employable graduates—in other words, making students fit predetermined molds. Instead, he believed one of the most important functions of higher education is to expand students' world views and to help them develop powerful and creative thinking skills—developing critical individuals who would then be a greater asset to society. Pete set out to write an essay with the potential audience of state college administrators for the purpose of convincing them that they should temper their current focus on higher education as a fast track to employment with a deeper, more intellectual goal. Quite a project! Clearly, this argument was going to require consulting a number of outside sources, the kind of argument that is the focus of Part II of this text. Pete began interviewing administrators and instructors, reading and studying state general education policy, and researching pertinent library and online materials.

As Pete learned more and more about this issue, he decided that one of the critical parts to his argument would be to address the opposition: businesses, parents, and students who believe a primary benefit of higher education is financial advancement in the workplace. According to this line of thinking, the "customer's" needs and desires should be addressed by a college. After all, haven't we all heard that college graduates have more earning power? Isn't that one of your expectations as you work your way through college? In the course of his reading, Pete ran across an article by Caroline Bird, "College is a Waste of Time and Money," from *The Case Against College*, published in 1975. In this article, Bird suggests that many students are encouraged to go to college to get a better job; her idea is that students who might do better going straight into the workforce are lured into the college environment with the promise that their lifetime earnings will be much greater if they have a college education. To the contrary, Bird says, many students would be financially better off if they got a job after graduating high school and began accumulating wealth. The following excerpt represents Bird's argument on this point that getting college education may not be the most efficient way to improve one's financial position.

1   If a 1972 Princeton-bound high-school graduate had put the $34,181 that his four years of college would have cost him into a savings bank at 7.5 percent interest compounded daily, he would have had at age 64 a total of $1,129,200, or $528,200 more than the earnings of a male college graduate, and more than five times as much as the $199,000 extra the more educated man could expect to earn between 22 and 64.

2   The big advantage of getting your college money in cash now is that you can invest it in something that has a higher return than a diploma. For instance, a Princeton-bound high-school graduate of 1972 who liked fooling around with cars could have banked his $34,181, and gone to work at the local garage at close to $1,000 more per year than the average high-school graduate. Meanwhile, as he was learning to be an expert auto mechanic, his money would be ticking away in the bank. When he became

28, he would have earned $7,199 less on his job from age 22 to 28 than his college-educated friend, but he would have had $73,223 in his passbook—enough to buy out his boss, go into the used-car business, or acquire his own new-car dealership. If successful in business, he could expect to make more than the average college graduate. And if he had the brains to get into Princeton, he would be just as likely to make money without the four years spent on campus. Unfortunately, few college-bound high-school graduates have the opportunity to bank such a large sum of money, and then wait for it to make them rich. And few parents are sophisticated enough to understand that in financial returns alone, their children would be better off with the money than with the education.

3   Rates of return and dollar signs on education are fascinating brain teasers, but obviously there is a certain unreality to the game. Quite aside from the noneconomic benefits of college, and these should loom larger once the dollars are cleared away, there are grave difficulties in assigning a dollar value to college at all.

4   In fact there is no real evidence that the higher income of college graduates is due to college. College may simply attract people who are slated to earn more money anyway, those with higher IQs, better family backgrounds, a more enterprising temperament. No one who has wrestled with the problem is prepared to attribute all of the higher income to the impact of college itself.

5   Christopher Jencks, author of *Inequality*, a book that assesses the effect of family and schooling in America, believes that education in general accounts for less than half of the difference in income in the American population. "The biggest single source of income differences," writes Jencks, "seems to be the fact that men from high-status families have higher incomes than men from low-status families even when they enter the same occupations, have the same amount of education, and have the same test scores."

6   Jacob Mincer of the National Bureau of Economic Research and Columbia University states flatly that of "20 to 30 percent of students at any level, the additional schooling has been a waste, at least in terms of earnings." College fails to work its income-raising magic for almost a third of those who go. More than half of those people in 1972 who earned $15,000 or more reached that comfortable bracket without the benefit of a college diploma. Jencks says that financial success in the United States depends a good deal on luck, and the most sophisticated regression analyses have yet to demonstrate otherwise.

Pete found this information, and he decided to use it in his first draft to show that for a certain segment of the population, the idea of making a better living by getting a college education is fiction rather than reality. Pete brought his first draft in to a conference with the Bird information included and was able to think through the logic of her argument and the viability of her evidence more thoroughly.

> **PASSIVE READING** *is the attempt to gain knowledge by simply recognizing what the words of a text say. The passive reader looks at a text as constructed of facts which, if committed to memory, will provide the reader with understanding.*

After reading through the first chapters, you probably already have some idea what problems he ultimately found with the material. First of all, he recognized this information is out of date. Updated material on this topic is certainly readily available (see the Also Note box on this page, for example). Pete also decided that using employment and income information from 1975 for a current argument is not going to inspire great confidence in his reader. This is not to say that a dated source might not ever be applicable. Pete might have, for example, said something like "Even as early as 1975, people like Caroline Bird were insisting that a college education was not necessarily a guarantee of more long-range earning power." Though there is certainly more recent material available, he might have had legitimate reason to use the material if he were to use it as historical perspective in this way.

However, Pete decided that being out of date might not be the greatest fault with the information. A larger problem was with some of the features of Bird's argument. Pete felt using it as support for his own point would discredit his case since, upon closer, analytical reading, he found some problems in the author's reasoning.

ALSO NOTE
OTHER IDEAS ON WHO SHOULD GO TO COLLEGE

William A. Henry's controversial book, *In Defense of Elitism*, has been required reading at some colleges and universities. This 1994 classic might have been a better source of information for Pete as he made his argument. In it, Henry argues we send too many young people to college and for the wrong reasons.

> . . . Those who stop their educations after earning a four-year degree earn about $1\frac{1}{2}$ times as much as those who stop at the end of high school. These outcomes, however, reflect other things besides the impact of the degree itself. College graduates are winners in part because colleges attract people who are already winners—people with enough brains and drive that they would do well in almost any generation and under almost any circumstances, with or without formal credentialing.
>
> The harder and more meaningful question is whether the mediocrities who have also flooded into colleges in the past couple of generations do better than they otherwise would have. And if they do, is it because college actually made them better employees or because it simply gave them the requisite credential to get interviewed and hired? The U.S. Labor Department's Bureau of Labor Statistics reports that about 20% of all college graduates toil in fields

(continued)

not requiring a degree, and this total is projected to exceed 30% by the year 2005. For the individual, college may well be a credential without being a qualification, required without being requisite.

ARGUMENT IN ACTION Advantages of Going to College

Many more recent arguments than Bird's have argued that attending college is a wise choice. Do you find this argument from a 2002 review of studies ("The Value of a College Degree," *ERIC Digest*) convincing?

The article includes evidence that during an adult's working life, the average amount earned was

- $1.2 million for high school graduates
- $1.6 million for graduates with an associate's (2-year) degree
- $2.1 million for those with bachelor's (4-year) degrees (Another study from the Center for Business Research at Arizona State University claims the differential is more like $1.27 million between high-school and college graduates.)

Other personal and social benefits are cited in the article:

- Greater savings
- Increased personal and professional mobility
- Better quality of life for children
- Wiser consumer decisions
- Increased participation in hobbies and leisure activity
- Better health for self and children
- More positive view of past and future
- Less dependence on government assistance

The report's conclusion:

> While it is clear that investment in a college degree, especially for those students in the lowest income brackets, is a financial burden, the long-term benefits to individuals as well as to society at large, appear to far outweigh the costs.

STUDENTS AT WORK: PETE ASKS CRITICAL QUESTIONS ABOUT HIS SOURCE

Following are the questions Pete developed about his source:

- $34,000 would be a little over $100,000 in today's dollars. How many uneducated, unemployed 18-year-olds have $100,000 in cash to invest?
- For her example, Bird chooses a "Princeton-bound" student. This tuition figure for an Ivy League school is a lot higher than for most college students. Bird's estimates are not really typical evidence.

- The Jencks source she cites talks about men. My other sources say today's college population has slightly more women than men. Would the case be different for women than men?
- Bird's made-up argument suggests that high-school graduates might often start out at entry-level positions (her mechanic) and move up to own the company, then use that advancement to move on to ownership of even a larger and more important corporation. How often does this really happen? Is her imaginary example enough evidence of this kind of job advancement? Would knowing just one person be enough evidence?
- Since 1975 when this was written, there have been big changes in the makeup of the workforce and in the types of jobs. Is Bird's argument as true today when there has been a shift from a manufacturing economy to an information economy?
- The Mincer source says that in 20–30% of the cases, earnings were not affected by a college education. That *could* mean that as much as 80% of the time, earnings *were* in fact improved. Wouldn't that be good odds?

Sometimes, a careful analysis of an argument will allow you to use the information with a caveat (a warning or expressed limitation) or as dated and now changed historical context. Pete decided the best choice was to look for more suitable material, and his final project certainly benefited from his decision, one that is often difficult to make once you have bought into an argument you've read.

So, if these problems were obvious upon Pete's more careful examination during his conference, why did this good student initially buy Bird's argument and choose to use it as support? Certainly, we have seen the same selection of material before and since with other students. Why does that happen?

CAUSES OF SUPERFICIAL, LESS THAN CRITICAL READING

As intelligent as Pete is, he was subject to the same problems as many other people are when they review initial, potential support for their arguments:

1. When people want to make a point, they are often willing to accept less compelling evidence if it agrees with their own point.

2. When people read arguments, they often look only for confirmation of their predetermined views. Consumers of arguments are not blank slates upon which thoughts can be written. Apply that concept rigorously to *yourself* as you review an argument just as thoughtfully as you apply it to your potential reader when you construct an argument of your own.

3. Understanding the words and information of an argument is not equivalent to understanding the purposes, potential biases, potential fallacious thinking, and basic assumptions underlying the argument.

Because these tendencies in assessing personal, public, professional, and academic arguments are so pervasive, we offer you the following hints on how to read and consume actively and critically rather than passively. Passive reading is just reading to understand the words and get the "facts." If you read an argument and can repeat it rather clearly in your own words, you still may have read passively. Active, or critical, reading, on the other hand, is practiced in order to analyze the argument of the writer and evaluate the quality of the argument. Active reading of an argument is a thoughtful process in which the reader engages with the material in order to break it down to its constituent parts and to see if the argument is both truthful and valid (see the discussion of deduction in Chapter 2 to review "truth" and "validity").

ALSO NOTE
THE WRITER'S "POSITION"

In Chapter 2, you read about the concept of *ethos*, the establishing of credibility as an arguer. Building that credibility begins early by carefully assessing the position from which you view the information you accumulate. What are the factors that determine how you make meaning of what you read? Age? Cultural heritage? Family background? Geographic location? Ethnicity? Socioeconomic status? Political persuasion? Religious tradition? How have those factors influenced your "take" on the material?

Your *position* will no doubt reflect in your reading as well as your writing. Being able to recognize that position and addressing it fairly will increase your credibility. Several different approaches, among others, are possible:

- Stepping away from your position temporarily in an attempt at objectivity
- Acknowledging and holding your position while attempting to learn about other positions
- Recognizing the strength of your position as a motivational force while being willing to examine its bases.

"ACTIVE" VERSUS "PASSIVE" READING PRACTICES

As you read actively and critically, keep the following suggestions in mind. Of course, based on the complexity, length, and sophistication level of the argument you are reviewing, you may need to use more or fewer of the activities to assure you have evaluated the argument adequately.

1. *Reserve judgment.* Approach all arguments with the intention of understanding the writer's (speaker's, creator's) line of discussion, and evaluate after you are sure you understand the argument fully. *If you read only to look for confirmation of your own perspective, you'll make some serious mistakes in reading.*

2. *Preview the reading if it is lengthy and complex.* Try reading the last paragraphs or pages to see what conclusions the writer will make, and then you can act as an investigator as you read, looking to see if the writer has used the proper logic and offered the necessary evidence to come to those conclusions. If the material has subheadings, read through those; they should be a guide to the organization of the argument's main points. Reviewing them first will make the argument more coherent upon a closer reading.

3. *Review key definitions from your preview.* If you have seen terms and concepts that you were unfamiliar with, look them up before reading, and you will not miss important meaning as you read.

4. *Ask yourself critical questions after your preview and as you read.* You might ask such questions as:

    - Is the claim of this argument clear and unambiguous? Is it explicit (evident in a specific sentence or sentences in the argument) or implicit (suggested or veiled)?
    - What kinds of appeals is this argument using, and are they appropriate? Is it trying to pull emotional strings (pathos)? Is the argument using an appeal to logic and reason (logos)? Is the argument based on the authority and integrity of its creator (ethos)? Are these appeals appropriate, or are they manipulative?
    - Has the writer made some assumptions in the argument that are not sound, or at least need more support? Are there "warrants," in Toulmin's language, that should be discussed or defended?
    - Does the argument adequately address reasonable opposition, or is it "preaching to the choir," a phrase used to describe an argument that will be convincing only to those who already believe it?
    - What kind of resources does the argument cite?
    - Is the argument current? Is the argument bringing up past issues that are resolved or from which we've moved on?
    - Do you notice any of the potential problems with argument mentioned in Chapter 5?

5. *Use highlighting and/or underlining judiciously.* We encourage you to highlight only on a second, very critical reading (note the few lines underlined in the example, "There's No Future in Lady Luck," on p. 138, for instance). Often, we review students' resource material and see material highlighted in every paragraph. Such overkill will not help you when you go back to the material later. You will probably only know what the most critical, and therefore highlight-worthy, parts of the argument are after reading the entire piece.

6. *Evaluate the typicality and sufficiency of the evidence provided* (see the section in Chapter 2 titled "Inductive Reasoning"). Also, be sure you are not tempted to accept opinions and assertions as evidence. Often, opinions are convincing, but just make sure you understand which type of development

the writer is offering and which type you are willing to accept as the basis of your judgments.

7. *After reading, make summary notes.* Making concise, written assessments forces you to evaluate the argument more carefully. Consider making bullet points of the main points the writer uses to convince you of the claim. (Had Pete done this, he probably would have seen that the evidence for Bird's argument was flawed before he came to his conference.) Most important, make written comments on how this argument compares and contrasts to other things you have read or experienced: for example, "This is the first argument I've seen that justified the large tax cuts of the early 2000s; all others have criticized them," or, in Pete's case: "This is pretty old information, but it does provide a historical context."

8. *Write out the Argument Concept the creator of the argument probably had in mind as he or she developed it.* Be thoughtful as you do this to think through the specific purpose of the argument (cause and effect, problem-solving, argument for quality, etc.). One of the essential judgments to make about an argument is if it meets the writer's intended purpose.

You may be tempted to look at these steps and reject them because they appear to take more time than you are used to giving to your reading. Before you make such a quick judgment, think not just about the initial reading time, but the time you will save later when you want to use some of the information. Remember, also, how easy it is to read passively and miss important parts of an argument. Also, when you are accumulating outside sources for arguments, without careful and analytical reading, you will probably find yourself having to reread much of your material. You may also fall into the same trouble Pete had when you are trying to use resource material. Even more seriously, without learning to read and think critically about arguments, you may be hoodwinked by fallacious arguments in your career and personal life.

"REVERSING" THE ARGUMENT CONCEPT

> **REVERSING THE ARGUMENT CONCEPT** *is the practice of analyzing a written, spoken, or visual argument to determine its creator's focus, intended reader, and purpose. Analyzing an argument in this way is a first good step in critical reading.*

One of the most effective ways to check your sense of the overall argument is to attempt to reconstruct the Argument Concept (focus, reader, purpose) from which the writer is operating. Of course, as we said earlier, professional and experienced writers may not write this concept out as a literal statement; they may just have those organizing principles in their consciousness as they approach their projects. But trying to articulate the argument in this way—by *reversing* the Argument Concept—is a very concrete method of teasing out those elements that you might otherwise ignore if you simply read passively.

To show you how reversing the Argument Concept works, let's return to Pete's argument from Carolyn Bird. Her Argument Concept may have been something like this:

> "*I will argue about* the misconception that a college education is an efficient path to building wealth *for* those who are considering using higher education as an occupational stepping stone *in order to* convince them that they should go directly into the workforce instead if that is their goal."

To evaluate the argument, then, ask yourself what methods the writer has used to construct this argument, if they are appropriate given the Argument Concept, and if they meet the tests of evidence discussed in Chapter 2 (sufficient and typical evidence). Looking at the way the argument is constructed—by using Toulmin's method of analysis (also in Chapter 2), for instance—will help you assess its quality. Had Pete applied these skills as he read, he probably would have found at least one problem in Bird's line of logic: few college freshmen have $100,000 at their disposal. The entire calculation is based on a faulty, and rather silly, assumption. With careful review, he might have discovered the additional problems with Bird's argument earlier.

What follows is an exercise in analyzing arguments ranging from the very obvious to the quite sophisticated. Some are explicit—arguments in which the writer, artist, or creator has put the claims in very clear and obvious terms. In most of these arguments, you will be able to find a statement or obvious image that needs no interpretation, one that conveys the claim unambiguously. Others are more subtle arguments where the claim is *implicit*. In these arguments, the claim is suggested only, and the reader or observer must interpret, must add up the evidence and come to his or her own understanding of the claim. You and your classmates may have some considerable disagreement about precisely what the claim is; sometimes that lack of clarity is intentional when a writer wants readers to think and project their own understandings on the argument, and sometimes it is unintentional when a writer simply does not communicate clearly enough. We encourage beginning writers of argument to be as explicit as possible so that they will avoid that second possibility.

Exercise 1
Group Analysis: Analyzing Arguments

As we have emphasized, arguments are everywhere around you; some are serious and life changing, some are used to keep business humming, some are in jest, and others are practical and simply help you get through each day more easily. You might be surprised to find the elements of argument in examples that are humorous, that are nonverbal, or that come from such everyday experience as a letter of complaint. In this exercise, you are asked to use the reading techniques listed previously to review several of the eight arguments actively and critically. Your instructor may want to assign one or more samples to each of several small groups and then ask you to report back on your findings to the class as a whole.

But first, to illustrate how you might analyze one of these arguments, we have provided a sample argument and analysis. The author, Linda Chavez, was the Executive Director of the U.S. Commission on Civil Rights from 1983 to 1985. This essay was originally published in *USA Today* in 1995.

There's No Future in Lady Luck
Linda Chavez

1. Remember when the American dream meant becoming a millionaire through talent, hard work, and thrift?

2. No longer.

3. Now it's hitting the lottery, with state governments spending millions of dollars a year to promote luck as the key to success.

4. In 1995, New York expanded the frontier of legalized gambling by offering a new, casino-style game called Quick Draw. Now, instead of a daily lottery, the state draws winning numbers every five minutes, thirteen hours a day, in bars and restaurants around the state.

5. It's a constant rush for compulsive gamblers.

    As one woman explained to the *New York Times*, "I play the daily number, but you have to wait until 7:30 P.M. to know. This is quicker—five minutes—it's like being in Atlantic City."

6. This same woman, interviewed at a Staten Island, N.Y., shopping center, had come into the place to buy milk and diapers. She won $1 in half an hour—and lost $7. "I have no more money for the diapers and the milk, but I had fun," she said in the interview.

These first three sentences are the argument's claim.

Argument Concept: <u>I will argue about</u> the targeting of the poor by state lotteries <u>for</u> poor people who buy tickets <u>in order to</u> convince them this is not the way to success. (Does this argument serve two potential readers and purposes? Is Chavez hoping to shame state lottery commissions as well?)

This example uses an appeal to emotion, pathos; Chavez is trying to get the reader to feel bad because a baby is being neglected. Yes, this one example seems bad, and the details of the specific example are convincing—still, it is just one example, not enough evidence from which to draw a conclusion.

"Reversing" the Argument Concept **139**

7   Yeah, well what about her baby? What fun will Junior have sitting in wet diapers all day, crying from hunger?

8   This woman isn't alone—in fact, she's typical of state lottery players.

9   If you doubt it, spend some time in any convenience store in an inner city in one of the thirty-seven states or the District of Columbia that sell state lottery tickets. The lines of men and women waiting to play their lucky numbers are filled with poor people, <u>many of them no doubt refunding to the state cash from welfare checks paid out for the care of dependent children</u>.

This is just an assertion on her part, not real evidence.

Stores are not allowed to use welfare checks in this way, so this is something of an exaggeration. Is Chavez losing some credibility here by trying to play on negative stereotypes of people on welfare?

10 In 1994, states sold $34 billion in lottery tickets. Lottery defenders—most prominently the state officials who oversee the games—claim this money brings in needed revenue for everything from education to health care.

This is damning evidence from the government plan.

11 But the fact is, the money is conned from the least educated, most gullible segment of the population. Joshua Wolf Shenk, writing in the *Washington Monthly* magazine, notes that state lotteries clearly target the poor as their best customers. He quotes an Iowa lottery media plan "<u>to target our message demographically against those that we know to be heavy users.</u>" <u>According to several studies on the subject, that means blacks, Hispanics, and poor whites.</u>

The last sentence is less convincing. The generic statement "several studies" is problematic. People often say things like "research shows" when they haven't really read it and can't cite any of the studies. If several studies exist, Chavez should easily be able to produce one.*

12 It's bad enough that the state sponsors lotteries, but what is worse is the huge state investment in promoting ticket sales. New York spends $30 million a year in advertising.

A convincing statistic here; could be stronger with addition of numbers from elsewhere.

---

*A quick look on the Web site of the Scientific Game Corporation shows that 65% of players have incomes of $45,000 to $75,000; least likely to play are people below $25,000. The Texas Lottery, possibly a biased source, says four surveys done by the University of Texas College of Communication found that "Contrary to well-known myths, Texans who earn the lowest income and who have the least amount of education are significantly less likely to buy a ticket. This finding is significant because it addresses one of the biggest misconceptions surrounding the Lottery."

13   And lottery ads are slick.

14   Virginia's Lady Luck commercials are among the most appealing on television. But their message is no different from all the other lottery ads. You've got to play to win, which means playing every week, every day—or, as now in New York, every hour. And adults who are legally permitted to buy tickets aren't the only targets of the ad campaigns. Kids are tomorrow's customers.

15   Recently, I went riding in Potomac, Md., with a little boy who visits me each summer from New York where he lives in a housing project. He had never seen houses like the huge homes that dot the affluent Washington suburb.

16   "Is that where people who win the lottery live?" he asked. No, I explained, most of the people in those houses are lawyers, doctors, or other professionals who had studied hard, gone to college, and worked many years before they could buy such homes.

17   Of course, my little New Yorker isn't likely to ever buy a house such as the ones he saw—nor am I, for that matter. But his chances of owning any house are certainly improved if he heeds my message rather than his own state government's.

An assertion here without any detail or description; however, Chavez may expect that readers of USA Today, *in which this argument was published, probably have seen lots of these ads.*

The specifics help make Chavez's first case: people (at least this one little boy) are looking to get rich quick on the lottery. The argument that governments are encouraging citizens to gamble is convincing. It is not clear that the evidence of players is typical, and it is certainly not sufficient, so Chavez's other charge that lotteries target the poor and minorities is questionable.

With this kind of thorough and careful analysis in mind, review some of the following sample arguments by addressing these activities in small groups:

- Decide which of the eight active reading activities listed on pp. 134–136 are most helpful in approaching each specific argument.
- For each argument, reverse the Argument Concept: write out the Argument Concept with which you think the creator of the argument was operating.
- Write out the sentence(s) or describe the image (in the poster, for example) in the selection that you think best encapsulates the writer's or creator's claim.

- Consider how the reader and writer are negotiating meaning in the argument. What is the writer expecting from the reader, and are those expectations reasonable? What warrants does the writer expect to share with the reader? What do you think the reader's mindset will be on the topic prior to reading or observing the argument? Where is a reader apt to go wrong in interpreting the argument based on those presuppositions?
- Can you see where any of the creators of these arguments are providing concessions and/or rebuttals in consideration of other perspectives?
- Explain why you think the argument is or is not convincing based on application of the principles of evidence and logic discussed in Chapters 2 and 3.

Questions are included after each argument to encourage your critical reading and analysis.

Sample 1—Environmental Poster Poster artists make their arguments with few words, but still the principles of argument apply to this form of visual rhetoric. *Traces of Man*, created by Cedomir Kostovic, was exhibited in 2003 at the Hatton & Curfman Gallery at Colorado State University. To give you some ideas about how to approach the analysis of visual argument, you may want to refer any or all of the following sections in Chapter 1:

- The questions listed in the Visual Rhetoric box on p. 5;
- The sample analysis of a W800: Walkman Phone advertisement on p. 12;
- The analysis of Frida Kahlo's painting on p. 20.

Questions About Sample 1

1. Writers or artists cannot control the consumer of their work. Although they may conceive of a specific reader, their work is broadly accessible. This is particularly true of the poster artist. What is the specific audience this artist is addressing? Will this poster be effective for a broader audience that may view the poster as well?
2. Simplicity is this poster's strength, yet there are details that reinforce the claim it makes. What are some of those details?
3. What effect is created by the lack of background or context for the images in the poster? How would the effect be different if there were more context for the tree trunks?
4. We have discussed the importance of being fair and of not alienating the opposition when making an argument. Is this poster fair or extreme?

Visual Rhetoric...
VISUAL "LANGUAGE" IN TRACES OF MAN

A *pun* in written or spoken language is a play on words that depends on different senses of the same word or on similar sounds of different words: "Everyone was crying at the wedding. Even the cake was in tiers." The same kind of visual language play is going on in *Traces of Man*. What two images are being confused purposefully?

Can it win over the opposition, or is it "preaching to the choir"? If it is just confirming already held views, is that a legitimate purpose for argument?

Sample 2—Argument in Poetry   In 1915, Edgar Lee Masters published *Spoon River Anthology*, a collection of poems about more than two hundred fictitious residents of Spoon River, a rural area where he grew up. He was a successful Chicago lawyer by that time, far removed from his country background. The book was unique: a "novel" about interrelated characters told through short first-person epitaphs, each either telling a character's secret, his downfall, her longings, or in some cases, keys to successful living. Some of Spoon River's inhabitants tell uplifting stories, and others make hard-edged social commentary. Sometimes the character's remarks have an implicit meaning. Sometimes the character is very explicit about the meaning of his or her life, as in this poem.

"Margaret Fuller Slack"
Edgar Lee Masters

1   I would have been as great as George Eliot
    But for an untoward fate.
    For look at the photograph of me made by Penniwit,*
    Chin resting on hand, and deepset eyes—
5   Gray, too, and far-searching.
    But there was the old, old problem:
    Should it be celibacy, matrimony or unchastity?
    Then John Slack, the rich druggist, wooed me,
    Luring me with the promise of leisure for my novel,
    And I married him, giving birth to eight children,
10 And I had no time to write.
    It was all over with me, anyway,
    When I ran the needle in my hand
    While washing the baby's things,
15 And died from lock-jaw, an ironical death.
    Hear me, ambitious souls,
    Sex is the curse of life!

Questions About Sample 2

1. Certainly, the last line is very explicit and expresses Margaret Fuller Slack's claim. But this poem is about much more than one woman's lost dreams.

---

*"Penniwit" is the town photographer who always tried to capture his subject in a pose that revealed his or her character.

144 Chapter 6 *Using the Argument Concept to Read the Arguments of Others*

One of the interesting aspects of reading literature is trying to sort out the character's actions, feelings, and statements from those of the writer. What is Masters's Argument Concept, looking at this poem as social commentary (remember, this was 1915)?

2. In a short poem like this, the "evidence" for the claim must be strong and condensed. What are some of the pieces of evidence that Margaret Fuller Slack cites to support *her* claim?

3. "Lock-jaw" (*tetanus*) was truly an ironic death for Masters to have chosen for this character. How does this choice illustrate further the claim he is making?

4. Is the emotional appeal in this poem convincing to you? Does it seem whining, or legitimate? What effect do you imagine this appeal would have on a reader in 1915? How does your experience nearly one hundred years later color your response to this character's claim?

Sample 3—A Student Argument This argument by John Gonzales, at the time a University of Southern California student, was published in the *Los Angeles Times*. Gonzales poignantly explains the difficulty he faced as he attempted to educate himself. (As you read, you may need to know that Proposition 187 was the watershed legislation passed in California and described in the official ballot argument as "the first giant stride in ultimately ending the illegal alien invasion." The proposition denied medical, educational, and other public services to undocumented residents of California.)

College Brings Alienation

John Gonzales

1 My decision to chase a dream, return to college at age 24 and take the liberal arts courses that will help me become a journalist has forced me to be two people. One face is for family and longtime friends, another is for my classes and college friends.

2 My homeboys have not read Marx, Nietzsche or Freud. They do not care to probe the economics behind their being paid less, despite working more, than their fathers. They don't want to hear about the Oedipus complex or the nature of good and evil. For them, intellectual theories are elaborate, unnecessary attempts to explain the inexplicable. Ideas do not feed their families and only seem to highlight the fact that I have begun to change. "That's enough. Don't read any more. I don't understand a word you're saying," Fidel, my *compadre*, said after I responded to his request to read him a paragraph from one of my textbooks. He had telephoned

while I was doing homework and jibed, "What the hell are you studying now?"

3   I also stumble to explain my studies to my parents. My father had a sixth-grade education. My mother earned her GED 15 years after leaving high school. I often reluctantly hand them my term papers they ask to see, knowing they won't truly comprehend them. After a careful reading, my mother's usual response: "You write so beautifully, *mijo*, I didn't really understand all the words you used but we can just tell how educated you are."

4   A senior at the University of Southern California, receiving a bachelor's degree in journalism and political science this May, I painfully realize the downside to education, a subtle alienation from friends and loved ones. I understand more clearly why Latinos approach higher learning with trepidation. For beyond the barriers of low income and racism lies another fight, the struggle to blend old and new identities.

5   It is not that education is discouraged; my family is proud of me and would be crushed if I were to quit. But disproportionately few Latinos acquire higher learning, and those who do often must balance an incompatible past and future.

6   I envision my old friends and new friends at my graduation party: Would they eat, drink and laugh together or huddle in separate groups? Which group would I join?

7   Who am I?

8   That is why many promising Latinos I know who attend college choose to major in business or other fields with more easily identifiable rewards for their parents and themselves. "I'm learning how to start and manage a restaurant" is certainly something my father, a part-time contractor, would grasp more clearly than the abstract knowledge I've obtained.

9   Noble careers that require no college sometimes seem even more attractive. My aunt, mother of an army sergeant, beams with pride at family gatherings when she recalls my cousin's boot-camp graduation. Yet my mother struggles to explain the value of my work as a journalist. Amid the music, food and drink of the get-together, a reporter is not a craftsman with words, not a guardian of democracy, not a voice against society's ills. Instead, journalists are perceived as the intrusive talking heads on the 11 o'clock news, the Latino ones pretentiously pronouncing their surnames with forced accents.

10   For other Latinos I know studying philosophy, sociology and literature, the struggle to retain identity is similar. In this political climate of Proposition 187, the demise of the Great Society and threats to affirmative action, analytical, creative Latino minds are needed more than ever. But the sacrifices are great indeed.

146 Chapter 6 *Using the Argument Concept to Read the Arguments of Others*

Questions About Sample 3

1. What is the purpose of Gonzales's essay? Why would he want to publish this personal perspective? Who is the audience? How are those two elements related?

2. Although the essay is narrative to an extent, it is explicit. What sentences(s) best explains the claim of this essay?

3. How do you feel about Gonzales, and what effect does that have on your reaction to the essay? How does he use the concept of *ethos* in attempting to relate to his audience?

4. Does Gonzales also use the concept of *pathos* in this essay? If so, why?

5. Gonzales mentions the "political climate of Proposition 187" in his conclusion. What does his personal struggle have to do with the political context in which this argument exists?

Sample 4—"A Hanging" In a somber mood, this essay, first published in *Adelphi* in London in 1931 and frequently appearing in classic essay anthologies, makes a moving comment on capital punishment. George Orwell (a pseudonym for Eric Arthur Blair) was born in India and spent five years working for the Indian Imperial Police in Burma, in which capacity he was exposed to great poverty and injustice, much at the hand of his British imperialist government. Many of his works were influenced by his experiences in Burma (currently called Myanmar). This essay is a classic example of argument made in narrative (story-telling) form.

A Hanging
George Orwell

1. It was in Burma, a sodden morning of the rains. A sickly light, like yellow tinfoil, was slanting over the high walls into the jail yard. We were waiting outside the condemned cells, a row of sheds fronted with double bars, like small animal cages. Each cell measured about ten feet by ten and was quite bare within except for a plank bed and a pot for drinking water. In some of them brown silent men were squatting at the inner bars, with their blankets draped round them. These were the condemned men due to be hanged within the next week or two.

2. One prisoner had been brought out of his cell. He was a Hindu, a puny wisp of a man, with a shaven head and vague liquid eyes. He had a thick, sprouting moustache, absurdly too big for his body, rather like the moustache of a comic man on the films. Six tall Indian warders were guarding him and getting him ready for the gallows. Two of them stood by with rifles and fixed bayonets, while the others handcuffed him, passed a chain through his handcuffs and fixed it to their belts, and lashed his arms tight to his sides. They crowded very close about him, with their hands always on him in a careful, caressing grip as though all the while feeling him to make sure he was there. It was like

men handling a fish which is still alive and may jump back into the water. But he stood quite unresisting, yielding his arms limply to the ropes, as though he hardly noticed what was happening.

3   Eight o'clock struck and a bugle call, desolately thin in the wet air, floated from the distant barracks. The superintendent of the jail, who was standing apart from the rest of us, moodily prodding the gravel with his stick, raised his head at the sound. He was an army doctor, with a gray toothbrush moustache and a gruff voice. "For God's sake hurry up, Francis," he said irritably. "The man ought to have been dead by this time. Aren't you ready yet?"

4   Francis, the head jailer, a fat Dravidian in a white drill suit and gold spectacles, waved his black hand. "Yes sir, yes sir," he bubbled. "All iss satisfactorily prepared. The hangman iss waiting. We shall proceed."

5   "Well, quick march, then. The prisoners can't get their breakfast till this job's over."

6   We set out for the gallows. Two warders marched on either side of the prisoner, with their rifles at the slope; two others marched close against him, gripping him by arm and shoulder, as though at once pushing and supporting him. The rest of us, magistrates and the like, followed behind. Suddenly, when we had gone ten yards, the procession stopped short without any order or warning. A dreadful thing had happened—a dog, come goodness knows whence, had appeared in the yard. It came bounding among us with a loud volley of barks, and leapt round us wagging its whole body, wild with glee at finding so many human beings together. It was a large woolly dog, half Airedale, half pariah. For a moment it pranced round us, and then, before anyone could stop it, it had made a dash for the prisoner and, jumping up, tried to lick his face. Everyone stood aghast, too taken aback even to grab at the dog.

7   "Who let that bloody brute in here?" said the superintendent angrily. "Catch it, someone!"

8   A warder, detached from the escort, charged clumsily after the dog, but it danced and gamboled just out of his reach, taking everything as part of the game. A young Eurasian jailer picked up a handful of gravel and tried to stone the dog away, but it dodged the stones and came after us again. Its yaps echoed from the jail walls. The prisoner, in the grasp of the two warders, looked on incuriously, as though this was another formality of the hanging. It was several minutes before someone managed to catch the dog. Then we put my handkerchief through its collar and moved off once more, with the dog still straining and whimpering.

9   It was about forty yards to the gallows. I watched the bare brown back of the prisoner marching in front of me. He walked clumsily with his bound arms, but quite steadily, with that bobbing gait of the Indian who never straightens his knees. At each step his muscles slid neatly into place, the lock of hair on his scalp danced up and down, his feet printed themselves on the wet gravel. And once, in spite of the men who gripped him by each shoulder, he stepped slightly aside to avoid a puddle on the path.

10   It is curious, but till that moment I had never realized what it means to destroy a healthy, conscious man. When I saw the prisoner step aside to avoid the puddle I saw the mystery, the unspeakable wrongness, of cutting a life short when it is in full tide. This man was not dying, he was alive just as we are alive. All the organs of his body were working—bowels digesting food, skin renewing itself, nails growing, tissues forming—all toiling away in solemn foolery. His nails would still be growing when he stood on the drop, when he was falling through the air with a tenth of a second to live. His eyes saw the yellow gravel and the gray walls, and his brain still remembered, foresaw, reasoned—reasoned even about puddles. He and we were a party of men walking together, seeing, hearing, feeling, understanding the same world: and in two minutes, with a sudden snap, one of us would be gone—one mind less, one world less.

11   The gallows stood in a small yard, separate from the main grounds of the prison, and overgrown with tall prickly weeds. It was a brick erection like three sides of a shed, with planking on top, and above that two beams and a crossbar with the rope dangling. The hangman, a gray-haired convict in the white uniform of the prison, was waiting beside his machine. He greeted us with a servile crouch as we entered. At a word from Francis the two warders, gripping the prisoner more closely than ever, half led, half pushed him to the gallows and helped him clumsily up the ladder. Then the hangman climbed up and fixed the rope round the prisoner's neck.

12   We stood waiting, five yards away. The warders had formed in a rough circle round the gallows. And then, when the noose was fixed, the prisoner began crying out to his god. It was a high, reiterated cry of "Ram! Ram! Ram!" not urgent and fearful like a prayer or cry for help, but steady, rhythmical, almost like the tolling of a bell. The dog answered the sound with a whine. The hangman, still standing on the gallows, produced a small cotton bag like a flour bag and drew it down over the prisoner's face. But the sound, muffled by the cloth, still persisted, over and over again: "Ram! Ram! Ram! Ram! Ram!"

13   The hangman climbed down and stood ready, holding the lever. Minutes seemed to pass. The steady, muffled crying from the prisoner went on and on, "Ram! Ram! Ram!" never faltering for an instant. The superintendent, his head on his chest, was slowly poking the ground with his stick; perhaps he was counting the cries, allowing the prisoner a fixed number—fifty, perhaps, or a hundred. Everyone had changed color. The Indians had gone gray like bad coffee, and one or two of the bayonets were wavering. We looked at the lashed, hooded man on the drop, and listened to his cries—each cry another second of life; the same thought was in all our minds: oh, kill him quickly, get it over, stop that abominable noise!

14   Suddenly the superintendent made up his mind. Throwing up his head he made a swift motion with his stick. "Chalo!" he shouted almost fiercely.

15   There was a clanking noise, and then dead silence. The prisoner had vanished, and the rope was twisting on itself. I let go of the dog, and it galloped immediately to the back of the gallows; but when it got there it stopped short, barked, and then retreated into a corner of the yard, where it

stood among the weeds, looking timorously out at us. We went round the gallows to inspect the prisoner's body. He was dangling with his toes pointed straight downward, very slowly revolving, as dead as a stone.

16   The superintendent reached out with his stick and poked the bare brown body; it oscillated slightly. "*He's* all right," said the superintendent. He backed out from under the gallows, and blew out a deep breath. The moody look had gone out of his face quite suddenly. He glanced at his wrist watch. "Eight minutes past eight. Well, that's all for this morning, thank god."

17   The warders unfixed bayonets and marched away. The dog, sobered and conscious of having misbehaved itself, slipped after them. We walked out of the gallows yard, past the condemned cells with their waiting prisoners, into the big central yard of the prison. The convicts, under the command of warders armed with lathis [clubs], were already receiving their breakfast. They squatted in long rows, each man holding a tin pannikin, while two warders with buckets marched round ladling out rice; it seemed quite a homely, jolly scene, after the hanging. An enormous relief had come upon us now that the job was done. One felt an impulse to sing, to break into a run, to snigger. All at once everyone began chattering gaily.

18   The Eurasian boy walking beside me nodded toward the way we had come, with a knowing smile: "Do you know, sir, our friend [he meant the dead man] when he heard his appeal had been dismissed, he pissed on the floor of his cell. From fright. Kindly take one of my cigarettes, sir. Do you not admire my new silver case, sir? From the boxwalah [a box of treasures], two rupees eight annas. Classy European style."

19   Several people laughed—at what, nobody seemed certain.

20   Francis was walking by the superintendent, talking garrulously: "Well, sir, all hass passed off with the utmost satisfactoriness. It was all finished—flick! like that. It iss not always so—oah, no! I have known cases where the doctor wass obliged to go beneath the gallows and pull the prissoner's legs to ensure decease. Most disagreeable!"

21   "Wriggling about, eh? That's bad," said the superintendent.

22   "Ach, sir, it iss worse when they become refractory! One man, I recall, clung to the bars of hiss cage when we went to take him out. You will scarcely credit, sir, that it took six warders to dislodge him, three pulling at each leg. We reasoned with him. 'My dear fellow,' we said, 'think of all the pain and trouble you are causing to us!' But no, he would not listen! Ach, he wass very troublesome!"

23   I found that I was laughing quite loudly. Everyone was laughing. Even the superintendent grinned in a tolerant way. "You'd better all come out and have a drink," he said quite genially, "I've got a bottle of whisky in the car. We could do with it."

24   We went through the big double gates of the prison into the road. "Pulling at his legs!" exclaimed a Burmese magistrate suddenly, and burst into a loud chuckling. We all began laughing again. At that moment Francis' anecdote seemed extraordinarily funny. We all had a drink together, native and European alike, quite amicably. The dead man was a hundred yards away.

150 Chapter 6 *Using the Argument Concept to Read the Arguments of Others*

Questions About Sample 4

1. After writing out the Argument Concept, find the paragraph in Orwell's essay that explicitly states his attitude toward the hanging.
2. Some of Orwell's evidence includes detail about the prisoner, detail of both his appearance and his behavior. How does this evidence help support his stance?
3. Orwell also spends a good deal of time describing the dog's behavior. What does the dog contribute to his argument?
4. After the hanging, even the other prisoners' moods improve. How can you explain the morbid laughter, and why does Orwell conclude his argument with the laughing and camaraderie?

Sample 5—Social Commentary with Reasons and Evidence from Personal Experience   H. Bruce Miller, a senior writer for *The Source Weekly*, makes a cause-and-effect claim about the violent inclinations of our society in this short essay. He does not pretend to offer hard evidence to support his claim, but expects the reader to buy in because of the reasonableness of his idea. Miller first made this argument in 1981. Is it still applicable to the prevalence of violence today?

Severing the Human Connection
H. Bruce Miller

1   Went down to the local self-serve gas station the other morning to fill up. The sullen cashier was sitting inside a dark, glassed-in, burglar-proof, bullet-proof, probably grenade-proof cubicle covered with cheerful notices. "NO CHECKS." "NO CREDIT." "NO BILLS OVER $50 ACCEPTED." "CASHIER HAS NO SMALL CHANGE." And the biggest one of all: "PAY BEFORE PUMPING GAS." A gleaming steel box slid out of the wall and gaped open. I dropped in a $20 bill. "Going to fill'er up with no-lead on Number 6," I said. The cashier nodded. The steel box swallowed my money and retracted into the cubicle. I walked back to the car to pump the gas, trying not to slink or skulk. I felt like I ought to be wearing striped overalls with a number on the breast pocket.

2   The pay-before-you-pump gas station (those in the trade call it a "pre-pay") is a response to a real problem in these days of expensive gas and cut-rate ethics: people who fill their tanks and then tear out of the station without paying. Those in the business call them "drive-offs." The head of one area gasoline dealers' association says drive-offs cost some dealers $500 to $600 a month. With a profit margin of only about a nickel a gallon, a dealer has to sell a lot of gallons to make up that kind of loss. The police aren't much help. Even if the attendant manages to get a license plate number and description of the car, the cops have better things to do than tracking down a guy who stole $15 worth of gas. So the dealers adopt the pre-pay system.

(continued on p. 152)

ALSO NOTE
CLIPS FROM *BOWLING FOR COLUMBINE*

In his 2002 film, *Bowling for Columbine*, Michael Moore investigates why America has so many more incidents of violence than other countries. In an argument some what similar to Miller's (pp. 150–153), his suggestion is that we are reacting to irrational fear that has been part of the American psyche for some time, a fear that is exacerbated by constant media focus on that which we should fear. The following are snippets of Moore's "evidence," some from interviews in the film:

- "Littleton [site of the Columbine tragedy] is painfully normal." (Matt Stone, Littleton High School graduate and originator of South Park cartoon series)
- One-year comparison of number of people killed by guns:

Germany	381
France	255
Canada	165
England	68
Australia	65
Japan	39
United States	11,127[*]

- Americans have feared others since the time of the Pilgrims, who feared the Native Americans. Americans traditionally and continually react by killing the objects of their fears. Suburbia, in particular, fears the cities and arms itself accordingly.
- Barry Glassner, author of *Culture of Fear*: "The most shocking statistic I came across is that while our murder rate has dropped 20%, the coverage of murders on the evening news has gone up 600%. . . . Why are we afraid of these things? It's because a lot of people are making a lot of money off of it [such as security companies, network news, and reality police programs]. And so there's vested interest, and lots of activity to keep us afraid. . . . The Media, corporations, and politicians have done such a good job of scaring the American public [that] it's come to the point that they don't have to give any reason at all."
- Arthur Busch, county prosecutor in Flint, Michigan, where a shooting of a six-year-old by her classmate took place: "People are conditioned by network TV and local news to believe that their communities are much more violent than they actually are. For example, in this county, crime has

(continued)

---

[*]There is much dispute over these numbers that Moore appears to have aggregated from a variety of sources including, possibly, The National Center for Health Statistics. What cannot be disputed, however, is the far greater rate of homicides and gun deaths in the United States than in any other industrialized nation.

decreased in every year in the past eight years, yet handgun ownership is on the increase. . . . In the suburbs, there is some fear that there is going to be some invading horde to savage their suburban community."
- Charlton Heston, celebrity spokesman for the National Rifle Association, when asked by Moore why he kept loaded weapons in his home:

"It's the comfort factor."

- Moore's comment: "Our children became something to fear . . . little time bombs are out there everywhere ticking."

3   Intellectually, I understand all of this, yet I am angry and resentful. Emotionally I cannot accept the situation. I understand the dealers' position, I understand the cops' position. But I cannot understand why I should be made to feel like John Dillinger every time I buy a tank of gasoline. It's the same story everywhere. You go to a department store and try to pay for a $10.99 item with a check and you have to pull out a driver's license, two or three credit cards and a character reference from the people—and then stand around for 15 minutes to get the manager's approval. Try to pay with a credit card and you have to wait while the cashier phones the central computer bank to make sure you're not a deadbeat or the Son of Sam or something. It's not that we don't trust you, they smile. It's just that we have to protect ourselves.

4   Right. We all have to protect ourselves these days. Little old ladies with attack dogs and Mace and 12-gauges, shopkeepers with closed-circuit TVs and electronic sensors to nab shoplifters, survivalists storing up ammo and dehydrated foods in hope of riding out Armageddon, gas station owners with pay-before-you-pump signs and impenetrable cashiers' cages—all protecting themselves. From what? From each other. It strikes me that we are expending so much time, energy and anguish on protecting ourselves that we are depleting our stock of mental and emotional capital for living. It also strikes me that the harder we try to protect ourselves, the less we succeed. With all the home burglar alarms and guard dogs and heavy armament, the crime rate keeps going up. With all the electronic surveillance devices, the shoplifters' take keeps climbing. The gas chiselers haven't figured out a way to beat the pre-pay system yet, but they will.

5   Is it that the people are simply incorrigibly dishonest, that the glue of integrity and mutual respect that holds society together is finally dissolving? I don't know, but I suspect that if something like this really is going on, our collective paranoia contributes to the process. People, after all, tend to behave pretty much the way other people expect them to behave. If the prevailing assumption of a society is that people are honest, by and large they will be honest. If the prevailing assumption is that people are crooks, more and more of them will be crooks.

6   What kind of message does a kid get from an environment where uniformed guards stand at the entrance of every store, where every piece of merchandise has an anti-shoplifting tag stapled to it, where every house has a burglar alarm and a .38, where the gas station cashiers huddle in glass cages and pass your change out through a metal chute? What can he conclude but that thievery and violence are normal, common, expected behaviors?

7   A society which assumes its members are honest is humane, comfortable, habitable. A society which treats everyone like a criminal becomes harsh, unfeeling, punitive, paranoid. The human connection is severed; fear of detection and punishment becomes the only deterrent to crime, and it's a very ineffective one. Somehow, sometime—I don't know when, but it was within my lifetime—we changed from the first type of society to the second. Maybe it's too late to go back again, but the road we are now on is a dark and descending one.

Questions About Sample 5

1. Review paragraphs 5 and 6 of Miller's argument. Often a writer tries to appeal to "common sense" to get readers to agree. The assertion that people and societies live up to expectations of them seems intuitively reasonable. But are there other options?

2. Is it logical to say that "If the prevailing assumption is that people are crooks, more and more of them will be crooks"? Paragraph 6 consists of two rhetorical questions—questions to which the writer assumes there is an obvious answer. Miller, with the last question, asks the reader to draw two conclusions from the fact that attempts at security are obvious everywhere:

   A. Violence is an "expected behavior."
   B. Because violence is expected, people fulfill that expectation.

   Can these conclusions logically be drawn from the observation that security is ubiquitous?

3. If Miller were to expand this essay and offer hard evidence for his opinion, what kind of evidence would you need to see to agree with his assessment?

Sample 6—Professional Essay with Illustrative Examples   Michael Medved is a well-educated (having graduated Yale with honors and then attending Yale Law School) and well-known film critic and nationally syndicated radio personality who, in the following article first printed in *Imprimis* in 1992, "Hollywood Poison Factory," objects to the graphic sex and violence in many movies. Among other publications, Medved has also collaborated with his wife, a clinical psychologist, on the 1998 book *Saving Childhood: Protecting Our Children from the National Assault on Innocence*. The Medveds argue in this later book that America's assault on childhood is from four sources: the media, the schools, children's peers, and parents themselves. They argue that children should be shielded during their formative years from the "poison" of their culture. What do *you* think?

154 Chapter 6 Using the Argument Concept to Read the Arguments of Others

---

ALSO NOTE
FURTHER INVESTIGATION ON MEDIA INFLUENCES

If the topic of media cultural influence on children interests you, you might look into the work of Neil Postman, who was, among many other things, a cultural and media critic. His approach is more satirical in some of his work, most notably *The Disappearance of Childhood* (1982) and *Amusing Ourselves to Death* (1985). He also writes about our society being controlled by technology in *Technolopy* (1993). The continuing discussion of this topic and the progression of thinking about cultural and media influences might be enhanced by looking at these articulate arguments from an earlier perspective.

One of the best starting places for good research on this topic is the Kaiser Family Foundation Web site that has published (January 2005) an overview of the history of research on the effects of electronic media on children up to six years old. You can find this valuable resource at http://www.kff.org/entmedia/7239.cfm.

Hollywood Poison Factory
Michael Medved

1   America's long-running romance with Hollywood is over. For millions of people, the entertainment industry no longer represents a source of enchantment, of magical fantasy, of uplift, or even of harmless diversion. Popular culture is viewed now as an implacable enemy, a threat to their basic values and a menace to the raising of their children. The Hollywood dream factory has become the poison factory.

2   This disenchantment is reflected in poll after poll. An Associated Press Media General poll released in 1990 showed that 80 percent of Americans objected to the amount of foul language in motion pictures; 82 percent of Americans objected to the amount of explicit sexuality, and by a ratio of 3 to 1 they felt that movies today are worse than ever.

3   Hollywood no longer reflects—or even respects—the values that most Americans cherish.

4   Take a look, for example, at the most recent Oscars. Five very fine actors were nominated for best actor of the year. Three of them portrayed murderous psychos: Robert DeNiro in *Cape Fear*, Warren Beatty in *Bugsy*, and Anthony Hopkins in *The Silence of the Lambs* (this last a delightful family film about two serial killers—one eats and the other skins his victims). A fourth actor, Robin Williams, was nominated for playing a delusional homeless psycho in *The Fisher King*. The most wholesome character was Nick Nolte's a good old-fashioned manic-depressive-suicidal neurotic in *The Prince of Tides*.

5   These are all good actors, delivering splendid performances, compelling and technically accomplished. But isn't it sad when all this artistry is lavished on films that are so empty, so barren, so unfulfilling? Isn't it sad when at the Academy Awards—the annual event that celebrates the highest achievement of which the film industry is capable—the best we can come up with is movies that are so floridly, strangely whacked out?

6   I repeat: the fundamental problem with Hollywood has nothing at all to do with the brilliance of the performers, or the camera work, or the editing. In many ways, these things are better than ever before. Modern films are technically brilliant, but they are morally and spiritually empty.

The Messages

7   What are the messages in today's films? For a number of years I have been writing about Hollywood's antireligious bias, but I must point out that this hostility has never been quite as intense as in the last few years. The 1991 season boasted one religion-bashing movie after another in which Hollywood was able to demonstrate that it was an equal-opportunity offender.

8   For Protestants there was *At Play in the Fields of the Lord*, a lavish $35 million rainforest spectacle about natives and their wholesome primitive ways and the sick, disgusting missionaries who try to ruin their lives. And then for Catholics there was *The Pope Must Die*, which was re-released as *The Pope Must Diet*. It didn't work either way. It features scenes of the Holy Father flirting with harlot nuns and hiding in a closet pigging out on communion wafers. For Jews there was *Naked Tango*, written and directed by the brother of the screenwriter for *The Last Temptation of Christ*. This particular epic featured religious Jews operating a brutal bordello right next door to a synagogue and forcing women into white slavery.

9   And then most amazingly there was *Cape Fear*, which was nominated for a number of the most prestigious Academy Awards. It wasn't an original concept. *Cape Fear* was a remake of a 1962 movie in which Robert Mitchum plays a released convict intent on revenge who tracks down his old defense attorney. Gregory Peck portrays the defense attorney, a strong , stalwart, and upright man who defends his family against this crazed killer. In the remake, by *Last Temptation* director Martin Scorsese, there is a new twist: The released convict is not just an ordinary maniac, but a "Killer Christian from Hell." To prevent anyone from missing the point, his muscular back has a gigantic cross tattooed on it, and he has Biblical verses tattooed on both arms.

10 When he is about to rape the attorney's wife, played by Jessica Lange, he says, "Are you ready to be born again? After just one hour with me, you'll be talking in tongues." He carries a Bible with him in scenes in which he is persecuting his family, and he tells people that he is a member of a Pentecostal church.

11 The most surprising aspect of this utterly insulting characterization is that it drew so little protest. Imagine that DeNiro's character had been

portrayed as a gay rights activist. Homosexual groups would have howled in protest, condemning this caricature as an example of bigotry. But we are so accustomed to Hollywood's insulting stereotypes of religious believers that no one even seems to notice the hatred behind them.

12   The entertainment industry further demonstrates its hostility to organized religion by eliminating faith and ritual as a factor in the lives of nearly all the characters it creates. Forty to fifty percent of all Americans go to church or synagogue every week. When was the last time you saw anybody in a motion picture going to church, unless that person was some kind of crook, or a mental case, or a flagrant hypocrite?

13   Hollywood even removes religious elements from situations in which they clearly belong. The summer of 1991 offered a spate of medical melodramas like *Regarding Henry*, *Dying Young*, and *The Doctor*. Did you notice that all these characters go into the operation room without once invoking the name of God, or whispering one little prayer, or asking for clergy? I wrote a nonfiction book about hospital life once, and I guarantee that just as there are no atheists in foxholes, there are no atheists in operating rooms—only in Hollywood.

14   Religion isn't Hollywood's only target; the traditional family has also received surprisingly harsh treatment from today's movie moguls. Look again at *Cape Fear*. The remake didn't only change the killer; it also changed the hero, and this brings me to the second message that Hollywood regularly broadcasts. As I mentioned, the original character Gregory Peck plays is a decent and honorable man. In the remake, Nick Nolte's character is, not to put too fine a point on it, a sleaze ball. He is repeatedly unfaithful to his wife; when his wife dares to question that practice, he hits her. He tries to beat up his daughter on one occasion because she is smoking marijuana. He is not a likable person. That a happily married, family-defending hero—the kind of person that people can identify with—is transformed into a sadistic, cheating, bitter man, says volumes about the direction of American movies.

15   Did you ever notice how few movies there are about happily married people? There are very few movies about married people at all. But those that are made tend to portray marriage as a disaster, as a dangerous situation, as a battleground—with a long series of murderous marriage movies.

16   There was *Sleeping with the Enemy*, in which Patrick Bergin beats up Julia Roberts so mercilessly that she has to run away. When he comes after her, she eventually kills him. There was also *Mortal Thoughts*, in which Bruce Willis beats up *his* wife and he is killed by his wife's best friend. In *Thelma and Louise*, there is another horrible, brutal, and insensitive husband to run away from. In *A Kiss Before Dying*, Matt Dillon persuades twin sisters to marry him. He kills the first one and then tries to kill the second but she gets to him first.

17   In *She-Devil*, Roseanne Barr torments her cheating husband Ed Begley, Jr., and in *Total Recall*, Sharon Stone pretends to be married to Arnold Schwarzenegger and tries to kill him. When he gets the upper hand, she

objects, "But you can't hurt me! I'm your wife." Arnold shoots her through the forehead and says, "Consider that a divorce." And then there was a more recent film, *Deceived*, starring Goldie Hawn. The advertisement for the movie says, "She thought her life was perfect," and, of course, her model husband turns out to be a murderous monster. *Deceived* is an appropriate title, because we all have been deceived by Hollywood's portrayal of marriage. It even applies to television. The *New York Times* reports that in the past TV season there were seven different pregnancies. What did six of the seven pregnancies have in common? They were out of wedlock. The message is that marriage is outmoded; it is dangerous, oppressive, unhealthy.

18   But is it true? Recently, I made an interesting discovery. The conventional wisdom is that the divorce rate in America stands at 50 percent. This figure is used repeatedly in the media. But the 1990 U.S. Census Bureau has a category listing the number of people who have ever been married and who have ever been divorced. Less than 20 percent have been divorced! The evidence is overwhelming that the idea of a 50 percent divorce rate is more than a slight overstatement; it is a destructive and misleading myth.

19   Yet for years Hollywood has been selling divorce. Remember *The Last Married Couple in America*, starring the late Natalie Wood? That may be a Hollywood prophecy, but it is not the reality of the American heartland. In this matter, as in so many others, by overstating the negative, the film industry leads viewers to feel terrified and/or insecure, and their behavior is adversely affected. I know many people who say, "I'm reluctant to get divorced." Wouldn't it make a difference if they knew there was an 80 percent chance of staying together?

Rekindling Our Love Affair with Hollywood

20   There are many indications that the entertainment industry may be eager to reconnect with the grass roots—and to entertain an expanded notion of its own obligations to the public. The industry has, in some areas, behaved responsibly. In the past five years it changed its message about drugs. No longer is it making movies in which marijuana, cocaine, and other drugs are glamorized. Hollywood made a decision. Was it self-censorship? You bet. Was it responsible? Yes.

21   We can challenge the industry to adopt a more wholesome outlook, to send more constructive messages. We can clamor for movies that don't portray marriage as a living hell, that recognize the spiritual side of man's nature, that glorify the blessings in life we enjoy as Americans and the people who make sacrifices to ensure that others will be able to enjoy them.

22   The box-office crisis put Hollywood in a receptive mood. Already two film corporations have committed to a schedule of family movies for a very simple reason: They are wildly successful. Only 2 percent of movies released in 1991 were G-rated—just fourteen titles—but at least eight of these fourteen proved to be unequivocally profitable. (By comparison,

158 Chapter 6 *Using the Argument Concept to Read the Arguments of Others*

of more than six hundred other titles, *at most* 20 percent earned back their investment.) Look at *Beauty and the Beast*, my choice for Best Movie of 1991. It was a stunning financial success. We need many more pictures like this, and not just animated features geared for younger audiences. Shouldn't it be possible to create movies with adult themes but without foul language, graphic sex, or cinematic brutality? During Hollywood's golden age, industry leaders understood that there was nothing inherently *mature* about these unsettling elements.

22   People tell me sometimes, "Boy, the way you talk, it sounds as though you really hate movies." The fact is that I don't. I'm a film critic because I *love* movies. And I want to tell you something: All of the people who are trying to make a difference in this business love movies and they love the industry, despite all its faults. They love what it has done in the past, and they love its potential for the future. They believe that Hollywood can be the dream factory again.

23   When I go to a screening, sit in a theater seat, and the lights go down, there's a little something inside me that hopes against all rational expectation that what I'm going to see on the screen is going to delight me, enchant me, and entice me, like the best movies do. I began by declaring that America's long-running romance with Hollywood is over. It is a romance, however, that can be rekindled, if this appalling, amazing industry can once again create movies that are worthy of love and that merit the ardent affection of its audience.

Questions About Sample 6

1. By writing out the Argument Concept, you will discover that Medved's purpose is more than to rail at Hollywood for making predominantly R-rated movies. What is his purpose? Do you agree?

2. Which kind of reasoning has Medved used in this article, inductive or deductive?

3. Which of Medved's examples is most convincing? Least convincing? Why?

4. In paragraph 20, the author says that responsible censorship is desirable. What, according to Medved, would "responsible censorship" be? Would Medved agree with government censorship? What does including the example of drug use in movies add to his argument?

5. Many people argue that movies are not creating negatives in society, but merely reflecting those that exist. What does Medved say about that opposition argument, and what kind of evidence does he offer for his perspective?

6. This article is over ten years old. What argument would you make about the content of movies today? Do you see a change from what Medved observed? What do you think is today's prime movie-going audience, and what do they want to see? What *should* they see? What would your arguments be?

Sample 7—U.S.–English "Op-Ads" are placed in a variety of media—television, magazines, and even roadside signs. These advertisements are an attempt to influence the attitudes of the readers on controversial topics. Analyze the argument in this op-ad that was published during the height of controversy around the "English only" movement in *National Review*, June 1997.

Mauro E. Mujica, Architect
Chairman/CEO, U.S.English

Why An Immigrant Heads An Organization Called U.S.English.

His name is Mauro E. Mujica. He immigrated to the United States in 1965 to study architecture at Columbia University. English was not his first language then – but he is perfectly bilingual today. Learning English was never an option. It was required for success. Now he is the Chairman of U.S.ENGLISH, the nation's largest organization fighting to make English the common language of government at all levels. Why? Because English is under assault in our schools, in our courts and by bureaucrats and self-appointed leaders for immigrant groups. The whole notion of a melting pot society is threatened if new immigrants aren't encouraged to adopt the common language of this country. We're not suggesting that people shouldn't hold onto their native languages.

We just don't believe the government should spend money providing services in multiple languages when money could be better used teaching new immigrants English.

Join us. Support us. Fight with us.

Because English is the key to opportunity for all new immigrants.

Speak up for America. Call 1-800-U.S.ENGLISH

U.S.ENGLISH

1747 Pennsylvania Avenue, NW, Suite 1100
Washington, DC 20006
http://www.us-english.org

160 Chapter 6 *Using the Argument Concept to Read the Arguments of Others*

Questions About Sample 7

1. What is the Argument Concept for this ad?

2. Does this ad use *ethos* effectively to support the argument, or is there a faulty implication that, because Mujica is Hispanic, he can speak for all Spanish speakers? Is the fact that Mujica is Hispanic relevant to the argument?

3. Examine the visual rhetoric of the image. What aspects of the picture of Mujica, for example, lend to his credibility as a spokesperson?

4. What do you think of the statement, "The whole notion of a melting pot society is threatened if new immigrants aren't encouraged to adopt the common language of this country"? Does this statement need support, even in this short ad? To whom is that line trying to appeal? What kind of an appeal is it?

5. Review the paragraph beginning, "We just don't believe the government should spend money...." Was this stance on the use of resources included in your Argument Concept? How important to the U.S. English organization do you think this money issue is? Is this paragraph relevant to the stated purpose of "fighting to make English the common language of *government* at all levels"? What do you think is the primary agenda of this organization?

Sample 8—"Erosion" Terry Tempest Williams is a Utah resident of the redrock desert and a passionate naturalist. On her professional Web site, Williams says, "I write through my biases of gender, geography, and culture," acknowledging what we have argued throughout this text, that all writers have a position—they are not coming at their arguments from the "view from nowhere." Currently, she is the Annie Clark Tannen Fellow in the Environmental Humanities Program at the University of Utah, and her work editing the 1996 book *Testimony: Writers Speak of Behalf of Utah Wilderness* was cited by President Clinton as making a difference in the eventual setting aside and dedication of the Grand Staircase-Escalante National Monument. In this nonfiction essay from *An Unspoken Hunger* (Pantheon Books, 1994), she makes a statement about a moment in American history.

Erosion
Terry Tempest Williams

1   In 1910, Tsuru and Kinji Kurumada left Japan and imigrated to Richfield, Utah. Kinji Kurumada was a farmer. He loved the Utah soil, which yielded robust harvests of potatoes, tomatoes, melons, and corn. Day after day, he worked the land. But perhaps Mr. Kurumada was best known for his canyon lettuce and for how he supplied neighboring counties each year with his greens. There were family priorities. Each spring, the lettuce was planted way into the night, as it had to be harvested before the Fourth of July. The moon would shine. The seeds would be folded into the earth. And as ritual would have it for more than thirty years, the canyon lettuce grew and was harvested early, just as the community had come to expect, year after year.

2   Mr. Kurumada also had an uncanny gift for recognizing soils. It grew out of his intimacy with the land. It was a game with residents, bringing the old man samples. They would hold out their hands, dirt in both palms, and ask, "Where are these from?"

3   He would look at them, mull them over in his own fingers, and then reply, "This is from Monroe Mountain—and this soil belongs to Capitol Reef."

4   And then other locals would come forth with two more handfuls. The old man would make a clod from the loose dirt. "Glacial till. Draper, Utah. And this—looks like Big Cottonwood Canyon."

5   He was usually right. Kinji Kurumada knew his ground, establishing a firm "sense of place" for himself and his family.

6   In the spring—March 15, 1942, to be exact—June Kurumada, son of Kinji Kurumada, was on a bus for California. He was traveling with members of the Japanese-American Citizens' League. The bus was stopped. June was pulled off, arrested, and jailed. It was the beginning of the process of interning Japanese-Americans in camps.

7   Had Kinji Kurumada been around to check the soils, he would have found two handfuls: one from Topaz, Utah; the other from Heart Mountain, Wyoming.*

Questions About Sample 8

1. Though the focus and purpose may be apparent for this essay, the reader may be difficult to define. Whom do you think Williams believes may benefit from this perspective?

2. The balance of detail is interesting in this short piece. Only the next to the last paragraph is devoted to the action Williams is most focused on. Why do you think she chooses to concentrate on the details of June Kurumada's father?

3. On which of the Aristotelian appeals (see Chapter 2) does Williams most depend?

4. In Chapter 11, we will discuss the question of whether numbers or depth of examples provide more convincing evidence for a reader. In this case, which helps sway you more: the fact that Americans watched 120,000 of their fellow citizens dispossessed of their belongings, or that you now understand the plight of one real family who was caught up in this nightmare?

5. Is Williams being unfair in this argument by not addressing the other side? Would it make her argument stronger or weaker if she mentioned the number of young soldiers killed at Pearl Harbor and the fear that "day of infamy" instilled in the population?

---

*In response to the attack on Pearl Harbor, nearly 120,000 Japanese Americans from primarily western states were "relocated" to internment camps across the country. Two of the first camps were Topaz and Heart Mountain. By the time the last internees were released in 1946, they had lost homes, businesses, and other possessions worth nearly 4 to 5 billion dollars in today's dollars.

6. Enough years may have gone by, now, to be able to reflect on the effects on our nation of September 11, 2001. Would you argue that we took actions at that time similar to this unwarranted internment of American citizens, or did we show restraint and wisdom?

DISCOVERING YOUR OWN ARGUMENTS: AN OVERALL ANALYSIS OF ARGUMENTS

1. After reading and analyzing one of the samples in Exercise 1 according to the suggestions given, write a critique of the argument. How does the creator of the argument attempt to satisfy the requirements of his or her Argument Concept? How satisfactorily has the author met the reader's needs? What appeals (ethos, pathos, logos) has the author chosen to use and are they both appropriate and effective? How convincing—typical and sufficient—is the evidence provided? What do you think would improve the author's argument?

2. Review several samples to see what information you find about the nature of the author or creator of the argument either from the introduction or from the work itself. You might want to investigate the biographies of George Orwell, Michael Medved, Terry Tempest Williams, and even Michael Moore, for example, on the Internet for more information. Which works might you cite in an argument about the impact of one's own background and position on the nature of the arguments he or she creates or supports? How can you relate these observations to potential arguments you will create?

3. Explain, as a summation and conclusive statement about your study of Part I of this text, how the reading and careful analysis of the arguments of others can give you insight into your own process of developing an argument.

REFLECTIONS ON THE CHAPTER

Using the critical reading techniques and the practice of reversing the Argument Concept are skills that will help you analyze and evaluate the arguments you come across. As you complete Part I of this text, consider how these skills will help you review research material that you accumulate on your topics and as you think about the form your own arguments might take. If you consider the strengths and weaknesses of the essays you analyzed, you may be able to see those features in your own work more easily. This application to your own composing process will be one of the best benefits of the reading and writing connection.

PART II

Developing Researched Arguments

In Part I, you concentrated on understanding the structure of argument well enough to *analyze* almost any argument you might come across. The writing you were asked to do in each chapter was designed to help you practice chapter concepts in relatively short pieces of writing usually focused on a single important feature of argument.

Part II focuses on the mirror image of analysis—*creation*. Think of a chemistry experiment. When you *analyze* a compound, you use tools to break it up into its component parts. To *create* a compound, you use many of those same tools to combine and unify those parts. Such is true of the tools of reading and writing. This section of the book concentrates on a useful and broadly required form of writing: the academic researched argument. As you dive into this task, you will use many of the skills and concepts discussed in Part I of the book in concert, not in isolation. You will create a coherent argument incorporating *and responding to* the ideas and arguments of others.

CHAPTER

7

Looking in the Mirror and Beyond—Generating Topics

This chapter starts you out in the writing process with a much more thorough consideration of "topic" than you may have made before, and it gives you a number of concrete suggestions about finding a topic for an argument that you are truly committed to make. The writing assignments in chapters of Part I were designed to isolate and emphasize the concepts included in each chapter. In Part II, you will be encouraged to work on a larger project, one about which you sincerely want to learn and write. If you have already determined a focus for such an argument, you can test it out against the standards that are set forward for a vital and workable topic (see "How to Generate a Productive Topic for an Argument," p. 167) to see how you might make it even stronger. If you are unsure of your topic, you can use the suggestions to evaluate the potential of several different ideas before making a commitment.

Some instructors may have class projects or may require the selection of your topic from a given list. With the idea of the recursive nature of the writing process in mind, use this chapter to your best benefit. Some students may have had rigorous experience in earlier classes with topic generation, and therefore may be tempted to overlook its value. We have found, however, productive topic selection to be deceptively difficult while being essential to the success of student arguments.

TERMS AND CONCEPTS TO WATCH FOR

- Clustering
- Free writing
- Looping

QUESTIONS TO GUIDE YOUR READING

- How can you discover a rich topic for argument?
- Which method of discovery works best for you?
- What do you want to look for and avoid in a topic?
- What are some productive topics you would like to pursue?

For writing and rhetoric teachers, thinking and reading about elements of argument is a life-long, vital interest—imagine that. Although it is probably hard for you to comprehend, we get excited talking (and arguing!) about the techniques a certain politician uses to gain advantage, the way a short story subtly suggests a claim, or the way a billboard on the way to school distorts the facts. For students, the elements of argument may seem just so much dry and artificial information to remember for a test until they apply them to a task they want to accomplish. Obviously, students have their own interests, and those just occasionally overlap with an instructor's. The way to get the most out of the ideas we present in the text is to think about them in context, in *your own* argumentative context, not your instructor's.

What are the issues and problems in your life that present the kind of urgency for argument that you can't resist?

- Are you and the financial aid office locked in mortal combat? Should the office find ways to be more student friendly?
- Have you been persuaded to lease a new car by some dealer that, as you think about it now, looked like a character in a *Saturday Night Live* skit? Are you now having to work too many hours just to support your car? Should other people in your situation understand how financially, personally, and educationally devastating such a poor choice can be?
- Are you a parent returning to school to try and make a better life for you and your family? Did you have to give up insurance and other benefits when you made that choice, and can you find no way to get reasonable health care for your children? Should Congress reconsider its rejection of some system of national health care?
- Has your employer asked you to behave in some way that compromises your personal sense of right and wrong in order to keep your job? What are the options open to you and other people in this situation, and what should you do?

> ### ALSO NOTE
> ### ARGUMENTS RELATED TO STUDENT ISSUES
>
> - Fitting in
> - Roommates
> - Attendance problems
> - Anxiety and stress
> - Homesickness
> - Day care
> - Discrimination and stereotyping
> - Alcohol abuse
> - Academic struggles
> - Money management
> - Balancing work and study
> - Eating right
>
> (You can also look for some help with any of these issues at *www.campusblues.com*.)

We don't pretend to know your lives, but we do know that they are rich with vital issues about which arguments need to be made.

Now is the best time to start thinking about some topics that light you up or, if you have already determined a general direction to go, think about how you can refine your focus on the topic. If you can use the concepts in this and succeeding chapters to begin developing an issue you *truly* want or need to argue—not just something your instructor selects as an example, or some topic you think might work for argument but you couldn't care less about—the concepts will not be lifeless facts, but essential tools that are immediately applicable.

So, what do you want to argue?

HOW TO GENERATE A PRODUCTIVE TOPIC FOR AN ARGUMENT

You have no doubt already heard that you should select a topic that you know about, or that you feel strongly about. That is good advice with which to start. But sometimes it is hard to know where to go from there. We offer you some advice in the following lists as you think about general topic areas for argument.

Topics to Avoid

- *Outdated arguments.* There is little reason, for instance, to argue that people should use seat belts when operating or riding in a vehicle. Make sure you are not just rehashing some already determined point. Otherwise, you might as well just talk to a mirror just to hear your own voice because there will be no reader interest or purpose in your discussion. When you read the discussion of "focus" that follows, however, you will see that you can often find a viable focus on a subject in which you are interested if you think about the most recent developments in that topic area. For example, if vehicle safety interests you, start thinking about current safety modifications and their efficacy. You and others could profit from knowing what types of side impact and "head curtain" bags are most effective.

- *Overused arguments.* You may have seen a file of "controversial topics" in the library, or maybe you have heard the same old battles refought in the lunchroom of your workplace. Topics such as capital punishment and abortion are classic examples. Though many people are still vitally interested in these issues, the typical arguments are like reruns of a bad sitcom—predictable and meaningless. Most people are aware of the arguments on both sides and the debates are stalled because there isn't anything fresh to add. Unless you can come up with that new angle, little can be gained by simply repeating the obvious dilemmas.
- *Arguments from personal preference.* Although you may be excited about Radiohead's newest CD, be careful about arguing that others should like it better than anything else they might listen to. Most preferences are just a matter of individual taste, and trying to make a reasoned argument about them is not profitable. However, you may find a way to argue that Radiohead has opened a new door in music similar to past innovations of ragtime, jazz, and rock groups.
- *Huge, unmanageable arguments.* We often refer to these as "thermonuclear war projects." Many areas of human concern are extremely important and interest in them is valid. The problem is that dealing with them in any significant way in a relatively short argument is simply impossible. You cannot say anything meaningful about thermonuclear war in 5 to 10 pages, or even in 20 to 30 pages. You might be able to discuss the recent (2004) shift by the Bush administration to the advocacy for, and further development of, tactical nuclear weapons. Still a rather large project, but more manageable. Students rightly see the interconnection of separate issues. Yes, the use of tactical nuclear weapons in a potential Middle Eastern conflict is related to the devastation in Hiroshima and Nagasaki, but remember that you can't tackle everything in one short argument.
- *Topics too complex for your current knowledge.* Some topics are very fertile ground for argument, but they will simply require that you learn so much to establish credibility that they must be left for another time. Unless you are a budding physicist, you should probably not try to make an argument against Newton's physical laws based on the phenomena of "dark energy" and "dark matter," as intriguing as those concepts are. Unless you are studying to be a genetic engineer or unless you know enough of the biology involved to understand the subtle differences in the different kinds and applications of genetic engineering, you risk arguing in a superficial, or worse, faulty fashion without even knowing it. Making a sophisticated argument can stretch your skills and knowledge as well as inform a reader, and we are not trying to steer students

away from difficult topics. There is a difference, however, between challenging and beyond one's reach.

Topics to Pursue

- *Arguments of personal concern.* Don't choose a topic because your cousin Larry wrote about it last semester. You'll hate every minute of developing that argument. Don't choose a topic because it seems easy or ready-made; you may end up writing a superficial or lifeless argument. The best topic is one of genuine personal interest, a topic of authentic urgency for the writer.
- *Arguments that begin in personal knowledge.* This can be a good news/bad news suggestion. The good news is that your knowledge on a subject can be the very best jumping off spot. You may already know some good reasons why we might develop hydrogen-powered vehicles, for instance. However, be cautious not to let your prior knowledge be your only guide. You will find out, for example, if you research that issue further that storage and distribution problems for hydrogen are extremely complex. Furthermore, there is a serious question about whether just putting more individually occupied vehicles on the road is any answer to our long-term transportation and environmental problems. So, although your level of knowledge going in to a project can be a great asset, make sure you don't let it turn into a liability. Stay open-minded to discovery.
- *Arguments of "local" interest.* Too often students think they need to develop arguments about national or international problems when the arguments they might make most successfully are about issues closer to home. "Home" can be viewed many different ways. What are the issues in your immediate family, your student government, your campus, your neighborhood, your city parks, or your state policy on gambling?
- *Arguments that match your personal style.* One of the best student arguments we've read recently was on the effect of belief in Santa Claus on children. This argument was convincing because it was a legitimate outgrowth of a mother's observation of her children. Jon Stewart's (The Daily Show) and Stephen Colbert's (The Colbert Report) arguments are fun to hear because their best mode is humor. For them to argue using an impersonal and formal style ("One should be cautious when attending to the seat belt use of one's children.") would be a serious mistake. Stewart and Colbert choose topics that are familiar in our everyday lives, not academic. A biology student might pick a much different topic, one about the fascinating appearance of recurring numbers in nature (the "Fibonacci sequence") because investigating issues of that type is more her style. Each of these endeavors is equally valid and can be approached with solid principles of argument.

As you develop a list of potential argument topics, think about these suggestions not as hardline dos and don'ts, but as cautionary principles. You can take almost any topic area and make it work if you keep these ideas in mind.

METHODS TO INSPIRE WRITERS' CHOICES

Entire books have been written on "invention strategies," the ways people come up with ideas. Many methods have been devised to help student writers discover ideas that will provide fruitful discussions and to help other writers discover what it is they are most interested in pursuing. Your instructor will no doubt have favorite methods to share. Trying several of these may help you bump into one that will work best for you. The following four methods are some of the methods we've found most helpful to students.

STUDENT AT WORK

Carmine, a student interested in politics, used a generating technique—clustering—to develop some topic areas she might want to pursue. Notice how, as the cluster moves away from the center, the topics get more focused, manageable, and arguable. She has a good start; even more limited ideas around the fringe of her cluster would probably give her a number of focused argument topics.

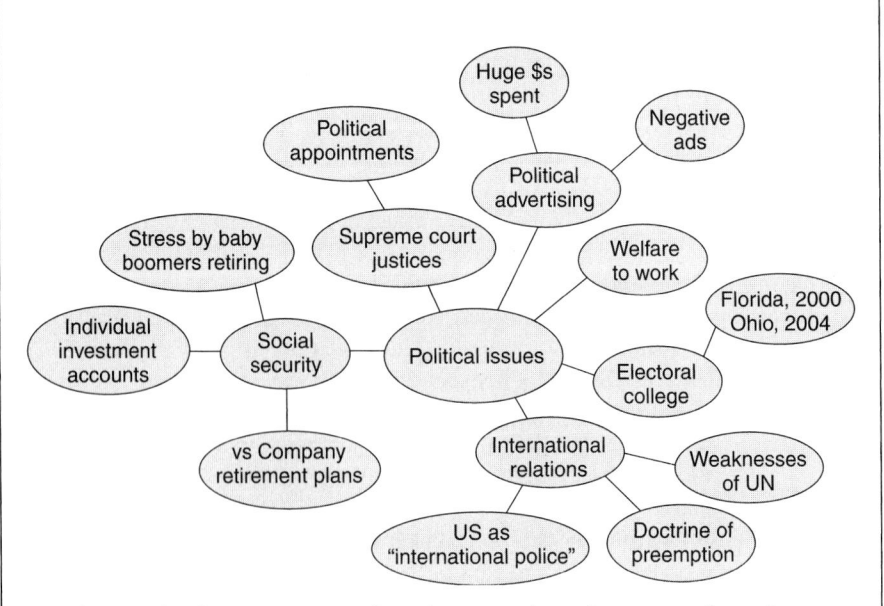

Notice how, as the cluster moves away from the center, the topics get more focused, manageable, and arguable.

Clustering

> **CLUSTERING** *is sometimes called* mapping *or* listing *and is a method for generating ideas by producing a large number of words or short phrases that represent more narrowed ideas springing from a more general, unfocused topic.*

You may have done this activity to discover topics to write about in a composition or English class. Since finding an issue for argument is a little different task than just thinking up a topic to write about, we suggest a slightly more focused method here. Without limiting your thinking in any way—try *NOT* to think about what you are going to write about at the moment—make a list of at least eight to ten things that come to mind as you think about each of the following categories. You can simply list ideas, but a method that sometimes works better for students is to start a blank page with the question in a circle in the middle. Then keep branching (clustering) ideas off the original circle until you have filled the page. Many students for whom this clustering technique works find that as they get to the edges of their clusters, the topics become more focused and more interesting (see the illustration of clustering).

What do you know?

- Make a list of issues that arise from your physical activity, either some activity at which you are proficient or in which you are interested. (For instance, have you had to learn to walk again after suffering a severe injury? Did you play Little League baseball while parents were screaming in the stands? Are you part of a Title IX women's sports program?)

> **ARGUMENT IN ACTION   A Potential Argument Inspired by Physical Activity**
>
> Are you a woman who had a career-ending ACL injury, only later to learn that sports scientists have discovered that women are up to eight times more apt to suffer this injury? Have you now read that women should be trained to jump differently than men?
>   You probably have an argument!

- Make a list of issues that arise from leisure time activities you pursue. (For instance, are you one of the new breed of classical music and opera lovers? Do you think your reading Stephen King novels has led to irrational fears? Does watching soap operas in your dorm cut into study time or create unrealistic expectations of relationships? Has the concept of dating changed significantly from your parents' time?)

> **ARGUMENT IN ACTION A Potential Argument Inspired by Leisure-Time Activities**
>
> Have you noticed that while parents, schools, politicians, and even church officials suggest that students of all ages should be spending more time in healthy, positive, non-television-based social activities, fewer and fewer of those opportunities are available in your community? Should there be more places for preteens, teens, and young adults to hang out and stay busy in an appealing and healthy way in your city?
>   You probably have an argument!

- Make a list of issues that arise from your family involvements. (For instance, do you have problems with child care? Are you from a "blended" family? What issues are involved in being an only child? If you are adopted, have you tried to contact a birth parent? Do you have trouble filling your role as a single father?)

> **ARGUMENT IN ACTION A Potential Argument Inspired by Family Involvements**
>
> Did you experience the loving chaos of a blended family? Do you think children in newly connected families can benefit from your experience?
>   You probably have an argument!

- Make a list of issues that arise from your most important school experiences. (For instance, why was that one special teacher pivotal in determining your career? Did you have to repeat a grade, or were you pushed ahead a level? Was your school's zero-tolerance policy effective? Was your history teacher biased?)
- Make a list of issues that arise from current issues with which you have had experience. (Have you had difficulty dealing with health insurance? Have

> **ARGUMENT IN ACTION A Potential Argument Inspired by Current Issues**
>
> Was a National Guard member in your family called to active duty, disrupting his or her life in unexpected ways? Has his or her family struggled unreasonably—and maybe unfairly—in this absence?
>   You probably have an argument!

you voted in the past few elections? Has financial aid for education been a challenge or an opportunity for you? Has quality, affordable housing been available for you? How has service in recent overseas conflicts affected your family?)

What do you want to learn?

- Make a list of issues that arise in your academic major. (For instance, how much should ethics restrain science? What is the best way to hire or fire an employee? Why wasn't Zora Neale Hurston appreciated in her own time? Are private prisons working well? What started the blacklisting of artists during the McCarthy era?)
- Make a list of issues that arise from questions you have about your community. (For instance, is photo-radar helping eliminate speeding in your community? Should wages in your community be raised to more closely match those in neighboring towns? Will the big new discount store hurt the local merchants, or is that a myth? Can another ice rink in a town this size be profitable?)
- Make a list of issues that arise from questions you have about family matters. (For instance, what is the best method of disciplining a two-year-old? How can a single mother find a good male role model for her teenage son, and is such a model necessary? Does premarital counseling improve the chances for success of a marriage? How do music lessons add to a child's developmental process? What is the best system for providing a child with an allowance?)

ARGUMENT IN ACTION A Potential Argument Inspired by Family Matters

Is your cousin obsessed with playing Mozart for her newborn, and do you wonder if she is helping her child grow intellectually or just following a fad? You probably have an argument!

- Make a list of issues that arise from current issues in the news you would like to know more about. (For instance, what states have term limits and how do they work? How much do companies pay to have their names on sports stadiums, and what do they hope to gain; *is* there a benefit from this practice to citizens? Should the companies that recruit and hire illegal immigrants be more thoroughly investigated? Should tax money go to subsidize tobacco growers? How many family farmers in your area are losing their property to corporate farming, and what will that mean? How much should HMOs control a doctor's medical decisions?)
- Make a list of issues that arise from questions you have about your culture. (For instance, why do you think reality shows have become so popular? What is your ancestry and how should it influence you? If 30-second television advertisements can influence our behavior, why can't hours of violence have an influence? Is the amount of money Americans spend on things like

Halloween costumes, cosmetics, and sports logo clothing unethical in a world where basic needs elsewhere are so great?)

What are the important issues in your world of work?

- Make a list of issues that involve coworkers, supervisors, and subordinates. (For instance, what changes would improve your immediate working environment? Is your supervisor's management style productive? How can you and your fellow employees improve your skills at giving and receiving instructions? Is the grievance procedure at your company satisfactory?)
- Make a list of issues that involve the company's structure or policies. (For instance, is your company's family leave policy reasonable? Is the "mission statement" a helpful tool to establish coherence in an organization? Does your company have a plan for including diverse workers? Is retirement impossible in a farming family like yours? What are the strengths and weaknesses of your company's insurance plan?)
- Make a list of issues related to business ethics. (For instance, is it ethical for CEOs to make nearly five hundred times the rate of pay of their employees? Should employees be able to use company equipment for private purposes? Do your supervisors encourage honesty with customers? Does your company have fair pricing policies? What company policies demonstrate a concern for the well-being of employees, and which ones seem to ignore the humanity of employees?)

ARGUMENT IN ACTION   A Potential Argument Inspired by Work Issues

Have you worked in a fast-food restaurant and been bothered by the incorrect and offensive stereotype of those workers?

You probably have an argument!

Exercise 1
Individual Analysis and Practice: Clustering or Listing

1. Choose one of the bulleted areas of interest on the previous pp. 171–174 and create a cluster. Put the area of interest, such as "What are the important issues in your world of work? Issues with coworkers" in a small circle in the center of a sheet of paper. Make branching "bubbles" or ideas as indicated in the student sample on p. 170 that extend clear to the edges of the paper.

2. Choose another of the areas of interest and create a rich and lengthy list of issues you might be interested in arguing about that spring from that general area. You should try to have at least 12 to 15 points in your list.

3. Circle the most compelling ideas you discovered in activities 1 and 2. Which method do you think worked best for you and why?

If you already have a couple of good ideas, you may want to use listing or clustering to limit and refine your topic more satisfactorily in line with the criteria for a solid argument topic on p. 169.

Free Writing

> **FREE WRITING** *is a method of generating ideas by writing whatever comes into your mind as you think about a very general topic with the purpose of discovering where you might go with that idea.*

To try this method, sit down at your computer or with a notebook and some uninterrupted time. You might start out with a sentence like "The thing I would most like to argue about is. . . ." and then see where that sentence takes you. Don't have any expectations, but just keep writing. Commit to writing for a certain amount of time or a certain length of text. If you have trouble getting started, you might look at the topic areas listed in the previous section as a jump start. The idea is to encourage ideas to come freely, maybe not even closely associated, and to release your brain from a linear or constricted way of thinking. For some people, the speed of typing on a computer aids the process; for others, the more personal and tactile experience of having a notebook or journal in their hands is more encouraging.

Advocates of free writing suggest that you keep your pen or cursor going, not letting yourself rest and that you write something when you are stumped, even if it is, "I'm stumped and I can't think of where to go next." A more directed way of "free" writing is to use a general topic area that you find interesting as a starting place and then let your ideas about that topic flow freely, not trying to make any point or create any coherent discussion, but just attempting to discover what you know, don't know, or may want to find out about the issue.

■■ Exercise 2
Individual Analysis and Practice: Free Writing
Choose one of the bulleted areas of interest on the previous pp. 171–174 that you did not address in Exercise 1. Using either paper and pen or your computer, write until you have filled two pages with writing on the topic. Remember, you need not worry about form or continuity. If an ideas comes to you, jump on it. Let your unrestricted thinking about the topic take whatever direction comes up. When you are finished, go back and circle ideas that might be worth pursuing for a researched argument.

Looping

> **LOOPING** *is a method for generating ideas by creating a number of "loops" of writing, each based on an intriguing idea from the previous loop.*

This is another version of free writing that some find helpful. Looping is practiced by starting with some phrase or sentence: "What I really want to look into is the paranormal; I've always wanted to know more about psychic phenomena." (Consider starting your first "loop" with one of the topics you found most interesting if you tried the listing method.) You write on that idea for three to five minutes and then you stop and review what you wrote. Maybe one of the things you wrote was, "I don't know much about it, but I've heard that people can bend spoons and move objects with their mind. I don't know if that's real, but I'd like to know how they think they can do it." As you review what you wrote in that first five-minute loop, you are most drawn to that one idea. You can circle the idea or rewrite a phrase that represents that most interesting or compelling idea in your first loop and then write on that new topic for another three to five minutes. In this case, your second loop may take you into thinking about different aspects of telekinesis, a more focused aspect of "psychic phenomena." You continue the process until you have completed six to eight (or more) successive loops. Usually, you will find the loops becoming more specific, and often you have written yourself into a topic that you are truly eager to pursue.

The difference between free writing and looping is that you let your free writing go wherever it may take you, whereas in looping, you will stop often, review what has taken place, find an element of interest, and start out anew. Looping may help you to go deeper into a issue, and while free writing may take you on a broader journey through a number of issues.

Exercise 3
Individual Analysis and Practice: Looping

Choose one of the bulleted areas of interest on the previous pp. 171–174 that you did not address in Exercises 1 or 2. Commit to creating at least six loops of writing, each lasting about five minutes. After each loop, review what you have written, circle the most interesting idea, and then write the next loop based on that idea. At the end of this 30-minute process, determine which of the ideas you have discovered would make the best topics for a researched argument.

If you already have a couple of good ideas, you may want to use one of the methods—listing, clustering, looping, free writing—to limit and refine your topic more satisfactorily in line with the criteria for a solid argument topic on p. 169.

DISCOVERING YOUR OWN ARGUMENTS: TOPIC EXPLORATION

Select the topic from those you developed in Exercises 1 through 3 that you are most interested in arguing about. Write an "argument proposal" to share with your classmates.

1. Explain why this issue is important to you and to your potential readers.

2. Explain what you think you already know about the topic and how you have come to that knowledge, including any examples you think are pertinent.

3. Discuss what you still need to learn about the topic in order to satisfy the readers' needs and to qualify as a credible writer on this subject.

4. Discuss two or three different approaches you might take to this topic by creating different Argument Concepts, being careful to detail the focus, reader, and purpose fully so that your classmates can discuss the opportunities and challenges in undertaking each of them.

5. Share your proposals with your classmates in small groups or as class presentations. Discuss how each proposal can be refined and/or further developed.

REFLECTIONS ON THE CHAPTER

The more carefully you work through this chapter at this point, the better start you will have on arguments you may want to develop throughout the course. Finding an issue to which you are truly committed will pull you through all the rest of the work; the work will still be arduous, but you will have a meaningful sense of accomplishment and you will probably learn a great deal related to an issue about which you really care. You can then approach the next chapters very productively, seeing always how the concepts discussed in them will directly apply to the project you have chosen—a project you feel passionate about and/or one you feel a sense of urgency to argue.

CHAPTER

8

Seeking, Sorting, and Selecting Outside Source Material

Once you have a refined and focused issue that you are interested in arguing, you will be on a quest. You will be reading many ideas of others about your topic, but just collecting articles that happen to mention your topic so you will have something to quote is far from a meaningful process for argument.

So, what is the quest *for*?

This chapter will help you think critically about what you are reading so that, from all you accumulate, you will recognize the sources upon which you feel comfortable basing your argument, those upon which you are willing to stake your credibility—your reputation.

TERMS AND CONCEPTS TO WATCH FOR
- Professional and scholarly journals
- Subscribed database
- Triangulation
- Author's credentials

QUESTIONS TO GUIDE YOUR READING
- Where can you find valid sources of support?
- How do you determine the *nature* of a source, and why is that important?

- What is the difference between an Internet search and a subscribed database search?
- How do you evaluate a source?
- How do you weed out—sort and select—the material you collect?

TURNING TO "OUTSIDE" SOURCES FOR SUPPORT

Your own voice is essential to your argument. Without it, the argument will be lifeless and sterile. An argument should present the writer's perspective. An academic argument in particular should demonstrate not only that you have read and understood sources, but that you are able to synthesize—to blend the ideas of others with your own. Although a writer should always have command of the argument and not be just a passive conduit for the ideas of others, many arguments demand that you look to sources outside yourself to add depth and strength. Your argument will be strongest when you approach outside (or "researched") sources to understand your argument more fully, not to find "sound bytes" to support your preconceived opinion. This approach is more difficult than it may seem. To some extent, we all sort and select every piece of information we take in based on what we like or dislike, approve or disdain, agree or disagree with, enjoy or abhor, and based on what we think will work for our purposes. Objectivity—the quality of being detached, unbiased, and impersonal—is probably impossible to obtain. However, a studied attempt at objectivity as you review the arguments of others will be to your advantage. Your own understanding can benefit from other perspectives by answering such questions as these:

- Who is truly involved in, and influenced by, the issue at hand? What are the different groups that have a stake in this issue, and what are their backgrounds?
- How do these various groups see the issue differently?
- Exactly who are the credible authorities for the issue at hand?
- What is the current stage of research or understanding on this issue? What are those principles or facts that are accepted by all interested groups, and what "facts" are still the object of debate?
- How might your own voice and thinking on this issue be affected by your personal experience?
- What are the *reasonable* arguments against your way of thinking?

When your reader will be best convinced by authoritative material and not just your own well-reasoned arguments and experience, when your purpose is dependent on the most recent and/or carefully researched findings, and when the sections you have envisioned for your argument demand, you should turn to outside sources.

> ### ALSO NOTE
> ### AN INTERNET CAUTION
>
> The television news magazine *60 Minutes* once aired a program on the Internet that focused on the difficulty of getting reliable information. One of the sources they chased down was J. Orlin Grabbe, Ph.D., from Harvard, who wrote several articles on the crash of TWA Flight 800 (in 1996) that were listed on a prominent online newsgroup. His articles appeared alongside articles from the *New York Times*, the *Wall Street Journal*, and other well-respected periodicals.
>
> Leslie Stahl, the *60 Minutes* reporter, finally found Grabbe drinking beer at a bar called Area 51 in Reno, Nevada. When she questioned him about the truth of his assertions that the plane was shot down by a guided missile, asking him if he really believed that argument, Grabbe replied in slurred speech, "Oh, I don't know; I don't believe much of anything." Pressed about the authenticity of any of his comments, Grabbe added, "The good news is that anybody can be a source on the Internet. The bad news is that anybody can be a source on the Internet."

HOW TO SELECT THE BEST OUTSIDE SOURCES FOR YOUR ARGUMENT

The intricacies of using a local or research library to find information for your argument and the best ways to navigate them is the subject of many a research handbook and is not included in the scope of this book. Our major concern is to provide help in evaluating and selecting source material to support an argument. If you are a novice at research, you may want to consult a handbook for additional hints on the technical aspects of accessing databases, using online library catalogs, conducting interviews with authorities, and other means of finding good information related to your issue. Many undergraduates are required to participate in an orientation to their library, and many instructors take their classes to the library for their own, class-specific orientation. Most college libraries have well-trained assistants whose job it is to help students find quality information, and although approaching them is sometimes a fearsome task for a new researcher, you will almost always find them as eager as you to find material. In addition, we have found that most students find it relatively easy to find books on their topics in the library's electronic catalog, and, anymore, you can do this search through most library catalogs from home on the Internet. It is much more difficult to use *wisely* the many electronic avenues available to get you to the wealth of popular, news, and scholarly articles written on your issue. We will stop, therefore, just a moment to recommend a couple of the places you might go for information and some of the questions to ask about information you find.

The bad news is that today, with the development and accessibility of the Internet, it is even easier for a student to write a poorly supported paper. The good news is that today, with the development and accessibility of the Internet, it is even easier for a student to write a *well*-supported paper. You are the one in charge of which way that will go. If you use online sources carefully and intelligently, you can expect good results. However, if you put your issue, "CEO compensation," for instance, into the search line of any of the popular search engines (Yahoo, MSN, Google) and look only at the first 10 to 12 of 200,000 potential Web sites with which you are presented, you may have less success.

> **PROFESSIONAL AND SCHOLARLY JOURNALS** *contain thorough and methodical original research that has passed through several stages of editing and has been approved for publication by experts in their fields.*

Most materials in a college library have been subject to an editorial process; some processes are very exhaustive, some less. But print sources have had the benefit of some outside decision that they were worthy of printing. If you are looking at scholarly journals such as the *American Journal of Nursing, Business Journal, Early Childhood Education Journal,* or *Journal of Applied Mechanics* (as opposed to a popular magazine such as *Newsweek* or *Vogue*) for material for your argument, you are seeing sources that are distinguished in several ways from other "popular" or news magazines.

- Scholarly journals are also called *peer-reviewed* or *refereed* periodicals, meaning that the articles have passed some established academic and professional standards.
- They are focused on the research and commentary on developments in specific disciplines.
- Articles are often lengthy, always signed, and most always have a bibliography.
- Few illustrations and almost no advertisements appear in these journals.
- They often have specialized vocabulary appropriate for a specific field.
- Their purpose is to inform, report, and make original research available.

Does less valid or biased information sometimes appear even in these sources? Yes. But the possibility is much smaller that you will be using questionable material than if you simply print off the first acceptable sources an Internet search engine has brought up. Here is the advice we give students, and those who follow it always succeed with their research: **Use your college or local library's electronic catalog and subscribed databases.** Your library will have a long list of databases for your use. Topics are well indexed in these databases, and your searches can be custom designed with very little effort. They are usually available at the library's home page under a button that says something like "Electronic Resources."

182 Chapter 8 *Seeking, Sorting, and Selecting Outside Source Material*

> *A* **SUBSCRIBED DATABASE** *is a service, usually quite expensive, provided by an academic library (and many public libraries) that provides access to broadly accepted sources in a broad variety of fields. These are such services as EBSCO, Galenet, Lexus, InfoTrac, Newsbank, Proquest, and so forth.*

You can't go to the library in your pajamas (or worse), like you can go to your bedroom and hunker down over your computer, but trying for convenience will not always pay off in the long run. You may actually be lucky and have student access to some of the databases from home, but sometimes that is not the case. Nevertheless, your time spent in direct use of subscribed databases will be more fruitful, you won't have so many wild goose chases in which you click down into the abyss of a Web site and still find nothing; and, most importantly, you will have something meaningful and valid to argue with less overall time spent. Although each school library has a slightly different collection of available databases, you will be able to use such subscribed databases as *EBSCO, Proquest*, and *Newsbank* for general article research. You will also have access to many discipline-specific databases such as *ERIC* for education-related topics, *GaleNet* for business, *Medline* for medical information, *Westlaw* for legal material, and even *Agricola* for agricultural issues.

We know those of you who follow this one major research tip will be extremely happy, even though the temptation to surf at home using just a major search engine is appealing.

ALSO NOTE
A WORD TO THE WISE

Write down or copy bibliographical information on all sources *as soon as you find them*, or at least as soon as you believe you may want to use them.

Particularly with electronic sources, you may have a difficult time finding the information later. You may have clicked 20 times to get to an item, and you either cannot retrace those clicks, or the information or even the entire site may have moved without creating a link to the previous location. This warning may be most applicable to material that you review in PDF (portable document format), an actual picture of the source, as PDF files often will not have any identifying access information when printed.

Save frustration! We don't know one student who has been angry because he or she copied down some publication information that turned out not to be fruitful, but we can tell lots of horror stories of those whose argument depended on some information that could not be verified and, therefore, had to be eliminated.

Exercise 1
Individual Analysis and Practice: Tapping into Subscribed Databases

Go to your school or local library and complete the following activities:

1. Ask the reference librarian about the databases that would be most helpful to an investigation of your issue.

2. Enter your issue into the search line of at least three subscribed databases and be prepared to report to the class about the nature of the material you found in this way. (Remember to focus the key terms you enter in the search line. For example, if you are interested in "year-round schools," don't put simply "education" in the search line. The more focused the key term, the better return you will receive.)

SOURCES OTHER THAN DATABASES

Although the immediate accessibility of electronic sources has great appeal, you may be missing a bonanza of information by not making a couple of forays to the library. Our experience is that students who are intent on only surfing the Web are frequently frustrated by what they find and the time they have spent. Particularly early in the process, committing to several hours in your college library will pay off. Following is a list of hints for success with that trip:

- *Check for your topic in the Library of Congress Subject Headings (LCSH).* This large, red, four-volume set will be close to the reference desk. You can look up your topic and find other terms associated with which to search the library catalog and databases. Sometimes you are simply not using the correct term in your search, so it appears there is not much information. For instance, a student once said that her university library had nothing on "endangered animals." We looked up the topic in the LCSH and found that the correct term was "extinct animals." Using the correct search term under which information is electronically "filed" provided access to a vast number of sources that were hidden to her under the first terms.

    One electronic option for doing an LCSH search is to use the *FirstSearch* service if your library subscribes to it. Choose *WorldCat* as the database you want to search and put LCSH in the search box. You can get the same fine detail as in the physical books at the library.

- *Use the specialized encyclopedias for your first exploration.* In the reference section of any library are a number of encyclopedias (sometimes row upon row) for specific topics. For example, you can find such references as the *Encyclopedia of Ecology,* the *Encyclopedia of World Art,* and the *Encyclopedia of Occupational Health and Safety.* Students can find a good introductory article in one of these encyclopedias. The articles cover the topic generally and are a good resource when you are trying to focus and refine your issue. They almost always have long bibliographies—lists of

associated articles and books—at the end of the articles that provide a starting place for quality research.
- *Identify the major authors associated with your issue.* You can often find names of people who are experts in the field in specialized encyclopedia articles and/or bibliographies or by finding a scholarly journal article and reviewing its bibliography. Notice the names cited in the sources you accumulate, and when one is mentioned frequently, start trying to find his or her publications. When looking in a database, use those names for an *author search* as well as searching for specific terms.
- *Find the section in the library dedicated to your issue.* You can most easily do this by looking in the electronic catalog and finding the call numbers (the number usually will be a three-digit number with decimals, for instance "321.465") most frequently associated with your topic. When you go to the stacks (the rows of books), you can then browse the shelves with those numbers. Often, you may not have found several books related to your issue because you didn't put in a search term that brought them up. Browsing the shelves lets you see the wide variety of materials available. Keep a record of the call numbers; you can use them in almost any library to walk right to the shelves of books in which you are interested.
- *Previewing a potential book source.* When examining books to use as potential sources, look at the table of contents to see if some of the aspects you have been interested in are covered, and to what depth. Look up a couple of key terms and authors' names, perhaps, in the index and read several short sections to see if the book is promising. Also, look at the first few pages of the book; frequently there will be a discussion of the author's credentials and other publications. Then thumb through the end of the book where you will probably find a bibliography. Even if the book is not quite what you wanted, you may find your best potential source in its bibliography.
- *Consider interlibrary loan.* Most college and public library catalogs are now connected to others through a library consortium. If your library does not have the material you are looking for, you can sometimes click at the top of the page to search for that information in another member library. If you locate the material, go to the interlibrary loan desk and inquire about getting the materials. You will have to fill out a form, and some materials take a good while to arrive from another library. However, if you have read a summary of a source or you have seen it referred to in several others, it may well be worth the wait. Some libraries charge for this service, so be sure to ask. Our advice, however, is not to plan completely on an interlibrary loan source. Keep looking for alternative sources so that you are not out of luck if, for some reason, the loan does not come through.

HOW TO SELECT THE BEST SOURCES

Once you have accumulated sources to help you understand your argument, you have the daunting task of selecting those you think will support the most sound argument. If you found 20 to 30 quality resources, you have a good chance of

> ### ALSO NOTE
> ### WHOM TO TRUST?
>
> "When an issue generates intense controversy . . . it can be difficult to determine who has the most scientifically credible, unbiased reasoning on their side."
>
> —Robert Behnke (Author of "About Trout," which appears later in this chapter)

selecting six to eight that will coalesce around your Argument Concept. Of course, this is just an estimate, and individual cases and topics will differ, but the general idea is that you cannot hope to use the first five things you put your hands (or mouse) on. The chances that someone organized the Internet or library with your specific argument in mind are slim. Arguments that try to use those first five or so sources can be spotted from a great distance; they are unfocused, and the source work usually is widely disparate rather than tightly knit around the Argument Concept.

Selecting quality source material can take some time. How are you to know what is valid material, who are the experts, and when you are close to the "truth"?

Imagine, for instance, that you love fly fishing, and you have seen signs put up by the campus chapter of PETA (People for the Ethical Treatment of Animals), claiming that fishing is one of the most inhumane of sports because of the repeated pain it causes the fish. You had never really thought about that problem, but you don't want to be a barbarian, so you decide to research and develop an argument about whether or not fish feel pain. Your hunch from your experience (and your hope) is that fish don't feel pain. Your first foray into the neurological makeup of fish is to visit the PETA Web site to see what information the organization bases its claim on. The PETA site refers you to *www.fishinghurts.com* and its summary of a study published in 2003 by the National Academy of Science of the United Kingdom. The research team was led by Dr. Lynn Sneddon of the Roslin Institute, and the study was published by the University of Edinburgh. The researchers injected either bee venom or acetic acid into the lips of trout and observed a number of differences in the behavior of the injected trout in contrast to a control group of noninjected trout, behaviors the researchers say demonstrate a pain response. The *fishinghurts.com* site lists five or six other sources that seem to corroborate the Sneedon study. This looks bad for your fishing career.

You are set about making an argument based on your experience and these sources. You form an Argument Concept:

> *I will argue about* fish feeling pain *for* other people who fly fish like myself who do not know that information *in order to* convince them that the "catch and release" method of fishing may not be as humane as we thought.

You reform this Argument Concept into a claim:

> People who fly fish and believe that "catch and release" fishing is a humane sport should reevaluate their activity in light of new scientific findings.

You plan a short but compelling argument:

- An introductory section developed with a generic example of what a good day fly fishing is like, how many fish might be caught, how the fish leap at the dry fly, and so on. The purpose of this section will be to connect with the reader who has no doubt enjoyed many days like this.
- A section detailing such a day, the day you fished the Grey Reef. This example will include an example of the large fish you caught that swallowed the hook, and how the fish struggled as you tried to extract it. The purpose of this section will be to remind the reader of the many times he or she has had to use pliers to extract a hook, and the damage it sometimes does to the fish.
- A section giving context for the claim, maybe including numbers of people who fly fish, the "kill rate" (ratio of fish that die to those caught), and other information to establish the scope of the problem. The purpose of this section is to draw the reader's attention to a problem that he or she may not have thought about while participating in this sport.
- A long section explaining the Sneddon study in detail as well as the other information on the PETA Web site. The purpose of this section is to show the reader that concern for the fish is not just the dream of animal activists, but that there is scientific backing to their claim.
- A concluding section suggesting that fishermen should use barbless hooks and that they should be the standard for flies, since they are so much easier to extract, and that fly fishing organizations such as Trout Unlimited should educate their members in the least damaging methods of fishing.

This sounds like a thoughtful and worthwhile argument. Can you see, however, a problem that you might have with this argument? The following exercise examines some of those problems.

Exercise 2
Collaborative Analysis: Evaluating the Strength and Validity of Sources

In small groups, address the following questions and be prepared to share your answers with the class as a whole. The following exercise examines some of those problems.

1. Although PETA is a foremost organization in the animal rights movement, what do you know about *www.fishinghurts.com*? What might be the problems of using only sources from the Web site of an organization such as this?

2. What do you know about Dr. Lynne Sneddon? What do you know about the Roslin Institute at which she works? How could you get that information, and what difference would it make to your argument? (The Roslin Institute has a Web site to investigate.)

3. Read the following article from the Spring 2004 issue of *Trout* by biologist Robert Behnke, author of *Trout and Salmon of North America*. Respond to the questions following the article and determine how Behnke's argument does or does not affect the confidence a writer might have in the Sneddon study.

About Trout
Robert Behnke

1   Laws and policies concerning such matters as listing of endangered species and controlling air and water pollution are supposed to be based on the best scientific evidence. This might be true in an ideal world, but rarely happens in the real world. In the real world, the best science may be ignored or called into question because of politics or ideology. This can be observed in the current debate over pollution laws and their enforcement. A consensus of the best scientific evidence unanimously agrees that the burning of fossil fuels is the major source of global warming. The strategy of the interest groups opposed to implementing expensive pollution controls on power plants or mandates for cleaner engines and better gas mileage for vehicles is to raise doubt by claiming that further research is necessary.

2   On a smaller scale, an understanding of how a self-interested point of view can override the best science can be applied to angling controversies. For instance, People for the Ethical Treatment of Animals (PETA) vigorously campaigns against angling (and all use or consumption of animals). PETA claims that angling is cruel and barbaric because fish feel pain. Their line of reasoning is that fish and humans are both vertebrate animals, humans feel pain, therefore fish must feel pain. This is a classic example of deductive reasoning; extrapolating from the general to the specific. For example, both humans and fish have the same general type of respiration in that both take in oxygen and expel carbon dioxide. More specifically, in regards to respiration in air and weather, without mechanical devices, we wouldn't last very long trying to breathe underwater.

3   PETA also uses the "scientists say" strategy—an effort to lend credibility to their position by quoting a supposed expert on a subject. Last year PETA widely publicized a report reputedly offering "scientific proof" that fish experience pain. Researchers associated with the University of Edinburgh and the Roslin Institute ran an experiment with rainbow trout. Test groups were injected in their "lips" (external surface of jaws) with either bee venom or acetic aid. Control groups were either "handled" or injected with a harmless saline solution. The test rainbows showed abnormal behavior, respiration rates increased and other indicators of stress were observed. The control groups, including the trout injected with saline solution, showed normal behavior. The

control fish resumed feeding sooner than the test fish. From all of this, it was concluded that fish experience pain because injections of bee venom or acetic acid produced abnormal behavior.

4 PETA ran a propaganda blitz for the news media trumpeting the "scientific proof" that fish experience pain and verifying their tenet that angling is cruel and barbaric—especially catch-and-release angling, which repeatedly subjects a fish to great pain. The story was widely covered in the media, but some authors overlooked or ignored the test trout that were injected with saline solution and behaved normally, showing no indication of pain or abnormal stress after being returned to their tank. Poking a hypodermic syringe (with saline solution) into the flesh around the mouth is similar to hook penetration. Thus, an obvious conclusion would be that hooking a fish doesn't cause pain unless the hook is somehow made into a hypodermic syringe, injecting a noxious substance such as bee venom or acetic acid.

5 I would also question the validity of associating abnormal behavior with pain. If a noxious substance is introduced into a medium with amoebae, abnormal behavior can be observed as the amoebae frantically move to escape the perceived threat. Are the amoebae experiencing true pain?

6 Attributing abnormal behavior to pain is another example of the "scientists say" strategy. Who are these scientists who say abnormal behavior must mean the fish are in pain? Are they qualified to make conclusions on the matter? Do they have the proper sort of scientific credentials?

7 In my column in the Summer 1999 *Trout*, I cited personal experience, common to many fly fishers, of hooking a trout, having it swim around a sunken limb and breaking my tippet. About 10 minutes later this same trout was caught by a companion, using the same fly pattern (an elk hair caddis). My fly and tippet were still carried by the trout when it couldn't resist gulping in another fake caddis. A logical conclusion is that this trout could not have suffered pain or significant trauma from being hooked the first time or it wouldn't have been fooled again so soon. Catch-and-release regulations, recycling fish again and again, would not work if each catching caused great pain and trauma. I defined my comments as "strong circumstantial evidence" that fish do not feel pain.

8 What's important here is that I am not expert on this question. Such expertise is found in the realm of those who specialize in comparative neurophysiology of the vertebrate brain. Dr. James Rose of the University of Wyoming has the credentials to be an expert witness on the question of pain reception in fishes. His recent paper, "The neurobehavioral nature of fishes and the question of awareness and pain," was published in *Reviews in Fisheries Science*, 2002, volume 10, number 1. Dr. Rose's conclusion is that fish have no awareness of pain because the fish brain lacks a neocortex that is responsible for pain awareness in higher vertebrate animals. A behavioral response to noxious stimuli is separate from the psychological experience of pain.

9   Many people will still question the morality of angling—humans obtaining pleasure from catching and releasing a less intelligent animal. The argument is that the fish feel something that makes them struggle when being caught and this makes angling morally wrong. Certainly, such people are entitled to their opinion; but, to at least be credible, they should no longer characterize angling as cruel and barbaric because of pain inflicted. Yes, fish "feel something" in their instinctive behavior to escape a threat, but it's not pain, according to the most qualified scientists.

10   When an issue generates intense controversy, polarization and strong emotion, it can be difficult to determine who has the most scientifically credible, unbiased reasoning on their side. This is true for all issues, from the consequences of global climate change to the question of whether fish feel pain. Scientists are not equal in regards to their qualifications and areas of expertise, and the influences of self-interest are pervasive. To lead the way on responsible fisheries policy, anglers must remain vigilant about questioning all the information they receive before making a decision.

Questions to Consider

A. Does the fact that Behnke is a fly fisherman disqualify the argument he makes in this article?

B. Behnke says that "a self-interested point of view can override the best science." How does this statement apply to the sources upon which the earlier hypothetical argument was based? What other scientific controversies can you imagine are subject to this same problem of self-interest?

C. In paragraph 2, Behnke questions the logic of the standard "fish pain" argument. How does he say the logic is incorrect?

D. Why does Behnke include a detailed summary of the study he is intending to criticize (paragraph 3)?

E. List the objections Behnke makes to the conclusions of the Sneddon study.

F. What do you think of the conclusion Behnke draws from his personal experience (paragraph 7)? Is the example Behnke uses in this section effective or not, and why?

G. What is the specific point the author makes by using Dr. Rose's work in paragraph 8?

H. How does Behnke explain fish behavior, if it is not "pain"?

I. Which do you now find more credible, Behnke's or Sneddon's argument? If you are more perplexed than ever, how would you go about resolving your quandary?

"TRIANGULATION"—AN ATTEMPT AT VALIDITY

> **TRIANGULATION** *is the practice of combining multiple observers, theories, methods, and materials in the hope of overcoming both the problems of bias inherent in the research process and the problems that come from single-method, single-observer, and single-theory studies. In simpler terms, it is the application and combination of several different research methods and sources to look at a phenomenon from a variety of angles.*

ALSO NOTE
TRIANGULATION IN PRACTICE

Triangulation broadens the base of your credibility. For instance, someone arguing for a specific method of teaching special education students might do well to look for multiple perspectives on any planned intervention. Statistics from a research study showing results would be only one piece of the puzzle. Interviews with students and parents would provide anecdotal information, specific examples of the impact of the method on real students. Finding testimony from teachers who actually implemented the method would give a necessary perspective on the opportunities and challenges of using the teaching method; such information might differ significantly from an article generated by a professor of education who advocates the method. And, of course, finding the opponents of the method is important to make sure you understand their criticisms.

Remember, you can always find a single source to agree with your preliminary stance if you look long enough. What you want to find is a number of different perspectives that start to come together around certain coherent "facts."

The word "triangulation" is taken from a practice in surveying whereby different measurable triangles from different perspectives are used to determine mathematically any distances that are physically immeasurable, usually because of distance or difficulty of terrain. Triangulation is now a term used in research to refer to the process of trying to get as clear a picture of an issue as possible by examining an idea (or physical phenomenon) from a variety of different perspectives and methods. If, in your process of reading about the issue you want to argue, you are confronted by opposing and often apparently equally convincing opinions, you should be encouraged rather than discouraged. Very seldom is the view from one standpoint satisfactory in searching for the "truth." Most often, if you have taken the time to read thorough and authoritative information on a subject, you will find that well-reasoned multiple perspectives are more common than some clear, monolithic right or wrong. Only when you have read broadly and have taken into consideration the qualifications and personal or professional agenda of the authorities that you have identified can you make a good inductive conclusion about whom you are willing to trust enough to base your own opinions on. Ultimately, the decision about what information rises to the top is up to you. Remember, all authors are people trying just like you to make valid arguments, and they are subject to the same personal, professional, political, philosophical, and religious influences. As you try to draw reasoned inductive conclusions, keep the following guidelines in mind to avoid the type of error made in the first conception of the argument on fish pain:

- *What is the nature or quality of the source in which the material was published?* Your readers have a right to know and respond to the authority behind your assertions, or the lack thereof. If the purpose of using *People* magazine information or concert-goer chatter is to provide the man-on-the-street thinking on the issue, then such a source may be appropriate. More convincing argument support is found elsewhere. If you are using information you overheard at a concert or that you read in *People*, a reader's response may be, "Don't bother me with gossip." Information from a lengthy *Discovery Channel* biography or from an article in *National Geographic* (or some other respected popular or academic source), however, will probably serve you better in two ways: (1) you will have more extensive background with which to understand your issue and on which to base your argument, and (2) your reader is more apt to respect the footwork you've done and, therefore, grant you more credibility.
- *Are you reading the most current thinking on your subject?* Reason may exist for you to use an older source if and when you want to supply historical perspective on your topic for readers or when it is still recognized as the best information around. Otherwise, you should consider carefully the publication date of the material you are selecting for support. Certainly, the nature of the issue has a bearing on this consideration. If you want to make an argument about downloading music or videos from the Internet, for example, you need information from the last three to six months, because the status of that issue changes almost daily. Knowledge builds on the ideas that have come before; students and professionals in all fields read what has been believed to be the best ideas, and then they create new hypotheses, policies, ideas, and concepts based on that information. Knowledge spirals onward in this way, and you want to offer support from the leading edge of the spiral, not from an earlier turn that is now in question or at least passé.

192 Chapter 8 *Seeking, Sorting, and Selecting Outside Source Material*

In this picture, Israeli Consul General Meir Romem is looking at an *ossuary*, a stone burial box, that its owner claimed once held the bones of the brother of Jesus. The engraving on the ossuary was "James, son of Joseph, Brother of Jesus." The artifact was valued at approximately $2 million because, if it was authentic, it would be a physical link with Biblical times. For a few weeks, the discovery was hailed as one of the most important finds of modern times. But upon closer examination, the inscription was proven to be a fake made of a homemade paste of crushed chalk and hot water.

Who knows why, but many people spend a great deal of time perpetrating frauds such as this. All the more reason for caution as you evaluate your sources!

> *An* **AUTHOR'S CREDENTIALS** *are the features of a writer's education level, professional history, career experience, and publication history that qualify or disqualify the writer as an expert on your topic.*

- *Have you examined the author's credentials?* The difficulty of evaluating appropriate authority is one way in which the Internet can cause you problems, as we explained earlier. If you cannot identify the author's professional connections, you may want to question whether the information is worthy of your time. When writers in authoritative sources refer to a certain person repeatedly, you may feel more comfortable that you have identified a dependable voice on the issue. As you read your material, try to detect any biases the author may have. Sometimes these biases are obvious, but more often you will have to analyze the material carefully to see if the author is trying to give a fair account, including different positions, or if the person's perspective is coming from only one direction. Also, ask yourself, "Do the author's credentials match the field in which he or she is commenting?" As Behnke noted, the most appropriate authority on fish pain would be an animal neurology specialist, preferably one concentrating in aquatic animals. If your brother is a computer whiz, his advice on computers would be beneficial, but his opinion on laparoscopic surgery is probably no more valid than ours.

- *Is this author familiar with the general expertise on this issue?* You can often tell if a writer is well-versed on a subject by examining the sources of information he or she uses. Is the author aware of most of the arguments for and against your claim? Does this material fit in reasonably with what you know and have read elsewhere, or does the information not seem to fit the developing pattern your multiple perspectives are starting to make?

To be comfortable that you can make these judgments, you will need to *triangulate*—try to find the most viable position by examining the issue from many perspectives. Without knowing much about your argument other than your own preconceived ideas, evaluating what you read is rather difficult. But the more you learn about your issue, the easier it will be to discern the quality of information and authorities you discover.

Exercise 3
Individual Analysis and Practice: Evaluating Sources for Your Potential Argument

1. Select five sources you may use to develop an argument (perhaps sources you uncovered during your search of databases in Exercise 1).

2. Which of these sources is current enough for potential use?

3. Note the credentials and authority of the author of each. Which seems the most reliable? Which should you consider rejecting or replacing? Why? If you have considered using Internet material that is compelling but not authoritative, what can you do?

4. What other potential authorities (either organizations or people) can you find in these sources?

5. Do these sources adequately reflect multiple perspectives on your topic, or have you purposely (or inadvertently) selected only sources that support your preconceived idea? If so, where should you look to find a reasonable argument that challenges this position in some way?

DISCOVERING YOUR OWN ARGUMENTS: A STATUS REPORT

Write a progress report: a short two- to three-page discussion of what you have discovered about the first few sources you have found on your topic. Include such things as major authorities you have discovered, arguments against your position that you didn't know about, points you may have to concede, source material you will choose not to use and why, what other avenues of research you believe you should pursue, and so on.

REFLECTIONS ON THE CHAPTER

Finding quality information to support your argument can be exhilarating. It does take some patience, however. We often tell students that the first few research sessions may not *seem* fruitful—sometimes you are eliminating possible focuses, trying to find the most productive search terms, and trying to find a gateway into good source material. If you are smart about your searching, however, that gate will open, and you will find fascinating and meaningful material that adds to your growing understanding of your argument. Many students change their direction slightly or significantly upon learning more. Don't hesitate to adjust your thinking to new information. Continue to search for more material as you think, in the next chapter, of how your preliminary plan—your Argument Concept—will also control the selection of outside source material for your argument.

CHAPTER

9

Envisioning the Complete Argument as a Prewriting Process

By now you have found a compelling issue, you have been reading a variety of views on your topic, and you have probably refined your Argument Concept, or maybe you are considering two or three. You have done some prewriting on your topic in the last couple of chapters, and you have probably discussed your preliminary plans with classmates. Now is the time to decide what shape your newly educated feelings and thoughts toward the issue will take.

This chapter will help you create a plan—maybe even several potential plans from which to choose. It will help you get an important overall (*holistic*) sense of your argument to assist you when you draft. *Thinking about your readers' needs is a shift away from thinking about the topic for your own understanding, the way you've thought as you reviewed and analyzed your source material.* Therefore, an important discussion of the reader's needs and position and why you should now turn your planning in that direction is included as one of the six processes involved in envisioning your argument.

Both a professional and a student argument at the end of the chapter offer examples of fully developed arguments and their structural, envisioned plan. Of course, as always, you can learn more about constructing arguments by reading them analytically.

TERMS AND CONCEPTS TO WATCH FOR

- Envisioning; envisioned plan
- Potential section of an argument

QUESTIONS TO GUIDE YOUR READING

- Why does the "I-write-best-under-pressure" attitude not work well for argument?
- Why is it particularly of value to establish a plan in argument?
- What are the parts of the envisioned plan?
- How does an envisioned plan differ from an outline?
- Why is it important to reflect, at this point, on the reader's needs at least as much your own?
- What is the reader's "position," and how should it drive your choices?
- What potential sections might an argument contain?
- How can including a statement of purpose for each section help with coherence and transition?

THE NEED FOR A PLAN

People develop arguments in many different ways according to the situation. You have no doubt tried to develop arguments on the fly. You may have tried to argue with your parents about some purchase you thought was important and they didn't. You may have received a grade on a project and argued with the professor about the evaluation of your work. You may have sat with friends late at night arguing about a political issue. If you are like most of us, you have probably had mixed results with such arguments. A good bet is that several times, the next day you have often shaken your head or slammed your forehead and thought, "Why didn't I say _____?"

You may also have made some of these personal arguments in a more planned and organized way. Because you knew your parents were going to think that a Harley was a little extravagant and dangerous for a 16-year-old just getting his license, you planned your argument to address those concerns. Otherwise, you knew instinctively that you would be laughed out of the family conference. In the second instance, you might also have been smart enough to look at your grade, go home and throw large objects, reread the section of the book that you think supports the answer that your professor counted wrong, and think of a reasonable way to approach him rather than questioning his parentage. Another good wager is that, if you took one of these paths instead of arguing on the fly, you probably fared better. Planning your argument carefully, then, has worked well for you in the past.

Professionals in the workforce would not consider walking into a meeting over an important issue and "just seeing how the discussion goes." An advertising executive needs to anticipate his client's desires and reactions when arguing that a certain ad campaign should be funded. A police chief needs to plan very cautiously what details will and will not be presented in a press conference about an investigation into an ongoing crime spree to convince the public that they are safe and that his department is managing the investigation properly and productively. You had better plan thoughtfully and provide believable evidence when you go to your boss and argue for a raise; don't try walking in, slumping in the chair, and saying "Let's chat about my wanting more money." The attorney for the defense reviews briefs written and researched by her law clerks, thinks about testimony she expects will be given at the trial, worries about evidence that may be introduced, and then decides with extreme care just how to approach the jury in her closing statement. And her innocent client is forever grateful.

Think of a good argument as this defense attorney's project with your potential reader as your jury. A solid, written argument differs from an argument on the fly in the same way the attorney's closing statement does. As you jab back and forth with your friends in that late night political argument, you hear a little of your friends' argument and you respond. One of them says, "What do you mean?" and you have a chance to clarify. You have the opportunity to change and restate your points and challenge your friends to do the same. Both you and your friends understand the convention—this will be a twisting, wandering argument that will probably double back on itself several times, and it will probably be dropped and picked up several times between other conversation about sports scores and newly released CDs. Written argument, however, does not provide you the advantage of these friendly conventions. You can't check to see if your reader needs further clarification. You can't say, "That's not what I meant," and try another sentence when you see the reader squinting hard and head-shaking at your prose. Your reader will lose patience quickly with meandering and diversions and will quickly discount your argument if he or she cannot follow it. Even though the defense attorney has the ability to use voice inflection, gestures, and body language, a competent and successful one is well aware of the disadvantage at which she is put by having only one shot at her jury. So is the competent writer.

An Ineffective Approach: Pasting Together a "Report"

Because of the many challenges presented to someone wishing to argue to an invisible and mute reader, the importance of planning the argument can never be overestimated. Many college students, when faced with these challenges, have only one experience with which to compare: the high school "research" paper. Having taught in high school and having had children who have written these papers, we think we have a good feel for that experience. We imagine the worst high school research paper experience is something like this:

> Matt has a paper due in five weeks—eight pages maximum, five sources minimum, rough draft due in three weeks. After approximately 19 days, Matt gets on the Internet to read up on his subject. He pulls down the first

five of 20,000 suggestions he found on Google and he scans through them, highlighting passages he thinks will work. He has to turn in source cards with his first draft, so he hurriedly makes out some 3 × 5 cards with the highlighted passages on them. On the night of day 20, Matt sorts the cards into some order, puts them beside his computer, and writes through them, adding some words of his own to tie some of them together. Early on Day 21, about 1:00 in the morning, Matt remembers. The outline! The outline was supposed to be made first, and then the paper written, but no sweat—he just goes through the paper and puts phrases from the paper into outline form, and voila, a completed assignment.

Hopefully, your experience was better than this. If you survived your experience—maybe you even received a B or an A—you may, in fact, have some wrong ideas and may have created bad habits. (For example, we can make a long list of unsuccessful college writers who have come to conferences and said they "write better under pressure.") Even the best of these experiences doesn't very often prepare a student well for organizing a sound college-level argument. Here's the major difference: The kind of researched "report" you may have completed in high school is primarily concerned with just accumulating information and presenting it to show you've done it. Other than the instructor, you have little sense of a reader, and no purpose other than showing that you've learned something. Of course, you will sometimes encounter the need to write such reports in college and in your personal and professional life; reports are an important part of the dissemination of information. But just be aware that because an authentic and thoughtful argument is something very different, you cannot accomplish it in the same way as you would a report.

A WRITER'S GUIDE TO THE ENVISIONED PLAN

The classic outline was assigned to Matt to try and help him organize the paper. Isn't it interesting that most students report that they created their outline *after* having written the paper rather than before? Why is that? We think it is because creating an outline as the first step in the writing process demands a level of detail and understanding that the writer is unprepared to produce. And the writer is unprepared because there is a step missing, a step that experienced writers often do "in their heads," and they may have been working on that first step for some time as they thought and thought about their arguments. The practice we are going to show you is a concrete way to help you with that missing step before an outline, and it may make a formal outline unnecessary. If your argument is lengthy and complex, an outline after this first step may be helpful, and because of that, many instructors will expect you to make one. However, if you first practice *envisioning* your paper holistically as we suggest, that outline process will be much easier, more productive, and more coherent. As an illustration of that point, we offer you the following "outline" that was submitted in one of our classes. (*Note:* One of the other problems with this outline is the imbalance of subheads and the lack of parallel structure in the items. Should your instructor assign an outline, make sure you attend to those requirements.)

Sample Student "Outline"

Neurolinguistic Programming

I. Basic background
   A. "Neuro"
   B. "Linguistic"
   C. "Programming"
II. Founders
   A. John Grinder
      1. Linguist
      2. Educational background
   B. Richard Bandler
      1. Mathematician, Gestalt therapist, computer expert
      2. 11 books
   C. Formed idea of NLP
      1. 2 basic concepts
      2. Directing our own nervous system
III. Modeling
   A. Adopting others' behaviors
   B. Internal process
   C. Organizing experience
IV. State
   A. Define: millions of neurological processes happen within us
   B. Produce different communication
   C. Firewalk
V. Cures
   A. Phobias
   B. Dysfunctional communicators
   C. Promotes personal achievement

ALSO NOTE

RELATIONSHIP OF ENVISIONED PLAN AND OUTLINE

Both practices have their value. An outline is more detailed and includes subsections and potential evidence. It is a midstep between an envisioned plan and drafting. Some people need that kind of detailed structure to be comfortable drafting, but others may do better with more latitude.

The envisioned plan is the substructure underneath such an outline, and it is helpful to either type of writer. The envisioned plan should be a flexible tool, not a restricting, artificial device.

Remember that you will discover more about your argument as you draft it. The idea that thinking, reading, and writing are integrally connected, that they are all reflections of each other, becomes most clear when you draft.

Use your plan as you draft to check your organization and coherence. Modify one or the other—or both—as you learn more through writing.

The student sample on p. 199 is recognizable as an outline because of its form, but it may be little help in writing a solid argument. Why? This particular outline is not helpful because it is not coherent, and it has no direction or purpose. Why, for instance, is anyone interested in the educational background of a founder of this process, or the fact that another wrote 11 books? The pieces of this outline are "factoids," meaningless bits of accumulated information. This is little more than Matt's outline: phrases put down representing material read and when to say it. What is missing is any purpose or connection in the phrases and most important, an author's perspective. Part of the problem is there appears to be no clear Argument Concept driving this outline: the title itself, "Neurolinguistic Programming," suggests the student has a topic area, but no sense of what to do with it. However, had this student first envisioned the argument as we will suggest, he could have then produced an outline with some meaning that would be a useful guide to drafting. If Matt doesn't like to get to the outline level of detail before he writes, then he has a solid plan from which to write what is sometimes referred to as a "discovery draft"—a first draft that fleshes out some of the weaknesses and strengths in his original plan and helps him think more freely about his topic than a traditional outline. Either way works, and both ways benefit by having some basic idea of the form the argument may take before tackling a first draft. After you practice this envisioning activity several times, you will find it makes your writing process much more efficient because you will not have those long moments of terror when you look at the paper or monitor and ask yourself what you should say, or even worse, "What in the world did I just write?" Also, as you revise, you can look at what you produced in your envisioning stage and decide if you still have a coherent thread of logic in your argument, or if you've taken some strange and reader-mystifying tangents. The following steps will help you envision your argument.

> **ENVISIONING** *is a concrete way to see the argument as a purposeful and coherent whole before attempting to write it by drafting an Argument Concept, a claim, and brief descriptions of potential sections. The envisioned plan is a guide that gives direction and order without confining the discovery that happens with drafting.*

The Envisioning Process

Step 1: Put away your source material and get a *holistic*, or overall, feel for your argument.

Step 2: Write out your Argument Concept in as much detail as possible; write out a corresponding, potential claim.

Step 3: Take time to consider your potential reader's needs in depth.

Step 4: Make a bullet list of sections necessary for the argument; *do not confuse sections with paragraphs*—each section may include any number of paragraphs, depending on the need.

Step 5: State the purpose of each section clearly.

Step 6: Include a last section that explains what you want the reader to take away from the argument.

Conceiving your argument in this way is an organic method. You are looking at each section *as it functions* within the whole argument to move your argument forward. Thorough guidance for envisioning your argument successfully is given in the next major divisions of this chapter, each of the six sections discussing one of the steps in detail.

STEP 1. *PUT AWAY ANY RESOURCES YOU MAY HAVE CONSULTED AND AVOID LOOKING AT THEM SO YOU CAN GET A HOLISTIC FEEL FOR YOUR ARGUMENT*

If you feel unprepared to think through your argument without looking at any material you have accumulated, then you probably do not know the topic well enough yet; return to your thinking and reading before trying to form a thoughtful argument. If you are trying to organize an argument by thumbing through resources or cards, you will not be able to get a holistic feel for the argument. You can always add any additional material later, but the idea here is to focus on the *overall* understanding you have of the argument from what you have read and what you know. Delving into the details of a source at this point has the potential to skew the big picture.

As an illustration of this very important point, move for a minute to the field of art. There is a practice in the art of drawing called "gesture drawing." The budding artist sits at a pad of newsprint and tries to capture the basic pose of a model. Hard enough, you might think, but the idea of gesture drawing is to do it in five to ten

---

ALSO NOTE
THE CONCEPT IN DRAWING

Gesture is the single most important element in the drawing. Glenn Vilppu, an artist and instructor, explains that getting the overall attitude and motion of a figure is essential for coherence of a drawing (just as that holistic feel is important for an argument):

> The drawings of the past were used primarily in planned stages toward the creation of paintings, sculptures, and murals. As such, they were *practical pragmatic steps in representing ideas* [emphasis added]. The classical approach of constructing forms in an effort to create the ideal perfect form, along with the desire for clarity, transition, and ease of understanding, are the same requirements of good animation drawing.

Vilppu's explanation can hardly be improved upon. The envisioned plan is a detailing of "planned stages"—the practical steps you will make in representing your argument ideas. The underlying structure of your argument, like a gesture drawing, is ultimately what its strength and coherence depends on.

seconds. Every five to ten seconds, the model moves and the student must capture that next pose. As you might imagine, this practice is difficult for beginners, and envisioning may be difficult for you in the beginning, also. But there is reason art students go through pad after pad of newsprint this way. Forcing the student to eliminate detail and concentrate only on critical structure is the best way to capture the *essence* of the pose and to keep the entire drawing in proportion. Concentrating on a leg, a turn of the neck, or the articulation of the fingers almost always produces a drawing in which there might be a nice or even brilliant moment or two, but the essence, the coherent feel for the pose, is missing and the overall representation is often distorted.

These images are gesture drawings by Glenn Vilppu. Even though they were executed in only five to ten seconds each, notice how they are proportionate and convincing. The reason artists use gestures to plan their works of art is so they can get an appropriate sense of the whole being before diving into the project. Otherwise, they lose coherence and power by being tied up in this or that detail.

Envisioning your argument allows you that same opportunity to conceive your argument holistically, proportionately, and convincingly. The details can always be added later. But without a powerful and strong *inner structure*, details will not hold together, no matter how accurate or compelling.

An important note to keep in mind: Just as an artist may need to adjust the original plan—the planned *practical, pragmatic steps in representing ideas*—you may also need to adjust your envisioned plan. As you write and think more about your project, you may discover some new approach you think will work. An envisioned plan should never be a concrete trap. Instead, it should be just like a map on an exciting road trip: it will get you where you want to go in an organized fashion, but it may not show all the fabulous sights along the way. When you make one of those stops along the way in your argument, review your plan and see how the new idea enhances your vision of your argument, how it may alter the overall plan, or how and where you can integrate the idea into your plan, and you will still maintain the sense of integrity of your argument that the plan helped you establish.

STEP 2: WRITE OUT YOUR ARGUMENT CONCEPT IN AS MUCH DETAIL AS POSSIBLE; WRITE OUT A CORRESPONDING CLAIM

As you do this, make sure you are clear in your mind of the kind of "thinking tools" you want to use to explore and develop your argument: arguing quality, arguing cause/effect, arguing solutions to problems, arguing to maintain or change policy (see Chapter 10). Although many arguments include more than one of these ways of thinking, it is important that you articulate for yourself what you are trying to accomplish. You would be surprised how often students, in conferences, say "I don't know what I was trying to do." If you can express your goal explicitly in your Argument Concept, then you will have a much better chance of accomplishing it in your full argument.

For example, following are an Argument Concept and claim that will probably not be very helpful in developing a meaningful argument:

> *I will argue about* affirmative action (AA) *for* those who are interested *in order that* they will know more about it.
> Claim: Everyone should know about affirmative action.

Starting out with such a vague road map as this is a guarantee you'll get lost.

Here are some more helpful potential Argument Concept statements and claims related to the same topic (see p. 70, Chapter 3, for more examples). Note how each has a clearly defined focus, reader, and purpose:

> *I will argue about* the Supreme Court's decision in the University of Michigan affirmative action case *for* white college-age students *in order to* convince them they will not be at much disadvantage because of college entrance practices such as these.

ALSO NOTE
ENVISIONING A PROJECT

Even builders, as detail-oriented as they are, begin with a loose, informal and holistic representation of a building they have in mind before they try to deal with the nitty-gritty of beams, wall width, electrical wiring, and so on. This drawing by structural engineer Blake Larsen is his "gesture drawing" of an addition he has been asked to envision.

The planning and engineering department of the city wouldn't be convinced by this drawing (they want to see every wall elevation, a wiring diagram, a foundation plan, and many more details) any more than a reader would be convinced by your envisioned plan. But without this overall conceiving of the project, the most detailed drawing Larsen might make of the cross-section of a wall would be meaningless.

The envisioned plan, just like Larsen's original drawing, provides guidance for the building of your argument. If you go on to make an outline—a detailed blueprint like Larsen will create before the addition is built—then you have one more aid to give form to your project.

Just remember . . . engineers like Larsen are well aware that they may need to make "change orders." As the building progresses, they have to alter their plans. You may also need to change your envisioned plan.

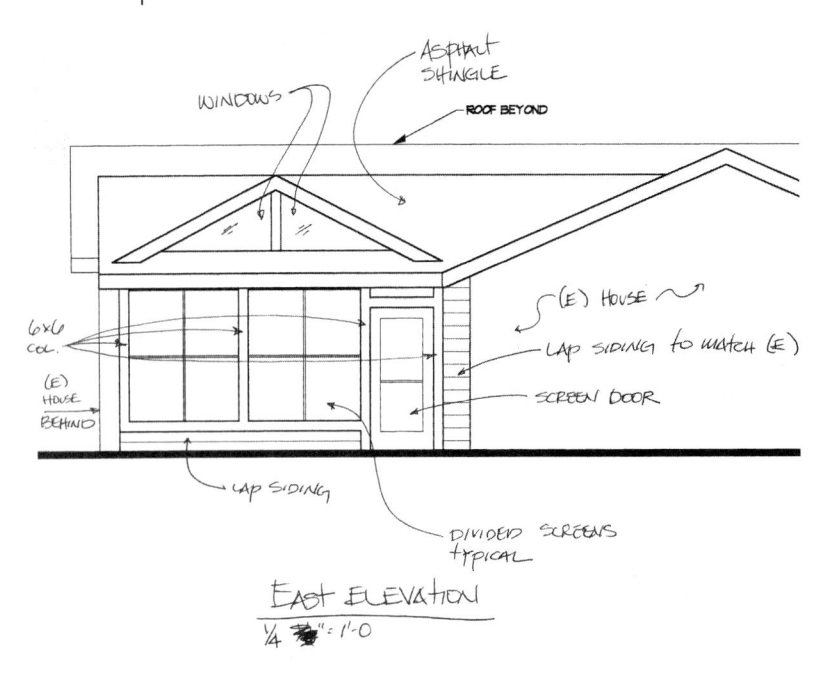

Claim: The affirmative action practices upheld by the Supreme Court decision on the University of Michigan case will not put white college students at a disadvantage.

I will argue about the Supreme Court's decision in the University of Michigan affirmative action case *for* college admissions officers who will now be creating their own entrance processes *in order to* convince them that, although the Court has said AA can be used in admission policies, it will be counterproductive and should be avoided.

Claim: College admission officers can legally use the type of affirmative action processes upheld by the Supreme Court in the University of Michigan case, but those practices may be counterproductive.

Only when you have a very precise Argument Concept are you ready to go to the next step. The very specific nature of the focus, reader, and purpose will tell you exactly what to do in the next step.

ALSO NOTE
THE NEED FOR HISTORICAL BACKGROUND

Often part of addressing both your needs as a communicator and the needs of potential readers is making a considered judgment about how much background information you will need to supply. This is not an easy call. Often, you will not be arguing in a limited context where you will be able to pinpoint your potential readers and assess their level of knowledge precisely.

Our best advice is this: do not start back at the beginning of time, but think in terms of the essential historical facts readers will need to put the issue in context. If you are arguing about rap music's potential influences, for instance, don't start with yawn-inducing information about the history of music and how cavemen probably sat around beating out rhythms on rocks with bones. You may find it important, however, to briefly discuss times in the past when music was feared to be a negative influence. Parents were scared to death of Elvis Presley's hip gyrations, and even Plato, as early as 400 B.C.E. warned that music had the power to overwhelm one's reason and that the wrong kind of music could be a corrupting influence. You may also want to provide information on when the first rap music was created that people found offensive, and by whom that music was created. Those pieces of historical context are directly relevant to your Argument Concept and will help your readers see the bigger picture within which your argument fits.

STEP 3: *TURN FROM WRITER-BASED TO READER-BASED THINKING—TAKE TIME TO CONSIDER YOUR READER IN GREAT DETAIL AND HOW MANY OF YOUR CHOICES FROM THIS POINT FORWARD SHOULD BE BASED ON THAT CONSIDERATION*

As you read and learned about your issue, your attention was primarily on your own understanding. But now, as you turn to composing your argument, your attention turns outward, toward your reader. After all, the reason you are writing is to communicate your new understanding and perspective to another. And remember, communication is not passive, but you are negotiating with an active reader.

Therefore, the next sections will concentrate heavily on reader "position" and needs. As we outline the facets of the reader's position (the mindset, previous knowledge, and values), think of your argument project and what position you might expect of your targeted readers. Also, think of the needs of your reader for clarity, balance, organization, and thoroughness as you draft your plan.

Considering Your Reader's Potential Knowledge

Unless you are writing to your life-long friend or your twin brother, and probably not even then, you will not be able to determine exactly what level of prior knowledge your reader has about your subject. However, you must think about the focus and the purpose of the argument you want to make and consider the potential level of understanding that a probable reader of your argument might bring to it. And don't be too quick to make assumptions about that level of knowledge. If you expect that a reader will understand certain principles and you don't review them for the reader, the reader will have many opportunities to go wrong. You don't want that. Look at the following paragraph, for example, from a student's first draft. This paragraph was the first paragraph in her argument:

> Due to recent legislation such as the Individuals with Disabilities Education Act, there is a great deal of discussion on the idea of the full inclusion of students with disabilities. One facet of the discussion is the uniqueness of each category of disability and the special needs each creates for the student. In the area of children who have emotional behavioral disorders, the debate heats up over the benefits full inclusion provides and what factors influence the achievement of those benefits.

Were you struggling for a while to adjust to the terms and concepts the writer is going to argue? This student's probable readers, as she designed the argument, were college students considering a career in special education who knew few details about the "mainstreaming" of special education students into traditional classrooms but who, at the minimum, understood the basic idea of "inclusion." She assumed that she could leap into her discussion because the issue is not technical and most of her probable readers would not need a review before starting. Was that a good decision? Can you see how, even if you have heard of "inclusion," you are not ready to go with her into the argument? What this student eventually decided was that her potential readers could probably connect more with the personal side of the problem. She thought that once they made a connection with the most essential part of the everyday problems for teachers and their behaviorally disordered students, possible future special education teachers would then want to know more about the policies and politics that define the issue and the potential solutions. She guessed that readers would have the most sympathy if they could relate to their own experiences in classrooms—their own knowledge about how classrooms work. Here is the human context, not the policy context, with which she then decided to start her paper:

> A teacher struggles to maintain order in her classroom of thirty students. Twenty-five students work quietly at their desks. Meanwhile, the other five students, her special education students, throw paper airplanes, talk loudly, and are generally disruptive. She has no control over the situation, for she did not receive the proper training before the special education students were included in her class. She has not received the resources necessary to handle the situation, whether in the form of an aide or just support from her supervisors. Unfortunately, this scene is not out of an educator's nightmare. This image replays itself over and over in classrooms across the country every day. The inclusion of children with disabilities was not intended to be a nightmare to any of the participants, but some confusion within the education system has caused it to be so.

Not only does the writer now link to a more appropriate level of reader knowledge, but also, in the course of doing so, she has emphasized the focus and purpose (the need for better preparation of special education teachers) that she had in mind, but that was certainly not evident from her off-putting first draft. Leaving out important steps because you assume a reader will follow you will destroy your chances for success. Unless you explicitly take those steps, even a brief acknowledgment, the reader thinks you've ignored them. The bridge between your argument and your reader may be the personal connection illustrated in this example, a current event connection to illustrate the urgency of your issue, or some historical context to properly situate your issue (see the Also Note box that discusses historical background on p. 205). *But somehow the steps must lead readers from their point of knowledge to your focus and stance on the issue.* Remember, the reader will go astray whenever given the chance.

Questions like these may help you think about addressing your probable reader's needs in sections of your argument:

- What is the general level of expertise of your probable reader?
- What context for your argument must you provide this reader?
- What important concepts and or terms must you review?
- What concepts, steps, policies, and so on must you acknowledge, maybe not in detail, but as assurance to this probable reader that you understand them fully?
- What current information is widely available that you might be able to use to connect to your reader's potential level of information? That is, is there some current case, problem, or scenario you can feel fairly sure your reader

208 Chapter 9 *Envisioning the Complete Argument as a Prewriting Process*

will be familiar with that will help you transmit the context of your argument satisfactorily to your reader?

▣ Exercise 1
Individual Analysis and Practice: Your Potential Readers
Who are your potential readers and what will they probably know about your argument?

1. Revise the Argument Concept statement that you have chosen to work from according to the previous discussion on specificity of the three elements.

2. Answer the questions in the bullet list immediately preceding this exercise as they regard your prospective reader.

3. Refine the reader definition in your Argument Concept as necessary and as possible after this analysis.

Considering Your Readers' Established Values
The fact that you may have come up with an argument about which your reader is totally neutral is not plausible. Even though you believe your probable reader may be a novice regarding your issue, remember that readers are loaded with

Both of the characters in this cartoon are exaggerated stereotypes, but the point is that readers come from a perspective. No reader is neutral: we all have a set of established values.

perspective. For instance, you may conceive your probable readers for your argument about school vouchers as people totally unaware of what vouchers are and how they may be used. Does this mean, then, that they are a blank slate on your topic? Hardly. In Chapter 2, we discussed Stephen Toulmin's idea of *warrants* in a more formal vision of argument. Think of these warrants, in this case, as the underlying values and beliefs your probable reader must have simply by virtue of having spent time in schools either as a student, parent, or teacher. These various groups will have quite different values and beliefs about schools, won't they? For students, an important value for schooling might be respect and interaction with peers. Parents might feel safety, compassion, and fairness for their children are extremely important values attached to schools. Teachers may believe that academic rigor, student responsibility, and teacher/student relationships are important. Of course, many values related to "school" will be shared to greater and lesser extents by these three groups. But to none of them is education a valueless, objective experience. To approach your argument with any of these groups in some antiseptic manner without acknowledging the power of their established values will probably not get you far. Acknowledging and respecting your own as well as your readers' values will make it easier for them to engage in a productive two-way process of communication with you.

To help recognize what those established values might be, ask yourself, as you begin to create the structure of your argument, questions like these:

- What are the belief systems you have that underlie the argument you feel compelled to make?
- What are the potential "hot button" issues that divide or unite groups on this topic?
- What are the most likely values your probable reader will have attached to the issue?
- What is the priority of those values? What ones are they apt to be willing to compromise, and which are they going to hang on to like a pit bull?
- Which of your values are you willing to compromise? Have you expected more flexibility of your reader than you are willing to give yourself?
- What values do you and your probable reader hold in common? Which are liable to get you to an impasse with your reader?
- What important values may your reader hold but not acknowledge?

Exercise 2
Individual Analysis and Practice: Your Readers' Values
What may be your readers' values that will affect the way they read and interpret your argument?

1. Write out your Argument Concept, including as refined a description of your potential reader (or readers) as possible.

2. Examine this description of your reader. Will there be groups of people within your potential readership base who will approach the issue with different values and beliefs?

3. Answer the questions in the preceding bullet list as they relate to your potential readers. When there may be several different value systems held, determine if you should refocus your reader description or whether you can adequately argue to both or all audiences at once.

ALSO NOTE
DON'T OVERLOOK YOURSELF!

Although it is critical to think about the reader, the seasoned writer is able to think critically about his or her own context. The writer is part of the process of negotiating meaning, not an objective provider of information. The writer's context colors the argument in many ways. What points he or she leaves out says as much about the writer's negotiating position as what is included. The selected evidence creates a distinct focus and perspective. As you develop your argument, monitor yourself to see that the lens with which you are viewing and then presenting your argument is not unreasonably clouded by your mindset and values.

Considering Your Readers' Opposition to Your Claim

Previously, we have talked about forming your claim, the statement that encapsulates your argumentative perspective on your topic. According to your purpose, you might want to lay out your claim to readers of like mind, so-called "preaching to the choir," in order to solidify their support or embolden them to action. Often, however, your probable reader will oppose your claim; the more frequent use of argument lies in the hope that doubting readers will see the logic behind your claim and acknowledge its worth. Therefore, one of the most critical preliminary activities you can do when developing a sound argument is to spend a great deal of time fleshing out the potential opposition to your claim. It is through understanding these arguments and dealing with them that you will be most effective.

Imagine the difference in approaches. The father, having read three books to his son, says, "Now it's time to go to bed." The son, still wanting more bedtime connection with the father, starts to whimper and whine for another story. "Go to bed NOW!" says the father, his argument for what the son should do. More tears ensue as the father tries to reassert his claim about the necessity to go to bed by simply repeating the claim: "Go to bed!" In the house next door, the father has finished his three books, and the same whimpering begins. The father says, "I know you were having a good time; so was I. We'll have more time like this tomorrow, but now it's bedtime." In the first case, the confrontation just escalates with more tears and yelling. In the second, there is at least a hope for compliance. Now, expand this line of thinking to social, academic, or political arguments. Failing to acknowledge an opposing argument leads to just such screaming and polarization. *Defending a claim without accepting that there might be other reasonable arguments from other reasonable people forces participants in the negotiations to protect their already held positions rather than convincing them to explore other possible perspectives.* To avoid alienating your probable readers in this way, ask questions such as these as you develop the structure of your argument:

- What is the best argument that can be made against your claim? Don't be tempted to use a weak argument that you can easily tear apart, a "straw man" argument. If your readers are opposed to your claim, they will be offended, and rightly so, if you associate them with such a weak argument.
- What is the best evidence to support arguments against your claim?
- What is the most well-known argument against your claim; what argument might you suspect that a probable reader would hold?
- Have you considered these arguments fully or dismissed them too readily?
- Should you accommodate part of this argument with yours, making it all the stronger?
- Where in your argument structure might you best deal with the reader's argument(s)? If they are exceptionally strong and well supported, should you discuss them first, acknowledging their strength, but holding that your claim is still superior?
- Can you truly ignore an argument that is potentially damaging to your own? What will be the effect on the reader if you avoid addressing such an argument?

Exercise 3
Individual Analysis and Practice: Your Opposition's Claims
How might you address the opposing ideas of your readers?

1. Write out your Argument Concept, including as refined a description of your potential reader (or readers) as possible.

2. By answering the questions in the preceding bullet list, explain the various opposing stances your reader may take and how you might best address them in your argument.

Deciding What to Include
Think how an argument takes on very different form when just that one factor in the Argument Concept—the reader—is changed. For example, imagine that you have just finished a class during your first year of college that involved "service learning," a requirement to spend a good number of hours volunteering for either a government or a nonprofit organization in the community related to the course.

You want to write an argument directed at incoming students to encourage them to get involved in one of the service learning classes. Imagine that you were using the following Argument Concept to guide the development of your argument:

> *I will argue about* the benefits of enrolling in service learning at State College *for* first-time students at the college *in order to* motivate them to enroll in a class that requires it early in their college career.

As you practiced earlier, this Argument Concept might be rewritten as a claim and appear in the written argument something like this:

> Because of the benefits to students as well as those to the community, new students at State College should take a class that requires service learning as early in their college career as possible.

To develop this argument, you might want to include the following sections aimed directly at motivating your probable readers, first-time State College students:

- A section introducing and defining the concept of service learning—*here, you are reviewing knowledge the reader may not have*
- A section giving the details of personal experience with service learning to show the reader what it is like in practice and to establish your credibility
- A section examining the pitfalls of such enrollment (sometimes excessive hours, difficulty of getting involved with an organization that is a good "match" for you, transportation, etc.)—*here, you are acknowledging the opposition arguments*
- A section describing the benefits to the community
- A section describing the benefits to new students (social network or students interested in the same things, connection to the community in which they will be living, appreciation of those less fortunate than themselves, real work in real time rather than just reading and talking about it, etc.)—*here, you are considering the values and needs of the student*
- A section explaining the different possibilities for service learning at State College and how they might fit into a student's general education requirements
- A concluding section encouraging new students not to miss this opportunity to enrich their classroom experience and possibly to determine the direction of their major or career

Now imagine how a change in reader would affect your argument plan. Another potential reader for this argument might be parents of new students. Using some preestablished form to argue to both groups would not be maximally effective because, though parents and students share some values and knowledge, different reasons will appeal more strongly to each group. You must think instead how the needs of this specific reader demand an altered plan such as this one.

Argument Concept

> *I will argue about* the benefits of enrolling in service learning at State College *for* parents of first-time students at the college *in order to* encourage them to have their students enroll in a class that requires it early in their college career.

Claim Statement

Because of the benefits to students as well as those to the community, parents may want to encourage their new students at State College to take a class that requires service learning as early in their college career as possible. The following sections may help you develop this argument for parents:

- A section introducing and defining the concept of service learning—*here, you are reviewing knowledge the reader may not have*
- A section giving the details of personal experience with service learning to show the reader what it is like in practice and to establish your credibility
- A section examining the pitfalls of such enrollment (sometimes excessive hours, difficulty of getting involved with an organization that is a good "match" for you, transportation, etc.)—*here, you are acknowledging the opposition arguments*
- A section describing the benefits to the community
- A section describing the benefits to new students (connection to the community in which they will be living, appreciation of those less fortunate than themselves, real work in real time rather than just reading and talking about it, etc.)—*here, you are considering the values and needs of the students that the parents also will share*
- A section explaining the tendency for students involved in service learning to avoid problems of first-time students (sleeping in and not attending class, getting involved in negative activities during leisure hours, wasting time in courses that seem irrelevant to their major)—*here, you are considering the values and needs of the parents*
- A section explaining the different possibilities for service learning at State College and how they might fit into a student's general education requirements

STEP 4: *MAKE A BULLET LIST OF THE SECTIONS YOU WILL NEED IN YOUR ARGUMENT TO CONVINCE THE SPECIFIED READER OF YOUR POINT*

It should be clear by reviewing the previous set of Argument Concepts that more than one paper can be written on service learning for college students. Such is true of all topics. Once you have your task spelled out clearly with a refined Argument Concept, then that concept demands its own sections out of necessity.

> **A POTENTIAL SECTION OF AN ARGUMENT** *serves a particular function in advancing the Argument Concept. A section might have multiple paragraphs, but it serves one purpose, which is spelled out clearly in the description.*

What you are trying to draw for yourself at this stage is the argument's logical and rhetorical inner structure. Imagine putting the finished argument in an x-ray machine so that only the structural elements that hold it all together are showing. That is what the drawing student is doing with a gesture drawing. That's what you are doing when you envision your argument's sections.

As an example, review the following three envisioned plans for different arguments about online coursework. Notice how the sections included for each are pertinent only to that particular Argument Concept. Some sections—definitions or background information, for example—may be necessary in almost all arguments about online courses. However, change one element in the Argument Concept, and, by necessity, the necessary sections change either somewhat or dramatically.

Plan 1:

Argument Concept

I will argue about taking online courses *for* first- and second-year college students *in order to* convince them to think carefully about their study ethic before enrolling in these classes.

Claim

First- and second-year college students should examine their study ethic carefully before they enroll in such classes that meet only online; this method of taking a course may not work well for students who are struggling to adjust to the rigors of college.

- A section of background information on online courses: the different kinds, the number available, and the growth in this method of "delivery." The purpose of this section is to acquaint new students with the many opportunities they may have to take online courses, and to distinguish totally online classes from "hybrid" classes in which students meet as often as once a week with the instructor.
- A section explaining the advantages of taking an online course: convenience and self-pace. The purpose of this section is to concede that online instruction works very well for certain circumstances.
- A section describing the kind of student who usually does well in this kind of class: a self-motivated and self-disciplined student with strong reading skills. The purpose of this section is to show by using

---

ALSO NOTE

An important mechanical note: When you are creating sections, do not confuse that with *paragraph* structure. Some sections will take several paragraphs—even pages—whereas others can be managed in one paragraph. You are thinking of logical structure, not paragraph structure, when you envision.

the available research that online instruction works better for some students than others.
- A section explaining the disadvantages of taking totally online courses for new college students. The purpose of this section is to explain that new students may not have developed the skills and behaviors necessary to be successful in a totally online environment.
- A section citing several examples of first-year students who took online courses thinking they would be easier and who did not complete the courses. The purpose of this section is to let the reader hear about the potential problems from their peers.
- A final section suggesting that the readers might take these courses later in their college careers, and that they will probably be more successful in online courses after they have adjusted socially and academically to the college environment.

Plan 2:
Argument Concept

I will argue about taking online courses *for* nontraditional students who have trouble balancing school, work, and family *in order to* show them that this choice will work very well for them if they understand and commit to the requirements of online coursework.

Claim

Online coursework will suit nontraditional students who have trouble balancing school, work, and family so long as they understand and commit to the self-discipline and study time these courses require.

- A section of background information on online courses: the different kinds, the number available, and the growth in this method of "delivery." The purpose of this section is to acquaint new students with the many opportunities they may have to take online courses, and to distinguish totally online classes from "hybrid" classes in which students meet as much as once a week with the instructor. (*This section would probably be necessary for most potential student readers. However, if the argument is about some change that needs to be made in online delivery for faculty who run these classes and obviously know this information, as in Plan 3 [following], the section is unnecessary.*)
- A section discussing the difficulties nontraditional students face when returning to school. The purpose of this section is to show identity with the readers and demonstrate why "regular" classes are often a challenge for them.
- A section discussing the advantages of online courses for students who have day care problems and work and parenting responsibilities. The purpose of this section is to demonstrate the convenience and self-pace features of these courses and how they might fit well into nontraditional students' schedules.

- A section explaining the disadvantages of online coursework. The purpose of this section is to warn readers that they must give an online class a good deal of time to be successful and that if they are thinking it is easier and less work, that it is not the best choice.
- A final section suggesting that these students might start out slowly to be most successful. The purpose of this section is to encourage them to go back to school by using this method, but that they might want to start with by taking maybe one "hybrid" class so that they will have more contact with an instructor as they begin their college careers.

Plan 3:

Argument Concept

I will argue about changes necessary in the way our school conducts online courses *for* instructors who conduct them *in order to* help them improve the success rate of students who take the classes.

Claim

Online instruction at our college could be improved with some rather simple changes in the way they are conducted.

- A section of background on the writer's experience with classes and observations of other fellow students who have taken online courses. The purpose of this section is to build credibility with the instructors.
- A section explaining what worked well for the writer and others in these classes. The purpose of this section is to acknowledge that much is going well so that the criticism seems balanced.
- A section detailing the first suggested improvement: having firm start and completion dates for these classes. The purpose of this section is to show that students who take these courses often procrastinate when they have no deadlines, and that the open enrollment policy does not provide enough structure for undergraduate students.
- A section detailing the second suggested improvement: meeting with instructor as a class, face to face, for at least one class session at the beginning of the semester. The purpose of this section is to explain that students need more direct instruction about how to take one of these classes. Also, they will feel more comfortable "talking" online with someone they have become acquainted with, and approaching the instructor either online or in person will be facilitated by this early meeting.
- A section explaining the third suggested improvement: more interactive content in the course materials. The purpose of this section is to

give examples of several courses that are primarily book reading and end-of-chapter question answering, and to give examples of the kinds of material other courses use to enliven the course and engage students.
- A final section assuring instructors that the writer appreciates the enormous effort it takes to put these courses together and then to communicate with all students regularly, but suggesting that the courses can be even better and the success rate can be increased with some additional procedures and materials.

After writing out your Argument Concept, spend a good deal of time deliberating about just exactly what that concept demands of you as a writer. Can you do everything your concept implies? Should you pare down your intentions? Have you used every tool at your disposal to make your case? And probably most important, what gaps will your reader see in your plan? What will be that reader's predisposition to the argument and have you addressed those concerns fully?

To help you as you first try this process of envisioning, it may be helpful to make a generic list of potential sections of arguments to spur your thinking. For example, you might make a list such as the following and then see, for your particular Argument Concept, which of these potential sections must be included to fulfill its promise:

- Claim statement
- Reasons in support of claim
- Potential reader opposition to the claim
- Refutation, or argument against the opposition
- Concessions to reader's opposition
- Critical definitions
- Historical perspective on the issue
- Policy descriptions
- Problem descriptions
- Explanation of alternative solutions
- Evaluation of alternative solutions
- Explaining a process
- Delineating causes or effects
- Categorizing or dividing: breaking a part of your argument into subgroups

Note that you are not spelling out in these sections the kind of *evidence* you will provide, but the logical or rhetorical step you are taking in that section. You will need to use examples, summary or others' opinions, facts, statistics, research study findings—a variety of types of evidence to develop each section. But that comes later.

> ### ALSO NOTE
> #### A BONUS USE OF THE PLAN
>
> One of the best things about having an envisioned plan is that you can get quality feedback from a classmate or your instructor before you have invested hours floundering in lack of direction. We have conferences with our students during which we talk over their envisioned plans, what they may have left out, how the organization seems coherent or scattered, and what kinds of evidence they may use in support of the sections.
>
> It is difficult, sometimes, for writers to commit to major change—throwing out whole sections they have spent time writing, for instance—even though they may agree the change will improve the argument! Adding, subtracting, or rearranging a few bullet points is not a great threat. In fact, many students find it fun to work with the "puzzle" of their argument in this form rather than in unwieldy (and sometimes pointless) text. We notice that they always can talk effectively about the paper's direction and purpose when they can see it holistically.
>
> Take advantage of the help available to you. Take your envisioned plan and some questions to your instructor or an expert in your Writing Center and talk your project over before you draft. You'll be surprised how much more flexible you'll be about possible alterations in the argument and how much more readily you can talk about the organization and *function* of each section.

STEP 5: *MAKE THE PURPOSE OF EACH SECTION CLEAR*

Include a statement in each bullet point that clarifies *why* you need that information. What will it accomplish for the reader? If you can't spell that out, do you really need the information? Remember, the worst thing to do in creating an argument is just to dump information for information's sake. Think back to the analogy of the defense attorney and the jury; what effect do you want this section to have on the jury/reader, and why do they need to know this to come to the same conclusion as you have?

The added benefit of spending time on this important step is that, when you write the argument, you will be surprised at how naturally coherent it is. Making good transitions between sections will be easy because you know why you are moving to the next section and you can then articulate that reason for the reader. Then, it will be very simple for the reader to follow your logic. (See the Also Note box on p. 219 about transitions.)

The following are examples of strong purpose statements in section descriptions:

- A section quoting and explaining our company's absence policy *so the reader can see how difficult it is to understand*

> ### ALSO NOTE
> ### TRANSITIONS MADE EASY
>
> The added benefit of spending time on Step 4 is that, when you eventually write the argument, you will be surprised at how naturally coherent it is. Making good transitions between sections will be easy because you know *why* you are moving to the next section and you can then articulate that reason for the reader. Then, it will be very simple for the reader to follow your logic. Transitions between sections of your argument typically occur near the beginning of paragraphs. The following transition using sections from the previous examples illustrate how easy writing transitions becomes when you know where you are going and why.
>
> Try your hand at writing transitions that might occur between the sections outlined in the examples of envisioning in Step 3. For example, here is a transition that might begin the third section of the first plan (p. 214):
>
> > The student who can take full advantage of these online course benefits must be self-motivated, self-disciplined, and have strong reading skills.
>
> Note how a good transition relates the new section to a previous one (or sometimes announces a whole new step in your plan and why you are taking it), making sure the reader sees the connection instead of guessing why you are starting on a new section. Understanding the inner structure of your argument by having an envisioned plan helps you as you guide the reader through the purpose of your sections.

- A section evaluating the zero-tolerance approach to weapons in school *to show the reader how unreasonable it is in actual application*
- A section explaining the unintended effects of discontinuing foreign aid to women's clinics *to show how many more health issues are affected than just abortion*
- A section conceding that welfare payments without obligations on the part of recipients have not been productive *to show the reader that I am aware of the major argument against providing free social services*

STEP 6: *INCLUDE A LAST SECTION THAT INDICATES WHAT YOU HOPE YOUR READER WILL CONCLUDE FROM YOUR ARGUMENT*

Make sure that this section is a true "conclusion" and not just a restatement of your topic and intent. Your conclusion is your "take-away message." Ask yourself, "After all these points I've made, what does it mean to my readers? How does it have any significance in their lives? How might I want them to act, implement, change their thinking, reconsider, and so on." After asking your readers to confront and examine your issue, you now want them to go beyond the essay—to internalize it. Your conclusion should help them do just that, and the careful analysis you made of their position and needs helps you know how to coax them into such thinking. You may make this section more powerful by reserving your most important example to drive home your point or by offering startling statistics to overpower the most compelling and normally accepted alternative opinion. Do not short this important section or think you have *concluded* by merely repeating your claim and/or major points. Your conclusion is the place for the swelling music and the high kicks.

ADJUSTING YOUR ENVISIONED PLAN

Now, before you practice envisioning an argument, one huge note of caution. As you write, you will understand your argument and its problems better and better. The purpose of the envisioning process is to give you an overall sense of your argument, not to work out the details. It is to help you establish a clear destination and some important roads to get you there. Just as a good road trip takes advantage of serendipitous moments—perhaps dodging off I-70 in Goodland, Kansas, to see the World's Largest Prairie Dog—so does a dynamic writing process. As you discover ideas through drafting, look again at your envisioned plan to see if you've found a way to enrich it, or if the new idea is a costly and destructive detour in your route. A thoughtful, nonconfining use of envisioning will help you set your sights and then arrive. Remember that tired but all-too-true adage, "If you don't know where you're going, you'll probably not arrive." The saying is true in life, road trips, and certainly in arguments.

Exercise 4
Collaborative Analysis: Envisioning Practice

Try working in groups on this activity. You will be surprised at how others' opinions, backgrounds, and knowledge of issues helps you get a more balanced feel for the argument. Also, you will turn up necessary sections you might not have thought of on your own.

Choose three of the following Argument Concepts that you know the most about or that you are most interested in. Determine what sections are needed to fully develop your chosen Argument Concepts. You might want to refer to the list of potential sections in Step 4 as you think through the argument.

   A. *I will argue about* the building of new golf courses around Santa Fe, NM, for residents of the area *in order to* motivate them to actively protest this use of resources during a prolonged time of drought.

   B. *I will argue about* the providing of social services, specifically health services, to illegal immigrants *for* state legislators *in order to* convince them that extending these services to immigrants will eventually be best for all the citizens of the state.

C. *I will argue about* the providing of social services, specifically health services, to illegal immigrants *for* state legislators *in order to* convince them that extending these services to immigrants is a misuse of taxpayers' money and that offering services will ultimately increase the need rather than decrease it.

D. *I will argue about* holding companies liable for acts of racial discrimination on the part of their employees *for* managers of large companies *in order to* convince them to take a proactive and zero-tolerance stance when training their employees.

E. *I will argue about* holding companies liable for acts of racial discrimination on the part of their employees *for* lawmakers who can change the policy *in order to* convince them that they should eliminate this corporate liability and hold only the employees themselves responsible.

F. *I will argue about* inconsistencies in our school's policy and practices on athletes' eligibility *for* faculty and administrators *in order to* correct the hypocritical treatment of "star" athletes.

G. *I will argue about* our school policies on athletes' eligibility *for* administrators *in order to* convince them to change to more lenient policies.

H. *I will argue about* requiring at least two years of foreign language study in high school *for* state curriculum directors *in order to* convince them that adopting the policy will prepare students more adequately for college and for interaction in a more diverse workplace.

I. *I will argue about* colleges and universities requiring all students to take general education curriculum classes (arts/sciences undergraduate requirements) *for* all degrees for state higher education curriculum directors *in order to* convince them that each discipline (biology, communications, art, for instance) should determine its own requirements.

J. *I will argue about* colleges and universities requiring all students to take general education curriculum classes (arts/sciences undergraduate requirements) *for* entering college freshmen *in order to* show them how beneficial these classes will be for them in their life beyond college.

K. *I will argue about* the horrors of "puppy mills" *for* potential dog owners *in order to* expose this inhumane practice and to keep them from buying a dog from a mill.

L. *I will argue about* access to adoption files *for* adult adopted children *in order to* convince them to investigate their rights and to demand access, at a minimum, to their natural parents' health histories.

M. *I will argue about* lack of family films other than animated features *for* film producers *in order to* convince them that producing more nonviolent, less sexually-obsessed movies will be financially as well as socially responsible.

DISCOVERING YOUR OWN ARGUMENTS: ENVISIONING YOUR ARGUMENT

Create an envisioned plan for your topic(s) to guide your drafting. The plan includes (1) the focused Argument Concept, (2) a claim, and (3) a list of specific sections you will need to fulfill that plan.

1. *The Argument Concept.* You probably have a workable, focused topic for argument now, and you have probably created several Argument Concepts related to it. You may have eliminated some to narrow your choices down to two or three, but you are not sure to which argument you want to commit; this practice can help you make a decision among several viable alternatives. You may want to sketch out two or three envisioned plans to see how your argument would work out if you change your focus, reader, or purpose. If you have not yet decided on a topic for your argument, return to your list of generated topics for argument that you made in Chapter 7 or 8 and select one to work with.

2. *The Claim.* Refer to Chapter 4, pp. 102–104, for a reminder about converting your Argument Concept into a claim. Make sure the claim has the same degree of specificity as your Argument Concept.

3. *List of Specific Sections.* This chapter has provided you several samples of such lists. You may want to review p. 217, which gives a list of potential sections to include so that you are as thorough as possible. *Remember the importance of providing a reason for the sections you create.*

Before you create your own plan, however, you may want to examine the following two samples, one a professional journalist's argument and one a student's academic argument.

PROFESSIONAL SAMPLE OF AN ENVISIONED PLAN AND FINAL ARGUMENT

Following is a professional argument that is coherent because it has direction and purpose. You can see how the final argument reflects organization and has a functional, organic quality to the sections of the argument; that is why it is easy to imagine what the author's plan for the essay might have been. Unfortunately, readers don't usually have access to a writer's many early generating thoughts, potential plans that may have been rejected, and preliminary drafts. Good writers, as we will discuss in Chapter 11, know that a quality product takes lots of process, as you can see in the "Other Writers' Process," Also Note box on p. 290. Your own argument will also certainly take a few, maybe even many, dry runs before it reflects this kind of coherence and competence. But for now, examine how the following final product reflects good planning.

Had we had access to an actual plan from the author, Jamie Fellner, it might have looked something like this:

Argument Concept
I will argue about the status of the death penalty for mentally retarded convicts *for* citizens who may believe mentally retarded convicts should be executed *in order to* convince such citizens that current law does, in fact, exclude the disabled from capital punishment and that the entire nation should discontinue this practice.

Claim
The United States should join the rest of the world and refrain from executing anyone who is mentally disabled; current law does exclude them from capital punishment, and life imprisonment is sufficient.

Potential Sections
- Introductory section using Penry's case to draw reader's attention to the problem with a real example
- A section describing the current status of the problem in the United States so that the reader knows the scope and depth of the issue
- A section defining "mentally retarded" so the reader will clearly see that Penry falls in this category
- A section focusing on the legal principle of blameworthiness to explain to the reader that the issue is not an all-or-nothing concept, that there is in the law a consideration of *degree* of responsibility
- A section giving reasons why the mentally retarded clearly do not fit into this category of extreme blameworthiness that justifies the death penalty so that readers will see why the mentally retarded should be excluded
- A section applying this same concept to Penry in specific
- A section explaining the Supreme Court's stance on executing the mentally retarded to show that we are out of step with the rest of the world
- A section conceding that there has been some progress to show the reader that some states are dealing with the problem and that a solution is possible
- A section explaining why changes are slow to be made
- A concluding section offering a better solution so that the reader will understand that he is not advocating letting the mentally retarded off with no punishment

Most of the time, in a lengthy argument, many sections will need several paragraphs to support them adequately. This short argument has a one-to-one correspondence of sections to paragraphs, but that is not the norm. Notice in the "Students at Work" sample, for instance, that one section needs six paragraphs of development.

Here are some prereading questions to consider as you evaluate the effectiveness of this essay:

1. What language choices does Fellner use that assume a certain stance against the practice of executing the mentally retarded? Are these language choices fair, or are they unnecessarily "loaded"?

2. What evidence has the author provided that the United States' allowing the execution of the mentally retarded is out of step with the rest of the world? Is this argument a "bandwagon" argument, or is it legitimate? Should the punishment practices of the United States conform to those of other nations?

3. Are you convinced by the reasons Fellner provides that the retarded are not extremely blameworthy? Why or why not?

4. What sections of the essay do you think are most convincing? Least convincing? Why?

5. What types of arguments would you make in opposition to Fellner's argument?

Mentally Retarded Don't Belong on Death Row
Jamie Fellner

1 Johnny Paul Penry won't get to see Hollywood's latest death row film, *The Green Mile*. That's because he is on death row himself, slated for execution in Texas on January 13. There's a chance, however, that the issues raised in the film will help people like Penry some day. Like the lead character in the movie, Penry has the mind of a child—and the government wants to execute him anyway. — *A section introducing an individual problem that brings up a larger issue of the execution of mentally retarded people*

2 The United States is almost alone in the world in allowing this barbaric practice. At least 33 mentally retarded men have been executed since the United States reinstated the death penalty in 1976. Some experts estimate that as many as 10 to 15 percent of the 3,000 men and women on the nation's death rows are retarded. A person is considered mentally retarded if he or she has significantly subaverage general intellectual functioning, which generally means recording an IQ score of lower than 70, and exhibiting deficits in adaptive behavior before the age of 18. An average IQ score is 100; Penry's measures at 54. — *A section providing background for the problem and current policy description*

3 Many of the mentally retarded on death row have committed terrible murders. Being guilty of a capital crime, however, is not enough to warrant the death penalty; U.S. law reserves it only for the most culpable or blameworthy offenders, based on consideration of their background, character, motivation, and circumstances of their crimes. — *A section further defining policy, bringing to reader's attention an important legal principle: blameworthiness*

4 The mentally retarded can never meet the criteria of extraordinary blameworthiness. People with retardation are incapable of calculated, mature evil. A retarded person is simply not the same as other adults. They are childlike in many of their limitations: their ability to reason and develop skills needed to navigate in the world are permanently stunted. They have grave — *A section offering reasons why the mentally retarded do not meet standards of blameworthiness*

Professional Sample of an Envisioned Plan and Final Argument **225**

difficulties with language, communication, learning, logic, foresight, strategic thinking, planning, and understanding consequences. They have problems with attention, memory and comprehension. They are limited in their ability to learn from experience, to control their impulses, to think in long-range terms or to understand causality. Children outgrow most of these limitations. Those who are retarded cannot.

5   Penry was physically abused as a child, has organic brain damage, and is mentally retarded. Twenty-two years old in 1979 at the time, he raped and murdered Pamela Mosely Carpenter in Livingston, Texas. He had then—and has now—the mental capacity of a 7-year-old.   *A section applying the criteria of "blameworthiness" to the specific case*

6   In a 5-to-4 decision, the Supreme Court overturned his conviction because the jury had not been allowed to fully consider his mental impairments. But the court stopped short of ruling that the Eighth Amendment's prohibition on cruel and unusual punishment precluded execution of the mentally retarded. It concluded that there was insufficient evidence that the national "standard of decency" had evolved far enough to reject such executions. It is a sad commentary that the standard of decency of almost every other country in the world exceeds that of the United States when it comes to the death penalty.   *A section providing the current status of the issue: Supreme Court does not think executing the mentally retarded violates current standards of decency*

7   There has been progress, however. The federal government and 12 states specifically exempt people with retardation from capital punishment. Polls consistently show that even death penalty supporters believe people who are mentally impaired should not be executed. But in some two dozen states, including California, such executions are permitted.   *A section acknowledging some movement toward a resolution of the problem*

8   Legislatures refuse to change state laws because of tough-on-crime sentiment, exacerbated by the grief and quest for vengeance of the murder victims' families, and the failure of officials and the public alike to understand the significance of mental retardation and the difference between guilt and culpability. The execution of the mentally retarded also continues because their mental limitations make them even more vulnerable than other defendants to the often arbitrary and unfair treatment inherent in capital trials. In their characteristic quest to please authority figures, for example, mentally retarded defendants are likely to waive their rights without fully understanding them. Almost invariably poor, they are usually represented by court appointed lawyers who lack the skills, resources and   *A section explaining why there is not more progress*

commitment to handle any capital case, much less one involving a defendant with mental retardation.

9 Penry, who was resentenced to death by another jury, now faces execution in less than two weeks. Lawyers pressing last-minute appeals hope to convince the federal courts that national standards of decency have evolved since the original Penry decision and that the execution of any defendant who is retarded should be prohibited as unconstitutional. No one argues that the mentally retarded should be free from criminal responsibility. But life imprisonment is sufficient to express society's outrage at horrible crimes, to hold offenders accountable and to protect society from further violence. It is time the United States join the world in recognizing the senseless cruelty of executing anyone with the mind of a child.*

A concluding section that offers a better alternative to capital punishment for these offenders

---

STUDENTS AT WORK: A STUDENT'S PLAN AND CORRESPONDING ARGUMENT

Student Debbie Stewart watched the debate in her state over the creation of an amendment to the constitution establishing a "living wage" for workers. Following are her envisioned plan and her final argument.

Argument Concept
I will argue about raising the minimum wage *for* legislators debating a potential state constitutional amendment to regulate the minimum wage *in order to* convince them that the current minimum wage is not a "living" wage and the amendment should be proposed.

Claim
An amendment increasing the state minimum wage should be proposed to raise the current rate to a living wage for our citizens.

Potential Sections
- Introductory section explaining the origin of the minimum wage with a real example to show that its purpose has been to improve living conditions of citizens
- A section comparing the rate of minimum wage as a percent of the median wage and poverty level in America over the years to demonstrate that the value of the minimum wage has decreased in recent years
- A section showing how many hours a minimum-wage earner would need to work to pay housing expenses to show the reader that it is impossible to subsist on the current wage

---

*As of the time of publication, Penry awaits a fourth trial on death row.

- A section showing how many hours a minimum-wage earner would need to work to pay food, household expenses, and child care to show the reader that it is impossible to subsist on the current wage
- A section suggesting a minimum wage figure to demonstrate how implementing that wage could benefit a worker
- A section exploring the opposition arguments and a refutation of each so that legislators would not be swayed by the arguments to the contrary
- A concluding section emphasizing that in a time when corporate profits are increasing, more and more Americans are falling below the poverty line, to appeal to the readers' sense of fairness

Here are some prereading questions to consider as you analyze Debbie's argument:

1. Why does the sixth section—the discussion of opposing argument—need to take such a large part of Debbie's argument?

2. Is the example given of the single mother in paragraphs 6–9 effective? Why or why not? Would an example of (or interview with) a real person struggling to survive on the minimum wage be more effective? Why or why not?

3. Debbie has chosen to write directly for the legislators who are debating the proposed amendment. In what ways do you believe the sections of the argument match that potential reader, and where does it seem that Debbie might be more focused on a citizen reader, one who will eventually vote for or against the amendment?

4. If you were one of the legislators in her state, what sections(s) would you like to see added to the argument? What more do you need to know before you could decide whether or not to propose this amendment?

5. The argument begins with a historical perspective on the minimum wage. In what way is this information a good connection for legislators? What other type of opening section might motivate this reader to consider Debbie's argument?

6. Which of Debbie's sections do you find most convincing? Least convincing? Why?

7. What do you think of the balance of source use and writer's voice in this argument? What effect do you think this balance will have on Debbie's intended readers?

Minimum Wage vs. Living Wage
Debbie Stewart

1   Our Colorado legislators are currently debating an issue that will have great impact on many of our citizens—an amendment to the constitution that will provide and

228 Chapter 9 *Envisioning the Complete Argument as a Prewriting Process*

regulate a raise in the minimum wage. A minimum guarantee has been in place for nearly seventy years since the Fair Labor Standards Act (FLSA) signed into law on June 28, 1938, by President Franklin Roosevelt. The FLSA was created as a means to restrict the long work hours that plagued women and children in the late nineteenth and early twentieth centuries. It also established a minimum wage for America's working class. The minimum wage implemented in 1938 at $.25 per hour with annual increases of $.05 until it reached $.40, which was the industrial standard at that time. According to the U.S. Department of Labor, minimum wage was originally designed only for those employees engaged in the "production of goods for interstate commerce" but was amended in 1961 to extend coverage to employees working in retail, service enterprises, local transit, construction, and gasoline service stations. In the article "Troubled Passage: The Labor Movement and the Fair Labor Standards Act," President Roosevelt's view of the law's importance is noted: "We are seeking, of course, only legislation to end starvation wages and intolerable hours. . . ."

Introductory section explaining the origin of the minimum wage with a real example to show that its purpose has been to improve living conditions of citizens

2   The minimum wage was introduced, as Roosevelt indicated, as a measure to create better living conditions for working class Americans. The amount was set at $.25 per hour and has increased 20 times in the past 68 years; however, the minimum wage has stayed static for the past 9 years even though the annual cost of living has not. *An amendment increasing the state minimum wage should be proposed to raise the current rate to a living wage for our citizens.*

Debbie includes her claim in this section

3   According to a Department of Labor report and the United States Census, in 1938 minimum wage was $.25 per hour, and the yearly median income was around $2000. The minimum wage averaged 25% of the average median income. In 1950, minimum wage was $.75 per hour while the median income was $6000. Again, the minimum wage was roughly 25% of the median yearly income. In 1969, the minimum wage was raised to $1.60 as the median income in America increased to $9586. A person on minimum wage earned 32% of the median income. In 1969, that placed minimum wage workers only $28 below the poverty line according to information on Oregon State University's Web site, "A Portrait of Poverty in Oregon."

A section comparing the rate of minimum wage as a percent of the median wage and poverty level in America over the years to demonstrate that the value of the minimum wage has decreased in recent years

4   The United States Census Bureau keeps income information on file dating back to 1966. Historically, from the Bureau's information, the minimum wage allowed American workers to stay at or slightly above the poverty line. Today, a minimum wage worker with two children is making roughly $8000 below the line of poverty and earning only 18% of the annual median income of $53,750. The gap between minimum wage and the annual median income is the largest in history due to the nine-year drought in minimum wage increases and the rising cost of goods and services.

5   With increasing housing, education, medical, and food costs in the United States, a person making minimum wage is falling further behind. A minimum wage worker would need to work an average of 70 hours a week making time and a half to rise slightly above the threshold of poverty. If a person worked two different minimum wage jobs he or she would need to work 76 hours to break $19,000, only $340 above the poverty level.

6   Taking into account housing costs, can a single mother with two children under five, for example, survive in America and still provide all the other necessities of life for her children? It is very difficult for her to live in a safe environment on minimum wage and still provide the other basic necessities of life for herself and her children.

A section showing how many hours a minimum wage earner would need to work to pay housing expenses to show the reader that it is impossible to subsist on the current wage

7   According to a Nov/Dec 2005 article published in *The Journal of Housing and Community Development*, the average income in America went unchanged since 2002, but the median housing price rose 22% in two years. According to apartmentguide.com the average rental for a two-bedroom, one-bathroom apartment in Fort Collins, Colorado, for instance, is $550. Annually that amounts to $6,600 not including utilities, which averaged $720 per year. If the hypothetical woman worked an average of 50 hours per week, she would make $13,598.40 per year. For this mother, housing plus utilities make up 53% of her annual gross income.

8   The cost of food is another increasing expense in America. In a 2002 United Stated Department of Agriculture Report, the average American family spent $37.50 per person per week on food. According to the United States Department of Agriculture, the average food stamp benefit for a single parent with two children is $345.00 per month, or 30% of monthly income. That is $105 below the national average. The monthly allowance of food stamps is 24% less than the average median

A section showing how many hours a minimum wage earner would need to work to pay food, household expenses, and child care to show the reader that it is

family spends, and the allowance only includes food and not toiletries or paper products. The single mother could spend upward of $150 per month on paper products if she has to buy diapers, amounting roughly to $1800 annually. So after housing, utilities, and groceries, a minimum wage worker working 50 hours per week is now left with $4,250.40 of her annual income. — *impossible to subsist on the current wage*

9   Another expense for a single mother is child care. According to the Colorado Division of Childcare, child care for poor working parents is subsidized, but still costs an average of $120 per child per month. For two children this amounts to $2880 annually. The single mother is left with a little over $1,202.40. With the average 5% social security tax withholdings from her pay, the mother is now $159.80 in the red, and she has yet to purchase clothing for her children or pay transportation costs to get back and forth to work.

10   The minimum wage needs to be increased to a "living" wage. What is a living wage? A living wage is the amount of money it would take to pay for the basic necessities of life such as housing, food, clothing, taxes, and transportation. So how much would the minimum wage need to be increased? If lawmakers take into account Medicaid benefits, child care subsidies, and food stamps, the minimum wage would only need to be raised to $8.15 per hour. This would place the minimum wage worker at 30% of the average median income. So, for a single mother with two children working fifty hours, she would make $21,526.00 per year. She would still be entitled to government assistance but be able to provide all the necessities for her children. — *A section suggesting a minimum wage figure to demonstrate how implementing that wage could benefit a worker*

11   Arguments against raising the minimum wage exist, however. Some opponents conclude that raising the minimum wage actually hurts the poor instead of helping them. The Joint Economic Committee Report released May 1996, argued that jobs would be lost and that raising the minimum wage would reduce the lifetime earnings of low-skilled workers. The report also stated that more students would drop out of high school to enter the work force. The Web site balancedpoliticsw.org, shows both sides to the minimum wage issue. However, there are more arguments against raising the minimum wage than for it: the minimum wage hurts nonprofit organizations; small companies are driven out of business by rising costs; price for consumer goods will increase; and unemployment will — *A section exploring the opposition arguments and a refutation of each so that a potential voter would not be swayed by the election arguments to the contrary*

rise. So would raising the minimum wage hurt America's economy and worsen the living conditions of the poor?

12   Richard Fisher, President of the Federal Reserve Bank of Dallas, argues that the American economy is still the growth engine of the world. According to Fisher, the U.S. economy grew 2.9 percent each year from 1995 to 1997 and grew 3.5 percent from 2000 to 2005 despite the 2001 recession. The Federal Reserve reports that the U.S. economy grew 3.25 percent over the decade between 1996 and 2006, while the growth from 1986 to 1996 was just three percent, and the United States Department of Labor reports that unemployment is currently at a rate of 4.7 percent, down from 5.3 percent in 1997. The unemployment rate has not increased significantly since 1997 when the minimum wage increased to $5.15 from $4.75 per hour. The argument that increasing minimum wage would increase the number of those unemployed and hurt the economy is unfounded according to historical data.

13   Another argument against raising the minimum wage is a risk of increasing the high school dropout rate. Opponents argue that an increase in the minimum wage would entice students to drop out of school in search of jobs. The high school dropout rate has increased in some states since 1997, but the variables are so complex a person is unable to argue with any certainty that a higher minimum wage is the cause.

Note that Debbie's envisioned plan had one section description for this lengthy discussion of opposition arguments.

14   The United States Department of Labor Employment Standards and Wage Division reports that California is one of thirteen states with a minimum wage higher than the $5.15 mandated by the federal government, and information from the Web site standup.org, created by the Bill and Melinda Gates Foundation, offers the opportunity to correlate a state's minimum wage with the state's dropout rate. Standup.org shows a map with each state and the state's educational data. California's 34% dropout rate is higher than the national average of 29%. Minnesota, another state that pays a higher minimum wage, however, records a dropout rate of only 14%, almost 20% lower than California's dropout rate, and 15% lower than the national average. Colorado and Nebraska, states with a standard minimum wage, have dropout rates of 28 and 14 percent, respectively. Then there are those states, such as South Carolina, that have abolished the minimum wage but have above average dropout rates of 40%.

15 Each state has a number of variables that increase the risk of high school dropouts, but it is not proven that increasing the minimum wage would worsen the high school dropout problem. A 2006 study by a Washington policy development group, Civic Enterprises, found the number one reason given by students who dropped out of high school was boring classes and lack of motivation. There are those students who drop out for financial reasons, but those students make up less than 20% of the total dropout rate.

16 If the variables of minimum wage and a higher rate of high school dropouts were positively correlated, then most of the states with higher than standard minimum wages would have the highest percentage of high school dropouts, but they don't. The statistics show there is no correlation between these two variables. A higher minimum wage does not necessarily increase the high school dropout rate.

17 One of the most powerful arguments against the minimum wage increase is the potential harm to small businesses and the increased risk of minimum wage workers losing their jobs in a highly competitive global economy. According to Employment Policies Institute, a study conducted by two Stanford University economists concluded that on the "poorest workers could be negatively impacted by a higher wage increase because small businesses are forced to either raise prices or decrease overhead." Since the world market is so competitive, price increases would threaten the business's very operation, so the business would most likely cut payroll expenses by reducing the number of employees. If small businesses are negatively affected by an increase in the minimum wage, millions of American workers could be affected. However, Jerold Waltman, Professor of Political Science reports in the *Journal of Economic Issues* that statistical analysis from 1928 to 1983 showed no correlation between business failures and increases in the minimum wage. According to the Economic Policy Institute, in states where the minimum wage exceeded the federal wage, small businesses grew by 3.4 percent while the average growth nationally was 1.6 percent. As long as small businesses continue to grow, there will be opportunities waiting for those workers affected by small business layoffs.

18 The minimum wage was established to improve the standards of living for working-class Americans. While the current minimum wage remains static, the

cost of living has steadily increased and more Americans than ever are slipping below the poverty line. The Center on Budget and Policy priorities claims that the "amount by which the average poor person fell below the poverty line in 2005—$3,236—remained the highest on record with data going back to 1975," and 43% of the poor are considered in "severe" poverty, below $7,788 income for a family of three. Arguments against increasing the minimum wage, such as adverse impacts to small businesses, don't hold up under scrutiny. As a matter of fact, a recent Gallup/Wells Fargo poll, 86% of small business owners reported that the rate of the minimum wage had no impact on their hiring policies. Some economists predicted a slowdown in America's economy at the last raise in the minimum wage, but corporate profits continue to soar.

A concluding section emphasizing that in a time when corporate profits are increasing, more and more Americans are falling below the poverty line, to appeal to the readers' sense of fairness

19   While the debate in America over whether to increase the minimum wage continues, millions of Americans are working harder than ever just to exist in the wealthiest nation on earth. A statement from 665 economists including four Nobel laureates and six past presidents of the American Economics Association concluded that ". . . modest increases in state minimum wages in the range of $1.00 to $2.50 and indexing to protect against inflation can significantly improve the lives of low-income workers and their families without the adverse effects that critics have claimed." Many states have taken steps to increase the living standards of their poorest residents by raising their state's minimum wage, while lawmakers in Washington D.C. argue the benefits and the consequences of such an action. Colorado could join these states and improve the lives of thousands of Coloradoans living in poverty, the majority of these being children. Colorado's lawmakers should follow in the footsteps of President Roosevelt and take steps to institute a minimum "living" wage for the most overlooked members of society, the working poor.

REFLECTIONS ON THE CHAPTER

With the thoughtful and comprehensive plan you've developed, you can more confidently launch into your draft instead of worrying, "Where do I start?" You may need to make a formal outline, and, if you do so, your envisioned plan will make it easier and more coherent. You may also need to consider more thoroughly just how each section will best be organized, and Chapter 10 will help you think through those possibilities. But best of all, when you are ready to tackle the drafting task, you needn't face the blank paper and panic. You know what to do, where to go next, and most important—why.

Your draft will take on life as you work through the argument; always realize your reader will be actively negotiating with you toward its meaning.

CHAPTER

10

Refining the Purposes for Your Argument

At this point, you have been crafting your overall argument and may now see that you need to look deeper into the structure of the varied sections in your paper and into the purposes of each. In your own argument, you want to lay down a clear path for your readers so that they will be led convincingly—and unswervingly—to your conclusion. You want your readers to come away with something, perhaps even feel changed in some manner when they finish reading your work.

As your reading has shown, authors employ a number of focused purposes in their work, in nearly all cases using an overlapping mesh of purposes to defend the significant claims in their work. This chapter examines the structures of the most common purposes used in arguments; but our unequivocal emphasis is that like all writers, *you should select those purposes that best serve the needs of your topic and claim's defense.* And the decisions you make about purpose(s) as you begin to draft your argument will depend on your understanding of your focus, reader, and ultimate goal—always.

TERMS AND CONCEPTS TO WATCH FOR
- Arguments evaluating quality
- Criterion
- Problem-solving argument
- Cause-and-effect argument

- False cause fallacy
- Post hoc ergo propter hoc fallacy
- Policy argument

QUESTIONS TO GUIDE YOUR READING

- What is the purpose of establishing criteria when arguing to evaluate?
- Why are evaluative criteria sometimes implied and sometimes explicitly stated?
- Why should you fully understand a problem before seeking a solution, or solutions, to it?
- Why must you "evaluate" solutions to problems?
- What are the two primary types of cause-and-effect reasoning?
- Why do most writers focus on either the causes or the effects of an issue?
- Why do many arguments about policy allow compromise?
- How are purposes most often intertwined in an argument?

As you become more experienced in reading and writing arguments, you will learn that few, if any, arguments are built upon a single purpose. When you examine the envisioned plan or plans you have written in earlier chapters, for example, you will see that different *sections* may require different means of organization and different types of development. Most writers use a medley of developmental purposes:

- Arguing for the quality of a product, behavior, or work of art;
- Arguing solutions to problems;
- Arguing for cause(s) and effect(s); and
- Arguing to maintain or change a policy.

Granted, some arguments may focus primarily (overall) on one of the above purposes, but writers rarely restrict themselves to just one, allowing instead that they will select the best course of action from the known possibilities. For example, let's say that your claim asserts that background checks should be conducted on all people who coach in your city's recreational athletic leagues. Such an argument may require that you concentrate some section (or sections) most on *changing the current policy* that allows anyone to coach a team without scrutiny of his or her legal background. In the course of your argument, however, another section will likely support the idea that background checks would help *solve the potential problems* of unethical behaviors of adult coaches toward their young athletes by *arguing the harmful effects* that sexual actions by a coach will have on children. Get the idea? Even though your argument centers mostly on a policy issue, you should not neglect any other purpose that will make your argument stronger and more persuasive.

In this chapter, we will discuss the various purposes *individually*, with the caution that *most arguments intertwine the options* as an issue dictates. Always ask yourself, "What tools will I need to build the sections of my argument for my selected focus, reader, and purpose?" Just like a carpenter who knows that building a new porch (one section of a house) may mostly require the use of a hammer, he or she would never disallow the use of a level, a drill, a saw, or any other tool necessary to complete the entire job.

ARGUING FOR THE QUALITY OF A PRODUCT, BEHAVIOR, OR WORK OF ART

> **ARGUMENTS EVALUATING QUALITY** *judge a subject (e.g., a person, an object, or an event) against a set of standards (criteria) that define an ideal subject of that type.*

When your issue requires that you support or reject the quality of something, you are evaluating its quality. Remember that it is not enough just to claim that you like or dislike something, such as stating, "I hated that movie" (see the Argument in Action box on movie reviews, p. 239). Such claims are rarely fruitful because they assert only your preference for something and do not make a statement about its quality. Although readers expect you to state your opinion about the quality of a product or behavior, to be sure, they also expect (and deserve) an explanation of why you feel the way you do. What standards of judgment did you use? What evidence can you provide that your judgment is reasonable and well supported? In short, your goal is to argue that your overall judgment of the product, behavior, or work of art is worth his or her consideration.

In its most skeletal form, the *thinking* process of evaluation will look something like this:

- You establish how something should be measured for quality (or how it is commonly measured) and often spend a portion of your argument discussing what each criterion is and why each is important (sometimes, of course, this discussion is unnecessary because your reader is familiar with the criteria).

> *A* **CRITERION** *(plural: criteria) is an established standard against which a behavior, product, or idea is measured and judged.*

- Next, you measure the product, idea, or behavior you are evaluating according to the criteria. In other words, how does a product, as an example, "stack up" against the criteria used to measure similar items? To do so, you must provide ample specific evidence of how your chosen item meets or does not meet each criterion you have established or are commonly accepted.

- You then conclude that the product, idea, or behavior does or does not meet the established criteria, and this conclusion serves as the *claim* your argument will defend.

Forming a criteria-based argument saves you from the dead end of trying to convince a reader something is good or bad simply because you like or don't like it (the "preference-based" or subjective argument).

Here are some examples of the evaluation system at work. The first one illustrates how the thinking process of an evaluative argument might work:

Evaluating a Product

Claim: The Macro 2900 car audio system offers the best sound quality for small car owners.

Criterion 1: Car audio systems should offer a variety of speaker options so that a small car owner can mount the speakers individually for the best sound quality.

Judgment and Evidence: The Macro 2900 system comes with low-range speakers (woofers), mid-range speakers, and high-range speakers (tweeters), with an external crossover device to synchronize the individual speakers. Such options allow the small car owner to place the tweeters up front and the mid-range and woofers in the rear, if desired.

Criterion 2: Car audio systems must provide "head units" (receivers) that offer not only radio and CD options, but also an amplifier with sufficient wattage from each channel to drive the speaker system.

Judgment and Evidence: The Macro 2900 head unit comes with radio and CD options and a choice of amplifiers up to 200 watts per channel. The small car owner can choose the desired amplifier power which is packaged in the 2900 that will best power the speaker system.

Evaluating a Behavior

Elementary school teachers who use fluent American Sign Language and have college training in teaching the hearing impaired are adequately trained to teach those hearing-impaired students they encounter in the classroom.

Three teachers at Westwood Elementary School—Marla Jameson, Jack Kirkpatrick, and Audrey Moreno—all use ASL fluently and have many hours of college work dedicated to teaching hearing-impaired students.

Claim: Thus, these three teachers are adequately prepared to teach those hearing-impaired students they may encounter, and parents of such students should feel comfortable that their children will receive a good education from teachers sensitive to their children's needs.

Evaluating a Work of Art

The timelessness and universality of novels whose powerful and beautiful prose portrays characters facing and overcoming the struggles of human life are often recognized as great literature. John Steinbeck's *The Grapes of Wrath* portrays timeless, universal characters who face and overcome the struggles of migrant workers during the Great Depression and does so with fervent dialogue and beautiful imagery.

Claim: Therefore, Steinbeck's *The Grapes of Wrath* deserves its oft-noted recognition as a great work of literary art.

ARGUMENT IN ACTION   Did They See the Same Movie?

Establishing objective criteria and judging a subject against them can help you avoid a biased and possibly invalid evaluation. Review these two conclusions about the 2004 movie *The Passion of the Christ*. No one can be entirely objective, but *does it appear individual beliefs and values may have more to do with these reviews than solid criteria?* Are these reviews simply "preference-based" assertions?

From "Flogged to Death" by J. Hoberman, film critic for the *Village Voice*, an alternative weekly in New York, for 24 years:

> X-ploitative though it may be, the spectacle of a man beaten and tortured to death seeks to be an object of contemplation. Serious questions are raised. Is there any other religion so rooted in the representation of human suffering? At last, the pain pageant ends—the heavens open, the earth quakes, and Satan's wig flies off. In the final moments, Jesus emerges from his grave, tanned, rested, and ready—accompanied by appropriately kick-ass martial music.
>
> Payback time.
>
> Sitting through the film's garishly staged suffering, one might well ponder the millions of people—victims of crusades, inquisitions, colonial conquests, the slave trade, political terror, and genocide—who have been tortured and killed in Christ's name.

From "This Is the Best Story Ever Filmed" by Cal Thomas, a conservative columnist syndicated in over five hundred newspapers, and a commentator for Fox News:

> I can say "The Passion" is the most beautiful, profound, accurate, disturbing, realistic, and bloody depiction of this well-known story that has ever been filmed. . . .
>
> Thirteen years ago, actor Mickey Rooney wrote an editorial for *Variety* in which he said, "The on-screen depiction of religion is less than flattering, and, as a Christian, I pray the era of denigrating religion on screen comes to a screeching halt. And soon!"
>
> Rooney's prayer has been answered with "The Passion." It is a soul-stirring film that deserves wide distribution and viewing. Its message is not just for Christians, but for everyone. I doubt a better film about Jesus could be made.

Exercise 1
Collaborative Analysis: Reading an Argument for the Quality of a Product, Behavior, or Work of Art

Read the following music review and be prepared to discuss these questions:

1. Who are the intended readers for this review?

2. The author contends that Los Lobos' album addresses the issue of immigration in a manner different from common social and political views of the topic. What is the author's purpose for such a claim?

3. What criteria does the author establish for his judgment of the album's quality? Where in the piece is each discussed? Or does the author assume the reader knows the criteria sufficiently that a formal discussion of criteria is unnecessary?

4. What phrases (or song lyrics) does the writer use to measure the individual songs and the entire album against the criteria? How do these phrases reflect the author's recognition of his audience?

5. Does the author defend or reject the quality of *The Town and the City*? Is it clear to you why the author reached this conclusion?

6. Besides evaluating the quality of the album, what other purpose(s) does the author use to defend his claim? Do you see why he chose to use another purpose or purposes?

Los Lobos Sing of Immigrants' Hopes, Heartbreaks
Agustin Gurza

1   While politicians and protesters were busy marching and making speeches on immigration in recent months, East Los Angeles' acclaimed Hispanic rockers were in a recording studio quietly preparing their own statement on the subject. The result is this outstanding new album, in stores this week. It's a subtle, suggestive and at times ambiguous look at an issue often drawn in trite extremes of pro and con, black and white. This set of 13 evocative songs is told from a clear immigrant point of view, as you might expect of four Mexican-Americans (and one Anglo fellow traveler) who have found fame and stature, if not fortune, while remaining loyal, artistically and personally, to their barrio roots.

2   But in a debate where talk is cheap, the strength of this work rests heavily on what's left unsaid. This is an album in the classic, pre-digital sense, in which the very sequence of songs suggests meaning and connection.

3   Los Lobos use lyrical images and moody soundscapes to convey what it feels like to be an immigrant. Buzz words—border, illegals, cheap labor,

homeland security—are banned. They speak of hope and heartache, ambition and disenchantment, sacrifices and healing.

4   Because immigration is always a journey, the album opens with "The Valley," which evokes the dawn of a new life in a promised land. But already, layers of sonic dissonance create an unsettling undercurrent. Dreams of arrival immediately turn into the droning, chain-gang blues of "Hold On," about the oppressive drudgery of low-skill work: "Killing myself just to keep alive/Killing myself to survive."

5   The songs then explore the unexpected changes immigration always brings to people who undertake it. The lively, carefree "Chuco's Cumbia," with its calo (slang) and hot sax, serves as transition to a cool new culture. But "Little Things" laments the loss of values and "Don't Ask Why" the emptiness of shattered illusions.

6   Near the end, the gospel-tinged "Free Up" urges a philosophical adjustment to a snappy beat. Happiness comes to those who wait, for the peace of death. "When it comes my time/You won't find me cryin'/When I'm gone/Everything will be fine."

7   Yet the album closes with the torn and unsettled yearning of "The Town." Where has the journey led us? Full circle to dreams of a better place, always out of reach: "I can go there when I dream/I close my eyes and it's all I see/The town where I come from."

Exercise 2
Individual Analysis and Practice: Planning the Argument for Quality of a Product, Behavior, or Work of Art

Select one of the following five options for evaluation. Specify a particular item or object in your selected category. Then decide the criteria you would choose to evaluate the quality of your selection. What conclusion about the item's quality would you draw? Discuss your criteria, measurements, and conclusion (claim) with the class. Write your evaluative plan in a manner similar to that given on p. 238.

For example, if you select the first option, determine what particular tool or gadget you are interested in evaluating—a car-top bike carrier, for instance. Then determine appropriate criteria by which such carriers should be judged as good or bad.

1. A piece of equipment you use on the job or for recreational purposes

2. A television drama or reality show

3. A governmental office: motor vehicles, Social Security, water department, Forest Service, or a similar bureaucratic organization

4. A restaurant whose clientele is primarily college students

5. A political decision: the war in Iraq or another country, a tax refund, limiting welfare recipients, sending aid to another country, building a border fence, or some other issue

Do Evaluative Arguments Allow for Fairness?

A quick reminder at this point: You probably remember from Chapters 1 and 2 that fair and reasonable arguments acknowledge (offer concessions to) opposing arguments with the understanding that because other people may disagree with your viewpoint, such disagreement stems from a differing perspective on an issue, not from intentional antagonism or ill will. In arguments about the quality of something, you may find that though a product, behavior, or work of art does not meet *all* of the standards you establish, it may meet *most* of them. Thus, you *concede* those qualities the product does not meet. In the earlier argument about the Macro 2900 car audio system, for example, your argument concentrates on the strengths of the system, but you may concede that in spite of these strengths, the Macro 2900 is more expensive than similar components. Doing so does not weaken your argument; rather, it indicates that you have studied the issue of car audio quality carefully. And as a reasonable person, you willingly admit that the Macro 2900 might not be the choice for people whose priority is an audio system that costs less.

How Evaluative Arguments Are Often Organized

Generally, organizing an argument of evaluation works best when you combine the criteria used to measure an item with aspects of the item itself. In the argument about the quality of three teachers' preparation to teach hearing-impaired students, you might organize a section of the paper similarly to the following. One caution, though: The following suggestion represents the *thought process* that often goes into evaluative argument. Your own paper or section(s) of this type may not appear to be so formulaic. For example, many writers of evaluative argument may not formally discuss a particular criterion and then move to the measurement in lock-step manner. Sometimes, the writer believes the reader is familiar with the criteria and so only alludes to the criteria without making them explicit. Likewise, you must consider carefully just what your purpose for the evaluation will be. What should the intended reader—determined in your envisioned plan—expect to gain from this section of your argument? When evaluating the qualifications of the three teachers, for instance, you would make sure that your readers (parents with hearing-impaired children) know that by reading your evaluation, they could make informed judgments of their own about what they require in such teachers, why the methods used to evaluate these teachers are necessary, and just how the evaluative information will prove useful in selecting a school, specific curriculum, specific teachers, and so forth. As with all other arguments, good arguments for quality arise from *real* questions that exist for writers and readers.

In the *planning* processes of their work, thinkers and writers of evaluation approach their arguments in a manner similar to this:

Criterion 1: Teachers of the hearing impaired must be fluent in ASL.

Discussion of Criterion 1: American Sign Language is often the communication choice of hearing-impaired students. Thus, teachers of these students must have the capability to speak with these children in a language common to them both. Many authorities in ASL and its use in education offer definitions of what ASL fluency entails.

Judgment and Evidence: Jameson, Kirkpatrick, and Moreno (perhaps discussed one by one) demonstrate the fluency defined by authorities as shown by documented annual evaluations of their classroom practice, reports of parental satisfaction, and in their college course work.

Criterion 2: Teachers of the hearing impaired must have adequate college education in teaching such students.

Discussion of Criterion 2: Although college education alone may not ensure success in teaching the hearing impaired, education of this type is imperative to understanding the nature of hearing impairment, background in the social and academic challenges for hearing-impaired students, and teaching theories geared specifically toward students with this disability.

Judgment and Evidence: Both Jameson and Moreno have master's degrees in teaching the hearing impaired, and Kirkpatrick majored in special education with a hearing-impairment emphasis and so are adequately prepared by their college course work.

Remember that you must provide ample evidence for how each teacher measures against the criterion. You cannot merely assert that he or she meets or does not meet the criterion as described. Exactly how does each teacher compare? Where did you get your information? Is it accurate? Complete?

The following are actual student arguments that have a primarily evaluative purpose. Keep in mind, however, that when writing his or her paper, each student used other types of developmental strategies as the need arose.

STUDENTS AT WORK: THE PRIMARILY EVALUATIVE PURPOSE

Laurie's Argument

> I will argue about Title IX regulations concerning equality in funding sports programs for concerned parents of student athletes in my local school district in order to demonstrate that our local school district complies very well with Title IX regulations.
>
> *Claim:* Lakeland County School District's compliance with Title IX regulations meets federal guidelines and serves all student athletes equally.
>
> *Developmental Strategies:* Laurie says, "Throughout my argument, I will use the federal Title IX guidelines as evaluative criteria. Though I know the *overall* purpose of my argument is evaluation, I may also use sections of policy (the school district should maintain its Title IX practices) and cause and effect (the current Title IX practices indeed allows [has the effect of] increased numbers of female athletes in school programs while not denying male athletes access to sports programs of their choosing)."

Brent's Argument

> I will compare our college's bookstore with two private bookstores in our community for students at our school in order to evaluate whether or not our college bookstore offers better service (prices, customer satisfaction,

organized layout) than the private stores so that students can understand their options when buying textbooks.

Claim: Two private bookstores in our community—Falcon Books and The Trinity Bookstore—offer better prices, customer satisfaction, and a comfortable shopping experience than our university bookstore does for students purchasing their required texts.

Developmental Strategies: Brent says, "I could see from my claim that my evaluative criteria are prices, customer satisfaction, and comfortable shopping, which I will use to evaluate the three bookstores in my investigation. My primary purpose is evaluation, yet I will include sections of cause and effect (the high prices of texts and the desire for courteous treatment at bookstores often cause students to look around for better options) and problem solving (students dissatisfied with the college's bookstore could solve their textbook dilemmas by seeking the services of the two private bookstores)."

Alejandra's Argument

I will evaluate the "bundling" of communication services offered by Qwest and other companies for small business owners in order to determine if real savings can be made by combining standard phone service, cell phone service, and Internet access with one company.

Claim: Small business owners should bundle their communication services, especially with Qwest Communications, in order to save money and time.

Developmental Strategies: Alejandra says, "Saving money and time for small businesses serve as my evaluative criteria, especially when applied to standard phone service, cell phone service, and Internet access. But I also need to evaluate the cost savings of bundling services and include sections of problem solving (I have concluded that bundling did indeed reduce small business costs [a problem solved] and reduced confusion created by using multiple communications companies for different business communications needs [another problem solved], and I will suggest that small businesses switch to bundling plans (alter their current policies)."

ARGUING SOLUTIONS TO PROBLEMS

> A **PROBLEM-SOLVING ARGUMENT** *analyzes a problem and its potential solutions, and it offers reasons why one or more of those solutions should be pursued.*

When you argue for a solution to a significant problem, you must first make it clear to your audience that a problem worth their consideration exists—again, that a significant question prompts your argument. And the phrase "worth their consideration" is crucial. Truly significant problems affect large groups of people who find such issues affect their work environments, their political views, their economic status, and so forth.

A story (perhaps an "urban legend") has floated around for years about a semi-trailer truck traveling under an overhead bridge. The truck, too tall for the bridge's dimensions, smashed into the structure and became wedged underneath it. The highway department brought in several engineers and charged them with removing the truck in a way that would do the least damage to the bridge. The engineers proposed a number of solutions, none of which seemed feasible to remove the truck efficiently. About this time, a young boy rode up on his bicycle, surveyed the engineers' problem, and suggested that they simply let the air out of the truck's tires to lower it enough to remove it from the bridge.

Like the red-faced engineers, we all seek the most workable solution(s) to our personal, employment, and academic problems—whether we see the solution(s) immediately or not. One purpose of argumentative thinking and writing, then, asks us to discover, focus upon, and evaluate the possible solutions to problems we encounter.

For example, assume you have encountered this problem: Over a period of time, you have attempted to study for exams and write important papers in your college library. However, on many occasions other students have distracted you with their talking, laughing, and shouting across the room. Now, though you do not always expect a library to be quiet as a tomb, you do believe that your tuition and fees entitle you to considerate library use. And recently, you have found the rude noise problem significant enough to yourself (and certainly to others) to write a letter to your college's library board. You must convince the board that a problem really exists by describing and dating the instances of "noise pollution" encountered in the library and then by explaining why you feel the problem should be addressed: the library should be a place for study, not socializing; your hard-earned dollars for college should guarantee the right to a quiet study space; the library seems understaffed to deal with noise problems when they occur. Doing so, you make it clear to the library board that not only does the noise problem exist, but it is one the board members should consider carefully. Once again, you establish context.

The point here is that even in our personal lives, we encounter a need for problem and solution arguments. Most such arguments follow a similar thought/planning process:

- Recognizing that a problem has occurred and identifying just what it entails
- Exploring the solutions to the problem and evaluating the weaknesses (objections to) and strengths of each
- Selecting and defending a solution to the problem

For instance, a solution to the library noise problem might be to hire additional library staff, perhaps work-study students, who could help maintain a quiet atmosphere. Doing so would alleviate some pressure from existing library staff and should—in a friendly manner, you hope—encourage noisy patrons to "put a sock in it." Or perhaps you might suggest that the library staff post warnings against excessive noise in conspicuous places throughout the library. In either case, of course, you must anticipate objections and be prepared to address them. The library board, you think, might argue that either additional personnel or posters would cost money. So you have to be ready: prepare for such an argument by asserting in your letter that the college's student government might be willing to grant the library money for such a good cause, the library budget might be adjusted to accommodate new employees, the number of the new "noise police" would not be excessive and so costs could be limited, and so forth.

Recognizing and Identifying a Problem

No one expects or experiences a problem-free life. It's how we respond to problems and seek solutions to them that helps us mature as thinkers. To do so, we must identify exactly what the problem is, who may be affected by the problem, and why they should be concerned.

For instance, perhaps you work at a local recreation center, and you have noticed a disturbing trend during some of the hockey matches and baseball games sponsored by the center for children under 12. Lately, it seems that the parents of the children have displayed rowdy and discourteous behaviors, including shouting at the referees and umpires, fighting with each other in the bleachers, and criticizing the play of the children themselves. The problem in your mind is that the intended healthy participation in sports has turned into an ugly, competitive confrontation. Those affected, of course, are primarily the children whose parents' unsportsmanlike conduct overshadows the pleasure of playing a game and may place people in harm's way.

Note here that you have recognized and identified the problem. It's not only that the parents at the games have lost their sense of positive sportsmanship (enough of a problem in its own right) but that the possibility of someone's getting hurt is real and unacceptable. And since both children and their parents are involved, you know to whom to address this problem. So, you have carefully identified the problem and who will most benefit from solving it.

ALSO NOTE

IDENTIFYING THE PROBLEM

In India, sonograms for sex determination have been banned because, if a sonogram showed that the fetus was female, the couple would often opt for an abortion. Still, well-connected couples have sonograms done surreptitiously by their medical friends just to determine the fetus's sex, even though that is against the law. The practice of providing a dowry (a substantial gift of money and/or property) to the family into which girls marry often makes for a heavy burden for already struggling families; the birth of a boy is met with great celebration and the mother is congratulated, whereas the mothers of girls frequently are ignored. In some villages, the men outnumber the women by nearly two to one.

To address this issue, the problem will have to be properly identified. Just dealing with the surface issue seldom truly solves a problem. Was the use of sonograms the problem? If so, banning them would have helped.

Often people try to resolve a dilemma by shifting the responsibility or solving a surface problem (see the caution about the law/school solution in the Also Note Box on p. 248) rather than by analyzing the problem carefully and dealing with the tough, underlying problem.

Exercise 3
Collaborative Analysis: Seeing and Identifying Problems

In each of the following scenarios, identify the problem that truly needs solving, identify who is directly affected by it, and discuss why they should be concerned.

1. You suspect that a friend may have an eating disorder.
2. Your business marketing course requires that you give an oral presentation to a local business group, but you are terrified of speaking in public.
3. You are doing poorly in your calculus course and need to speak with the professor; however, the professor intimidates you.
4. You have learned that a group of parents wants to ban three books from a local library, but you believe the books have literary merit.
5. A close friend confides that his father sometimes physically abuses his mother.

Exploring and Evaluating the Possible Solution(s) to a Problem

You may be tempted to believe that a problem has only one solution, and if you are simply smart enough, you will discover it. Or you may fail to solve a problem because you can see only one solution; and since it seems unacceptable, you cannot force yourself to commit to it. Try to set these potentially limiting attitudes aside for a moment. Like the problem of library noise discussed previously, most problems have varying solutions. Allow yourself the flexibility of exploring multiple options so that you do not limit the possibilities too soon and risk overlooking what may be a simple, efficient solution (remember the engineers and the bridge?). Granted, not all solutions will work equally well, but in the beginning stages of your thinking, you should consider them all—and do so at this point without passing judgment about effectiveness, cost, and so on.

248 Chapter 10 *Refining the Purposes for Your Argument*

> ### ALSO NOTE
> ### WHO SHOULD BEST IMPLEMENT YOUR SOLUTION?
>
> One note of caution on problem solutions. Many students attempt to defend solutions that require enacting a new law or adding another program to the public school curriculum. People often desire the "law/school" solution when they simply don't want to change a more local or personal behavior or habit. Perhaps such "solutions" seem the easiest, but if you truly think about the difficulty of passing a law to solve a particular problem or the increased pressure on schools already overloaded with educational and social pressures, such solutions may indeed prove untenable. Be careful to assess whether the new law or school curriculum decision is truly the best alternative.

Let's say that you have approached your boss at the recreation center with the problem of the ill-mannered parents. She assigns you the task of solving the problem before anyone gets hurt. What are your options?

1. Maybe the recreation center could hire security guards for each sporting event.

2. Maybe the recreation center could sponsor forums for parents, during which the problem could be illustrated and discussed.

3. Maybe the recreation center could distribute flyers that list unacceptable behaviors by spectators. Parents would be required to sign the flyer indicating that they have read it and accept its terms. Failure to do so would disallow their child's participation in the center's sporting events.

4. Maybe the recreation center could adopt a policy stating that participating teams will be disqualified from their games or matches if parents display unacceptable behaviors.

Perhaps you can think of other solutions as well, but the idea is that you lay out as many ideas as you can, hoping that by doing so, you will discover one or more that may indeed work. Keep in mind that rarely is there a "perfect solution," even though people look for one all the time.

Evaluating potential solutions requires careful thought about why you eventually select one (or more) and reject the others. You can ask yourself a set of common questions about each solution as a test of its effectiveness:

1. Is this solution too costly in light of current budget constraints?

2. Is this solution unfeasible in that it violates a law, accepted policy, or value?

3. Are there sufficient resources (space, equipment, personnel) to allow this solution to work?

4. Will the target reader accept the solution? What changes does the proposed solution require in terms of the reader's values, current practices, job security, and so forth?

5. Is there sufficient time to implement the solution?

Do Problem/Solution Arguments Allow for Fairness?

Like all arguments, those focused upon finding solutions to problems may require that you concede points to the opposing viewpoint. In these types of arguments, concessions will most likely be those that acknowledge that other possible solutions to a problem—other than the one you are defending—may have merit. Linea, a student, whose problem/solution strategies can be found later in this chapter, argued in her paper that airline flight attendants should be trained in self-defense to help solve problems with potential terrorists on airliners. But she willingly acknowledged the many other solutions that have been proposed to combat this problem. She admitted that some have had at least some success. Such concessions in no way weakened Linea's argument. Indeed, the opposite is true. Readers found that she had studied the problem fairly and fully; she just did not believe the other solutions to preventing terrorist actions went far enough to protect flight crews and passengers.

Exercise 4
Collaborative Analysis: Brainstorming Solutions

In small groups, see what solutions you might discover for the scenarios listed in Exercise 3. Make no judgments about anyone's contributions; just see how many possibilities there may be.

Selecting and Defending a Solution to a Problem

Once you have considered a good number of potential solutions to a problem, you must decide which seems the most reasonable and defend it. Doing so may require that you discuss with your readers what other options are available but eliminate them (perhaps one by one) because they are ineffective or inefficient. Then, of course, you spell out the reasons for your selected solution, offering ample evidence and examples that you hope will persuade your readers that out of all the possible solutions, this one is best.

STUDENTS AT WORK: THE PRIMARILY PROBLEM/SOLUTION PURPOSE

Linea's Argument

I will write about training flight attendants in self-defense techniques for the managers of major airlines in order to argue that self-defense training would provide another safeguard against terrorists' actions on airliners.

Claim: Major airlines should provide self-defense training for all flight attendants to help prevent terrorist actions on airliners.

Developmental Strategies: Linea says, "Overall, I will propose a solution to a problem I have encountered; however, my argument will also contain sections of evaluation (I will concede that other solutions to potential terrorist threats on airliners have been tried, but demonstrate—evaluate—that the other solutions have had too little effect) and a section on policy (I will argue that the policy of neglecting self-defense training for flight attendants must be changed)."

Harlan's Argument

I will write about "drag race" car acceleration (when a driver "floors" the accelerator pedal when a traffic light turns green or when the driver leaves a stop sign) for drivers of low-gas-mileage vehicles in order to argue that eliminating the "drag race" acceleration would greatly improve personal gas mileage and help save gasoline overall.

Claim: Drivers of all vehicles, but especially those of low-mileage vehicles, should discontinue rapid acceleration from stop lights and stop signs to increase their gas mileage and decrease air pollution.

Developmental Strategies: Harlan says, "My primary purpose is to show that eliminating drag race acceleration would help solve some of drivers' gas mileage woes etc., but I will also use sections of my argument to demonstrate cause-and-effect issues (improper acceleration uses more gasoline and, directly or indirectly, causes increased consumption and pollution)."

Martine's Argument

I will write about the dangers of online dating for college women in order to argue that this type of dating may lead to serious physical, emotional, and financial troubles.

Claim: College women should avoid online dating services because of real possibilities that their physical, emotional, and financial health could be seriously compromised by unscrupulous "dates."

Developmental Strategies: Martine says, "I will focus on the problems created by online dating as my primary purpose, but I will probably also overlap my discussion of the problems—physical, emotional, financial—by discussing various factors in some young women's lives that may cause them to see online dating as a viable option in their social lives."

ARGUING CAUSE(S) AND EFFECT(S)

> A **CAUSE AND EFFECT ARGUMENT** *usually focuses on either the causes or effects of a particular phenomenon in order to draw attention to complicated, unclear, or controversial causal relationships.*

Some issues you will encounter require that you examine and argue the cause(s) and/or effect(s) of those issues. How or why did some effect come into being? What are the possible results of particular causes? Like other thinking purposes, cause-and-effect reasoning ranges from the common ("My car's engine froze because I neglected to keep sufficient oil in it") to the more complicated ("Spanking a child will lead to the child's acceptance of violence as a means to solve problems"). Your first task in such arguments is to decide if you will focus on the cause(s) of an effect or on the effect(s) created by a particular cause.

As an example, think again of the problem of ill-mannered parents at the recreation center where you work. You might choose to compose an argument focusing on the causes of the parents' behaviors (they have become too competitive over the years, the structure of the children's leagues encourages a "winning at all costs" attitude, parents have lost their perspective on the value of sportsmanship such athletic events were originally meant to foster, and so forth). Or you may focus on the effects (children learn that winning is the only purpose of sporting activity, children adopt more violent behaviors toward opponents, children learn that disagreements should be resolved not by reasonable discussions but by outbursts of shouting and fighting, and so forth). Your professor may agree that attempting to concentrate on both causes and effects in one paper often creates an unwieldy and unfocused argument.

Keep in mind, too, what we have encouraged throughout this chapter: You may find that some intertwining of purposes may make the most effective paper. Should you argue that parents' poor behaviors ultimately harm children (an effect that is also a problem), your paper might then argue that a solution must be found before real harm is done. In truth, both causes and effects can often be viewed as problems in need of solutions, and those solutions must be evaluated for their effectiveness. First, make sure you know exactly what it is you want to accomplish (a clear Argument Concept will help you clarify this for yourself as well as your reader) and then seek the best tools to fulfill the argument you have in mind.

Cause-and-effect reasoning generally occurs in two manners. One way to consider causes and effects might be labeled "linear" causation, in which an effect is shown to be the result of a series of causes linked in a line. Consider an effect (your car runs out of gas on the way to class) in this way:

A hurricane strikes the U.S. southern coast where many oil refineries exist.

Those oil refineries are shut down for several days.

Local gas stations significantly raise the price of gasoline.

You only put five gallons of gas in your car two days ago (because of the high prices) but drove many miles running errands and going to work.

Your car runs out of gas on the way to class.

The ultimate effect (running out of gas) is obvious. What you now must consider the true cause of your running out of gas. Should you claim that the hurricane striking the U.S. southern coast caused you to run out of gas, you would be arguing on tenuous grounds. The hurricane only has a remote causative value. The real, or most defensible and immediate, cause of your car running out of gas is your failure to put in more than five gallons two days ago and then driving many miles. After all, the linear causes of your gas shortage could be taken back, if you wished, as far as your own birth (if you hadn't been born, you would not have run short of gas driving to class!). Surely you would not blame a lack of gasoline on your own birth. The point is that you must seek substantial and likely causes for effects, and the more remote those causes, the weaker your cause-and-effect argument becomes.

Of course, you face the same reasoning hurdles with remote effects:

Your car runs out of gas on the way to class.

You miss the exam review for your upcoming geography exam.

You take the geography exam and earn only a D.

The D on the exam lowers your GPA.

Because of your lower GPA, the college places you on academic probation.

In this case, claiming that your running out of gas created the effect of your being placed on academic probation is at best absurd. The effect of academic probation is too remote from the cause cited. The most immediate effect of running out of gas of course, is the missing of the exam review.

The second form of cause-and-effect reasoning might be termed "coordinate" causation (keep in mind that the following principles can also be applied to coordinate effects), in which you cite a number of necessary causes, all of which work together to create the effect. Lacking just one of the coordinate causes will disallow the effect. The causes of the American Civil War illustrate coordinate causation. Many historians believe that several causes *working together* led to this terrible conflict: the issue of states' rights, the differing social and economic bases of the North and South, the centralization of the federal government, and the issue of slavery. A common theory asserts that the war may not have happened should one or more of the given causes not have occurred. A diagram of coordinate causation and coordinate effects might help:

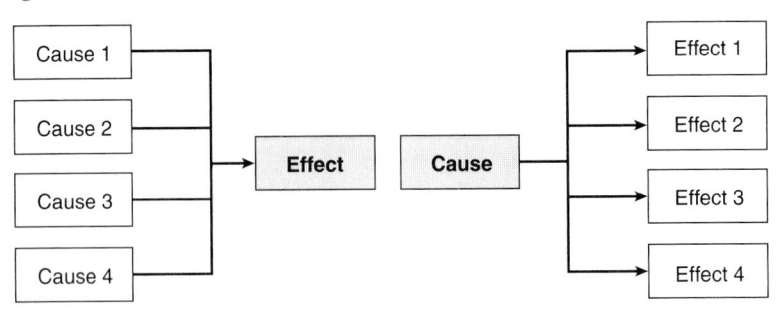

```
  Cause 1 ─┐                              ┌─→ Effect 1
  Cause 2 ─┤                              ├─→ Effect 2
           ├─→ Effect      Cause ─────────┤
  Cause 3 ─┤                              ├─→ Effect 3
  Cause 4 ─┘                              └─→ Effect 4
```

      Coordinate Causes   Coordinate Effects

If your issue (or a section of your paper) requires cause and effect reasoning, be sure that you offer ample evidence for the cause(s) you assert (if this is your focus) or for the effect(s) you claim. Readers expect you to demonstrate a reasonable connection between a cause and an effect. Thus, you must avoid the logical fallacies associated with cause-and-effect thinking. The **fallacy of false cause** occurs when the cause you claim for an effect has no direct or meaningful relation to the effect. For instance, if you speak with your aunt on Sunday and then lose your favorite jacket on Monday—and blame your aunt for your loss—you have committed the false cause fallacy. Such thinking is relatively common because no one likes to take blame when blame can be shifted elsewhere. A more reasonable thought process would show that you lost the jacket due to leaving it in the cafeteria, letting an irresponsible roommate borrow it, and the like.

> *The* **FALSE CAUSE FALLACY** *is a logical problem that occurs when the cause the writer claims for an effect has no direct or meaningful relation to the effect.*

Another form of false cause is called the **post hoc ergo propter hoc** ("after this, therefore because of this") fallacy. You commit this error by assuming that simply because one event precedes another (all causes, of course, come before their effects) that the first event *must* have necessarily caused the second but without proof. But think about this. Because a black cat crosses your path before you fall down some stairs, does this mean the cat *caused* your bad luck? After all, didn't other events take place between the cat's crossing your path and your crashing down the stairs, such as you ate a sandwich, passed by a yellow house, and watched an episode of *Survivor*? Why not blame those events? Again, you must be certain that a distinct, logical connection exists between an effect and your claimed cause, and not simply *assume* that some previous event caused a later event to occur.

> *A* **POST HOC ERGO PROPTER HOC FALLACY** *is a problem in logic caused by assuming without proof that simply because one event precedes another, the first event must have necessarily caused the second.*

Do Cause-and-Effect Arguments Allow for Fairness?

Arguments for cause(s) and effect(s) often demand that you offer concessions to differing viewpoints. To do so, you will acknowledge that while you are defending a particular cause or effect for an issue, other people believe that other causes or effects may be at work. Or others may assert, especially in coordinate causation, that not all of the causes were necessary to create the effect. For example, some historians have recently downplayed the importance of the slavery issue in causing the Civil War. They believe the war would have taken place even without the moral underpinnings of the antislavery movement at the time. A fair argument about the motives for the Civil War, then, would grant that the historians might have a point. As always, though, such concessions indicate more about your thorough study of the issue and willingness to be fair than they indicate some potential weakness in your reasoning.

Exercise 5
Individual Analysis and Practice: Searching for Causes and Effects

Write responses to the following cause-and-effect scenarios. Can you discover more than one cause or effect for the given situation?

1. Offer potential, yet reasonable, causes for the following effects:

    A. The jobless rate in your city has gone up.
    B. You did not get a job you applied for in spite of the fact that you have the proper qualifications.
    C. Your research paper in anthropology received only a C.
    D. Your college recently adopted a "no alcohol on campus" policy.
    E. Some college students believe they are "entitled" to good grades.
    F. A family member recently quit smoking.
    G. Your state decreased its funding for cultural arts programs.

2. Now, consider the issues in section 1 to be causes. What effect(s) may accrue as a result of each cause?

ALSO NOTE
POST HOC FALLACY IN THE MOVIES

Michael Moore, the controversial director of such documentaries as *Roger and Me* and *Bowling for Columbine*, was criticized soundly for some of the cause-and-effect relationships he tried to establish in his 2004 movie, *Fahrenheit 9/11*. Among other charges he leveled at the Bush administration, he tried to persuade viewers that the Bush family and administration were collaborating inappropriately with the ruling family of Saudi Arabia. His evidence? A long series of video clips and photos of both George H.W. Bush and George W. Bush walking and talking with members of the Saudi family in both casual and state-sanctioned situations.

Moore's implication was that since all of these meetings and conversations had taken place in the past (cause), there must now be some conspiratorial relationship between the families that influence oil prices and supplies (effect).

Presidents often meet with heads of state. Powerful families in a number of countries interact. What kind of evidence would be necessary to make the causal link Moore insinuates?

Exercise 6
Collaborative Analysis: A Thoughtful Investigation of Cause(s)

One day in your sociology course, the professor has you read a 2000 *Washington Post* article by Michael Fletcher, and you are disturbed by some of the data. Fletcher's article reveals apparent inequities (noted by the Human Rights Commission) in the way different racial groups are treated in the court system for nonviolent drug-related crimes. You read that in the state of Virginia, for example, 82 percent of convictions are of African-American citizens, but only 20 percent of the Virginia population is black. In Maryland, according to Fletcher's research, 90 percent of those sent to prison on drug charges are black, but they make up 27 percent of the Maryland population. Nationally, 62 percent of those imprisoned for drug use in state institutions are black, but the national population is 12 percent black. Also, Fletcher says that Department of Health and Human Services statistics for 1991–1993 show that "about five times as many whites had used cocaine than African Americans."*

Is this disparity changing or is it still the same? Can you immediately determine the cause of this apparent inequity? Is it discrimination? Are more African Americans actually guilty of this crime? Could it have to do with the fact that sentencing structures differ for powder and crack forms of cocaine? Could it have to do with poverty and the ability of defendants to afford a powerful defense? Might there be overlapping causes? Can your class discover any answers?

STUDENTS AT WORK: THE PRIMARILY CAUSE/EFFECT PURPOSE

Kimberly's Argument

> I will write about the government's "No Child Left Behind Act" for our state's legislators in order to argue that the NCLB Act ignores four real causes of a poor student achievement: low parental income, the difficulties faced by ESL students, high ethnic diversity in some schools, and a lack of students' exposure to what is tested in some schools.
>
> *Claim:* The federal government's "No Child Left Behind Act" is intended to ensure that all students have equal opportunities to succeed in school; however, the act fails to address four prominent causes of poor student achievement.
>
> *Developmental Strategies:* Kimberly says, "I plan to point out four coordinate causes for the effect of poor student performance. I believe my issue has a primarily cause-and-effect focus, yet I will also include sections of problem solving (the fact that the NCLB ignored the real causes of poor student achievement that leads to long-term problems in many students' academic and work lives) and of policy (the government needs to rethink

---

*Fletcher, M. (June 8, 2000). "More Whites Use Drugs, More Black Imprisoned." *Washington Post*. http://www.manpinc.org/drugnews/v00.n771.a03.html.

its policies about student testing) and evaluation (the government needs to explore and evaluate alternative means of student testing)."

Ephraim's Argument

I will write about "over scheduling" children under 12 for the parents of these children in order to argue that having nearly every hour of a child's life scheduled for participation in a sport, musical activity, and so forth causes the child to miss many of the important and fun activities of just "being a kid."

Claim: In an attempt to provide a nurturing atmosphere for their children, many parents overschedule their children's time. Doing so may prevent these children from the social and emotional activities important to a healthy childhood.

Developmental Strategies: Ephraim says, "I will concede that many activities that parents schedule for their children—music lessons, karate lessons, museum tours, and so on—have positive effects. However, my primary cause-and-effect purpose is to show that such activities can be overdone, leading children to potentially negative effects: they may become overly competitive or may miss the benefits of using their imaginations. I will also include sections of problem solving (the effects of overscheduling are potential problems) and suggest that parents reevaluate their 'policies' of scheduling a child's every moment of free time."

Cassie's Argument

I will write about the coach for our school's women's basketball team for our school's athletic director to argue that the coach's lack of experience, poor practice scheduling, and harsh reaction to violations of team rules caused the team's low morale and poor record this year. (I will name the coach in my introduction and so will not do so in my claim.)

Claim: The low morale and poor team record displayed by our school's women's basketball team this year were direct results of the coach's actions.

Developmental Strategies: Cassie says, "I recognize the overall cause-and-effect purpose of my argument, but I will also include sections of problem solving (the low morale and poor team record may prove problematic for the following year's team and for recruitment of future players) and evaluation (this year's coach did not compare favorably to coaches at other schools in terms of the other coaches' experience, practice scheduling, and reaction to athletes' rules violations)."

ARGUING TO MAINTAIN OR CHANGE A POLICY

> A **POLICY ARGUMENT** *provides reasons that certain rules or practices should be kept or changed.*

Another common purpose in argument is whether to maintain or to change a policy. We see such argument everywhere: about governmental practices and programs, about work-related practices, about school-related practices, about home-related practices—even questions such as how a local children's theater program goes about its business.

Arguments about policy are those concerning how or why something is done, and whether a new policy would create better conditions for people, whether an existing policy works well in spite of questions of its efficiency, or if a current policy should be maintained with modifications. A professor, for instance, may have a policy in which students are kicked out of a class if their cell phone rings during the class. The students, though, wonder if the policy is fair. They might argue that sometimes they simply forget to turn off their cell phones before class or that on occasion they must keep the phone on because of potential family emergencies and the like. However, when two students poll their classmates, they learn that most other students support the policy because of the disruptions cell phones create in class. Thus, the students overall agree that the policy should be maintained.

Of course, the students might also argue that the cell phone policy could be made more workable if the professor would agree that, upon notification from a student with a potential emergency situation, that student could be allowed to keep his or her phone on, in "silent mode," during class. Such modifications—compromises agreed to by all parties concerned—often work well in policy arguments.

Because of their usefulness and importance within the argumentative context, arguments about policy employ all the other purposes of argument discussed in this chapter. Perhaps a group of parents dislikes a local school's

---

ARGUMENT IN ACTION   Policy Argument in the Political World

One of the biggest battles in the U.S. Senate in 2005 was an argument over policy: the right to filibuster. A filibuster is the act of holding the floor in the Senate by talking on and on—not necessarily about the issue at hand—to forestall a vote.

Policy battles such as this take place in the business world, in schools, in churches, in nonprofit organizations—and in families.

Just as in the Senate, however, writers making policy arguments should make sure they have not just set their feet as a power play, or that they are not arguing for a certain policy only because of what they stand to gain. Neither should they argue to keep a policy just because it has always been around. A change in policy should come from a legitimate reappraisal and it should stand up to the challenges presented by hypothetical future cases.

policy about book selection for the library. The parents want the policy changed. Now, to effect such change, the parents might argue that the current policy is a problem in need of solution because the current policy allows the library to purchase books that the parents believe may have a negative effect on students. But the parents know they cannot merely say, "Change the policy or else!" They have to offer alternatives—solutions—and, of course, these possible solutions must be evaluated for their effectiveness. As you can see, then, arguments about policy often use other argumentative purposes to be most persuasive.

Do Policy Arguments Allow for Fairness?

As we have maintained throughout this book, you will likely have to offer concessions to perspectives different from your own. Although you believe your reasons to maintain or change a policy are strong, a fair argument of this type acknowledges that no policy is perfect. In the argument for maintaining the cell phone ban, the students may concede that cell phones do indeed allow students to maintain contact with family members, for example, in the event of family emergencies. Again, such a concession does not weaken the argument to maintain the cell phone ban policy. It just allows multiple viewpoints among reasonable people who recognize that arguments of all types produce differing perspectives.

Claims of policy that you defend will nearly always contain the words "should" or "should not" as in these examples:

- Women should be allowed to participate in military combat.
- Olympic athletes should face mandatory drug screening.
- American wheat farmers should receive government subsidies to protect their profits in the likelihood of increasing imported wheat products.
- Bookstores should not be required to release customer information to the police even during a police investigation of a customer.
- Girls under the age of 16 should not participate in beauty pageants.

The use of "should" or "should not" specifies your stance on an issue. Of course, readers may not agree with your stance, but they know exactly which side of the issue you intend to defend in your argument.

When you claim that something "should" or "should not" be the case, your readers will expect well-considered reasons and ample specific evidence to support your reasons. In arguments about policy, you must take extreme care not to give the impression that only because you (or others) believe or have always believed your stance on an issue that that alone serves as the basis for your claim. Readers will truly desire to see how and why you have come to the conclusions you have. As an example, consider the claim "Girls under the age of 16 should not participate in beauty pageants." (Note that in this policy argument, there is a hint of cause-and-effect reasoning, another example of how the argumentative purposes often interact to form a persuasive whole.) What reasons might we offer to support this claim?

- Beauty pageants promote the idea that a young girl's most important characteristic is her appearance. It is unethical to promote the idea that to be successful, females must appear "sexy." Young girls may not be prepared for such behavior.
- Beauty pageants foster an atmosphere of competition that many young girls are not mature enough to handle.
- To compete in a beauty pageant, a young girl must spend hours in preparation: how to walk and smile for judges, how to put on makeup and style her hair, how to select "proper" clothing. So much time dedicated to a vain and commercial pursuit would be better spent in more "child-like" activities, such as riding a bicycle, reading, playing with other children, or doing crafts.
- Parents of young girls in beauty pageants may be living vicariously through their daughters' competitions, hoping to fulfill some missing need in their own lives.

Now before any reader will suddenly adopt your perspective on girls in beauty pageants, that reader must see your evidence. You never want a reader to say, "Oh, come on! You just don't like beauty pageants and have a personal agenda against them." So, what types of evidence must you provide?

- Testimony from former beauty pageant participants, parents, psychologists, teachers and so forth (evidence from varied authorities is invaluable here) that an emphasis on appearance over other personal characteristics is indeed the focus of beauty pageants and that such emphasis has harmful effects on a young girl's healthy emotional and mental development.
- Evidence that winning, not having fun, is the main point of a beauty pageant and that a "winning above all else" attitude may lead to later self-esteem and self-image problems for young girls.
- Specific evidence from participants and others about the number of hours spent in dress and makeup preparation as well as classes in singing, dancing, and elocution. Evidence that these hours do take away time for more traditional children's activities in which children learn valuable social and emotional skills.
- Testimony and other evidence from former beauty pageant parents, psychologists, and perhaps even beauty pageant promoters, that the parents of young female competitors encourage their daughters' participation more to fill some emotional need of their own rather than to help their daughters mature in a healthy manner.

You can probably tell that any argument lacking these types of evidence would fall flat, perhaps causing a backlash in your reader who might think that your motives come more from some unfortunate experience you or a family member had in a beauty pageant than from some real and defensible evidence of the harm of such pageants. So, in arguments about policy, we cannot emphasize enough the value of carefully considered reasons and specific, reliable evidence to make your point.

260 Chapter 10 *Refining the Purposes for Your Argument*

Here, too, you will probably need to concede at least one point to those who find beauty pageants valuable for young girls. For example, you might acknowledge that some girls benefit from the poise and confidence gained through competition. And it's quite likely this is the case. Over time, some participants (particularly those fortunate to win often) learn lessons in dealing with others, in handling pressure, and in finding success. You might rebut such points, however, with your evidence that not all young girls find fame and fortune in the pageants and that successive losses in the competitions may cause more harm than good.

Exercise 7
Individual Analysis and Practice: Analyzing an Argument of Policy

In her article, "Tort Reform at Gunpoint," *Newsweek* writer Anna Quindlen argues that pending legislation (governmental policy) in the U.S. Congress concerning lawsuits against the gun manufacturing and selling industries is improper. Read the article and write out your answers to the following questions:

1. What Argument Concept do you believe Quindlen had in mind?
2. What exactly is the pending legislation that Quindlen opposes?
3. What reasons does she give for her opposition?
4. Can you cite examples of specific evidence that Quindlen offers in support of her claim?
5. What does Quindlen concede in her argument? Does it add to the argument's sense of fairness?
6. Besides focusing upon an impending policy decision, what other purposes (as discussed in this chapter) does Quindlen use? Why?

Tort Reform At Gunpoint
Anna Quindlen

1   Under cover of darkness—or a relentless media focus on the Iraqi war, which amounted to the same thing—the House of Representatives recently passed a bill that made a single industry largely immune from lawsuits.

2   That industry is the one that makes and sells guns.

3   If a hospital leaves a sponge in your midsection, you can sue. If a car dealer sells you a clunker it hadn't properly inspected, you can sue. Of course, it may be that your suit will get nowhere. Witness the jurists who threw out the action by parents who argued that fast food made their kids fat, and who did it faster than you can say, "Do you want fries with that?"

4   But judges and juries and responsible litigants will be out of the loop and out of luck if what the National Rifle Association likes to call the "Reckless Lawsuit Preemption Legislation" passes the Senate. The people whose

loved ones were allegedly shot by the D.C. snipers can forget about holding responsible the gun shop that was the chief enabler. Even though both the sniper suspects were legally banned from buying guns. Even though they had a Bushmaster rifle that came from a store in Tacoma, Wash. Even though federal agents couldn't find required sales records for the rifle. Even though the store is run in such a haphazard fashion that an audit can't account for more than 200 guns that were supposed to be on the premises.

5   "Frivolous lawsuits" is one reason Sen. Max Baucus of Montana gave for his support of what I like to call the Cover Your Butt or They'll Target It in the Next Election legislation. Is that really how easily senators can dismiss the widow of the bus driver shot in the back during the sniper spree, who was flabbergasted to discover that the gun industry may get special protections that no other business enjoys?

6   Like most Americans, that poor woman had no idea whom she was really dealing with. Not only does the NRA make things difficult for any elected official who doesn't go along with it; it does the same for gun manufacturers who don't toe the line. Take the case of Smith & Wesson, which made a deal with the government to adopt safety measures in exchange for an end to some lawsuits. Those measures were scarcely radical: hidden serial numbers, a trigger lock, and a plan for better smart-gun technology, which allows a weapon to be fired only by authorized users. These are precisely the sort of efforts that might have led to fewer lawsuits down the road.

7   That's not how the all-or-nothing leadership of the NRA saw this treasonous display of compromise. In the aftermath of the agreement, Smith & Wesson lost an estimated 40 percent of its business. Dealers refused to stock its guns. The National Shooting Sports Foundation attacked the company as "foreign-owned." Under new ownership this year, Smith & Wesson prostrated itself at the feet of the real chief executive of the industry; its new chairman's first action was to glad-hand at the NRA convention.

8   The interesting thing about the organization's dominance is that it not only doesn't represent the views of many gun owners, it doesn't represent the views of some of its own members. It's easy to find NRA members who say they have no problem with gun licensing or registration, or the strict policing of negligent dealers. Lots of them welcome a smart gun. It would mean a child couldn't accidentally fire or a teenager commit suicide with a weapon kept for protection; a thief would wind up with a useless hunk of metal instead of a lethal weapon.

9   But the sensible attitudes of the average gun owner are lost in the relentless far-right positions of the NRA. What Congress gets instead is the rhetoric of the most successful extremist pressure group in America. And what Congress is now prepared to pass is its most extremist legislation ever.

10   Let's say that the members of the House commemorated the anniversary of the Columbine massacre by giving negligent gun dealers a free pass not out of fear of the NRA, but out of purer motives. Let's say this is really about fighting back against a ridiculously litigious culture. Ought tort reform to begin with firearms? Ought the gun industry,

of all businesses, be the only one to be exempted wholesale from exercising reasonable care to prevent injury to others?

11   The man who taught my kids everything they need to know about gun safety taught them a one-word mantra: redundancy. The gun is not put away loaded. But even if the gun is not loaded, you put on a trigger lock. And even if you put on a trigger lock, you put the gun in the gun safe. Layers of protection between them and an accident, them and a mistake, them and injury or death.

12   There used to be redundancy in the system, too. Good manufacturers. Good dealers. If not, sanctions. Even lawsuits. If the NRA manages to intimidate the Senate into making its industry the only one in the nation with blanket protection from most lawsuits, what will be the premium in building a safer gun, in taking care when selling one? Not much. And the message from Congress will be clear: it's the NRA's country. The rest of us just live in it.

Exercise 8
Individual Analysis and Practice: Envisioning the Policy Argument

Consider the following policy issues. Write out a stance, or claim, that you might defend if you selected the issue for a paper. Then, list your reasons and the potential evidence you would provide for the stance you take. What might you reasonably have to concede to a different viewpoint?

1. Moving from gasoline-powered automobiles to hydrogen-powered vehicles.
2. Offering monetary compensation to American descendants of slaves.
3. Parking fees in college parking lots.
4. Ensuring privacy on the Internet.
5. Requiring college students to complete volunteer work as a graduation requirement.
6. Providing scholarships for first-generation college students.

STUDENTS AT WORK: THE PRIMARILY POLICY PURPOSE

Adam's Argument

I will argue about the policy against working overtime for my restaurant's manager in order to convince him that overtime pay is essential to some college students' budgets and allows the manager the freedom of not having to hire additional personnel.

Claim: The manager of La Casa Restaurant does not allow his wait staff and cooks to work overtime hours. He should reverse this policy.

Developmental Strategies: Adam says, "I will explain the current policy against overtime hours at the restaurant and name the manager in my introduction. My primary purpose in this argument, of course, is to argue for a policy change. However, I expect to include sections on problem solving (the mostly college-student wait staff and cooks could earn more money [a solution to their ever-present financial shortages] and the manager could solve his problem of having to hire additional staff) and evaluation (I might compare my manager's policy to that of other similar restaurants to show that when the other restaurants allowed their personnel to work overtime, the workers were happier [more money, after all] and more loyal to the business)."

Lyndell's Argument

I will argue in support of our school's "no alcohol on campus" policy for our college's administrators in order to demonstrate that the policy helps immature students avoid alcohol-related problems.

Claim: Because some students lack the discipline to avoid alcohol-related problems, our college should maintain its "no alcohol on campus" policy.

Developmental Strategies: Lyndell says, "My primary purpose in to argue in support of a policy, but I may need to include sections on problem solving (such as discussing various alcohol-related problems some students face and arguing that the current policy against alcohol on campus helps resolve the problems) and cause-and-effect (the immaturity of some students managing the relative "freedom" of being in college and away from home, and these students' lack of control when consuming alcohol and its effects on their academic achievement and health)."

Renae's Argument

I will argue to alter our school's policy against taking final exams early for the dean of Arts and Sciences in order to show that outside circumstances such as summer jobs, family crises, and scheduled medical procedures should be allowed as exceptions to the policy.

Claim: To account for individual students' needs, our college should reconsider its policy against taking final examinations before the regularly scheduled times.

Developmental Strategies: Renae says, "I intend to argue against an existing policy by defending my claim with sections of evaluation (some students' reasons for taking exams early are legitimate in light of family, health, and financial matters), and cause-and-effect (the current policy against early exams affects students' abilities to be with family when needed or to secure satisfactory employment, especially during the summer)—all of which may create problems for students in their ability to continue their college careers."

DISCOVERING YOUR OWN ARGUMENTS: REFINING YOUR ENVISIONED PLAN

Look again at the envisioned plan you developed in Chapter 9. What purposes for argument might each section express? Look back at the parts of this chapter dedicated to those purposes and include a note to yourself in specific sections of your plan that demand a certain type of organization. Remind yourself what things and organization you may want to think about as you draft that section. For instance, you may make a note similar to this: "I need to remember in this section to acknowledge the potential difficulty of instituting my proposed policy change so that the reader will know I have thought about this and have some ideas about how to overcome the challenges."

REFLECTIONS ON THE CHAPTER

We cannot emphasize enough the importance of considering the purpose(s) of each section when writing argument. The better your understanding of exactly what you want to accomplish, then the better your thought processes in finding relevant evidence, defending your claim, and persuading your reader that your argument has merit. Remember, as well, that many—if not most—arguments will have overlapping purposes. As you conceive and plan your arguments, take the time to consider whether you need, in the subsections of your paper, purposes beyond your primary one to defend your claim. Can you identify what these supportive purposes might be and how they may function within your overall goal? Your job is to think carefully about exactly what your focus, reader, and purpose require and permit you to do. Even professional writers quiver at the thought of a reader finishing a piece and wondering, "Why did I spend time reading that?"

CHAPTER

11

Drafting the Sections of Your Argument— Illustration, Detail, and Outside Sources

You have created a working plan for your draft. You have refined the purposes of its sections and thought about what those purposes require of you. Now what? Since you now know that argument is much more than just repeating what you've read, how should you proceed to craft the sections of your argument?

This chapter explains some tools at your disposal to reflect your argument picture at least somewhat accurately in your reader's mind—tools for *developing* the plan you have made into draft form. Remember, there are so many possible interpretations your reader can cast on your material that you have the burden of developing your sections comprehensively so that the reader will not go wrong.

Not to worry. You have some very powerful methods to use. As you begin your draft (or revise and improve it if you have already started), using these techniques will help you as you and the reader negotiate the meaning of your text.

TERMS AND CONCEPTS TO WATCH FOR

- Illustration
- ID tags
- Informal documentation or "in-text" documentation
- Formal documentation
- Authority of a source
- Blind quotation

QUESTIONS TO GUIDE YOUR READING

- What is the difference between hypothetical, generic, specific, and extended examples?
- What can examples accomplish in your argument?
- How can you use your own experience in an argument?
- What is the difference between the authority and identity of a source?
- How can you combine the ideas of others with your own?

THE NEED FOR SUPPORT—GETTING YOUR READER TO "BUY IN"

In the 1990s, the Nike corporation began a very expensive and slick advertising campaign—Just Do It! By most measures, the campaign was extremely effective. The Center for Applied Research (CFAR) explains that "Just Do It!" was a very clearly targeted production. The intent was to challenge Reebok, the shoe company that had been the world leader in the 1980s. And the campaign "did it." Nike "was able to increase its share of the domestic sport-shoe business from 18 percent to 43 percent, from $877 million in worldwide sales to $9.2 billion in the ten years between 1988 and 1998. . . . The success of the campaign is that much more remarkable when one considers that an estimated 80 percent of the sneakers sold in the U.S. are never used for the activities for which they have been designed."*

Successful advertising campaigns like this do not just happen by accident. Much thought and market research goes into such things as the purchasing power of demographic groups and growing or dwindling trends. One of Nike's gambles in the campaign was that people, in the CFAR's words, "would accept sneakers as fashion statements." Nike capitalized on the growing jogging and fitness focus in that gamble. The campaign was also developed to appeal not only to traditional buyers of high-tech athletic shoes (18- to 40-year-old males), but to the expanding market of female and teenage consumers. These market considerations went into determining

---

*Center for Applied Research. "Mini-case Study: Nike's 'Just Do It' Advertising Campaign." 17 June 2004. http://www.cfar.com.

the "reader" and "purpose" for their advertising argument. Their "focus" was to associate the Nike swoosh logo with grit, passion, and determination—qualities that new sneaker purchasers would aspire to, or at least imagine in themselves.

Once the campaign was envisioned, the real work began: How to get this good image into the viewer's/reader's head. You no doubt have seen the answer. Nike did not just purchase billboards and air time to print "Just Do It!" in black and white next to the swoosh. Neither did they simply tell consumers, "We think you should *just do it* and buy our sneakers." What followed their clear envisioning of their argument was a long and vivid series of successful sports star images (and then, after that, sports star wannabees) showing the sneaker-buying public what sweaty grit, determination, and passion are, and graphically demonstrating that one could best achieve those character traits in Nike shoes. Nike used humor in the later versions: Tour de France winner Lance Armstrong boxed; Olympic runner Marion Jones did gymnastics; and baseball ace Randy Johnson bowled, further advancing the "anything is possible" image. Fortunately for Nike, most people were not smart or savvy enough to see the faulty reasoning in this appeal, so they bought the idea of a clear causal link between wearing Nikes and becoming a noble sports hero. Millions of advertising dollars and many strong visual images later, Nike can now simply print "Just Do It!" in small letters on a screen and those powerful and effective images float back in your memory. Their argument has been exceptionally effective.

Visual Rhetoric. . .
DOONESBURY/NIKE

Alternative responses to the Nike ad campaign: Although this successful business tale serves as a good example of the power of illustration, not everyone became a convinced sneaker buyer in response to the ads. As a matter of fact, there is now considerable reaction against the campaign (called Don't Do It!) calling for a boycott of Nike products because they reportedly have been made in "sweatshops" in foreign countries, sometimes by youth workers. In response to the outcry, Nike now claims to have an "over 18 policy" for hiring foreign workers. This recent cartoon, however, is a strong visual argument that the controversy is not yet resolved.

THE POWER OF ILLUSTRATION

> **ILLUSTRATION** *is the process of providing images for a reader to demonstrate your points vividly and memorably.*

Now that you have envisioned the framework for an argument to which you are hopefully as committed as Nike was, you are lucky to have the same means of developing a powerful and lingering message in your reader's head: **illustration**. These illustrations provide images that portray the experience of people, yourself or others, involved in the issue at the center of your argument.

Imagine, for a moment, you are trying to argue that four-wheelers should not be allowed on state park land. You will also explain the potential damage, give reasons why land should be preserved, and maybe suggest a specific policy change, but one of the most powerful tools you have is illustration. In one section of your essay, you can describe in detail "Lost Forest Road" that used to be a sheltered walk among dense blackberry bushes and other undergrowth beneath a thick canopy of cedars. You could describe the ruts and mangled vegetation that now exist, including the many spots where four-wheelers have ventured off the trail through the trees, breaking new saplings and creating erosion of thin and fragile soil cover. You can finish your example with a description of the creek bed that used to be the scene of a soft trickle of clear water that was audible but barely visible from the trail, showing your readers how it has now become muddy, the banks crushed into the former rocky bed, by the invasion of four-wheelers in search of a cool splash. That image of a specific, real instance of degradation will go much farther than just saying "Don't Do It!"

Types of Examples

As you try to develop and support the sections of your argument, think which points might best be illustrated, and what kind of illustration will be most appropriate for your audience and purpose. Several different types of examples offer different levels of support, and they are listed with brief descriptions in the Also Note box on p. 269. *Hypothetical examples*, for instance, are made-up examples to show an imaginary case that helps make the writer's point. (You can read an extreme case of this kind of example in Unit 3 of the additional readings, Part IV of this text, in "The Singer Solution to World Poverty.") You can often recognize hypothetical examples by words included in them such as *might, may, if, could*, and *would*. You see visual hypothetical examples every day on television: a hypothetical homemaker is thrilled when the faked grass stains on her son's baseball pants come out in the wash; a hypothetical husband is nervous as he enters the office of a pretend doctor to discuss the possibility of taking Viagra (and he appears happy when he goes home); a sleek, stylish two-door vehicle races along at mach speed on hypothetical, computer-generated curves created to "demonstrate" the handling and flashy nature of the car. Remember, however, that the

> ### ALSO NOTE
> ### THE TYPES OF ILLUSTRATION
>
> Illustration, as you have learned, is the practice of showing examples to create a mental picture of what the writer is trying to communicate. Illustration is effective because it is vivid, memorable, and concrete evidence for your point. There are four main types of illustration you can use to support your argument:
>
> - Hypothetical Examples are a writer's guess at what an appropriate example might be. They are made up to suggest what the writer's point would look like in action. Words such as *might, may, if, could,* and *would* are some of the words typically used in hypotheticals.
> - Generic Examples are "collected" examples in which many experiences are condensed into one. These generalizations are tipped off by such words as *always, whenever, seldom, every time,* and *never*.
> - Specific Examples are distinct, real instances to which you can refer for hard evidence that your claim is true. A specific example is convincing because it includes such things as *times and places, details of actions, exact quotations or statements, accurate numbers*, and so on.
> - Extended Examples are lengthy, almost storylike examples giving the total picture of one incident. Such examples are convincing because of the level of detail and the extent to which a reader can identify with narrative explanations.

fine print below those illustrations usually tells you not to try this at home! Those statements remind you that the examples *are* hypothetical, not real.

Some occasions in an argument that you might be considering may call for a hypothetical example. For instance, if you are suggesting a change in the sick leave policy for your place of work, you cannot give a real example of how the new policy might work out because, of course, it isn't in place yet. You could, however, give a hypothetical example of a case that would be dealt with more equitably under the new policy, taking the time to give the details of exactly how the policy might apply in that instance. On the other hand, if you are trying to argue that the war in Afghanistan was worth the effort, you don't want to say, "Probably most of the Al-Qaeda fighters trained in Afghanistan were eliminated by this offensive." "Probably" just isn't good enough in that argument. The key to using hypothetical examples effectively is to use them when a reader will understand and accept that you are just suggesting an image, not claiming the truth of a situation. Also, your reading of arguments will benefit from an assessment of the types of examples you are being offered and the power they should rightly have to convince.

Generic examples are another frequently used means of illustration. Generic examples have no individual identity; they are "collected" examples in which many experiences are condensed into one. When you read the words *always, whenever,*

270 Chapter 11 *Drafting the Sections of Your Argument*

seldom, every time, or *never* in an example, the author is most likely offering you a generic example. Therese, for example, decided to offer the following critique of the studio classes (classes in which students are working at their art) in her program.

STUDENTS AT WORK

Therese's First Argument

> Whenever I took a painting class, the instructor would come in for the beginning of the period and suggest something we might work on, but then he would either spend the rest of the time working on a project of his own, talking with a colleague, or doing research for a new project of his own. He hardly ever offered criticism as we were working, comments we might have been able to use to refine or remodel our paintings, but he waited until we were finished to evaluate our work.

This type of example that compresses experience into an overall interpretation is valuable for just that, to give a general impression. However, think critically about this kind of example. What is the writer depending upon for acceptance of this interpretation of the quality of instruction for studio courses in the fine arts program? The reader has to believe that the student's inductive process, her accumulation of evidence and her drawing a conclusion from that evidence, was sound. The reader has to depend on the fact that every instructor operated in the same way, and that evaluating these studio courses based on the student's judgment is valid. That kind of trust is more than a writer should expect, and more than a reader should give. If a generic example is in fact valid, there should be many instances of evidence from which that generic interpretation is derived. The way to use a generic example effectively, then, is to follow it (or precede it) with specifics so that a reader can rightfully trust the writer's judgment. Also, it may be necessary to qualify a generic example to make it accurate and not an exaggeration. The following revision of the student's criticism should be much more effective.

STUDENTS AT WORK

Therese's Revision

<u>Often</u> when I took a painting class, the instructor would come in for the beginning of the period and suggest something we might work on, but then he would either spend the rest of the time working on a project of his own, talking with a colleague, or doing research for a new project of his own. <u>Introduction to Oil Painting 201, for example</u>, was a class of beginning painters most often in their first semester. <u>Few students knew the principles of setting up a still life model from which to paint and none had taken basic design, yet we were given the</u>	A qualifier—in the earlier draft, Therese said "Whenever..." meaning always. The specific instance to

advice to "Paint something in the room you find interesting." The instructor would walk around the room occasionally looking at our canvasses but offering no comments. This particular instructor, as were most of the instructors in undergraduate painting classes, was a graduate assistant who had work of his own to focus on. He had an easel set up in an adjoining room and spent at least 75% of the class periods working on his own painting. This experience in 201 was not unique. Instructors for 202, 203, and 204 were graduate assistants also who seemed preoccupied with their work and research, not with their teaching.

follow the generalization. Details to support the judgment about this instructor. Information to show the writer is not relying on one aberrant experience.

One problem consistent in all studio classes—painting, sculpting, jewelry making, and figure drawing—appears to be so consistent as to be a department-wide policy that should be reexamined. The instructors in all these classes adopt a policy of reserving any criticism until the end of the class when projects are evaluated in a group setting. While the idea of allowing a student free reign to express herself seems a good idea, the evaluations (and therefore the grades) do not match that ideal. In Painting 204, for instance, one of my fellow students was having a particularly difficult time getting the layers of paint in his landscape to appear transparent and thin, not muddy and thick. He asked for the instructor's help with this problem, and was told "Just work with the paint" and was given no technical suggestions. He was frustrated and ended up repainting that part of the painting several times, each time making it more muddy rather than less. When our projects were evaluated during the last session, the instructor told him much of the painting had promise, but that his grade was unsatisfactory because he had not learned to avoid "dirtying up" his glazes. Either the evaluation criteria should match the teaching philosophy, or instructor should give more practical advice during the process rather than after the fact.

A concession that there may be some reason for the policy.

Detail to support the assertion about this practice.

This use of *specific examples*—exact, real cases of the point in question—to back up the generic interpretation is effective. To recognize specific examples, notice the use of detail such as names, accurate numbers, places, times, and direct quotations. Your writing teachers have probably always stressed that you should have "fully developed" sentences and paragraphs. "Fully developed" means detailed, well-supported, and well-explained. Your professors don't want you to develop something "fully" just so they will have more to read. The reason good detail is important, as we stressed in earlier chapters, is whenever readers can go wrong, they will. This is true of reader comprehension of examples as well. If you want a reader to glean a certain thing from an example, you must give those details to assure your desired interpretation. Too often a writer mentions an example in passing but fails to give adequate detail and explanation, assuming that the reader will take the case at face value. Remember our discussion of critical reading, and that your reader, if he or she is any good at all, will be analyzing your argument as carefully as we asked you to examine the arguments of others. A good reader takes nothing at face value. As in Therese's art class situation, specific examples and detail take less pressure off the writer's judgment. In the student's first version, she says, "He hardly ever offered criticism as we were working. . . ." The reader must decide, based solely on her opinion, whether her assertion is accurate or not. This is the "Trust Me" school of arguing, and readers are right to reject conclusions based on assertions. Instead of simply giving the bottom-line generalization (or the inductive conclusion) as the student does in the first draft, using specific examples as in the improved paragraphs provides enough representative evidence that the reader can draw the same conclusion as the writer. That evidence is what will be convincing, not the "trust me" statement of a generic example.

Occasionally, you may read, or have the need to use, an *extended example* as support for an argument. An extended example is a lengthy and detailed single example of a case in point. Writers often use such detailed "stories" very effectively to win over readers; stories help a reader identify with a situation, and the detail is usually compelling evidence. A classic example of this method is the essay in Chapter 6, "A Hanging" by George Orwell (p. 146). Orwell's essay is about a point much larger than this one case of capital punishment, but the stirring details of contrast between the casual manner of the observers of the hanging (even that of a stray dog), and the horror of the individual's experience make for a memorable image that is hard to shake. Sometimes a writer has a personal experience or has observed some incident that is so moving, aggravating, enlightening, heartwarming, or in some other way powerful, that he or she rests an entire argument on that one extended example.

ALSO NOTE
DEVELOPMENT VS. LENGTH

Snoopy, the canine hero of Charles Schultz's cartoon strip *Peanuts*, often has cliché school experiences. In one strip, he turns in his essay to the teacher. It has one sentence: "It was a very dark night." He gets it back with the cryptic note from his teacher, "Underdeveloped."

He scribbles and scribbles, and then he resubmits the revised essay: "It was a very, very, very, very dark night."

Students often wonder why teachers require a minimum length for an essay. It is not so that they can read versions of Snoopy's revised essay. Instead, the length requirement often encourages students to give adequate, specific, and convincing evidence rather than just the "bottom line."

Such arguments can be extremely compelling, but they are not without their risks. On what does this kind of argument depend? Again, your study of inductive reasoning can help you answer. Such an argument implies that the extended example used is representative of all cases, and the conclusion drawn from this one example is sound for all other similar examples. A reasonable response from a reader to a single, narrative example is, "Well, Bob's case was devastating, yes. But that was just Bob." The strength of this kind of argument depends upon the degree to which the writer has been able to build trust with the reader, the extent to which the writer presents the example as legitimately representative, and the degree to which the writer has qualified his or her claim to fit the range and scope of this single example. Arguments based on extended examples can be strengthened by using other means of support to contextualize and reinforce the example.

A lengthy example of one school's struggle for survival in a depressed area of East St. Louis opens Jonathan Kozol's fine book-length argument, *Savage Inequalities*. That story is followed by excruciating detail from school budgets, interviews with school board members, and discussion with parents. Detailed comparisons are made between the management of East St. Louis schools and other wealthier districts. Kozol's argument has a clear Argument Concept: he intends *to argue about* schools in poverty-stricken areas *for* those who believe the behavior of people in those areas is to blame for the predicament of their schools *in order to* convince them that money does matter, that the schools are chronically underfunded and that such prejudice against the poor is often politically acceptable. To force a reluctant reader to attend to this problem, he begins his argument with a vivid picture the reader can't turn away from, a picture of children going to school in rooms with sewage dripping down the walls and in rooms where the rain comes in through holes in the ceiling. He asks his reader if blame can reasonably be put on students for not wanting to go to school in that environment, and he asks what sense a reader should make of a society that offers such vastly unequal opportunities to different groups. Only after he has reeled the reader in does he begin the other more scholarly sections of his argument.

The Impact of Extended Example From Savage Inequalities

Jonathan Kozol

1   The problems of the streets in urban areas, as teachers often note, frequently spill over into public schools. In the public schools of East St. Louis this is literally the case.

2   "Martin Luther King Junior High School," notes the *Post-Dispatch* in a story published in the early spring of 1989, "was evacuated Friday afternoon after sewage flowed into the kitchen.... The kitchen was closed and students were sent home." On Monday, the paper continues, "East St. Louis Senior High School was awash in sewage for the second time this year." The school had to be shut because of "fumes and backed-up toilets." Sewage flowed into the basement, through the

floor, then up into the kitchen and the students' bathrooms. The backup, we read, "occurred in the food preparation areas."

3   School is resumed the following morning at the high school, but a few days later the overflow recurs. This time the entire system is affected, since the meals distributed to every student in the city are prepared in the two schools that have been flooded.

* * * * *

[While visiting Clark Junior High, Kozol asks a question about what the "I Have a Dream" speech of Martin Luther King means to students, and he gets the following response from a student.]

4   Christopher approaches me at the end of class. The room is too hot. His skin looks warm and his black hair is damp. "Write this down. You asked a question about Martin Luther King. I'm going to say something. All that stuff about 'the dream' means nothing to the kids I know in East St. Louis. So far as they're concerned, he died in vain. He was famous and he lived and gave his speeches and he died and now he's gone. But we're still here. Don't tell students in this school about 'the dream.' Go and look into a toilet here if you would like to know what life is like for students in this city."

5   Before I leave, I do as Christopher asked and enter a boy's bathroom. Four of the six toilets do not work. The toilet stalls, which are eaten away by red and brown corrosion, have no doors. The toilets have no seats. One has a rotted wooden stump. There are no paper towels and no soap. Near the door there is a loop of wire with an empty toilet-paper roll.

6   "This," says Sister Julia, "is the best school that we have in East St. Louis."

Illustration is one of the most influential of the tools you have when you argue. Understanding the kind of examples you are planning to use and the weight of evidence they will carry is important. To use this tool in the most advantageous way, consider the following guidelines as you select examples to support the various sections of your argument:

- Use *hypothetical examples* when you want to suggest what might occur, or what is the most probable case, not when you are trying to "prove" a point.
- Use *generic examples* to establish an overview or general interpretation, but not as hard evidence for your claim.
- Use *specific examples* either to back up a hypothetical or generic example, or whenever you need vivid and memorable "proof" of a point. Remember, the best part of a source you have read may be the specific examples you can use, of course carefully giving credit to the source for those examples. Also, explaining a research source and the results that were achieved instead of just saying "research shows . . ." employs the strength of specifics.
- Use an *extended example* when you can demonstrate that it is representative of the issue you are developing and when its power will compel the reader to relate positively or negatively to the example, or compel the reader to examine your argument further. Be cautious about making an argument, however, that rests on one example.

Exercise 1
Individual Analysis and Practice: Generating Examples for Your Argument

1. Review a draft you are developing. Determine which sections of your argument will benefit most from a greater use of illustration. Make a list of examples you have observed or read that will help you support those sections. As you do so, think about the impact of these examples on the reader.

   - What purpose will each accomplish, and will the reader see the same things in those examples as you do?
   - What important details will you have to include to ensure the reader interprets the examples in the way you want?
   - Review the guidelines provided for the use of examples to evaluate the potential of this material as support for your argument.
   - Discuss your decision about detail use with a classmate or with your instructor in a conference. Do they share your enthusiasm for your intended detail use?

2. Revise a section of the draft you reviewed to include one of your best illustrative ideas.

Examples from Personal Experience

The previous discussion was primarily focused on the kinds of examples you have observed, incidents you have seen, heard, or read. Students often discount a potentially effective source of examples, however: themselves. One of the reasons students are sometimes hesitant to include their own experience in their arguments is because that old (and incorrect) saying echoes in their heads, "Don't ever use 'I' in your paper." That advice is as appropriate as saying, "Don't ever take painkillers." Of course there is an appropriate time and situation for taking a painkilling drug. Certainly, using it too often and in the wrong circumstances can make you incoherent and self-absorbed. So can the overuse of "I." There is, for example, no reason to continually say, "I believe that . . . ," "In my opinion, . . . ," "I think that . . . ," etc. When you are writing an argument, the ideas are assumed to be yours unless you have credited others (see Chapter 12 on assigning credit for the ideas of others.) If the old adage keeps you from overusing such phrases, it has done some good. But don't interpret the saying as meaning you should not include your own *reasoned* perspectives and your own *pertinent* experience in an argument.

That said, we offer a stern guideline for including your own experience in an argument: *Use your own experience to enhance your argument, but not as its sole basis.* We bet that you know several friends or relatives who have a somewhat distorted world view based on their experiences. Do you have a friend, for example, who will never again eat seafood because she had a bad shrimp once? Do you have a dad that will never buy a Ford (or Chevy, or Dodge) truck again because the one he bought in 1972 was a dog? Do you have an Uncle Delwood who refuses to vote because he knew a crooked politician back in Cincinnati? In Chapter 4, we said, "It is human nature that what we learn first, we believe as truth. Everything else that comes to us is measured against that standard." When you use *only* your own experience, you run the risk of making a blind argument, or an argument from at least very limited vision. You may believe deeply in a certain subject simply because that is all you have experienced. Though that basis may be enough for you (we hope not, however), such narrow vision will not be enough for your reader. If you apply rigorous standards of evidence to the personal experience you intend to use as support for your argument and it measures up, then examples from your own life can add credibility to your argument. You can be recognized not as Uncle Delwood, but as a thoughtful and valued expert because of your experience. We offer you some guidelines to think about when considering the use of personal experience:

- Use personal experience as a way to enhance your credibility and/or to help connect your reader to the personal side of your issue.
- Rethink your experience in light of what you have now read or learned about your issue. Does your original interpretation of your experience bear reevaluation?
- Make sure your experience is typical (see Chapter 2, p. 52).
- Contextualize your experience in the larger issue. How can you show your reader that your experience is representative?
- Feel free to use "I" when talking about your own experience. You need not use "I" to identify your opinions, as your written argument is acknowledged to be your personal expression. Give credit (as discussed in the next section of this chapter) to others for their opinions, and everything else is considered yours.

Exercise 2
Individual Analysis and Practice: Generating Personal Examples for Your Argument

1. Review the draft you developed further in Exercise 1. Determine if any sections of your argument will benefit from the use of examples from personal experience. Make a list of experiences you have had that will help you support those sections. As you do so, think about the impact of these examples on the reader.

    - What purpose will each accomplish, and will the reader see the same things in those examples as you do?
    - What important details will you have to include to ensure the reader interprets the examples in the way you want?
    - Review the guidelines provided for the use of personal experience to evaluate the potential of these examples as support for your argument.

2. You may have thought of good personal examples to add dimension to your draft, or you may have a draft in which personal experience is inappropriate. If personal experience will accomplish a goal in your plan, revise a section to include such experience.

INTEGRATING OUTSIDE SOURCE MATERIAL WITH YOUR ARGUMENT

You may certainly want to add examples you have read during your research process to your draft. Your source material may also offer statistics, discussion of studies, reasoned arguments both for and against your claim, and beautifully worded passages that you believe will be compelling to your reader. The question now is how best to insert this material into your argument. Three options exist for integrating sources: (1) using summaries, (2) using paraphrases, and (3) using direct quotations. In a lengthy argument, you might use each of these methods, and you might use them in combination. Deciding which to use is a reader-oriented decision, for a reader's needs. Think about what level of detail the reader will need to be convinced of the support and choose the type of source use that best fits that need. The following sections illustrate the differences among these three ways of sharing source material with your reader and demonstrate how to incorporate this material into your text.

Using Summary, Paraphrase, and Direct Quotation

Following is an excerpt from Harold Kushner's book, *Living a Life that Matters (2001)*. Kushner talks about bringing integrity to one's everyday life, and how difficult that is in today's world. A student writer, Stephen, wanted to use this information in an argument about personal decision making in the business world, and you will read Stephen's summary of this excerpt later in the chapter (p. 278).

> We human beings are such complicated creatures. We have so many needs, so many emotional hungers, and they often come into conflict with each other. Our impulse to help needy people or to support medical research conflicts with our desire to have the money to buy all the things we are attracted to. My commitment to doing the right thing impels me to want to apologize to people I have offended, but my desire to protect my image and nourish my sense of righteousness persuades me that the problem is their hypersensitivity, not my behavior. What happens when our need to think of ourselves as good people collides with our need to be recognized as important? Is it possible to do both? How often do we find ourselves betraying our values, violating our consciences, in our struggle to have an impact on the world? Political candidates compromise their values to raise funds and gain votes. Salesmen exaggerate the virtues of their wares. Doctors, lawyers, and businessmen neglect their families in the pursuit of professional and financial success. Often we don't like what we find ourselves doing (although it is remarkable how easily we get used to it after the first few times), but we tell ourselves we have no choice. That is the kind of world we live in, and that is the price we have to pay for claiming our space in it.

This may well be the central dilemma in the lives of many of us. We want—indeed, we need—to think of ourselves as good people, though from time to time we find ourselves doing things that make us doubt our goodness. We dream of leaving the world a better place for our having passed through it, though we often wonder whether, in our quest for significance, we litter the world with our mistakes more than we bless it with our accomplishments. Our souls are split, part of us reaching for goodness, part of us chasing fame and fortune and doing questionable things along the way, as we realize that those two paths may diverge sharply.

Writing an Accurate and Adequate Summary

Using a summary can accomplish several different purposes. You may believe an author's idea is so central to your argument that you want to convey it in total. You may want to establish some background information, as Robert Behnke does in "About Trout" when he summarizes the work of two researchers, Sneddon and Rose (Chapter 8, pp. 187–188), or you may think that summarizing a specific example you have read will illustrate a situation clearly for your reader. When you summarize, you include all of the major points of a passage but in a much condensed version. You *do not* use the words of the author, but you explain the passage in your own words. Students often plagiarize inadvertently when summarizing, and this practice is important to avoid. *Picking up strings of words from the original, even though you change the words around them, is still plagiarism.* A summary may include a correctly punctuated direct quotation from the original if that quotation is particularly powerfully stated. Following is Stephen's summary of the Kushner excerpt.

STUDENTS AT WORK

Stephen's Summary

Kushner explains that because humans are so complex, we have many conflicting desires. We want to be successful, but that desire is sometimes counter to our desire to care about other people. Many of us, as we strive for successful professional careers, do not pay attention to our values. Devotion to family, for instance, may take second place to our drive to become the best doctor, politician, or lawyer. Kushner argues that we talk ourselves into certain behaviors: "Often we don't like what we find ourselves doing (although it is remarkable how easily we get used to it after the first few times), but we tell ourselves we have no choice." Unfortunately, we end up tearing ourselves apart because we cannot find a way to make our desire to be good mesh with our desire to be important.

Notice that in a good summary, the writer uses "**ID tags**," frequent mention of the original author's name to clarify that the summary is continuing, and that the writer is still talking about source material, not giving his or her own ideas. Tags in this summary are "Kushner explains . . ." and "Kushner argues. . . ." *Summarizing does not alleviate the responsibility of giving credit for information or ideas.*

> ### ALSO NOTE
> **SUMMARY AND REVERSING THE ENVISIONING PROCESS**
> In Chapter 6 you practiced using the Argument Concept idea to look for the organizing concept and intention of writers of many different kinds of communication, explicit and implied. We referred to it as "reversing the Argument Concept process." This process, shown on p. 224 as applied to the Jamie Fellner article, can be an equally productive tool for reading more critically and analytically, particularly as you approach the task of summarizing your source material. If you are reading an essay, for example, you can, after thinking through the writer's Argument Concept, reverse the envisioning process as a way of clarifying the writer's logic for yourself. This practice is particularly helpful when reading long and complex articles, but it is also helps avoiding being "bamboozled" by advertising, political speeches, whining friends, and salespersons. What is the arguer doing to try to convince you?

> **ID TAGS** *are phrases in your text that identify the source of ideas and information from outside sources. These tags help the reader, particularly in a summary, sort out your words from the words of your source.*

Creating a Paraphrase

When paraphrasing, a writer is using the same level of detail as in the original, but using a sentence or sentences of his own rather than those of the original authors. Paraphrases are usually approximately the same length as the original, but ideally even the structure of the sentence is different than the original. The reason to use a paraphrase is that all the information from the source is necessary, but it is not extraordinarily stated and your text will read more smoothly if you do not chop it up with a quotation. Examine Kushner's sentence, an example of a poorly constructed paraphrase, and Stephen's more successful paraphrase that follows.

> *Original:* Often we don't like what we find ourselves doing (although it is remarkable how easily we get used to it after the first few times), but we tell ourselves we have no choice.
>
> *Poor Paraphrase:* Often people don't enjoy what they find themselves doing (even though they can get used to it), but they convince themselves they have to do it. (*Note that this is not competent recasting of the sentence, but just word substitution; the structure is identical to the original.*)

STUDENTS AT WORK

Stephen's Better Paraphrase

> Sometimes people do things they are not proud of because they delude themselves into thinking they *have* to; after compromising themselves like this several times, it gets easier.

Be sure to remember that a paraphrase needs to be attributed to the original author just like any other kind of borrowing. Just because you have changed all the words, you cannot claim the idea as your own.

Using Direct Quotations

Quoting a source is maybe the easiest method of using outside material, but *it should be used more sparingly*. You should primarily use paraphrasing and summarizing when you integrate source material. First of all, your argument will not read smoothly if it is broken up frequently with the words and styles of other writers. Second, an argument should articulate your thinking and your interpretation of what you have read; it should not just repeat the ideas and words of others. Use a direct quotation only when you believe it is so powerfully stated that those exact words will add credibility to your argument. (Unfortunately, we often see quotations used in student arguments because the writer doesn't understand the sentence fully enough to write a good paraphrase. That's a lousy reason to quote!)

When quoting, almost always avoid using what we call a "blind quotation," a quotation dropped into your text without any introduction, identification of the author, or interpretation. Too often, students are unaware of how to integrate a direct quotation, and their text might read something like this:

> It's not that young people don't want to do the right thing, but that they are torn between two alternatives. "Our souls are split, part of us reaching for goodness, part of us chasing fame and fortune and doing questionable things along the way, as we realize that those two paths may diverge sharply."

> A **BLIND QUOTATION** *is a string of words or sentences taken directly from a source and inserted in a writer's text with no acknowledgement of source or without any expressed connection to the text.*

Instead, use some kind of tag (indicated below in bold) to identify the quotation appropriately and provide the context for it:

> It's not that young people don't want to do the right thing, but that they are torn between two alternatives. **Harold Kushner, author of the**

popular book *When Bad Things Happen to Good People*, describes this difficulty of maintaining integrity while trying to be important in the world: "Our souls are split, part of us reaching for goodness, part of us chasing fame and fortune and doing questionable things along the way, as we realize that those two paths may diverge sharply."

> **INFORMAL DOCUMENTATION** *(used for the most part in Part I of this text), also called "in-text" documentation, refers to the kind of source identification found in popular, general interest sources such as magazines and newspapers.*

> **FORMAL DOCUMENTATION** *(appropriate for research-based writing emphasized in Part II of this text) refers to the academic practice of documenting papers according to an established style sheet.*

When using source material in an argument, your responsibility is to identify the original author (or artist, speaker, musician, etc.). This chapter focuses on the skills involved in integrating this material smoothly and ethically. In many of the arguments you have read and will read—those in magazines, newspapers, business transactions, many of the samples in Part I of this book, and so forth—you will see only informal or *in-text documentation* of a source. In-text documentation notes the source of the information for the reader in the flow of the argument. Formal academic documentation, the subject of Chapter 12, includes the additional practice of providing a list of sources cited in the argument. Contrary to what a student might think, quality documentation is truly more difficult than merely adding a list of sources at the paper's end and requires attention as you work through your drafts. The responsibility to a reader is great. Just as you should be alert to the source of a newspaper's quotation about the battle at last week's city council meeting, your reader should be alert to your sources, and you should be cognizant of his or her needs. Therefore, we offer some detailed advice about how to meet this need.

ALSO NOTE
YOUR WRITING PROCESS: TRACKING SOURCES AS YOU DRAFT

In this text, we have reserved a discussion of formal academic documentation until Chapter 12. This was an intentional choice because it often seems a student becomes obsessed with that process and focuses

(continued)

on documenting outside source material as the core of an argument or research writing course.*

If an argument is unsound, however, no amount of proper documentation can save it—and therefore our decision about the priority of documentation.

That said, learning the academic skill of documentation is an important objective. Our approach is to ask you to focus first on all of the rhetorical, structural, and logical issues that will make or break your argument. In this chapter, we focus on the *development* and *integration* of source material. Once you have integrated valid and productive information from outside sources into your argument in a reader-oriented way (see the next section, "Guidelines for Integrating Source Material"), then the documenting of these sources takes on its appropriate weight.

Here is a practical suggestion to help you accomplish all of these tasks: If you are to document your paper using MLA or APA style (or some other accepted academic style), then *as you write*, you may want to have a system of noting the source of the material, so that you can go back later and complete the proper formal documentation. It is easy, for instance, to just put the author's name and the page number of the information in parentheses when you incorporate source material:

> Kushner (p. 14) describes the difficulty of maintaining integrity while trying to be important in the world: "Our souls are split, part of us reaching for goodness, part of us chasing fame and fortune and doing questionable things along the way, as we realize that those two paths may diverge sharply."

Why do this instead of documenting formally as you go? Your paper will morph many times before it is finished. You may put in sources, take out sources, and change the nature of what you use from a source (using a paraphrase instead of a direct quotation, for instance). If you are spending all of your time and focus on documenting rather than making your argument coherent, reader-friendly, and logically sound, you are emphasizing the wrong task at the drafting stage of your process. Additionally, if you have invested heavily in documenting in a draft, you will probably be hesitant to make necessary changes.

Chapters 12 (documentation) and 13 (revision and editing) are the last chapters in the text because they discuss activities that most often, and most effectively, are undertaken after you have created what you think is a structurally sound, well-supported draft.

*Some instructors may want students to discuss and practice documentation skills at an early stage to make sure they are aware of the requirements and methods as they find their sources. If so, working through Chapter 12 earlier is a good and reasonable practice. Remember the recursive nature of the writing process: there is no lock-step order to the activities necessary for producing a well-conceived, organized, developed, and documented argument.

GUIDELINES FOR INTEGRATING SOURCE MATERIAL

Any time you integrate source material, there are three features to keep in mind:

1. *Identify the authority that lends credibility to the source material.* Think about what provides authority, not just identity. For instance, let's say you wanted to use some information from the American Heart Association on the newest treatment for post–heart attack patients. You found the information in an article in *Newsweek*, written by a staff writer, Alexis Carson. What is the authority behind the information? Is it Alexis Carson? Will her name add any credibility to the information? Should you say, "According to an article in *Newsweek*, . . ."? The authority behind this information is the American Heart Association, a long-standing and respected national institution that studies all angles on heart disease and is up to date on the most recent innovations. If instead you say "According to Alexis Carson . . ." you still will not provide authority for the information. You may have satisfied the formal need to avoid plagiarism, but your reader's desire for authoritative evidence remains unfulfilled since he or she hasn't the foggiest idea who Alexis Carson might be. On the other hand, identifying the information as coming from the American Heart Association takes care of both of your obligations—to scholarship and to your reader.

    Each time you want to use a source, you need to go through this same thought process to determine how best not just to identify your source, but to give authority to it. Remember your responsibility to your reader's needs. Also, remember that the source of *all* direct quotations, summaries, or paraphrases must be identified or you have plagiarized.

> The **AUTHORITY OF A SOURCE** *refers to the information about the origin of the material that will provide credibility to the reader when used in your internal documentation. Be thoughtful not to confuse the* authority *with the identity—the "location"—of the source, which you will also need for the external bibliographical citations.*

2. *Enclose any exact words of the source in quotations marks and include enough summary of the source to be both fair to the original author and clear to the reader about the tone, intent, and scope of the original source.* Don't just use a "sound bite," but represent your source material fully and accurately. Two of the frequent problems of integrating source material are taking things out of context and failing to give enough of the information for a reader to be convinced.

3. *Interpret, evaluate, and connect the source material to the point you are making.* Don't use a **blind quotation** that expects the reader to guess how the information is related to the purpose of your paragraph or to the overall

claim of your argument. Connections that seem obvious to you because you read the material will not be so clear to a reader who it trying to piece them together from a brief summary or quotation.

Exercise 3
Collaborative Analysis: Identifying the Elements of Source Integration

Following is an excerpt from a student's paper on "profiling." Marie argued that young black males are often profiled—selected for special attention—when they are in retail shops. The material the student uses in this passage comes from an article by Clarence Page, a black parent and a well-known columnist for the *Chicago Tribune*, about a real instance of profiling. A reader would not appreciate the power of the reference by just reading a short, disconnected quotation. Analyze how Marie has paid close attention to the three guidelines for integration by answering the following questions:

1. Where does the writer identify the authority behind this information (there may be several places)? Has the writer selected the appropriate elements to include in this identification? The quotation from Chris Rock was included in the Clarence Page article. Is Rock's authority identified adequately and appropriately? The writer chooses to identify Page as a black parent. How does that identity add to a reader's understanding?

2. Where has the writer used summarized information from the article and where has she used direct quotations? Were those appropriate choices in this case?

3. Where do you see the interpretation of the information; where is the writer explaining the impact of this information on her argument?

> The discrimination many young black men faced earlier in our history is perhaps even more insidious today, and the suspicion is directed toward younger men in very nonthreatening environments such as retail establishments in the form of "profiling," the practice of singling out persons of a certain identifiable group for special attention or investigation. Clarence Page of the *Chicago Tribune* tells of an incident when an 18-year-old black man and his friend were accosted in an Eddie Bauer store. The man was wearing an Eddie Bauer jacket and was spotted by a security guard who immediately assumed the jacket was being shoplifted. The guard confronted the young man and his friend and demanded he take off the jacket. The suspected shoplifter was later able to produce a receipt for the jacket, but before he was allowed to provide that evidence, "a second guard ordered the two young men to a corner of the store and threatened to 'lock them up' if they moved." Page, one of many black parents who have to address such stereotyping with their sons, says the two young men were "guilty" of a typical American crime: "They were SWB—shopping while black." Others have been guilty of DWB—driving while black, or even HATWB—hailing a taxi while black. In these situations, the young black male is "born to be a suspect," according to black comic Chris Rock.

Adolescent males like these boys in the Eddie Bauer incident are still frequently prejudged on the basis of their race.

Exercise 4
Collaborative Analysis: Analyzing Source Integration in Popular Media

1. Pick up any newspaper or magazine that you have available at home or at work. Browse through the articles and locate several different places where "outside" source material is integrated into the articles. You will find examples everywhere—the sports section, editorials, feature articles, music reviews, and so forth.

2. Bring at least three samples to class.

3. In groups of three, analyze each other's examples of source integration, identifying the three parts of good source integration. Find one good example and one example that is not so strong to share with the class.

Exercise 5
Collaborative Analysis: Examining the Development and Source Use of an Argument

Read the following argument regarding the effect of computer use (addiction?) on the behaviors of college students. After reading, discuss the questions following the essay about the types of examples used, the apparent validity of sources, and the integration of outside source material.

Surfing's Up and Grades Are Down
Rene Sanchez

1   A new campus support group called "Caught in the Web" is being formed at the University of Maryland to counsel students spending too much time on computers. At the Massachusetts Institute of Technology, students unable to break their addiction to playing computer games on campus terminals have new help. At their request, the university will deny them access whenever they try to sign on.

2   Faculty studying the freshman dropout rate at Alfred University in New York have just found that nearly half the students who quit last semester had been logging marathon, late-night time on the Internet. Nationwide, as colleges charge into the digital age with high-tech libraries, wired dormitories, and computerized course work, faculty and campus counselors are discovering a troubling side effect: A growing number of students are letting computers overwhelm their lives. It is hardly a crisis on any campus—yet. Some college officials say it is merely a fad, and not nearly as harmful as other bad habits students often fall prey to on campuses—such as binge drinking of alcohol. But concern over the issue is spreading.

3   Some universities now are imposing limits on the time students spend each day, or each week, on campus computers. Other colleges are debating whether to monitor the time students spend on computer games and chat rooms, then program a warning to appear on their screens when it gets excessive. Some college counselors are creating workshops on the subject and planning to include them in freshman orientation programs. Others already are urging students not to plunge into on-line relationships with strangers.

4   "More and more students are losing themselves in this," says Judith Klavans, the director of Columbia University's Center for Research on Information Access. "It's very accessible on campuses, and students have time on their hands. We're seeing some of them really drift off into this world at the expense of practically everything else."

5   Campus officials say that comunicating on the Internet or roaming the huge universe of information on the World Wide Web holds an especially powerful lure for many college students because it takes them into a vast new realm of learning and research, usually at no cost. But for students having trouble establishing social ties at large universities, or who are on their own, unsupervised, and facing adult pressures for the first time, it also poses an array of new risks.

6   At the University of California's Berkeley campus, counselors say they are dealing with a small but increasing number of student cases linked to excessive computer use. Some students, they say, are putting too much emphasis on electronic relationships, are neglecting course work, and, in a few instances, are even being swindled out of money by e-mail strangers they have come to trust. "There can be a real sense of isolation on a large campus, and for young students or new students, this seems like a safe, easy way to form relationships," says Jeff Prince, the associate director of counseling at UC-Berkeley. "But some go overboard. It becomes their only way to connect to the world. One of the things we're really working on now is helping students balance how many social needs they try to have fulfilled by computers."

7   Linda Tipton, a counselor at the University of Maryland, which limits students to forty hours a week on campus terminals, says she began noticing some of the same problems arise last year in individual and group therapy sessions. Some of them, she says, spoke of spending more than six hours a day on-line and considered a computerized forum the only setting in which they could express themselves or relate well to others. A few students told her of dropping or flunking courses partly because they were so preoccupied with the Internet. Others confessed to trying to get multiple computer accounts with the university to circumvent its forty-hour-a-week rule. "Obviously, this is a wonderful tool, and for many students it's perfectly fine," says Tipton, who is trying to form a campus support group and develop a workshop on Internet addiction. "But for others it's becoming a tremendous escape from the pressures of college life. Students can become whomever they want, for as long as they want, and many other things in their lives, like classes, start to suffer."

8   Nathaniel Cordova, a graduate student at Maryland, says his problems are not that severe—but he is nevertheless heeding Tipton's advice and trying to cut back on the time he spends on computers. And he says he routinely talks to other students on campus also trying to break habits like his. "I don't think I'm an addict," Cordova says. "But I admit, sometimes I'll be in my office at eight o'clock at night, and then the next thing I know it's three A.M., and I realize I forgot to eat. It's so easy to get drawn in, and not just in research, but talking to people. You tell yourself, 'Okay, just one more link-up.' But you keep going."

9   Other college officials, however, say the concern seems exaggerated. Some say they see few signs of trouble, and others say student interest in computer games or the Web is often intense at first, then fades. One of the venerable rites of college, they contend, is for students to find distractions from their academic burdens. They say this one is much safer than many others causing campus problems. "There will always be something like this on college campuses," says Richard Wiggins, who manages information systems and teaches computer courses at Michigan State University. "In my day, in the 1970s, it was pinball. We played that all the time to get rid of stress. Usually things like this are not that harmful." "For some people, it's just a great new way to waste time," says Jeff Boulier, a senior at George Washington University who spends several hours a day on the Internet. "And college students have always been quite dedicated to wasting time."

10   At MIT, Patrick McCormick, an undergraduate who helps administer computer game systems for the university, says he sees both sides of the trend. A few students in his residence hall dropped classes, or saw their grades sink, after they lapsed into intensive computer use. "But others stay up all night with this stuff and still get 4.0s," he says. "It's very easy to get sucked in, but it isn't always bad."

11   Still, McCormick notes one problem he spots consistently: Classmates who trust virtually everyone they meet, or everything they read, on-line. "Some people think if it's on a computer screen, it must be true, and they get burned," he says. "You hear them talking about flying their dream lover up, and of course they never show."

12   This spring, Alfred University in upstate New York decided to examine what the students who dropped out last semester had in common. What prompted the inquiry was that twice as many students as usual—seventy-five, mostly freshmen—did not return for classes there this spring. Every student at Alfred receives a campus computer account, which is free. So Connie Beckman, the director of Alfred's computer center, decided to check the account records of all the students who had dropped out. She found that half of them had been logging as much as six hours a day on computer games or the Web, usually late at night. "It was the only thing that correlated among so many of them," Beckman says. University officials say they doubt that is the only, or even the primary, reason many of those students quit. But the discovery has led to several new policies.

288 Chapter 11 *Drafting the Sections of Your Argument*

13   Next fall, for the first time, freshmen at Alfred will be told about the dangers of heavy computer use as soon as they arrive on campus. Residence halls, all of which have computer rooms, also will each have a full-time, professional counselor to keep a close eye on late-night computer addicts. Other campuses are studying similar moves. "We've dealt with alcohol and drugs; we've dealt with TV and video games. Now this looks like the latest pitfall for college students," Beckman says. "They're doing this all night instead of doing their homework, or eating, or sleeping. When they're up until five A.M. playing around on the Web, they're not going to make their eight A.M. classes."

Questions to Consider

1. What is Sanchez's Argument Concept? Why do you think the evidence she provides will, or will not, be convincing to this reader? Although the purpose doesn't appear to be a persuasive one, there are many clues that this argument has a certain perspective. What is that perspective, and what are some of the words and phrases you see that reveal the writer's take on this issue?

2. Sanchez uses testimony from two different groups of "experts" on her topic. What are those groups? In general, what perspective does each group share? Which perspective do you find most convincing, and why?

3. What is your experience with Internet surfing, and how might that affect your reading of this argument?

4. Sanchez discusses two loosely conceived "studies," the information collected by Tipton at the University of Maryland, and the Alfred University investigation. How does Sanchez choose to share this information with her reader: paraphrase, summary, direct quotation, or combination? What detail from these investigations does she provide? Is the level of detail satisfactory?

5. What kind of examples of student computer involvement does the author provide—hypothetical, generic, or specific? How could you tell what kind they are? Why is her choice more effective than using either of the other two types? How many examples of this type has she used? Are there enough, and are they the right kind of examples, to draw a reasonable inductive conclusion about student computer behaviors (is the evidence *sufficient* and *typical*)?

6. Examine the identification of sources in paragraphs 4, 6, 8, 9, 10, and 12. Has she given the reader enough information to provide authority for her material? Notice the second identification of Tipton in paragraph 7. Why does the author offer this additional identification of Tipton rather than just saying, "Tipton also says"?

7. Examine the identification of the students in the examples. What does it add to the argument to know some information about the students? Look at the identification in paragraph 10 for Patrick McCormick, which is quite lengthy. Why give all that information? (And notice where the author remarks that McCormick "sees both sides of the trend." Here, she is

interpreting his remarks and connecting the information to her argument—the third important part of effective source integration.)

DISCOVERING YOUR OWN ARGUMENT: PRACTICE IN INTEGRATING OUTSIDE SOURCE MATERIAL WITH YOUR VOICE

1. Find a passage of two to three sentences from one of your sources that you intend to use in your argument in a draft. *Paraphrase* this passage according to the guidelines in this chapter.
   A. Exchange passages and paraphrases with a classmate.
   B. Does each person's paraphrase adequately and completely characterize the original passage? Where do you think the paraphrase does not adequately reflect the original?

2. Find a passage of three to four paragraphs from one of your sources that you may want to use in a draft. *Summarize* this passage according to the guidelines in this chapter. Exchange passages and summaries with a classmate.
   A. Does each person's summary adequately and completely characterize the original passage? Where are your partner's words too close to those of the original?
   B. What changes can you suggest to improve the summary?

3. Review passages you might quote directly in your draft. Which ones are truly dramatic or particularly masterfully stated and, therefore, deserve to be quoted? On the other hand, which ones would be better paraphrased or summarized to match the tone and voice of your own writing?

4. Examine the three strongest sources you have collected. What is the quality of the evidence provided? What kind of examples have the authors used, and how convincing are they? Which examples, if summarized and included in a draft, would improve its quality?

DISCOVERING YOUR OWN ARGUMENT: DRAFTING YOUR ARGUMENT

Create a fully developed draft of your argument, incorporating the techniques discussed in this chapter for rich illustration and effective use of outside sources.

Set aside some time when you are not rushed, and start a first—or second—draft of your argument. You have created a guideline that you have thought through carefully, so you know where to start and approximately where you want to go. You have thought more fully about what type of organization and what reader needs might be associated with each section. You have considered where illustration will help you draw vivid word pictures for your reader.

Keep this enriched plan in mind to help you on your journey, but don't feel restricted when a good idea hits you. The drafting process is still a discovery process for you. As you think and write, write and think, you will probably come up with dramatic new ideas or at least a few additions. You also may find that one section you had conceived simply doesn't work with the rest. That's what drafts are for. But you can approach the process with a sense of confidence that you have at least one good idea of how it may go.

ALSO NOTE
OTHER WRITERS' PROCESS

As you start your first draft, RELAX! This draft is not even close to a finished product. You are writing as much to feel out your plan and discover what that road is like rather than to arrive, perfectly on time, at your fantasy destination. Maybe the experience of other writers will confirm what the encouragement of two textbook writers cannot.

The classic example of multiple drafts as the way to success comes from Ernest Hemingway. Using a word other writers seem to repeat, Hemingway said that "The first draft of anything is ****." In a *Paris Review* interview, he described his drafting process:

Interviewer: "How much rewriting do you do?"
Hemingway: "It depends. I rewrote the ending of *Farewell to Arms*, the last page of it, 39 times before I was satisfied."
Interviewer: "Was there some technical problem there? What was it that had you stumped?"
Hemingway: "Getting the words right."

Anne Lamott, a more contemporary author, expresses the same thought in her book, *Bird by Bird*: "For me and most of the other writers I know, writing is not rapturous. In fact, the only way I can get anything written at all is to write really, really ****ty first drafts."

Experienced professionals are not the only writers who understand this important concept of multiple drafts. A university student, Diane Mason, was the winner, out of 3000 other entries, of a *Story* literary magazine short fiction contest for which she earned $1000 plus another $950 for publication rights. Mason talks about being a "café writer"; she headed to a comfortable café location with her pen and paper, and furiously wrote out the first draft of her story. However, the winning story, "Feast," went through 15 drafts before she submitted it.

The University Writing Center at Western Carolina University says, on its Web site, that ". . . we think of the first draft as *potentially* useful, even if it gets tossed into the compost bin, because the best way to start writing is when the stakes are low, using whatever words you have at the time, because the act of writing *what* you think of *as* you think it can lead you to both better thinking *and* better writing."

Mike Resnick, a prolific science fiction writer, demonstrates this process aspect of writing in one of his books, titled *Putting It Together: Turning Sow's Ear Drafts into Silk Purse Stories*.

So think of your first draft, of that first attempt to put flesh on the structural bones of your envisioned plan, as a low-stakes enterprise. You are doing it as a trial run to learn, by writing, what you are thinking, and as a mirror image, to improve your thinking about your topic and plan by writing.

REFLECTIONS ON THE CHAPTER

As you draft and redraft your argument, practicing the different ways of providing vivid examples and integrating credible outside source material will make it easier to vividly develop the sections you have planned.

You are trying to paint a word picture so detailed, so accurate and unambiguous, that your reader will follow readily and fit the pieces of the argument together as you direct. As you write, you may find places where you do not have adequate material to develop a section. At that point, you have several options. You can skip over that part during the drafting process, leaving yourself a note in your draft. You can look at your plan and assess whether the section is so critical that you must do some more research. You can write what you know at this point and return to the section later. You might have included a poorly developed section in your final draft, hoping the reader won't notice; such a passage might destroy your credibility and leave a gaping hole in an otherwise convincing argument. You might even decide that the section was just "gravy" on an already sound argument, and that leaving it out will not affect the quality of your argument.

A coherent plan and the knowledge of how to flesh out its sections makes working on an argument an intriguing voyage of discovery rather than a frustrating, stalled—or what's worse, aborted—trip.

PART III

Documenting and Polishing Arguments

Part III is about preparing your draft to meet its reader. You do not want to be dismissed after all your hard work because you have neglected the nitty gritty of preparing a final document. You want to eliminate any surface interference between your fine thoughts and the reader. Chapter 12 will cover the basics of internal and external source documentation and provide samples of the most frequently used citations. It also includes a serious warning about plagiarism and the ways to avoid it. Chapter 13 will help you with the most common developmental and mechanical errors you may have made while drafting your paper.

CHAPTER

12

Documenting Outside Sources

You have done all the good work of setting up a coherent and deeply developed argument. Now you also want to provide the reader information about your sources that will add even more to your credibility. Particularly in the academic world, presenting yourself as a writer who knows the conventions of presenting and documenting outside source information is essential. As a reader, you appreciated all the good documentation in your sources that helped you in your research. You picked up names of experts, titles of the most important works on your issue, even specific articles considered to be the most authoritative and revealing (often referred to as "seminal articles"). Now is the time for you to extend that courtesy to *your* reader.

This chapter will help you meet the academic requirements for ethical, effective, and credible source documentation.

TERMS AND CONCEPTS TO WATCH FOR

- Style manual
- Plagiarism
- Internal documentation
- External documentation
- Works Cited and References pages

QUESTIONS TO GUIDE YOUR READING

- How do informal and formal documentation differ?
- What are the four purposes for formal documentation?
- Are unintentional breaches of documentation guidelines still plagiarism?
- What is the relationship between internal and external documentation?
- If you read a source for background information but did not use it in your argument, should the source appear on your list of references?
- What are the specific problems of using Internet sources, and how do you deal with them?

THE PURPOSES OF DOCUMENTATION

If you are writing a researched argument, you may be tempted to look at the documentation process as a nit-picking, "teacherly" requirement: an exercise in meaningless hoop-jumping. Before discussing the admittedly detail-oriented task, we would like to first convince you that the act of documenting your sources, giving credit where credit is due, is much more than just a formality. It is an important, meaningful part of making an argument. If you have crafted your Argument Concept carefully and thoughtfully, you have become convinced by now that your reader's needs are central to the development of your argument. Skillful documenting of sources is one of the technical tasks late in the writing process that attends most directly to a reader's needs.

> ### ALSO NOTE
> #### THE INTELLIGENT USE OF INFORMATION
> Knowing a great deal is not the same as being smart; intelligence is not information alone but also judgment, the manner in which information is collected and used.
> —Carl Sagan

By now, if you have taken the rest of the book seriously, you have probably heard or observed arguments that suffered from many of the problems we've discussed such as logical fallacies or weak evidence. You may have also noticed another very prevalent problem if you've listened closely to arguments among your friends or coworkers. When arguing, people often want to give weight to their side by claiming some kind of authority. Too often, that urge comes out in one of the following ways:

"*They* say that . . ."
"Research has confirmed that . . ."
"A source close to the White House tells us that . . ."

Two serious problems occur with this kind of weak allusion to authority. First, "they" or "research" is most often some mixture of information that the speaker/writer has compressed in a form convenient to the point he or she is trying to make. The arguer expects the consumer of the argument to trust the memory, interpretation, consolidation, and representation of the information. Second, the arguer is appealing to some unidentified authority to add credibility to the point being made; without any access to the authority, however, the consumer of the argument might be skeptical. After all, if the source is some hastily put together Web site or a talk-radio program, careful readers *should* be wary. If the source of information regarding the Geneva Conventions and the World Court is an interview with your little brother, your reader *should* expect more and discredit you as a serious arguer. That sort of critical reading is what we've asked from you throughout the book.

Revealing and explaining the context of your sources is an integral part of your argument, not just "window dressing."

Documenting sources of information serves the following purposes in your argument:

1. *Providing authority for your claims.* This is intentionally number one on the list. Along the lines of the "garbage in–garbage out" saying, the quality of your argument will be as good as the quality of your information. You can convince your reader of your claim by supplying authoritative material and revealing its source. Formal documentation is just a more uniform method of providing authority than the informal method discussed earlier. (Recall, for example, how important the nature of the source of scientific information was in Behnke's discussion of whether or not fish feel pain, Chapter 8.)

2. *Providing access to your sources for your reader.* Because careful consumers of arguments should check the quality of sources, and because many readers may want to pursue more detail from those sources, styles of documentation have been established to systematize the process. Imagine how difficult it would have been, for instance, for you to find information if every writer used any method he or she wished to document material, or, even worse, if you had no references or names to guide you. You would only know that you wanted to find some research that was done on the feeding habits of porpoises, but you would have no place to start finding it! Understanding how helpful references were to *you* may help you look at the system as a friendly mechanism rather than as a barrier to get through.

    You will hear these systems referred to as "style sheets," or "style manuals," or "documentation manuals," and there are many. Professionals who write for different journals have to adjust the style of documentation they are using to the publication in which their work will appear. Students are luckier. Only two style manuals are used most often in writing and argument courses: the *Publication Manual of the American Psychological Association* (APA) and the *MLA Handbook for Writers of Research Papers* (MLA). The APA style is used in social sciences, education, psychology, sociology, and many other social sciences as well as biology and other sciences. The MLA style is used in English and other arts. Because writing teachers usually have an English background, MLA is frequently the style of choice for writing classes, simply because that is what the instructor is most familiar with. However, students may actually have more need during their academic and professional careers to use and understand the APA system. Therefore, we are going to give some elementary guidance in both systems.

> **A STYLE MANUAL** *is a reference handbook that provides detailed guidelines regarding a broadly accepted documentation style; the handbook will include specifications for formatting the text, citing sources, and making lists of sources to accompany a paper.*

This book will not go into great detail on some of the more unusual sources of information you might come across. Instead, we will concentrate in this chapter on the design of these systems and the connections they provide for readers, the importance of providing authority in the appropriate way, and the method of citing the main types of sources undergraduate students usually need. Nearly every library has copies of these two manuals if you need to find further information; we will simply demonstrate the general idea of documentation to familiarize you with their methods.

3. *Giving credit where credit is due.* Intellectual property is an important concept. For those who spend their lives studying, researching, and writing, their words and ideas are both their product and their livelihood. Acknowledging their work is simply the right (and legal) thing to do.

> **PLAGIARISM** *is the intentional or unintentional use of another's words or ideas while presenting them as if they were your own. Altering, creating, or manipulating sources (e.g., leaving out critical parts of quotations) are all methods of plagiarism.*

4. *Avoiding plagiarism.* Not acknowledging the words *and ideas* of others is the wrong thing to do. We emphasize *ideas* because students often think if they change a few, or even many, words of a source, they can then present them as their own. This is not so. Failure to acknowledge the ideas of another is plagiarism. Note in the definition on this page that *unintentional* use of another's words or ideas is still plagiarism. Sarah Jenkins explains in her 2004 article in the *Yakima Herald-Republic* on the current plague of plagiarism that unintended incidents can happen, sometimes easily:

It's easy to understand how it can happen; in an editorial I wrote last week about the Rattlesnake Peak fire, I used information from two newspaper archives (ours and *The Seattle Times*), background from the National Park Service, the U.S. Forest Service and the Wilderness Society (all available on the Internet), and statistics from the state of Washington and Yakima County. I believe it was all properly credited, but it could have gotten combined or confused if I had been gathering it over several

---

ALSO NOTE
PLAGIARISM DOESN'T PAY

Students aren't the only people who are tempted to shave the rules of conduct for using source material. Unfortunately, famous people and people just like you have lost their careers and credibility by such ethical lapses.

- Most colleges and universities have honesty policies that require, at the least, failure in any class in which the student has plagiarized. Dismissal from the school is also an option.
- The business world takes plagiarism extremely seriously. Michael Bolton, the singer/songwriter, had to pay $5.4 million when he was found guilty of "stealing" from an Isley Brothers song. Just as in writing, Bolton's product didn't have to be exactly like the original, but it demonstrated clearly unauthorized and/or unacknowledged borrowing.
- Several journalists have lost promising careers due to moments of unethical behavior. In the 1980s, Janet Cook invented the young ghetto hero of her *Washington Post* article, "Jimmy's World." She created a character from pieces of many different interviews and presented him as a real child in the Pulitzer Prize-winning story. The prize was, of course, rescinded, and she will never work in the industry again.
- In 2004, Jayson Blair, a writer for the *New York Times*, and Jack Kelly at *USA Today*, lost their careers over plagiarizing and sometimes fabricating sources. Maybe more significantly, their actions have cast doubts not only on their own truthfulness, but on that of their peers. Students who plagiarize also jeopardize the complete trust that should exist between all learners and teachers.

The point here is that plagiarism is an ugly form of dishonesty and theft. It erodes your character, compromises your current and future credibility, and you fail to learn skills that you will need for success in school and in the workplace. Don't be tempted to fall into what is now, with the Internet, a very open trap.

Instructors are, and should be, merciless in the face of such dishonesty.

days or weeks and working on it in the midst of several other projects. . . . It's no excuse, but it is an explanation.

If professionals have trouble managing information competently, it is not hard to see the challenge for a student who has to balance the demands of several courses, multiple exams, part-time work, perhaps family obligations, and some remote glimpse of a social life.

Nevertheless, *it is a writer's responsibility to use outside material ethically and accurately; it is part of a student's job and a course requirement to learn the process and to avoid either intentional or unintentional misuse of source material.*

Today, students are fortunate to have vast amounts of original sources and commentary a click away. Students are unfortunate that much of this information is also ready to swipe, copy, and paste. We would be remiss not to inform you that while using information unethically is easier than ever, it is also much easier to discover and chase down plagiarism. Because of the ready availability of essays both free and for purchase on the Internet, as well as the proliferation of dishonest use of electronic information, many sources have popped up to help teachers when they suspect improper source use. Often, simply "Googling" information will pop up the source. Remember, if you found it, your instructor, who is an expert researcher, will find it even more quickly. (And, by the way, that teacher will not be happy to have spent time this way!) Also, there are programs such as *turnitin.com* that will find the source of plagiarism very readily.

Carefully use the methods provided in Chapter 11 and Chapter 12, and you will be able to take great pride in your accomplishment rather than having a frustrating and humiliating experience with plagiarism.

AN IMPORTANT CAUTION ABOUT DOCUMENTATION

To accomplish the four important tasks of documentation, follow one of the established style manuals closely. Understanding the principles and format is not hard. Addressing your reader's needs for coherence while using proper documentation is not so easy a task. But attention to a reader's needs is the first concern. *The MLA Handbook* (the official publication of the Modern Language Association) provides the best advice we have ever seen for readability and documentation:

> Keep parenthetical references as brief—and as few—as clarity and accuracy permit. Give only the information needed to identify a source, and do not add a parenthetical reference unnecessarily.

This excellent advice should echo each time you start to document a source. It is easy to get carried away with the detail and formality of citing sources in an attempt to accomplish the four goals listed previously. If that happens, however, you have lost sight of the purpose of your argument: conveying a clear and coherent message to a reader. Proper citation of sources should *enhance* your argument, *not detract* from it.

THE BASIC PROCESSES OF DOCUMENTING SOURCES

Formal documentation involves two different but interrelated processes: internal documentation (or in-text citations), and external documentation (or "Works Cited" lists in MLA style, "References" in APA).

> **INTERNAL DOCUMENTATION** *is the information included in the text of a paper that identifies both the authority and location (and date in APA style) of any direct quotations or paraphrased ideas of outside sources.*

- **Internal documentation** is the information included in the text of your paper that identifies both the *authority* and *location* of any direct quotations or ideas of outside sources (see Chapter 11). The order and type of this information varies with different style manuals. We will illustrate both MLA and APA styles. *The purposes of internal documentation are to identify the authority (and date in APA style) of the material you are using, to give the page location of any direct quotation (and additionally, any paraphrased material in MLA style), and to refer a reader efficiently to the bibliographical information at the end of the paper (the external documentation) for further research.* Some of this information is included in parentheses. Internal documentation is also referred to as "in-text citation" and the material in parentheses is often called "parenthetical citation."

> **EXTERNAL DOCUMENTATION** *is the publication information of all sources used in a paper, listed as prescribed in the style manual on a separate "Works Cited" page (MLA) or a "References" page (APA).*

- **External documentation** is the bibliographical (publication information) description of the sources that appear in a researched paper. This information is listed on a page (or pages) at the end of the paper. The order and type of this information varies with different style manuals. We will illustrate MLA ("Works Cited") and APA ("References") styles. *The purpose of external documentation is to provide readers with a complete and uniform listing of the publication information necessary to find the source, should they want to find the book or article for further research.*

> **WORKS CITED AND REFERENCES PAGES** *are the final, separate pages that follow the last page of a paper. They list alphabetically all of the sources used in a paper. Materials the writer read for background knowledge do not appear on the list unless they have been used specifically in the paper.*

These concepts and their relationship are so important that we offer you the following visual clarification. Study these pages to see how the internal documentation leads a reader to the external bibliographical information. Also, you may want to use these pages as a rough guide when you are documenting your own paper. Extremely detailed sample papers are included in both the APA and MLA manuals, and we have included student sample arguments at the end of this chapter, one in APA format and the other in MLA.

MLA Sample Page

Parker 8

Some of the ideas from research that was done in the late 1980s and early 1990s might help create better experiences in college for Hispanic students. **In 1993, for example, Alexander Astin in his book**, *What Matters in College?*, identified many of the things that help students adjust to college and those that encourage them to stay in school. What he found was that, first of all, a meaningful relationship with a faculty member was one of the strongest motivators for students to continue with their education. Also, anything that keeps students on campus longer and makes them feel more a part of the school is helpful. Meeting in study groups in campus locations, participating in extracurricular activities of any type, and socializing with peers in campus lounges or food operations can accomplish the goal of connecting students to their school (**68–72**). Setting up connections with faculty for Hispanic students and encouraging them to take advantage of campus activities could satisfy those needs that Astin points out and maybe overcome their feeling of isolation from the campus culture.

Another practice that could help Hispanic students adapt more easily to college is something called "cohort enrollment" (**Levine and Shapiro 89**). A "cohort" is a group of students that usually share some feature such as age, background, career interest, etc. Some schools are showing good success when enrolling students with some common feature (or features) in the same sections of several classes so that they create a social and academic bond that acts as a safety net when a student is struggling. If the students know one another better and are being exposed to the same material and teaching techniques, they can better assist each other. Also, students are more apt to ask good questions in class and ask for help from their peers when they are more closely bonded in this way (**89–96**). Sometimes, cohorts even live together on campus on special floors of dorms dedicated to this practice.

Notice how the internal documentation in bold links to the "Works Cited" page that follows.

MLA "Works Cited" Sample Page

>Parker 12
>
>**Works Cited**
>
>**Astin, W. Alexander.** ***What Matters in College: Four Critical Years Revisited.*** **San Francisco: Jossey-Bass, 1993.**
>
>Avalos, Juan, and D. Michael Pavel. "Improving the Performance of the Hispanic Community College Student." (1993). ERIC Document Service ED 358907. University of Kansas Library. 11 May 2007.
>
>Banathy, Bela. "We Enter the Twenty-first Century with Schooling Designed in the Nineteenth." *Systems Research and Behavioral Science* 18.4 (2001): 287–299.
>
>Gandara, Patricia. "Passing Through the Eye of the Needle: High-achieving Chicanas." *Hispanic Journal of Behavioral Science* 2 (1992): 167–179.
>
>"Hispanic Educators Call for Record Spending Increases." *Black Issues in Higher Education* 18.5 (2001): 9.
>
>Kinser, Jeri, Brenda Pessin, and Patricia Meyertholen. "From the Fields to the Laptop." *Learning & Leading with Technology* 28.5 (2001): 5.
>
>Pidcock, Boyd, Judith L. Fisher, and Joyce Munsch. "Family, Personality, and Social Risk Factors Impacting the Retention Rates of First-year Hispanic and Anglo College Students." *Adolescence* Winter 2001. LookSmart: FindArticles. <http://findarticles.com/p/articles/mi_m2248/is_144_36/ai_84722702>.
>
>**Levine, Jody, and Nancy Shapiro**. ***Creating Learning Communities***. **San Francisco: Jossey-Bass, 2000**.
>
>Swail, Watson Scott., Alberto F. Cabrera, and Chul Lee. "Latino Youth and the Pathway to College." Pew Hispanic Center. Pew Charitable Trusts and USC Annenberg School for Communication. 23 June 2004. <http://pewhispanic.org/files/reports/31/pdf>.

ALSO NOTE
ITALICS

You may want to ask your instructor how titles should appear if you are using MLA documentation. All titles are in *italics* in this text for consistency; in APA style, italics is suggested, and in MLA either is acceptable.

Underlining was originally the way of indicating to a printer that a title should be set in italics. Examples of citations in the sixth edition of the MLA handbook still have underlining. Now that word processors can

(continued)

italicize words, either underlining or italics is often acceptable. Consider this advice from the MLA Web site:

> Most word-processing programs and computer printers permit the reproduction of italic type. In material that will be graded or edited for publication, however, the type style of every letter and punctuation mark must be easily recognizable. Italic type is sometimes not distinctive enough for this purpose. In printed material submitted for grading and editing, therefore, words that would be italicized in a publication are usually underlined to avoid ambiguity. If you wish to use italics rather than underlining, check your instructor's or editor's preferences.

APA Sample Page

Hispanic success 8

Some of the ideas from research that was done in the late 1980s and early 1990s might help create better experiences in college for Hispanic students. For example, **Astin (1993) in his book**, ***What Matters in College?***, identified many of the things that help students adjust to college and those that encourage them to stay in school. What he found was that, first of all, a meaningful relationship with a faculty member was one of the strongest motivators for students to continue with their education. Also, anything that keeps students on campus longer and makes them feel more a part of the school is helpful. Meeting in study groups in campus locations, participating in extracurricular activities of any type, and socializing with peers in campus lounges or food operations can accomplish the goal of connecting students to their school. Setting up connections with faculty for Hispanic students and encouraging them to take advantage of campus activities could satisfy those needs that Astin points out and maybe overcome their feeling of isolation from the campus culture.

Another practice that could help Hispanic students adapt more easily to college is something called "cohort enrollment" (**Levine & Shapiro, 2000**). A "cohort" is a group of students that usually share some feature such as age, background, career interest, etc. Some schools are showing good success when enrolling students with some common feature (or features) in the same sections of several classes so that they create a social and academic bond that acts as a safety net when a student is struggling. If the students know one another better and are being exposed to the same material and teaching techniques, they can better assist each other. Also, students are more apt to ask good questions in class and ask for help from their peers when they are more closely bonded in this way. Sometimes, cohorts even live together on campus on special floors of dorms dedicated to this practice.

Notice how the internal APA style documentation links (in bold type) to the following "References" page. Also note that APA style does not require a page citation for paraphrased material as does MLA. Both styles require page citations for direct quotations.

APA "References" Sample Page

Hispanic success 12

References

Astin, A. W. (1993). *What matters in college?* **San Francisco: Jossey-Bass.**
Avalos, J., and D. M. Pavel. (1993). Improving the performance of the Hispanic community college student. ERIC Document No. 358907.
Banathy, B. (2001). We enter the twenty-first century with schooling designed in the nineteenth. *Systems Research and Behavioral Science 18* (4), 287.
Gandara, P. C. (1992). Passing through the eye of the needle: High achieving Chicanas. *Hispanic Journal of Behavioral Sciences, 2,* 167–179.
Hispanic educators call for record spending increases. (2001). *Black Issues in Higher Education, 18*(5), 9.
Kinser, J., Pessin, B, & Meyertholen, P. (2001). From the fields to the laptop. *Learning & Leading with Technology, 28* (5), 5.
Pidcock, B., Fisher, J., and Munsch, J. (2001 Winter). Family, personality, and social risk factors impacting the retention rates of first-year Hispanic and Anglo college students. *Adolescence*. Retrieved May 11, 2007, from http://findarticles.com/p/articles.com/mi_m2248/is144_36/ai_84722702
Levine, J., and Shapiro, N. (2000). *Creating learning communities.* **San Francisco: Jossey-Bass.**
Swail, W. S., A. F. Cabrera, and C. Lee. (2004). Latino youth and the pathway to college. Pew Hispanic Center. Pew Charitable Trusts and USC Annenberg School for Communication. Retrieved April 20, 2007, from http://pewhispanic.org/files/reports/31/pdf

EXTERNAL DOCUMENTATION (BIBLIOGRAPHICAL INFORMATION)

Creating your "Works Cited" or "References" list is one of the easier but maybe more tedious tasks of writing with researched sources. Many students who read that sentence may disagree because they have neglected in the past to follow the advice most instructors give students: find and keep the publication data for *all* material you acquire as you go (or, as some writers prefer, make a copy of the title page of each source), then simply listing them and polishing up the detail is truly a minor job. If, however, you neglected to get some of the information about several sources, thinking you would do it later or that you probably won't use that source, and you cannot readily locate that information later, you will waste valuable time at the end of your project hunting down sources when you could be paying attention to the quality of your final text. We have had some students who found extremely valuable sources in professional Internet journals, for example, who could not find the publication material again the day before their papers were due. The only correct action in that case is to take the information out of your paper since you cannot adequately document it. You don't want to face that eventuality.

As you can see in the previous sample pages, the MLA and APA formats are different for external documentation. Regardless of the format you are required to use, you have three important responsibilities as you construct your list of sources.

The Three Responsibilities of External Documentation

1. The formats required by MLA or APA are quite specific, so be sure you follow them to the letter. This includes such specifics as alphabetizing, margins, spacing of entries, use of commas, placement of dates, and so forth. One prerequisite of academic work is the attention to detail you bring to your writing. Follow your chosen format carefully. Competent research requires that you follow the conventions of documenting as closely as you will the conventions of English usage. Occasionally a student will think his or her title will look more "cool" in a fancier font. What that choice says to a reader is that the student doesn't yet understand the value of uniformity in the MLA and APA worlds.

2. Your final list should contain *only* those sources from which you actually cited information in your paper. You may have read hundreds of sources during your search for support for your argument, but only those that appear in your paper should be on the list.

3. Be sure, however, that every source you do use in your paper (internally) has a matching external citation on your works cited or reference list.

Samples of the Most Frequently Used Citations   Having a style manual handy as you complete your source list is almost a necessity because of the wide variety of sources available. You may find information in everything as diverse as a college lecture to an obscure government document. We provide you with a list of the citation formats most frequently used by college writers; for more unusual sources, you will need to consult your style manual. The following hypothetical citations can be used as models for many of your most straightforward citations, but if the bibliographical information varies from that in the sample, we suggest checking with the manual for finer detail.

Book with One Author*

MLA   Gordon, James A. *Beyond the Reef.* Rochester, MN: Major House Publishing, 1993.

APA   Gordon, J. A. (1993). *Beyond the reef.* Rochester, MN: Major House Publishing.

---

*Note the difference between MLA and APA style in capitalization of titles and placement of date.

> ### ALSO NOTE
> #### ONLINE DOCUMENTATION ASSISTANCE
>
> The art of documenting electronic sources is a work in process. As this book is being published, decisions and changes are made to try to deal with the difficult issues of creating a uniform and satisfactory system of documenting information from a chaotic and inconsistent (while empowering) source: the Internet. You can, however, find updated guidance at several quality OWLs (Online Writing Labs) and commercial Web sites for the latest information on online citation as well as documentation for more traditional sources. The following sites are particularly helpful:
>
> http://owl.english.purdue.edu/owl/resource/557/08/
> Fine source for examples of citation
>
> http://www.bedfordstmartins.com/online/cite5.html#1
> Excellent site for online citations
>
> http://www.dianahacker.com/resdoc/
> Good, reliable source for a variety of styles of documentation
>
> http://www.liu.edu/CWIS/CWP/library/workshop/citation.htm
> Concise, use-friendly, color-coded examples of citations

Book with Two or Three Authors*

MLA Gordon, James A., Christopher Sheafor, and Marni Norris. *Beyond the Reef*. Rochester, MN: Major House Publishing, 1993.

APA Gordon, J. A., Sheafor, C., & Norris, M. (1993). *Beyond the reef*. Rochester, MN: Major House Publishing.

Book with More than Three Authors*

MLA Gordon, James A., et al. *Beyond the Reef*. Rochester, MN: Major House Publishing, 1993.

APA Gordon, J. A., Sheafor, C., Smith, M., & Norris, M. (1993). *Beyond the reef*. Rochester, MN: Major House Publishing.

Book with Corporate or Group Author

MLA American Association of Enviornmental Ethics. *Saving the Panther*. Chicago: American Association of Enviornmental Ethics, 1993.

APA American Association of Environmental Ethics. (1993). *Saving the panther*. Chicago: American Association of Environmental Ethics.

---

*Note that MLA style does not list more than three authors individually. However, in APA style, all authors are listed. Authors in both styles are listed in the order their names appear on the title page as in this case, not necessarily alphabetically.

Book in an Edition Other than the First
MLA   Gordon, James A. *Beyond the Reef.* 5th ed. Rochester, MN: Major House Publishing, 1993.

APA   Gordon, J. A. (1993). *Beyond the reef* (5th ed.). Rochester, MN: Major House Publishing.

Book with Editor
MLA   Brennan, Grace, and Linda Aldrich, eds. *Poetry from the Heart.* Ottawa, Canada: Maple Leaf Inc., 1993.

APA   Brennan, G., & Aldrich, L. (Eds.) (1993). *Poetry from the heart.* Ottawa, Canada: Maple Leaf Inc.

Book from an Author Already Listed
MLA   Gordon, James A. *Beyond the Reef.* 5th ed. Rochester, MN: Major House Publishing, 1993.
—*Denizens of the Deep.* Boston: Smith & Sons, 2001.

APA   Gordon, J. (1993). *Beyond the reef.* 5th ed. Rochester, MN: Major House Publishing.
Gordon, J. (2001). *Denizens of the deep.* Boston: Smith & Sons.

Essay or Chapter from a Book with Essays or Chapters by Different Authors*
MLA   Norris, Jill M. "Dogs and Their Owners." *Bonding Between Animals and Humans.* Ed. Laura Brennan. New York: Fowler Books, 2001. 88–103.

APA   Norris, J. M. (2001). Dogs and their owners. In Laura Brennan (Ed.), *Bonding between animals and humans* (pp. 88–103). New York: Fowler Books.

Encyclopedia Article
MLA   "Bangladesh." *The New Encyclopaedia Britannica*: Macropaedia. 1990 ed.

APA   Bangladesh. (1990). In *The new encyclopaedia Britannica* (Vol. I, pp. 866–868). Chicago: Macropaedia.

Article Published in a Scholarly Journal (each issue not beginning with page 1)
MLA   Shpancer, Noam. "What Makes Classroom Learning a Worthwhile Experience?" *Thought & Action* XIX (2004): 23–35.

APA   Shpancer, N. (2004). What makes classroom learning a worthwhile experience? *Thought & Action*, XIX, 23–35.

---

*Again, note the difference in capitalization and punctuation between the two styles: no punctuation is necessary for article titles in APA citations.

Article Published in a Newspaper, Author Given*
MLA   Dubrow, Josh. "Huskies Respond to Challenge, Reach Sweet 16."
      The Coloradoan 23 March 2003: D5+.
APA   Dubrow, J. (2003, March 23). Huskies respond to challenge,
      reach Sweet 16. *The Coloradoan*, pp. D5, D7.

Article Published in a Newspaper, No Author Given
MLA   "Judge Rules against NFL." *The Wichita Eagle* 6 February 2004: D1.
APA   Judge rules against NFL (2004, February 6). *The Wichita Eagle*, p. D1.

Editorial in a Newspaper
MLA   "Gay Opponents on Right Side of History?" Editorial. *The
      Wichita Eagle* 12 May 2004: 9A.
APA   Gay opponents on right side of history? (2004, May 12).
      [Editorial]. *The Wichita Eagle*, p. 9A.

Unpublished Interview
MLA   Brennan, Sadie. Personal interview. 7 December 2004.
APA   No citation appears in "References" for an original interview since
      it is not recoverable. Cite the interview in the text only.

External Documentation of Electronic Sources

Documenting electronic sources is a problem all its own, and therefore this special section attending to the issue. Both the MLA and APA manuals explain that because publication information for electronic sources has no consistency—or worse, is nonexistent in some cases—the task of documenting these sources is formidable. They also explain that your citations will often need to include more, not fewer, elements because of that lack of consistency: for instance, some electronic sources have numbered paragraphs, some numbered pages, and some have no numbering system of any kind. Recall that one of the main goals of careful documentation is to provide your readers a path to your original sources. Unlike the publication information for print sources, frequently the electronic path changes and/or the information is archived, changed, or even deleted. Nevertheless, your responsibility doesn't change. Since electronic sources have become more and more popular, and sometimes more valid as well, a consistent system will probably evolve, hopefully soon. In the meantime, the following recommendations will help you meet your responsibilities in either MLA or APA format.

Electronic Source with Print Form   If an electronic source has an alternative print form, the reference for that print form is preferable because, as of this time, print references are more dependable and enduring. Use the same format for the

---

*Note the different way MLA and APA treat newspaper page numbers. In MLA, an article on more than one page is indicated by a "+" after the page number. In APA, however, the "pp." symbol is used and if pages are consecutive, a dash is used: pp. D5–D6. If an article continues on a nonconsecutive page, a comma is used: pp. D5, D7.

material as you would any other source and then add the electronic publication material and access information to indicate how you were able to find the information. For example, an article from *Time* that you found online would appear in one of these two ways:

Samples of Citations from Electronic Sources
Magazine Article Found Online

MLA   Gibbs, Nancy. "Faith, God, & the Oval Office." *Time* 17 June 2004, 29 Sept. 2004 <http://time.com/time1101040621/story.html>.
                                    Date of your search

APA   Gibbs, N. (2004, June 17). Faith, God, and the Oval Office. *Time* [Online]. Retrieved Sept. 29, 2004, from <http://time.com/time/1101040621/story.html>.

Electronic Source with No Print Form If the electronic source does not have an alternative print form, you must then search the Web site carefully to provide as much electronic publication information as you can. *Keep in mind that if you cannot identify the source very thoroughly, you might reconsider your decision to use the information.* If, after all, you cannot determine who has published the material or any of the author's credentials, what organization sponsors the Web site, the date of the information, and so on, then you may be repeating outdated gossip rather than supporting your argument with credible information. Following the general MLA or APA order of author, date, and publication information, include as many of these elements as possible:

1. Author (editor, compiler, translator, etc.)
2. Title
3. Title of the Internet site (database, scholarly site, online periodical, etc.)
4. Editor or manager of the site
5. Date of electronic publication (frequently listed as "last updated [date]," "posted [date]," or a copyright date)
6. Names of subscription sources. (These are frequently used sources that you should distinguish from broadly available search engines such as Yahoo, Excite, or Google. Services such as EBSCO, InfoTrac, Galenet, and Newsbank are available only at libraries that have paid for access for their patrons [and students at school libraries]. Search engine names will never appear in your citations; that would be like saying "My Car" in a citation for a library source. A search engine is just a way to get to an electronic "place" where you can find information. That place [EBSCO, Newsbank, etc.], on the other hand, is an important piece of information because your reader will know that such a subscribed service is a way to find

access to the information since you found it that way.) Information retrieved from such a subscribed database should follow this general pattern:

Material Found in a Subscribed Database

MLA   Norris, Kelly. "Poisonous Frogs of the Tropics." *Amphibians* 23 Dec. 2001, 115–117. Info Trac. University of Kansas Library. 8 Oct. 2004.

    Date of your search   Subscribed database   Library in which you used database

APA   Norris, K. (2001, Dec. 23). Poisonous frogs of the tropics. *Amphibians*. 115–117. Retrieved Oct. 8, 2004, from Info Trac database.

7. The number of pages or paragraphs, if they are numbered

8. Date the information was accessed

9. URL (Internet address) of the source. (This is listed as http://www.time.com, for instance.) Note that some individual URLs are extremely long. If the site has a search option or "links" to click on to get to the item, you need only give the home page URL. MLA suggests listing the "path" or sequence of links upon which you clicked to reach the item after the URL. For instance, your MLA citation might include the following information: http://www.time.com. Path: Archives; Special Issues; Man of the Year; Issue: 3 Jan. 2001.

When you first locate a promising online source, write down as many of the pieces of its identity listed here as you can, or print the home page if it contains full bibliographical information. Also, you may want to go the bottom of the electronic file, as authors, authors' credentials, copyright dates, and so forth, often appear there. As with all source citations, refer to your style manual when any irregularity comes up or for further detail. The citation for information found on a Web site provided here is a very general example; you should remember three cautions as you create your own list of electronic references:

1. Each site provides publication in a different format, and your responsibility to get it right will take some patience and digging.

2. Since electronic documentation is an evolving art, your instructor may have specific preferences about what must be included in your online citations.

3. If you are careful, these citations will probably contain more information than traditional print citations. Better to err in favor of too much information than to have your credibility questioned because your reader (or instructor!) thinks your information may have come from some unverifiable Internet source.

312 Chapter 12 *Documenting Outside Sources*

The sample on p. 311 demonstrates one type of electronic entry for material found on the Web site of the American Cancer Society. Notice where the elements of the citation (copyright date) occur on the page; there are no uniform locations for this information, so you will need to be resourceful in hunting them down. Also, note the "About ACS" link at the bottom of the page; this helpful "About Us" link is available on most quality Web sites, and at that location you will find information that will help you determine the reliability of the Web site as well as publication data.

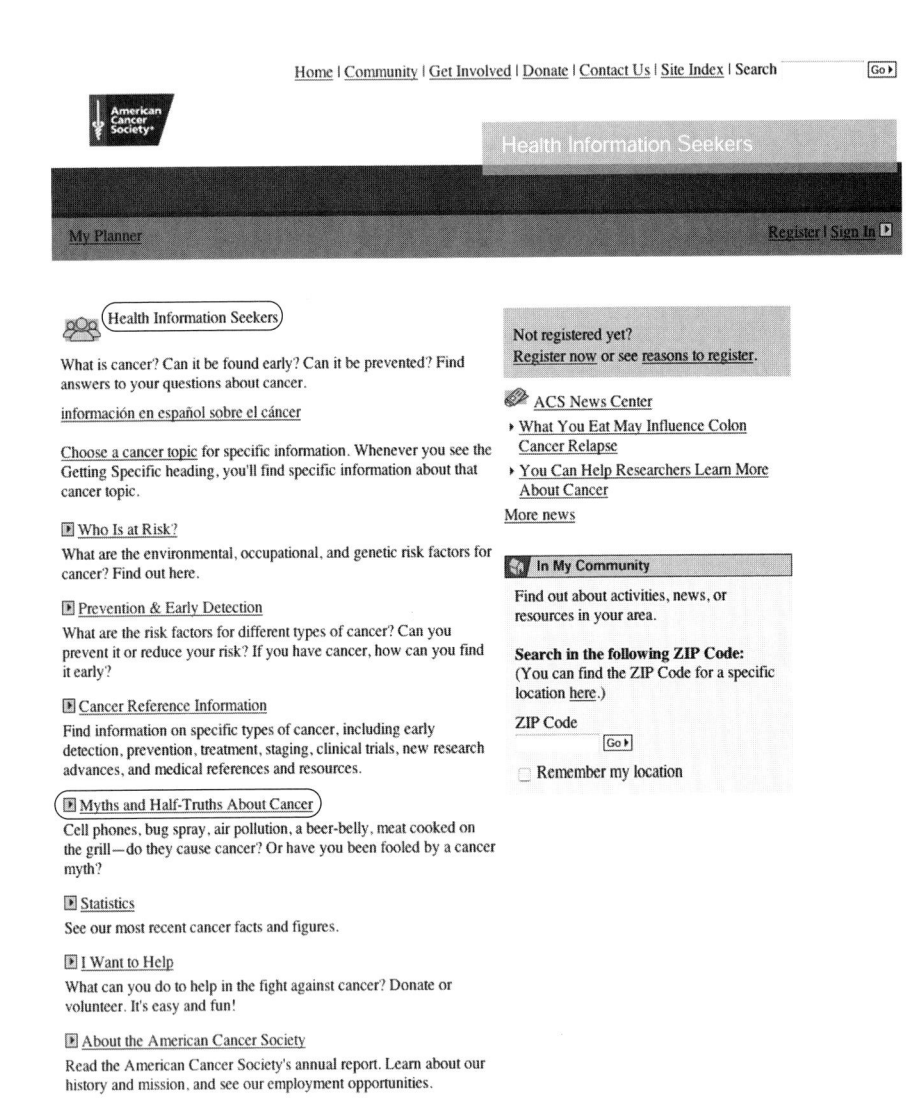

Used with Permission of the American Cancer Society, Inc. All rights reserved.

Material Found on Internet Site

MLA "Myths and Half-Truths About Cancer" Cancer. org. 2007. American Cancer Society, Inc. 1 Sept. 2007. <http://www.cancer.org>. Path: Health Information Seekers.

                        Date of your search   Copyright date on site

APA American Cancer Society, Inc. (2007). Myths and half-truths about Cancer. [Electronic database] Retrieved September 1, 2007, from http://cancer.org.

Type of electronic source: "database," "online posting" (newsroom, for instance), or "online periodical," etc.

Copyright date on site, or date of access if date of copyright or "last updated" or "posted" is not available

Internal (In-Text) Documentation

As we noted earlier, the three purposes of good in-text documentation are as follows:

- To refer a reader efficiently to the bibliographical information at the end of the paper (the external documentation) for further research
- To give the page location of any direct quotation (and paraphrase in MLA style)
- To identify the authority of the material you are using

    The trick is to do all this while not alienating a reader. Nothing is more difficult to read than an argument chopped up with bulky citations (what some writers call "documentation clutter"). You may want to review the last section of Chapter 11 regarding the integration of source material and the proper use of authority, as the information in this section builds on that concept of providing authority. The question discussed in Chapter 11 was, "What constitutes authority and when should it be included it in the text?" In informal documentation (used in arguments in Chapters 1–11) all the necessary identifying material for your sources must appear in the text. The benefit of using formal MLA or APA citations is that you can now make even more subtle decisions about what authority identification you will use in your text because you can take care of plagiarism concerns by using parenthetical citations. Done correctly, this option is a distinct advantage for readability. Done incorrectly, you can clutter up an otherwise nicely written paper.

    What, then, is the process for efficiently and effectively making in-text citations? Internal documentation requires that you cite the source (and date in APA) for every indirect quotation, paraphrase, or summary of an outside source. Additionally, for any direct quotation, you must give the page number(s) for the location of the quotation. Again, we defer to the MLA Handbook for a clear and succinct statement of the major principle in meeting those requirements and in crafting your in-text documentation:

> Remember that there is a direct relation between what you integrate into your text and what you place in parentheses. If, for example, you include an author's name in a sentence, you need not repeat the name in the parenthetical page citation that follows, provided that the reference is clearly to the work of the author you mention.

This simple but essential concept can be illustrated in the sets of sentences in the following examples. Notice that making a list of references first makes the task of in-text citation simpler because the words or phrase in the parentheses should match the first word or phrase in the "Works Cited" or "References" list; the internal and external documentation are always linked in this way. Therefore, to discuss in-text citation, it is important to have some sample external citations from which to derive the internal documentation.

Samples of In-Text Documentation

Hypothetical Citations for Sources from Which Example Material Is Taken

MLA   Norris, Jill M. "Dogs and Their Owners." *Bonding between Animals and Humans*. Ed. Laura Brennan. New York: Fowler Books, 2001. 88–103.

APA   Norris, J. M. (2001). Dogs and their owners. In Laura Brennan (Ed.), *Bonding between animals and humans* (pp. 88–103). New York: Fowler Books.

Examples of In-Text Citations for a Paraphrase or Summary*

MLA   Professional breeder Jill Norris claims that her pugs may be difficult to train, but that they are the smartest and most loyal of breeds; they just don't want to sit (92).

APA   Professional breeder Norris (2001) claims that her pugs may be difficult to train, but that they are the smartest and most loyal of breeds; they just don't want to sit.

Of course, this is just one of several ways to take care of documentation responsibilities in this passage. To decide how much of the authority disclosure you will include is an individual decision in each case. Let's say you have none of Norris's credentials. In that case, you have little reason for including her name in your text; to do so will only clutter your argument, as we have cautioned. In that case, your citation might look more like this:

Examples of In-Text Citations**

MLA   Pugs may be difficult to train, but they are the smartest and most loyal of breeds; they just don't want to sit (Norris 62).

APA   Pugs may be difficult to train, but they are the smartest and most loyal of breeds; they just don't want to sit (Norris, 2001).

Not unusually, two or more works from the same author may help support your argument. If so, you will need to be careful to indicate from which of those

---

*Although you finish your use of source material with a page number in MLA style (or range of pages, 63–67, for instance), you include a page number in APA only when you are using a direct quotation or when you are referring to a specific part of the source (specific chapter, for example).

**Note the different use of commas in parenthetical citations: no comma between name and page number in MLA; use a comma and the abbreviation "p." or "pp." in APA. Also, note that APA style includes a date, whereas MLA does not.

works you are taking your material. Formal citation makes this rather easy. Just include the title (or a short abbreviation of a long title) of the appropriate work in the parenthetical citation:

In-Text Citation for Author from whom You Are Using Multiple Works

MLA   Pugs may be difficult to train, but they are the smartest and most loyal of breeds; they just don't want to sit (Norris, "Dogs and Their Owners" 62).

APA   Pugs may be difficult to train, but they are the smartest and most loyal of breeds; they just don't want to sit (Norris, "Dogs and their owners," 2001, p. 62).

Sometimes you may have not multiple works, but instead, multiple authors for the same bit of information. Be careful not to overdo this citation, however. If you have read, for example, in almost all of your sources that mixed breed dogs are easiest to train, you may accept that as a point of "common knowledge" in the field and you need not cite a source. On the other hand, if only two of your sources make that assertion, then you should cite both of them:

In-Text Citation for Multiple Sources

MLA   Even though each owner often claims the superiority of their breed, almost every professional agrees that mixed breed dogs, the common Humane Society type, is actually the easiest to train (Norris 62; Carson 344).

APA   Even though each owner often claims the superiority of their breed, almost every professional agrees that mixed breed dogs, the common Humane Society type, is actually the easiest to train (Norris, 2001; Carson, 1999).

Imagine yet another case in which Norris is a very witty writer and you think her words will spice up your paper. You decide to use a direct quotation:

In-Text Citation for Direct Quotation*

MLA   Professional breeder Jill Norris explains how "smart" and training fit together for at least one breed: "My pugs are terribly smart and loyal, counter to what you may think because they look disobedient. Who do you think is smarter, the child who obediently takes her chair when asked, or the pug that looks at you and thinks 'Make me!' or 'Why?'" (62).

APA   Professional breeder Jill Norris (2001) explains how "smart" and training fit together for at least one breed: "My pugs are terribly smart and loyal, counter to what you may think because they look disobedient. Who do you think is smarter, the child who obediently takes her chair when asked, or the pug that looks at you and thinks 'Make me!' or 'Why?'" (62).

---

*Of course, you may want to omit Norris's name as illustrated earlier, which would call for adding the name (and date in APA) in the parentheses.

One of the other needs you may have for internal documentation is a situation in which you are using a quotation by a source that has been cited in another document. The MLA manual refers to this case as an "indirect source." Fortunately, a very clear way exists to credit the correct person for the exact words:

In-Text Citation for an Indirect Source (one source quoting another)

MLA Fourth-time poodle owner Marion Schultz argues, "My dogs have always been perfectly trained by the time they were a year old. I don't know any mutt that can do that" (qtd. in Norris 217).

APA Fourth-time poodle owner Marion Schultz argues, "My dogs have always been perfectly trained by the time they were a year old. I don't know any mutt that can do that" (cited in Norris, 2001, p. 217).

As you refine your in-text citations, vary the methods you use. If, every time you introduce a source, you say "According to . . . " your reader will feel monotony rather than interest when you start to provide support for your arguments. Also, remember our advice from Chapter 11. Your text will read best when you use paraphrases and summaries of your source material. Use quotations sparingly and only when well explained, contextualized, and/or interpreted. Most significantly, think about the power of the authority behind the information and use it to establish your credibility with your reader. Strong sources of evidence—well selected, judiciously quoted, and well documented—will enhance the coherent structure you've worked so hard to establish.

Exercise 1
Collaborative Analysis: Practice in Citing and Integrating Source Material

Two instances are given here of argument scenarios using outside source material. The first, Scenario A, is rather simple and straightforward. Scenario B is challenging as it brings up some more complicated skills for citing and integrating source material, but they are issues you will often encounter. In small groups, complete the following tasks for each scenario:

1. Create both an APA "References" and an MLA "Works Cited" listing for the source.

2. Determine what method of in-text documentation will work to integrate the material and write out two different forms of the paragraph, one that would appear in a final APA draft and one that would appear in a final MLA draft. Be sure that all three purposes of good in-text documentation (see pp. 313–316) are addressed.

Scenario A   You are writing an argument to include more readings by women authors in traditional introductory history classes. In your conclusion, you want to use the following quotation from page three of Sue Monk's book, *The Dance of the Dissident Daughter*, published by HarperCollins in 1996 (publisher located in New York): "If women don't tell our stories and utter our truths in order to chart ways into sacred feminine experience, who will?" Monk is described on the book cover as a "'conventionally religious, churchgoing woman, a traditional wife and mother' with a thriving career as a Christian writer until she began to question her role as a woman in her culture, her family, and her church."

The part of your conclusion into which you want to merge Monk's words is as follows:

> Since ancient history, men have been speaking for the experience of women. What has been claimed to be some generic version of human history is anything but objective. The history of Man has been just that, and not the history of Humanity. As long as we continue to use predominantly male perspectives and voices to present history, the unique value of the voices of women will be excluded.

Scenario B You are arguing that restrictions should be put on the amount of fish taken from the sea by commercial fishing operations. You have read predictions of marine biologists around the world that say the supply of fish is rapidly diminishing because of overfishing. You want to use a quotation from Stephen Palumbi that appeared in November 13, 2006, issue of *Time*. The article on p. 56, "Oceans of Nothing," was written by Unmesh Kher. In the article, Palumbi, who is a marine biologist at Stanford University, says, "None of us regular working folk are going to be able to afford seafood. It's going to be too rare and too expensive."

The passage into which you want to merge Palumbi's words is as follows:

> If the environmental issue of losing so many species of seagoing creatures is not enough to encourage action, the impact on personal diet and budget should be. Seafood has become more attractive to many people because of its low calorie content and high nutritional value. For a long time, seafood has been a reasonably priced staple in a healthy diet, but we may not be able to depend on that for long.

Exercise 2
Individual Analysis and Practice: Practicing and Assessing Your Own Documentation

Carefully craft the "Works Cited" (MLA) or "Reference" (APA) entry for one of your sources. Integrate the material smoothly and accurately into your text, using either summary, paraphrase, or direct quotation. Be sure to include the three parts of good internal documentation as you do so.

Exchange the citation and the paragraph(s) with the integrated source material with a classmate. Discuss the strengths and weaknesses of the documentation choices you have made.

318 Chapter 12 *Documenting Outside Sources*

STUDENTS AT WORK: SAMPLE MLA AND APA PAPERS

Following are two sample papers, one in MLA style, one in APA style. They are very different in style and rhetoric and demonstrate two different types in a range of possibilities for academic argument. The first argument against the appropriateness and effectiveness of the No Child Left Behind Act is lengthy because it depends for its power on heavy empirical evidence—numbers, observations, and research studies. An academic paper in this MLA documentation style might be written for any humanities class. The second paper depends on a different type of "evidence." The APA paper against hate crime legislation uses reasons against the rationale for hate crimes to argue against different sentencing based on the motivation of the criminal. An APA-documented paper is preferred in social science disciplines such as sociology and psychology, for example.

Dillon's and Bergford's Argument Concepts are extremely different, not only in topic, but in rhetorical intent. Examine the papers for their documentation technique, but also for their rhetorical and logical soundness. Questions for consideration follow each essay.

MLA Sample Paper

Dillon 1

Kimberly Dillon
Professor Aldrich
Eng122
April 28, 2006

Set Up to Fail

1   The level of education our nation's population receives is a fundamental factor in our nation's prosperity and our ranking among other countries. Our status in the global economy is directly affected by the quality of workers that we put into the work force. When we improve our educational system, we directly improve our standing in the global economy and our nation's prosperity. It is common knowledge that the level of education a person obtains plays a key role in the type of employment he or she has. In fact, a report by the U.S. Department of Education explains that those with a master's degree or higher experienced an increased employment rate of over 3.2 million from March of 1993 to March of 2003. In contrast, those with only a high school diploma experienced a meager increase of only 460,000. The report also suggests that significant advances in our nation's educational system could in turn produce a 4 percent increase to the Gross Domestic Product over the next 20 years (*A Guide* 2).

2   Because the education of our population has such a dynamic effect on our nation, it is no wonder that such an emphasis is put on improving the United States' educational system. One of the most recent of these attempts is seen in President Bush's No Child Left Behind Act

(NCLB) of 2002. This act encompasses the idea that standardized testing is the best way to weed out the successful schools from the "failing" ones. In 1999, the National Research Council put out a report suggesting that the principle behind standardized testing is that if a test were made to challenge every student and the curriculum taught in schools was designed around those tests, "then student learning would improve" (Buly and Valencia 5).

3   Due partially to the United States' non-traditional communities, including variables such as low-economic backgrounds and various ethnic groups, an educational gap has grown between students all over the country. The level of education received from one child to the next often varies. When the education gap grows, so does the employment gap. Reports show that the gap in education is responsible for two-thirds of the income gap between Mexican-Americans and Caucasians (Mehring 2). Bush's plan is an attempt to close the educational gap that has grown over the years. His main focus is using standardized tests, mandated in every state, to measure the level and quality of education being provided to students in this country. After the passage of NCLB, each state set up a system that labeled educational proficiency standards for children. A report put out by the United States Department of Education states that "the first principle of accountability for results involves the creation of standards in each state for what a child should know and learn in reading and math. . . . With those standards in place, student progress and achievement will be measured according to state tests designed to match those state standards and given to every child, every year" (*Stronger Accountability* 1). The goal of these standards is to have every child meet that proficient level set by each state by the year 2014. To accomplish this, adequate yearly progress (AYP) toward those standards must be shown by every school, so every school is given an AYP goal to meet each year (Novak and Fuller 2).

4   To ensure that a school's AYP goals are met, various forms of accountability have been put into effect all over the country. One form of accountability is seen in high school exit exams, given to students their senior year, and which students are required to pass in order to receive their high school diplomas. Other states require tests be given at the end of a school year to show that a student has gained the education needed to merit promotion to the next grade level. However, most tests given do not affect the students directly, but instead the accountability is placed on the schools. If a school does not meet AYP goals for three consecutive years, the school is marked as "failing" and becomes subject to state and national sanctions. These include reduced federal aid, "privatizing school management, firing staff, state takeovers, and similar measures . . ." (Guisbond and Neill 14). At this time, federal funding is removed from the school and given to individual students to pay for private school or tutoring.

5   Since education reform is a very controversial issue, due recognition should be given to the Bush administration for taking on such a task;

however, No Child Left Behind is not the answer for improving our nation's schools. Parents, teachers, and school administrators need to take a closer look at President Bush's NCLB school reform program. In doing so, they will find that the very plan that is meant to improve a child's education may be doing more harm than good. The "one-size-fits-all" solution seen in NCLB hurts those schools that are already achieving at an above average rate. Also, NCLB takes time away from "higher level" thinking and forces teachers to focus their time only on those subjects that are seen on the standardized tests. In addition, the score a school receives as a result of standardized tests may not be accurate because they do not reflect the school's non-traditional population: children from low-economic backgrounds, minority children, and children with disabilities.

6   One major flaw in NCLB is that it relies too heavily on a "one-size-fits-all" solution, which hurts those schools that are already achieving at an above average rate. No Child Left Behind leaves no room for "higher-order thinking" or creativity (Guisbond and Neill 13). Many schools are already excelling far beyond the mandatory levels set by state governments; therefore, the Bush Administration should not generalize a solution to a problem that for some is non-existent. However, because of the new tests and laws implemented, educators have to go backwards and work more on testing skills and the information on those tests instead of going forward to learn new things. Teachers and administrators are putting less of an emphasis on subjects such as "art, music, social studies, and physical education" because the standardized tests do not cover those topics (Amerim and Berliner 2). Teachers all over the country voice their opinion that standardized tests put too much stress on the subject matter of the tests as opposed to other essential information children should be learning. Half of the teachers surveyed in a study done by anthropologist Lesley Bartlett at the University of North Carolina in 1998 said that they had spent at least 40% of the school year focusing on studying for end of the year tests (8).

7   One unnamed parent expresses her concerns by saying, "Our children have always possessed a love of learning. This law is creating an environment where their love is being reduced to a quest for the highest scores" (qtd. in Zmiewski 1). One seventh grader explained his feelings well when he said that "the test is taking away the real meaning of school. Instead of learning new things and getting tools for life, the mission of the schools is becoming to do well on the test" (qtd. in Guisbond and Neill 13). Spending time preparing for standardized testing does not allow teachers and administrators to spend time on other important aspects of education or to focus on the individual needs to the students.

8   The graduation rates of upper-middle-class communities are also being affected. John Jennings, President of the Center on Education Policy, reports, "Upper-middle-class communities are generally

satisfied with their schools. Their kids are going to college. They feel they control their schools. And they don't want high school exit exams interrupting their kids' path to college" (qtd. in "Testing in Schools" 3). However, one argument for NCLB is that graduation rates are so low that reform and higher standards are vitally needed in schools ("Leave No Grades" 1). Therefore, because of the NCLB school reform plan, new laws are now being implemented that require students to pass the standardized tests given in order to graduate; eighteen states have already instituted them. If a student does not pass the test, he or she has the potential of needing to repeat the senior year of high school. These new tests ensure that the average graduation rate will be lower than ever (Bartlett 11). "Some children just don't perform well on multiple-choice tests," says professor Theodore R. Sizer of Brown University, founder of the Coalition of Essential Schools. "To try to nail down the quality of a school after a few hours of paper and pencil tests seems, to me, pretty hard to defend" (qtd. in "National Education Standards" 2). Multiple-choice tests do not accurately reflect a child's education. They are a very limited way to assess knowledge and learning. Many children do not do well on multiple-choice tests, and many more are poor test takers overall. Assessing a student through such a limited source of information has the potential of being inaccurate and unfair to a student who may very well have received a high-quality education but who does poorly on standardized tests.

9 Last, No Child Left Behind gives schools with non-traditional populations a biased score. In schools around the country, children are put into subgroups to ensure that no child is being "left behind." These groups include various ethnic backgrounds, English as a Second Language students, disabled students, and children from low-economic backgrounds (Novak and Fuller 1). "The idea is to prevent schools [from] neglecting harder-to-teach groups such as students from low-economic backgrounds, minority children, and children with disabilities" ("Progress and Confusion" 2). Because each of these factors is not accounted for in the scores a school receives, many scores given to schools with non-traditional communities are unfair and do not reflect the schools' students' knowledge accurately.

10 In 1992, the National Assessment of Educational Progress issued a report stating that 89% of the difference in scores was due to four main factors: the education of the parents, the "number of parents in the home," the community the children live in, and the economic background of the children (Bartlett 8). Schools with kids from low-income families are likely to be hurt by standardized tests. Family income plays a large role in the quality of education children receive. A study by the Common Sense Foundation shows evidence that there is a direct correlation between the number of students receiving free or reduced lunches and the grades received on standardized tests by schools (Bartlett 9). "Many critics fear that without major financial investments,

poor students will be hit by a double whammy. First they will be tested without first being given the same benefits as rich kids, and then poor test results will be used to cut funding in their schools" ("National Education Standards" 8).

11   In 1999, officials reviewed the results for a standardized test issued in Colorado, the Colorado State Assessment Program (CSAP). The results showed that the correlation between the scores achieved on the CSAP test and the percentage of low-income students attending those schools is strong. A report in the *Denver Post* in 2000 regarding CSAP scores stated that "schools with a lot of kids receiving federally subsidized lunches generally did worse than more affluent schools" (Illescas and Bingham 1). That same report showed a graph demonstrating the statistics more clearly: 76% of the fourth grade students in a school with a mere 0-10% of low-income students were graded as "proficient or above" in reading. In contrast, only 25% of fourth graders in a school with 91-100% of low-income students were given a proficient or above. The report went on to say that if the grades received were "based solely on 1999 fourth-grade reading results, 66 of 789 schools would get an A. Of those, 45 have fewer than 10 percent low-income students. Seventeen schools would get an F. All but two have poverty rates of more than 75 percent" (1). In other words, those schools with a high population of students from low-income families achieved scores far lower than those schools which served children in more wealthy communities.

12   The CSAP models the type of tests required by the government. These statistics reasonably reflect the achievement levels of underprivileged children as compared to those in more affluent households on any standardized test taken. Average Yearly Progress standards are, on average, less likely achieved by those schools that have children from low-income families (Novak and Fuller 4).*

13   Those who feel that the No Child Left Behind school reform program will improve our nation's educational system need to rethink their positions in this matter and more closely examine the evidence that suggests otherwise. The Bush Administration's plan imposes a "one-size-fits-all" solution on schools all over the country. While standardized testing may seem to be the only way to test school improvement, attempting to judge a child's learning and a school's performance through such a limited source of information has the potential of giving inaccurate and unfair scores to schools that very well may be providing

---

*In the interest of conserving space, a multiple-paragraph section has been omitted here that provides reasons and statistics demonstrating that schools with highly diverse populations (minority children, children with disabilities, and children from low economic backgrounds) have the lowest chance of reaching the required goals of NCLB and are, therefore, at an unfair disadvantage.

a high-quality education to their students. Also, NCLB is a biased attempt to ensure that every child is receiving the best education possible. Resources and money need to be provided to schools at the federal level in order for schools to be able to achieve the standards mandated by the state governments. Only when these failings are addressed will our country be on its way to improving the education of, not just a few but, every child in our nation.

Works Cited

A Guide to Education and No Child Left Behind. Oct. 2004. United States Department of Education. Office of the Secretary. Office of Public Affairs. 2 March 2005 <http://www.ed.gov/print/nclb/overview/intro/guide/html>.

Amerim, Audrey, and David C. Berliner. *Executive Summary: An Analysis of Some Unintended and Negative Consequences of High-Stakes Testing*. Dec. 2002. Arizona State University. 19 April 2005 <http//www.asu.edu/educ/epsl/EPRU/documents/EPSL-0211-125-EPRU-exec.pdf>.

Bartlett, Lesley. *The Tyranny of the Test: The Social Implications of North Carolina's Accountability Program*. 2001. U. of North Carolina. 9 April 2005 <http://www.unc.edu/depts/antrho/talks/bartlett.pdf>.

Buly, Marsha Riddle, and Sheila W. Valencia. "Below the Bar: Profiles of Students Who Fail State Reading Assessments." *Educational Evaluation and Policy Analysis*, 19 April 2005 <http://www.reading firstohio.org/worddocs/Salinger_Below_the_Bar1.pdf>.

Guisbond, Lisa, and Monty Neill. "Failing Our Children: No Child Left Behind Undermines Quality and Equity in Education." *Clearing House* 78.1 (2004): 12. Academic Search Premier. EBSCOhost. Jerry A. Kiefer Library. 2 March 2005 <http//www.epnet.com>.

Illescas, Carlos, and Janet Bingham. "Is the Testing Fair to Poor Students?" *Denver Post* 27 Feb. 2000. 19 April 2005 <http// 63.147.65.175/testing/test0227b.htm>.

Mehring, James. "Latinos' Education Gap." *Business Week* 2 Aug. 2004. Academic Search Premier. EBSCOhost. Jerry A. Kiefer Library. 23 April 2005 <html://www.epnet.com>.

"National Education Standards." *The CQ Researcher Online* 9/18 (1999). 22 April 2005 <http://library.cqpress.com/cqresearcher/cqreserre 10000514000>.

Novak, John R., and Bruce Fuller. *Policy Brief: Penalizing Diverse Schools?* Dec. 2003. Arizona State University. 19 April 2005 <http://www.asu.edu.educ/epsl/EPRU/documents/EPRU-o312-48-RW.pdf>.

"Progress and Confusion." *Economist* 27 Sept 2003. Academic Search Premier. EBSCOhost. Jerry A. Kiefer Library. 25 March 2005 <http://search.epnet.com/login/aspx?direct=trie&db=aph&an=10953689>.

Sage, Kathy. Personal interview. 23 April 2005.

Stronger Accountability: Testing for Results. Jan. 2002. United States Department of Education. Office of the Secretary. Office of Public Affairs. 2 March 2005 <http://www.ed.gov/print/nclb/accountability/ayp/testingforresults. html>.

"Testing in Schools." *The CQ Researcher Online.* November 15, 2001. Jerry A. Kiefer Library. 21 April 2005 <http://library.cqpress.com/cqresearcher/cqresrre2001041000>.

Zmiewski, Barbra. "'No Child' Quest for High Scores Leaves Good Sense Behind." *USA Today* 1 March 2005. Academic Search Premier. EBSCOhhost. Jerry A Kiefer Library. 4 March 2005 <http://www.epnet.com>.

Questions for Consideration

1. Dillon uses a "blind" quote—one with no "ID tag" or identifying material. How could she write a better lead-in to that quotation? Where else in her argument do you see blind quotes?

2. Review Dillon's "Works Cited" list. Does it seem authoritative? Balanced? Dillon has used mostly sources she found electronically. What is the nature of these sources, and how can you tell from the citations if they are probably reliable or not? Review the section in this chapter titled "External Documentation of Electronic Sources." Has Dillon created appropriate "Works Cited" references for these sources?

3. Where does Dillon give credit to the opposition? Does this strengthen or weaken her argument?

4. What is Dillon's most convincing evidence in her argument? Why is it so?

5. Has the author used a good balance of summary, paraphrase, and direct quotation? If not, what would you suggest? Find a place where Dillon has used a detailed summary of one of her sources instead of just saying, "Research shows that I'm right."

APA Sample Paper (by student writer Brad Bergford)

Justly accused 1

Justly Accused—Unjustly Sentenced*

1   In this country, we tout our rights to think and believe as we wish—right or wrong. One notable exception to these rights occurs when thoughts and beliefs are shown to have catalyzed a crime. So-called "hate crime" laws criminalize and effectively revoke the rights to think and believe

---

*Papers in APA style begin with a title page with the following features in the same font as the text, double-spaced and centered: title, student name, course number and title, instructor's name, and date.

freely. Jeannine Bell (2002), an associate professor of law from Indiana University and a PhD in political science, points out that "the political and intellectual debate on hate crime is dominated by three main concerns: 1) that hate crime legislation is special protection for minorities; 2) that hate crime legislation will be enforced in a way that violates the First Amendment; and 3) hate crime law is redundant" (p. 181). This argument will address the last two issues.

2   The Violent Crime Control and Law Enforcement Act of 1994 defines *hate crime* as "a crime in which the defendant intentionally selects a victim, or in the case of a property crime, the property that is the object of the crime, because of actual or perceived race, color, religion, national origin, ethnicity, gender, disability, or sexual orientation of any person" (Altschiller, 1999). Enhanced sentencing is the corresponding increase in the sentence for a given crime due to its classification as a hate crime. The sentence enhancement for a violator of this act's provisions is "not less than three offense levels for offenses that the finders of fact at trial determine beyond a reasonable doubt are hate crimes" (p. 17).

3   Hate crime sentencing must be examined from a practical standpoint to determine whether it can satisfy any of the moral requirements of sentences: that they contain some element of retribution, rehabilitation, deterrence, and/or punishment ("Sentencing Alternatives" 2004). When a criminal's personal bias is being sentenced, how would any of these requirements be properly applied? How would a criminal pay his debt to his victim and to society (provide retribution) for thinking the way he does? Or how can we change his thoughts (rehabilitate) and dissuade (deter) him from these thoughts in the future? What penalty (punishment) would fit this crime? Most importantly, how could success in any of these areas be measured? We know how victims recover from broken arms and theft, but how do they recover from hate? In any free society, laws cannot and never have been intended to govern the thoughts of people—only their actions. The notion that we could determine the appropriate severity of a sentence for criminal thoughts, or conversely, to think that we could predict the degree to which such a sentence will be efficacious is ridiculous. For these reasons, only criminal actions—not opinions or motives—should be prosecuted and sentenced.

4   Some proponents of enhanced sentencing for hate crimes maintain that hate crimes are unique because there are not only direct victims of these crimes, but indirect victims as well. Indirect victims are those belonging to the same group as the victim who, by virtue of their inclusion in this group, are indirect mental and/or emotional casualties of the crime in question. Those belonging to the same group as the victim are said to feel that an attack against one member of the group is an attack against all members of the group. Frederick Lawrence, Associate Dean and Professor of Law at Boston University School of Law and author of *Punishing Hate: Bias Crimes Under American Law* (2002),

discusses the justifications frequently made for hate crime legislation. According to Lawrence, indirect victims are also believed to be traumatized by the fear that they may suffer a fate like that of the direct victim some day (Lawrence, 2002). For two reasons this rationale is unsound. First, according to this assertion, people perceiving their inclusion in the same group as a particular crime victim could be considered direct victims of that crime regardless of whether they are aware of the criminal's motive. Carried to its outer limits, this argument means that anyone perceiving any commonality with any victim is an indirect victim of the given crime. Second, the potentially broad scope of indirect victims of hate crimes may appear to give justification to a more severe punishment for the convicted; however, these indirect victims are to some extent hypothetical. There is no way to know the number of indirect victims resulting from a particular crime, nor can we quantify or qualify indirect damage to indirect victims. This type of thinking where hypothetical builds on hypothetical works well in science fiction movies, but has no place in the American criminal justice system.

5 Hate crime laws also fail in upholding our standards of jurisprudence. There is often no way to see into the mind of any person and prove that a belief he or she holds is what motivated a particular crime, as opposed to some other factor. For example, someone who hates people of Asian descent may rob an Asian-American. It may be proven by testimony and even admitted by the offender that he hates Asian-Americans, and yet he may have been otherwise motivated to steal. That someone hates is not equivalent to being motivated to injure. Consider the case of a local ex-gang member I know. Joe, who prefers anonymity, used to perpetrate crimes against strangers for the purpose of acquiring money or possessions he or the gang desired. Rival gang members were fair game at any time and place, and they were the objects of unspeakable violence. Such crimes against other gangs were undoubtedly motivated by hate, although probably not the kind of hate directed at those who are different from the perpetrator as the criteria for "hate crimes" intend. Other times, the gang would cruise the streets on Saturday night having decided that, after bowling and a bite at a fast food joint, they might, for example, find someone in a red car to beat up as a sort of recreational activity. In this case, if the driver was, incidentally, of a different racial background than the attackers, a prosecutor might argue for hate crime sentencing when the victim targeted was in fact absolutely random. Finally, Joe said some crimes (mostly theft) were committed against complete strangers. In these instances, someone might conclude again, if the victims were in a different demographic group from the gang members, that they had chosen to steal from these people because of the perception of their membership in some group when the gang was totally unaware of this circumstance.

The outward appearance of each of these crimes might be that they were hate-motivated. However, only in the first was hate remotely part of the motivation. The inability to clearly determine hate as a motivator and the degree to which it motivated a crime is one of the glaring weaknesses of hate crime laws.

6   Another weakness of this type of legislation is the idea that a motive for a crime may or may not be punishable. This is absurd because it suggests that while some motives are not acceptable, some are. What criminal's motive is good? What victim approves of his offender's motive? I doubt any daughter whose father had been stabbed to death for reasons other than the perpetrator's bias would find consolation in knowing so. Further, by allowing more serious punishment under hate crime laws, we may be sending a message to victims of non-hate crimes that their lives and well-being are valued less than those of hate crime victims.

7   Hate crime laws are made less necessary by the relative strength of existing sentencing laws which provide for judicial discretion based on aggravating factors. If a judge believes there is some reason to hand down a sentence in excess of the minimum for any crime, she has the authority to do so without having to meet the additional requirements of hate crime legislation.

8   Hate crime laws are well-intentioned, but as singer/songwriter Michael W. Smith put it, "the road of good intentions doesn't lead to anywhere." Despite the unpalatability of hate, it is not in and of itself a crime and should not be treated as criminal under any circumstances. The prospect of accurately and fairly dispensing justice for hatred is strictly subjective, eluding the laws of logic and common sense. We must undertake only the prosecution of crimes and not of Constitutionally protected rights of freedom of thought. It is time we abandon the irony of preferring some criminals (and subsequently, their victims) to others because they think of people differently, and provide criminals and victims the equal justice they deserve.

References

Altschiller, D. (1999). *Hate crimes*. Santa Barbara, CA: ABC-CLIO.

Bell, J. (2002). *Policing hatred: Law enforcement, civil rights, and hate crimes*. New York: New York University Press.

Lawrence, F. (2002). Punishing hate: Bias crime under American law. Boston: Harvard University Press.

Sentencing alternatives: From incarceration to diversion. Retrieved July 14, 2004, from Nolo.com. <http://www.nolo.com/lawcenter/ency/article.cfm>.

Smith, M. (1992). Give it away. In *Change Your World*. Los Angeles: Geffen Records.

Questions for Consideration

1. Bergford's intention is to assail the justification of hate crime laws, so he does not include any illustrations of these crimes. Three of his sources, Altschiller, Bell, and Lawrence, include copious examples of this type of crime as well as a historical perspective. Would it strengthen or weaken Bergford's argument to include any of these examples?

2. What effect did the information from "Joe" have on you? What effect will it possibly have on Bergford's reader?

3. One of Bergford's sources, Frederick Lawrence's book, is a strong argument in favor of hate crime legislation. Would Bergford's argument be strengthened or weakened by more inclusion of the opposition's argument?

4. Which type of argument, the heavily researched Dillon argument, or the logical attack of Bergford, do you find more compelling? Which approach do you think would be more effective for the readers each writer has in mind?

5. Which writer's voice seems more authentic, less sterile? Is that an advantage or disadvantage? Does the voice fit each writer's Argument Concept, or should there be some adjustment?

DISCOVERING YOUR OWN ARGUMENTS: REVIEWING AND REVISING YOUR SOURCE USE

Considering the skills of documentation discussed in this chapter and the examples you have analyzed, review your researched argument carefully to see where you can improve the integration and citation of your sources. Remember, even though you may have cited sources correctly and accurately, you may be able to improve on the readability of your internal documentation, and such improved coherence will lead to more clarity for your reader. You don't want all the good work you have done in constructing and developing your argument to be obscured by cumbersome documentation.

REFLECTIONS ON THE CHAPTER

Taking the time to acknowledge your sources carefully and thoroughly is important. If you think about the way you would want someone to treat your prized possessions, you'll feel an obligation to use the ideas of others appropriately and accurately. High quality use of material serves you as well. Your reader recognizes that you are competent and ethical, two characteristics that should add to your credibility as an arguer. In the last and critical chapter, you will practice two final ways of increasing your credibility as a writer: revision and editing.

CHAPTER

13

Revising Your Written Argument

We often encourage students to reread an essay or some other school assignment that they wrote some time in the past. We want to know if they still believe the piece is as good as they thought when they first composed it. Most students admit they would make substantial changes if they were to write the paper again. But when we ask those students why they didn't make major changes in the first place, a common response (and a fair one, we believe) is that they didn't really know *how* to revise with any confidence. And like the old adage that even professional writers live by, "A paper is never really *done*; it's just *due*."

Chapter 13 provides you with a method of revision—real *revision*, not mere *editing*—that will help you improve your arguments. However, all effective writers know that making significant changes to a draft is sometimes like cutting off a limb. After all, a writer has spent hours gathering materials, sweating over a draft, worrying about its quality—and now it needs to be changed? Do not fear the revision process. We show you step by step how effective writers go about making necessary changes to increase an argument's persuasive appeal.

TERMS AND CONCEPTS TO WATCH FOR

- Revising
- Editing

QUESTIONS TO GUIDE YOUR READING

- Why does effective revising entail more than just error correction?
- What are some tips to make your revising more effective?
- Why will the four steps to revising a draft generally overlap?
- Why should a writer revise "big stuff" before revising "small stuff"?
- What "Top Ten Editing Errors" most commonly hurt a writer's credibility?

BASIC REVISING ADVICE

Experienced writers will tell you that revising a piece of writing is as important—if not more so—than writing an original draft. Such writers recognize that early drafts are never the polished products that they would allow friends or publishers to see, in spite of how long those early drafts took to compose or how hard the author worked. Experienced writers would never allow themselves the indulgence of saying, "Hey, I worked on this draft for nearly an hour. It ought to be good by now!"

We have learned that novice writers tend to hope and believe that their early drafts of an argument are better than they are. Still, when they are not—and the writers willingly admit this—many become too easily discouraged too soon. "Why," they wonder, "do my early drafts not sparkle with brilliance and calls for publication? Why is this writing thing so hard?" If this sounds like you, it is time to dispel some myths about how truly effective arguments come into play. Maybe you believe, for instance, that published writers must be people born with a computer and thesaurus in their hands. These writers merely sit down, rub their hands together, and watch as words leap onto the computer screen. Rubbish. Effective writers at all levels experience the same frustrations you do; they just approach the revising of their early work differently.

For one thing, effective writers do not confuse "revising" with "editing." Real revision is not mere error correction, those times when you strike out a comma or correct a misspelled word. Although such corrections must be made to maintain your credibility, of course, focusing on such errors in early drafts may limit your chances to make substantive and necessary changes in the work as a whole. And if your argument's primary flaws are its lack of evidence or focus upon the issue, changing a comma or eliminating a fragment alone will not increase its persuasive appeal. Revision, on the other hand, calls for you to examine a draft realistically for its focus, amount of evidence, organization, and, finally, its correct punctuation, spelling, and so forth. Consider the following tips to improve any draft of an argument. See if they help you rethink and recast what you really want to say.

Basic Revising Advice 331

> **REVISING** *is the practice of reviewing the* global *aspects of a paper — its focus, evidence, and organization.*

> **EDITING** *is the practice of finding and correcting errors in mechanics and grammar.*

1. *Allow a draft to "cool off."* A good tip, one that professional writers use all the time, is to allow a draft to "cool off" before making changes to it. This practice is easy: shut down your computer and do not look at your draft for a period of time, anywhere from a few hours to a few days, if possible. If you are like us, you become so wrapped up in a draft that pretty soon you cannot really see it for what it is. You begin to reread your argument for what you think it says (or is supposed to say) rather than for what it actually says. Putting a draft away for a while will allow your throbbing brain and bloodshot eyes to refocus. You need to regain your objectivity before you run screaming into the night. And, of course, this advice is one more reason that professors admonish you not to put your writing off until the last minute.

   After a time, pull out your draft and read it, this time with the eyes of someone refreshed and ready to be honest. What you will see may amaze you. "Did I really write this? How could I conclude such a thing based upon this evidence? How could I allow such a sentence in my paper? I must have had my eyes crossed." Accept that your paper needs changes. It happens to all writers. But at least with a more rested view, you have a better chance of improving the argument and increasing its persuasive power.

2. *At first, trust your own vocabulary.* Students often feel less than confident about the level of their vocabularies. They believe that they do not possess sufficient words to sound "academic" or "expert" enough. So, many turn to "thesaurus surfing" to find words with more syllables or words they believe will make them sound more mature. Unfortunately, using a thesaurus for this purpose may create more hilarity from your reader than credibility. Perhaps you want to use the word *building* in a draft but believe it sounds too mundane, so you turn to your trusty thesaurus where you find the word *edifice* and replace *building* with it: "The arsonist ran from the now-burning edifice." Ask yourself, though, if *edifice*, not currently in your usable vocabulary, is really "you." Does the use of a word with which you were formerly unfamiliar really increase your reader's trust and positive response? Really?

   We subscribe to the common writing adage of the K.I.S.S. principle—meaning "Keep It Simple, Stupid." Readers rarely find overblown, inflated language to their liking, preferring instead a straightforward, simple-to-read piece of writing. Our advice is this: Be yourself. Be as clear and concise with your language choices as possible. Of course, your vocabulary will grow over the years, and turning to a thesaurus is sometimes a good idea, especially when you have used the same word many times in a draft or when the perfect word really *is* in your vocabulary, but for whatever reason your vocabulary is on vacation. In these cases, the thesaurus may indeed help. Just do not select any word you find as a synonym merely because it sounds more "authoritative."

3. *Start revising with larger concerns and move to smaller concerns.* Though the notion of "larger" and "smaller" concerns within a piece of writing may be new to you, think about how effective writers go about changing an argument for the better. If you correct all the punctuation and spelling errors in an early draft—a draft that remains unfocused or underdeveloped—will that draft really be any better? The draft will certainly be more "correct" but probably not more effective.

Consider this analogy: When you rearrange the furniture in a room, where do you begin? Most likely, you move the "larger" pieces first (piano, couch, loveseat) before concerning yourself with the "smaller" items (plants, lamps, knickknacks), right? The same principle applies to revising. Begin with examining an argument's whole focus, for example, before revising the focus of a single paragraph or individual sentence. Be sure the argument is persuasive overall before worrying about a verb in sentence five. Then, move progressively. Rethink the whole argument, then whole sections one by one, then whole paragraphs, and then whole sentences.

Following this pattern, you not only enhance the effectiveness of your argument, but you may save time as well. After all, why worry about a misplaced apostrophe in a sentence if your primary concern should be for the entire sentence? Why work early in the process to change items that may not remain in later drafts anyway?

4. *Turn to "outside" help.* We often suggest to students that they print out their entire argument before revising it. Since most computer screens only allow you to see part of a single page, printing the whole piece provides you with the chance to see your entire piece of writing in all its groaning glory at this point. This way, you can look at how whole sections connect to others, how individual paragraphs support a larger reason, how individual pieces of evidence line up in support of smaller conclusions, and so on.

Here is yet another tip: At some point in your revising process, ask someone unfamiliar with your topic (but willing and able enough) to read your paper aloud. Turn away from the reader and just listen to how your argument sounds. Hear any clinks and clanks? If so, have your reader mark the offending spot and continue. You may be amazed at how an argument sounds "choppy" or disconnected in places, something you may not detect by reading the piece over and over to yourself.

> **ALSO NOTE**
>
> **HELP FROM ANOTHER READER**
>
> The suggestion that you ask another reader to give you feedback on your argument can be one of the best aids to revision. Your argument was intended to be read, and someone other than you can let you know how close your intentions are to the actual effect.
>
> But you will only get what you ask for. Unless you set up the experience correctly, you may have the frustrating experience some of our students have when they ask a friend to read their papers. The friend says, "Looks good to me," and the student thinks the argument is in good shape. The reader may not have wanted to offend a friend with criticism or may not have understood enough about what the writer was trying to accomplish to give competent feedback.
>
> You may get more helpful feedback if you use these suggestions to set up the experience:
>
> - Ask specific questions ("I'm not sure if the information on the third page is fair to the opposition") instead of saying, "Would you read this and tell me what you think?"
> - Explain that this is just a draft and you know it needs work. Ask readers to mark spots where they are confused or where they question your assertions.
> - Ask a reader to point out your weakest and strongest points.
> - Ask if the reader had an objection to a point that you have not considered.
> - Ask the reader to underline any words or phrases that caused problems.
> - Ask the reader to write out the main argument that he or she thinks you made in the paper. You may be surprised!
>
> Asking for the kind of help that will help you revise rather than asking for confirmation from a friend will get you much better information.

5. *Revise from most important to least important.* One of the most meaningful ways to revise an argument is to follow the same four-step revision process that most effective writers do. Granted, not everyone follows these steps in the same manner, and generally the steps will overlap as your argument becomes more fully formed. Nonetheless, having a plan to change the effectiveness of your argument is better than just saying, "Well, I guess I should try to make this better somehow." Follow these steps in order as much as possible when you rethink a draft, with the caveat that you may have to repeat some steps. In other words, because you have revised for focus (step 1) does not mean that once you have revised the quality of your evidence

(step 2) that you may not have to reconsider the breadth of your focus. This revising process is not some plan set in stone; it just gives you a plan by which you can improve an argument's power.

ALSO NOTE
A WORD TO THE WISE REVISER

Take advantage of the many people who are eager to help you with your revision process.

1. *Writing teachers* are ecstatic when a student comes in with a legitimate and thoughtful question. Check on your instructor's office hours, or talk to him or her after class about an appointment. Don't wait until the hour before the paper is due—you may not get a positive response at that point.
2. Most schools have excellent *Writing Centers* where trained writing tutors are available to help you with your project at any stage. If you are having trouble narrowing your topic, writing an introduction, supporting a point, developing alternative arguments, or even learning how to avoid comma splices, the Writing Center is there to help. Sometimes you will have to make an appointment, but often there is drop-in tutoring. Check with your center for policies.
3. *OWLS—Online Writing Labs—*are another option for help. They range from the clever, interactive "Virgil" site at the University of Texas at Austin (uwc-server.fac.utexas.edu/) to the Virtual Writing lab at Rensselaer Polytechnic Institute (rpi.edu/dept/llc/writecenter/web/online.html) that provides a visitor with a wide range of possible avenues for help. One of the most popular and widely used is the Purdue University Owl (owl.english.purdue.edu/). You can find many more online options by searching "online writing labs."

REVISING THE FOCUS ON READER AND PURPOSE

One of your most crucial concerns when revising your argument is its focus upon your intended reader and purpose. If you have formed an Argument Concept, you have already worked to narrow your focus upon a reader and his or her needs and to ensure that the purpose for your argument is clear and doable. In any case, when you begin to revise an argument, you want to make sure that you can fulfill the promise of your claim. A focused claim is one that you can defend with ample evidence and examples within the targeted limits of your assigned paper or professional task.

Your claim is too broad, too ambiguous, if you cannot defend it with rich and proportioned reasons and evidence to your reader's satisfaction. For example, a claim that purports, "Public schools should move to year-round scheduling because of the many advantages of doing so" leaves a reader scratching his or her head, wondering exactly where this argument will go. What exactly does "because of the many advantages" mean? What precise reasons and evidence might you offer? It would be better to refocus the claim to something like this: "Public schools should move to year-round scheduling to ensure that students maintain their basic skills in reading and writing." Now, the reader sees the direction of the argument and anticipates that you will provide reasons and evidence that year-round scheduling shows promise in basic skills retention. Plus, *you* now understand the limits of your argument much better than when you conceived a preliminary Argument Concept and claim. You will include evidence specifically aimed at basic skills and longer school years while excluding reasons and evidence concerning how year-round schools use building space more efficiently, provide greater flexibility in scheduling, reduce overcrowding, and so forth. Although the excluded reasons are certainly significant, your focus is upon basic skills—leaving the other advantages of year-round schools for another argument, another time.

Though building an argument from an Argument Concept probably helped you focus well before you drafted, you may have gotten sidetracked in your eagerness to include everything you learned while preparing to argue. A careful and self-critical second (or third, or . . .) look at your focus may reveal sections that simply don't belong in this argument.

Questions to Help Revise Focus

1. Can my claim be fully and significantly defended in the length and in the time I have for my argument? How might I narrow its scope if I decide it commits me to more than I can support?

2. Is it possible that one of my major sections in my current draft might serve as the focus for my entire argument?

3. What do I know about my reader's needs concerning my current focus? Can I define necessary terms, provide ample evidence, and illustrate relevant examples without writing a library-length argument?

4. Is my claim clearly stated in clear, concise language?

5. Is every reason and piece of evidence (in every paragraph) in my current draft necessary to defend my claim? Is every piece of information in individual paragraphs relevant to that paragraph's point? Are there places in my draft where I seem to go on a tangent, including some preplanned section that now seems less than relevant?

STUDENTS AT WORK: REVISION BEGINS

Throughout this chapter, we will follow a student's step-by-step revision process. This demonstration comes from student Rachel Morales's argument concerning health care for seasonal migrant workers. We will follow Rachel as she revises

336 Chapter 13 *Revising Your Written Argument*

only a single paragraph, but such an example illustrates how the four steps of revision help Rachel strengthen her argument.

Rachel had studied the issue of health care for migrant workers for some time, and she finally decided to defend this claim: "States should adopt policies that ensure quality health care for their seasonal Spanish-speaking migrant workers." Granted, this stance may itself be revised at a later time, but for now Rachel had a working claim for her piece. At one point in her first draft, Rachel composed the following paragraph:

> Migrant workers needing health care often find access to such care very limited. Transportation to and from health care facilities poses a major obstacle. Most migrant workers, of course, come to this country without personal transportation and must rely on buses or taxis (which they often cannot afford) to get to a doctor's office. This means they must know the bus schedule in an area or have access to a telephone to call a taxi—both options in English only. But even if they work out their transportation needs, once at the health care facility, migrants encounter health care workers who do not speak their language. How does a person who speaks no English tell a doctor what their health care needs are? Most health care facilities that treat migrant patients have no translators available, reducing the discussion between patient and doctor to hand gestures and eventual frustration. Simply because someone does not speak English should not keep them from getting the medical help they need.

Comments on the First Draft

- Though Rachel's initial draft reads blandly, she has the opportunity to improve it as she revises further. At least she has a start.
- Note here that even if Rachel corrected the punctuation and sentence errors in this draft, it still would not read convincingly.
- The primary problem with this paragraph is that it has a split focus. Rachel includes two problems of health care access for migrant workers: transportation and language differences. She would be wise to select one of these topics and develop it fully for more effectiveness.

■ STUDENTS AT WORK: SECOND DRAFT

Rachel revised her paragraph to resolve some of the problems she discovered with the focus of her argument (step 1 in the revision process):

> Should migrant workers needing health care resolve their transportation needs, they still encounter difficulties with health care workers who speak no Spanish. One can only imagine the difficulties for a migrant worker attempting to explain to a doctor what health care needs they have when that doctor speaks only English. Without a translator available, for

> example, how would a woman tell her doctor she is having stomach cramps, abnormal periods, or depression? All medical conditions not apparent from a visible examination. She would have to resort to hand gestures, perhaps drawings, both of which are less than perfect and certainly which would lead to frustration on the part of patient and doctor alike. If health care facilities would anticipate the language needs of migrant workers by providing Spanish-speaking interpreters, those migrant workers could receive the medical help they deserve.

Comments on the Second Draft

- Rachel's second draft of her paragraph is improved in that she has selected only the issue of language difficulties for its focus. She has also decided to place the transportation problem in the paragraph immediately preceding this one, evident from her transition in the first sentence.
- Here again, Rachel's paragraph contains a few sentence-level errors, but fixing them at this point still would not improve her piece significantly.
- Perhaps you can see that the real problem with Rachel's persuasiveness is her lack of real examples and evidence. She needs to provide more specific comment, perhaps, from authorities in the issue of migrant health care. Doing so would add the weight of experts to her argument, lessening the reader's impression that Rachel may simply be arguing for a point only she believes to be true.

REVISING THE AMOUNT AND QUALITY OF EVIDENCE

When you believe your argument has a focused stance (keep in mind that you may still reexamine your focus later), you must evaluate the evidence in your draft. In our experience, many student-written arguments fail to be persuasive not because the issue is uninteresting or insignificant, but because the evidence used by a student is too "thin" to be convincing. So, begin by asking yourself if your evidence is sufficient. Do you provide enough reasons, evidence, interviewee remarks, quotations, statistics, exact dates, etc. to be persuasive? In early drafts, your response will probably be "no." Many students new to writing argument too often assume that they have written a convincing argument because of the "well, it seems convincing to me" syndrome. Be wary. Remember the thinking error of subjectivism studied in Chapter 5. Do not be too quick to assume that because you have done some research and have included it in your argument that a reasonable reader will find it equally persuasive. Let your draft "cool off" for a time (or show it to another person not familiar with your issue) to help determine if your evidence supports your stance.

Likewise, ask yourself if every reason and piece of evidence is relevant to your stance. When you research an issue, you will locate all sorts of interesting and powerful information. Do not be overly tempted, though, to include that information merely because you went to the trouble of finding it, and it seems really interesting to you. Always question whether you need the information for its persuasive appeal.

At this stage of your revising process, too, take care to examine how your evidence and your conclusions from it relate. You want to avoid committing any of the thinking errors discussed in Chapter 5. Be honest. Have you reasonably drawn your conclusions, or have you done so because you *want* something to be a certain way, or you have always believed that a certain effect must have the cause you cite? Your reader just wants a forthright and interestingly evidenced discussion of your issue. He or she wants to trust you. Try not to betray that trust.

Questions to Help Revise Evidence Use

- Does my argument contain a sufficient number of body paragraphs to make a convincing case? In its current form, does each paragraph offer a relevant argument in support of my claim?
- Does each paragraph say anything? Have I relied only on assertions rather than real evidence? Does it contain enough illustrative, specific, concrete evidence? Would the addition of another example, another statistic, another fact improve the persuasive power of this paragraph?
- Is the point of each paragraph (each reason provided) apparent to my reader? Do I make clear *why* I say what I do?
- Does my argument overall contain a healthy combination of facts, examples, statistics, authoritative comment, and personal experience to make my case convincingly? Does the overall argument sound too stuffy, too formal for my reader's needs? Should I add more of my own comments and conclusions?

STUDENTS AT WORK: REVISING THE EVIDENCE

Rachel reviewed the evidence that she needed to support her argument in step 2 of the revision process and then wrote the third draft of her paragraph:

> Should migrant workers needing health care resolve their transportation needs, they still encounter difficulties with health care workers who speak no Spanish. One can only imagine the difficulties for a migrant worker attempting to explain to a doctor what health care needs they have when that doctor speaks only English. Speaking at a U.S. Department of Health and Human Services forum in Boston, Wilson Augustave, a migrant farm workers representative for the National Migrant Health Advisory Council, reported on some of the barriers faced by non-English-speaking migrants: "Sometimes farm workers go into their local communities to be seen at the emergency room . . . and they don't have someone on staff to translate. Many times they [farm workers] have to have their kids, who may not know the medical terminology, translate for them." Such was the case for Emilia Zamora, a field worker in rural New Mexico. Zamora entered a health care facility suffering from a painful bent back, a condition she assumed resulted from long hours stooping to weed onions and cauliflower. The doctor, however, diagnosed her as having osteoporosis.

> A condition of having too little calcium in Zamora's body severely affected her spine. Zamora speaks no English, so the doctor attempted to describe her condition to her nine-year-old son. One can imagine the difficulty of a young boy trying to understand a term such as osteoporosis, a word for which he had no Spanish equivalent. He told his mother she had "bad bones." A University of Tennessee report noted that like Zamora's son, ". . . untrained translators are acting as interpreters under the most difficult of circumstances. The translators are asked to accurately convey crucial information in life or death situations." We must sympathize with the feelings of cultural isolation that such migrant workers face when they seek medical care in non-Spanish speaking facilities. Most people find a doctor's visit uncomfortable enough without having language barriers to deal with also.

Comments on the Third Draft

- Rachel has improved her argument in this paragraph significantly by citing two credible authorities. She now demonstrates that others who have studied the problem of migrant health care share her concern that language differences set up barriers to quality health care.
- The use of the Zamora example makes the problem of language barriers more real and personal. Now, Rachel must reconsider the organization of her paragraph.

REVISING ORGANIZATION

If you are determined to compose an effective argument, you probably wrote an outline or a bulleted list of envisioned sections (or both) before writing your first draft. And being the reasonable person you are, you have grouped related information and have drawn early connections between your thoughts and conclusions. So, when you reconsider the organization of early drafts, keep your reader and purpose clearly in mind. Readers expect you to keep them "filled in" as the argument progresses. Readers need to sense some pattern in your work; they need each sentence, each paragraph to be logically connected to the one before and after. They even hope to anticipate what you may say next.

In most cases, your argument will follow one of the regular patterns of organization that follow. Select and evaluate the pattern(s) most likely to fit your reader and purpose.

- *Moving from general to specific.* In this pattern, your argument proceeds from its claim (general statement of opinion) to more specific reasons and evidence to solidify your thinking. Even within paragraphs, you will move from topic sentence to sentences of very specific information.
- *Moving from least important reason to most important reason.* Many writers use this pattern because first, it gives their argument a sense of growing

importance: each argument, each page gets more interesting and persuasive. Second, since readers tend to remember best what they read last, placing your most convincing material near the end of your argument serves the purpose well.

- *Moving from most important reason to least important.* Some writers and speakers will adopt this pattern again for two reasons. One, they hope that beginning an argument "with a bang" will immediately garner the reader's interest and trust. Two, this pattern may work well if you perceive that your intended readers will be antagonistic to your claim. In this way, at least those reluctant readers will encounter your strongest information before tuning you out.

When you revise your argument's organization, you should simultaneously reconsider its coherence, that quality of writing in which all pieces of information seem reasonably connected to each other. Ask yourself, for example, if you could explain to another person just why paragraph three follows paragraph two and precedes paragraph four. Any difficulty explaining the order of your paragraphs is reason alone to rethink their order. Maybe paragraphs two, three, and four indeed belong in your paper—somewhere—just not in the order they reside in this early draft. Consider the concept of coherence between these two sentences.

Original Draft

> Schools often recommend the use of Ritalin for students with Attention Deficit Disorder. The drug may have serious side effects.

Do you see that the two sentences may indeed belong in the same paragraph together, but they have a logical "disconnect" between their thoughts? The leap from schools' use of Ritalin to the drug's danger is a huge one, perhaps too much of a leap to enable your reader's understanding of your point. So, you rethink the coherence between the two sentences (sometimes such revising means that you must add one or more complete sentences to make the connection between ideas clear):

Revised Version

> Schools often recommend the use of Ritalin for students with Attention Deficit Disorder. However, parents of ADD children should carefully consider this recommendation because the drug may have serious side effects.

In the revised version, the connection between the school's recommendation and your point about the drug's danger becomes apparent—and actually makes your point in a more direct manner as well.

Keep in mind when it comes time to revise an argument's draft that you have studied the issue carefully for a length of time. Thus, the connections and conclusions you draw seem reasonable. But your reader has had no such opportunity. It becomes your obligation as writer, then, to "fill in the gaps" for the reader's benefit. You will not only increase the reader's understanding of your argument, but you will find that the reader is more likely to trust that you know what you are talking about.

Questions to Help Revise Organization

1. Does each of my major sections (primary reasons) in my argument appear in a logical, obvious, and predictable manner? Have I left my reader "hanging" or uncertain about why I have arranged my reasons and evidence in the manner I have? Do my transitions provide enough guidance?

2. If asked, could I explain why one reason follows another and precedes yet another?

3. Have I ordered the evidence within each paragraph in some reasonable manner?

4. Will a reader be able to read my entire argument without the need to reread or look back to find out what I'm doing? Whom might I allow (who might be objective enough) to read my paper for comment?

STUDENTS AT WORK: REVISING ORGANIZATION

For her fourth draft, Rachel concentrated on improving the organization of her argument, step 3 of the revision process:

> Should migrant workers needing health care resolve their transportation needs, they still encounter difficulties with health care workers who speak no Spanish. We must sympathize with the feelings of cultural isolation that such migrant workers face when they seek medical care in non-Spanish-speaking facilities. Most people find a doctor's visit uncomfortable enough without having language barriers to deal with also. Speaking at a U.S. Department of Health and Human Services forum in Boston, Wilson Augustave, a migrant farm workers representative for the National Migrant Health Advisory Council, reported on some of the barriers faced by non-English-speaking migrants: "Sometimes farm workers go into their local communities to be seen at the emergency room . . . and they don't have someone on staff to translate. Many times they [farm workers] have to have their kids, who may not know the medical terminology, translate for them." Such was the case for Emilia Zamora, a field worker in rural New Mexico. Zamora entered a health care facility suffering from a painful bent back, a condition she assumed resulted from long hours stooping to weed onions and cauliflower. The doctor, however, diagnosed her as having osteoporosis. A condition of having too little calcium in Zamora's body had severely affected her spine. Zamora speaks no English, so the doctor attempted to describe her condition to her nine-year-old son. One can imagine the difficulty of a young boy trying to understand a term such as osteoporosis, a word for which he had no Spanish equivalent. He told his mother

> she had "bad bones." A University of Tennessee report noted that like Zamora's son, ". . . untrained translators are acting as interpreters under the most difficult of circumstances. The translators are asked to accurately convey crucial information in life or death situations." Surely states that employ large numbers of migrant field workers should mandate that health care facilities in their state employ Spanish-speaking interpreters to insure quality health care for these important people.

Comments on the Fourth Draft

- Interestingly, Rachel has decided to move her comments on cultural isolation to the first part of the paragraph, reserving the more direct problems of health care and language for the ending. She decided to place what she believes to be the more powerful evidence at the end for greater emphasis.
- Note too that Rachel has modified the beginning of her paragraph from her third draft so the cultural isolation comments fit more smoothly into her paragraph.
- Rachel also decided to place a "tie-up" sentence at the paragraph's end in an attempt to relate her paragraph's point more directly to her overall stance.
- Now, believing that her paragraph better conveys what she really wants to say, Rachel must address the sentence-level problems (including some word choices) to increase her correctness and credibility.

Exercise 1
Collaborative Analysis: The Anticipation Exercise

Testing the Organization and Coherence of Your Argument   One characteristic of effective readers is that, while reading, they can often anticipate what an author may likely say next, especially if the author has carefully structured his piece according to a specific focus, reader, and purpose. This exercise, often called an "Anticipation Exercise," allows you to ascertain if your readers can come reasonably close to anticipating where your argument is going.

First, gather into groups of three or four. From the draft of your argument, select what you consider to be one of its best paragraphs. Next, read your primary claim to the group and discuss where your selected paragraph fits into the overall paper. Then, read the paragraph's first two sentences and stop. Have your group members tell you what the believe may come next. Did they anticipate a piece of specific evidence? Did they think you would move right into an example? Did they anticipate your offering a definition? Then, read the next sentence and discuss how accurate your group members' guesses were. If they were reasonably accurate, you know you have "set up" the paragraph with some of your readers' needs in mind. If the groups' guesses were *distinctly* different from what you actually wrote, discuss with them why you did what you did and if some revision to the paragraph is in order. Then, continue the process, sentence by sentence, with the group's anticipations after each. Did you learn anything about readers? Do this with everyone's paragraphs.

ALSO NOTE
THE SURFACE APPEAL OF YOUR ARGUMENT

Lynne Truss is the author of three novels and numerous radio comedy and drama programs. She is a television critic and has worked as an editor. The subtitle of her book *Eats, Shoots and Leaves* is *The Zero Toleration Approach to Punctuation*, and it probably explains why she is affectionately referred to as the "Nazi grammarian." In her book that, believe it or not, was a best seller in 2004, she shares many humorous examples about punctuation gone bad. The following is an excerpt in which she discusses the value of proper punctuation.

> Punctuation has been defined many ways. Some grammarians use the analogy of stitching: punctuation as the basting that holds the fabric of language in shape. Another writer tells us that punctuation marks are the traffic signals of language: they tell us to slow down, notice this, take a detour, and stop. I have even seen a rather fanciful reference to the full stop and comma as "the invisible servants in fairy tales—the ones who bring glasses of water and pillows, not storms of weather or love." But best of all, I think, is the simple advice given by the style book of a national newspaper: that punctuation is "a courtesy designed to help readers to understand a story without stumbling. . . ."
>
> The reason it's worth standing up for punctuation is not that it's an arbitrary system of notation known only to an over-sensitive elite who have attacks of the vapours when they see it misapplied. The reason to stand up for punctuation is that without it there is no reliable way of communicating meaning. Punctuation herds words together, keeps others apart. Punctuation directs you how to read, in the way musical notation directs a musician how to play. As we shall see in the chapter on commas, it was first used by Greek dramatists two thousand years ago to guide actors between breathing points—thus leading to the modern explanation of why a cat is not a comma:
>
>> A cat has claws at the ends of its paws.
>> A comma's a pause at the end of a clause.
>
> Words strung together without punctuation recall those murky murals Rolf Harris used to paint, where you kept tilting your head and wondering what it was. Then Rolf would dip a small brush into a pot of white and—to the deathless, teasing line, "Can you guess what it is yet?"—add a line here, a dot there, a curly bit, and suddenly all was clear. Good heavens, it looked like just a splodge of colours and all along it was a kangaroo in football boots having a sandwich! Similarly, take a bit of unpunctuated prose, add the dots and flourishes in the right place, stand back, and what have you got?

TOP TEN EDITING ERRORS TO AVOID

Unfair as it may seem, some readers will choose to disqualify your credibility if they notice even one error in your language use. In spite of all your hard work, research, and revision, such readers detect even a single spelling error, for instance, and discount the quality of your argument. What follows, then, is a checklist of what we have found to be the most common sentence-level errors in student writing. Study each carefully and examine your later drafts to eliminate any problem that may harm your credibility and persuasiveness with your reader. Why allow errors of this type to harm the power of your hard work?

Error One: Fragmented Sentences

Readers find it difficult and annoying when they encounter incomplete sentences within your argument (and frankly, fragmented sentences make writing professors wish they had gone into refrigerator repair). So, at some point in your revision process, take the time to examine each sentence to be sure it is complete, with a subject, a verb, and complete sense. Here are some examples:

Incorrect: *Students often fear visiting their professors during office hours. Even though doing so is one of the best ways to get needed help.*

Note here that the phrase "Even though doing so is one of the best ways to get needed help" is incomplete. It is "fragmented" from the main clause of the sentence and needs to be connected to the main clause. Ask yourself if you would understand the fragmented section if someone said it to you. (One way to check this is to place the phrase "It is the case that" in front of the fragment. Does it make sense? No? Then, you have a fragment on your hands.) The fragment can be easily corrected:

Correction: *Students often fear visiting their professors during office hours even though doing so is one of the best ways to get needed help.*

Incorrect: *Although Israelis and Palestinians face continued warfare.*

Note again that placing "It is the case that" in front of this set of words would not produce a complete thought, and so a fragment occurs. Such fragmented sentences may be corrected a couple of ways:

Correction: *Although Israelis and Palestinians face continued warfare, ambassadors from the embattled countries hope for a peaceful resolution.*

Or

Alternate Correction: *Ambassadors from the embattled countries hope for a peaceful resolution although Israelis and Palestinians face continued warfare.*

Error Two: Comma-Spliced and Run-on Sentences

Comma-spliced and run-on sentences fail to signal clearly to a reader exactly where one sentence ends and the next sentence begins. The only real difference between a comma splice and a run-on is that a comma-spliced sentence connects two complete sentences with only a comma, whereas a run-on connects two complete sentences with no punctuation whatever.

Incorrect: *Many farmers believe they are helping the environment, they are actually harming it when they overfertilize their land.* (Comma splice)

Incorrect: *Many farmers believe they are helping the environment they are actually harming it when they overfertilize their land.* (Run-on)

Note that in the comma-spliced sentence, two full sentences hook to one another with only a comma, forcing the reader, not the writer, to make the connection clear. Basically, the same problem appears in the run-on sentence. These sorts of sentences can be corrected in a number of ways:

> Correction: *Many farmers believe they are helping the environment. They are actually harming it when they overfertilize their land.*
>
> Or
>
> Alternate Correction: *Many farmers believe they are helping the environment; they are actually harming it when they overfertilize their land.*
>
> Or
>
> Alternate Correction: *Many farmers believe they are helping the environment, but they are actually harming it when they overfertilize their land.**
>
> Or
>
> Alternate Correction: *Many farmers believe they are helping the environment; however, they are actually harming it when they overfertilize their land.*

Error Three: Subject/Verb Agreement Errors

Occurring only in the present tense use of verbs, errors in subject/verb agreement occur when the subject is plural but the verb that goes with it is singular—or vice versa. The point here is to be consistent.

Incorrect: *None of the students in the AP English course write poorly.*

Although this is a common and confusing error sometimes, you must recognize that the subject of the sentence is *none*, not *students* (which is actually the object of the preposition *of*). *None* ("not one") is singular, and so the verb must likewise be singular.

> Correction: *None of the students in the AP English course writes poorly.*

Here is another example:

Incorrect: *There is several reasons for the nation's economic downturn.*

---

*Only seven words can be used with a comma in this way to combine two complete sentences: for, and, nor, but, or, yet, so.

346 Chapter 13 *Revising Your Written Argument*

In a sentence of this type, the subject is *reasons*, a plural word, so the verb that attends it must be plural as well.

Correction: *There are several reasons for the nation's economic downturn.*

Error Four: Pronoun Problems

The system of pronoun use in English causes occasional problems for any writer. Generally speaking, such errors occur under three conditions: (1) a pronoun and its antecedent (the word to which a pronoun refers) do not match in number (both singular or both plural); (2) the antecedent for a pronoun is unclear; or, (3) the pronoun use may be sexist.

Condition 1: *A pronoun and its antecedent do not match in number.*

Incorrect: *Any student who does not study for each test will probably have trouble with their grades.*

In this sentence, the problem occurs in the "agreement in number" between the pronoun *their* (plural) and its antecedent *student* (singular). You must be consistent in making a pronoun and antecedent match. Ask yourself how one student becomes more than one by the end of a sentence, and you should see the logic here. Errors of this type can be corrected easily:

Correction: *Any student who does not study for each test will probably have trouble with his or her grades.*

Or

Alternate Correction: *Students who do not study for each test will probably have trouble with their grades.*

We recommend the second option because plural pronouns are often easier to handle than singular ones; and if the singularity or plurality of pronouns and antecedents does not alter the meaning you intend, why not write as many plural matches as possible? That way, you avoid having to write *he or she, him or her,* and so on, throughout your argument.

Condition 2: *The antecedent for a pronoun is unclear.*

Incorrect: *The teachers' behaviors were actually worse than the students' actions. They should be censured.*

In this situation, ask yourself to whom *they* refers. Is it the teachers or the students? A reader will be confused about your intent to censure someone without knowing just whom you intend.

Correction: *The teachers' behaviors were actually worse than the students' actions. The teachers should be censured.*

Incorrect: *An instructor may have a problem getting a student to complete a project if they perceive the project as artificial.*

This sentence has a combination of problems. First of all, the pronoun *they* is plural, but no plural antecedent appears anywhere in the sentence. Even fixing the singular/plural problem, however, would not fully clarify the sentence. Ask yourself who perceives the project as artificial, the instructor or the student? Such a vague reference must be clarified.

> Correction: *An instructor may have a problem getting a student to complete a project if the student perceives the project as artificial.*

Condition 3: *The pronoun use may be sexist.*

Incorrect: *The math teacher frequently found his students ill prepared for calculus.*

Perhaps from previous sentences, we know that the math teacher in question is indeed male. If so, the use of *his* would be acceptable. Should we not know the teacher's gender, however, then using the pronoun *his* is unnecessarily sexist in that a math teacher could be of either gender. Some of your readers may find this usage offensive, so take care to avoid such constructions when you can.

> Correction: *Math teachers frequently find their students ill prepared for calculus.*

Incorrect: *Everyone knows just how difficult his first day on a job can be.*

In a sentence such as this one, the pronoun *his* actually agrees in number with the singular antecedent *everyone*. However, using the masculine pronoun has no real purpose in that all people, regardless of gender, may find the first day on a job confusing and embarrassing.

> Correction: *Everyone knows just how difficult the first day on a job can be.*

Error Five: Common Comma Problems

As you probably know, using commas correctly can be challenging, because the comma serves so many purposes in writing sentences. So, we list below the three most common types of comma errors we have seen students and even experienced writers commit.

Condition 1: *Missing commas following introductory sentence parts.*

Incorrect: *Because prescription drug costs have risen over the years many people now purchase their prescribed drugs in Canada.*

This sentence essentially has two parts—an introductory part and the main clause of the sentence—and needs a comma to separate them. The best way to avoid such errors is first to find the main clause of the sentence, "many people now purchase their prescribed drugs in Canada." Do you see that this clause could actually be a complete sentence unto itself? So the other words, "Because prescription drug costs have risen over the years," serve as some form of introductory matter. Separate the two sections of such sentences with a comma:

> Correction: *Because prescription drug costs have risen over the years, many people now purchase their prescribed drugs in Canada.*

Incorrect: *Before the start of each class session the professor calls roll.*

In this sentence, introductory matter again occurs before the main clause, "the professor calls roll," and so a comma must be placed between the introductory matter and the main clause:

Correction: *Before the start of each class session, the professor calls roll.*

Condition 2: *Commas missing around sentence "interrupters."*

Incorrect: *The new software however was too complicated to learn quickly.*

This sentence contains a main clause, "The new software was too complicated to learn quickly," and an interrupting word—generally used for transition. Interrupting words like this should be preceded and followed by a comma:

Correction: *The new software, however, was too complicated to learn quickly.*

Incorrect: *John's excuse for his late paper though unique made the professor chuckle all day.*

This sentence again contains an "interrupting phrase" that should be separated from the main clause with commas:

Correction: *John's excuse for his late paper, though unique, made the professor chuckle all day.*

Condition 3: *Commas missing between coordinate adjectives.*

Incorrect: *The mad scientist wore an evil frightening grin.*

In this sentence, the words *evil* and *frightening* both equally describe the scientist's grin and so should be separated with a comma. A trick here is to ask if the word *and* can be placed between the two adjectives without altering the sentence's meaning. If so, the comma is necessary:

Correction: *The mad scientist wore an evil, frightening grin.*

Incorrect *The wedding took place at a large, city park.*

Note in the above sentence that adding *and* between the two adjectives would alter the sentence's meaning: "The wedding took place at a large and city park." Thus, a separating comma is unnecessary.

Error Six: Apostrophe Problems

Like commas, apostrophes occasionally trouble writers. The following examples show these errors in action. Our best advice when you use apostrophes is to use common sense in expressing your meaning.

Condition 1: *Confusing plural words with possessive words.*

Incorrect: *A sign in a grocery store reads, "Five onion's for a dollar."*

The apostrophe in *onion's* makes it appear that the vegetable owns something. And what would that be? The word *for*? How can an onion own the word *for*? The sign should refer only to more than one onion for a dollar:

Correction: *"Five onions for a dollar."*

Incorrect: *The professor noted a number of error's in my paper.*

In this sentence, once again the term *errors* is plural only; it does not possess anything in the sentence.

Correction: *The professor noted a number of errors in my paper.*

Condition 2: *Leaving out necessary apostrophes.*

Incorrect: My roommates mind must have come unhinged.

In this sentence, we can surely assume that the roommate owns his or her mind. But omitting the necessary apostrophe makes the word appear plural only.

Correction: *My roommate's mind must have come unhinged.*

Condition 3: *Confusing singular possessive words with plural possessive words.*

Incorrect: Four student's names were added to the waiting list.

This sentence uses the apostrophe before the "s," making the word possessive, to be sure, but also singular. Common sense points out, however, that since four students are mentioned, the possessive word should then be plural. *Tip: Form the plural first; then add the apostrophe.*

Correction: *Four students' names were added to the waiting list.*

Error Seven: Quotation Marks and Italics in Titles

The titles of books, articles, poems, movies, and so forth must be punctuated correctly to indicate exactly what they are. Here is our best advice: If you could purchase the titled item independently at a bookstore (a book, a music CD, a movie, a magazine), then its title should appear in italics. If the item cannot be purchased independently (a magazine story or a chapter of a book), then its title should appear in quotation marks:

Correct: I read *War and Peace* during spring break.

Correct: I gave Usher's album, *Confessions,* to my youngest sister.

Correct: The article, "Seven Means to Inner Happiness," appeared in *Ebony*.

Correct: This chapter is entitled "Revising Your Written Argument."

Error Eight: Writing Equal Items in Equal Grammatical Form ("Parallelism")

Writers should place "equal" items in similar grammatical forms. Doing so helps to indicate the equality of the items' meaning:

Incorrect: My brother thinks it best to eat, to drink, and be merry.

This sentence lists three items in a series, each having equal importance to the brother. Therefore, each should be cast in similar grammatical form:

Correction: *My brother thinks it best to eat, to drink, and to be merry.*

Incorrect: My favorite activities include surfing the Web, studying the genealogy of my family, and to meet friends for lunch.

Here again, the three items—apparently equal in importance to the writer—should be written in a similar manner:

Correction: My favorite activities include surfing the Web, studying the genealogy of my family, and meeting friends for lunch.

Error Nine: Mixing up Similar Words

Words called "homophones" are those that sound the same but have differing meanings, such as *air* and *heir*. An incorrect use of similar sounding words will harm your effectiveness and credibility with your reader. An additional caution is important here: Your computer's spellcheck program will not catch these errors, so you must carefully read through your work to find them.

Incorrect: *Mavis paid her electrical bill on time each month to insure continued service.*

In this sentence, the word *insure* would work only if Mavis had some form of insurance on her bill. What the writer intended was *ensure*, meaning to guarantee that something will occur:

Correction: Mavis paid her electrical bill on time each month to ensure continued service.

Incorrect: *When his job was outsourced, Artie worried that the loss of income would effect his family.*

In this sentence, *effect* should be *affect*. Generally, *effect* is a noun, and *affect* is a verb; and since the writer needs a verb following "would," the sentence should read this way:

Correction: When his job was outsourced, Artie worried that the loss of income would affect his family.

Other commonly confused homophones include to/too; they're/their/there; waist/waste; which/witch; and weather/whether.

Error Ten: Misplaced Modifiers

Often a source of hilarity for professors, misplaced modifiers are those in which a sentence's modifier describes the wrong word. Common sense should rule here.

Incorrect: *Hanging in the closet, Reggie found his jacket.*

Note in this sentence that the modifier, "hanging in the closet," modifies "Reggie," making it sound as though poor Reggie has somehow gotten hung in the closet. What a spot to be in when he suddenly spies his jacket. Make sure the modifier rests next to the logical word:

Correction: Reggie found his jacket hanging in the closet.

Incorrect: *Arriving in Tucson, my skin began to feel dry.*

In this sentence, it would appear that someone's skin arrived in Tucson before he or she did! Does this construction make sense? The sentence is easily corrected:

Correction: When I arrived in Tucson, my skin began to feel dry.

Incorrect: *Having a faulty memory, the professor became frustrated with her computer.* Now, in this sentence, it is possible the professor is the one with the faulty memory. However, if your intent is to show that the professor's frustration is due to her computer's faulty memory, then the sentence should read this way:

Correction: *The professor became frustrated with her computer's faulty memory.*

STUDENTS AT WORK: REVISING FOR LANGUAGE CORRECTNESS

After Rachel had revised her paragraph's focus, evidence, and argument, she still had some work to do. In her fifth draft, Rachel completed step 4 of the revision process—she corrected the errors in language and punctuation that she had found:

> Should migrant workers needing health care resolve their transportation needs, they still encounter difficulties with health care workers who speak no Spanish. We must sympathize with the feelings of cultural isolation such migrant workers face when they seek medical care in non-Spanish speaking facilities. Most people find a doctor's visit uncomfortable enough without facing language differences also. Speaking at a US Department of Health and Human Services forum in Boston, Wilson Augustave, a migrant farm workers representative for the National Migrant Health Advisory Council, discussed some of the barriers faced by non-English speaking migrants: "Sometimes farm workers go into their local communities to be seen at the emergency room . . . and they don't have someone on staff to translate. Many times they [farm workers] have to have their kids, who may not know the medical terminology, translate for them." Such was the case for Emilia Zamora, a field worker in rural New Mexico. Zamora entered a health care facility suffering from a painful bent back, a condition she assumed resulted from long hours stooping to weed onions and cauliflower. The doctor, however, diagnosed her as having osteoporosis, a calcium deficiency in her bones severely affecting her spine. Zamora speaks no English, so the doctor attempted to describe her condition to her nine-year-old son. One can imagine the difficulty of a young boy trying to understand a term such as *osteoporosis*, a word for which he had no Spanish equivalent. He told his mother she had "bad bones." A University of Tennessee report noted that like Zamora's son, ". . . untrained translators are acting as interpreters under the most difficult of circumstances. The translators are asked to accurately convey crucial information in life or death situations." States that employ large numbers of migrant field workers should mandate that health care facilities in their state employ Spanish-speaking interpreters to ensure quality health care for those needing such care.

Yes, Rachel wrote five drafts of her paragraph before considering it reasonably credible and convincing. Such effort is admirable on her part, especially if you now look back at Draft One and compare it to Draft Five. Rachel followed the recommended four stages of revision and found that each gave her direction toward improving what otherwise would have read as an ineffective reason in support of her stance.

Do not be intimidated by the work it sometimes takes to improve a draft. Even professional writers find this the case more often than not. Give yourself time to discover exactly what you want to say and how to say it. You, too, will find that your argument improves over time.

DISCOVERING YOUR OWN ARGUMENTS: EXAMINING DRAFTS FOR LANGUAGE CORRECTNESS

Sitting in circles of four to five students, pass your draft to the student on your left. Now read the first page of your classmate's paper and put a check mark in the margin by a sentence you believe needs editing. In the margin, briefly note what correction you think might be necessary. Pass the papers, read the second page, and repeat the activity. Keep passing the papers until they have gone around the circle.

Retrieve your own draft, and read the comments your classmates have made. Take enough time to talk to each other about the corrections. As with any writing advice, consider it carefully, review the section titled, "Top Ten Editing Errors to Avoid," and make sure you and your reading partners are correct about the suggestions.

You can learn about editing in two ways from this practice. First, you will have another set of eyes to help you find your own errors that you often gloss over when drafting. Second, by reading the draft of another and seeing the kind of errors others are prone to make, you become more aware of those errors in your own work.

REFLECTIONS ON THE CHAPTER

As writers ourselves, we recognize the challenges of revising our writing. Let us assure you that in the writing of this text, we revised, revised again, talked things over, revised some more—all to the point that we were nearly ready to run away with the circus. Even now, we would probably look at places in this text that we believe we could revise further. Our point, though, is that having to revise many times is not some negative reflection on your writing ability. Just because it takes you several drafts to achieve a truly readable piece, such experience does not mean you don't know what you're doing. In fact, it means that *you do know what you're doing.* Try to accept that early drafts of any piece of writing rarely demonstrate a writer's full abilities; but luckily for us all, revision offers us unlimited chances to improve our work before we face that all-important reader.

PART IV

Additional Readings for Analysis

Each of the next five units contains a set of essays inspired by a very general topic. As this book has emphasized, there are many angles to any topic, and competent writers focus narrowly on one of those angles. The sets of essays are not pro-con pairings, although they do often provide differing perspectives. More than anything, they demonstrate a range of possibilities for writers addressing contemporary issues.

These readings can be used in two main ways. First, of course, they provide more practice in analyzing arguments. A cautionary note to students as you read these essays: Don't return to your previous ways of passive reading. Use the devices you have learned to delve into the rhetorical structure of these essays, and you will understand them much more completely. Second, you may want to write about one of these topics after reviewing the corresponding set of essays. The essays can act as a springboard for you. You may want to use paraphrases, quotations, or summaries of them; you may find other good sources mentioned in them; you may just find an angle that you want to investigate on your own. At the end of each unit, you will find questions to encourage your careful and critical thinking about the essays individually and as a group.

As you read, try to monitor the way you bring your own meaning to the essay by your mindset, your previous experience, your political persuasion, your religious affiliation, and all of the other influences that have molded you.

UNIT

1

Business Ethics

In the first few years of the twenty-first century, America's economy was shaken by business scandals of a greater scope than in practically any other time in our history. The CEOs of large companies were walking away with great sums of money as their companies collapsed in their wake. Gary Winnick, chairman of Global Crossing, bought the most expensive single-family estate in America, valued at approximately $62 million, and he planned on making $15 million in improvements to the property. Shortly before the company he presided over fell apart, putting workers out of their jobs, Winnick made $735 million on his sale of stock while workers lost the money they had in their retirement accounts. Arthur Andersen, the long-term, well-respected international accounting firm, folded under legal scrutiny* when it became clear that its employees had given unethical and often even illegal advice to its clients, advice that made money for Arthur Andersen and the company officials. On Arthur Andersen's advice, corporate worth was often overstated, which increased stock value and encouraged public purchases of the stock. When the public realized the value of these companies was substantially lower than had been stated, they tried to sell their stock but took great losses; many lost their entire retirement accounts. The CEOs, meanwhile, had usually sold their stock much earlier and walked away as multimillionaires. These are just a few of a long list of examples of corporate misconduct that has led to some serious soul-searching in business and academic communities.

What accounts for such misconduct? Is it just a short step from taking home a box of paper clips to bilking thousands of employees and naïve investors out of their life savings? Would you do the same thing if you were in the CEO's position? Is that just the way capitalism works, and the point is to make sure you are on the winning side?

What kind of ethical standards should we be able to hold our business leaders to? If we like our system, how can we improve it to avoid such disasters? These questions need answers if our economy is to stay healthy and our personal financial futures are to be secure. This unit includes essays by writers who argue

---

*Although Arthur Andersen went out of business and was found guilty of illegal accounting practices in the courts, that conviction was overturned by the Supreme Court in June 2005. It is left to determine which of their actions were, in fact, illegal and which actions were unethical.

about the cause of the problems, the correct standards business leaders should live by, and different ways of conceiving leadership.

> ### ALSO NOTE
> #### THE FAILURE OF ETHICS
>
> At one point or another in the Great Bull Market, Jack F. Welch Jr., the chairman and CEO of the General Electric Co.; Ronald O. Perelman, the chairman of the Revlon Corporation; Leo D. Kozlowski Jr., the chairman and CEO of Tyco International, Inc.; and Albert J. Dunlap Jr., the chairman of Sunbeam Corp. were all lionized in the press and celebrated by the public as larger than life figures—true heroes of American culture. In some cases, the praise, such as for Welch's financial helmsmanship of GE, was warranted, too. Yet in the end, each in turn suffered ridicule and rebuke—and in the case of Kozlowski and Dunlap, even worse—when internal guidance systems of all four men regarding what is decent behavior and what is not, simply failed them.
>
> —Christopher Brown, *Testosterone, Inc.*

The Ethics of Business Schools
Katherine S. Mangan

> This short excerpt from a long and very thoroughly researched article in *The Chronicle of Higher Education* (September 20, 2002) highlights the relationships between professors and companies that suggest problems of influence. The argument is subtle and informative in purpose. Mangan's investigation suggests that business schools may have a good deal to do with corporate ethical failures.

1 Looking relaxed and confident as he leans back in an armchair in his spacious Houston office, Jeffrey K. Skilling gives M.B.A. students a lesson in integrity.

2 When the Enron Corporation works on a project, customers have nothing to worry about, says the company's then-president. "They know that it's clean, absolutely clean, because Enron's involved. That's the way we do business."

3 Mr. Skilling's words were recorded in a case study on a CD-ROM used last year by the University of Virginia's Darden Graduate School of Business Administration, before his company went bankrupt and scandal forced him from his job. The statement may have drawn nods of respect from students last year, but now it is likely to elicit groans of disbelief from those viewing the repackaged case study. The first half

> ### ALSO NOTE
> ## MBAS WOULD RATHER QUIT THAN FIGHT FOR VALUES
>
> Faced with a clash between their own values and those of their employers, most MBA students have learned that it's easier to quit than to fight. That's one of the lessons business schools are unwittingly passing along to students, according to a study by the Aspen Institute's Initiative for Social Innovation Through Business.
>
> The nonprofit policy-research group studied nearly 2,200 MBA students from 13 major business schools—nine from the United States and four from elsewhere—between the summer of 1999 and the spring of 2001 to determine the students' view of the role that business plays in society, and how their business school experience has shaped that view.
>
> Students who had started their two years of graduate school thinking that a company's top priorities were customer needs and product quality said that by the time they graduated, their own top priority had shifted to "shareholder value."
>
> They also said they didn't feel it was possible to change a company's values, and that, faced with a stressful conflict, they'd leave.
>
> "There is a flaw in business-school education if students say they will leave a company when faced with a values conflict," says Stephen A Stumpf, a professor of management at Villanova University. "Business schools are supposed to be training leaders . . . teaching them to raise the issues—not bail out."
>
> (Study can be found at http://www.aspeninstitute.org/isib/student_att.html.)
>
> —Katherine S. Mangan, *The Chronicle of Higher Education*

of the new version includes the upbeat interviews from Enron's executives, while the second half—hurriedly added between semesters last year—chronicles the company's collapse.

4   Not since the days of the insider-trading poster boy Ivan F. Boesky and the junk-bond king Michael R. Milkin have M.B.A. programs been so assailed for their role in preparing future corporate executives. Many of the schools are scrambling to rewrite case studies, dust off their ethics lessons, and defend professors who have worked for the very companies now under scrutiny.

5   Among the questions being raised: Were business professors merely duped like everyone else? Or does the bottom-line–first ethos that many of them promote in the classroom help create a system that breeds corruption? And are some professors letting their own close ties

and financial relationships with companies taint the way they write and teach about the corporate world?

Many Conflicts

6   Business schools and their faculty members alike benefit from the largess of friendly companies.

7   The school at the University of Arkansas at Fayetteville, for example, beefed up faculty salaries, created new programs, and improved its curriculum after receiving $50-million in 1998 from the family of Sam M. Walton, founder of Wal-Mart. The school's new name is the Sam M. Walton College of Business. Not every business school can boast a $50-million gift, but corporate contributions are common.

8   Many faculty members collect fat paychecks for serving on corporate boards or working as consultants—sums that can rival their faculty salaries. The benefits, they argue, include real-world experience that they can draw on in the classroom. The danger, critics respond, is that the same corporate entree can lead to conflicts of interest when the companies they work for show up on their syllabuses.

9   "If you're writing a case on a particular company, you have to be detached and objective—as any good researcher is. If the company is paying you, that's obviously a conflict of interest," says Amitai Etzioni, a sociologist at George Washington University who taught ethics at Harvard Business School from 1987 to 1989.

10 Even if most business professors resist the temptation to skew their studies, "why put them in that situation in the first place?" Mr. Etzioni asks.

11 "It's not like they're underpaid and poor. We're not asking them to take vows of chastity and poverty in order to write case studies."

12 Thomas A. Bausch, a professor of management and former dean of the Marquette College of Business, echoes those sentiments: "I think a lot of business professors didn't see anything wrong with what was going on," says Mr. Bausch, a former president of the AACSB International Association to Advance Collegiate Schools of Business. "They were part of the 'greed is good' culture. Many business professors make far more money consulting than they do teaching. . . ."

Cooking The Books

13 Michael R. Lissack, a former investment banker who used to lecture on business ethics, caused a furor when he sent out e-mail messages to members of the Academy of Management, a national association of business professors, urging them to approve a resolution that business schools are largely at fault for "the current crisis of confidence in corporate America marked by evidence of fraud and greed."

14 Mr. Lissack, who has an M.B.A. from Yale University, insists that cooking the books and misleading shareholders are by-products of business schools' emphasis on the bottom line. "When I was an M.B.A. student the very things that WorldCom is accused of doing we were being taught to

15 Yale accounting professors dismissed his claim as "outrageous," adding, in a prepared statement, "perhaps Mr. Lissack was asleep in class when we discussed the differences between assets and expenses."

16 Jean Bartunek, president of the business-professors' group, calls Mr. Lissack's charges unfair. "The idea that business schools are to blame for decisions that people make in the workplace 20 years later is naive," says Ms. Bartunek, who is a professor of organizational studies at Boston College's Carroll School of Management.

17 It's not that business schools are not teaching ethics. They must in order to become accredited. But the accrediting body, AACSB International, doesn't spell out how the subject should be taught. A school could integrate lessons about ethics into existing courses, for instance, or offer a separate course.

18 On the other hand, argues Neal M. Stoughton, a professor of finance at the University of California at Irvine, ethics has no place in a business school. "The whole notion of business is about profit and competition and trying to defeat your opponent," he says. "Ethics implies that there's some social good at stake. If you worry about social good, you'll end up being clobbered by the competition."

19 Irvine has no required ethics courses in its M.B.A. program, although ethical issues are addressed in a variety of classes. Perhaps none will scrutinize them with the intensity of "The Enron Case," a new, six-week course that started this fall. The speakers will include Sherron Watkins, the former Enron employee who became a whistle-blower.

20 Darden's revised case study, with its follow-up on the company's downfall contrasting with the ebullient tone of the account of its rise, will probably be used in some classes at Virginia. Instead of cozy interviews with Mr. Skilling and Enron's former chief executive officer, Kenneth Lay, the added material is mostly about embarrassing revelations, high-profile resignations, and the events leading up to the nation's largest corporate bankruptcy.

21 Events are charted along a graph that follows the plunge in Enron's stock price over the course of 2001. The revision ends with reflections on the lessons learned from the Enron debacle.

22 The backlash against the fallen company "comes as a bitter reminder that the market forces that Mr. Lay once worshipped can prove a double-edged sword," the study notes.

23 It's a lesson that business schools are learning as well.

They Call Their Boss a Hero
Michael Ryan

Aaron Feuerstein has become nearly legendary because of the way he handled a catastrophic fire at his company, Malden Mills. He has operated under very different ethical guidelines than the other CEOs mentioned so far. This *Parade* feature article is an example of a narrative argument that is quite different from the type of argument we have discussed most frequently in this book. What Michael Ryan provides his reader is one long, extended example of Feuerstein's and his employees' experience to argue that Feuerstein's actions were in fact a model for corporate and individual responsibility. Instead of structuring an analytical argument, Ryan lets the power of the story, along with Feuerstein's words, convince the reader.

Are CEOs like Feuerstein typical? Are the CEOs of Enron, WorldCom, and Global Crossing just a few bad examples?

1   Bill Cotter has known his boss, Aaron Feuerstein, for a long time. In 19 years as a factory worker and sometime union official, Cotter has dealt with the chief executive officer of Malden Mills across a bargaining table and chatted with him on the shop floor. But Bill Cotter never really knew Aaron Feuerstein until Dec. 11, 1995, when a catastrophic fire nearly destroyed all of the textile company's manufacturing plant in Lawrence, Mass., and seemed certain to put its 3000 employees out of work.

2   "We had just spent $1000 on Christmas presents," Cotter recalled. "We thought we'd just collect our last check and then go on unemployment," added his wife, Nancy, a production supervisor at the mill. "Most of us would have lost everything."

3   But that week, Aaron Feuerstein did something that astonished his workers—something so impressive that he was invited to sit with Hillary and Chelsea Clinton during the President's State of the Union Address this year. Feuerstein announced that he would keep all of his 3000 employees on the payroll for a month while he started rebuilding the 90-year-old family business. In January, he announced he would pay them for a second month. In February, he said he would pay them for a third month.

4   "When he did it the first time, I was surprised," said Bill Cotter. "The second time was a shock. The third . . . well, it was unrealistic to think he would do it again." Nancy Cotter finished her husband's thought: "It was the third time that brought tears to everyone's eyes." By March, most of the employees had returned to full-time work. Those who hadn't were offered help in making other arrangements. "Aaron gave us a chance," said Bill Cotter, 49, who went back to the mill last month. That chance cost Feuerstein several million dollars. "Another person would have taken the insurance money and walked away," said Bob Fawcett, the security director. "I might have done that. But he's not that type of person."

5   Like many successful businessmen, Feuerstein has a reputation for being demanding but fair. "He wants what he wants when he wants it," said Fawcett.

6   When I visited the mill, I asked Feuerstein, 70, what set him apart from other CEOs. "The fundamental difference is that I consider our

workers an asset. Not an expense," he told me. Indeed, he believes his job goes beyond just making money for shareholders, even though the only shareholders of Malden Mills are Feuerstein and his family. "I have a responsibility to the worker, both blue-collar and white-collar," Feuerstein added, his voice taking an edge of steely conviction. "I have an equal responsibility to the community. It would have been unconscionable to put 3000 people on the streets and deliver a deathblow to the cities of Lawrence and Methuen. Maybe on paper our company is worthless to Wall Street, but I can tell you it's worth more. We're doing fine."

7 It is complicated, perhaps impossible, to explain why Feuerstein did what he did. He is a deeply religious man whose command of biblical Hebrew is impeccable. He quoted Hillel, the first century Talmudic scholar, twice in our conversation: "Hillel said, 'In a situation where there is no righteous person, try to be a righteous person.' Before that, he said, 'Not all who increase their wealth are wise.'" Yet Feuerstein said his love of Scripture was just part of what makes him a successful CEO: "If you think the only function of a CEO is to increase the wealth of shareholders, then any dime he spends on scripture or Shakespeare or the arts is wasteful. But if you think the CEO must balance responsibilities, then he should be involved with ideas that connect him with the past, the present and the future."

8 After hearing this, I was not surprised, in a day of walking around the plant, to learn about the heart-bypass operations Feuerstein had arranged for several workers or about the free soft drinks and breaks he offers employees when the summer heat drives up temperatures to more than 90 degrees on the manufacturing lines.

9 As a company, Malden Mill stands out in the Lawrence area, once a thriving center for the textile industry. "When I came here, there were quite a few mills, but most of them are gone," said Bill Angelone, 62, a 38-year employee and one-time union president. He has watched business after business move away in search of lower labor costs. Even among companies that stayed in Lawrence, said Angelone, there has been downsizing, as textile firms have laid off workers in attempts to stay profitable.

10 "That goes straight against the American Dream," Feuerstein said when I raised the subject. "You work hard and should make a good living and have a good retirement. I could get rid of all the workers who earn $15 an hour and bring in a contract house that will pay their laborers $7 an hour. But that breaks the spirit and trust of the employees. If you close a factory because you can get work done for $2 an hour elsewhere, you break the American Dream."

11 Skeptics say Feuerstein's practices are sentimental, not businesslike. However the mill's history suggests otherwise. Like scores of other textile manufacturers, the company went through hard times in the 1970s and '80s, filing for bankruptcy protection in 1981. "We had to lay off workers," said Feuerstein. "That was very painful." Yet, explained Bill Cotter,

"Aaron came out stronger than he went in. He went heavy into research and development, and that's where Polartec® and Polarfleece® came from." These two synthetic fabrics, produced exclusively by Malden Mills, are used in outdoor wear by upscale clothing manufacturers like Patagonia and L.L. Bean. Malden Mills holds patents not only for the fabrics but also for the machines used to make them. Before the fire, factory lines ran 24 hours a day to keep up with demand. Over the years, the company's profits rose steadily.

12   "The quality of our product is paramount," said Feuerstein, "and it's the employee who makes that quality. If the quality slips, the employee is in a position to destroy your profit."

13   Feuerstein saw his loyalty repaid the moment the fire began. "Aaron was standing in the parking lot," recalled Bob Fawcett. "He was saying, 'This is not the end.' You could see him fighting back tears. But he convinced us he wasn't quitting. If he had the guts to rebuild, we decided we would try to save whatever we could." What happened next was one of hundreds of acts of courage that night, beginning with the rescue of 33 injured workers by fellow employees and volunteer fire fighters. Bob Fawcett, Fire Marshall Al Potter and a handful of fire fighters dashed into the mill's last and smallest manufacturing plant. Propane tanks began exploding around them, and a deputy fire chief raced in to order everyone out. But Potter and Fawcett convinced him they could save the building. The next morning amid the rubble of the other buildings the small one remained standing. Ten days later, its production was back in operation.

14   Investigators today remain uncertain about what caused the fire. Yet Feuerstein's employees left little doubt about what they thought of him. Using new equipment, they set up a temporary manufacturing plant in a warehouse and quickly began working again. "Before the fire, that plant produced 130,000 yards a week," Feuerstein said "A few weeks after the fire, it was up to 230,000 yards. Our people became very creative. They were willing to work 25 hours a day."

15   By midsummer, Feuerstein had broken ground for a new production plant, and 85 percent of his employees were back at work. That still left some 400 jobless, but Feuerstein refused to abandon them. He extended their health benefits, designated a fulltime employee to help them find work and guaranteed them their old jobs back when the new plant opens in 1997.

16   Walking around the shop floors, I was struck by the devotion with which Malden Mills' employees approached their tasks. "It is these workers," said Feuerstein, "who are responsible for his company's recovery. They wanted a miracle to happen, and it did," he said. "That's all I can tell you: It did."

Michael Ryan, "They Call Their Boss a Hero." © 1996 Michael Ryan. Initially published in *Parade Magazine*, September 8, 1996. All rights reserved. By permission of Parade Publications.

Executive Decisions
Russell Mokhiber and Robert Weissman

Statistics accumulated by the Fair Economy Web site (www.FairEconomy.org) demonstrate the extreme disparity between CEO and worker pay. Although there has been a slightly downward trend in the proportion since 2000, CEOs are paid a great deal more than workers in organizations. In 2000, the average CEO made 525 times the average worker's salary, and in 2005 this number decreased to 411 times the average worker's wage. As a demonstration of how management compensation has outpaced that for workers, the average worker's salary in 2005 was $28,315. If this wage had increased at the same rate that management compensation has increased over the past few years, that figure would be $106,138. As Bud Crystal, a leading compensation consultant, argues, CEOs are now compensated extraordinarily for any kind of performance, not just excellence. As you will see from the specific example of Michael Eisner, CEO of Disney, offered in this Internet editorial from the *Multinational Monitor*, an argument is often made that such compensation comes at great social and financial expense.

1   If greed is good, as Michael Douglas infamously stated in the movie *Wall Street*, then Disney CEO Michael Eisner must be a saint. Last year, the Disney executive received compensation of more than $575 million. On top of his $750,000 salary, Eisner claimed a $9.9 million bonus and cashed in on $565 million in stock options. This is not the first mega-pay haul for Eisner. From 1991 to 1995, he took in $235 million. In 1988, his $40 million take prompted shrieks of outrage.

2   In Eisner's defense, it can be said that giant pay grabs are increasingly the norm among big company CEOs. Among the heads of the largest U.S. corporations, CEO average compensation is $5.8 million. CEO pay rose 54 percent from 1995 to 1996 (final 1997 figures are not yet in) and have risen almost 500 percent since 1980.

3   Skyrocketing CEO pay does not represent a massive expansion of the economic pie from which all corporate stakeholders are benefiting. While executive pay increases partly reflect rising returns to shareholders, workers have received almost none of the benefits showered on those at the top. Average hourly earnings for working people have actually dropped since 1980, from $12.70 (in 1996 dollars) in 1980 to $11.81 in 1996. The ratio of big company CEO pay to factory workers' wages has ballooned from 44-to-1 in 1965 to more than 200-to-1 today. There is no sharing of the economic pie here.

4   As severe as the wage disparity is between U.S. executives and U.S. workers, however, the differential between the executives and Third World workers at whose expense they increasingly profit is staggering. Disney, to its everlasting shame, has in recent years outsourced production of Disney

(Continued on p. 365)

ALSO NOTE
FROM *BUSINESS AS WAR*

CEOs, senior managers, and other business leaders need to understand and apply some truths not covered during their MBA education or executive experiences up to now:

- Strategy is a matter of balance, and sometimes that's tough: choosing between two equally unpalatable alternatives, for example, or calibrating what you may be forced to do one day against your original motivation—or, for that matter, your ultimate objectives.
- CEOs have to be leaders above all else, and if they can't lead, then they shouldn't be in the job. The same thing goes double for every member of the board of directors—and every member of the leadership team, from corporate offices to line or project managers.
- To be a real leader, vision and competence are prerequisites: but the defining characteristic is to put everyone else's interest ahead of your own. And in business, those interests include the shareholders, the employees, the customers, and even the firm itself. Or simply get the hell out of Dodge.
- What we are really hearing in these endless waves of corporate scandals is pure and simple bad leadership—the natural end product of a self-centered mentality that starts at the top and quickly comes to pervade an organization.
- Leadership is about planning and direction, but it is also about setting an absolute moral and ethical standard that puts the greater good before any individual, in any position.
- The sorry examples of Enron and all the rest should have tipped off corporate America that its leaders simply aren't living right, that they need to spend less time and money on their lawyers, lobbyists, and lackeys, and more in leading their organizations.
- Today's business leaders are doing much less than what is expected of them if they fail to return to the values of leadership, selflessness, and giving back that have been the hallmark of the American way—and American greatness.
- What leadership comes down to is character; and although character can be defined in many ways, my favorite is the one my pastor taught me many years ago: The real test of character is what you do when no one is looking.

—Kenneth Allard

clothing and toys to sweatshops in Haiti, Burma, Vietnam, China, and elsewhere. Last year, the Asia Monitor Resource Center, a labor monitoring organization based in Hong Kong, reported on the operations of Keyhinge Toys, a factory based in Da Nang City, Vietnam, that makes giveaway toys based on characters in Disney films which are distributed with McDonald's Happy Meals. According to the Asia Monitor Resource Center, the approximately 1000 workers in the Keyhinge factory in Vietnam earn six to eight cents an hour, far below the subsistence wage estimated at 32 cents an hour. The workers—90 percent of them young women 17- to 20 years-old—are required to work mandatory overtime, with 9- to 10-hour shifts required seven days a week. On an annual basis, the workers at Keyhinge are making approximately $250 a year.

5   Less than one-fifth of Michael Eisner's compensation package—$100 million—would be enough to quintuple the wages of each of the 1000 Keyhinge workers—giving them a still inadequate, but at least living wage—and to pay them for 100 years! That would leave Eisner with $465 million for 1997 alone. To call this kind of disparity "Dickensian" is to understate the nature of the problem dramatically. Globalization has wrought unprecedented and unconscionable spreads in income and wealth.

6   Devising remedies for this situation is not a simple matter. Eliminating the U.S. corporate tax incentive to provide executives with stock options would help a bit. Income tax surcharges on super-income—say more than $1 million a year—would also help level the pay playing field. Raising the minimum wage and pegging it to the inflation rate would help raise workers' wages.

7   The ultimate solution to the domestic problem, not now on the political horizon, would be a legislative mandate that executive salaries not exceed firms' lowest paid and average employees by more than a designated ratio. Crafting legislation to enforce this mandate would be tricky, but doable. Much more difficult would be generating political support in an era when the intellectual apologists for Michael Eisner and his ilk indeed argue that "greed is good," and are taken seriously.

8   If enough CEOs start taking home Eisner-like wages, then public outrage may lead to some palliative measures to curb executive compensation. But it is hard to imagine a concerted effort to rectify the imbalance in executive and worker pay in the absence of a resurgent labor movement. There are no signs of self-restraint or enlightened generosity among the employer class.

9   None of this begins to address the global gaps in income. Although measures to raise income levels in the Third World are needed and desirable, asking how to close the global wage gaps may be the wrong question for the long term. Bettering the lives of people in Vietnam and elsewhere in the Third World is unlikely to turn on improving the conduct of Disney or other rich country corporations, and more likely to depend on sustainable development approaches that emphasize self-reliance.

Greed Despoils Capitalism
Barbara Wilder

This newspaper column demonstrates a phenomenon that happens all the time in the developing thinking about a controversy. One author makes an argument, and another reads it and responds with another argument. On the opinion pages of a newspaper, this process sometimes goes on and on and on. This sort of back and forth argument, however, helps readers better judge an argument's validity and come to improved, more tenable positions. After reading Wilder's argument, do you believe that conscience and character are an essential part of capitalism, or do you believe, as Rob Reuteman suggested, that capitalism lends itself to ruthlessness and corruption?

Editor's Note

On July 13, business editor Rob Reuteman wrote a column [for the *Rocky Mountain News*] titled "Conscience, Capitalism? Coexistence an Anomaly." In part, it read:

"*Listening to President Bush's Wall Street speech on Tuesday, I was stunned to hear him say, 'There can be no capitalism without conscience, there is no wealth without character . . .'*

"No capitalism without conscience? No wealth without character? In fact, there is—and always has been—plenty of both. From Jay Gould to J.P. Morgan, from Andrew Carnegie to John D. Rockefeller to William Randolph Hearst, you simply cannot write U.S. history without citing the stupendous financial accomplishments of capitalism's ruthless pioneers. Modern-day counterparts abound."

What follows is a rebuttal [written by Barbara Wilder].

1   I could never be accused of supporting President Bush, but all the same I find merit in his call for conscience and character in capitalism, whether he means it or not.

2   The idea that conscience, character, and morality are incongruent with capitalism, as Rob Reuteman mentions in his July 13 column, flies in the face of the social contract. In fact, capitalism's origins are deeply rooted in ethics and human dignity. Adam Smith, the father of western capitalism, wrote, "What improves the circumstances of the greater part can never be regarded as an inconveniency to the whole. No society can surely be flourishing and happy, of which the far greater part of the members are poor and miserable." Smith would turn over in his grave if he could observe the antics of the Enron CEOs and their fellows.

3   It is no mere coincidence that American democracy and capitalism's founding document, *The Wealth of Nations*, were conceived in the same year. These two philosophies are inextricably interwoven, based as they are on beliefs in the inherent right of the individual to life, liberty, and the pursuit of happiness.

4   Capitalism does not rely on the whims of despots, or even benign governments, for its leadership, but on the genius and talent of the brightest and most visionary citizens. Capitalism is a system of economics, guided by the people willing and able to build businesses that create wealth for all. This is done by creating more jobs, which creates more products, which creates more profit which then is meant to be reinvested to create more jobs more product and more profit ad infinitum. And the system works for everyone—if there is integrity and vision in the people at the top. But when the people at the top are driven by greed and line their pockets with the profits instead of reinvesting in the production of goods for the benefit of all, the system fails.

5   And when the system fails it fails for all of us. No human being stands alone. We are all part of the world economy. We all have to take the fall when the guys at the top decide to keep all the marbles.

6   But capitalism, of itself, is not the culprit. Capitalism has the potential to bring the most good to the most people, if it is directed by people of conscience.

7   What we lost in the '80s and '90s juggernaut of bottom-line profits is the understanding that industry is about labor and product and profits and reinvesting those profits in the labor and the production of products. And most importantly, we lost the connection to the human element. We have created a bottom line that does not consider anything but profit for profit's sake, and therefore the bottom line has no substance.

8   We have created an economy based on fear and greed that is unprecedented, and in so doing we have alienated both our enemies and our friends around the world. The nation that was created on the most moral foundations of any nation in history has become, or is quickly becoming, the most immoral. And it is all because of greed.

9   To change this—to turn back to a path toward goodness, prosperity, and peace—we must all make a moral commitment. We must call not only for the punishment of those who have been caught, because there are many who have sinned against the world marketplace who will go unpunished; but we must call for all participants in the market, from corporate leaders to small investors to workers, to realign with a standard of integrity.

10   We must create a new bottom line. We must move out of an economy based on fear and greed and move into an economy based on integrity and love and caring for our fellow human beings. Over-the-top market prices may go down as we struggle to give up our fear and greed, but the market will readjust itself as we all begin to invest more of our attention in integrity.

11   Money and the economy are directed by all of the peoples' thoughts and feelings. When love, caring and integrity replace greed, fear, anger and disrespect, the economy will do more than recover, it will transform.

But for this to happen we must all begin to believe in a new kind of bottom line.

12   When we as individuals think in terms of love, caring and integrity, we will expect it of others, and that expectation will demand corporate integrity and the creation of a new bottom line on Wall Street and in the world marketplace. America wasn't founded on greed—it was founded on freedom for all. And that means economic freedom for all.

The Upside of Downsizing
Art Buchwald

> Throughout his long career in journalism, humorist Art Buchwald (1925–2007) commented on politics, society, culture, and practically everything. His column was syndicated in over 550 papers, he wrote some 30 books, he was awarded the Pulitzer Prize for Outstanding Commentary in 1982, and he was elected to the American Academy and Institute of Arts and Letters in 1986. This short essay appears in his book, *We'll Laugh Again*, and provides an example of a sarcastic, tongue-in-cheek argument against corporate excess.

1   I hadn't planned to write anything about downsizing for a while until I read in the papers that Robert Allen, the CEO of AT&T, received $16 million in salary and stock option compensation. He was given $16 million at the time his company laid off 40,000 workers. When questioned about it, he said he deserved every penny.

2   One of my friends who doesn't understand downsizing was outraged. I tried to explain to him how it works.

3   "It takes a very talented executive to lay off forty thousand employees, and sixteen million is not out of the ballpark if you want someone to play hardball."

4   MacDougal asked, "What is Allen going to do with sixteen million?"

5   I told him. "He has to buy milk and bread, and cornflakes and yogurt, just like everybody else. You have to remember that sixteen million isn't what it used to be. What's important about the layoffs is that Wall Street now views AT&T as a serious company. The people who were pink-slipped don't count. If Wall Street sees that the phone company is paying its chief sixteen million, they have confidence in the management.

6   "They know that you don't hand paychecks like that to the big guys unless the company has great plans for the future. Wall Street is in the tea-leaf reading business, and they consider big salaries for big people to be a good sign, even if middle management is asked to walk the plank."

7   MacDougal was not to be persuaded.

8   "I still don't understand what he can do with the whole sixteen million. How many cordless phones can Allen have in his house? How

many cellular phones can he use in his Mercedes-Benz? How many golf balls does a CEO need?"

9   I tried to be patient and replied, "Allen has to buy shoes for his children, bus tokens for his wife, and he probably has a big heating bill. I very much doubt that any of the money will be spent on luxuries."

10 MacDougal had the poor taste to bring up the 40,000 people who had been laid off. "Don't you think they feel wounded to see the man who dumped them receiving sixteen million for being their executioner?"

11 "When you downsize, you can't be sentimental about people. Allen claims he had to fire the forty thousand to save the company. If this is true, we Americans have to bless him for saving our long-distance lines."

12 "Do you trust him?" MacDougal asked.

13 "Maybe he was laying it on a bit thick, but he has to say something or the AT&T Credit Union would have refused to cash his sixteen million check."

14 MacDougal wasn't giving up. "Who decides how much a CEO is going to get for laying off thousands of people?"

15 "The board of directors."

16 "Who chooses the board of directors?"

17 "The CEO."

Unit 1
Questions to Guide Analysis

1. Mangan's article makes a case for increasing the study of ethics in business schools. What is her most impressive evidence? The UC–Irvine professor says, "If you worry about social good, you'll end up being clobbered by the competition." Write out an Argument Concept supporting the professor's opinion, and try to envision the sections of an argument based on this perspective. What kind of evidence would you need for the reader you imagine?

2. Aaron Feuerstein's story did not turn out quite as well as one might hope. Because of the monumental debt the company had to take on to rebuild after the fire, the company filed for bankruptcy. Malden Mills is still operating and has several new large contracts for its Polartec fleece, but the road has been very difficult and costly for Feuerstein. In a *60 Minutes* interview, he was asked if, knowing all the problems he was to have, would he have done the same thing. His answer: "Yes, It was the right thing to do."

    Write out the Argument Concept for the original narrative in *Parade*. If you were to write the story today, would the focus and purpose have to change, knowing what difficulties Feuerstein has had? Would the argument the example makes be more or less effective?

3. Imagine an argument you might make about ethics education and the field of study in which you are interested. What kind of ethical training is needed

for students who are studying anthropology, animal biology, political science, medicine or nursing, education, theatre, economics, or computer science, for instance? What kind of evidence might you provide that such an education is important?

4. The *Multinational Monitor* editorial claims that Michael Eisner is grossly overvalued in relationship to workers. What arguments can you find for and against this position on the Internet? For example, Edward Jay Epstein in *Slate* online magazine says, "He [Eisner] turned a faltering animation-and-amusement-park company into one of the world's most successful purveyors of home entertainment." Epstein cites several areas in which Disney grew 3000 percent under Eisner's leadership. Is such performance grounds for extraordinary compensation, or does such disparity cause some of the problems Wilder suggests in her essay?

5. Wilder's argument has a problem-solving purpose; her last four paragraphs offer her idea of how we can turn capitalism "back to a path toward goodness, prosperity, and peace." What is her solution, and are you convinced by it? What kind of evidence does she offer that her "new bottom line" can work? What kind of examples might she offer to demonstrate that her solution is viable?

6. Many essayists use the kind of sarcasm Buchwald employs in his short argument to highlight social or political problems. What pieces of hard evidence does Buchwald use even in this humorous commentary? Buchwald refers to the CEO's needing to buy milk, bread, cornflakes, yogurt, and shoes for his kids. How is that reference directed to his reader?

7. After reading these arguments, you might be interested in business ethics as an argument topic. How might you develop an argument inspired by two or more of the articles in this unit?

   A. Create three hypothetical Argument Concepts that you might pursue on the topic of business ethics.

   B. What are the most compelling arguments from this set of essays that could be used as support for one of the Argument Concepts you conceived in activity A, and why do you think they are strong?

   C. What is the weakest argument you read in these articles, and why do you think it is not convincing?

   D. What type of outside source material would you seek to further develop your argument?

UNIT

2

Our Body Images

Many Americans, both male and female, seem to be obsessed with their body shape. Statistics* abound that demonstrate this fixation:

- Eating disorders affect 7 million girls and women and 1 million boys and men.
- 25 percent of men and 45 percent of women at any one time are on some kind of diet.
- 80 percent of women are unhappy with the way they look.
- 51 percent of nine- and ten-year-old girls report a better self-image if they diet.
- 35 percent of "normal dieters" eventually take on unhealthy diet habits.
- 42 percent of first, second, and third graders wish they were thinner.
- 80 percent of ten-year-olds fear being fat.
- 40 percent of women and 20 percent of men would give up three to five years of their lives to reach what they believe is their ideal weight.
- Women overestimate the size of their hips by 16 percent and their waists by 25 percent, but they could correctly estimate the size of a box.
- Young girls report fearing overweight more than nuclear war, cancer, or losing their parents.
- The diet industry makes over $40 billion yearly.

The unrealistic images in the media are often cited as an important factor in this American obsession:

- Almost half of the most popular U.S. video games give "unhealthy" messages for girls; 38 percent of female game characters have large breasts and 46 percent have abnormally small waists.
- Most fashion models are thinner than 98 percent of American women.
- The average American model is 5'11" and weighs 117 pounds; the average American woman is 5'4" and weighs 140 pounds.

---

*Information is taken from the following sources: The National Eating Disorders Association; CUHealth@Colorado.edu; Office for National Statistics, Mintel, *The Adonis Complex.*

Visual Rhetoric...
ARGUMENTS FROM ABOUTFACE.ORG

About-Face.org is an Internet Web site with the following mission: "About-Face's mission is to equip women and girls with tools to understand and resist the harmful stereotypes of women that the media disseminates." About-Face has assembled galleries of positive and negative images such as the one below to demonstrate the ubiquitous—ever present—nature of these images. Often an image presents a claim that is nearly as literal as a written argument. What would be the Argument Concept for this image?

Image from *About-Face.org*.

- After seeing pictures of female fashion models, seven out of ten women felt more depressed and angry than before they saw the pictures.
- The popular media standard for the "perfect" woman depicted by models, Miss America, Barbie Dolls, and screen actresses is 5'5", 100 pounds, and size 5.

Because of this national interest, many people argue about the issue of body shape and what we should do about it. Are we a nation of obese citizens? Most estimates agree that nearly 13 percent of children and two-thirds of American adults are overweight, including one-third who are considered obese (at least 30 pounds overweight). Are we destructively focused on outward appearances? What causes this obsession? What extremes—early and frequent cosmetic surgery, for example—will we go to in order to look "perfect"? Included in this unit are diverse arguments from male and female perspectives on such questions.

I'm a Barbie Girl
Karen Epstein

> This argument by a female student at Tufts University in 1997 is a different angle on the influence of popular culture on the development of an unhealthy body image. "Barbie" has been blamed for setting an unrealistic standard for beauty for young girls, and sometimes the argument extends to Ken for boys. Barbie's maker, Mattel, took the loud criticism into consideration and decided to alter her image to mimic a more "real" or "normal" woman. Currently, Mattel has also issued Barbies that may more appropriately reflect broader women's roles than "clothes horse"; one of the newest models, for example, is "Pediatrician Barbie." Epstein played with Barbies when she was a child, and she thinks that blaming Barbie is a faulty cause-and-effect claim.

1   It wasn't her curvaceous hips. Or her Scarlett O'Hara–esque waist. Or even her unnaturally voluptuous bustline. The only things that bothered me were her feet. Those tiny little plastic feet were bent up in this permanent high-heel position that was extremely aggravating because

---

ALSO NOTE

A DIFFERENT LOOK FOR BARBIE

So, I'm at this conference with a very different looking Barbie in my lap. I made her look more real and a bit more like me. I gave the doll a set of drastic re-constructive surgeries before I took her to the conference. I stripped away her unrealistic chest with a power sander, I took two inches off her legs with a pair of ultra-strong scissors, I chopped off her golden locks, and using child's modeling clay, added a lot of weight to her waist and behind. She didn't look half bad.

If only it were that easy to reconstruct ourselves . . . if we could just slap some clay on . . . or off . . . to accentuate or downplay certain natural attributes. My most important discovery came while I was sanding down my Barbie . . . deconstructing her dreamy body. This doll, this image I spent my early years trying to live up to, was hollow inside.

—Tamara Keith, "Remaking Barbie," About-Face.org

I could never get those itsy-bitsy high-heel pumps to stay on. Ah, but the handsome Ken: he had these big, wide, "manly" feet that were perfectly flat. Those sensible shoes never fell off. Poor Barbie, on the other hand, never got to wear shoes in my house.

2   To my dismay, the Mattel toy company has not yet announced whether they will bring in their podiatry experts to examine thirty-eight-year-old Barbie's feet before her upcoming surgery. Earlier this week, the company told the world that the shapely Barbie is scheduled for some extensive nips and tucks—a wider waist, slimmer hips, and a smaller bustline. She's even getting a new face, minus the toothy grin.

3   Many who felt that the pop icon Barbie doll upheld an unrealistic standard of beauty are hailing Mattel's decision to make her look more like a real woman. And her highly unrealistic 38-18-34 figure (according to some estimates) gives girls a negative body ideal from a young age. "I actually think it's healthy because we are surrounded by cultural icons that create unrealistic expectations in adult women. . . . Barbie's change is a wholesome step in the right direction," retired plastic surgeon Sharon Webb told the *Boston Globe*.

4   I don't know about you, but for me, Barbie was always, well, a doll. When Barbie's skinny plastic legs popped out of their sockets, I knew she wasn't real. When my friend Lauren's bratty, semicannibalistic six-year-old neighbor chewed off Barbie's foot, and Barbie kept up that same cheery grin, I knew she wasn't real. I never deluded myself into thinking we little girls were supposed to grow up to have 38-18-34 figures. My mom didn't look like that. My teenage sisters didn't look like that. NO women I knew looked like Barbie. She was fun. She was a fantasy. And she sure did have some nice clothes.

5   I've always been a big fan of Barbie. I'm not alone. According to M.G. Lord, the author of *Forever Barbie*, the average American girl owns eight Barbie dolls—eight gals, that is, to "one pathetic, overextended Ken," she says. That was the case with me, although I think the number far exceeded eight. I don't remember all of their official names anymore, but I remember many in the lineup: there was punk-rocker Barbie, bride Barbie, "day-to-night" Barbie (her outfit converted from a work suit to evening wear, tres yuppie 1980s), the Barbie that came with an assortment of "fashion wigs," the Barbie with the funky hair-curler, birthday Barbie, ballerina Barbie, and, my favorite, permanently puckered kissing Barbie, who, at the push of a button on her back, would give Ken a big smooch. I was very upset when Barbie's kissing button stopped working. Looking back on it, I realize perhaps she just didn't, like Ken anymore.

6   My Ken was a busy fella. He was forced to play to boyfriend, brother, father, husband, "insert male role here" role in every one of my Barbies' adventures. What a nice guy. And, oh, those adventures. I could dress her in fancy clothes and send her on a romantic date with Ken, give her a bath in my Barbie bubble bath, put her to bed in the Barbie dream

house (I didn't actually have one, but I could pretend). It was a fantasy. "I mean, they say Barbie is unrealistic. But she's got a Ferrari, a Malibu dream house, and big plastic boobs. Here in LA, you can't get more realistic than that," said late-night TV host Jay Leno earlier this week.

7   Don't get me wrong. I do understand the concern many have with Barbie's current look. And, although her incredibly unrealistic body image did not affect me consciously as a child, there is a good chance it did affect me unconsciously. There is no one cause of the obsession with body image in this country and the rampant eating disorders young girls and women develop. While I place more of the blame on unattainable images of sickly thin women in advertising, movies, and television for the perpetuation of unrealistic standards of beauty, I must say that, despite my love for the Barbie I grew up with, Mattel is making the right move. If it helps one girl to not internalize the ridiculous ideal of big-busted thinness as perfection, it's worth it. But I'll never forget my Barbie.

8   Even Christina Hoff Sommers, the author of a book entitled *Who Stole Feminism*, told the *Boston Globe*, "The new Barbie is more attractive, and she did need a makeover. But I didn't mind the fact the older one reflected earlier ideals of feminine beauty. I liked Barbie as a child. She was glamorous. And part of being a child is fantasy and play, not an exercise in self-esteem."

9   In the end, she's a doll. A fantasy. An unanatomically correct piece of plastic with a ridiculously extensive wardrobe. And funny feet.

Wearing Tights
From *Real Boys' Voices*

> William Pollack is a clinical psychologist who is interested in the social situation of young men in our culture. He is particularly vocal about bullying and our society's tolerance of it. He has traveled the United States, even going to Littleton, Colorado, to talk to survivors of the Columbine disaster, talking to boys in hopes of getting to their true feelings about their lives and the society in which they live. This excerpt from Pollack's book is a transcript from Pollack's conversation with Roland, 17, a boy from a city in the Northeast. Although Roland's words are not a carefully constructed essay, revised and reworked to his best advantage, they certainly present a clear argument that boys are insecure and concerned about their image.

1   I've been dancing since I was six years old. I've always liked to dance at parties and everything. In elementary school and at junior high I joined a community dance group. It wasn't ballet or modern dance, just a community dance program. Then I took a modern dance class later in junior high school. It has beautiful choreography. With modern, you put your spirit into it. It's like you're flowing through the dance.

You do different things with your arms. You're organized and steady. You're synchronized with everybody else. In high school, I began taking tap. Then hip-top. With hip-hop, you're doing a lot of jumping around, lots of pumping. You do anything you want with your arms and legs. Hip-hop is energy. Later I did a little bit of classical. But I never did ballet, not yet. I don't want to do that. I'm not ready for the tights.

2   I'm not ashamed of my body. I think my body is fine. But I feel embarrassed, especially in front of guys, to dance in tights. I don't like the negative energy that I'm gonna get back. And I've seen shows that guys have done in tights and the other guys just act ridiculous toward them. I was thinking: "Why are you laughing at him? He's doing something that you can never possibly do, so you shouldn't be laughing at him!" I mean, it takes a lot to get up there, first of all, and dance in front of a lot of people; and second, to be dancing in tights and being probably the only guy up there. I was really upset and that kind of pushed me away from getting up there and dancing in tights. With the negative feedback they were giving, I was just like "No, I'm not getting up there."

3   It's easy to dance in front of strangers, but it's hard to dance in front of your friends. It's such a nerve-racking experience. If I were running the ballet class, and a boy in the class didn't want to put on his tights, I would tell him, "I've been there, it's okay to feel embarrassed."

4   I am worried about my upper body and arms. I want to look nice with my muscles and things like that. Most of the guys do. A young person like me, I'm really not that toned. I don't feel insecure but I feel like I'm kind of skinny. I want to be more bulked up, not to impress anybody, but just for me. Just to feel good about myself. But I think for a lot of guys it's mostly for the look, so they can impress girls and other guys.

5   I think boys and men are concerned about their bodies and the way they look. One time I went to this audition at a nearby high school and this guy—it was so funny because he had tights, and he put socks in his tights to make it look bigger, and I was like "Why are you doing that?" And he was like "Because it's not big enough!" And it was so funny, but I was like, who cares? The thing about him, he wasn't insecure about dancing, but he didn't like the way he looked in his tights.

6   The other guys think that girls are the only ones who can dance and girls are the only ones who are supposed to be wearing tights. They don't know that guys can do it, too. You can do whatever you want! I think that guys are insecure about themselves, basically. They don't know what they are or what they want. Whenever you're judging somebody, I think that you are insecure about yourself. Because you wouldn't be judging other people if you didn't think there was something wrong with yourself.

7   Maybe they're insecure about their body, maybe they're insecure that they can't dance. It could be a lot of things. Their bodies. Their personality. Do people like them? How well are they liked? Things like that can make you act stupid, really. If you don't know where you stand

> **ALSO NOTE**
> ## MEN AND ANOREXIA
>
> - More studies on men and boys are emerging in medical publications such as the *International Journal of Eating Disorders Research*.
> - One in six men may have anorexia and bulimia, according to a 1999 study in *Psychiatric Annals*, by Dr. Arnold E. Andersen, an eating-disorder researcher at the University of Iowa.
> - The number of men with eating disorders may be greater than 3 to 5 million, according to Roberto Olivardia, clinical psychologist at McLean Hospital in Belmont, MA, and coauthor of *The Adonis Complex: The Secret Crisis of Male Body Obsession*. ". . . Male eating disorders are underdiagnosed because society lacks awareness of them and men are less likely to admit they have this medical problem and seek help," Olivardia said.
> - Researchers have coined a term for one type of male body obsession: body dysmorphia disorder (BDD). An example is of BDD is muscle dysmorphia, sometimes called "reverse anorexia" or "biggerexia." This disorder occurs when normal-size or big, muscular men think of themselves as thin and scrawny. Some men with muscle dysmorphia may be workout-aholics, or users of steroids or muscle-enhancing supplements.
>
> —Lisa Liddane, *Orange County Register*

among your peers, you can act stupid. I think it's mostly boys, because girls, they have this freedom, that's why I admire them so much. Girls have this freedom to be like "Yeah, I can do whatever I want." I'm not saying that all girls are secure. But most guys have a problem with being insecure, that's what I'm saying.

Fat Girls (Don't) Dance
Sharleen Jonasson

> Although she is a business journalist by trade, Jonasson's first novel, *It's My Body and I'll Cry If I Want To*, is a story about a journalist who infiltrates the beauty industry to uncover its secrets and to protect unsuspecting women. During the course of her research for the book, she was mud-wrapped, put naked into a body tube, zapped by weird lights, and pummeled by a computerized bathtub. In this article, Jonasson evaluates an unusual performance designed to stimulate the audience's thinking about body image.

1   It's a Saturday night in Victoria, B.C., Canada, home base of the Big Dance dance troupe, "where the large body is inspiration and vessel to the art of dance," and I'm sitting on a hard chair waiting for their performance to begin.

2   In an audience of over 100, predominantly female, I count six bodies that are what Big Dance people might call "super-size" and only a handful mildly to moderately obese. I wonder why my fellow audience members are here. Support for the cause? Curiosity about what obese bodies can do to music? Just an interest in modern dance? Maybe a combination of all of the above, the same reasons I bought a ticket. A young woman passes around a sheet of paper with the program. "It's a test," she jokes. But as far as I'm concerned, it is: will I respond the way I know I should? I am, after all, the author of a novel that takes a scalpel (with hopefully some humor) to the arbitrariness and tyranny of the beauty industry. I have a reputation to uphold, if only in my own mind.

3   I'm already on their side, even before I've seen them, but that doesn't mean I know what to expect. I'm thinking of the ballerina dolls I had as a kid, Barbies with fewer curves, and I know what I'm going to see is going to be way off this stereotype. We may have magazines and fashionable shops for large-size women now, but we simply don't see the obese female body celebrated in dance, an art form in which women are if anything even thinner than the average model. What I'm really wondering is, will I soon be saying to myself, Oh, how beautiful these bodies can be in their abundance! Because in a fair, far gentler world, that'd be the case.

4   Somebody's turned out the lights. A muted blue spotlight shines onto the center of the floor and, to hauntingly beautiful music, into this circle of light come The Four Graces—four women who arrange themselves in a group pose that looks like a Renaissance sculpture. They're wearing only skin-colored tights. Recently in San Francisco, they performed this number naked. (Yes, naked; I asked.) And these women are not merely Rubenesque. One—not even the biggest—will joke during the evening that she resented being referred to recently as weighing 300 pounds: "I'm not an ounce over 299!"

5   The light goes off. The light goes on: the mass of abundant flesh has rearranged itself into another form, some arms and legs outstretched, others wrapped round other limbs, one spine curled forward into a fetal position. Each pose is a harmony of bodies pulling, pushing, straight, bent, open, closed.

6   Now as I watch this I am 10 pounds heavier than I really want to be (in case you were wondering—bet you were) which is to say, probably average for a 40-something North American woman, but I've weighed more, and I know that to be inside a large female body is to try to make yourself smaller, to take up as little space as you can. Arms in, legs together, head down. So my overwhelming reaction to this series of poses is wonder, admiration—not so much for the dance, or even for what the bodies do as part of it, but simply because they're here, they move, they stretch, they reach. And they're doing it under a spotlight.

7   The next piece is a solo of a woman battling a chair, and is both funny and poignant. Other pieces are jauntier (brocade vests and fedoras to the music of Duke Ellington), or make a more overt statement about fat and attractiveness with the use of props such as popular women's magazines, a bathroom scale, and red high heels.

8   But what rouses the crowd most is the Broccoli Bride. With a white half-slip over her head like a bridal veil and apron-like garment simulating a dress, the dancer holds a bunch of broccoli like a bouquet, gazes at it, then tosses it. No, not tosses it: hurls it across the room. Then she produces, from the pocket of her "wedding dress," a chocolate bar she eats with exaggerated lust. She closes her eyes, she swoons, she smears melting chocolate over her cheeks. It's defiant, it's over-the-top funny . . . but there's a part of me that finds the idea of rubbing chocolate over your body to the sounds of Gershwin on a Saturday night just a bit sad. I know I'm not supposed to be thinking this; everyone else is cheering.

9   There's a final number in which all four dancers, with pink tutus over black tights, perform a comic send-up to the hippo dance in *Fantasia*. I'm laughing with the best of them, now.

10 The struggle for acceptance of the female body in all its forms won't be won by one evening's dance or one dance troupe. I think it happens gradually, with our exposure to different body types shown in different ways changing our attitudes in tiny increments. But tonight, I think everyone in this audience has moved a big dancing leap forward. As the dancers turn and take a bow—you cannot see a row of fat, black, bent-over bums rimmed with pink tutus and not laugh—I'm thinking the point isn't whether or not fat women can be beautiful. The point tonight is simply whether fat women can make physical poetry with their bodies.

11 These women can.

12 This city I live in has an annoying habit of giving a standing ovation to everything (these people would rise for the winning cabbage at a fall fair) and except for performances that really move me, I make it a point to remain stubbornly in my seat. But as this performance ends and everyone stands, I'm up there with them, hollering and clapping. Because one thing I truly admire is people who take great personal risks for the sake of their art—and these women have taken a huge risk (no pun intended) and turned it into entertainment that's thought-provoking, humorous, and touching. What courage. Beautiful.

Just One Look
Kim Campbell

The newest wave in America's focus on beauty is cosmetic surgery. "Reality" shows such as *The Swan, Extreme Makeover*, and *Nip and Tuck* feature contestants who undergo surgical procedures to "improve" their appearance in hopes of winning the honor of having the most successful makeover. Contestants also receive the services of cosmetic dentists, eye surgeons, hair and makeup artists, and personal trainers. *Extreme Makeover* received over 10,000 written applications for their last casting call. Kim Campbell of *The Christian Science Monitor* argues in this article that the popularization of cosmetic surgery will create standards of "aesthetic sameness" and will alter the way we think about identity.

1. Plastic surgery is common enough in American culture that people don't think twice when they see it on The Learning Channel or in the pages of Oprah's magazine. But *Extreme Makeover*, a reality series launched recently by ABC, may be adding some edge to the question of where society is headed with all the nipping and tucking. The fact that the prime-time show has drawn about 12 million viewers per episode—and that participants say their experience is an "education process" for those considering procedures—focuses the concerns: What would it be like if everyone had cosmetic surgery? Would we all start looking alike?

2. Changing your features is not as controversial as, say, being cloned (unless, perhaps, you're Michael Jackson). And some people, including a few on *Extreme Makeover*, do it to fix serious problems. But as cosmetic surgery becomes more mainstream, unique noses and untucked tummies might be increasingly hard to come by, much the way braces have made crooked teeth largely a thing of the past.

3. "By the year 2020, no one will ask you whether you've had aesthetic surgery, they will ask you why you didn't have aesthetic surgery," predicts Sander Gilman, a University of Chicago professor who has studied the history of plastic surgery. Today, he says, it's acceptable to live in a world where you can change your looks but choose not to. But in 20 years or so, he says, "in certain societies—Brazil, Argentina, more and

---

ALSO NOTE
COSMETIC PROCEDURES BECOMING MORE POPULAR

- Both surgical procedures and other practices such as Botox injections have increased by 100 percent in five years.
- In 2002, 6.9 million cosmetic procedures accounted for a 228 percent increase since 1997.
- Women account for 6.1 million of the procedures in 2002; men underwent 800,000 procedures such as liposuction, nose reshaping, eyelid surgery, and Botox injections.
- According to a survey by the American Society for Aesthetic Plastic Surgery, 54 percent of their respondents approved of cosmetic surgery, and 24 percent said they would consider it for themselves.

—From "Cosmetic Surgery Comes Out of the Closet," MSNBC

4   more the UK, South Korea, Japan—the [question will be], 'Why didn't you take advantage? Why are you walking around bald?'" he says.

4   Reversing society's fascination with quick fixes could be difficult. Cultural observers say that surgery, now viewed as a viable option, is always in the back of people's minds, even if they never act on it. And it's not just self-assessment—more people now look at one another with what Virginia Blum calls "the surgical gaze." In her forthcoming book, *Flesh Wounds: The Culture of Cosmetic Surgery*, the University of Kentucky professor suggests that America's potent celebrity and consumer cultures are driving people to want to alter their bodies as quickly as fashions change. "Beauty is now as disposable and short-lived as our electronic gadgetry," she writes, "more impermanent than even the flesh it graces. . . ." In the few years since Professor Gilman wrote his 1999 book, *Making the Body Beautiful*, for example, women in Brazil have gone from wanting to reduce their breasts in order to look less primitive, to wanting to enlarge them to conform to what's perceived as the Western norm. "That's something that's just unbelievable to me, because it happened so quickly," he says.

5   Settling on one standard of beauty may be one of the biggest hurdles to having a society of Barbies and Kens—who or what would be the model? Blum argues it's a moving target, where people are constantly trying to look "better," but what defines better-looking is always changing. And, of course, until the aging process is reversed or teens start wearing tents, there will likely always be some pressure to look younger or have a tank-top body.

6   For one *Extreme Makeover* participant, the key to keeping people from all looking alike lies in the responsible behavior of plastic surgeons. Kine Corder, a Chicago barber who had corrective work done on her lips, says doctors, like the one on the show, are the gatekeepers, making sure changes are simply an extension of a person's natural look. "You can't bring him a picture and say 'I want Halle Barry's nose,' or 'I want Michelle Pfieffer's lips,'" she says. "He's going to say, 'I'm going to give you Kine's lips, the best Kine's lips I can give you.' So as long as we have doctors like [him] then no, we won't all end up looking alike."

7   If the day did come when everyone looked like a movie star, Gilman says an 18th-century philosopher named M.F.X. Bichat could offer guidance. Hundreds of years ago he pondered what would happen when every woman was beautiful according to some social standard. His answer, Gilman says, is the exact correct one: "We will find ever more subtle ways of defining beauty." The tiny differences between people will be the new scale of beauty, he says. "Freud called this the narcissism of minor differences, and, taken together with the radical shifting beliefs over time as to what beautiful is, we may desire uniformity, but it will always elude us."

8   Plastic surgeons throw cold water on the idea that a standard, societal "look" could emerge—even though observers say there is already often a "sameness" to the surgery done by particular doctors. People's

genes and bone structure would keep them from really looking the same, argue the professionals. That's the same argument experts offer for why face transplants—grafting the face of a deceased donor onto a burn victim, for example—will not produce people who look alike. Still called science fiction by some surgeons, such dramatic procedures are now being pursued in some medical circles.

9   If plastic surgery does become as common as braces, then the concern over its impacts on society could fade, says Blum: "The emphasis will be different. It won't be as big a deal. And if it's not a big deal, the sense of its extremity is diminished."

10   The number of people having plastic surgery is still a small portion of the nation's roughly 300 million people. Last year, those having procedures fell by 12 percent from the year before, dropping to 6.6 million people from 7.5 million in 2001, according to the American Society of Plastic Surgeons. The ASPS blames the poor economy for the decline. But the number of procedures performed—ranging from nose reshaping to nonsurgical chemical "peels"—is still dramatically higher than a decade ago, with more men and younger patients involved.

11   *Extreme Makeover* reflects this demographic shift. Participants offer a range of reasons for their decision: finding better dating and job prospects, having inner youth reflected in their outward appearance, fixing flaws they've had since birth. Most say they just want to look like better versions of themselves. "You can see some changes in my new look, but they're not to the point where you can't recognize David," says David Patteson, a noncommissioned officer in the Virginia National Guard who lives in Farmville, Va. Interested in having a look he felt would make it easier for him to get promoted, his changes included a nose job, chin enlargement, and work around his eyes. Rather than worry about what the people in his rural town might think, he explained, "I looked at it and I said, well, what do you want, and what's going to improve yourself and your family's life?"

12   That attitude may be a natural offshoot of living in a society where self-direction is prized in all areas, and increasingly simple for some to achieve. Appearance—and by extension, identity—is simply an area in which the potential for control has surged, says Carl Elliott, professor of bioethics and philosophy at the University of Minnesota: "[Identity has] changed from something that's largely given to you, to something that you have the responsibility for creating yourself."

The Muscle Mystique
Barbara Kingsolver

> The pressure to "work out" is sometimes hard to resist in our appearance-oriented culture. Health club statistics collected by *Fitness Management* in 1999 showed industry revenues of $9.6 billion; 22.5 million members

belonged to fitness clubs. The National Sporting Goods Association reports that the number of health clubs and gyms rose 14 percent in 2004. In this humorous argument, novelist and essayist Kingsolver discusses her giving in to fitness pressure even though she is admittedly "embarrassed by all this . . . unproductive sweat." She ultimately cannot get into the workout routine that seems artificial and somewhat silly to her.

1   The baby-sitter surely thought I was having an affair. Years ago, for a period of three whole months, I would dash in to pick up my daughter after "work" with my cheeks flushed, my heart pounding, my hair damp from a quick shower. I'm loath to admit where I'd really been for that last hour of the afternoon. But it's time to come clean.

2   I joined a health club.

3   I went downtown and sweated with the masses. I rode a bike that goes nowhere at the rate of five hundred calories per hour. I even pumped a little iron. I can't deny the place was a lekking ground: guys stalking around the weight room like prairie chickens, nervously eying each other's pectorals. Over by the abdominal machines I heard some of the frankest pickup lines since eighth grade ("You've got real defined deltoids for a girl"). A truck perpetually parked out front had vanity plates that read: LFTWTS. Another one PRSS 250, I didn't recognize as a vanity plate until I understood the prestige of bench pressing 250 pounds.

4   I personally couldn't bench press a fully loaded steam iron. I didn't join the health club to lose weight, or to meet the young Adonis who admired my (dubiously defined) deltoids. I am content with my lot in life, save for one irksome affliction: I am what's known in comic-book jargon as the ninety-eight-pound weakling. I finally tipped the scales into three digits my last year of high school, but "weakling" I've remained, pretty much since birth. In polite terminology I'm cerebral; the muscles between my ears are what I get by on. The last great body in my family was my Grandfather Henry. He wore muscle shirts in the days when they were known as BVDs, under his cotton work shirt, and his bronze tan stopped midbiceps. He got those biceps by hauling floor joists and hammering up roof beams every day of his life, including his last. How he would have guffawed to see a roomful of nearly naked bankers and attorneys, pale as plucked geese, heads down, eyes fixed on a horizon beyond the water cooler, pedaling like bats out of hell on bolted-down bicycles. I expect he'd offer us all a job. If we'd pay our thirty dollars a month to *him*, we could come out to the construction site and run up and down ladders bringing him nails. That's why I'm embarrassed about all this. I'm afraid I share his opinion of unproductive sweat.

5   Actually, he'd be more amazed than scornful. His idea of fun was watching Ed Sullivan or snoozing in a recliner, or ideally, both at once. Why work like a maniac on your day off? To keep your heart and lungs in shape. Of course. But I haven't noticed any vanity plates that say GD LNGS. The operative word here is vanity.

6   Standards of beauty in every era are things that advertise, usually falsely: "I'm rich and I don't have to work." How could you be a useful farmhand, or even an efficient clerk-typist, if you have long, painted fingernails? Four-inch high heels, like the bound feet of Chinese aristocrats, suggest you don't have to do *anything* efficiently, except maybe put up your tootsies on an ottoman and eat bonbons. (And I'll point out here that aristocratic *men* wore the first high heels.) In my grandmother's day, women of all classes lived in dread of getting a tan, since that betrayed a field worker's station in life. But now that the field hand's station is occupied by the office worker, a tan, I suppose, advertises that Florida and Maui are within your reach. Fat is another peculiar cultural flip-flop: in places where food is scarce, beauty is three inches of subcutaneous fat deep. But here and now, jobs are sedentary and calories are relatively cheap, while the luxury of time to work them off is very dear. It still gives me pause to see an ad for a weight-loss program that boldly enlists: "First ten pounds come off free!" But that is about the size of it, in this strange food-drenched land of ours. After those first ten, it gets expensive.

7   As a writer I could probably do my job fine with no deltoids at all, or biceps or triceps, so long as you left me those vermicellisized muscles that lift the fingers to the keyboard. (My vermicellis are *very* well defined.) So when I've writ my piece, off I should merrily go to build a body that says I don't really have a financial obligation to sit here in video-terminal bondage.

8   Well, yes. But to tell the truth, the leisure body and even the GD LNGS are not really what I was after when I signed up at Pecs-R-Us. What I craved, and long for still, is to be *strong*. I've never been strong. In childhood, team sports were my most reliable source of humiliation. I've been knocked breathless to the ground by softballs, basketballs, volleyballs, and once, during a wildly out-of-hand game of Red Rover, a sneaker. In every case I knew my teammates were counting on me for a volley or a double play or anyhow something more than clutching my stomach and rolling upon the grass. By the time I reached junior high I wasn't even the last one picked anymore. I'd slunk away long before they got to the bottom of the barrel.

9   Even now, the great mortification of my life is that visitors to my home sometimes screw the mustard and pickle jar lids back on so tightly *I can't get them open!* (The visitors probably think they are just closing them enough to keep the bugs out.) Sure, I can use a pipe wrench, but it's embarrassing. Once, my front gate stuck, and for several days I could only leave home by clambering furtively through the bougainvilleas and over the garden wall. When a young man knocked on my door to deliver flowers one sunny morning, I threw my arms around him. He thought that was pretty emotional, for florists' mums. He had no idea he'd just casually pushed open the Berlin Wall.

10   My inspiration down at the health club was a woman firefighter who could have knocked down my garden gate with a karate chop. I still dream about her triceps. But I've mostly gotten over my brief fit of muscle envy. Oh, I still make my ongoing, creative stabs at body building: I do "girl pushups," and some of the low-impact things from Jane Fonda's pregnant-lady workout book, even if I'm not. I love to run, because it always seems like there's a chance you might actually get somewhere, so I'll sometimes cover a familiar mile or so of our country road after I see my daughter onto the school bus. (The driver confessed that for weeks he thought I was chasing him; he never stopped.) And finally, my friends have given me an official item of exercise equipment that looks like a glob of blue putty, which you're supposed to squeeze a million times daily to improve your grip. That's my current program. The so-called noncompetitive atmosphere of the health club whipped me, hands down. Realistically, I've always known I was born to be a "before" picture. So I won't be seen driving around with plates that boast: PRSS 250.

11   Maybe: OPN JRS.

■■ Unit 2
■■ Questions to Guide Analysis

1. Epstein, in "I'm a Barbie Girl," relies mostly on her own experience to argue that Barbie dolls don't influence young women's concept of body image. What logical problem could therefore be connected to the conclusion she draws? Reread paragraph 7. Does this paragraph alleviate, to some extent, the logical problem, or does it just point to the problem in her argument?

2. Of his experiences talking to many boys, Pollack says, "When boys speak about 'being themselves,' many describe a double life in which they are one person in public—a cool guy who plays fast and lives by the rules of the Boy Code—and somebody completely different in his private life, often a much more creative, gentle, caring sort of guy." Who was Roland's audience when he was discussing "Wearing Tights"? How might the argument he makes be different if he were talking to his peers? Are we hypocritical when we change our purpose and focus for different readers or audiences, or are we just "sensitive to the argumentative context"?

3. Of the specific purposes for argument discussed in Chapter 10, which purpose drives Jonasson's argument, "Fat Girls (Don't) Dance"? Is there perhaps a double purpose to this argument? Who is Jonasson's reader, and will this argument be effective for that reader?

4. Why has the author used much more vivid detail in "Fat Girls (Don't) Dance" than the author of "Just One Look" has included?

5. Does Campbell, in "Just One Look," present a balanced or one-sided argument? Would the argument be strengthened or weakened by discussing the positive value of cosmetic surgery for some patients? What kind of examples might connect the reader more strongly to the argument?

6. Why does Kingsolver use the image of the vanity plates repeatedly in her essay? What point is she trying to make by those references? How does her example of her Grandfather Henry add to that point?

7. At the end of Kingsolver's argument, she lists the fitness activities that she will still participate in. What is the significant difference between these activities and those in her aborted health club attempt? Why would she choose to end her essay with these activities and her reference to opening jars?

8. After reading these arguments, you might be interested in body images as an argument topic. How might you develop an argument inspired by two or more of the articles in this unit?

   A. Create three hypothetical Argument Concepts that you might pursue on the topic of body images.
   B. What are the most compelling arguments from this set of essays that could be used as support for one of the Argument Concepts you conceived in activity A, and why do you think they are strong?
   C. What is the weakest argument you read in these articles, and why do you think it is not convincing?
   D. What type of outside source material would you seek to further develop your argument?

UNIT

3

Poverty and Wealth

In his 2002 Nobel Peace Prize lecture, former President Jimmy Carter made the following statement:

> At the beginning of this new millennium I was asked to discuss, here in Oslo, the greatest challenge that the world faces. Among all the possible choices, I decided that the most serious and universal problem is the growing chasm between the richest and poorest people on earth. Citizens of the ten wealthiest countries are now seventy-five times richer than those who live in the ten poorest ones, and the separation is increasing every year, not only between nations but also within them. The results of this disparity are root causes of most of the world's unresolved problems, including starvation, illiteracy, environmental degradation, violent conflict, and unnecessary illnesses that range from Guinea worm to HIV/AIDS.
>
> Most work of The Carter Center is in remote villages in the poorest nations of Africa, and there I have witnessed the capacity of destitute people to persevere under heartbreaking conditions. I have come to admire their judgment and wisdom, their courage and faith, and their awesome accomplishments when given a chance to use their innate abilities.
>
> But tragically, in the industrialized world there is a terrible absence of understanding or concern about those who are enduring lives of despair and hopelessness. We have not yet made the commitment to share with others an appreciable part of our excessive wealth. This is a potentially rewarding burden that we should all be willing to assume.

The disparity between rich and poor is nowhere more evident than in the United States. Of all industrialized countries, we rank the lowest (twenty-second) in equality between rich and poor. The accompanying charts show the distribution of wealth in America, an imbalance that has grown dramatically in the last 15 years. From 2003 to 2004, for example, the number of millionaires increased by 14 percent during a time when many wage earners could not find jobs. One way to simplify the figures so they are more digestible is to imagine, as the Web site *therationalradical.com* suggests, the wealth of the nation to be $100 and the population to be 100. In that case, the $100 would be distributed, according to the current proportions of wealth, as follows:

1 person would have	$ 38.10
4 people would have	$ 5.32
5 people would have	$ 2.30
10 people would have	$ 1.25
20 people would have	$ .60
20 people would have	$ .23
40 people would have	$ .005 (1/2 cent.)

The top 1 percent of our population owns 38.1 percent of the wealth, the top 10 percent owns 70.9 percent, and the other 90 percent of the population owns 29.1 percent. Seen historically, this disparity is even more dramatic. Income of the top 1 percent has risen 201 percent from 1979 to 2000, while the income of the middle 20 percent rose 15 percent, and income of the lowest 20 percent went up only 9 percent.*

Many people argue that an imbalance of this proportion is a danger to the strength and health of the country, just as Carter argues that the uneven distribution of wealth worldwide accounts for many of our global problems. Some wealthy Americans have even taken a "Responsible Tax Pledge" and will turn down their share of the $69 billion tax cuts that went into effect in 2004.

Included in this unit of readings are arguments on how the American imbalance has developed, how complex poverty is, what obligations we have or don't have to the less fortunate, and how we should solve the problems.

Wealth Statistics Stack Up Unevenly

Rick Montgomery

> This article appeared in the *Kansas City Star* on December 19, 2006. Montgomery investigates a recent phenomenon related to the inequity of distribution of wealth in the United States. His argument is that the "somewhat wealthy," who are now seeing separation even between themselves and the ultrarich, may be a group who has the power and voice to bring this issue to the proper attention.

1   In a case of bonus envy, even the well-to-do find six-figure incomes don't impress like they used to. Goldman Sachs had a good year. The investment house is giving its top employees $16 billion in bonuses.
2   Sixteen. Billion. Bucks. In bonuses.
3   The author Tom Wolfe, himself very wealthy, didn't call Wall Street bankers "masters of the universe" for nothing. Why, it's enough to make the less rich—say, the half-million-a-year crowd—stew this Christmas in their Vail chalets. Or so we're told. "A New Class War: The Haves vs. the Have Mores," declares the *New York Times*. "Revolt of the Fairly Rich," says *Fortune* magazine. And just last week, Anne Taylor Fleming, an essayist on

---

*Data and graphs are from United for a Fair Economy (UFE), www.faireconomy.org, an organization dedicated to the pursuit of social and economic justice. If you are interested in this issue, you might also want to investigate the Responsible Wealth Project, which can be found on the UFE home page.

Visual Rhetoric...
THE GRAPHIC STORY OF POVERTY AND WEALTH

What claims might the data in these graphs support? What is the difference in impact between the pie chart and the bar chart? What is the difference in effect between reading this data in paragraph and text format and reading it in a chart?

—Graphs from www.faireconomy.org

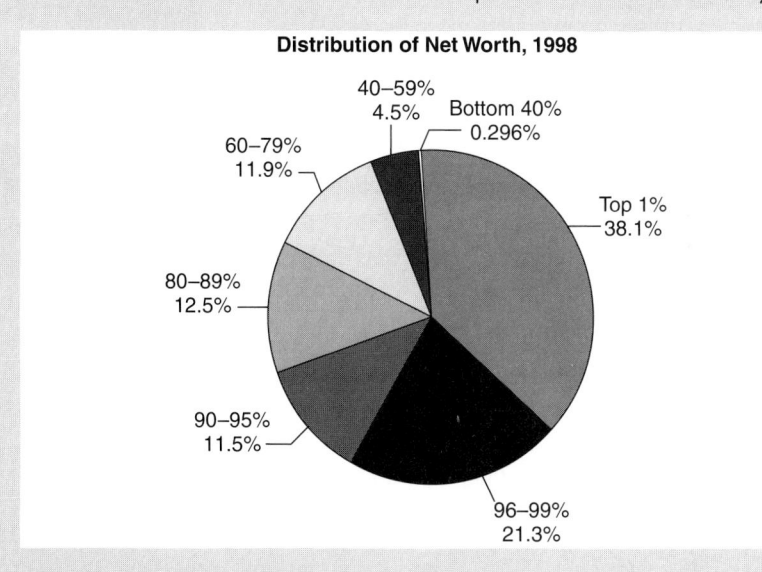

Distribution of Net Worth, 1998

- Top 1%: 38.1%
- 96–99%: 21.3%
- 90–95%: 11.5%
- 80–89%: 12.5%
- 60–79%: 11.9%
- 40–59%: 4.5%
- Bottom 40%: 0.296%

Data from United for a Fair Economy (www.faireconomy.org)

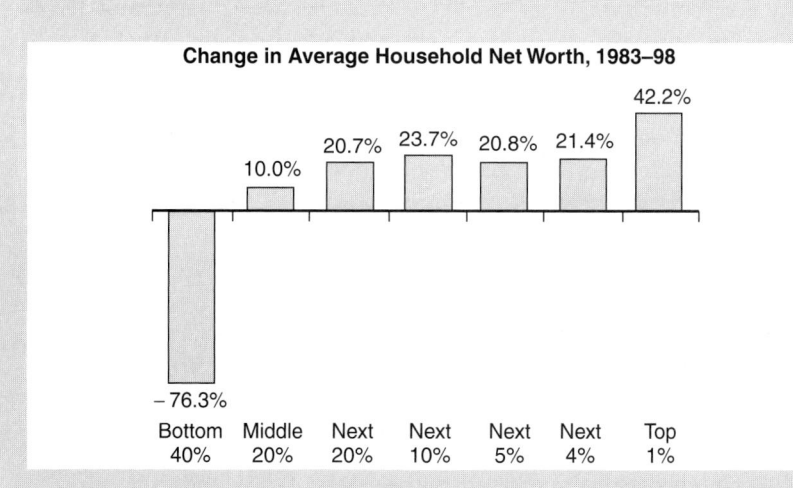

Change in Average Household Net Worth, 1983–98

- Bottom 40%: −76.3%
- Middle 20%: 10.0%
- Next 20%: 20.7%
- Next 10%: 23.7%
- Next 5%: 20.8%
- Next 4%: 21.4%
- Top 1%: 42.2%

Data from Economic Policy Institute/Center on Budget and Policy Priorities (www.cbp.org)

PBS *NewsHour*, voiced indignation at gift catalogs selling $26,000 handbags, and she said: "I hear it all the time, people making $300,000 a year saying they are having a hard time keeping their boats afloat." While the rest of America rolls its eyeballs at such injustice, a spate of new studies and statistics throws a blinding spotlight on just how concentrated the world's wealth has become. The richest of the rich are getting much richer, and ascending quicker, than are the rather wealthy.

4 And Average Joe? He appears stuck in the mud. According to data recently prepared by the Center on Budget and Policy Priorities, the bottom 90 percent of U.S. households saw an increase in real household income of 2 percent between 1990 and 2004. That's adjusted for inflation.

5 Two. Percent. In 14 years.

6 Now creep up the income ladder to the top 1 percent of households. There, says the center's Aviva Aron-Dine, real income shot up 57 percent in the same period. Climb higher. For the top 0.1 percent—where incomes average about $4.5 million a year—the jump was 85 percent. For the top .01 percent, 112 percent. "The increasing gulf between the rich and super rich is a reflection of the greater chasm throughout society," says Aron-Dine. "What's going on is an increasingly skewed assessment of wage and income over the long term."

7 Not since the 1920s—the era of F. Scott Fitzgerald's rollicking Jay Gatsby—has such a small slice of America hoarded so much of the nation's income, her findings show. Globally, the richest 2 percent of adults now own more than half of the personal wealth, says a new study by U.N. researchers. The bulk of the world's valuables are not just controlled by relatively few people, but those people live in relatively few places—North America, Europe, and some nations in the Asia Pacific region. "There's definitely a vicious cycle at work," said New York University economist Edward N. Wolff, who studies wealth accumulation. "Once this process starts, it feeds on itself. When one industry bids up CEOs' salaries, they all follow and the pay just keeps increasing."

8 The splintering of the affluent—a demographic once loosely regarded as one—is profoundly evident in the medical industry. The spectacular lifestyles accorded to some doctors specializing in tummy tucks and facelifts lure gifted surgeons who feel they aren't earning

---

ALSO NOTE
UNEQUAL DISTRIBUTION OF RESOURCES

The world's 358 billionaires together possess as much money as the poorest 50 percent of the world's population. Their combined assets roughly equal the assets of the world's poorest 2.5 billion people.

—Affluenza.org

enough reattaching severed limbs. Spiraling costs of medical schooling and the temptation of specialists' pay drive doctors away from family practice or pediatrics and straight up the "E—ROAD." That's the fraternal acronym for emergency, radiology, ophthalmology, anesthesiology or dermatology. "A person looking at huge medical-school debt says, 'I can be a primary-care physician and make $150,000 a year, or I can invest the same amount of time and be a radiologist, making $400,000,'" said Perry A. Pungo, director of medical education for the Kansas City–based American Academy of Family Physicians.

9   And those pay figures are peanuts to physicians such as Robert H. Glassman, who left a lucrative practice to rake in millions more managing health-care investment funds for Merrill Lynch. In a recent *Times* story headlined "Very Rich are Leaving Merely Rich Behind," Glassman, 45, spoke of being self-conscious at the 20th reunion of his Harvard class. His medical peers "remained true to their ethics . . . and saw that somebody else who was 10 times less smart was making much more money."

10   But experts say if such disparities are, in fact, fueling "class warfare" within the well-to-do, then it is a cold war—a whispered frustration over a meritocracy out of whack. "There are pathways to becoming rich and pathways to becoming super rich, and they don't take the same amount of work, talent or credentials," said Jared Bernstein, senior economist at the Economic Policy Institute. In the push for record-upon-record profits, "many high-end white-collar people are being beset by the same trends that affected blue-collar people 20 years ago. An economy that had always divided the middle from the bottom, and the middle from the top, is now differentiating the top from the upper top." Part of that is due to more Americans being at the top, or near it: In 2005 the number of millionaire U.S. households jumped for a third straight year to a record 8.9 million, according to the market-research firm TNS Financial Services.

11   But these days having a net worth of at least $1 million, not counting your home, places you in a universe light years from, say, Warren Buffett's. In June, the Omaha businessman's gift of $31 billion to the Bill and Melinda Gates Foundation crystallized growing concern in philanthropic circles that donations of the ultrarich could stifle the giving of lesser benefactors who think their $50 checks—or even $10,000 checks—won't make much difference. "There is some of that rumbling out there," said Laura McKnight of the Greater Kansas City Community Foundation. "I do believe that there is some degree of a chilling effect . . . on people who give at lower levels, potentially feeling disenfranchised."

12   Across the income spectrum, Americans are sending mixed messages about the widening wealth gaps, according to recent opinion polls. Almost three-quarters of those surveyed this month in a Bloomberg/*Los Angeles Times* poll said the divide between rich and poor is a "serious" issue, versus 24 percent who didn't think so. Still, a Gallup Poll suggests the very rich remain more admired than despised: A majority of Americans agree that "people who make lots of money deserve it" and "almost anyone can get rich if they put their

mind to it." And, in survey after survey, one of America's uberrich—Oprah Winfrey—also is one of its most admired.

13   "Look, there's always been a sense that Horatio Alger's alive and well in America," said economist Bernstein. "But I also think there's a sense that fair play has been violated in the present economy. . . This idea of 'You're on your own—try making it big in this market,' I think, has given rise to a sense that we've gone too far on that path," he said.

14   And whether reform means prohibiting corporations from deducting executive pay, or your usual redirecting of wealth through taxation, Bernstein raises a provocative point: Who better to get policymakers' attention than the frustrated masses earning six figures? "It's hard to believe they wouldn't have some effect on social change."

ALSO NOTE
FALLING BEHIND

Here's how real income grew between 1990 and 2004:*

- Up 2% for the bottom 90 percent of U.S. households
- Up 57% for the top 1 percent of households
- Up 85% for the top 0.1 percent of households
- Up 112% for the top .01 percent of households

*Source: The Center on Budget and Policy Priorities

What Is Poverty?

Jo Goodwin Parker

Parker's widely anthologized speech was first delivered in Florida in 1965, but its power to put a face on poverty is timeless. By thinking about the Argument Concept for this argument, you will be able to see how Parker's speech is about much more than her own experience. Her purpose is much larger than just to complain about her situation. How does her argument reveal the complexity of poverty that we often fail to recognize?

ALSO NOTE
CHILDREN IN POVERTY

In 2003, 12.9 million American children younger than 18 lived below the poverty line and more than one out of every six American children (17.6 percent) were poor. That is more children living in poverty today than 30 or 35 years ago. A child in America is more likely to live in poverty than a child in any of the 18 other wealthy industrialized nations for which data exist.

—The Children's Defense Fund

1   You ask me what is poverty? Listen to me. Here I am, dirty, smelly, and with no "proper" underwear on and with the stench of my rotting teeth near you. I will tell you. Listen to me. Listen without pity. I cannot use your pity. Listen with understanding. Put yourself in my dirty, worn out, ill-fitting shoes, and hear me.

2   Poverty is getting up every morning from a dirt- and illness-stained mattress. The sheets have long since been used for diapers. Poverty is living in a smell that never leaves. This is a smell of urine, sour milk, and spoiling food sometimes joined with the strong smell of long-cooked onions. Onions are cheap. If you have smelled this smell, you did not know how it came. It is the smell of the outdoor privy. It is the smell of young children who cannot walk the long dark way in the night. It is the smell of the mattresses where years of "accidents" have happened. It is the smell of the milk which has gone sour because the refrigerator long has not worked, and it costs money to get it fixed. It is the smell of rotting garbage. I could bury it, but where is the shovel? Shovels cost money.

3   Poverty is being tired. I have always been tired. They told me at the hospital when the last baby came that I had chronic anemia caused from poor diet, a bad case of worms, and that I needed a corrective operation. I listened politely—the poor are always polite. The poor always listen. They don't say that there is no money for iron pills, or better food, or worm medicine. The idea of an operation is frightening and costs so much that, if I had dared, I would have laughed. Who takes care of my children? Recovery from an operation takes a long time. I have three children. When I left them with "Granny" the last time I had a job, I came home to find the baby covered with fly specks, and a diaper that had not been changed since I left. When the dried diaper came off, bits of my baby's flesh came with it. My other child was playing with a sharp bit of broken glass, and my oldest was playing alone at the edge of a lake. I made twenty-two dollars a week, and a good nursery school costs twenty dollars a week for three children. I quit my job.

4   Poverty is dirt. You say in your clean clothes coming from your clean house, "Anybody can be clean." Let me explain about housekeeping with no money. For breakfast I give my children grits with no oleo or corn-bread without eggs and oleo. This does not use up many dishes. What dishes there are, I wash in cold water and with no soap. Even the cheapest soap has to be saved for the baby's diapers. Look at my hands, so cracked and red. Once I saved for two months to buy a jar of Vaseline for my hands and the baby's diaper rash. When I had saved enough, I went to buy it and the price had gone up two cents. The baby and I suffered on. I have to decide every day if I can bear to put my cracked, sore hands into the cold water and strong soap. But you ask, why not hot water? Fuel costs money. If you have a wood fire it costs money. If you burn electricity, it costs money. Hot water is a luxury. I do not have luxuries. I know you will be surprised when I tell you how

young I am. I look so much older. My back has been bent over the wash tubs every day for so long. I cannot remember when I ever did anything else. Every night I wash every stitch my school-age child has on and just hope her clothes will be dry by morning.

5   Poverty is staying up all night on cold nights to watch the fire, knowing one spark on the newspaper covering the walls means your sleeping children die in flames. In summer poverty is watching gnats and flies devour your baby's tears when he cries. The screens are torn and you pay so little rent you know they will never be fixed. Poverty means insects in your food, in your nose, in your eyes, and crawling over you when you sleep. Poverty is hoping it never rains because diapers won't dry when it rains and soon you are using newspapers. Poverty is seeing your children forever with runny noses. Paper handkerchiefs cost money and all your rags you need for other things. Even more costly are antihistamines. Poverty is cooking without food and cleaning without soap.

6   Poverty is asking for help. Have you ever had to ask for help, knowing your children will suffer unless you get it? Think about asking for a loan from a relative, if this is the only way you can imagine asking for help. I will tell you how it feels. You find out where the office is that you are supposed to visit. You circle that block four or five times. Thinking of your children, you go in. Everyone is very busy. Finally, someone comes out and you tell her that you need help. That never is the person you need to see. You go see another person, and after spilling the whole shame of your poverty all over the desk between you, you find that this isn't the right office after all—you must repeat the whole process, and it never is any easier at the next place.

7   You have asked for help, and after all it has a cost. You are again told to wait. You are told why, but you don't really hear because of the red cloud of shame and the rising black cloud of despair.

8   Poverty is remembering. It is remembering quitting school in junior high because "nice" children had been so cruel about my clothes and my smell. The attendance officer came. My mother told him I was pregnant. I wasn't, but she thought that I could get a job and help out. I had jobs off and on, but never long enough to learn anything. Mostly I remember being married. I was so young then. I am still young. For a time, we had all the things you have. There was a little house in another town, with hot water and everything. Then my husband lost his job. There was unemployment insurance for a while and what few jobs I could get. Soon, all our nice things were repossessed and we moved back here. I was pregnant then. This house didn't look so bad when we first moved in. Every week it gets worse. Nothing is ever fixed. We now had no money. There were a few odd jobs for my husband, but everything went for food then, as it does now. I don't know how we lived through three years and three babies, but we did. I'll tell you something, after the last baby I destroyed my marriage. It had been a good one, but could you keep on bringing children in this dirt? Did you ever think how much it costs for any kind of birth control? I knew my

husband was leaving the day he left, but there were no good-bys between us. I hope he has been able to climb out of this mess somewhere. He never could hope with us to drag him down.

9. That's when I asked for help. When I got it, you know how much it was? It was, and is, seventy-eight dollars a month for the four of us; that is all I ever can get. Now you know why there is no soap, no needles and thread, no hot water, no aspirin, no worm medicine, no hand cream, no shampoo. None of these things forever and ever and ever. So that you can see clearly, I pay twenty dollars a month rent, and most of the rest goes for food. For grits and cornmeal, and rice and milk and beans. I try my best to use only the minimum electricity. If I use more, there is that much less for food.

10. Poverty is looking into a black future. Your children won't play with my boys. They will turn to other boys who steal to get what they want. I can already see them behind the bars of their prison instead of behind the bars of my poverty. Or they will turn to the freedom of alcohol or drugs, and find themselves enslaved. And my daughter? At best, there is for her a life like mine.

11. But you say to me, there are schools. Yes, there are schools. My children have no extra books, no magazines, no extra pencils, or crayons, or paper and the most important of all, they do not have health. They have worms, they have infections, they have pink-eye all summer. They do not sleep well on the floor, or with me in my one bed. They do not suffer from hunger, my seventy-eight dollars keeps us alive, but they do suffer from malnutrition. Oh yes, I do remember what I was taught about health in school. It doesn't do much good. In some places there is a surplus commodities program. Not here. The county said it costs too much. There is a school lunch program. But I have two children who will already be damaged by the time they get to school.

12. But, you say to me, there are health clinics. Yes, there are health clinics and they are in the towns. I live out here eight miles from town. I can walk that far (even if it is sixteen miles both ways), but can my little children? My neighbor will take me when he goes; but he expects to get paid, *one way or another*. I bet you know my neighbor. He is that large man who spends his time at the gas station, the barbershop, and the corner store complaining about the government spending money on the immoral mothers of illegitimate children.

13. Poverty is an acid that drips on pride until all pride is worn away. Poverty is a chisel that chips on honor until honor is worn away. Some of you say that you would do *something* in my situation, and maybe you would, for the first week or the first month, but for year after year after year?

14. Even the poor can dream. A dream of a time when there is money. Money for the right kinds of food, for worm medicine, for iron pills, for toothbrushes, for hand cream, for a hammer and nails and a bit of screening, for a shovel, for a bit of paint, for some sheeting, for needles and thread. Money to pay *in money* for a trip to town. And, oh, money for hot water and money for soap. A dream of when asking for help

does not eat away the last bit of pride. When the office you visit is as nice as the offices of other governmental agencies, when there are enough workers to help you quickly, when workers do not quit in defeat and despair. When you have to tell your story to only one person, and that person can send you for other help and you don't have to prove your poverty over and over and over again.

15   I have come out of my despair to tell you this. Remember I did not come from another place or another time. Others like me are all around you. Look at us with an angry heart, anger that will help you help me. Anger that will let you tell of me. The poor are always silent. Can you be silent too?

Helping Binyam, When His Mother Won't
Nicholas D. Kristof

> Whereas Parker argues poverty in America is a much more difficult problem than we might think looking on from the outside, Kristof discusses the cultural, economic, and political factors that complicate solutions to poverty in less developed countries. This opinion piece from the *New York Times* (May 20, 2003) was filed from Adi Keih, Eritrea, where Kristof was traveling and where he experienced poverty and starvation beyond what we can imagine. An important and unusual feature of his focus is that he acknowledges the responsibility of the countries and their folkways that sometimes exacerbate the problems, yet, he argues, we should still help.

1   Alas, there are several good reasons not to help starving Africans.

2   I wish the famine were as simple as the local governments portray it: as a drought that has left 40 million Africans at risk of starvation. But after jouncing over rumors of roads in Ethiopia and Eritrea, I've met too many children like Binyam Berhane. Binyam is a 14-month-old boy in this town in southern Eritrea who came within a whisker of starving to death. But before you reach for your checkbook, I should add that his mother, a 20-year-old woman named Senait Derhane, looks healthy and plump. She was wearing a nice dress and had purple nail polish on her toenails. She acknowledges that the reason she doesn't have food for Binyam is that the Eritrean government drafted her husband to fight a (senseless) war still simmering with Ethiopia. In his absence, she has no income and no one to work the fields.

3   So sure, there is a severe drought. But it has only aggravated a chronic shortage that is the fault of governments and individual families.

4   What breaks your heart is the sight of healthy parents cradling skeletal children. Petros Loka, for example, is a young man with the hint of a potbelly—yet he was at an Ethiopian clinic with his 7-year-old son, David, who was admitted at 31 pounds and looked like a ghost. Trying to puzzle out how this could happen, I asked how the family ate.

"The man eats first, and then the children and the wife eat together," Mr. Loka explained. Others confirm that across rural Ethiopia, the father eats first and the mother and children get leftovers—with the smallest kids mostly squeezed out. To address that problem, we need not just more food but, above all, education, so that, as in Ethiopia's cities, families eat together and understand the need to look out for their youngest members.

5   Moreover, even in a good year five million Ethiopians need food aid, and Georgia Shaver, head of the World Food Program in Ethiopia, says that "normal" may need to be redefined as 10 million in need. So the problem goes beyond the weather and includes insecure land tenure, the 29 million Africans with AIDS or HIV, and the lack of irrigation. I talked to members of one family who were hungry because their crops had failed from the drought, just 100 yards from a lake. Why hadn't they irrigated? The risk of being stomped by hippos was one factor, but another was that carrying water is women's work and tending the fields is men's work, and this cultural impasse left them stymied—and starving.

6   Another problem is that food aid solves immediate problems but adds to the underlying one. U. S. gifts of grain save lives—but also lower local food prices. This reduces incentives for farmers and leaves them poorer, and thus arguably more vulnerable in the next famine.

7   So there are plenty of reasons not to help the 40 million at risk of starvation in Africa. And yet . . .

8   I've never seen anything like the wizened children dying of starvation in Ethiopia. Even if we do our part, perhaps 100,000 Ethiopian children will die of malnutrition-related ailments in 2003, as they do in a typical year. But if the drought persists and we don't do more, the toll will rise to several hundred thousand or more. When children are dying in front of you—or at risk of permanent brain damage if they survive—practical objections to food aid lose their force. And it's not true that giving such aid is always pouring food aid down a rathole. In the 1970s, Bangladesh perpetually seemed in famine and was famously dismissed by Henry Kissinger as an "international basket case." Since then, Bangladesh has grown economically faster than the U.S.

9   So just because famine is chronic doesn't mean that we shouldn't help. This fact simply underscores the importance of focusing not just on relief, but also on longer-term development. While preventing today's famine with food, we can prevent tomorrow's with irrigation ditches, schools and AIDS education campaigns.

10   It's astonishing how easy it is to save lives here. Give a starving kid a bit of milk and high-nutrition grain, and within a few days the eyes shine again and a smile reappears. At a Catholic-run clinic near Awassa, Ethiopia, the Italian medical director, Dr. Isabel Arbide, suddenly dashed over and embraced a small boy. "Oh, look at this child!" she gushed delightedly as the boy beamed back. "I thought he was going to die. I wouldn't have given five centimes for his life. Now look at him!"

11   We also hold these lives in our hands. And while there may be several good reasons to turn our backs, kids like Binyam provide 40 million even better reasons to help.

The Singer Solution to World Poverty
Peter Singer

> Peter Singer is one of the currently best-known utilitarian philosophers (utilitarians argue that we ought to do that which maximizes pleasure and minimizes pain). Singer is a strident ethicist, one who does not compromise his values for personal or national convenience. His well-known argument for personal responsibility for others is developed in this article in his strong, in-your-face way of pushing the moral component of a question. Although you may see him as an extremist, few students read this argument without questioning their stance on obligation to others.

1   In the Brazilian film *Central Station*, Dora is a retired schoolteacher who makes ends meet by sitting at the station writing letters for illiterate people. Suddenly she has an opportunity to pocket $1,000. All she has to do is persuade a homeless 9-year-old boy to follow her to an address she has been given. (She is told he will be adopted by wealthy foreigners.) She delivers the boy, gets the money, spends some of it on a television set, and settles down to enjoy her new acquisition. Her neighbor spoils the fun, however, by telling her that the boy was too old to be adopted—he will be killed and his organs sold for transplantation. Perhaps Dora knew this all along, but after her neighbor's plain speaking, she spends a troubled night. In the morning Dora resolves to take the boy back.

2   Suppose Dora had told her neighbor that it is a tough world, other people have nice new TVs too, and if selling the kid is the only way she can get one, well, he was only a street kid. She would then have become, in the eyes of the audience, a monster. She redeems herself only by being prepared to bear considerable risks to save the boy.

3   At the end of the movie, in cinemas in the affluent nations of the world, people who would have been quick to condemn Dora if she had not rescued the boy go home to places far more comfortable than her apartment. In fact, the average family in the United States spends almost one-third of its income on things that are no more necessary to them than Dora's new TV was to her. Going out to nice restaurants, buying new clothes because the old ones are no longer stylish, vacationing at beach resorts—so much of our income is spent on things not essential to the preservation of our lives and health. Donated to one of a number of charitable agencies, that money could mean the difference between life and death for children in need.

4   All of which raises a question: In the end, what is the ethical distinction between a Brazilian who sells a homeless child to organ peddlers

and an American who already has a TV and upgrades to a better one—knowing that the money could be donated to an organization that would use it to save the lives of kids in need?

5   Of course, there are several differences between the two situations that could support different moral judgments about them. For one thing, to be able to consign a child to death when he is standing right in front of you takes a chilling kind of heartlessness; it is much easier to ignore an appeal for money to help children you will never meet. Yet for a utilitarian philosopher like myself—that is, one who judges whether acts are right or wrong by their consequences—if the upshot of the American's failure to donate the money is that one more kid dies on the streets of a Brazilian city, then it is, in some sense, just as bad as selling the kid to the organ peddlers. But one doesn't need to embrace my utilitarian ethic to see that, at the very least, there is a troubling incongruity in being so quick to condemn Dora for taking the child to the organ peddlers while, at the same time, not regarding the American consumer's behavior as raising a serious moral issue.

6   In his 1996 book, *Living High and Letting Die*, the New York University philosopher Peter Unger presented an ingenious series of imaginary examples designed to probe our intuitions about whether it is wrong to live well without giving substantial amounts of money to help people who are hungry, malnourished, or dying from easily treatable illnesses like diarrhea. Here's my paraphrase of one of these examples:

7   Bob is close to retirement. He has invested most of his savings in a very rare and valuable old car, a Bugatti, which he has not been able to insure. The Bugatti is his pride and joy. In addition to the pleasure he gets from driving and caring for his car, Bob knows that its rising market value means that he will always be able to sell it and live comfortably after retirement. One day when Bob is out for a drive, he parks the Bugatti near the end of a railway siding and goes for a walk up the track. As he does so, he sees that a runaway train, with no one aboard, is running down the railway track. Looking farther down the track, he sees the small figure of a child very likely to be killed by the runaway train. He can't stop the train and the child is too far away to warn of the danger, but he can throw a switch that will divert the train down the siding where his Bugatti is parked. Then nobody will be killed—but the train will destroy his Bugatti. Thinking of his joy in owning the car and the financial security it represents, Bob decides not to throw the switch. The child is killed. For many years to come, Bob enjoys owning his Bugatti and the financial security it represents.

8   Bob's conduct, most of us will immediately respond, was gravely wrong. Unger agrees. But then he reminds us that we, too, have opportunities to save the lives of children. We can give to organizations like Unicef or Oxfam America. How much would we have to give one of these organizations to have a high probability of saving the life of a child threatened by easily preventable diseases? (I do not believe that children are more worth saving than adults, but since no

one can argue that children have brought their poverty on themselves, focusing on them simplifies the issues.) Unger called up some experts and used the information they provided to offer some plausible estimates that include the cost of raising money, administrative expenses, and the cost of delivering aid where it is most needed. By his calculation, $200 in donations would help transform a sickly 2-year-old into a healthy 6-year-old—offering safe passage through childhood's most dangerous years. To show how practical philosophical argument can be, Unger even tells his readers that they can easily donate funds by using their credit card and calling one of these toll-free numbers: (800) 367-5437 for Unicef; (800) 693-2687 for Oxfam America.

9   Now you, too, have the information you need to save a child's life. How should you judge yourself if you don't do it? Think again about Bob and his Bugatti. Unlike Dora, Bob did not have to look into the eyes of the child he was sacrificing for his own material comfort. The child was a complete stranger to him and too far away to relate to in an intimate, personal way. Unlike Dora, too, he did not mislead the child or initiate the chain of events imperiling him. In all these respects. Bob's situation resembles that of people able but unwilling to donate to overseas aid and differs from Dora's situation.

10   If you still think that it was very wrong of Bob not to throw the switch that would have diverted the train and saved the child's life, then it is hard to see how you could deny that it is also very wrong not to send money to one of the organizations listed above. Unless, that is, there is some morally important difference between the two situations that I have overlooked.

11   Is it the practical uncertainties about whether aid will really reach the people who need it? Nobody who knows the world of overseas aid can doubt that such uncertainties exist. But Unger's figure of $200 to save a child's life was reached after he had made conservative assumptions about the proportion of the money donated that will actually reach its target.

12   One genuine difference between Bob and those who can afford to donate to overseas aid organizations but don't is that only Bob can save the child on the tracks, whereas there are hundreds of millions of people who can give $200 to overseas aid organizations. The problem is that most of them aren't doing it. Does this mean that it is all right for you not to do it?

13   Suppose that there were more owners of priceless vintage cars—Carol, Dave, Emma, Fred, and so on, down to Ziggy—all in exactly the same situation as Bob, with their own siding and their own switch, all sacrificing the child in order to preserve their own cherished car. Would that make it all right for Bob to do the same? To answer this question affirmatively is to endorse follow-the-crowd ethics—the kind of ethics that led many Germans to look away when the Nazi atrocities were being committed. We do not excuse them because others were behaving no better.

14   We seem to lack a sound basis for drawing a clear moral line between Bob's situation and that of any reader of this article with $200

to spare who does not donate it to an overseas aid agency. These readers seem to be acting at least as badly as Bob was acting when he chose to let the runaway train hurtle toward the unsuspecting child. In the light of this conclusion, I trust that many readers will reach for the phone and donate that $200. Perhaps you should do it before reading further.

15   Now that you have distinguished yourself morally from people who put their vintage cars ahead of a child's life, how about treating yourself and your partner to dinner at your favorite restaurant? But wait. The money you will spend at the restaurant could also help save the lives of children overseas! True, you weren't planning to blow $200 tonight, but if you were to give up dining out just for one month, you would easily save that amount. And what is one month's dining out, compared with a child's life? There's the rub. Since there are a lot of desperately needy children in the world, there will always be another child whose life you could save for another $200. Are you therefore obliged to keep giving until you have nothing left? At what point can you stop?

16   Hypothetical examples can easily become farcical. Consider Bob. How far past losing the Bugatti should he go? Imagine that Bob had got his foot stuck in the track of the siding, and if he diverted the train, then before it rammed the car it would also amputate his big toe. Should he still throw the switch? What if it would amputate his foot? His entire leg?

17   As absurd as the Bugatti scenario gets when pushed to extreme, the point it raises is a serious one: only when the sacrifices become very significant indeed would most people be prepared to say that Bob does nothing wrong when he decides not to throw the switch. Of course, most people could be wrong; we can't decide moral issues by taking opinion polls. But consider for yourself the level of sacrifice that you would demand of Bob, and then think about how much money you would have to give away in order to make a sacrifice that is roughly equal to that. It's almost certainly much, much more than $200. For most middle-class Americans, it could easily be more like $200,000.

18   Isn't it counterproductive to ask people to do so much? Don't we run the risk that many will shrug their shoulders and say that morality, so conceived, is fine for saints but not for them? I accept that we are unlikely to see, in the near or even medium-term future, a world in which it is normal for wealthy Americans to give the bulk of their wealth to strangers. When it comes to praising or blaming people for what they do, we tend to use a standard that is relative to some conception of normal behavior. Comfortably off Americans who give, say, 10 percent of their income to overseas aid organizations are so far ahead of most of their equally comfortable fellow citizens that I wouldn't go out of my way to chastise them for not doing more. Nevertheless, they should be doing much more, and they are in no position to criticize Bob for failing to make the much greater sacrifice of his Bugatti.

19   At this point various objections may crop up. Someone may say: "If every citizen living in the affluent nations contributed his or her share, I wouldn't have to make such a drastic sacrifice, because long before

such levels were reached, the resources would have been there to save the lives of all those children dying from lack of food or medical care. So why should I give more than my fair share?" Another, related objection is that the government ought to increase its overseas aid allocations, since that would spread the burden more equitably across all taxpayers.

20   Yet the question of how much we ought to give is a matter to be decided in the real world—and that, sadly, is a world in which we know that most people do not, and in the immediate future will not, give substantial amounts to overseas aid agencies. We know, too, that at least in the next year, the United States government is not going to meet even the very modest target, recommended by the United Nations, of 0.7 percent of gross national product; at the moment it lags far below that, at 0.09 percent, not even half of Japan's 0.22 percent or a tenth of Denmark's 0.97 percent. Thus, we know that the money we can give beyond that theoretical "fair share" is still going to save lives that would otherwise be lost. While the idea that no one need do more than his or her fair share is a powerful one, should it prevail if we know that others are not doing their fair share and that children will die preventable deaths unless we do more than our fair share? That would be taking fairness too far.

21   Thus, this ground for limiting how much we ought to give also fails. In the world as it is now, I can see no escape from the conclusion that each one of us with wealth surplus to his or her essential needs should be giving most of it to help people suffering from poverty so dire as to be life-threatening. That's right: I'm saying that you shouldn't buy that new car, take that cruise, redecorate the house, or get that pricey new suit. After all, a $1,000 suit could save five children's lives.

22   So how does my philosophy break down in dollars and cents? An American household with an income of $50,000 spends around $30,000 annually on necessities, according to the Conference Board, a non-profit economic research organization. Therefore, for a household bringing in $50,000 a year, donations to help the world's poor should be as close as possible to $20,000. The $30,000 required for necessities holds for higher incomes as well. So a household making $100,000 could write a yearly check for $70,000. Again, the formula is simple: whatever money you're spending on luxuries, not necessities, should be given away.

23   Now, evolutionary psychologists tell us that human nature just isn't sufficiently altruistic to make it plausible that many people will sacrifice so much for strangers. On the facts of human nature, they might be right, but they would be wrong to draw a moral conclusion from those facts. If it is the case that we ought to do things that, predictably, most of us won't do, then let's face that fact head-on. Then, if we value the life of a child more than going to fancy restaurants, the next time we dine out we will know that we could have done something better with our money. If that makes living a morally decent life extremely

arduous, well, then that is the way things are. If we don't do it, then we should at least know that we are failing to live a morally decent life—not because it is good to wallow in guilt but because knowing where we should be going is the first step toward heading in that direction.

24   When Bob first grasped the dilemma that faced him as he stood by that railway switch, he must have thought how extraordinarily unlucky he was to be placed in a situation in which he must choose between the life of an innocent child and the sacrifice of most of his savings. But he was not unlucky at all. We are all in that situation.

Are You Too Rich If Others Are Too Poor?
Marjorie Kelly

> Kelly's argument first appeared in the March/April 1992 issue of *Business Ethics* and was then reprinted in the September/October 1992 issue of *Utne Reader*. A businesswoman herself, Kelly questions the kind of responsibility we have to the less fortunate, and she questions the idea that if some people have more wealth, others must suffer because of that unequal distribution. Although Kelly believes we have some duty to care, her solution would be extremely different than Singer's proposal.

1   Can you never be too rich or too thin, as the saying goes? It seems to make sense from a personal point of view, doesn't it? You simply can't be too rich.

2   Wanting money above all else is an obsession unique to our times, says Jacob Needleman in *Money and the Meaning of Life* (Doubleday, 1991). It's not that the forces of nature have changed, for we live on the same human plane on which Moses lived. Rather, the forces that once took various channels today act uniformly through money. Needleman writes:

3   "In other times and places, not everyone has wanted *money* above all else; people have desired salvation, beauty, power, strength, pleasure, propriety, explanations, food, adventure, conquest, comfort. But now and here, money—not necessarily even the things money can buy, but *money*—is what everyone wants. The outward expenditure of mankind's energy now takes place in and through money."

4   One of the consequences of our single-mindedness is that we have come to lack a sense of financial obesity: a cultural consensus that enough is enough and too much is grotesque. As a society we do have such a feeling about food (you *can* eat too much), and many of us have it about fitness (weight lifters *can* be grossly muscle-bound). But we lack any such revulsion to vast sums of money.

5   That's beginning to change, and the issue that's driving the change is excessive CEO pay. But I note that people react less to the *absolute* level of executive pay than to pay in relation to performance, or in

relation to workers' wages. Among the pieces of legislation on CEO pay currently circulating, for example, the most prominent would tie executive pay to worker pay—eliminating the tax deductibility for any salary more than 25 times that of the lowest-paid worker. Surprisingly, a recent poll found that such a move had the support of three out of five voters. And it was favored more highly by Republicans than Democrats.

6   Here we approach the nub of what I hope is an emerging new consensus on wealth: Can you be too rich when others are so poor? It's a question that prosperous Americans might be called upon to face in the years ahead, and it is a question that is distinctly uncomfortable.

7   The other morning, as I sat in the warmth of my apartment, hot coffee in hand, reading my morning *New York Times*, I saw on page one a photo of a refugee mother stumbling ashore, with four small children in tow. Clearly she owned nothing but the clothes on her back—and there I was, preparing to go off and plot how to bring more money into my business, and not incidentally how to bring more money into my life. At such moments I ask myself: Has my money got anything to do with her poverty? Am I or my nation or my business colleagues somehow responsible for this woman's plight?

8   The question enters territory governed by one of our unconscious but profound beliefs about money, that it is a zero-sum game, and that for one person to have more means another has less. In short, that wealth is made on the backs of the poor.

9   There's a kind of reflexive reaction in us that says this might be true, and there are some very caring people who are quite convinced that it is true. Their redistribution argument: Wealth generates poverty, therefore you solve poverty by redistributing wealth. For those of us concerned with social justice, this scenario has a kind of siren-song appeal, based as it is on compassion—an irresistible motive—and offering as it does a manageable solution to an age-old problem.

10   But there's an assumption here that is only partly accurate, and that is that money is a physical commodity that can be moved about, something like a pile of marbles. This assumption was central to the 70-year experiment in redistribution that we know as communism—the experiment that so tragically and so disappointingly failed. Yet it seemed to be based on such a good idea: If capitalists are hoarding all the wealth, take it from them and spread it around. Yet what happened is that instead of being redistributed, the wealth somehow dissipated, and whole nations sank into poverty.

11   I suspect the truth is that money has a dual nature. For if the zero-sum theory holds part of the truth of money, the other part is this: that prosperity can beget prosperity.

12   There is no denying that at times wealth has been made on the suffering of others—as in the slave trade, or sweatshops. But if we are truly to understand the magic of money, we must equally acknowledge the times it does not behave in a zero-sum fashion—as when a company develops computer software that becomes popular, or starts a consulting

service that takes off. Such products or services can enrich the clients who use them, make the companies who developed them wealthy, and allow both to pay excellent wages to their employees. There are no losers here, and no plunder—and not much more environmental damage than we all do in the normal course of living. Such creation of wealth does not cause anyone's poverty. For indeed, such businesspeople create the successful society in which many may flourish.

13   I do not mean here to justify the trickle-down theory, for I don't support it. But I am groping for a genuinely difficult truth about money, a truth that may come hard to those of us working for greater fairness in the world—that perhaps we must allow individuals to pursue vast wealth. Perhaps we never can have equality of wealth, any more than we can have an end of suffering. It is a sobering thought, but it may be a comforting one as well: that we must allow ourselves an ethically earned prosperity, for denying it to ourselves will not enrich anyone else.

14   But if our guilt may be at an end there, our obligation is not. For even if wealth doesn't cause poverty, I believe it does have some relationship to it, and that relationship takes the form of a duty to care. Those with money have an obligation to care for those without, just as the healthy have a responsibility to care for the sick, or the young to care for the old. And if it's not as simple as sharing the marbles, perhaps it's the role of the fortunate to find a way to share the magic.

Unit 3
Questions to Guide Analysis

1. Although the main argument of Montgomery's article, "Wealth Statistics Stack Up Unevenly," suggests there is a problem with the unequal distribution of wealth, he offers an opposing view. Where does he offer this opposition, and what examples does he use to illustrate that view? What is his rebuttal of that opposition?

    In two places, Montgomery sets off statistics in purposely incomplete sentences: "Sixteen. Billion. Bucks. In bonuses," and "Two Percent. In 14 years." What is the impact he achieves with this device, and is it effective? Why does he set of these two sets of numbers in this way?

2. One of the great characters in literature, Atticus Finch in *To Kill a Mockingbird*, says you can't really understand other people until you walk around in their shoes. How does Parker ("What Is Poverty?") establish credibility with an intended reader who cannot possibly walk in her shoes? What is her purpose in this speech? She uses detail from her own experience but wants her listeners to accept her experience as representative. Does she accomplish this task? Why or why not?

3. How would you describe Parker's tone in her argument? Does her tone establish a connection with the reader, or is it off-putting?

4. The last three essayists—Kristof, Singer, and Kelly—all argue about the level of responsibility we should have toward others who are poor. Define the specific purpose for each of these writers.

5. What solution(s) does Kristof suggest for the cultural practices in less-developed countries that add to the difficulty of helping the poor and starving children? Why does Kristof include the examples from Bangladesh and Awassa, Ethiopa? What mindset of the opposition do they address?

6. Examine the logic Singer applies in his argument for sharing resources. In paragraphs 9 and 10, is Singer asking you to make an *inductive* or *deductive* conclusion to sacrifice your own wealth? Do you think the argument is valid? Is it truthful? (Refer to Chapter 2.)

7. What opposition arguments does Singer consider, and how does he answer them? What additional opposition can you think of to Singer's argument?

8. What is the effect of Singer's providing the reader with the telephone numbers and organization information for donations that could save lives? Why does he offer the specifics rather than just allude in general to organizations to which one can contribute?

9. Although Kelly ("Are You Too Rich If Others Are Poor?") disagrees with Singer about the nature of our obligation and the effectiveness of redistributing wealth, the first nine paragraphs of her argument talk about the problem of "financial obesity." Why does she start her argument agreeing that Americans, in particular, have much more wealth than is necessary? What is the effect of this opening on the specific reader she has in mind?

10. Where does Kelly spell out her solution to the problem of poverty? What does she mean by "sharing the magic"? She says she is interested in greater fairness in the world. Will her purpose be realized for her intended reader, or is there a chance that her argument can be used to justify ignoring the unfortunate?

11. After reading these arguments, you might be interested in poverty and wealth as an argument topic. How might you develop an argument inspired by two or more of the articles in this unit?

    A. Create three hypothetical Argument Concepts that you might pursue on the topic of poverty and wealth.
    B. What are the most compelling arguments from this set of essays that could be used as support for one of the Argument Concepts you conceived in activity A, and why do you think they are strong?
    C. What is the weakest argument you read in these articles, and why do you think it is not convincing?
    D. What type of outside source material would you seek to further develop your argument?

UNIT

4

Visual Rhetoric

Many students are considered part of "Generation X," a category of people born sometime between 1965 and 1980, now between the ages of 17 and 35. This generation—often referred to as "X-ers"—has been stereotyped in many ways, but one of the main influences on this group has been an intense visual environment. Cliff Zukin, Professor of Political Science and Public Policy at Rutgers University and a consultant to the Pew Research Center for the People and the Press, describes this characteristic of Generation X:

> This is not a generation that has grown up on the written word. Far from it: They grew up on visual images. They are the product, in perhaps its purest form, of television where for a generation producers have picked compelling visuals and then assigned writers to match words to the video. It is a generation that scans information quickly; information that can be graphic or text, and one that is more than adept at picking quick meaning out of pictures. It grew up "reading" visual images rather than text.

But some critics are not so sure that the messages X-ers and others pick up *quickly* from visual arguments are well-reasoned and thoughtful. Instead, the argument is often made that people, and particularly X-ers who are subject to a more exclusively visual context, are *passive consumers* of visual argument rather than *active analysts*—the kind of readers of argument that we have encouraged. Generation X has been raised on television, movies, advertising, Internet images, and now, text messages and picture phones. Therefore, according to this line of argument, they are less critical, less able to rationally discern the control many of these images are trying to exert over them because they are not a literate—not a well-read—generation. To feed into this argument, a survey, *Reading at Risk*, published by the National Education Association in 2004, found that all levels of American society are reading much less than in the past. The change from the 1980s to today for 18- to 24-year-olds was 55 percent greater than for the total adult population. But is this argument valid? Might people in this visually saturated culture be more adept at analysis? And even if it is valid, haven't people *always* been inclined to more emotional, less intellectual responses to visual arguments than to text? Are these arguments just an historically repeated rant of one generation about the deterioration of the generations younger than they?

What is the power of visual argument, where do we see it, how is it used to influence us, and how savvy are we about "reading" it? These are some of the subjects of the essays and visual rhetoric in this unit.

An Argument for the Superiority of Printed Media over Visual Media
Scott Aniol

> Scott Aniol (1980–) earned his undergraduate degree in music at Bob Jones University; he was awarded a master's degree in musicology from Northern Illinois University and is currently working on an advanced degree in theology. He is associate pastor at First Baptist Church in Rockford, Illinois. Aniol's argument is a counter to the optimism of Zukin.

1   The purpose of this essay is not to argue that visual media is inherently evil. Nor is its purpose to contend that visual media lacks any value. The purpose of this essay is to prove that printed media is simply better than visual media, and then faced with the choice to choose one or the other for educational or recreational purposes, a conscientious person should choose printed media over visual media in most cases. With each of the following points the possibility of immoral content is erased, quality in each form is assumed, and each medium is evaluated for its own inherent worth. Expressions of fiction are the primary focus of this essay, though these points could apply to other forms as well. An application of these points might be a comparison between reading Jane Eyre by Charlotte Brontë or viewing the film version. Another poignant example might be to compare reading the gospel accounts of the death of Christ or viewing *The Passion of the Christ* by Mel Gibson.

2   1. Printed media communicates through logic and analysis; visual media communicates only through images. The very nature of visual media prevents its capacity for profound depth. Visual media cannot thoroughly evaluate the human condition like printed media can. Printed media can literally burrow into the hearts and minds of its characters, thus enabling the reader to understand and benefit from the development of each character and his relationship to the overall moral of the work. Visual media can explore character development to some extent, but due to time constraints and the nature of the visual, it cannot reach the potential of printed media in these respects. "Words communicate in linear, logical form; something communicated in words can thus be judged to be true or false. But an image cannot be true or false."[*]

---

[*]Kenneth A. Myers, *All God's Children and Blue Suede Shoes* (Wheaton, IL: Crossway, 1989), 162.

3   2. Printed media demands skill and work; visual media encourages mindless consumption. Visual media is certainly more popular because it requires little if any active participation. In fact, visual media is attractive primarily because it is "easy." Understanding, appreciating, and benefitting from printed media takes discipline and requires a certain amount of skill. This occurs, of course, on different levels, but each level encourages aspirations toward higher adeptness.

4   3. Printed media stimulates imagination; visual media discourages creativity. Printed media allows the reader to fill in gaps with his mind, while visual media leaves little room for imagination, painting every picture for the viewer. Visual media can encourage a degree of creativity, but certainly not to the magnitude of printed media.

5   4. Printed media promotes education; visual media invites vicarious participation. While many defenders of visual media insist that exposure to realistic visual imitations of life benefits the viewer, the nature of the medium actually solicits vicarious participation in the events. For instance, a boy watching a violent war film in order to "appreciate the seriousness of war" will more likely delight in the gratuitousness of the violence than weep over the depravity of the human condition. Because printed media demands more skill and lacks the sensationalism of visual media, such benefits as a healthy hatred for sin are more plausible.

6   5. Printed media develops the whole person; visual media cannot. Reading increases vocabulary, develops attention span, fosters imagination, cultivates reasoning skills, and stimulates the ability to articulate thoughts and ideas. Any of these benefits that are possible with visual media are never as extensive as with printed media, and visual media often discourages them.

7   6. Visual media inhibits the ability to appreciate printed media. Because participating in visual media is effortless, it is addictive, and with its discouragement of qualities such as attention span or depth of understanding, it actually inhibits the ability to appreciate and therefore benefit from superior printed media. Participation in visual media is not necessarily sinful. But all other factors being equal, printed media is superior to visual media in its ability to develop important qualities. All things being equal, those concerned with their education and betterment should choose printed media over visual media as a their regular practice.

A Modern Perspective on Graffiti

Killian Tobin

The following essay by Killian Tobin is frequently mentioned on the Internet in discussions of graffiti, even though his identity and any credentials that might give clues to his authority on this subject are absent. The reason this argument is often discussed is that Tobin takes a provocative view: graffiti is an art form with some social value. Notice how he distinguishes graffiti art from other types of graffiti, and how this distinction is a critical piece of his argument.

1. For as long as people have been able to write they have been writing on walls. The Romans wrote on the buildings of the towns they conquered, and even before words were used, the cave men painted on walls. This writing was first called graffiti in Roman times and holds the same name now. But as the times have changed, so have the forms that this writing on the walls have taken. Today, there are quite a few different classifications that separate graffiti. There is the gang graffiti that street gangs use to mark their turf, graffiti that people write to express political views, and a new form of graffiti that has just emerged in the past twenty-five years. This new form is artistic graffiti. Artistic graffiti is a modern day offspring of traditional graffiti that has elevated itself from just scrawling words or phrases on a wall, to a complex artistic form of personal expression.

2. This new form of graffiti first took form in the inner city of New York. It started with people writing their names and street numbers on public buildings, street signs or more commonly public transportation. These graffiti artists started experimenting with different styles, colors, and mediums once they grew tired of writing just their names in plain letters. Soon this new form of graffiti blossomed into intricate artistic works. Contemporary graffiti involves much more than just a spur of the moment defacement; it is now a skillful display from each particular graffiti artist. At first, the New York citizens were amazed when a train rolled past with a huge colorful spray painted work on it. The first reaction of the liberal New York public was to take pictures of this art work.

3. For a while, this graffiti was tolerated in New York by the law and the public which helped spread this novel form of graffiti to other cities. Artistic graffiti grew by leaps and bounds as younger aspiring graffiti artists became attracted to this mode of artistic expression. The majority of graffiti artists were young boys from the city looking for some way to express themselves; painting graffiti became an artistic form of rebellion. Eager to show everyone their artistic skills and earn respect from other graffiti artists, this new generation of graffiti artists enlarged the circle of people who did artistic graffiti to include all sorts of races and economic classes.

4. As modern artistic graffiti expanded, a graffiti subculture filled with young artists emerged. This subculture became fused with a rising music culture now known as hip-hop. This connection came about mainly because hip-hop started in New York about the same time as modern graffiti took root; hence, many people were involved

in both areas. As hip-hop and graffiti spread to other cities a large underground group of graffiti artists started to solidify. Making up this group were kids whose childhood hangout was the city, kids who knew the ins and outs of the transit lines and neighborhoods where this art form lived.

5   Unfortunately, artistic graffiti grew to a point where it invaded personal property. Graffiti artists had to compete for space, and it inevitably offended property owners. This combined with the common misconception that all graffiti represented gang activity led to community pressure on politicians. These politicians responded by ordering police pressure and other measures on graffiti writers. New York led the way with such constraints and other cities followed suit. Most politicians saw this problem as much easier to solve then [sic] a drug or gang problem. They realized that most graffiti writers are young and don't have the same resources as a gang might. Also the effects of graffiti can be painted over, while the effects of a drug problem take much more effort to "erase."

6   Instead of trying to work with the youth who are doing the graffiti, the various politicians have taken the classic stance and declared war on graffiti writers. This approach is outdated and accomplishes little as far as fixing the problems that motivate these kids to do graffiti in the first place. This strategy only breeds resentment from the youth who perpetrate these crimes. The fines, imprisonment, and police tactics against graffiti writers continue to escalate as the law proceeds with its attack on graffiti. This reaction has come to a point where the police in many cities have formed special task forces in an attempt to trap graffiti writers. Various bans on the sale and possession of markers and spray paint have also been implemented. In some cases, the penalties for having a can of spray paint can be equal to the penalties for possessing a handgun.

7   At the advent of artistic graffiti, it was a new and accepted art form. Since then, the public outlook on graffiti has been changed greatly. This change occurred mainly because of reports to the public which equated artistic graffiti with gang graffiti. Soon people became scared whenever they saw any form of graffiti in their neighborhoods. This misinformation also gave graffiti an undying reputation of gang affiliation which contributed to community pressure against graffiti.

8   It is unfortunate that artistic graffiti has been given such a negative undertone. The positive conceptions of this form of graffiti would be restored if the public were more knowledgeable of what this graffiti really consisted of. This creative outlet for many people would be more accepted, and graffiti artists would have a better chance of achieving something beyond their neighborhoods if only the public perception of graffiti is changed (see Also Note, "Murals of Philadelphia," p. 423).

> ### ALSO NOTE
> #### THE MURALS OF PHILADELPHIA
>
> To see the positive effect of working with graffiti artists that Tobin is suggesting, visit the Web site for the Philadelphia Mural Arts Program: www.muralarts.org. You can see samples of the city-wide murals and you will find a link to a slide show of the murals featured on Time.com. The Mural Arts Program, started in 1984, was originally part of an anti-graffiti plan. It has now become an educational and training organization that has encouraged the creation of some 2700 murals throughout the Philadelphia area. Governor Edward G. Rendell endorses the program in this quotation on the Web site:
>
> "There is no program anywhere that better realizes the potential and value of art to our culture. As much as these murals have contributed to the beautification and revitalization of the City, the Mural Arts Program must be congratulated even more for engaging the youth of Philadelphia."

Learning to Love PowerPoint
David Byrne

> The next two essays in this section argue about the most well-known image creation tool in business, education, and many other fields: PowerPoint. This software is broadly available, and we find that most students are quite skilled in its use. If you have not been exposed to it, you may want to investigate the program in your school library or writing center. In this first argument, David Byrne—former lead singer for the Talking Heads, an artist, and film director—talks about his conversion experience with PowerPoint in this article from *Wired*, September 2003. Note what particular qualities he believes the program offers and then compare his perspective with the argument of the next author.

1. A while ago, I decided to base the book-tour readings from my pseudoreligious tract *The New Sins* on sales presentations. I was going for a fair dose of irony and satire, and what could be better than using PowerPoint and a projector, the same tools that every sales and marketing person relies on?

2. Having never used the program before, I found it limiting, inflexible, and biased, like most software. On top of that, PowerPoint makes hilariously bad-looking visuals. But that's a small price to pay for ease

and utility. We live in a world where convenience beats quality every time. It was, for my purposes, perfect.

3   I began to see PowerPoint as a metaprogram, one that organizes and presents stuff created in other applications. Initially, I made presentations about presentations; they were almost completely without content. The content, I learned, was in the medium itself. I discovered that I could attach my photographs, short videos, scanned images, and music. What's more, the application can be made to run by itself—no one ever needs to be at the podium. How fantastic!

4   Although I began by making fun of the medium, I soon realized I could actually create things that were beautiful. I could bend the program to my own whim and use it as an artistic agent. The pieces became like short films: Some were sweet, some were scary, and some were *mysterioso*. I discovered that even without text, I could make works that were "about" something, something beyond themselves, and that they could even have emotional resonance. What had I stumbled upon? Surely some techie or computer artist was already using this dumb program as an artistic medium. I couldn't really have this territory all to myself—or could I?

David Byrne comments on his PowerPoint creation: "This is Dan Rather's profile. Expanded to the nth degree. Taken to infinity. Overlayed on the back of Patrick Stewart's head. It's recombinant phrenology [a theory whereby one can determine character and personality traits by examining the shape of, and bumps on, the head] . . . ." You can view other examples of Byrne's PowerPoint art on his Web site: www.davidbyrne.com.

PowerPoint Is Evil
Edward Tufte

> Edward Tufte, who teaches statistics, graphic design, and political economy at Yale University, argues that presentations created with PowerPoint software are often more about the graphics than the content. Although Byrne and Tufte approach the issue with different arguments, what is the point of connection between the two? What ideas can you carry forward from one or both of them as you think about using PowerPoint for your own presentations? If you are interested in visual rhetoric with presentations in particular, you might want to consult Tufte's books, *The Cognitive Style of PowerPoint* (2006) and *Envisioning Information* (1997).

Power Corrupts.
PowerPoint Corrupts Absolutely.

1   Imagine a widely used and expensive prescription drug that promised to make us beautiful but didn't. Instead the drug had frequent, serious side effects: It induced stupidity, turned everyone into bores, wasted time, and degraded the quality and credibility of communication. These side effects would rightly lead to a worldwide product recall.

2   Yet slideware—computer programs for presentation—is everywhere: in corporate America, in government bureaucracies, even in our schools. Several hundred million copies of Microsoft PowerPoint are churning out trillions of slides each year. Slideware may help speakers outline their talks, but convenience for the speaker can be punishing to both content and audience. The standard PowerPoint presentation elevates format over content, betraying an attitude of commercialism that turns everything into a sales pitch.

3   Of course, data-driven meetings are nothing new. Years before today's slideware, presentations at companies such as IBM and in the military used bullet lists shown by overhead projectors. But the format has become ubiquitous under PowerPoint, which was created in 1984 and later acquired by Microsoft. PowerPoint's pushy style seeks to set up a speaker's dominance over the audience. The speaker, after all, is making power points with bullets to followers. Could any metaphor be worse? Voicemail menu systems? Billboards? Television? Stalin?

4   Particularly disturbing is the adoption of the PowerPoint cognitive style in our schools. Rather than learning to write a report using sentences, children are being taught how to formulate client pitches and infomercials. Elementary school PowerPoint exercises (as seen in teacher guides and in student work posted on the Internet) typically consist of 10 to 20 words and a piece of clip art on each slide in a presentation of three to six slides—a total of perhaps 80 words (15 seconds of silent reading) for a week of work. Students would be better off if the schools simply closed down on those days and everyone went to the Exploratorium or wrote an illustrated essay explaining something.

5   In a business setting, a PowerPoint slide typically shows 40 words, which is about eight seconds' worth of silent reading material. With so little information per slide, many, many slides are needed. Audiences consequently endure a relentless sequentiality, one damn slide after another. When information is stacked in time, it is difficult to understand context and evaluate relationships. Visual reasoning usually works more effectively when relevant information is shown side by side. Often, the more intense the detail, the greater the clarity and understanding. This is especially so for statistical data, where the fundamental analytical act is to make comparisons.

GOOD

Estimates of relative survival rates, by cancer site

	% survival rates and standard errors			
	5 year	10 year	15 year	20 year
Prostate	98.8 0.4	95.2 0.9	87.1 1.7	81.1 3.0
Thyroid	96.0 0.8	95.8 1.2	94.0 1.6	95.4 2.1
Testis	94.7 1.1	94.0 1.3	91.1 1.8	88.2 2.3
Melanomas	89.0 0.8	86.7 1.1	83.5 1.5	82.8 1.9
Breast	86.4 0.4	78.3 0.6	71.3 0.7	65.0 1.0
Hodgkin's disease	85.1 1.7	79.8 2.0	73.8 2.4	67.1 2.8
Corpus uteri, uterus	84.3 1.0	83.2 1.3	80.8 1.7	79.2 2.0
Urinary, bladder	82.1 1.0	76.2 1.4	70.3 1.9	67.9 2.4
Cervix, uteri	70.5 1.6	64.1 1.8	62.8 2.1	60.0 2.4

A traditional table: rich, informative, clear.

6   Consider an important and intriguing table of survival rates for those with cancer relative to those without cancer for the same time period. Some 196 numbers and 57 words describe survival rates and their standard errors for 24 cancers.

7   Applying the PowerPoint templates to this nice, straightforward table yields an analytical disaster. The data explodes into six separate chaotic slides, consuming 2.9 times the area of the table. Everything is wrong with

these smarmy, incoherent graphs: the encoded legends, the meaningless color, the logo-type branding. They are uncomparative, indifferent to content and evidence, and so data-starved as to be almost pointless. Chartjunk is a clear sign of statistical stupidity. Poking a finger into the eye of thought, these data graphics would turn into a nasty travesty if used for a serious purpose, such as helping cancer patients assess their survival chances. To sell a product that messes up data with such systematic intensity, Microsoft abandons any pretense of statistical integrity and reasoning.

BAD

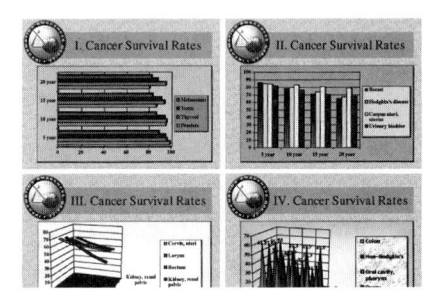

PowerPoint chartjunk: smarmy chaotic, incoherent.

8   Presentations largely stand or fall on the quality, relevance, and integrity of the content. If your numbers are boring, then you've got the wrong numbers. If your words or images are not on point, making them dance in color won't make them relevant. Audience boredom is usually a content failure, not a decoration failure.

9   At a minimum, a presentation format should do no harm. Yet the PowerPoint style routinely disrupts, dominates, and trivializes content. Thus PowerPoint presentations too often resemble a school play—very loud, very slow, and very simple.

10 The practical conclusions are clear. PowerPoint is a competent slide manager and projector. But rather than supplementing a presentation, it has become a substitute for it. Such misuse ignores the most important rule of speaking: Respect your audience.

Visual Culture and Health Posters: Anti-Smoking Campaigns
From *Profiles in Science,* National Library of Medicine

This article comes from a series of articles on the method and effect of visual rhetoric regarding public health issues. You might be interested in looking at the other groups of posters on environmental health, HIV/AIDS, infectious disease, and historical health issues. This article discusses the use of visual images in anti-smoking campaigns, and while it is an informative article, there is a clear judgment on the role of tobacco companies in persuading their audience. What is the argument concerning this role? The British Tobacco Control journal recently published a study that found 10- to 19-year-old Americans whose favorite movie stars smoked in their films were more inclined to smoke than those whose movie idols never smoked publicly. Think of the images you've seen in the media of smokers from Cruella DeVille (the villain in *100 Dalmatians*) to Leonardo DiCaprio. What message do you think these images are sending? How do you think the audience reads these messages; are they passive consumers or active analysts? (View the other ads referred to in this article at http://profiles.nlm.nih.gov/VC/Views/Exhibit/other/visuals.html.)

1   This section of the exhibit on anti-smoking campaigns scrutinizes the political, social, and psychological messages utilized by anti-tobacco educators since the 1960s in print advertisements, posters, and billboards, in order to examine how traditional values, cultural conditions, and medical knowledge are conveyed in print media. The exhibit includes images of the cigarette, the smoker, the nonsmoker, smoke-free environments, and celebrities in a variety of campaigns created by voluntary organizations, professional advertising firms, and governmental organizations.

2   In the first half of the twentieth century, anti-smoking messages emphasized primarily moralistic and hygienic concerns. Anti-tobacco crusaders saw the cigarette as ungodly and unhealthy. Although medical objections to smoking remained implicit in their arguments, activists did not have any medical consensus behind them. In fact, medical opinion was generally noncommittal until the 1964 Surgeon General's Report on Smoking and Health, which consolidated and legitimized 15 years of growing evidence of the dangers of smoking to health.

3   The 1964 Surgeon General's report marked the beginning of a transformation in attitudes and behaviors related to cigarettes, but smoking norms and habits yielded slowly and incompletely. Despite legislative restrictions on advertising in the late 1960s and early 1970s, the persistent and pervasive marketing of cigarettes continued in different forums. Still, grassroots activists, professional consumer advocates, and the public health bureaucracy remained inspired by scientific and social interest in the hazards of smoking. Their collective anti-smoking campaigns have employed a variety of educational, clinical, regulatory, economic, and counter-advertising strategies.

The Cigarette

4   In the first half of the twentieth century, cigarette smoking became a widespread habit firmly engrained in American culture. Ennobled by its heroic association with soldiers in each of the World Wars, associated with a new sense of freedom and equality by young women in the 1920s, and generally considered a slightly illicit but forgivable moral transgression, cigarette smoking has remained ubiquitous in popular forms of visual media such as movies, art, and advertising, past and present. As a

result, antismoking campaigners since the 1960s have been compelled to challenge the perception that the behavior is commonplace and integral to everyday life. Anti-smoking advertisements often use what might be called "deglamorization" and "denormalization" strategies, designed to work against the allure of cigarettes and upset their routine presence in popular culture. By using negative or denunciatory images of the cigarette, for example, they send messages that discourage the aura, appeal, and attractiveness of tobacco use. These messages warn viewers that the cigarette is dangerous, addictive, and deadly. An alternative, moralistic strategy features the cigarette as a threat to traditional social values such as deferred gratification, self-control, and personal responsibility.

The Smoker

5   Despite the pervasive presence of cigarette smoking in popular culture, and its role as a generational marker, historians have argued that the marketing efforts of tobacco giants never fully legitimized the image of the smoker, with some suspicion that they never intended to. In fact, the seductive quality of smoking cigarettes has often been used as a subtle marketing strategy, emphasizing an association with transgression, defiance, and rebellion. Visual representations of smokers have frequently underscored the guilty pleasure they experience by associating smoking with committing an illicit act. The images of smokers in this section illustrate how anti-smoking campaigns have countered this phenomenon by using three main strategies: 1) appealing to individual and social responsibility; 2) emphasizing evidence from medical research; and 3) deglamorizing the smoker. These images showcase a variety of marketing techniques used to reduce tobacco use by combining information, images, emotional appeals, and psychological tools to influence viewers.

The Non-Smoker and Smoke-free Environments

6   As the images in this section [of the Web site] demonstrate, smoking has long played an important role in popular culture and the shaping of personal identity. This relationship helps explain smoking's persistence, despite widespread anti-smoking campaigns, and also functions as a limit on government intervention in our everyday consumption decisions. Informed by this relationship, anti-smoking advertisers have combined negative representations of smokers with positive portraits of non-smokers as far more appealing or desirable. In some cases this involves emulating the strategies of tobacco advertisers by using the same glamorization and normalization strategies in the depiction of non-smokers as popular or heroic and smoke-free environments as invigorating or therapeutic. These images employ the following techniques: 1) emphasizing the psychological, social, economic, and health benefits of smoking cessation (or regaining non-smoker status); 2) stressing a sense of personal or social responsibility as motivation for choosing to be a non-smoker; 3) using

deglamorization strategies to suggest that the non-smoker is more fashionable; and 4) appropriating idealistic or romanticized environmental images as symbolic representations of health and the decision not to smoke.

The Celebrity

7   The tobacco industry has long capitalized on the ability of the entertainment industry to create, reinforce, and normalize messages. The invaluable marketing advantage this creates for the tobacco companies has allowed them to overcome legislative restrictions on cigarette advertising since the late 1960s. In movies and on television, celebrities facilitate the normalization of cigarette smoking by increasing the perception that the behavior is commonplace and integral to everyday life. Capitalizing on this power, tobacco companies have frequently paid

producers and actors to feature their cigarette brands. In Superman II, for instance, Phillip Morris paid 20,000 pounds (about $40,000) for the Marlboro brand name to appear some 40 times in the film. Understanding the power of celebrities as spokespersons for smoking, anti-smoking campaigns have employed counter-marketing strategies to promote smoking cessation and decrease the likelihood of initiation. An integral part of this approach has involved a deglamorization strategy that de-emphasizes and discourages the aura, appeal, and attractiveness of tobacco use through its portrayal of smokers in advertisements.

Cartoons from the Time of the Spanish-American War

Because of the current interest in the field of visual rhetoric, you can find a number of interesting studies of visual argument in politics, advertising, movies, television, and even in dance. For example, one recent documentary, *Drawing Conclusions: Editorial Cartoonists Consider Hillary Rodham Clinton*, looks at this politician and how she is portrayed. The classic historical case of visual rhetoric is the selling of the Spanish-American War by what has been called "yellow journalism." The United States supported Cuba and the Philippines in their wars for independence against Spain with the intention, many might argue, that the ultimate result would be annexation and an expansion of the American "Empire." Newspapers (some 28 newspapers by the 1920s) and magazines owned by William Randolph Hearst were famous for using cartoons with their stories to whip up a pro-war sentiment in the public. Following are just a few of the images that were used in this campaign and immediately after the war to argue for what is known as "American Imperialism." Also included is a less typical cartoon of that period that questions America's choice of war. Examine the images and see how the United States is portrayed and how Cuba, the Philippines, and Hawaii are portrayed. How would you expect a reader of the images in the late 1890s would respond? How do we respond today? What makes the difference?

The White Man's Burden appeared in *The Journal* in Detroit. The allusion in the title is to a poem by Rudyard Kipling, first published in 1889. The poem was an argument for the United States to develop the Philippines after the Spanish-American War. It included sentiments similar to this, its first stanza:

Take up the White Man's burden—
Send forth the best ye breed—
Go bind your sons to exile
To serve your captives' need;
To wait in heavy harness,
On fluttered folk and wild—
Your new-caught, sullen peoples,
Half-devil and half-child.

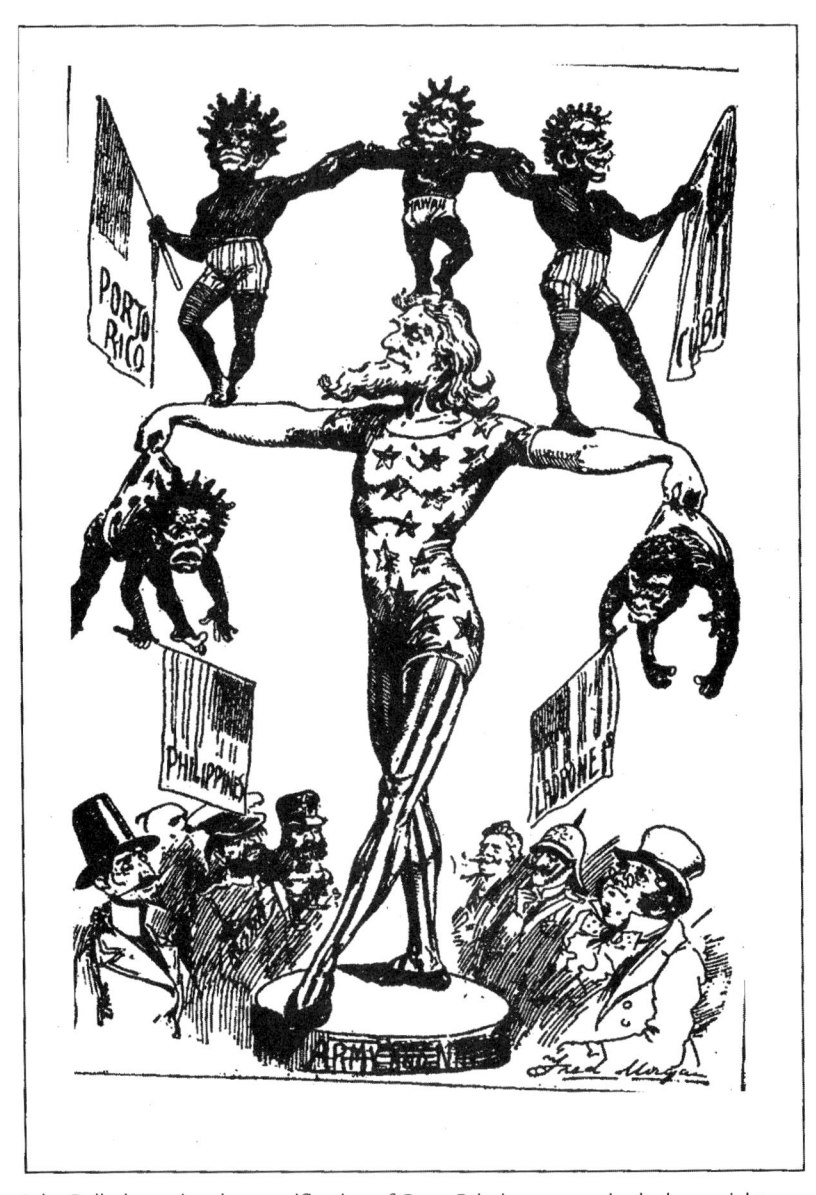

John Bull, the national personification of Great Britain, appears in the lower right corner of this cartoon from the Philadelphia Inquirer in 1898. He says, "It's really most extraordinary what training will do. Why, only the other day I thought that man was unable to support himself." What is the irony John Bull refers to? Is his statement a positive or negative comment?

"Uncle Sam Teaches the Art of Self-Government" appeared in 1889. Leader of the Philippines, Emilio Aguinaldo, is the dunce figure who hasn't learned from the teacher; Puerto Rico and Hawaii (where no uprisings took place) are the passive figures in the right background, and the unruly students are rebels.

424 Unit 4 *Visual Rhetoric*

"CIVILIZATION BEGINS AT HOME."

"Civilization Begins at Home" was published in 1898. The message is decidedly different than in the other cartoons in this collection, demonstrating that there were conflicting arguments about the United States' responsibilities. What are the messages of this strong visual rhetoric?

American Progress
John Gast

Visual rhetoric isn't limited to the press or electronic media. Over the years, art has been a tool for argument. One of the most famous paintings of the time leading into the Spanish-American War was this representation from 1872 of Manifest Destiny, the idea that the certain future—destiny—of the United States was ordained. Manifest Destiny meant that the United States would eventually spread from Atlantic to Pacific, and then the term was picked up to advocate for further annexation of territory. Examine the images in this painting in detail and consider their implications.

Unit 4
Questions to Guide Analysis

1. Scott Aniol argues that

   > Printed media communicates through logic and analysis; visual media communicates only through images. The very nature of visual media prevents its capacity for profound depth. Visual media cannot thoroughly evaluate the human condition like printed media can.

   Examine Aniol's argument, thinking about the graphics in this unit and other images that you can find in print media or on the Internet. Examples might be the famous picture of a student confronting an armed tank in Tiananmen Square during the Beijing student revolt in 1989. Another might be the vivid image of a fireman carrying a wounded child from the wreckage of the bombed Alfred P. Murrah Federal Building in Oklahoma City in 1995. Others might be pictures from the Iraq War, a family wedding, or a movie. What kind of an argument can you create using these images as evidence that either contradicts or agrees with Aniol?

2. In his discussion of graffiti, Killian Tobin argues that officials should take a more positive view of some graffiti and "work with" these artists instead of making war on them. Is Tobin's solution well-enough developed to convince you of his somewhat controversial position? Look at some of the antigraffiti program links at http://www.dougweb.com/grlinks.html. If you were Tobin, what details would you suggest for a program to work with these artists?

   Also, Tobin seems to suggest that as long as graffiti was confined to public space, it was acceptable and almost admired, but that once it attacked personal property, the public's attitude changed. Do you agree there should be room in the public arena for this kind of personal artistic expression? How is it the same and how is it different from other means of rebellion and antiestablishment rhetoric such as T-shirt messages, activist demonstrations and parades, student sit-ins in the 60s, political signs, etc.?

3. You may have many opportunities to evaluate PowerPoint presentations while you are in classes. Many instructors use this program and often student presentations in class are created with PowerPoint. Maybe you have been exposed to such a presentation at work. The next time you experience such a presentation, take notes not just on the content but the way it is graphically represented. Read over Byrne's and Tufte's arguments and decide if you think the creator of the presentation used the power of this form of visual argument well, or if, as Tufte suggests, the presentation did not enhance the content. What specific details from the presentation would you use in defense of your position?

4. Examine the images in an advertising campaign or public service campaign that you have seen. For example, during professional football games, a strong "stay in school" message is often run. In some women's magazines today, ads sometimes try to encourage readers to be comfortable with their size and body shape. Analyze the message in the images you see as in the antismoking analysis. Is there a particular way you can categorize or generalize the message (e.g., "deglamorization" in the antismoking campaign)?

5. Collect at least six cartoons or still images that make a statement about a particular issue. You can easily do this now by putting "Cartoons: cartoons + [subject]" in the Google Images search box on the Internet. For example, try searching for "Cartoons + Abu Ghraib" and you will see some very strong visual rhetoric about the indecencies that took place in that prison. Try "Cartoons + Football" and you'll see a potential argument about its players. Try a search for Internet images on a topic of interest to you. Do you think the images you have found reflect the thinking of the times in a way similar to the cartoons in this chapter from the Spanish-American War era? Are the images you found one-sided and exaggerated? Do you think they present a fair or unfair image of your topic?

6. After reading these arguments, you might be interested in visual rhetoric as an argument topic. How might you develop an argument inspired by two or more of the articles in this unit?

    A. Create three hypothetical Argument Concepts that you might pursue on the topic of visual rhetoric.
    B. What are the most compelling arguments from this set of essays that could be used as support for one of the Argument Concepts you conceived in activity A, and why do you think they are strong?
    C. What is the weakest argument you read in these articles, and why do you think it is not convincing?
    D. What type of outside source material would you seek to further develop your argument?

UNIT

5

Working in America

In 1997, the National Study of the Changing Workforce by the Families and Work Institute was published. This study is done every five years to determine trends of many kinds: The status of dual-income earners, relative wages of men and women, time spent *with family* compared to time at work, work stress, hours worked, and other important issues. Supported by 15 large corporations and foundations, among them the Ford Foundation and the Sloan Foundation, this survey is considered the authoritative source on work trends. In 1997, one of the major focuses of the survey was changes in hours worked. Some of the highlights are listed here:

- Women worked 44 hours per week, up from 39 in 1977.
- Men worked 49.9 hours compared to 47.1 in 1977
- 64 percent of all workers would have liked to cut their work time an average 11 hours a week compared to 47 percent in 1992. (Reasons most often given for not reducing working time: Needing money, employer pressure, or wanting to contribute to company success.)
- 70 percent of parents believed that they didn't have enough time with their children compared to 66 percent in 1992.
- Almost half of all workers had to work overtime once a month, sometimes with no prior notification; 18 percent worked overtime as much as once a week.

Juliet Schor, author of *The Overworked American*, points out that this change has been an escalating trend for the last three decades, but that the increase is now seriously affecting the quality of life for American workers and families. "Take Back Your Time Day" was started on October 24, 2003. This date, nine weeks before the end of the year, symbolizes the additional nine weeks Americans work compared to most Western European workers. Because many business and economic writers believe this issue is so important, many arguments such as the ones in this unit have appeared about the quality and quantity of work and how the way we work changes our lifestyle.

All Work, No Play
Claudia Smith Brinson

> In this article she wrote as a Knight Ridder/Tribune columnist for *The State* (South Carolina), Brinson's argument builds on the data about hours worked. Her focus is to look at the differences between working in America and working in other industrial countries, to see what we have given up in our drive to work more and more. Strong parts of her argument are the sections that address the opposition, those who might argue that we have a better life by working more than people in other countries. As you read, you may be prompted to think about what you have given up for the extra hours you spend at work, and if those things truly enhance your life. If you have not seen the *Affluenza* program she refers to, you may want to visit the Web site (www.affluenza.org).

1   What is an economy for? Consider before you answer. Consider your life. Consider whether you feel like a tiny cog in a very large, indifferent machine. Consider the daily grind. You might, then, begin to wonder whether the U.S. economy exists for you—or for itself. Or for American CEOs, who 30 years ago made 30 times more than the average worker and now make 500 times more.

2   If it feels as if you work all the time for "the economy," you're right. In the United States, the 40-hour week is just a fond memory. American men average more than 49 hours a week at work, women more than 42. Yet men and women say they would like to work about 11 fewer hours each week. Americans work more than medieval peasants did. We work more hours per day, more days per year than citizens of any other industrialized nation.

3   John de Graff wants us to reconsider the grind. De Graff, who spoke at USC recently, is known for his PBS documentary films "Affluenza" and "Escape from Affluenza." The films, and an accompanying book, are about the American desire for stuff and more stuff. De Graff can rattle off statistics about work because he has done the research for a new project, Take Back Your Time Day. He is national coordinator. On Oct. 24, those interested, or curious, will celebrate the first Take Back Your Time Day with forums, community meetings, study groups, potluck suppers. The date, nine weeks before the end of the year, represents "how much more, on average, Americans work each year than Western Europeans," de Graff said.

4   The idea arose in a 2002 meeting of The Simplicity Forum, a collection of leaders in the simple living or voluntary simplicity movement. Aspirants to a simple life pare down, eliminating consumer goods, debt, clutter in their homes, overwork, learning to live on less with less. In other words, they don't think the good life is a TV in every room; they think it's enough time to hang out in the park with the kids. And that's

not where the American culture is headed. Their model for this event is the first Earth Day. Take Back Your Time Day is aimed at redirecting our attention and, perhaps, our energy.

Not Enough Time

5   In 1996, Americans surpassed the Japanese in our long work hours, becoming the workaholics of the world. Over a lifetime, we end up with 10 years less leisure time than Europeans—10 years less with our children, traveling, reading, playing. Through national agreements and labor unions, most Europeans reduced their work weeks while we were expanding ours. Workers in the Netherlands average 36 hours a week; Denmark, 37; Norway, 37.5; Portugal, 40. In 2000, France set 35 hours as a legislated standard. Americans achieved a workaholic high by making "an unconscious choice" to take all "productivity gains in the form of more money, more stuff if you will, and none of them in the form of more time," de Graaf writes in a handbook for Take Back Your Time Day.

6   And what do we have to show for it? American families eat, at most, two meals a week together. Dual-income couples report 12 minutes a day to talk to each other. Nearly half of Americans report they're so sleepy it interferes with work and safety. America possesses one of the highest infant-mortality rates and lowest life expectancies of the world's industrialized nations. A fifth of the people who could have but didn't vote in the 2000 presidential election said they didn't have the time. De Graaf's handbook for Take Back Your Time Day deals with such woes in essays by various experts on work, leisure, transportation, health and other pertinent subjects. Juliet Schor, a Harvard economist and author of "The Overworked American," tackles expanding hours on the job. During the past 30 plus years, Americans added 199 hours a year, on average, to the work day and week, Schor writes. For the middle class, the increase takes away breath and sleep. Work increased 660 hours a year.

7   We could have bought time. Productivity increased 80 percent between 1969 and 2000 in the United States. That means the average worker produces nearly twice as much now. If we had applied that to time rather than money, the average American could work a little more than 20 hours a week, Schor writes.

Busier And Sicker?

8   You have to wonder how we got here, when other cultures took the route to the beach. De Graaf's handbook notes that American companies have decided it is more cost-effective to pay employees overtime than hire more workers and pay benefits. And it is legal here for employers to require, without advance notice, more work when shifts end and to take disciplinary action if a worker refuses. De Graaf said, "We got the technology, but we didn't get the time." Technology may

be just another way to crack the whip: 26 million Americans are monitored by the machines they use, according to de Graaf.

9 The global economy adds a dab of irony to this fix. Many countries in the European Union mandate by law 25 days of vacation. So if you're an American working for a company with a division in Germany, you'll get off four to six weeks you wouldn't get back home. Americans average 10.2 days of vacation annually—after three years on the job. We're the only industrialized country without a minimum-paid-leave law.

10 Thanks to paranoia about layoffs and down-sizing, a quarter of Americans don't take any vacation, Joe Robinson writes in the handbook. He leads a national campaign for paid vacation. Passing on vacations doesn't pay off in productivity, Robinson argues. Being present but exhausted won't get the work done: productivity decreases as stress and fatigue increase. Robinson cites several productivity studies, the most revealing dealing with health: Annual vacation reduces risk of heart attack by 30 percent for men and 50 percent for women. That's a statistic to ponder in a larger context. In the 1950s, the United States was one of the healthiest countries in the world. Now, we rank 25th, behind almost all other rich countries.

More Problems

11 We may have convinced ourselves this single-minded devotion to work is meaningful and necessary. But de Graaf's handbook reveals our work-dominated lives don't provide the national benefits we imagine. Countries such as Belgium, France, the Netherlands and Norway, where fewer hours are worked, are more productive per hour of labor. Norway, for example, has an hourly productivity rate 10 percent higher than that of the United States, and its poverty rate is a quarter lower. So what are the personal benefits for the overworked American? Consumption has doubled during the past 30 years. Families are smaller, but the average house size is 50 percent larger. New homes offer three times the closet space as homes of the 1950s. We use 40 times more commercial storage than in the 1970s. We buy stuff, instead of time, 120 pounds of stuff a day, according to the handbook. It takes, on average, 24 acres of natural resources to sustain this standard of living. The planet, by the way, has available 5 acres per person.

12 The handbook includes a study of people working as many as 95 hours a week, with personal incomes up to a quarter million. Income was not related to satisfaction with life, as other studies have shown. And "people who worked fewer hours reported being more satisfied than those who worked many hours," report psychologists Tim Kasser and Kirk Warren Brown. The toll is high. People working more than 50 hours a week report severe work-family conflicts. Marriages are at greater risk of separation or divorce when a husband and/or wife works

nights or rotating shifts. American children have lost 12 hours a week in free time, thanks to day care and organized activities.

13   And, of course, we're all tired—all the time.

14   Again, what is an economy for?

15   "The purpose of an economy is to help us live fully and well," writes David Korten, a former business professor at Harvard and Stanford Universities and founder of the Positive Futures Network. The handbook does offer remedies: eliminate mandatory overtime or increase overtime pay. Make the minimum wage a "living wage," enough for two parents to support a family. Instead of laying off workers, companies can reduce the hours of all employees, a job-sharing technique used by Presidents Herbert Hoover and Franklin Delano Roosevelt. Provide public transportation, thus reducing commuting costs in money—20 percent of a family income and time. Legislate paid vacation. Adopt full cost pricing, which takes into account all relevant production costs, thus exposing the real price tag to factory farming or suburban sprawl.

16   "It didn't have to be this way," de Graaf told his audience at USC. For this first Take Back Your Time Day, de Graaf proposes, "Say no. Take part of the day off." He hopes local campaigns will spring up, and he expects, on Oct. 24, 2004, to challenge candidates, including presidential nominees, to address the issue.

17   "We're not against work, but American life has simply gotten way out of balance," de Graaf said. "We need to think about what we're losing."

The Work Addict in the Family
Diane Fassel

> Diane Fassel, Ph.D., in organizational behavior, is president and CEO of New Measures, a company that develops and administers employee and management surveys. This excerpt comes from Fassel's 1990 book, *Working Ourselves to Death: The High Cost of Workaholism and the Rewards of Recovery*. The section we have included is from her chapter discussing workaholism and its effects on the family. Fassel agrees with Brinson about the toll overworking takes and goes into detail about those effects. As you read this argument, think about the kind of evidence upon which Fassel defends. How is it different, in general, than the evidence provided by Brinson?

1   Work addicts have trouble restricting their disease to the job. After all, they are work addicts, not job addicts. Therefore the addiction does not stop at the front door of the house or the apartment. It comes with you wherever you go.

2   The workaholic lacks appropriate boundaries. Thus the workaholic process pervades everything. There is no difference between the workplace and the home. Workaholics take work to bed, take it home on

weekends, and take it on vacation. The workaholic is never without work, because work is the fix.

3   Vacations are stressful for the families of workaholics. First of all, it is difficult to get addicts to agree to a vacation ahead of time, because they never know what might be happening at work six months hence. Then, if work addicts do agree to vacations, they may be totally unavailable emotionally because they take work with them. Many children of workaholics describe vacations as whirl-winds of activity. Their parents do vacations the way they do work.

4   One boy told me of a trip to Hawaii in which his father woke him up at the crack of dawn to run on the beach. Then it was breakfast on the deck. Next a boat cruise around the coast. Lunch was on the run; hit the beach when the surf is up; dash back to the rental shack with the surfboards, gulp an island snack on the way back to the hotel, shower, drive madly to the end of the road to watch the sun go down over the ocean, meet friends for dinner, drop exhausted into bed.

5   Every day of vacation was similar until the boy pleaded, then demanded a day off to do what he wished to do. He wanted to lay around and read and watch videos and maybe hang out around town. His father, who saw the vacation as a chance to spend "quality time" with his son, grumbled and paced the hotel room. Finally, after mild threats to his son that he would be missing some fun, the father took off to see a waterfall.

6   The boy was racked with guilt over the vacation. He missed contact with his father and longed for time with him. He felt confused and conflicted. He was doing wonderful things, and he was spending more time with his father than he ever dreamed possible. Yet, by the end of the trip, he felt further removed from his father than before the vacation.

7   The boy's father was not present emotionally. He had not brought work along on the trip, he just transferred his workaholic pace to the leisure activities. The boy was as isolated as if the father had dropped him in the hotel and left; only it felt more confusing, because there was a body there but no person to relate to.

8   Workaholics are simply not available to their loved ones. Their disease tends to make them self-centered, but the disease is tricky enough that work addicts go through the motions of relating. If family members are at all aware, they know the relationship is superficial at best, nonexistent at worse.

9   Still, not all workaholics are totally removed from loved ones. When work addicts are present, they can be intensely present. They can be great lovers when they are aware. It is the inconsistency that is maddening. The workaholic does come home on time occasionally, so the family never knows if this is going to be one of those times. When confronted, the addict always has those times to use in defense of the denial about the addiction.

10   I believe that the lack of a significant emotional connection is the most devastating aspect of this disease for families. Workaholic families resemble families that have suffered the death of a loved one. You can see them going through the stages of denial ("This isn't happening to us"); bargaining ("If I do this, will you spend time with me?"); anger ("I'm furious that you've left me"); resignation ("This is just the way he is. I may as well get used to it"). The only problem is that the loved one is still walking around, a constant reminder of what could have been.

11   Work addicts have hobbies, but rarely are the hobbies a source of playfulness. Hobbies are turned into money-making ventures. Hobbies generate anxiety, deadlines, and more work. A young man told me about his father, who was a physician in the northwest and became interested in smoking salmon. He was handy with his hands, so first he built a smoking shed. Then he recruited the children to help fish for salmon. Since the shed was quite large, he decided to smoke enough fish to give to neighbors as gifts. This project then turned into a roadside stand with demands for more fish, more time in the smoking shed, and more of the family's time to take their turn working.

12   "The odd thing about it," said the young man, "was that we didn't need the money. My father made enough as a doctor. My family didn't like salmon that much. This was just a lark of my father's that we all got trapped in."

13   The father was rarely available to his family due to his medical practice. Now any free time was spent with the salmon venture. It became a source of anger and resentment for the family and a way to keep the father busy every "free" minute.

14   Sometimes workaholics become irritated with family members who have priorities other than work. Workaholic parents can set a tone in families in which incessant busyness is rewarded; staring into space, dreaming, and playing around aren't. Almost all adult children who are second-generation work addicts either learned their workaholism in the family or come from families where other addictions were present. The clue to these families is that busyness and work become a substitute for feeling.

15   A story of generational work addiction was shared with me by Amy, a woman who was on a fast track all her life. Her grandfathers were adventurers and frontier entrepreneurs. Her father was never at home nor at the births of any of his children. He wasn't capable of waiting. Amy discounted her mother, because Amy got all her strokes from her father for doing. She played tennis, skied, sang for the church, volunteered, and worked a regular job.

16   All of Amy's life decisions were dictated by work. She moved to cities she hated, because of work. She never considered staying in a locale she liked. She looked for social connections in work-related groups. She did not have a separate social life. During a depression over her inability to form close relationships with men, she confided her

sadness to a colleague. He shot back, "How are you going to meet anyone but the janitor?"

17   Amy continued working. She joined a large company, optimistic that she could reorder her life; but really her world was collapsing. To meet the objectives her boss set took eighty hours a week. He asked her to sign a sheet of objectives specifying that she would do the work, and she knew she was done for. "I had no support system. No caring person to fall back on. I had worked myself to a skeleton and there was no flesh left. I was out of reserves. The corporate values were things I didn't believe in. Inside I was emotionally bankrupt. I couldn't be who they wanted me to be."

18   Amy dropped out of work completely, left all civic involvement, and took time to discover who she was and what she wanted to do with her life. During this time her generational connection with her workaholic father became painfully clear. Her father was the one person to whom she related, because they talked about work. Now she was trying to drop work—her only tangible connection with him. When she met with him to share developments in her life, he was silent. He had nothing he could ask her now that she wasn't working. When Amy queried her father about this, his only reply was: "Well, what else is there?"

19   Amy has many memories of her father, but the one she cherishes most is the time they were on a deserted road and the car broke down. Far from help, they had to wait several hours for a tow truck. "It was the best time," she said. "He was always fixing and doing and here we were with a forced wait. He did something he never did before or since: He sat in the front seat, he gazed out the car window, he looked at me, and we just talked."

20   Listen to the themes in these stories. They are all the same, and the desires are so simple. Children just want a little time with parents. They want to *be with* someone they love and trust. They don't necessarily want anything from the parents. They don't seem to need activities, they just need to be with. But being with is impossible for work addicts, because they aren't capable of being with themselves, much less someone else. Even when they are trying hard, they can only do what they know best, their addiction.

21   Undeniably, work addiction is destroying families. Children and spouses are resigning themselves to making appointments to spend time with the workaholic. We now have the prevalence of "quality time," which in the addictive system is an excuse for too little time or preoccupied time. *Time* magazine ran a cover article on how America is running itself ragged. Their conclusions? "Kids understand that they are being cheated out of childhood. Eight-year-olds are taking care of three-year-olds. There is a sense that adults don't care about them."[*] Increasingly, children are scheduled into multiple activities and pushed

---

[*]Gibbs, Nancy, "How America Has Run Out of Time." *Time*, April 28, 1989: 61.

by their parents in order that the parents may protect their own work addiction. The result is a generation of workaholic kids.

Other Factors More Important in Job Stress
Melissa C. Stöppler, M.D.

> A different view on the stress Americans experience from working comes from Melissa Stöppler, a pathologist, researcher, and writer with an interest in stress and its effect on the human body, particularly its role in illness. The study Stöppler discusses concludes that worker stress comes from different causes than long hours. Are you convinced by this argument that other arguments about the effects of the longer American work week are incorrect?

1. Downsizing and increased productivity goals mean longer work hours and higher stress for many workers. But University of Arkansas researcher Dan Ganster has found that the longer hours are not the cause of the stress experienced by workers and their families. "We found that it is not how long you work, it is how you are working that causes stress," explained Ganster, professor of management and department chairman in the Walton College of Business. "The impact of work hours was dwarfed by factors related to the job itself, such as schedule flexibility and autonomy."

2. Ganster and graduate student Collette Bates conducted their study by using data from the 1997 National Study of the Changing Workforce (NSCW). The 2,842 respondents were at least 18 years old and worked for pay but were not self-employed. The researchers presented their findings recently at the annual meeting of the Academy of Management in Seattle. American workers spend more time on the job than workers in other industrialized countries. Many people believe that this increased time at work leads to work-family conflicts and increased stress. Elements like number of hours worked, the amount of overtime or the work schedule are said to have an impact on general well-being, work-family conflict and job stress. "When we started to look at the research, we found what little research had been done on the topic gave an ambiguous picture of the role of working hours," Ganster explained. "In addition the samples studied were not adequate to draw sound conclusions. Some research looked at a single company, while others considered a single type of job or socio-economic group."

3. Ganster's study included both salaried and hourly workers and looked at work interfering with family, family interfering with work, job stress, job satisfaction, absenteeism, illness absences, stress symptoms and life satisfaction. The size of the data set allowed the researchers to control for conditions that might affect the results, including demographic characteristics, occupation, non-work demands and non-linear effects.

4   To see if there were effects on subgroups, the researchers used nine control variables: gender, age, race, education, total family income, occupation, hourly/salaried, length of time with the employer and union membership. In addition, they looked at four variables – non-work demands, job quality, scheduling support and fringe benefits – that might moderate the effect of the number of work hours. Non-work demands included marital status, the number of children living in the household, children's ages, number of hours spent on chores and the number of hours spent on elder care; fringe benefits included benefit flexibility, the ability to work from home and dependent care benefits. Job quality comprised autonomy, learning opportunities and job pressure, while scheduling support included the organizational culture of "unwritten rules" pertaining to work and family, supervisor support and control over scheduling work hours. After the data were coded, the researchers examined how the control and moderating variables might interact with work hours.

5   They also examined how work hours might impact subgroups, such as women with children, workers in jobs with low autonomy or workers with traditional fringe benefits. "We kept getting zero. We tried different groups. We asked ourselves what we had missed. But despite every conceivable test, we couldn't find any significant interactions. We were forced to conclude that long work hours are not an important contributor to life satisfaction or feelings of well-being," said Ganster.

6   However, Ganster is quick to point out that work-family conflict does have an impact on life satisfaction, but that conflict is shaped by factors related to the work environment. Work autonomy, learning opportunities, supportive supervisors and scheduling flexibility are more important influences on work family conflict and the satisfaction than are long work hours. "We don't want to downplay the importance of work-family conflict," Ganster said. "Employer policies do matter. Flexibility is a good thing no matter how many hours you work. But it's not how long you work that matters, it's how you are working."

A Working Community
Ellen Goodman

> Ms. Goodman is an accomplished journalist. She won the Pulitzer Prize for Distinguished Commentary in 1980 and has a long list of other national awards. Her ability to identify and humanize emerging public and private trends has helped her become a widely read columnist. She thinks that readers should be "less alienated from the editorial pages" where arguments fly at each other regularly. Whereas the first readings in this unit focused on rather immediate effects of the American way of working, Goodman discusses a more global effect. Goodman's argument is that the differences in the way

we work are changing our sense of community and our idea of self-identity. Her observation was made in 1985; do you think her observation of a trend is borne out by the times since 1985, or have our working lives evolved in another direction?

1. I have a friend who is a member of the medical community. It does not say that, of course, on the stationery that bears her home address. This membership comes from her hospital work.

2. I have another friend who is a member of the computer community. This is a fairly new subdivision of our economy, and yet he finds his sense of place in it.

3. Other friends and acquaintances of mine are members of the academic community, or the business community, or the journalistic community. Though you cannot find these on any map, we know where we belong.

4. None of us, mind you, was born into these communities. Nor did we move into them, U-Hauling our possessions along with us. None has papers to prove we are card-carrying members of one such group or another. Yet it seems that more and more of us are identified by work these days, rather than by street. In the past, most Americans lived in neighborhoods. We were members of precincts or parishes or school districts. My dictionary still defines community, first of all in geographic terms, as "a body of people who live in one place." But today fewer of us do our living in that one place; more of us just use it for sleeping. Now we call our towns "bedroom suburbs," and many of us, without small children as icebreakers, would have trouble naming all the people on our street.

5. It's not that we are more isolated today. It's that many of us have transferred a chunk of our friendships, a major portion of our everyday social lives, from home to office. As more of our neighborhoods work away from home, the workplace becomes our neighborhood. The kaffeeklatsch of the fifties is the coffee break of the eighties. The water cooler, the hall, the elevator, and the parking lot are the back fences of these neighborhoods. The people we have lunch with day after day are those who know the running saga of our mother's operations, our child's math grades, our frozen pipes, and faulty transmissions. We may be strangers at the supermarket that replaced the corner grocer, but we are known at the coffee shop in the lobby. We share with each other a cast of characters from the boss in the corner office to the crazy lady in Shipping, to the lovers in Marketing. It's not surprising that when researchers ask Americans what they like best about work, they say it is "the schmooze [chatter] factor." When they ask young mothers at home what they miss most about work, it is the people.

6. Not all the neighborhoods are empty, nor is every workplace a friendly playground. Most of us have had mixed experiences in these environments. Yet as one woman told me recently, she knows more about people she passes on the way to her desk than on her way around

the block. Our new sense of community hasn't just moved from house to office building. The labels that we wear connect us with members from distant companies, cities, and states. We assume that we have something "in common" with other teachers, nurses, city planners.

7   It's not unlike the experience of our immigrant grandparents. Many who came to this country still identified themselves as members of the Italian community, the Irish community, the Polish community. They sought out and assumed connections with people from the old country. Many of us have updated that experience. We have replaced ethnic identity with professional identity, the way we replaced neighborhoods with the workplace.

8   This whole realignment of community is surely most obvious among the mobile professions. People who move from city to city seem to put roots down into their professions. In an age of specialists, they may have to search harder to find people who speak the same language.

9   I don't think that there is anything massively disruptive about this shifting sense of community. The continuing search for connection and shared enterprise is very human. But I do feel uncomfortable with our shifting identity. The balance has tipped and we seem increasingly dependent on work for our sense of self. If our offices are our new neighborhoods, if our professional titles are our new ethnic tags, then how do we separate our selves from our jobs? Self-worth isn't just something to measure in the marketplace. But in these new communities, it becomes harder and harder to tell who we are without saying what we do.

Reprinted with the permission of Simon & Schuster Adult Publishing Group, from *Keeping in Touch* by Ellen Goodman. Copyright © 1985 by The Washington Post Company. All rights reserved.

Good-bye to the Work Ethic
Barbara Ehrenreich

We have chosen to include in this unit two works by one of America's most respected investigative reporters, political essayists, and social critics. She has 12 books to her credit and has written for many of the prominent, respected magazines in the United States. These two pieces exhibit very different writing styles and demonstrate the ability of a fine writer to adjust her writing "register" to the specific focus, reader, and purpose she is addressing at the moment. This first article was written in 1988 for *Mother Jones*, an independent, nonprofit magazine committed to social justice and high quality investigative journalism.

To analyze the Argument Concept of this article, it is probably helpful to know more about the potential reader of *Mother Jones*, and to do that you might best know a little about the real "Mother Jones" (Mary Harris Jones, 1830–1930), whose life symbolized the spirit of the magazine. During her life, she led strikes, gave dramatic speeches, interviewed presidents and business tycoons, organized miners, and championed the working people and the downtrodden. She was dedicated to the idea that citizens of a democracy need to take part vigorously in the affairs of government and society. She was one of the strongest women in the American tradition of protest, so much so that Elliott J. Gorn has published a biography of her, *Mother Jones: The Most Dangerous Woman in America*.

What kind of a reader do you think Ehrenreich can expect for this argument, and how does her choice of language, tone, and evidence appeal to that reader?

1. The media have just buried the last yuppie, a pathetic creature who had not heard the news that the great pendulum of public consciousness has just swung from Greed to Compassion and from Tex-Mex to meatballs. Folks are already lining up outside the mausoleum bearing the many items he had hoped to take with him, including a quart bottle of raspberry vinegar and the Cliff Notes for *The Wealth of Nations*. I, too, have brought something to throw onto the funeral pyre—the very essence of yupdom, its creed and its meaning. Not the passion for money, not even the lust for tiny vegetables, but the *work ethic*.

2. Yes, I realize how important the work ethic is. I understand that it occupies the position, in the American constellation of values, once held by motherhood and Girl Scout cookies. But yuppies took it too far; they *abused* it.

3. In fact, one of the reasons they only lived for three years (1984–87) was that they *never* rested, never took the time to chew between bites or gaze soulfully past their computer screens. What's worse, the mere rumor that someone—anyone—was not holding up his or her end of the work ethic was enough to send them into tantrums. They blamed lazy workers for the Decline of Productivity. They blamed lazy welfare mothers for the Budget Deficit. Their idea of utopia (as once laid out in that journal of higher yup thought, the *New Republic*) was the "Work Ethic State": no free lunches, no handouts, and too bad for all the miscreants and losers who refuse to fight their way up to the poverty level by working eighty hours a week at Wendy's.

4. Personally, I have nothing against work, particularly when performed, quietly and unobtrusively, by someone else. I just don't happen to think it's an appropriate subject for an ethic. As a general rule, when something gets elevated to apple-pie status in the hierarchy of American values, you have to suspect that its actual *monetary* value is skidding toward zero.

5. Take motherhood: nobody ever thought of putting it on a moral pedestal until some brash feminists pointed out, about a century ago, that the pay is lousy and the career ladder nonexistent. Same thing with work: would we be so reverent about the "work ethic" if it wasn't for the fact that the average working stiff's hourly pay is shrinking, year by year, toward the price of a local phone call?

6   In fact, let us set the record straight: the work ethic is not a "traditional value." It is a johnny-come-lately value, along with thin thighs and nonsmoking hotel rooms. In ancient times, work was considered a disgrace inflicted on those who had failed to amass a nest egg through imperial conquest or other forms of organized looting. Only serfs, slaves, and women worked. The yuppies of ancient Athens—which we all know was a perfect cornucopia of "traditional values"—passed their time rubbing their bodies with olive oil and discussing the Good, the True, and the Beautiful.

7   The work ethic came along a couple of millennia later, in the form of Puritanism—the idea that the amount of self-denial you endured in this life was a good measure of the amount of fun awaiting you in the next. But the work ethic only got off the ground with the Industrial Revolution and the arrival of the factory system. This was—let us be honest about it—simply a scheme for extending the benefits of the slave system into the age of emancipation.

8   Under the new system (aka capitalism in this part of the world), huge numbers of people had to be convinced to work extra hard, at pitifully low wages, so that the employing class would not have to work at all. Overnight, with the help of a great number of preachers and other well-rested propagandists, work was upgraded from an indignity to an "ethic."

9   But there was a catch: the aptly named *working class* came to resent the resting class. There followed riots, revolutions, graffiti. Quickly, the word went out from the robber barons to the swelling middle class of lawyers, financial consultants, plant managers, and other forerunners of the yuppie: Look busy! Don't go home until the proles have punched out! Make 'em think *we're* doing the work and that they're lucky to be able to hang around and help out!

10   The lawyers, managers, etc., were only too happy to comply, for as the perennially clever John Kenneth Galbraith once pointed out, they themselves comprised a "new leisure class" within industrial society. Of course, they "work," but only under the most pleasant air-conditioned, centrally heated, and fully carpeted conditions, and then only in a sitting position. It was in their own interest to convince the working class that what looks like lounging requires intense but invisible effort.

11   The yuppies, when they came along, had to look more righteously busy than anyone, for the simple reason that they did nothing at all. Workwise, that is. They did not sow, neither did they reap, but rather sat around pushing money through their modems in games known as "corporate takeover" and "international currency speculation." Hence their rage at anyone who actually works—the "unproductive" American worker, or the woman attempting to raise a family on welfare benefits set below the average yuppie's monthly health spa fee.

12   So let us replace their cruel and empty slogan— "Go for it!"—with the cry that lies deep in every true worker's heart: "Gimme a break!" What this nation needs is not the work ethic, but a *job* ethic: If it needs

doing—highways repaired, babies changed, fields plowed—let's get it done. Otherwise, take five. Listen to some New Wave music, have a serious conversation with a three-year-old, write a poem, look at the sky. Let the yuppies Rest in Peace; the rest of us deserve a break.

From *Nickel and Dimed: On (Not) Getting by in America*
Barbara Ehrenreich

> Ehrenreich, as mentioned in the introduction to the previous argument, is renowned for her meticulous and deep research into her topics. For the 2001 bestselling book from which this excerpt comes, she decided to test whether it was possible to live on minimum wage. She applied for jobs at Wal-Mart and other entry-level positions and tried to pay for all her living expenses from just those paychecks. The book is a searing and bleak insight into struggling for survival in the 21st century in America.
>
> In this excerpt from the conclusion to her 2001 book, Ehrenreich discusses the conclusions about housing and wages that she drew from her experience. Note that she did exhaustive academic research, also, to support her own experience. How are elements of the Argument Concept different in this selection and the previous essay? How has Ehrenreich adjusted her style and tone to this changed plan?

1   The problem of rents is easy for a noneconomist, even a sparsely educated low-wage worker, to grasp: it's the market, stupid. When the rich and the poor compete for housing on the open market, the poor don't stand a chance. The rich can always outbid them, buy up their tenements or trailer parks, and replace them with condos, McMansions, golf courses, or whatever they like. Since the rich have become more numerous, thanks largely to rising stock prices and executive salaries, the poor have necessarily been forced into housing that is more expensive, more dilapidated, or more distant from their places of work. Recall that in Key West, the trailer park convenient to hotel jobs was charging $625 a month for a half-size trailer, forcing low-wage workers to search for housing farther and farther away in less fashionable keys. But rents were also skyrocketing in the touristically challenged city of Minneapolis, where the last bits of near-affordable housing lie deep in the city, while job growth has occurred on the city's periphery, next to distinctly unaffordable suburbs. Insofar as the poor have to work near the dwellings of the rich—as in the case of so many service and retail jobs—they are stuck with lengthy commutes or dauntingly expensive housing.

2   If there seems to be general complacency about the low-income housing crisis, this is partly because it is in no way reflected in the official poverty rate, which has remained for the past several years at

ALSO NOTE
A FEW PERTINENT RESEARCH NOTES FROM *NICKEL AND DIMED*

- In 1996 the number of persons holding two or more jobs averaged 7.8 million, or 6.2 percent of the workforce. It was about the same rate for men and for women (6.1 percent versus 6.2 percent). About two-thirds of multiple jobholders work one job full-time and the other part-time. Only a heroic minority—4 percent of men and 2 percent of women—work two full-time jobs simultaneously (John F. Stinson, Jr., "New Data on Multiple Jobholding Available from the CPS," *Monthly Labor Review*, March 1997).
- For the affluent, houses have been swelling with no apparent limit. The square footage of new homes increased by 39 percent between 1971 and 1996, to include "family rooms," home entertainment rooms, home offices, bedrooms, and often a bathroom for each family member ("Détente in the Housework Wars," *Toronto Star*, November 10, 1999). By the second quarter of 1999, 17 percent of new homes were larger than three thousand square feet, which is usually considered the size threshold for household help, or the point at which a house becomes unmanageable to the people who live in it ("Molding Loyal Pamperers for the Newly Rich," *New York Times*, October 24, 1999).
- [Ehrenreich] could find no statistics on the number of employed people living in cars or vans, but according to a 1997 report of the National Coalition for the Homeless, "Myths and Facts about Homelessness," nearly one-fifth of all homeless people (in twenty-nine cities across the nation) are employed in full- or part-time jobs.
- The *National Journal* reports that the "good news" is that almost six million people have left the welfare rolls since 1996, while the "rest of the story" includes the problem that "these people sometimes don't have enough to eat" ("Welfare Reform, Act 2," June 24, 2000, pp. 1, 978–93).

a soothingly low 13 percent or so. The reason for the disconnect between the actual housing nightmare of the poor and "poverty," as officially defined, is simple: the official poverty level is still calculated by the archaic method of taking the bare-bones cost of food for a family of a given size and multiplying this number by three. Yet food is relatively inflation-proof, at least compared with rent. In the early 1960s, when this method of calculating poverty was devised, food accounted for 24 percent of the average family budget (not 33 percent even then, it should be noted) and housing 29 percent. In 1999, food took up only 16 percent of the family budget, while housing had soared to 37 percent.[1] So the choice of food as the basis for calculating family budgets seems fairly arbitrary today; we might as well abolish poverty altogether, at least on paper, by defining a subsistence budget as some multiple of average expenditures on comic books or dental floss.

3   When the market fails to distribute some vital commodity, such as housing, to all who require it, the usual liberal-to-moderate expectation is that the government will step in and help. We accept this principle—at least in a halfhearted and faltering way—in the case of health care, where government offers Medicare to the elderly, Medicaid to the desperately poor, and various state programs to the children of the merely very poor. But in the case of housing, the extreme upward skewing of the market has been accompanied by a cowardly public sector retreat from responsibility. Expenditures on public housing have fallen since the 1980s, and the expansion of public rental subsidies came to a halt in the mid-1990s. At the same time, housing subsidies for home owners—who tend to be far more affluent than renters—have remained at their usual munificent levels. It did not escape my attention, as a temporarily low-income person, that the housing subsidy I normally receive in my real life—over $20,000 a year in the form of a mortgage-interest deduction—would have allowed a truly low-income family to live in relative splendor. Had this amount been available to me in monthly installments in Minneapolis, I could have moved into one of those "executive" condos with sauna, health club, and pool.

4   But if rents are exquisitely sensitive to market forces, wages clearly are not. Every city where I worked in the course of this project was experiencing what local businesspeople defined as a "labor shortage"—commented on in the local press and revealed by the ubiquitous signs saying "Now Hiring" or, more imperiously, "We Are Now Accepting Applications." Yet wages for people near the bottom of the labor market remain fairly flat, even "stagnant." "Certainly," the *New York Times* reported in March 2000, "inflationary wage gains are not evident in national wage statistics."[2] Federal Reserve chief Alan Greenspan, who spends much of his time anxiously scanning the horizon for the slightest hint of such "inflationary" gains, was pleased to inform Congress in July 2000 that the forecast seemed largely trouble-free. He went so far as to suggest that the economic laws linking low unemployment to wage increases may no longer be operative, which is a little like saying that

---

[1] Jared Bernstein, Chauna Brocht, and Maggie Spade-Aguilar, "How Much Is Enough? Basic Family Budgets for Working Families," Economic Policy Institute, Washington, D.C., 2000, p. 14.
[2] "Companies Try Dipping Deeper into Labor Pool," *New York Times*, March 26, 2000.

the law of supply and demand has been repealed.[3] Some economists argue that the apparent paradox rests on an illusion: there is no real "labor shortage," only a shortage of people willing to work at the wages currently being offered.[4] You might as well talk about a "Lexus shortage"—which there is, in a sense, for anyone unwilling to pay $40,000 for a car.

5   In fact, wages *have* risen, or did rise, anyway, between 1996 and 1999. When I called around to various economists in the summer of 2000 and complained about the inadequacy of the wages available to entry-level workers, this was their first response: "But wages are going up!" According to the Economic Policy Institute, the poorest 10 percent of American workers saw their wages rise from $5.49 an hour (in 1999 dollars) in 1996 to $6.05 in 1999. Moving up the socioeconomic ladder, the next 10 percent–sized slice of Americans—which is roughly where I found myself as a low-wage worker—went from $6.80 an hour in 1996 to $7.35 in 1999.[5]

6   Obviously we have one of those debates over whether the glass is half empty or half full; the increases that seem to have mollified many economists do not seem so impressive to me. To put the wage gains of the past four years in somewhat dismal perspective: they have not been sufficient to bring low-wage workers up to the amounts they were earning twenty-seven years ago, in 1973. In the first quarter of 2000, the poorest 10 percent of workers were earning only 91 percent of what they earned in the distant era of Watergate and disco music. Furthermore, of all workers, the poorest have made the least progress back to their 1973 wage levels. Relatively well-off workers in the eighth decile, or 10 percent-sized slice, where earnings are about $20 an hour, are now making 106.6 percent of what they earned in 1973. When I persisted in my carping to the economists, they generally backed down a bit, conceding that while wages at the bottom are going up, they're not going up very briskly. Lawrence Michel at the Economic Policy Institute, who had at the beginning of our conversation taken the half-full perspective, heightened the mystery when he observed that productivity—to which wages are theoretically tied—has been rising at such a healthy clip that workers should be getting much more.[6]

7   The most obvious reason why they're not is that employers resist wage increases with every trick they can think of and every ounce of

---

[3] "An Epitaph for a Rule That Just Won't Die," *New York Times*, July 30, 2000.
[4] "Fact or Fallacy: Labor Shortage May Really Be Wage Stagnation," *Chicago Tribune*, July 2, 2000; "It's a Wage Shortage, Not a Labor Shortage," *Minneapolis Star Tribune*, March 25, 2000.
[5] I thank John Schmidt at the Economic Policy Institute in Washington, D.C., for preparing the wage data for me.
[6] Interview, July 18, 2000.

strength they can summon. I had an opportunity to query one of my own employers on this subject in Maine. You may remember the time when Ted, my boss at The Maids, drove me about forty minutes to a house where I was needed to reinforce a shorthanded team. In the course of complaining about his hard lot in life, he avowed that he could double his business overnight if only he could find enough reliable workers. As politely as possible, I asked him why he didn't just raise the pay. The question seemed to slide right off him. We offer "mothers' hours," he told me, meaning that the work-day was supposedly over at three—as if to say, "With a benefit like that, how could anybody complain about wages?"

8   In fact, I suspect that the free breakfast he provided us represented the only concession to the labor shortage that he was prepared to make. Similarly, the Wal-Mart where I worked was offering free doughnuts once a week to any employees who could arrange to take their breaks while the supply lasted. As Louis Uchitelle has reported in the *New York Times*, many employers will offer almost anything—free meals, subsidized transportation, store discounts—rather than raise wages. The reason for this, in the words of one employer, is that such extras "can be shed more easily" than wage increases when changes in the market seem to make them unnecessary.[7] In the same spirit, automobile manufacturers would rather offer their customers cash rebates than reduced prices; the advantage of the rebate is that it seems like a gift and can be withdrawn without explanation.

9   But the resistance of employers only raises a second and ultimately more intractable question: Why isn't this resistance met by more effective counterpressure from the workers themselves? In evading and warding off wage increases, employers are of course behaving in an economically rational fashion; their business isn't to make their employees more comfortable and secure but to maximize the bottom line. So why don't employees behave in an equally rational fashion, demanding higher wages of their employers or seeking out better-paying jobs? The assumption behind the law of supply and demand, as it applies to labor, is that workers will sort themselves out as effectively as marbles on an inclined plane—gravitating to the better-paying jobs and either leaving the recalcitrant employers behind or forcing them to up the pay. "Economic man," that great abstraction of economic science, is supposed to do whatever it takes, within certain limits, to maximize his economic advantage.

10   I was baffled, initially, by what seemed like a certain lack of get-up-and-go on the part of my fellow workers. Why didn't they just leave for a better-paying job, as I did when I moved from the Hearthside to Jerry's? Part of the answer is that actual humans experience a little more "friction"

---

[7]"Companies Try Dipping Deeper into Labor Pool," *New York Times*, March 26, 2000.

than marbles do, and the poorer they are, the more constrained their mobility usually is. Low-wage people who don't have cars are often dependent on a relative who is willing to drop them off and pick them up again each day, sometimes on a route that includes the babysitter's house or the child care center. Change your place of work and you may be confronted with an impossible topographical problem to solve, or at least a reluctant driver to persuade. Some of my coworkers, in Minneapolis as well as Key West, rode bikes to work, and this clearly limited their geographical range. For those who do possess cars, there is still the problem of gas prices, not to mention the general hassle, which is of course far more onerous for the carless, of getting around to fill out applications, to be interviewed, to take drug tests. I have mentioned, too, the general reluctance to exchange the devil you know for one that you don't know, even when the latter is tempting you with a better wage-benefit package. At each new job, you have to start all over, clueless and friendless.

11   There is another way that low-income workers differ from "economic man." For the laws of economics to work, the "players" need to be well informed about their options. The ideal case—and I've read that the technology for this is just around the corner—would be the consumer whose Palm Pilot displays the menu and prices for every restaurant or store he or she passes. Even without such technological assistance, affluent job hunters expect to study the salary-benefit packages offered by their potential employers, watch the financial news to find out if these packages are in line with those being offered in other regions or fields, and probably do a little bargaining before taking a job.

12   But there are no Palm Pilots, cable channels, or Web sites to advise the low-wage job seeker. She has only the help-wanted signs and the want ads to go on, and most of these coyly refrain from mentioning numbers. So information about who earns what and where has to travel by word of mouth, and for inexplicable cultural reasons, this is a very slow and unreliable route. Twin Cities job market analyst Kristine Jacobs pinpoints what she calls the "money taboo" as a major factor preventing workers from optimizing their earnings. "There's a code of silence surrounding issues related to individuals' earnings," she told me. "We confess everything else in our society—sex, crime, illness. But no one wants to reveal what they earn or how they got it. The money taboo is the one thing that employers can always count on."[8] I suspect that this "taboo" operates most effectively among the lowest-paid people, because, in a society that endlessly celebrates its dot-com billionaires and centimillionaire athletes, $7 or even $10 an hour can feel like a mark of innate inferiority. So you may or may not find out that, say, the Target down the road is paying better than Wal-Mart, even if you have a sister-in-law working there.

13   Employers, of course, do little to encourage the economic literacy of their workers. They may exhort potential customers to "Compare Our

---

[8]Personal communication, July 24, 2000.

Prices!" but they're not eager to have workers do the same with wages. I have mentioned the way the hiring process seems designed, in some cases, to prevent any discussion or even disclosure of wages—whisking the applicant from interview to orientation before the crass subject of money can be raised. Some employers go further; instead of relying on the informal "money taboo" to keep workers from discussing and comparing wages, they specifically enjoin workers from doing so. The *New York Times* recently reported on several lawsuits brought by employees who had allegedly been fired for breaking this rule—a woman, for example, who asked for higher pay after learning from her male coworkers that she was being paid considerably less than they were for the very same work. The National Labor Relations Act of 1935 makes it illegal to punish people for revealing their wages to one another, but the practice is likely to persist until rooted out by lawsuits, company by company.[9]. . .

* * * * *

14   Guilt, you may be thinking warily. Isn't that what we're supposed to feel? But guilt doesn't go anywhere near far enough; the appropriate emotion is shame—shame at our *own* dependency, in this case, on the underpaid labor of others. When someone works for less pay than she can live on—when, for example, she goes hungry so that you can eat more cheaply and conveniently—then she has made a great sacrifice for you, she has made you a gift of some part of her abilities, her health, and her life. The "working poor," as they are approvingly termed, are in fact the major philanthropists of our society. They neglect their own children so that the children of others will be cared for; they live in substandard housing so that other homes will be shiny and perfect; they endure privation so that inflation will be low and stock prices high. To be a member of the working poor is to be an anonymous donor, a nameless benefactor, to everyone else. As Gail, one of my restaurant coworkers put it, "you give and you give."

15   Someday, of course—and I will make no predictions as to exactly when—they are bound to tire of getting so little in return and to demand to be paid what they're worth. There'll be a lot of anger when that day comes, and strikes and disruption. But the sky will not fall, and we will all be better off for it in the end.

Unit 5
Questions to Guide Analysis

1. Brinson ("All Work, No Play") and Stöppler ("Other Factors More Important in Job Stress") both seem to be very credible writers and they use well-documented and authoritative sources, yet their conclusions are

---

[9]"The Biggest Company Secret: Workers Challenge Employer Practices on Pay Confidentiality," *New York Times*, July 28, 2000.

contradictory. What would you do if you confronted these two arguments as you were searching for evidence for an argument regarding American workers and hours worked? Why do you think one or the other is a stronger argument?

2. What specific purpose (refer to Chapter 4) drives Brinson's argument? Stöppler's? Fassel's?

3. Review the type of evidence used in the Brinson and Fassel ("The Work Addict in the Family") arguments. On what type of evidence does each author rely? What is the strength of each type of evidence? Which is more compelling to you? Which do you think would be more compelling to other readers and why?

4. Ehrenreich's book, *Nickel and Dimed*, gives excruciating detail of her poorly paid jobs, her arrogant and noncaring supervisors, the low-nutritional food she could afford on minimum wage, and the dilapidated housing in which she had to live. Why do you think she includes detailed research (and there is much of it) along with her narrative?

5. Would you have guessed that the two Ehrenreich works were written by the same person? What are the most striking similarities and differences between the two pieces? Make a list of words and phrasing in "Good-bye to the Work Ethic" that are crafted particularly for the *Mother Jones* reader.

6. After reading these arguments, you might be interested in working in America as an argument topic. How might you develop an argument inspired by two or more of the articles in this unit?

   A. Create three hypothetical Argument Concepts that you might pursue on the topic of working in America.
   B. What are the most compelling arguments from this set of essays that could be used as support for one of the Argument Concepts you conceived in activity A, and why do you think they are strong?
   C. What is the weakest argument you read in these articles, and why do you think it is not convincing?
   D. What type of outside source material would you seek to further develop your argument?

Credits

Text Credits

Chapter 1

Graph "Real Hourly Wages by Education" reprinted from the speech "Economic Inequality in the United States," the 2006–2007 Economics of Governance Lecture to the Center for the Study of Democracy, University of California, Irvine by Janet L. Yellen, President and CEO, Federal Reserve Bank of San Francisco. The opinions expressed do not necessarily reflect the views of the management of the Federal Reserve Bank of San Francisco or of the Board of Governors of the Federal Reserve System. By permission.

Mike Rosen, "Road Tests for Seniors," *Rocky Mountain News*, July 25, 2003. Reprinted by permission of the author and the Rocky Mountain News.

Bruce Wexler, "Poetry Is Dead. Does Anybody Really Care?" from *Newsweek*, May 5, 2003. © 2003 Newsweek, Inc. All rights reserved. Reprinted by permission.

Sarah M. Lowe, from *Frida Kahlo*. New York: Universe, 1991. Used with permission from Rizzoli International Publications.

James Reel, "Border Calling," *Sojourners Magazine*, March 2005. Reprinted with permission from Sojourners, (800) 714-7474, www.sojo.net.

Kurt Williamsen, from "Not Giving Up on Immigration Control," *The New American*, October 31, 2005. Reprinted by permission of The New American.

Rubi Reyes, "Children Born in the U.S. Serve as Means to Get Parents, Family Here," *The South Texan*, Texas A & M University at Kingston, October 24, 2006. Reprinted by permission of the author.

Hector Avalos, "Issue Looks Different Through Latino Eyes," *The Des Moines Register*, January 2, 2007. Reprinted by permission of the author.

Mike Pearson, review of "Assault on Precinct 13" from Video Reviews: "'Life' Sails Along on Oddball Energy," *Rocky Mountain News*, May 13, 2005. Reprinted with permission of the Rocky Mountain News.

Chapter 2

Dana Priest, "Report Says CIA Distorted Iraq Data," *Washington Post*, July 12, 2004.
William Lutz, *Doublespeak*. New York: Harper & Row, 1989.

Chapter 3

From "Top Ten Reasons to Keep the Penny" from the Americans for Common Cents website, http://www.pennies.org. Reprinted by permission.

Chapter 4

Amy Tan, "Mother Tongue," *The Threepenny Review*, 1990.

"Letters to the Editor" from *Time*, February 5, 2007. Copyright © 2007 Time Inc. Reprinted by permission. TIME is a registered trademark of Time Inc. All rights reserved.

Chapter 6

Caroline Bird, from "College Is a Waste of Money," *The Case Against College*, ed. by Helene Mandelbaum. New York: D. McKay, 1975.

William A. Henry, III, *In Defense of Elitism*. New York: Doubleday, 1994.

Linda Chavez, "There's No Future in Lady Luck," *USA Today*, September 13, 1995. Reprinted by permission of the author.

Edgar Lee Masters, "Margaret Fuller Slack,"*Spoon River Anthology*, 1915.

John Gonzales, "College Brings Alienation from Family, Friends," *Los Angeles Times*, January 20, 1996. Reprinted by permission of the author.

George Orwell, "A Hanging" from *Shooting an Elephant and other Essays* by George Orwell. Copyright © 1950 by Sonia Brownell Orwell and renewed 1978 by Sonia Pitt-Rivers. Reprinted by permission of Harcourt, Inc.

Clips from *Bowling for Columbine*, a 2002 documentary film written, produced, and directed by Michael Moore.

H. Bruce Miller, Severing the Human Connection," *San Jose Mercury News*, August 4, 1981. Reprinted by permission of Reprint Management Services.

Michael Medved, "Hollywood's Poison Factory: Making It the Dream Factory Again," *Imprimis*, November 1992. Reprinted by permission from Imprimis, the monthly journal of Hillsdale College.

Terry Tempest Williams, from *An Unspoken Hunger: Stories from the Field*. Copyright © 1994 by Terry Tempest Williams. Used by permission of Pantheon Books, a division of Random House, Inc.

Chapter 8

Robert Behnke, "The Best Science" from "About Trout" in *Trout*, Spring 2004. Reprinted by permission of the author.

Chapter 9

Jamie Fellner, "Mentally Retarded Do Not Belong on Death Row," *San Francisco Chronicle*, January 4, 2000. Reprinted by permission of the author.

Glenn Vilppu, 3 drawings as appeared in Animation World Magazine, Issue 3.3, June 1998, based upon the *Vilppu Drawing Manual*. Reprinted by permission of Glenn V. Vilppu.

Chapter 10

J. Hoberman, from "Flogged to Death," a film review in *The Village Voice*, February 25–March 2, 2004. Copyright © 2004, Village Voice Media. Reprinted with permission of the Village Voice.

Cal Thomas, from "The Greatest Story Ever Filmed," August 5, 2003. © Tribune Media Services. All rights reserved. Reprinted with permission.

Agustin Gurza, Pop Album Review of Los Lobos "The Town and the City," *Los Angeles Times*, September 12, 2006, E. 8. Copyright © 2006 Los Angeles Times. Reprinted by permission.

Anna Quindlen, "Tort Reform at Gunpoint," *Newsweek*, May 5, 2003. Reprinted by permission of International Creative Management, Inc. Copyright © 2003 by Anna Quindlen.

Chapter 11

Center for Applied Research. "Mini-Case Study: Nike's 'Just Do It' Advertising Campaign," June 17, 2004. http://www.cfar.com.

Jonathan Kozol, *Savage Inequalities*. New York: Crown Publishers, 1991.

Harold Kushner, *Living a Life That Matters*. New York: Alfred A. Knopf, 2001.

Harold Kushner, *When Bad Things Happen to Good People*. New York: Schocken Books, 1981.

Rene Sanchez, "Surfing's Up and Grades Are Down," *Washington Post National Weekly Edition*, June 3-9, 1996. © 1996, The Washington Post. Reprinted with permission.

From Interview by George Plimpton with Ernest Hemingway, *The Paris Review*, 18 (Spring 1958).

University Writing Center at Western Carolina University web site, http://www.wcu/writingcenter/

Anne Lamott, *Bird by Bird*. New York: Pantheon, 1994.

Carl Sagan, quote.

Chapter 12

Sarah Jenkins, from "Plagiarism by Some Damages All Journalists," *Yakima Herald-Republic*, August 29, 2004. Reprinted by permission.

Walter S. Achert and Joseph Gibaldi, *MLA Handbook for Writers of Research Papers*, Second Edition. New York: The Modern Language Association of America, 1984.

American Cancer Society web page "Health Information Seekers" http://www.cancer.org/docroot/HOME/skr/skr_0.asp

Chapter 13

Lynne Truss, *Eats, Shoots & Leaves: The Zero Tolerance Approach to Punctuation*. London: Profile Books, 2003.

Unit 1

Katharine S. Mangan, "MBAs Would Rather Quit Than Fight for Values," *The Chronicle of Higher Education*, September 20, 2002. Reprinted by permission of The Chronicle of Higher Education.

Katherine S. Mangan, "The Ethics of Business School," *The Chronicle of Higher Education*, September 20, 2002. Reprinted by permission of The Chronicle of Higher Education.

Michael Ryan, "They Call Their Boss a Hero." © 1996 Michael Ryan. Initially published in *Parade Magazine*, September 8, 1996. All rights reserved. By permission of Parade Publications.

"Executive Decisions." Editorial from *Multinational Monitor*, March 1, 1998. Reprinted by permission of Multinational Monitor.

Kenneth Allard, excerpt from *Business as War: Battling for Competitive Advantage*. Copyright © 2004 by Kenneth Allard. Reprinted by permission of John Wiley & Sons, Inc.

Barbara Wilder, "Green Despoils Capitalism," *Rocky Mountain News*, August 3, 2002. Reprinted with permission of the Rocky Mountain News.

Art Buchwald, "The Upside of Downsizing" from *We'll Laugh Again* by Art Buchwald. Copyright © 1991, 1992, 1993, 1994, 1995, 1996, 1997, 1998, 1999, 2000, 2001, 2002 by Art Buchwald. Used by permission of G.P. Putnam's Sons, a division of Penguin Group (USA) Inc.

Unit 2

Christopher Byron, *Testosterone, Inc.* Hoboken, NJ: John Wiley & Sons, 2004.

About-Face, "Mission Statement" from http://about-face.org. By permission.

Karen Epstein, "I'm a Barbie Girl," *The Tufts Daily Online*, November 21, 1997. Reprinted by permission of the author.

Tamara Keith, excerpt from "Remaking Barbie," first published in *The Berkeleyan*, 4/1/98, and aired on National Public Radio's Weekend Edition Sunday. Reprinted by permission of the author.

William Pollack, from *Real Boys' Voices*. Copyright © 2000 by William Pollack. Used by permission of Random House, Inc.

Lisa Liddane, excerpts from "Man in the Mirror"; Mental Health: "More Males Are Joining the Ranks of People with Distorted Body Images and Eating Disorders," *The Orange County Register*, August 29, 2001. Reprinted by permission of The Orange County Register.

Sharleen Jonasson, "Fat Girls (Don't) Dance" from the About-Face web site, http://www.about-face.org. Copyright © Sharleen Jonasson 2002. Reprinted by permission of the author.

Kim Campbell, "Just One Look." Reproduced with permission from the May 8, 2003 issue of *The Christian Science Monitor* (www.csmonitor.com). © 2003 The Christian Science Monitor. All rights reserved.

Barbara Kingsolver, "The Muscle Mystique" from *High Tide in Tucson: Essays from Now or Never* by Barbara Kingsolver. Copyright © 1995 by Barbara Kingsolver. Reprinted by permission of HarperCollins Publishers.

Unit 3

Jimmy Carter, from the 2002 Nobel Peace Prize Lecture, Oslo, December 10, 2002. © The Nobel Foundation 2002. Reprinted by permission.

Income distribution quotes from http://www.therationalradical.com: "The Daily Diatribe," subject "Income/Wealth Inequality," September 4, 2001.

From United for a Fair Economy website: Graphs "Distribution of U.S Wealth Ownership, 2001" and "Change in Average Household Net Worth, 1993-98" from http://www.faireconomy.org/research/wealth_charts.html. Reprinted by permission.

Rick Montgomery, "Wealth Statistics Stack Up Unevenly," *Kansas City Star*, December 19, 2006. Reproduced by permission of the Kansas City Star. © Copyright 2007 The Kansas City Star. All rights reserved. Format differs from original publication. Not an endorsement.

Quote from The Children's Defense Fund, www.childrensdefense.org.

Jo Goodwin Parker, "What Is Poverty?" from *America's Other Children: Public Schools Outside Suburbia* by George Henderson. Copyright © 1971 by University of Oklahoma Press, Norman. Reprinted by permission of the publisher. All rights reserved.

Nicholas D. Kristof, "Helping Binyam, When His Mother Won't," *The New York Times*, May 20, 2003. Copyright © 2003 by The New York Times Co. Reprinted with permission.

Peter Singer, "The Singer Solution to World Poverty," first published in *The New York Times Magazine*, September 5, 1999. Reprinted by permission of the author.

Marjorie Kelly, "Are You Too Rich if Others Are Too Poor?" from *Business Ethics*, March/April 1992. Reprinted by permission of New Mountain Media LLC.

Cliff Zukin, "How Generation X Watches Television," 1997, www.rtnda.org/resources/genx/genhow.htm.

Unit 4

Scott Aniol, "An Argument for the Superiority of Printed Media over Visual Media." http://religiousaffections.org/content/view/80/31. Reprinted by permission of the author.

Killian Tobin, "A Modern Perspective on Graffiti." http://sunsite.icm.edu.pl/graffiti/faq/tobin.html. ©1995 by Killian Tobin. Reprinted by permission of the author.

David Byrne, from "Learning to Love PowerPoint," as appeared in *Wired*, September 2003. Reprinted by permission of Todo Mundo Ltd.

Edward Tufte, "PowerPoint is Evil." Reprinted by permission, from Edward R. Tufte, *The Cognitive Style of PowerPoint* (Cheshire, Connecticut: Graphics Press, 2003), as appeared in *Wired* Magazine, September 2003.

"Visual Culture and Health Posters: Anti-Smoking Campaigns" from *Profiles in Science*, National Library of Med., http://profiles.nlm.nih.gov.

"In/Out" poster published by the United States Department of Health and Human Services, 1994.

"You're Bright Enough to Learn 40 Different Football Plays" poster published by Centers for Disease Control (U.S), 1998.

454   *Credits*

Unit 5

Claudia Smith Brinson, "All Work, No Play," *The State*, June 10, 2003. Reprinted by permission of The State Newspaper.

Diane Fassel, excerpt from "The Work Addict in the Family." From *Working Ourselves to Death* by Diane Fassel, © 1990. Used by the permission of The Lazear Agency, Inc.

"Stress Test: Long Work Hours Are Not the Culprit" from University of Arkansas press release, August 20, 2003, found at www.Newswise.com. Reprinted by permission of the University of Arkansas, Fayetteville.

Barbara Ehrenreich, "Good-bye to the Work Ethic," *Mother Jones*, 1998. Reprinted by permission of International Creative Management, Inc. Copyright © 1998 by Barbara Ehrenreich.

Barbara Ehrenreich, excerpts from *Nickel and Dimed: On (Not) Getting By in America* by Barbara Ehrenreich. © 2001 by Barbara Ehrenreich. Reprinted by permission of Henry Holt and Company, LLC.

Photo Credits

p. 4: Cheryl Gerber/AP/Wide World Photos
p. 6: © Zits Partnership, King Features Syndicate
p. 12: The Advertising Archives
p. 14: Courtesy State Farm
p. 20: © 2008 Banco de Mexico Diego Rivera & Firda Museums Trust. Av. Cinco de Mayo No. 2, Col. Centro, Del. Cuauhtemoc 06059, Mexico, D.F. Digital Image © The Museum of Modern Art/Licensed by SCALA /Art Resource, NY.
p. 24: © King Features Syndicate
p. 25: Pearson Learning
p. 44: Lowe Worldwide
p. 46: Substance Abuse and Mental Health Service Administration
p. 48: American Council on the Teaching of Foreign Languages
p. 78: John Severson/The Arizona Republic
p. 88: The Advertising Archives
p. 110: Mike Baldwin/Cartoon Stock
p. 119: United Features Syndicate
p. 143: Cedomir Kostovic
p. 159: Courtesy U.S. English
p. 192: James Gunn/AP/Wide World Photos
p. 208: Steve Brodner
p. 267: DOONESBURY © G.B. Trudeau. Reprinted with permission of Universal Press Syndicate. All Rights Reserved.
p. 372: Sarah Hamilton/aboutface.org
p. 413: "Physiognomies," David Byrne, 2007 (courtesy Pace/MacGill Gallery)
p. 414: AP/Wide World Photos

Credits

p. 419: National Institutes of Health
p. 420: National Institutes of Health
p. 421: Courtesy of OAH Magazine
p. 423: Library of Congress
p. 424: C.G. Bush, American Social History Productions, The Graduate Center, CUNY
p. 425: Library of Congress

Index

Note: Page numbers followed by *f* refer to figures.

A
"About Trout" (Behnke), 187–189, 278
Academic argument, synthesis of sources in, 179
Active reading. *See* Critical (active) reading
Ad hominem attacks, 116–117
Advertising
 appeals to emotions in, 45, 46*f*
 appeals to personal credibility in, 43, 44*f*
 appeals to reason in, 48*f*
 argument in, 11–14
 visual rhetoric in, 11–14
 "weasel words" in, 60
Allard, Kenneth, 364
"All Work, No Play" (Brinson), 428–431
"American Progress" (Gast), 424
Analysis of argument
 with argument concept
  construction of meaning, 87–89
  overview, 68–69, 136–137
  rubric (plan of action) for, 8, 66–67
  sample analyses, 79–81, 137–140
 with critical reading
  causes of failures in, 133–134
  definition of, 128, 134
  need for, 128–131
  sample analysis, 132–133
 sample analyses, 79–81, 132–133, 137–140
 with Toulmin system, 57–63
"Anchor Babies" (Reyes), 34–35, 91
Aniol, Scott, 408–409
APA style manual. *See* Publication Manual of the American Psychological Association (APA)
Appeals. *See* Persuasive appeals

"Are You Too Rich If Others Are Too Poor?" (Kelly), 403–405
Argument. *See also* Analysis of argument; Construction of argument; Context(s) of argument; Revision; Writing of argument
 vs. assertion, 22–23, 138–139
 confrontation *vs.* persuasion, 9, 24–25
 as critical thinking, 22–24
 personal voice in, 179, 331–332
 as thought process, 6–8, 22–24
Argument concept. *See also* Focus of argument; Purpose of argument; Reader (audience)
 in analysis of argument
  construction of meaning, 87–89
  overview, 68–69, 136–137
  rubric (plan of action) for, 8, 66–67
  sample analysis, 79–81, 137–140
 and claim
  distinctions between, 102–104
 in construction of argument, 89–100
  and defining of argument boundaries, 87, 90–91, 102
  overview, 40–41, 67–68
 definition of, 8
 in envisioned plan creation, 200, 202–205, 209–210, 212
 evaluation of, 217
 in revision, 334–335
 Rhetorical Triangle and, 66–69
"An Argument for the Superiority of Printed Media over Visual Media" (Aniol), 408–409

Aristotle
 on persuasive appeals, 40
 and Rhetorical Triangle, 66
 on successful argument, 66–67
Art
 as context for argument, 18–22
 evaluation of, as purpose of argument, 237–244
"Assault on Precinct 13" (Pearson), 19
Assertion, *vs.* argument, 22–23, 138–139
Attack(s)
 personal, as logical fallacy, 116–117, 124
 unfair, and personal credibility, 42
Atypical evidence, as logical fallacy, 109, 112–113
Audience. *See* Reader
Author. *See* Writer(s)
Authority, of source, 283, 297, 316
Avalos, Hector, 36–37

B
Background information, amount needed, 205
Backing, in Toulmin system of argument, 58–59, 60–61, 62
Begging the question, as logical fallacy, 118–119, 124
Behnke, Robert, 185, 187–189, 193, 278
Bergford, Brad, 324–328
Bias
 and critical reading, 133–134
 evaluation essays and, 237–239
 and examples from personal experience, 275–276
 and fallacy of improper authority, 113–114
 and personal credibility, 44–45, 134
 and source selection, 113–114, 184–189, 193

457

Index

Bibliography. *See* External documentation; References list (APA style); Works Cited list (MLA format)
Bird, Caroline, 129, 131, 137
Black/white fallacy. *See* False dilemma
Blind quotation, 280
Body image, readings on, 371–386
"Border Calling" (Reel), 28–31
Bowling for Columbine (film), 151–152
Brennan, Jim, 77, 79–81
Brinson, Claudia Smith, 428–431
Buchwald, Art, 368–369
Bullet list of potential sections, in envisioned plan, 200, 213–218
Business as War (Allard), 364
Business context, argument in, 8–11
Business ethics, readings on, 355–370
Byrne, David, 412–413

C

Campbell, Kim, 379–382
Capital punishment, debate on, 146–150
Carter, Jimmy, 387
Cause and effect
  as claim type, 70
  coordinate causation, 252
  false cause fallacy, 117–118, 253
  linear causation, 251–252
  post hoc, ergo propter hoc fallacy, 118, 253, 254
Cause-and-effect arguments, 250–256
  definition of, 250
  evidence in, 252–253
  fairness in, 253–254
  logical fallacies in, 117–118, 253
  reasoning process in, 251–252
Chavez, Linda, 138–140
"Children Born in the U.S. Serve as Means to Get Parents, Family Here" (Reyes), 34–35, 91
Claim(s)
  and argument concept
    distinctions between, 102–103
    turning argument concept into claim, 103–104
  definition of, 69
  development of, 200, 202–205, 212

role of, 69–70
subclaims, 69
support of. *See* Evidence; Reasons
tightening of, in revision, 334–335
in Toulmin system of argument, 58–59, 60–61, 62
types of, 70–71
Clustering, as idea-generation strategy, 170–175, 170f
"College Brings Alienation" (Gonzales), 144–146
College education, debate on value of, 129–133, 137, 144–146
"College Is a Waste of Time and Money" (Bird), 129, 131, 137
Comma problems, common, 347–348
Comma splices, 344–345
Computer addiction, debate on, 285–289
Concessions
  definition of, 75
  and personal credibility, 42–43, 75, 242, 249, 253–254, 258, 260
  in Toulmin system of argument, 62
  use of, 75–76, 81
  words that signal, 76
Confrontation, *vs* persuasion, 9, 24–25
Context(s) of argument
  argument concept applied to, 86
  and construction of argument, 40, 41–42, 99–100
  definition of, 85
  importance of, 85
  types of
    advertising context, 11–14
    art context, 18–22
    business context, 8–11
    social commentary context, 14–18
Coordinate causation, 252
"Cosmetic Surgery Comes Out of the Closet" (MSNBC), 373
Credibility. *See also* Personal credibility; appeal to (ethical appeal) of sources, 283
Crime, debate on impact of, 150–153
Criteria, for evaluation arguments, 237–239, 242–243
Critical (active) reading
  causes of failures in, 133–134

definition of, 128, 134
example of, 132–133
need for, 128–131
practices, 134–136
Critical thinking
  argument as, 22–24
  Toulmin system, 57–63
"Culture of Fear" (Glassner), 151

D

Dangling modifiers, 350–351
Deductive reasoning, 54–57
  definition of, 54
  reliable conclusions, methods for achieving, 56–57
Dillon, Kimberly, 318–324
Direct quotation
  documentation of, 315
  uses of, 280–281
The Disappearance of Childhood (Postman), 154
Discovery drafts, 200
Diversion, as logical fallacy, 120
Documentation
  of electronic sources. *See* Electronic sources
  external. *See* External documentation
  formal (*See also* External documentation; Internal documentation)
    definition of, 281
    as final step of draft, 281–282
    of online sources, 307
    importance of, 295, 296–297
  informal
    definition of, 281
    during drafting process, 282
  internal. *See* Internal documentation
  purposes of, 296–300
  reader's needs and, 300–301, 313
  responsibilities of, 306
Documentation manuals, 297–298, 306. *See also MLA Handbook for Writers of Research Papers* (MLA); *Publication Manual of the American Psychological Association* (APA)
Drafts. *See also* Revision; Writing of argument
  discovery drafts, 200
  multiple, as norm, 290
  suggestions for writing, 289–291

Index **459**

E
"Eats, Shoots and Leaves" (Truss), 343
Editing
 grammatical errors. *See* Grammatical errors
 vs. revision, 330–331
Ehrenreich, Barbara, 438–447
Either/or fallacy. *See* False dilemma
Electronic sources
 documentation of, 309–313
  cautions about, 311
  sources without print form, 310–311
  sources with print form, 309–310
  subscribed databases, 311
  Web sites, 312–313
 Internet research
  author's credentials, difficulty of identifying, 192
  bibliographic information, recording of, 182
  reliability of information, 180, 181, 312
  subscribed databases, 181–182
Emotions, appeals to (pathetic appeals), 45–47
 dangers of, 45–47
 in Rhetorical Triangle, 66
Encyclopedias
 citation format, 308
 specialized, as research tool, 183–184
Environmental poster, analysis of, 141–142, 143f
Envisioned plan
 analyzing from reader's perspective, 195, 200, 205–211
  reader's knowledge, 206–208
  reader's opposition to claim, 210–211
  reader's values, 208–210
 argument concept in, 200, 202–205, 209–210, 212
 bullet list of potential sections, 200, 213–218
 conclusion, 201, 219
 envisioning process, 200–206
 examples of, 214–217, 222–233
 need for, 196–200
 vs. outline, 198–200
 points to include, deciding on, 211–219

revision of, 202, 204, 217, 220–221
sections in
 bullet list of, 200, 213–218
 generic list of, 217–218
 vs. paragraphs, 214
 purpose, clarity of, 200, 218
Epstein, Karen, 373–375
"Erosion" (Williams), 160–161
Ethical appeal. *See* Personal credibility, appeal to
"The Ethics of Business Schools" (Mangan), 356–359
Ethos. *See* Personal credibility, appeal to
Evaluative arguments, 237–244
 criteria in, 237–239, 242–243
 definition of, 237
 examples of, 238–239, 243–244
 fairness in, 242
 organization of, 242–244
 thinking process of, 237–238
Evidence
 atypical, as logical fallacy, 109, 112–113
 in cause-and-effect arguments, 252–253
 definition of, 72
 effectiveness of, evaluating, 66–67, 135–136, 138–140, 337–339
 insufficient (hasty generalization), as logical fallacy, 52, 109, 110–111
 misuse of. *See* Logical fallacies
 in policy arguments, 258–259
 revision process and, 337–339
 in Toulmin system of argument, 58–59, 60–61, 62
 types of, 73–74
 use of, 72–73, 79, 80
Examples
 from personal experience, 275–276
 types of, 268–274
"Executive Decisions" (Mokhiber and Weissman), 363–365
Expert opinion, and fallacy of improper authority, 113–114
Extended examples, 269, 272–274

External documentation, 305–317. *See also* References list (APA style); Works Cited list (MLA format)
 definition of, 301
 of electronic sources, 309–313
  cautions about, 311
  sources without print form, 310–311
  sources with print form, 309–310
  subscribed databases, 311
  Web sites, 312–313
 purpose of, 301
 responsibilities of, 306

F
Fairness
 in cause-and-effect arguments, 253–254
 in evaluative arguments, 242
 and personal credibility, 42–43, 75
 in policy arguments, 258–260
 in problem-solving arguments, 249
Fallacies. *See* Logical fallacies
False cause, as logical fallacy, 117–118, 253
False dilemma, as logical fallacy, 120–121
Fassel, Diane, 431–435
"Fat Girls (Don't) Dance" (Jonasson), 377–379
Fellner, James, 222–226
Filibuster rights, debate on, 257
Fishing, debate on, 185–189
Fletcher, Michael, 255
"Flogged to Death" (Hoberman), 239
Focus of argument. *See also* Argument concept; Topic selection
 in argument analysis, 8, 9, 12, 66–67
 in argument construction, 41, 67–68, 89–91, 99
 and boundaries of argument, 90–91
 definition of, 89
 tightening of, in revision, 334–337
Ford, Gerald, 93–94
Fragmented sentences, 344
Free writing, as idea-generation strategy, 175–176
Frida Kahlo (Lowe), 20–21
"From Nickel and Dimed: On (Not) Getting by in America" (Ehrenreich), 441–447

G
Gast, John, 424
Gellman, Barton, 53
Generic examples, 269, 270–271, 274
Gesture drawing, 201–202, 203f, 204f
Gonzales, John, 144–146
"Good-bye to the Work Ethic" (Ehrenreich), 438–441
Goodman, Ellen, 436–438
Grammatical errors
  apostrophe misuse, 348–349
  comma misuse, 347–348
  comma splices, 344–345
  fragmented sentences, 344
  homophone substitution, 350
  misplaced modifiers, 350–351
  parallelism errors, 349–350
  pronoun errors, 346–347
  run-on sentences, 344–345
  subject/verb agreement, 345–346
  titles, format of, 349
"Greed Despoils Capitalism" (Wilder), 366–368
Gun control, debate on, 93–94
Gurza, Augustin, 240–241

H
"A Hanging" (Orwell), 146–150, 272
Hasty generalization. *See* Evidence, insufficient
Hate crime laws, debate on, 324–328
"Helping Binyam, When His Mother Won't" (Kristof), 396–398
Henry, William A., 131
Hoberman, J., 239
Holistic feel for argument, and envisioned plan, 200, 201–202
"Hollywood Poison Factory" (Medved), 153–158
Homophones, substitution of, 350
Hurricane Katrina and appeals to emotions, 46f
Hypothetical examples, 268–269, 274

I
I, use of, 275–276
Idea-generating strategies, 170–176
  clustering, 170–175, 170f
  free writing, 175–176
  looping, 176

ID tags, 279
Illustration, 268–276
  choice of example type, 274
  definition of, 268
  examples from personal experience, 275–276
  types of examples, 268–274
"I'm a Barbie Girl" (Epstein), 373–375
Immigration, debate on, 27–37
Improper authority, as logical fallacy, 113–114
Indirect sources, documentation of, 316
Inductive reasoning, 51–54
  definition of, 51
  example of, 80
  inductive leap in, 53
  reliable conclusions, methods for achieving, 51–54
Informal documentation
  definition of, 281
  during drafting process, 282
  overview, 38
Internal documentation, 304–305, 313–317. *See also MLA Handbook for Writers of Research Papers* (MLA); *Publication Manual of the American Psychological Association* (APA)
  citation forms
    author of multiple works, 315
    direct quotations, 315
    general form, 314
    indirect sources, 316
    multiple sources, 315
  definition of, 301
  documentation clutter, 313
  linking to Works Cited or References list, 314
  purposes of, 301, 313
  reader's needs and, 300–301, 313
  responsibilities of, 306
Internet research. *See also* Electronic sources, documentation of
  author's credentials, difficulty of identifying, 192
  bibliographic information, recording of, 182
  reliability of information, 180, 181, 312
Interviews, unpublished, citation format, 309
In-text citations. *See* Internal documentation

Iraq, Weapons of mass destruction in, debate on, 53
"Issue Looks Different Through Latino Eyes" (Avalos), 36–37

J
Japanese-American internment, debate on, 160–161
Jenkins, Sarah, 298–300
Jonasson, Sharleen, 377–379
"Just Do It!" ad campaign, 266–267
"Justly Accused—Unjustly Sentenced" (Bergford), 324–328
"Just One Look" (Campbell), 379–382

K
Kahlo, Frida, 19–21, 20f
Keith, Tamara, 373
Kelly, Marjorie, 403–405
Kingsolver, Barbara, 382–385
Kostovic, Cedomir, 141–142, 143f
Kozol, Jonathan, 273–274
Kristof, Nicholas D., 396–398
Kushner, Harold, 277–280, 280–281

L
Larsen, Blake, 204
LCSH. *See Library of Congress Subject Headings*
"Learning to Love Power-Point" (Byrne), 412–413
Library of Congress Subject Headings (LCSH), 183
Library research
  interlibrary loan, 184
  overview of, 180
  previewing of books, 184
  reliability of information, 181
  research handbooks, 181
  resources, 183–184
Liddane, Lisa, 373
Living a Life that Matters (Kushner), 277–280
Logical appeals (appeals to reason), 47–49, 66
Logical fallacies
  appeal to majority, 115–116
  atypical evidence, 109, 112–113
  begging the question, 118–119, 124
  cause-and-effect arguments and, 253
  diversion, 120
  false cause, 117–118, 253

false dilemma, 120–121
improper authority, 113–114
insufficient evidence (hasty generalization), 52, 109, 110–111
irrelevant evidence, 109, 112–113
non sequiturs, 119–120
personal attacks, 116–117, 124
post hoc, ergo propter hoc, 118, 253, 254
subjectivism, 114–115
Logos. *See* Reason, appeal to
Looping, as idea-generation strategy, 176
"Los Lobos Sing of Immigrants' Hopes, Heartbreaks" (Gurza), 240–241
Lotteries, state, debate on, 138–140
Lowe, Sarah M., 20–21
Lutz, William, 60

M

Majority, appeal to, as logical fallacy, 115–116
Mangan, Katherine S., 356–359
"Margaret Fuller Slack" (Masters), 142–144
Masters, Edgar Lee, 142–144
Media influence, debate on effects of, 151–152, 153–158
Medved, Michael, 153–158
"Mentally Retarded Don't Belong on Death Row" (Fellner), 224–226
Miller, H. Bruce, 150–153
"Minimum Wage *vs.* Living Wage" (Stewart), 227–233
Misplaced modifiers, 350–351
MLA Handbook for Writers of Research Papers (MLA), 298
  internal documentation, 313–317
    author of multiple works, 315
    direction quotations, 315
    general form, 314
    indirect sources, 316
    multiple sources, 315
    sample page, 302–303
    on readability, 300
  sample paper, 318–324
  on titles, format for, 302
Works Cited list
  citation formats
    articles, electronic, 310
    articles, print, 308–309
    books, 306–308
    electronic sources, 309–313
    encyclopedias, 308
    essays, 308
    newspaper articles, 309
    subscription databases, 311
    unpublished interviews, 309
    Web sites, 313
  definition of, 302
  sample of, 303–304, 323–324
"A Modern Perspective on Graffiti" (Tobin), 409–411
Modifiers, dangling, 350–351
Mokhiber, Russell, 363–365
Montgomery, Rick, 388–392
Moore, Michael, 151–152, 254
"Mother Tongue" (Tan), 92
Movies, debate on sex and violence in, 153–158
"The Muscle Mystique" (Kingsolver), 382–385

N

Newspaper articles, citation format, 309
No Child Left Behind (NCLB) program, debate on, 124, 318–324
Non sequiturs, as logical fallacy, 119–120
"Not Giving Up on Immigration Control" (Williamson), 31–34

O

Objectivity, and credibility of evidence, 113–115
Occasion, for argument, 66
Oil drilling, debate on, 23, 75–77
Online Writing Labs (OWLs), 307, 334
Opposing viewpoints, acknowledging. *See* Concessions
attacking, and credibility, 42, 75
attacking holder of (*ad hominem* attacks), 116–117, 124
Orwell, George, 146–150, 272
"Other Factors More Important in Job Stress" (Stöppler), 435–436
Outlines, *vs.* envisioned plan, 198–200
OWLs (Online Writing Labs), 307, 334

P

Parallelism errors, 349–350
Paraphrase, 279–280
Parenthetical citations. *See* Internal documentation
Parker, Jo Goodwin, 392–396
The Passion of Christ (film), 239
Passive reading
  causes of, 133–134
  definition of, 130
Pathetic appeal. *See* Emotions, appeals to
Pathos. *See* Emotions, appeals to
Pearson, Mike, 18–19
Pennies, debate on, 72–74
Personal attacks, as logical fallacy, 116–117, 124
Personal credibility, appeal to (ethical appeal), 42–45
  and author's credentials, 192–193
  biases and, 44–45, 134
  concessions and, 42–43, 75, 242, 249, 253–254, 258, 260
  in Rhetorical Triangle, 66
Personal experience, examples from, 275–276
Personal voice, in argument, 179, 331–332
Persuasive appeals
  appeals to emotion (pathetic appeals), 45–47
    dangers of, 45–47
    example of, 138
    in Rhetorical Triangle, 66
  appeals to personal credibility (ethical appeal), 42–45
    and author's credentials, 192–193
    biases and, 44–45, 134
    concessions and, 42–43, 75, 242, 249, 253–254, 258, 260
    in Rhetorical Triangle, 66
  appeal to reason (logical appeal), 47–49, 66
    (*See also* Logical fallacies)
  classical appeals, 40
  context and, 41–42
Plagiarism
  avoiding, 298–300
  definition of, 298
  detection of, 300
  penalties for, 299
  summary and, 278–279
  unintentional, 298–300

"Poetry Is Dead. Does Anybody Really Care?" (Wexler), 17–18
Policy arguments
  definition of, 256
  evidence in, 258–259
  fairness in, 258–260
  in political world, 257
Pollack, William, 375–377
Popular magazines, as source, 181
Post hoc, ergo propter hoc fallacy, 118, 253, 254
Poverty and wealth, readings on, 387–406
"PowerPoint Is Evil" (Tufte), 414–416
Problem-solving arguments, 244–250
  definition of, 244
  fairness in, 249
  problem exploration and evaluation, 247–249
  problem recognition and identification, 246–247
  solution selection and defense, 249–250
  thought/planning process for, 245–246
Product, evaluation of, as purpose of argument, 237–244
Professional journals, as source, 181
Pronoun errors, 346–347
Publication Manual of the American Psychological Association (APA), 298
  internal documentation, 313–317
    author of multiple works, 315
    direction quotations, 315
    general form, 314
    indirect sources, 316
    multiple sources, 315
    sample page, 304–305
  References list
    citation formats
      articles, electronic, 310
      articles, print, 308–309
      books, 306–308
      electronic sources, 309–313
      encyclopedias, 308
      essays, 308
      newspaper articles, 309
      sample of, 305
      subscribed databases, 311
      unpublished interviews, 309
      Web sites, 313
    definition of, 302
    sample of, 305, 327
    sample paper, 324–328
    on titles, format for, 302
Punctuation
  comma problems, common, 347–348
  comma splices, 344–345
  importance of, 343
Purpose of argument.
  types, 236
    argument for cause and effect. *See* Cause-and-effect arguments
    argument for quality of product, behavior, or work of art. *See* Evaluative arguments
    argument for solution to problem. *See* Problem-solving arguments
    arguments on policy. *See* Policy arguments
    mixing of, 236

Q

Qualifier
  in Toulmin system of argument, 58–59, 60–61, 62
  "weasel words" as, 60
Quality of thing, evaluation of
  as purpose of argument. *See* Evaluative arguments
  as type of claim, 70–71
Quindlen, Anna, 260–262
Quotation
  blind, 280
  direct
    documentation of, 315
    uses of, 280–281
  indirect (paraphrase), 279–280
  integrating into text, 280, 283, 316

R

Racial profiling, debate on, 284–289
Reader (audience). *See also* Argument concept
  analyzing envisioned plan from perspective of, 195, 200, 205–211
    reader's knowledge, 206–208
    reader's opposition to claim, 210–211
    reader's values, 208–210
  in argument analysis, 8, 10, 12–13, 66
  and argument construction, 41, 43, 91–96, 99, 339
  definition of, 92
  and documentation, 300–301, 313
  preconceptions of, 92–95
  in Rhetorical Triangle, 66–67
  and source selection, 277
Reading
  See Critical and Passive Reading
"Reading Ability: Why Males Fall Behind," 122–124
Reason, appeal to (logical appeals), 47–49, 66. *See also* Logical fallacies
Reasoning
  deductive, 54–57
    definition of, 54
    reliable conclusions, methods for achieving, 56–57
    three parts of argument, 55–56
  inductive, 51–54
    definition of, 51
    example of, 80
    inductive leap in, 53
    reliable conclusions, methods for achieving, 51–54
Reasons. *See also* Evidence
  definition of, 72
  exercises, 74–75
  use of, 72–73, 79
Rebuttals
  definition of, 77
  exercises, 81
  use of, 77, 81
Recursive process, argument construction as, 25–26
Reel, James, 28–31
Referred periodicals, as source, 181
References list (APA style)
  citation formats
    articles, electronic, 310
    articles, print, 308–309
    books, 306–308
    electronic sources, 309–313
    encyclopedias, 308
    essays, 308
    newspaper articles, 309
    sample of, 305
    subscription databases, 311
    unpublished interviews, 309
    Web sites, 313
  definition of, 302
  linking internal citations to, 314
  sample of, 305, 327

"Remaking Barbie" (Keith), 373
Resnick, Mike, 290
Reversing the argument concept, 136. *See also* Argument concept, in analysis of argument
Revision
basic advice, 330–334
vs. editing, 330–331
of envisioned plan, 202, 204, 217, 220–221
of flawed argument, necessity of, 25–26
four-step process for, 333–334
evidence, amount and quality of, 335–337
focus, tightening of, 334–337
organization, tightening of, 339–344
sources of help, 333, 334
Reyes, Rubi, 34–35, 91
Rhetorical Triangle, and argument concept, 66–69
"Road Test for Seniors" (Rosen), 15–17
Rogerian analysis, and persuasion *vs.* confrontation, 24–25
Rosen, Mike, 14–17
Run-on sentences, 344–345
Ryan, Michael, 359–362

S
Same-sex marriage, debate on, 23
Sanchez, Rene, 285–289
Savage Inequalities (Kozol), 273–274
Scholarly journals, as source, 181
Sections
drafting of. *See* Drafts; Writing
in envisioned plan
bullet list of, 200, 213–218
generic list of, 217–218
vs. paragraphs, 214
purpose, clarity of, 200, 218
organization of, revision process and, 340–341
Self-Portrait with Cropped Hair (Kahlo), 20–21, 20*f*
Service learning, debate on, 211–213
"Set Up to Fail" (Dillon), 318–324
"Severing the Human Connection" (Miller), 150–153

Sex and violence in movies, debate on, 153–158
Singer, Peter, 398–403
"The Singer Solution to World Poverty" (Singer), 398–403
Social commentary, as context for argument, 14–18
Solutions to problems, arguments for. *See* Problem-solving arguments as type of claims, 71
Sony Walkman W800i, advertisement for, 11–13, 12*f*
Sources. *See also* Documentation
authority of, 283, 297, 316
author's credentials, 192–193
bibliographic information, recording of, 182
currency of, 191
electronic. *See* Electronic sources
general citation of ("research shows..."), 139, 297
integration into argument, 277–284
guidelines for, 283–284, 316
ID tags and, 279
via direct quotation, 280–282
via paraphrase, 279–280
via summary, 277–279
on Internet
author's credentials, difficulty of identifying, 192
bibliographic information, recording of, 182
frustrations of, 183
reliability of information, 180, 181, 312
in library
interlibrary loan, 184
overview of, 180
previewing of books, 184
reliability of information, 181
resources, 183–184
popular magazines, 181
professional journals, 181
scholarly journals, 181
search terms and, 183
selection of
credibility and, 283
evaluating strength and validity, 184–189, 191–193
objectivity in, 179

readers' needs and, 277
subscribed databases, 181–182
triangulation of, 190–192, 193
types of, 180–183
use of, 38
Spanish-American War, cartoons from, 421–424
Specific examples, 269, 271–272, 274
Spoon River Anthology (Masters), 142–144
Stereotypes, as logical fallacy, 108–109, 111
Stewart, Debbie, 226–233
Stöppler, Melissa C., 435–436
Style manuals, 297–298, 306. *See also MLA Handbook for Writers of Research Papers* (MLA); *Publication Manual of the American Psychological Association* (APA)
Subjectivism, and credibility of evidence, 113–114, 337
Subject/verb agreement errors, 345–346
Subscribed databases
citation format, 311
as source, 181–182
Summary, of source
and plagiarism, 278–279
uses of, 278
writing of, 277–279
"Surfing's Up and Grades Are Down" (Sanchez), 285–289

T
"Tagged on the Job" (Brennan), 70–81, 77
Tan, Amy, 92
Tattoos, debate on, 78*f*, 79–81
"Tax Increase for New Jail May Face Opposition," 61–62
"There's No Future in Lady Luck" (Chavez), 138–140
"They Call Their Boss a Hero" (Ryan), 359–362
"This Is the Best Story Ever Filmed" (Thomas), 239
Thomas, Cal, 239
Titles, format for, 302, 349
Tobin, Killian, 409–411
Topic selection. *See also* Focus of argument
idea-generating strategies, 170–176
clustering, 170–175, 170*f*
free writing, 175–176
looping, 176

(continued)
    personal issues and knowledge in, 166–167, 169
    topics to avoid, 167–169
    topics to pursue, 169
"Tort Reform at Gunpoint" (Quindlen), 260–262
Toulmin system, 57–63
Traces of Man (Kostovic), 141–142, 143*f*
Transitions
    envisioned plan as aid to, 218, 219
    revision process and, 340–341
Triangulation, of sources, 190–192, 193
Truss, Lynne, 343
Tufte, Edward, 414–416

U
Unpublished interviews, citation format, 309
"The Upside of Downsizing" (Buchwald), 368–369
U.S.-English, debate on, 159–160

V
Vilppu, Glenn, 201, 203*f*
Violence and sex in movies, debate on, 153–158
Violence in society, debate on, 150–153
"Visual Culture and Health Posters: Anti-Smoking Campaigns" (National Library of Medicine), 416–420

Visual rhetoric. *See also* Advertising
    in advertising, 11–14
    argument concepts of images, 372
    arguments from data, 15, 15*f*, 389
    definition of, 5
    environmental poster, analysis of, 141–142, 143*f*
    readings on, 407–426
    simile and metaphor, 13–14
    Spanish-American War cartoons, 421–424
    tattoos, 78*f*, 79–81
    U.S.-English advertisement, 159–160
Voice, personal, in argument, 179, 331–332

W
Warrant
    reader's values and, 209
    in Toulmin system of argument, 58–59, 62, 63
Wealth and poverty, readings on, 387–406
"Wealth Statistics Stack Up Unevenly" (Montgomery), 388–392
Weapons of mass destruction in Iraq, debate on, 53
"Wearing Tights" (Pollack), 375–377
"Weasel words," in advertising, 60
Web sites, citation format, 312–313

Weissman, Robert, 363–365
Wexler, Bruce, 17–18
"What Is Poverty?" (Parker), 392–396
When Bad Things Happen to Good People (Kushner), 280–281
Wilder, Barbara, 366–368
Williams, Terry Tempest, 160–161
"With These Words I Can Sell You Anything" (Lutz), 60
"The Work Addict in the Family" (Fassel), 431–435
"A Working Community" (Goodman), 436–438
Working in America, readings on, 427–448
Works Cited list (MLA format)
    citation formats
        articles, electronic, 310
        articles, print, 308–309
        books, 306–308
        electronic sources, 309–313
        encyclopedias, 308
        essays, 308
        newspaper articles, 309
        subscribed databases, 311
        unpublished interviews, 309
        Web sites, 313
    definition of, 302
    linking internal citations to, 314
    sample of, 303–304, 323–324
Writing centers, as source of help, 334